Fodor's
2ND EDITION

GREAT AMERICAN VACATIONS

ACURA

Fodor's Travel Publications, Inc.
New York • Toronto • London • Sydney • Auckland

ISBN 0–679–02576–6

Fodor's Great American Vacations

Editor: Scott McNeely

Editorial Contributors: Steven K. Amsterdam, Greg Bailey, Tom Barr, David Brown, Robert P. Blake, Deke Castleman, Andrew Collins, Don Davenport, John Filiatreau, Elizabeth Gardner, Jonathan Gelber, Patricia Gibson, Kimberly Grant, Tara Hamilton, David Hepler, Sylvia Higginbotham, Anthony Howard, Wayne Humphries, Stephanie Joyce, Bud Journey, Steve Kane, Jeff Kuechle, Karl Luntta, Cynthia Maddox, Jillian Magalaner, Bob McCord, Dave McDaniel, Nat Moss, Candy Moulton, Hilary Nangle, Honey Naylor, Eddie Nickens, Kristen Perrault, Ron Potvin, Carolyn Price, Marcy Pritchard, Andres Puhvel, Gene Rebeck, Bill Roberts, Anne Rogers, Linda Romine, M. T. Schwartzman, Donna Singer, George Snyder, Bill Suber, Marty Wentzel, Tom Wharton, Sandra Widener, Dick Willis, Anne Wright, Karie Youngdahl

Art Director: Fabrizio LaRocca

Cartographers: David Lindroth, Maryland Cartographics

Illustrator: Karl Tanner

Cover Photograph: American Flag: Nicholas Devore, Photographers/Aspen; San Francisco: Phil Schermeister, Photographers/Aspen; Monument Valley, Arizona: Craig Aurness, Westlight; Statue of Liberty: Larry Lee, Westlight

Cover Design: Tigist Getachew

Special Sales

CONTENTS

While every care has been taken to ensure the accuracy of the information in this guide, the passage of time will always bring change, and consequently the publisher cannot accept responsibility for errors that may occur.

All prices and opening times quoted here are based on information supplied to us at press time. Hours and admission fees may change, however, and the prudent traveler will avoid inconvenience by calling ahead.

Fodor's wants to hear about your travel experiences, both pleasant and unpleasant. When a hotel or restaurant fails to live up to its billing, let us know and we will investigate the complaint and revise our entries where the facts warrant it.

Send your letters to the editors of Fodor's Travel Publications, 201 E. 50th Street, New York, NY 10022.

The 50 destinations we cover in this book span the map, from sea to shining sea. We'll take you to the great American metropolises—New York, Miami, Chicago, Los Angeles—as well as to our nation's capital, Washington D.C., and those twin cradles of liberty, Boston and Philadelphia. We'll stroll around New Orleans's French Quarter and ride a cable car up and down the hills of San Francisco. We'll listen to blues and country music in Memphis and Nashville, and we'll visit the antebellum mansions of Charleston and Savannah, not to mention the Colonial buildings in Williamsburg, Virginia, and lavish turn-of-the- century summer "cottages" in Newport, Rhode Island.

But every American knows that there's a lot of land out beyond the cities, too, and so we'll view some awe-inspiring natural wonders—thundering Niagara Falls, mysterious Mammoth Cave, the majestic Grand Canyon, and the towering Grand Tetons. From the sands of Cape Cod to the wilderness of Alaska's Denali National Park, from the Wisconsin Dells to the Texas Gulf Coast, we'll visit America's favorite vacationlands.

And tucked in among all the busy spots like Disney World and Honolulu and Las Vegas are charming corners of the country where small-town America reveals itself—places like Pennsylvania Dutch Country, the rocky Maine coast, Virginia's Shenandoah Valley, and the Ozarks heartland near Hot Springs, Arkansas.

We'll tell you where to stop along the road for a wholesome bite to eat, and where to lay your head down after a full day of touring and tramping around. You'll find out where to walk and stretch your legs, where to pedal a bike, and where to splash in the water. If you're looking for some gifts to buy—something one-of-a-kind you could never find at home—we'll point you toward the best local specialty shops, too.

There are enough vacations here to keep you busy every summer for the next half-century (although plenty of these trips are even more fun in other seasons—think of a blooming springtime along the Natchez Trace, blazing autumn in New Hampshire, or wintertime in Taos, New Mexico). Whether you take off for far-flung states or rediscover your own backyard, this book will be a faithful companion as you hit the highways.

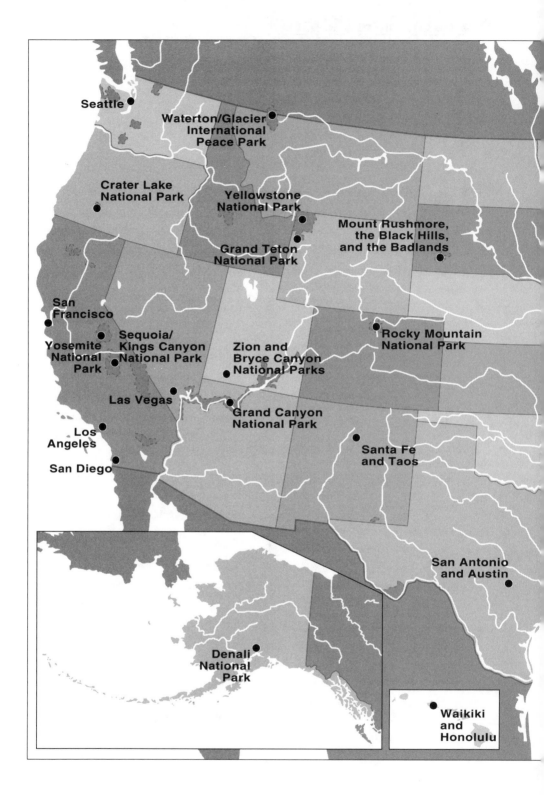

Seattle ●

Waterton/Glacier
International
Peace Park ●

Crater Lake
National Park
●

Yellowstone
National Park
●

Grand Teton
National Park
●

Mount Rushmore,
the Black Hills,
and the Badlands
●

San
Francisco
●

Yosemite
National
Park
●

Sequoia/
Kings Canyon
National Park
●

Zion and
Bryce Canyon
National Parks
●

Rocky Mountain
National Park
●

Las Vegas
●

Grand Canyon
National Park
●

Los
Angeles
●

Santa Fe
and Taos
●

San Diego
●

San Antonio
and Austin
●

Denali
National
Park
●

Waikiki
and
Honolulu
●

The
Maine
Coast

The White
Mountains

Boston

Minneapolis
and St. Paul

Niagara
Falls

Newport

Cape
Cod

Wisconsin
Dells

Pennsylvania
Dutch Country

New York
City

Chicago

Gettysburg

Philadelphia

The Lincoln
Trail

Washington, D.C.

Shenandoah
Valley and
Charlottesville

Williamsburg

Mammoth Cave
National Park

Nashville

The Outer
Banks

Memphis

Great Smoky
Mountains
National Park

Hot Springs
and the Ozarks

Charleston

The Natchez
Trace

Savannah and
the Golden Isles

Walt Disney World
and the Orlando Area

New
Orleans

Greater
Miami

The Texas
Gulf Coast

Everglades
National Park

THE UNITED STATES

Essential Information

No matter what your destination, your vacation can run more smoothly with advance planning. What follows are a few things to consider to make your trip easier.

LODGING ALTERNATIVES Consider religious retreats, guest houses, college dormitories, and home exchange. The directory *U.S. and World Accommodations Guide* lists college dorms and university apartments that can cost as little as $15 a night. It can be ordered for $12.95 from Campus Travel Service (Box 5486, Fullerton, CA 92635, tel. 714/525–6625). For first-class postage, add $2.55 in the U.S., $3.05 in Canada or Mexico. *A Guide to Monastic Guest Houses* by Robert J. Regalbuto (published by Morehouse, Box 1321, Harrisburg, PA 17105, tel. 800/877–0012) lists mostly Roman Catholic and Episcopalian guest houses and is available at bookstores for $13.95. For home exchange, go through an established organization. The Vacation Exchange Club (Box 650, Key West, FL 33041, tel. 800/638–3841) and Loan-a-Home (2 Park La., 6E, Mount Vernon, NY 10552, tel. 914/664–7640) specialize in home exchange.

The following are toll-free numbers for the major hotel chains: Adams Mark (tel. 800/231–5858); Best Western (tel. 800/528–1234); Clarion (tel. 800/252–7466); Colony (tel. 800/777–1700); Comfort (tel. 800/228–5150); Days Inn (tel. 800/547–7878); Doubletree (tel. 800/528–0444); Four Seasons (tel. 800/332–3442); Hilton (tel. 800/445–8667); Holiday Inn (tel. 800/465–4329); Hyatt & Resorts (tel. 800/233–1234); Intercontinental (tel. 800/327–0200); Marriott (tel. 800/228–9290); Meridien (tel. 800/543–4300); Quality Inn (tel. 800/228–5151); Radisson (tel. 800/333–3333); Ramada (tel. 800/228–2828); Red Lion (tel. 800/547–8010); Ritz-Carlton (tel. 800/241–3333); Sheraton (tel. 800/325–3535); Stouffer (tel. 800/468–3571); Westin Hotels & Resorts (tel. 800/228–3000); Wyndham (tel. 800/822–4200).

WHAT TO PACK If you're on any kind of medication that needs to be taken regularly, prevent a disaster by packing two sets—one in your carry-on bag and one in your larger suitcase. Also, make sure you take your doctor's phone number. Make sure you bring an extra pair of glasses or your prescription.

If you're traveling in summer, bring some sort of insect repellent, especially if you plan to be hiking or walking.

HINTS FOR OLDER TRAVELERS Many senior discounts are not advertised, so before you pay for anything, be sure to mention your age—if you're over 50, you're probably eligible for reduced rates on rooms, fares, packages, admission prices, and more. While 65 is the age most people associate with the term senior citizen, you can be a lot younger and still obtain certain discounts offered to older travelers. Just by joining certain organizations (*see below*), most of which you need only be 50 years old to join, you can be eligible for many discounts.

The Golden Age Passport is a lifetime pass to all parks, monuments, and recreation areas run by the federal government. Permanent U.S. residents 62 or older may pick them up in person at any of the national parks that charge admission; there is a one-time $10 fee. The passport covers the entrance fee for the holder and anyone accompanying the holder in the same private vehicle. It also provides a 50% discount on camping, boat launching, and parking. Proof of age is required. The Golden Eagle Pass offers similar advantages to people under 62 for $25 a year. Call the National Park Service (tel. 202/208–4747).

Publications: *The Senior Citizens Guide to Budget Travel in the United States and Canada,* by Paige Palmer, is available for $4.95, plus $1 for shipping, from Pilot Books (103 Cooper St., Babylon, NY 11702, tel. 516/422–2225).

Associations: The American Association of Retired Persons (AARP, 601 E St. NW, Washington, DC 20049, tel. 202/434–2277) has two programs for independent travelers: (1) the Purchase Privilege Program, which offers discounts on hotels, airfare, car rentals, RV rentals, and sightseeing; and (2) the AARP Motoring Plan, provided by Amoco, which furnishes emergency road-service aid and trip-routing information for an annual fee of $39.95 per person or couple. AARP members must be 50 years or older; annual dues are $8 per person or couple.

If you're allowed to use an AARP or other senior-citizen identification card to obtain a reduced hotel rate, mention it when you make your reservation. At participating restaurants, show your card to the maître d' before you're seated, because discounts may be limited to certain menus, days, or hours. When renting a car, be sure to ask about special promotional rates.

The nonprofit **Elderhostel** (75 Federal St., 3rd floor, Boston, MA 02110-1941, tel. 617/426–7788) offers inexpensive study programs for people 60 and older. Courses cover everything from marine science to cowboy poetry. Participants usually attend lectures in the morning and spend afternoons sightseeing or on field trips. Fees for programs in the United States, which usually last one week.

Tour Operators: Saga International Holidays (222 Berkeley St., Boston, MA 02116, tel. 800/343–0273) specializes in group travel for people over 60. If you want to take your grandchildren, look into **GrandTravel** (6900 Wisconsin Ave., Suite 706, Chevy Chase, MD 20815, tel. 301/986–0790 or 800/247–7651).

Discount Travel: In the U.S., Amtrak offers senior citizens (65 and over) a 15% discount on all round-trip travel. This discount is available without restrictions except for during holiday periods of heavy travel. Check the price of excursion tickets first as these are often cheaper. Call Amtrak (800/USA–RAIL) for more information.

Greyhound (tel. 800/231–2221) offers senior citizens (64 and older) a 10% reduction on regular fares Mondays through Thursdays, and a 5% reduction on weekends.

HINTS FOR TRAVELERS WITH DISABILITIES All U.S. citizens and permanent residents with mobility problems or vision or hearing impairments are entitled to a $10 lifetime pass to all federally operated parks, monuments, historic sights, recreation areas, and wildlife refuges that charge entrance fees. The Golden Access Passport, which must be obtained in person from a federally operated park or recreation area, also provides a 50% discount on federal fees charged for facilities and services, such as camping and parking.

Organizations: Several organizations provide travel information for people with disabilities, usually for a membership fee, and some publish newsletters and bulletins. Among them are the **Information Center for Individuals with Disabilities** (Fort Point Pl., 27–43 Wormwood St., Boston, MA 02210, tel. 617/727–5540 or 800/462–5015 in MA between 11 and 4, or leave message; TDD 617/345–9743); **Mobility International USA** (Box 3551, Eugene, OR 97403, tel. and TDD 503/343–1284), with affiliates in 30 countries; **MossRehab Hospital Travel Information Service** (tel. 215/456–9603, TDD 215/456–9602); the **Travel Industry and Disabled Exchange** (TIDE, 5435 Donna Ave., Tarzana, CA 91356, tel. 818/368–5648); and **Travelin' Talk** (Box 3534, Clarksville, TN 37043, tel. 615/552–6670).

Travel Agencies and Tour Operators: Directions Unlimited (720 N. Bedford Rd., Bedford Hills, NY 10507, tel. 914/241–1700) has expertise in both tours and cruises. **Evergreen Travel Service** (4114 198th St. SW, Suite 13, Lynnwood, WA 98036, tel. 206/776–1184 or 800/435–2288) operates Wings on Wheels Tours for travelers using wheelchairs and tours for people with hearing impairments and makes group and independent arrangements for travelers with any disability.

Publications: Several free publications are available from the U.S. Consumer Information Center (Pueblo, CO 81009): "New Horizons for the Air Traveler with a Disability" (include Dept. 608Y in the address), a U.S. Department of Transportation booklet describing changes resulting from the 1986 Air Carrier Access Act and those still to come

from the 1990 Americans with Disabilities Act, and the Airport Operators Council's *Access Travel: Airports* (Dept. 5804).

Twin Peaks Press (Box 129, Vancouver, WA 98666, tel. 206/694–2462 or 800/637–2256) publishes the *Directory of Travel Agencies for the Disabled* ($19.95); *Travel for the Disabled* ($19.95), listing some 500 access guides and accessible places worldwide; the *Directory of Accessible Van Rentals* ($9.95) for campers and RV travelers; and *Wheelchair Vagabond* ($14.95), a collection of personal travel tips. Add $2 per book for shipping. The Sierra Club publishes *Easy Access to National Parks* ($16 plus $3 shipping; 730 Polk St., San Francisco, CA 94109, tel. 415/776–2211). Fodor's publishes *Great American Vacations for Travelers with Disabilities* (available in bookstores, or call 800/533–6478).

Discount Travel: Amtrak (tel. 800/USA–RAIL; TDD 800/523–6590) offers all disabled passengers a 25% discount on regular fares (disabled children two to 11 get a 25% discount on already lower children's fares). However, it is wise to check the price of excursion tickets first. These often work out much cheaper than disabled reductions on regular tickets. All trains and all large stations have accessible toilets, though some of the region's smaller, unmanned stations do not. Reserve tickets 48 hours in advance.

While Greyhound buses have no special facilities, an attendant can ride for free if a written request is presented. For additional information contact Greyhound (tel. 800/231–2221; TDD 800/345–3109).

Avis (tel. 800/331–1212), Hertz (tel. 800/654–3131), and National (tel. 800/328–4567) can provide hand controls with advance notice.

CREDIT CARDS The following credit card abbreviations are used throughout this guide: AE, American Express; D, Discover; DC, Diner's Club; MC, MasterCard; V, Visa. It's always a good idea to call ahead and confirm an establishment's credit card policy.

Boston
Massachusetts

 ew England's largest and most important city, the cradle of American independence, Boston, Massachusetts, is 364 years old—far older than the republic it helped to create in the days of its vigorous youth. Its most famous buildings are not merely civic landmarks but national icons; its great citizens are not the political and financial leaders of today but the Adamses, Reveres, and Hancocks who lived at the crossroads of history and myth.

At the same time, Boston is a contemporary center of high finance and higher technology, a place of granite-and-glass towers rising along what were once rutted village lanes, dwarfing the commercial structures that stood as the city's largest just a generation ago. In this other Boston, Samuel Adams is the name of a premium beer and the price of condominiums is as hot a topic as taxation without representation ever was. The city's enormous population of students, artists, academics, and young professionals has made it a haven for foreign movies, late-night bookstores, racquetball, sushi restaurants, and unconventional politics. Happily, these elements peacefully coexist alongside the more subdued bastions of Yankee sensibilities.

Best of all, Boston is meant for walking. Most of the city's historical and architectural attractions are located within compact areas, and Boston's varied and distinctive neighborhoods only begin to reveal their character and design to visitors who take the time to stroll through them.

ESSENTIAL INFORMATION

WHEN TO GO The best times to visit Boston are late spring and the months of September and October. Like other American cities of the Northeast, Boston can be uncomfortably hot and humid (75°–80°) in high summer and freezing cold (25°–30°) in the winter. Yet the city is not without its pleasures in these seasons. In summer there are Boston Pops concerts on the Esplanade, harbor cruises, and a score of sidewalk cafés. In winter there is Christmas shopping on Newbury Street, the symphony, the theater, and college drama and music seasons.

Each September, Boston and Cambridge welcome thousands of returning students, along with the perennially wide-eyed freshmen beginning their four-year (or longer) stays in Boston. University life is a big part of the local atmosphere.

Autumn is a fine time to visit the suburbs. The combination of bright foliage and white church steeples may have been photographed countless times, but it will never become clichéd. The shore routes are less crowded in spring and fall, nearly all the lodging places and restaurants are open, and the Atlantic is as dramatic as ever.

BARGAINS Although most Boston museums charge admission, several offer a period when admission is free or reduced: the Museum of Fine Arts (tel. 617/267–9300), Wednesdays, 4–10; the Museum of Science (tel. 617/723–2500), November–April, Wednesdays, 1–5; the Gardner Museum (tel. 617/734–1359), Wednesdays, noon–5; the Aquarium (tel. 617/973–5200), October–March, Thursdays, 4–8; the Children's Museum (tel. 617/426–8855), Fridays, 5–9; and in Cambridge, the Harvard Museum (tel. 617/495–1910), Saturday mornings.

TOURIST OFFICES Greater Boston Convention & Visitors Bureau (800 Boylston St., Prudential Plaza, Boston 02199, tel. 617/536–4100). Boston Common Information Kiosk (Tremont St., tel. 617/426–3115) is at the beginning of the Freedom Trail. National Park Service Visitor Center (15 State St., Boston 02109, tel. 617/242–5642) is across from the Old State House.

EMERGENCIES **Police, fire,** and **ambulance:** Dial 911. **Hospitals:** Massachusetts General Hospital (55 Fruit St., tel. 617/726–2000). **Doctors:** MGH Physician Referral Service (tel. 617/726–5800). **Dentists:** Dental emergencies

(tel. 508/651–3521). **Pharmacies:** CVS (Porter Square Shopping Plaza, Massachusetts Ave., Cambridge, tel. 617/876–5519); Walgreens (Gallivan Blvd., Dorchester, tel. 617/282–5246).

ARRIVING AND DEPARTING

BY PLANE Logan International Airport (tel. 617/973–5500) is served by most major airlines.

Between the Airport and Downtown. Only 3 miles—and Boston Harbor— separate Logan International Airport from downtown, yet it can seem like 20 miles when you're caught in one of the many daily traffic jams at the two tunnels that go under the harbor.

By Subway: The MBTA Blue Line (tel. 800/235–6426) from Airport Station travels to downtown 5:30 AM–1 AM daily, for 85¢; allow 45 minutes' travel time to downtown. Free shuttle buses connect the subway station with all airport terminals.

By Water Shuttle: The Airport Water Shuttle (tel. 800/235–6426) takes 7 minutes and charges $8 to cross Boston Harbor and arrive at Rowes Wharf downtown; from here, though, you'll need to hail a cab to your final destination. The shuttle leaves every 15 minutes on weekdays and every 30 minutes on weekends. Free shuttle buses connect the ferry terminal with all airport terminals.

By Taxi: Cabs can be hailed outside any terminal; fares are $12–$15 downtown assuming moderate traffic, and travel time is 20–40 minutes. Call 617/561–1769 for cab information.

By Minibus: City Transportation (tel. 800/235–6426), leaving every 30 minutes at a cost of $6.50, and Airways Transportation (tel. 617/442–2700), leaving every 30 minutes at a cost of $7.50, serve major downtown hotels.

By Bus: Logan Link (tel. 800/23–LOGAN) connects all airport terminals to train and subway services at South Station. The link

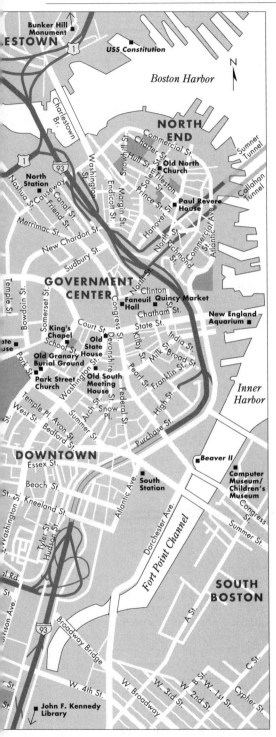

Boston Harbor

N

departs every 30 minutes and costs $5 one-way.

BY CAR Boston is reached via I–93 (also called the Southeast Expressway or the John F. Fitzgerald Expressway) from the south, via the Massachusetts Turnpike (I–90, a toll road) from the west, and via I–93 and U.S. 1 (from I–95) from the north. Traveling between Boston and Cambridge, Storrow Memorial Drive runs along the Charles River on the Boston side (the busier and faster route) and Memorial Drive (affording more scenic views of Boston) on the Cambridge side.

BY TRAIN Amtrak (tel. 800/USA–RAIL) stops at South Station (at Atlantic Ave. and Summer St., tel. 617/482–3660) from points south and west of Boston. North Station (Causeway and Friend Sts., tel. 617/722–3200) is used by commuter trains serving points within the state north and west of the city.

BY BUS Greyhound Lines (tel. 800/231–2222) connects Boston's South Station (tel. 617/423–5810) with all major U.S. cities. Peter Pan Bus Lines (Atlantic Ave. opposite South Station, tel. 617/426–7838) connects Boston with points in New England and New York. Plymouth & Brockton Buses (opposite South Station, tel. 508/746–0378) serve towns on Cape Cod.

GETTING AROUND

Boston is a walker's city; you're likely to move faster and see more when you stay on foot. If you get tired, the city's subway and trolley systems are efficient. And if it's late, taxis are plentiful.

BY CAR If you must bring a car into the city, stick to the major thoroughfares and park in a lot—no matter how expensive ($10–$15 for a few hours or a full day)—rather than on the streets. Meter maids in Boston are ruthless, and the maze of one-way streets drives even the locals crazy. Major public parking lots are located at Post Office Square, Government Center, Faneuil Hall, the Prudential Center, and Copley Place.

BY SUBWAY The MBTA (tel. 617/722–3200 or 617/722–5125), commonly called the T, operates subways, elevated trains, and trolleys along four connecting, color-coded lines. The Park Street station is the major transfer point for the Red and Green lines; the Orange and Blue lines intersect at State Street. Trains operate from 5:30 AM to 12:30 AM and the fare is 85¢. Tourist passes, which cost $5 for one day, $9 for three days, and $18 for seven days, can be purchased at the Park Street or airport stations, as well as at Bostix and the Boston Common Information Kiosk.

BY BUS MBTA bus routes crisscross the metro area and extend farther into the suburbs than the trolleys or subway. But for the uninitiated or those in a hurry, routes and stops on the street are difficult to pinpoint. Local fares are 60¢ paid on board with exact change, and buses operate weekdays 6:30 AM–11 PM, weekends 9 AM–6 PM. Pick up a map at the Park Street station.

BY TAXI Cabs are easily hailed on the street and can also be found at hotel taxi stands. Companies offering 24-hour radio-dispatched taxi service include Checker (tel. 617/536–7000) and Independent Taxi Operators (tel. 617/426–8700). The rate is about $1.60 per mile.

REST STOPS Public rest rooms can be found in Quincy Market and the newly renovated South Station downtown, and in the Copley Place shopping area on Copley Square.

GUIDED TOURS **Orientation:** The Brush Hill Transportation Company (439 High St., Randolph, tel. 617/986–6100 or 800/343–1328) and Gray Line Tours (275 Tremont St., tel. 617/426–8805) offer three-hour narrated introductory coach tours of Boston's principal sights for $21 and $18, respectively. Both tours are specifically designed for first-time visitors and provide an excellent way for you to get your bearings, both historically and geographically.

Special-Interest: Boston Park Rangers (tel. 617/522–2639) lead nature walks through the city's almost 200 parks. Samuel Adams Lager Brewery (Jamaica Plain, tel. 617/522–9080) offers 90-minute tours with a tasting at the end. The New England Aquarium (Central Wharf, off Atlantic Ave., tel. 617/973–5277) sponsors five-hour cruises May to early October, and Boston Harbor Cruises (1 Long Wharf, tel. 617/227–4320) offers sightseeing tours and trips to the Harbor Islands from mid-April through December.

Walking Tours: The Historic Neighborhoods Foundation (2 Boylston St., tel. 617/426–1885), a nonprofit educational foundation, offers informal guided walking tours of Beacon Hill, the North End, and Chinatown for $5. For more information on walking tours of Boston, *see* Outdoor Activities, *below.*

EXPLORING

Boston can be seen as a series of concentric circles, with the oldest and most famous attractions clustered within easy walking distance of the State House. Many attractions are on the well-marked Freedom Trail; none is far off the track. Boston's remarkable compactness is a boon for the pedestrian explorer; indeed, in central Boston there should be no other kind.

Back Bay, a neighborhood 11 blocks long by 6 blocks wide, properly begins with the Public Garden, the oldest botanical garden in the United States. Its pond has been famous since 1877 for its swan boats, which cruise during the warm months of the year. While Commonwealth Avenue resembles a Parisian boulevard, Newbury Street is Boston's equivalent of New York's Fifth Avenue. On Boylston Street, the commercial spine of Back Bay, is Copley Square, a civic space that is defined by the stately Copley Plaza Hotel, Trinity Church (Henry Hobson Richardson's masterwork of 1877), and the Boston Public Library. A few blocks farther down Boylston Street is the **Prudential Center Skywalk** with an observatory offering fine views of Boston, Cambridge, and the suburbs to the west and south. *800 Boylston St., tel. 617/236–3318. Open daily. Admission charged.*

Beacon Hill, a residential neighborhood behind and to the west of the State House, is full of classic Federal-style brick row houses, brick sidewalks, and gas lanterns. Search out Chestnut and Mt. Vernon streets, two of the prettiest streets in America; Louisburg Square, a stunning 1840s town house "development"; and Acorn Street, a narrow span of cobblestones lined with tiny row houses and doors to private gardens.

Boston Common is the oldest public park in the United States and undoubtedly the largest and most famous of the town commons around which all New England settlements were once arranged. On the north side of the Common is the **State House,** arguably the most architecturally distinguished of American seats of government. At the **Park Street Church,** on the corner of Tremont and Park streets, the hymn "America" was first sung, and William Lloyd Garrison began the campaign against slavery. Next door is the **Old Granary Burial Ground,** where Samuel Adams, John Hancock, and Paul Revere are buried. *State House: Park and Beacon Sts., tel. 617/727–3676. Open weekdays. Admission free. Park Street Church: Open late June–late Aug., Tues.–Sat. Admission free. Old Granary Burial Ground: Open daily. Admission free.*

Cambridge (actually its own city, reached from Boston via the Red Line to Harvard Square), is home to Harvard University and the Massachusetts Institute of Technology (MIT). Harvard's **Fogg Art Museum** includes art from every major period and from every corner of the world. Walking-tour brochures for Revolutionary and Old Cambridge can be obtained at Cambridge Discovery (tel. 617/497–1630), an information booth near the entrance to the Harvard MBTA station. *Fogg Art Museum: 32 Quincy St., tel. 617/495–9400. Open Tues.–Sun. Admission charged.*

Charlestown, over the Charlestown Bridge, is home to the undefeated **USS *Constitution*** (nicknamed "Old Ironsides"), the oldest commissioned ship (1797) in the U.S. Navy. She is moored at the Charlestown Navy Yard, a national historic site. Take Main Street to Monument Street and walk straight uphill to reach the historic **Bunker Hill Monument.** Ascend the 295 steps (there is no elevator) for a view worth the climb. *USS Constitution: tel. 617/426–1812. Open daily. Admission free. Bunker Hill Monument: Monument St. Open daily. Admission free.*

The Christian Science Church Center is the mother church of the Christian Science faith, established here in 1879. The 670-foot reflecting pool is a pleasant place to stroll around, and the Maparium, a 30-foot stained-glass globe, gives you the feeling of walking through the world on a glass bridge. *175 Huntington Ave., Back Bay, tel. 617/450–3790. Church open daily, Maparium open Tues.–Sat. Admission free.*

Downtown Boston—the financial district—is off the beaten track for visitors who are concentrating on following the Freedom Trail, yet there is much to see in a half-hour's walk. At the corner of Tremont and School streets stands **King's Chapel,** where Paul Revere's largest, and in his opinion his sweetest-sounding bell, chimes. Two blocks from King's Chapel (down School Street, with the Parker House Hotel on your right), on Washington Street at the corner of Milk, is the **Old South Meeting House.** Samuel Adams called a town meeting here to discuss dumping dutiable tea into Boston Harbor. A right turn onto Washington Street from the doorstep of the Old South will take you to the **Old State House,** the seat of the Colonial government from 1713 until the Revolution. *King's Chapel: Open Tues.–Sat. Admission free. Old South Meeting House: Open daily. Admission charged. Old State House: Washington and Court Sts., tel. 617/720–3290. Open daily. Admission charged.*

Faneuil Hall (pronounced Fan'l), on Merchants Row in downtown Boston, was erected in 1742 to serve as both a place for town meetings and a public market. Inside Faneuil Hall are dozens of paintings of famous Americans and the headquarters and museum of the Ancient and Honorable Artillery Company of Massachusetts. **Quincy Market,** right behind Faneuil Hall, consists of three structures that originally served as a retail and wholesale meat and produce distribution center; today the area is a model of urban renewal, with specialty foods, restaurants, bars, market stalls, and shops. *Open daily. Admission free.*

Isabella Stewart Gardner Museum is a monument to one woman's taste (and despite the loss of a few masterpieces in a daring 1990 robbery, still a trove of paintings, sculpture, furniture, and textiles) housed in an Italian-style villa. The collection includes works by Titian, Matisse, Van Dyck, Rubens, and Botticelli. *280 The Fenway, tel. 617/566–1401. Open Tues.–Sun. Admission charged.*

John F. Kennedy Library, south of the city but accessible on the Red Line, is the official repository of this native Bostonian's presidential papers, desk, and other personal belongings. *Columbia Pt., South Boston, tel. 617/929–4523. Open daily. Admission charged.*

Museum of Fine Arts has holdings of American art that surpass those of all but a few other American museums, plus the most extensive collection of Asiatic art under one roof, and a European collection representing the 11th through the 20th centuries. *465 Huntington Ave., tel. 617/267–9300. Open Tues.–Sun. Admission charged.*

Museum of Science has more than 400 exhibits covering astronomy, anthropology, and earth sciences. Also housed here are the Hayden Planetarium and the Mugar Omni Theater. *Science Park, across the Charles River on Green Line, tel. 617/523–6664. Museum open Tues.–Sun.; Planetarium open Fri.–Sun.; Omni open daily. Admission charged.*

The **North End** has been Italian Boston for more than 60 years; Italian grocers, cafés, festivals honoring saints, and encroaching gentrification characterize the narrow and winding streets of the present-day neighborhood. Salem and Hanover streets are particularly active and colorful. Off Hanover Street is the oldest house in Boston, the **Paul Revere House,** built nearly 100 years before Revere's midnight ride through Middlesex County.

Head right on Hanover Street and make a left onto Tileston Street. At the end of Tileston Street make a right on Salem Street to find the **Old North Church** (the oldest church in Boston), where two lanterns in its steeple signaled Paul Revere on the night of April 18, 1775. *Paul Revere House: 19 North Sq., tel. 617/523–1676. Open Apr.–Dec., daily; Jan.–Mar., Tues.–Sun. Admission charged. Old North Church: tel. 617/523–6676. Open daily, except Thanksgiving. Admission free.*

The **Waterfront** is home to several popular Boston attractions. Behind Quincy Market and to the south is the **New England Aquarium,** where you'll find more than 2,000 species of fish. Walk along Atlantic Avenue to the Congress Street Bridge to board the Boston Tea Party Ship, **Beaver II,** a replica of one of the ships that was forcibly boarded and unloaded on the night Boston Harbor became a teapot. Across the bridge is the **Computer Museum,** with exhibits chronicling the development of computers. Next door, the **Boston Children's Museum** has a multitude of hands-on exhibits designed with kids in mind. *Aquarium: Central Wharf, tel. 617/973–5200. Open Wed.–Sun. Admission charged.* Beaver II: *Open Mar.–Nov., daily. Admission charged. Computer Museum: 300 Congress St., tel. 617/426–2800. Open May–Aug., daily; Sept.–Apr., Tues.–Sun. Admission charged. Children's Museum: 300 Congress St., tel. 617/426–6500. Open Tues.–Sun. 10–5. Admission charged.*

HOTELS AND INNS

Lodging in Boston will be your biggest expense. Some expensive hotels offer reasonably priced weekend packages, but availability varies. If you choose a hotel in Cambridge but plan to spend most of your time in Boston, remember that it will take 25 minutes to get to downtown Boston by public transportation. Lastly, with all the colleges, businesses, conventions, and historic attractions in the area, hotels generally maintain a very high rate of occupancy; to avoid frustration, do not arrive without a confirmed reservation. Keep in mind that hotel prices generally do not include parking fees. Price categories for double occupancy, without 9.7% tax, are *Expensive*, $95–$125; *Moderate*, $70–$95; and *Inexpensive*, under $70.

AIRPORT **Hilton.** This high-rise chain hotel, with completely refurbished and soundproof modern rooms, has relatively easy access to the city. *75 Service Rd., Logan International Airport, East Boston 02128, tel. 617/569–9300 or 800/445–8667. 542 rooms. Outdoor pool, baby-sitting service, free parking, free shuttle to airport terminals. AE, DC, MC, V. Expensive.*

BACK BAY **57 Hotel/Howard Johnson's.** The location is part Park Square and part theater district, which makes this clean and serviceable property popular with both business travelers and tourists. *200 Stuart St., 02116, tel. 617/482–1800 or 800/654–2000. 354 rooms. Heated indoor pool, sauna, sun deck, baby-sitting service, free indoor parking. AE, DC, MC, V. Expensive.*

Beacon Guesthouses. These furnished studio apartments in converted town houses (similar to European pensions) offer basic accommodations in a few buildings on Newbury Street. *248 Newbury St., 02116, tel. 617/266–7276. 20 rooms in summer, 10 rooms in winter. MC, V. Moderate.*

CAMBRIDGE **Cambridge House.** This antiques-filled gracious old home, listed on the National Register of Historic Places, offers rooms in several buildings, full breakfast, and afternoon tea and sherry—and it's only a short walk to the MBTA Red Line. *2218 Massachusetts Ave., 02140, tel. 617/491–6300 or 800/232–9989. 12 rooms. Free parking. MC, V. Expensive.*

Harvard Manor House. This functional and clean five-story motel in Brattle Square, minutes from Harvard Square, offers the largest rooms in the area for the price. *110 Mt. Auburn St., 02138, tel. 617/864–5200 or 800/458–5886. 72 rooms. AE, DC, MC, V. Expensive.*

Susse Chalet Cambridge. Rooms at the Susse Chalet are clean but sparse, and the location is a bit isolated from most shopping areas and sights. However, you're only a 10-minute car ride from Harvard Square and within walking distance of the MBTA Red Line terminus. *211 Concord Tpke., 02140, tel. 617/661–7800 or 800/258–1980. 78 rooms. Free parking. AE, DC, MC, V. Inexpensive.*

DOWNTOWN **Copley Square Hotel.** One of Boston's oldest hotels and best values, this centrally located hotel has a European flavor and rooms of various sizes—from singles to family suites. *47 Huntington Ave., 02116, tel. 617/536–9000 or 800/225–7062. 143 rooms. Use of health club (for a small fee). AE, DC, MC, V. Expensive.*

SOUTH END **Terrace Townhouse.** Only a few blocks from Copley Square, this elegantly appointed and meticulously restored brick town house offers a rooftop deck, afternoon tea in the library, and a delectable full breakfast brought to your room. *60 Chandler St., 02116, tel. 617/350–6520. 4 rooms. Full breakfast included. MC, V. Expensive.*

THEATER DISTRICT **Tremont House.** The lobby, with its high ceilings, marble staircase, lots of gold leaf, and four-tiered chandelier, denotes a grandeur that is not reflected in the rooms themselves; both the guest rooms (furnished with 18th-century Thomasville reproductions) and the bathrooms are small. Many special packages are available. *275 Tremont St., 02116, tel. 617/426–1400 or 800/331–9998. 281 rooms. Laundry service, no-smoking floor. AE, DC, MC, V. Expensive.*

MOTELS

MODERATE **Comfort Inn** (Rte. 1, Saugus 01906, tel. 617/324–1900 or 800/228–5150). 117 rooms; free parking. **Holiday Inn** (55 Ariadne Rd., Dedham 02026, tel. 617/329–1000 or 800/HOLIDAY). 200 rooms; free parking.

INEXPENSIVE **Red Roof Inn** (650 Cochituate Rd., Framingham 01701, tel. 508/872–4499 or 800/843–7663). 170 rooms; free parking.

DINING

The main ingredient in Boston's restaurant fare is still the bounty of the North Atlantic, the daily catch of fish and shellfish that appears somewhere on virtually every menu. Seafood or no, the choice of dining experience in Boston is unusually wide. Between the extremes lies an extensive range of American, French, Italian, and other national and ethnic cuisines, their variety ample enough to create difficult decisions at mealtime. Price categories per person, not including 5% tax, service, and drinks, are *Expensive,* over $25; *Moderate,* $15–$25; and *Inexpensive,* under $15.

BACK BAY **Legal Sea Foods.** The atmosphere at Legal's is bustling and the cuisine simple but delectable—choose from raw, broiled, steamed, or baked seafood. *64 Arlington St., Park Sq., Boston Park Plaza Hotel, tel. 617/426–4444. AE, DC, MC, V. Moderate.*

Miyako. Small in size, large in ambition, and with remarkably personable waitresses, this basement restaurant serves up some of the most exotic sushi in town, as well as such Japanese standards as shrimp fritters, yellowtail teriyaki, and fried bean curd. *279A Newbury St., tel. 617/236–0222. MC, V. Moderate.*

Thai Cuisine. This restaurant offers well-prepared Thai food that goes beyond mere exotica for the uninitiated. The half duck is the only entrée on the menu you might manage to eat by yourself; the rest are the kind you order and share. *14A Westland Ave., tel. 617/262–1485. AE, DC, MC, V. Inexpensive.*

Turner Fisheries. This tastefully decorated fish house offers a wide selection of broiled, grilled, fried, baked, or blackened seafood, but any meal should begin with the rich chowder, which has been inducted into the city's Chowderfest Hall of Fame. *10 Huntington Ave., Westin Hotel, tel. 617/424–7425. AE, DC, MC, V. Moderate.*

CAMBRIDGE **Iruna.** This popular Spanish restaurant serves up paella, fresh seafoods, and great salads to large crowds of mostly students. There is outdoor dining in warm weather. *56 John F. Kennedy St., tel. 617/868–5633. No credit cards. Moderate.*

Grendel's Den. Housed in a former Harvard College fraternity building, Grendel's has an unusually warm and clubby atmosphere, a downstairs bar, and an eclectic assortment of cuisines, including Middle Eastern, Greek, Indian, and French. *89 Winthrop St., tel. 617/491–1160. AE, DC, MC, V. Inexpensive–Moderate.*

CHINATOWN **Imperial Teahouse Restaurant.** Its lively second floor is a large, airy dining room with the most extensive dim sum selection in Chinatown; dim sum denotes both the meal (a Chinese brunch served daily 9–3) and the variety of dumplings and buns, tiny chicken, shrimp, and other foods that you select from passing carts and pay for by the item. *70 Beach St., tel. 617/426–8543. AE, DC, MC, V. Inexpensive–Moderate.*

FANEUIL HALL **Union Oyster House.** The best feature of Boston's oldest restaurant, established in 1826, is the shellfish bar where the oysters and clams are fresh and well chilled—a handy place to stop for a dozen oysters or cherrystone clams on the halfshell. *41 Union St., tel. 617/227–2750. AE, DC, MC, V. Moderate.*

NORTH END **Felicia's.** A place for solid Italian home cooking (good enough for Luciano Pavarotti when he's in town), Felicia's serves up such specialties as chicken verdicchio, angel-hair pasta, and cannelloni in a dark, second-floor, traditional Italian restaurant. *145A Richmond St., tel. 617/523–9885. AE, DC. Moderate.*

Daily Catch. This tiny restaurant, with long lines after 6:30 PM, has an open kitchen and its menu posted on blackboards. Dishes include calamari cooked every way imaginable and healthy servings of other fresh seafood and pasta. *323 Hanover St., tel. 617/523–8567. No credit cards. Inexpensive.*

SOUTH END **Hamersley's Bistro.** Rave reviews and chic black-and-white decor are the norm here, where specialties include a garlic and mushroom sandwich served as an appetizer, bouillabaisse (ingredients change with the season), and roast chicken with garlic, lemon, and parsley. *578 Tremont St., tel. 617/267–6068. MC, V. Moderate.*

Botolph's on Tremont. The atmosphere here is pure bistro, with black high-gloss chairs with red upholstery, black tables, lush plants, and contemporary paintings hung on the high white walls; the food is gourmet Italian. *569 Tremont St., tel. 617/424–8577. AE, MC, V. Inexpensive–Moderate.*

THEATER DISTRICT **Joyce Chen Restaurant.** In a gracious setting with an extensive menu of Mandarin, Shanghai, and Szechuan cuisine, specialties include hot and cold soups, Szechuan scallops, and moo shu dishes. The lunch buffet on weekdays is a good value. *115 Stuart St., tel. 617/720–1331. AE, MC, V. Moderate.*

SOUTH STATION **Blue Diner.** This original 1945 diner has genuine diner food as well as more sophisticated offerings to please the mixture of blue-collar workers, architects, and artists that frequent the Blue. *178 Kneeland St., tel. 617/338–4639. AE, DC, MC, V. Inexpensive–Moderate.*

WATERFRONT **Cornucopia.** The chef is a master of traditional New England cuisine and more innovative New American cuisine; but both taste superb at this intimate restaurant overlooking the harbor. *100 Atlantic Ave., tel. 617/338–4600. AE, MC, V. Moderate–Expensive.*

Weylu's Wharf. With a view of the Boston skyline, this restaurant serves up not only traditional Mandarin and Szechuan cuisine but also such specialties as fu yong three-treasure (shrimp, chicken, scallops, and vegetables in white wine sauce). *254 Summer St., tel. 617/423–0243. AE, MC, V. Moderate.*

No-Name Restaurant. Beginning as a nameless hole-in-the-wall for Fish Pier workers, the No-Name now attracts suburbanite families, tourists, and businesspeople—but the staples still include such seafood as boiled lobster, broiled scallops, and the fish of the day. *15¹/₂ Fish Pier off Northern Ave., tel. 617/338–7539. No credit cards. Inexpensive–Moderate.*

SHOPPING

Boston has its fair share of places to spend money, and its two daily newspapers, the *Globe* and the *Herald,* are the best places to learn about sales. Most of Boston's stores and shops are located in an area bounded by Quincy Market, the Back Bay, downtown, and Copley Square. There are few outlet stores in the area, but there are plenty of bargains, particularly in the world-famous Filene's Basement. Cambridge has a new indoor mall with outdoor seating and myriad smaller shops in Harvard Square.

SHOPPING DISTRICTS Back Bay is home to Newbury Street, Boston's version of New York's Fifth Avenue (where the trendy gives way to the chic and expensive), and Boylston Street, with more than 100 stores spread out over a seven-block area. Cambridgeside Galleria (tel. 617/621–8666), a beautiful new three-story mall between Kendall Square and the Museum of Science in Cambridge, has more than 60 shops, including the larger anchor stores of Filene's, Lechmere, and Sears. The indoor shopping area is accessible via the Green Line.

Copley Place (tel. 617/375–4400), an indoor shopping mall connecting the Westin and Marriott hotels near Copley Square, is a blend of the elegant, the unique, the glitzy, and the overpriced. The Neiman Marcus department store anchors 87 stores, restaurants, and cinemas. Prices in the shops on the second level tend to be a bit lower.

Downtown Crossing (on Washington St. across from Boston Common), is the city's traditional shopping area. Here are Filene's, Jordan Marsh, and the Jewelers' Building (with many fine discount jewelers) as well as a pedestrian mall with outdoor food and merchandise kiosks, street performers, and benches.

Faneuil Hall Marketplace, between Government Center and the waterfront, has hundreds of small shops, kiosks of every description, street performers, and Quincy Market, with more than a hundred international food stalls. Be prepared for crowds, especially on the weekends. On Fridays and Saturdays, Haymarket—a crowded jumble of outdoor fruit and vegetable vendors, meat markets, and fishmongers—is in full swing.

Harvard Square in Cambridge has more than 150 stores within a few blocks, including, in the middle of it all, Out-of-Town News (Harvard Sq., tel. 617/354–7777) with dozens of current international periodicals. In addition to the surprising range of items found in the square, Cambridge is a great place to find new and used books.

DEPARTMENT STORES Filene's (426 Washington St., tel. 617/357–2100), a full-service department store, is famous for its two-level bargain basement, where items are automatically reduced in price according to the number of days they've been on the rack. Competition for goods can be stiff down here, so if you see something you want, buy it—it probably won't be there the next day. Harvard Coop Society (1400 Massachusetts Ave., Cambridge, tel. 617/492–2000), established in 1882 as a nonprofit service for students and faculty, is now a full department store best known for its extensive collection of records and books. Jordan Marsh Company (450 Washington St., tel. 617/357–3000) has been New England's largest department store for more than 130 years.

SPECIALTY STORES **Antiques:** Charles Street on Beacon Hill offers a full range of antiques for browsers and buyers. **Books:** The Brattle Bookstore (9 West St., tel. 617/542–0210) is Boston's best used and rare bookshop; if the book you want is out of print, the Brattle either has it or can probably find it. **Clothing:** Brooks Brothers (46 Newbury St., tel. 617/267–2600) offers men's traditional formal and casual clothing, correct and durable down through the ages. Ann Taylor (18 Newbury St., tel. 617/262–0763; Faneuil Hall, tel. 617/742–0031) has high-quality women's clothing, shoes, and accessories for both classic and trendy dressers. **Crafts:** The Society of Arts and Crafts (175 Newbury St., tel.

617/266–1810) offers an excellent assortment of quality handicrafts. **Food:** Savenor's (160 Charles St., tel. 617/723–6328) carries outstanding cheeses, breads, and produce for picnic fixings. **Jewelry:** Shreve, Crump & Low (330 Boylston St., tel. 617/267–9100), one of Boston's oldest and most respected stores, offers a complete line of the finest jewelry, china, crystal, and silver.

OUTDOOR ACTIVITIES

The mania for physical fitness is big in Boston. Lots of people bicycle to work, and runners and roller skaters are seen constantly on the Storrow Memorial Drive Embankment, which flanks the Charles River. Most public recreational facilities, including swimming pools and tennis courts, are operated by the Metropolitan District Commission (MDC, tel. 617/727–5215).

BIKING Boston's flat terrain and well-marked bike paths are well suited for bicycling. The Dr. Paul Dudley White Bikeway, approximately 18 miles long, runs along both sides of the Charles River from Watertown Square to the Museum of Science. Free bike-route maps are available from the Boston Area Bicycle Coalition (Box 1015, Cambridge 02142, tel. 617/491–7433). Bikes may be rented at the Community Bike Shop (490 Tremont St., tel. 617/542–8623).

JOGGING A jog along the grassy shores of the winding Charles River, from the Hatch Shell on the Esplanade to the Harvard/JFK Street Bridge and then back again on the Cambridge side, is a popular 7- or 8-mile circular route for conditioned city joggers. For shorter trips, many hotels provide jogging maps for guests. Another excellent source of information is the Bill Rodgers Running Center (Faneuil Hall Marketplace, tel. 617/723–5612).

SWIMMING Two convenient and clean public swimming pools are located downtown: Lee Pool (tel. 617/523–9746), off Charles Street on the banks of the Charles River, and a city-operated pool (tel. 617/523–9746) off Commercial Street in the North End, which overlooks Boston Harbor and the USS *Constitution*. Both pools are open in July and August only.

TENNIS Charlesbank Park (Charles St.) is open from April to November and has lighted courts. Permits are issued at Lee Pool next door (tel. 617/523–9746).

WALKING The grandmother of all historical walks is the Freedom Trail, a 3¹/₂-mile walk that winds past 16 of Boston's most important historic attractions, including the Old State House, the Paul Revere House, and the USS *Constitution*. Its path is delineated by a red line marked on the sidewalk, beginning on Boston Common and ending in Charlestown. The 1¹/₂-mile self-guided Harborwalk traces Boston's maritime history. The 1.6-mile Black Heritage Trail explores the history of the city's 19th-century black community. The Women's History Trail celebrates notable contributions by Bostonian women. Maps for each of these four trails are available at the Boston Common Information Kiosk (146 Tremont, tel. 617/426–3115) and the National Park Service Visitor Center (15 State St., tel. 617/242–5642).

ENTERTAINMENT

Boston is a paradise for patrons of all the arts, from the symphony orchestra to experimental theater and dance to Orson Welles film festivals. Thursday's *Boston Globe* Calendar and the weekly *Boston Phoenix* provide comprehensive listings of events for the coming week. If you want to attend a specific performance, it would be wise to buy tickets when you make your hotel reservations. Bostix (Faneuil Hall Marketplace, tel. 617/723–5181) is Boston's largest official entertainment information center. Half-price, cash-only tickets are sold here for the same day's performances.

DANCE The Boston Ballet (tel. 617/695–6950 or 617/931–2000 for tickets) is the city's premier company, dancing at the Wang Center for the Performing Arts October through May. Dance Umbrella (tel. 617/492–7578) is one of New England's largest presenters of

contemporary dance; performances are scheduled throughout Boston and throughout the year.

FILM The Loews Nickelodeon Cinema (606 Commonwealth Ave., tel. 617/424–1500) presents first-run independent and foreign films as well as revivals. In Cambridge, try the Brattle Theater (40 Brattle St., tel. 617/876–6837), a restored landmark cinema, for classic movies.

MUSIC For its size, Boston is the most musical city in America. Of the many contributing factors, perhaps most significant is its abundance of universities and other institutions of learning, which are a rich source of performers, music series, performing spaces, and audiences. Boston's churches also offer outstanding, and often free, music programs; early music, choral groups, and chamber groups also thrive here. Check Saturday's *Boston Globe* for listings of musical events.

Classical. One of the world's most perfect acoustical settings, Symphony Hall (301 Massachusetts Ave., tel. 617/266–1492) is home to the Boston Symphony Orchestra September–April. On Wednesday evenings the orchestra has open rehearsals, and tickets for these evenings are less expensive and easier to obtain. From May through July, the Boston Pops take over Symphony Hall with their upbeat, lighter renditions of the classics.

Jazz. The Boston Jazz Line (tel. 617/787–9700) reports area jazz events. The Plaza Bar (Copley Plaza Hotel, Copley Sq., tel. 617/267–6495) is Boston's answer to New York's Oak Room at the Plaza Hotel. In Cambridge, Scullers (The Guest Quarters Suite Hotel, 400 Soldier's Field Rd., tel. 617/783–0811) has made a strong name for itself by hosting such well-known acts as Herb Pomeroy and the Victor Mendoza Quintet, and at the Regattabar (The Charles Hotel, Bennet and Eliot Sts., tel. 617/864–1200), top names perform in a spacious and elegant club.

THEATER Boston has long played the role of tryout town, a place where producers shape their productions before taking them to

Broadway. While many shows come to Boston this way, there is an equally strong tradition of local theater. Commercial theaters clustered in the Theater District include the Colonial (106 Boylston St., tel. 617/426–9306), the Shubert (265 Tremont St., tel. 617/426–4520), the Wang Center (270 Tremont St., tel. 617/482–9393), and the Wilbur (246 Tremont St., tel. 617/423–4008). Highly regarded smaller companies include the American Repertory Theatre (Loeb Drama Center, Harvard University, 64 Brattle St., tel. 617/495–2668); the Huntington Theatre Company (264 Huntington Ave., tel. 617/266–3913), affiliated with Boston University; and the Charles Playhouse (74 Warrenton St., tel. 617/426–5225), a local institution producing *Shear Madness;* and the Theater Lobby (216 Hanover St., tel. 617/227– 9872), which produces the long-running *Nunsense.*

SPECTATOR SPORTS Sports are as much a part of Boston as codfish and Democrats, and the zeal of Boston fans can be witnessed year-round. April through September, the Boston Red Sox (tel. 617/267–8661 or 617/267–1700 for tickets) play baseball at Fenway Park, accessible via the Kenmore stop on the Green Line. The Boston Celtics (tel. 617/523–3030 or 617/931–2000) shoot hoops on the parquet at Boston Garden on Causeway Street from November through April. The Boston Bruins (tel. 617/227–3223) are on the ice (under the Celtics' parkay) at Boston Garden, accessible via the North Station stop on the Orange and Green lines, from October through April. From September through December, the New England Patriots (tel. 800/543–1776) play football at Sullivan Stadium in Foxboro (best reached by car), 45 minutes south of the city.

Cape Cod
Massachusetts

The craggy peninsula called Cape Cod—jutting into the open Atlantic and separated from the Massachusetts mainland by the 17.4-mile Cape Cod Canal—offers the visitor both a ruggedly beautiful coast and well-preserved towns and farmscapes dating from Colonial times. Provincetown, with its bright, gay, muscular nightlife, is another story altogether.

The Cape is only about 70 miles from end to end and no more than 20 miles wide; you can make a cursory circuit of it in a day. Most visitors, however, prefer to settle into a hotel or bed-breakfast and wander no farther than the nearest beach or clam bar. Though overdevelopment has bred some ugly strip malls and tourist traps, much of the land is now permanently protected. Paved trails wander through nature preserves, protecting the natural beauty of the pine forests, marshes, swamps, and cranberry bogs. Thanks to the establishment of the Cape Cod National Sea-shore, one can walk for almost 30 miles along the dune-backed Atlantic beach virtually without seeing a trace of human habitation.

Through the creation of many national historical districts, similar protection has been extended to some of the area's oldest and loveliest settlements. Along tree-shaded country roads you'll see traditional saltboxes and Cape Cod–style cottages, their shingles weathered to a silvery gray, with soft pink roses spilling across them or massed over low, split-rail fences. You'll also pass many working windmills and white-steepled churches, taverns, and village greens that epitomize old New England. The onetime artists' colony of Provincetown—still alive with art, and the Cape's prime people-watching town—offers a cheerful, back-to-back mix of tiny waterfront shops.

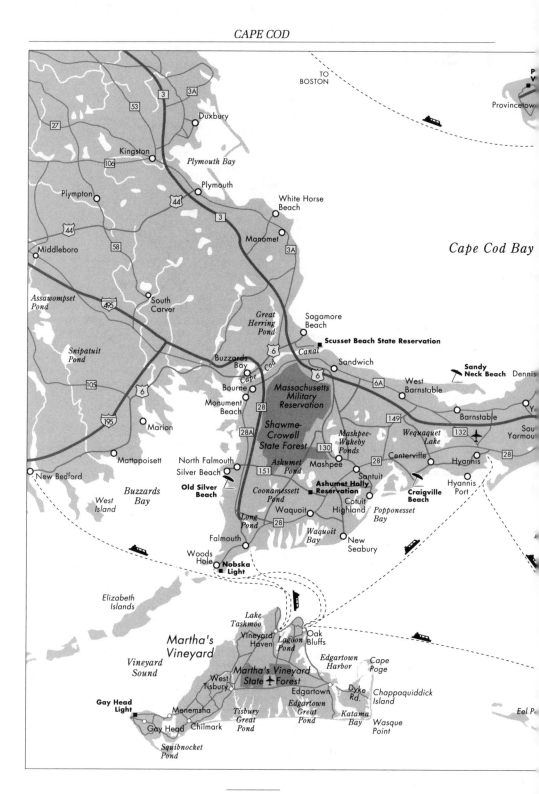

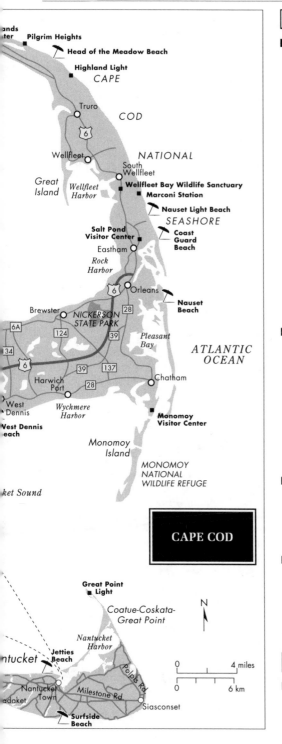

CAPE COD

ESSENTIAL INFORMATION

WHEN TO GO Cape Cod's climate is milder than the mainland's, with average minimum and maximum temperatures of 63°–78° in July and 25°–40° from December through February. Winter sometimes brings bone-chilling dampness and winds, but very little snow as a rule. Memorial Day through Labor Day (and in some cases through Columbus Day) is the high season, when the weather makes you think nothing but "beach" and everything is open; unfortunately, it is also a time of high prices, crowds, and traffic. In fall, the moorland turns rich autumn colors and the mild weather and thinned-out crowds make exploring a pleasure. Unpredictable spring arrives late. Though winter is a time when many activities and facilities shut down, romantic country inns offer cozy rooms with canopy beds and fireplaces at as much as 50% below summer rates.

BARGAINS Factory outlets are scattered throughout the Cape, a number of them along Rte. 28 east of Hyannis. The visitor centers of the Cape Cod National Seashore offer free slide shows, exhibits, and free or inexpensive nature-oriented programs and tours. Most of the historical museums throughout the Cape charge only nominal fees. In the off-season especially, many restaurants offer early-bird specials and weekend buffets.

TOURIST OFFICES Massachusetts Office of Travel & Tourism (100 Cambridge St., 13th floor, Boston 02202, tel. 617/727–3201). Cape Cod Chamber of Commerce (junction of Rtes. 6 and 132, Hyannis 02601, tel. 508/362– 3225).

EMERGENCIES **Police:** Dial 0 for an operator. **Fire** and **ambulance:** tel. 800/352– 7141. **Hospitals:** Cape Cod Hospital (27 Park St., Hyannis, tel. 508/771–1800). Falmouth Hospital (100 Ter Heun Dr., Falmouth, tel. 508/548–5300).

ARRIVING AND DEPARTING

BY PLANE Barnstable Municipal Airport (Rte. 28 rotary, Hyannis, tel. 508/775– 2020) is the Cape's main air gateway, with frequent flights to Martha's Vineyard and Nantucket islands. Provincetown Municipal Airport (Race Point Rd., tel. 508/487–0241) offers year-round scheduled flights to Boston, plus charters anywhere (regular charters from New York arrive on summer weekends). Both airports are only a few minutes from the town center. There are private airports in Falmouth, Marstons Mills, and Chatham.

BY CAR From Boston (60 miles), take Rte. 3, the Southeast Expressway, south to the Sagamore Bridge. From New York (220 miles), take I–95 north to Providence; change to I–195 and follow signs for the Cape to the Bourne or Sagamore bridges. At either bridge, take Rte. 6 to reach the central and eastern towns fast. At the Bourne Bridge, Rte. 28 leads south to Falmouth and Woods Hole.

BY TRAIN Amtrak (tel. 800/USA–RAIL) offers limited weekend service to the Cape; the rest of the year, there is connecting bus service from the Boston train station.

BY BUS Bonanza Bus Lines (tel. 508/548–7588 or 800/556–3815) serves the Cape from several East Coast cities, with connections from points beyond. Plymouth & Brockton Street Railway (tel. 508/775–5524 or 800/328–9997 in MA) has routes from Boston and Logan International Airport.

BY BOAT From Memorial Day into October, passenger ferries to Provincetown are operated by Bay State Cruise Company in Boston (tel. 617/723–7800 or 508/487–9284; 3 hours) and by Capt. John Cruises in Plymouth (tel. 508/747–2400 or 800/242–2469 in MA; 1½ hours).

GETTING AROUND

BY CAR AND RV For touring the Cape, a car is necessary; public transportation is very limited. Traffic in summer can be maddening, especially on Rte. 28 along the busy south shore and on Rte. 132 near Hyannis center. Rte. 6 is a limited-access highway running the entire length of the Cape through the sparsely populated center. During summer, Rte. 6 is often congested at the bridges with incoming traffic on Fridays and Saturdays and outgoing traffic on Sundays. On the north shore, the Old King's Highway, or Rte. 6A, is a scenic country road paralleling Rte. 6. When you're in no hurry, use the back roads.

BY BUS The Cape Cod Regional Transit Authority (tel. 800/352–7155) provides bus service between Hyannis and Woods Hole, with many stops, Mon.–Sat. Plymouth & Brockton Street Railway (tel. 508/775–5524) has service between Sagamore and Provincetown, with stops, and Bonanza Bus Lines (tel. 508/548–7588 or 800/556–3815) plies the route between Bourne, Falmouth, Woods Hole, and Hyannis.

BY BOAT The Steamship Authority (tel. 508/540–2022) runs car ferries to Martha's Vineyard out of Woods Hole (45 minutes) and to Nantucket out of Hyannis (2¼ hours) year-round. Hy-Line (tel. 508/778–2600) carries passengers only to both islands, May–October, out of Hyannis. Both lines offer interisland travel May–September.

REST STOPS The Herring Run visitor center, on Rte. 6 between the Bourne and Sagamore bridges, has rest rooms, a good view of the Cape Cod Canal, picnic tables, and access to the canal bike path. The Cape Cod National Seashore visitor centers have public rest rooms as well as picnic areas.

GUIDED TOURS Domenico Tours (751 Broadway, Bayonne, NJ 07002, tel. 800/554–8687) offers three- to five-day escorted tours (Apr.–Oct.), including visits to Hyannis, the National Seashore, Provincetown, and the islands. Hy-Line (Ocean St. Dock, Pier 1, tel. 508/778–2600) offers one-hour narrated tours of Hyannis Port Harbor. Cape Cod Scenic Railroad (Main and Center Sts., Hyannis, tel. 508/771–3788) runs 1¾-hour excursions between Sagamore and Hyannis, with stops at Sandwich and the Canal. In season, Cape Cod National Seashore (*see* Exploring, *below*) has guided walks, nature trips, self-guided trails, and more.

EXPLORING

Rte. 6A from Sandwich east (about 50 miles) is part of the Old King's Highway historic district. Among the charms of this tree-shaded country road are beautifully preserved saltboxes and Cape Cod–style cottages, a number of small museums, and fine crafts, book, and antiques shops. In fall, foliage along 6A is bright because of the many ponds and marshes, and in Sandwich you can watch the berries being harvested in flooded bogs. The Cape Cod National Seashore offers dramatic and unspoiled ocean vistas. For outdoors enthusiasts, the Cape offers walking, bicycling, and horseback-riding trails through diverse environments, as well as a number of nature preserves.

Sandwich is the oldest town on the Cape. A pleasant stroll through its center, a perfectly preserved old New England village just off Rte. 6A, offers the **Sandwich Glass Museum** and the **Thornton W. Burgess Museum,** dedicated to the children's-book author and his Old Briar Patch characters. At the center of it all is idyllic **Shawme Pond** and the waterwheel-operated **Dexter Gristmill.** *Glass museum: 129 Main St., tel. 508/888–0251; open Apr.–Oct., daily; Nov., Dec., Feb., and Mar., Wed.–Sun.; admission charged. Burgess museum: 4 Water St., tel. 508/888–4668; open daily (may close Sun. and/or Mon. Jan.–Mar.); donations accepted.*

Heritage Plantation, reached from Sandwich center via Grove Street, is a complex of museums devoted to classic cars, military memorabilia, Americana, and more, all set on 76 beautifully landscaped acres. Walking paths weave through the extensive daylily, herb, rhododendron, and other gardens. *Intersection of Grove and Pine Sts., tel. 508/888–3300. Open Mother's Day–Oct., daily. Admission charged.*

Sandy Neck Beach, farther east on 6A (take a left across from Michael's at Sandy Neck restaurant), is a 6-mile stretch of sand and dunes that makes for excellent beach walks, including a glimpse of a privately owned, nonoperational lighthouse.

Yarmouth Port, east of Barnstable Village on 6A, boasts impressive former captains' homes, some now bed-and-breakfasts; **Hallet's Store,** a still-operating country drugstore preserved as it was in 1889; and **Parnassus**

Bookshop, an old barn brimming with books. Behind the post office are the **Botanical Trails of the Historical Society of Old Yarmouth,** 50 acres of woodlands, a pond, an 1873 chapel, and marked trails with benches (small admission to trails). A left off 6A onto Centre Street (follow signs to Gray's Beach) leads to **Bass Hole Boardwalk,** over a marshy creek.

Dennis hosts the **Cape Museum of Fine Arts,** an exhibition gallery that hosts works by local and international artists, as well as lectures and avant-garde films at the nearby Reel Art Cinema. *Rte. 6A, on the grounds of the Playhouse, tel. 508/385–4477. Open daily. Admission charged for nonmembers.*

Brewster, farther east on 6A (past Dennis, whose back streets have a well-preserved Colonial charm) has a number of attractions scattered along 6A. Among them are the **Sydenstricker Glass,** a gallery and glass decoration facility; and the **New England Fire & History Museum.** *Sydenstricker Glass: tel. 508/385–3272; open mid-May–Oct., daily; Jan.–mid-May, Tues.–Sun. Fire and history museum: tel. 508/896– 5711; open mid-May–Labor Day, daily; Labor Day–Columbus Day, weekdays. Admission charged.*

Cape Cod Museum of Natural History offers nature and marine exhibits, as well as self-guided walking trails through 80 acres of forest, marshland, and ponds. *Rte. 6A, Brewster, tel. 508/896–3867. Museum open daily. Admission charged for museum; trails free.*

Hyannis, on the south shore's Rte. 28, is the busy commercial hub of the Cape, with a lively downtown and the John F. Kennedy Memorial, a quiet esplanade with a fountain pool overlooking boat-filled Lewis Bay. The John F. Kennedy Museum (Main St., tel. 508/775–2201; donations accepted) displays photographs, memorabilia, and historical documents from the Kennedy era. Nearby, in Hyannis Port, is the Kennedy family compound (closed to the public).

Chatham, east of Hyannis on Rte. 28, sits at the bent elbow of the Cape, with water on three sides. A traditional town, it boasts gray-shingled houses with tidy awnings and cheerful flower gardens, an attractive Main Street with crafts and antiques shops, and scenic walking and biking loops around coves and ponds. Chatham Light, a working lighthouse, offers a view of the harbor, the offshore sandbars, and the ocean beyond.

The Cape Cod National Seashore is a 30-mile stretch between Eastham and Provincetown that is protected from development. It includes spectacular beaches, dunes, and other habitats, making for excellent swimming, fishing, bicycling, horseback riding, bird-watching, and nature walks. The nine self-guided walking trails include the moderately difficult 1¼-mile Atlantic White Cedar Swamp Trail in Wellfleet and two easy ones in Truro—the ¾-mile Pilgrim Spring Trail (through wild woodland leading to the spring where a Pilgrim expedition once stopped) and the ½-mile Cranberry Bog Trail. Visitor information, slide shows, and many programs are centered at the **Salt Pond Visitor Center** (Rte. 6, Eastham, tel. 508/255–3421; open Mar.–Dec., daily; Jan.–Feb., weekends) and the **Province Lands Visitor Center** (Rte. 6, Provincetown, tel. 508/487–1256; open Apr.–Thanksgiving, daily).

Provincetown, at the farthest tip of the Cape, is reached via Rte. 6 East, past the fishing-and-art village of Wellfleet and Truro's Highland Light (Thoreau slept here), high atop an eroding cliff. A place of creativity and infinite diversity, Provincetown mixes Portuguese fishermen with painters, poets, writers, and tourists, many of whom come to enjoy the freedom of a town with a large, visible gay population. In summer, crowds throng the many art galleries, shops, restaurants, and night spots that line Commercial Street, the 3-mile main street. Get a good overview of it all from atop the **Pilgrim Monument,** a 252-foot granite tower with a museum of local history at its base. *Tel. 508/487–1310. Open Dec.–mid-Mar., weekends only; mid-Mar.–Nov., daily. Admission charged.*

Martha's Vineyard, an island off the south shore, has six towns, varying from the tidy, polished former whaling port of Edgartown, with its fashionable shops and well-pre-

served architecture; to Oak Bluffs, where 300 tiny cottages trimmed in Victorian gingerbread are gathered around the open-air tabernacle of the Methodist Camp Ground; to the sparsely developed towns of Chilmark and Gay Head, where scenic roads lead to the dramatically striated Gay Head Cliffs, high above the ocean.

Nantucket, once the whaling capital of the world, is a smaller island farther south than the Vineyard, giving it a more remote feeling. It is blessed with a remarkably preserved 17th- to 19th-century town, where cobblestone streets are lined with hundreds of weathered gray-shingled antique houses. Along with more than a dozen historical museums, the island offers the seaside village of Siasconset, where tiny cottages are dressed in masses of climbing pink roses. Several paved bike paths traverse the island, a third of which is open moorland and other protected conservation land. Like the Vineyard, Nantucket boasts excellent white-sand beaches and coastal scenery.

THE NATURAL WORLD   Whale-watch tours are offered from spring into fall. At the main center, Provincetown's MacMillan Wharf, Dolphin Fleet (tel. 508/255–3857 or 800/826–9300; Apr.–Oct.) and Portuguese Princess (tel. 508/255–3857) have tours narrated by scientists. From Barnstable Harbor, there's Hyannis Whale Watcher Cruises (Mill Way, tel. 508/362–6088 or 800/287–0374 in MA; Apr.–Nov.).

Monomoy National Wildlife Refuge (tel. 508/945–0594), two barrier-beach islands off Chatham, provide nesting and resting grounds for 285 bird species. White-tailed deer also live on Monomoy, and harbor seals frequent the shores in winter. Tours to the islands are offered by the **Cape Cod Museum of Natural History** (tel. 508/896–3867) and the **Massachusetts Audubon Society** (tel. 508/349–2615). The Audubon Society's 750-acre **Wellfleet Bay Wildlife Sanctuary** (off Rte. 6, South Wellfleet, tel. 508/349–2615) is a more accessible spot for bird-watching and offers evening bat watches.

HOTELS AND INNS

With a tourism-based economy, the Cape abounds in lodging choices. A number of appealing bed-and-breakfasts in old sea captains' houses are located along Rte. 6A from Sandwich to Brewster, as well as in Falmouth. Rte. 28, in the very commercial section between Hyannis and Orleans, has many motels in all price ranges. Price categories for double occupancy, excluding 9%–10% tax, are *Expensive,* $100–$150; *Moderate,* $75–$100; and *Inexpensive,* under $75. (B&Bs listed here have no TVs or phones in guest rooms.)

BREWSTER **Isaiah Clark House.** Colonial decor and homey antiques echo the flavor of this B&B's 18th-century main house, set on 5 acres of gardens, fruit trees, and a pond in a rural stretch of Rte. 6A; full breakfast is served. *1187 Rte. 6A, Box 169, 02631, tel. 508/896–2223 or 800/822–4001. 7 rooms. Turndown service, bikes, piano. AE, D, MC, V. No smoking in bedrooms. Inexpensive–Moderate.*

Old Sea Pines Inn. This B&B in a former girls' school features a broad front veranda, a spacious common room with fireplace, antiques-furnished guest rooms (many large, some with fireplace or enclosed sun porch, a few tiny and very cheap singles), full breakfasts, and afternoon tea in winter. *2553 Main St. (Rte. 6A), Box 1026, 02631, tel. 508/896–6114. 19 rooms, 2 suites. AE, DC, MC, V. Smoking discouraged. Inexpensive–Moderate.*

CHATHAM **Moses Nickerson House.** This inn, situated in an 1839 house, is characterized throughout by superb taste in decorating, a love of fine antiques, and warm, thoughtful service (including full breakfast and afternoon wine or tea). *364 Old Harbor Rd., 02633, tel. 508/945–5859 or 800/628–6972. 7 rooms (some with fireplaces). Turndown service. AE, MC, V. No smoking. Closed Jan. Moderate–Expensive.*

FALMOUTH **Coonamessett Inn.** Complemented by fine, gracious dining New England style (heart-healthy dish offered each night), suites are nicely decorated in bleached woods or pine with antique and reproduction furnishings and set in five Cape Cod–style buildings arranged around a landscaped lawn near a wooded pond. *Jones Rd. and Gifford St., Box 707, 02540, tel. 508/548–2300. 25 suites, 1 cottage. 2 restaurants, clothing shop. AE, DC, MC, V. Expensive.*

Capt. Tom Lawrence House. A prim white house with cupola, set back on a lawn shaded by old maple trees, this 1861 whaling captain's house is an intimate B&B (full breakfast) with rooms romantically decorated in antique and painted furniture, French country wallpapers, and queen canopy or king beds. *75 Locust St., 02540, tel. 508/540–1445. 6 rooms. MC, V. No smoking. Moderate.*

Village Green Inn. This B&B, set in a turreted Victorian facing the green, offers spacious guest rooms with antique beds, lovely wallpapers and hardwood floors, elaborate woodwork, and some working fireplaces, as well as full breakfasts. *40 W. Main St., 02540, tel. 508/548–5621. 4 rooms, 1 suite. AE, MC, V. No smoking. Closed Jan.– Mar. Moderate.*

HYANNIS AREA **Harbor Village.** Set in pine/woods by a swimming beach is this family-oriented community of Cape Cod–style cottages, most with a water view and all homey, nicely furnished, clean, and fully equipped, including fireplaces, barbecue grills, and decks. *Marstons Ave., Box 635, Hyannis Port 02647, tel. 508/775–7581. 20 units. Maid service, playground. No credit cards. Closed Nov.–Apr. Expensive.*

Inn on Sea Street. A charming, relaxed B&B a walk away from the beach and downtown, this 1849 Victorian home is furnished with country antiques and lacy fabrics and offers excellent breakfasts served with china, silver, and crystal. *358 Sea St., Hyannis 02601, tel. 508/775–8030. 6 rooms. AE, D, MC, V. Smoking discouraged. Closed mid-Nov.– Mar. Inexpensive–Moderate.*

PROVINCETOWN **The Masthead.** Unpretentious but cheerful seaside accommodations offer cooking facilities, cable TV, phones, air-conditioning, and decks, some overlooking the beach. *31–41 Commercial St., 02657, tel. 508/487–0523 or 800/395–5095. 8 rooms, 6 apartments, 3 efficiencies, 4 cottages. AE, D, DC, MC, V. Moderate–Expensive.*

Fairbanks Inn. Guest rooms in the 1776 main house and other buildings offer four-poster and canopy beds, antiques, and Oriental rugs on wide-board floors; some have TVs, fireplaces, or kitchens. *90 Bradford St., 02657, tel. 508/487–0386. 14 rooms, some with shared bath. Continental breakfast included, rooftop sun deck. AE, D, MC, V. Moderate.*

SANDWICH **Dan'l Webster Inn.** This large, traditional New England inn in the center of town has an excellent restaurant as well as guest rooms recently redecorated with reproduction furnishings—some with canopy beds, fireplaces, or whirlpools, and one with a baby grand piano. *149 Main St., 02563, tel. 508/888–3622 or 800/444–3566; fax 508/888–5156. 46 rooms and suites. Gift shop, pool, access to health club and golf club, room service, turndown service, air-conditioning, gift shop. AE, D, DC, MC, V. Moderate–Expensive.*

MOTELS

MODERATE **Captain's Quarters** (Rte. 6, Box Y, North Eastham 02651, tel. 508/255–5686 or 800/327–7769; fax 508/240–0280). 75 rooms; Continental breakfast included, pool, beach shuttle, bikes, tennis courts. **Hampton Inn Cape Cod** (1470 Rte. 132, Hyannis 02601, tel. 508/771–4804 or 800/999–4804; fax 508/790–2336). 104 rooms; Continental breakfast included, pool, saunas, fitness room. **Wellfleet Motel & Lodge** (Rte. 6, Box 606, South Wellfleet 02663, tel. 508/349–3535 or 800/852–2900). 65 rooms; breakfast room, bar, pool.

INEXPENSIVE **Handkerchief Shoals Motel** (Rte. 28, Box 306, South Harwich 02661, tel. 508/432–2200). 26 rooms; pool. **Sandy Neck Motel** (669 Rte. 6A, corner of Sandy Neck Rd., East Sandwich 02537, tel. 508/362–3992 or 800/564–3992 in MA). 11 rooms, 1 efficiency; minifridges.

CAMPGROUNDS

For a listing of the Cape's many private campgrounds, contact the Cape Cod Chamber of Commerce. No camping is permitted on the Cape Cod National Seashore itself.

Bourne Scenic Park. Sites are in a wooded area by the Bourne Bridge and the Cape Cod Canal. Amenities include a saltwater swimming pool and summer recreation programs. *Near Bourne Bridge underpass, north side of Canal (Scenic Hwy.), Bourne 02532, tel. 508/759–7873. 472 RV and tent sites, hookups ($20), no hookups ($18), showers, bathrooms, LP gas available, picnic tables and barbecue areas, store. No reservations. No credit cards.*

Nickerson State Park. The most popular site for those who like camping closest to nature, Nickerson is almost 2,000 wildlife-filled acres of white pine, hemlock, and spruce forest, dotted with opportunities for trout fishing, walking or biking along 8 miles of paved trail, canoeing, sailing, motorboating, and bird-watching. *Rte. 6A, Brewster 02631, tel. 508/896–3491. 418 RV and tent sites, no hookups ($13), showers, bathrooms, picnic tables and barbecue areas, store. No reservations. No credit cards.*

Scusset Beach State Reservation. The reservation is 450 acres near the canal, with a beach on the bay. Sites are behind dunes in an open area. Its pier is a popular fishing spot; other activities include biking, hiking, swimming, and hunting. *140 Scusset Beach Rd., off Rte. 3, Sandwich (Buzzards Bay 02532), tel. 508/888–0859. 104 RV and tent sites, hookups ($18), no hookups ($13), showers, bathrooms, picnic tables and barbecue areas. No reservations. No credit cards.*

DINING

The area offers a wide variety of fresh fish and shellfish. Each restaurant has its version of New England clam chowder, a milk- (sometimes cream-) based soup including chunks of potatoes and salt pork. Other area specialties are Wellfleet oysters and buttery-sweet bay scallops. A long history of Portuguese immigration accounts for the variety of Portuguese dishes encountered, such as kale soup or *linguiça* (a spicy sausage). Though most Cape restaurants serve traditional Yankee fare in casual settings, a few offer haute cuisine; virtually all will honor special dietary requests. Price categories per person, excluding 5% tax, service, and drinks, are *Moderate,* $15–$27, and *Inexpensive,* under $15.

BREWSTER **Brewster Fish House.** Traditional New England cuisine with a contemporary, light touch is the specialty of this small, intimate restaurant in the center of Brewster; besides salmon and swordfish, indulge in poached sole, lobster, and a variety of fresh-made chowders. The building, which falls into the "very old" category, used to be a carnation farm and fish market. *2208 Main St., Rte. 6A, tel. 508/896–7867. MC, V. Inexpensive–Moderate.*

DENNIS **Gina's by the Sea.** An intimate—and sometimes crowded—fireplace-warmed bistro by the bay, Gina's serves some of the tastiest northern Italian and seafood dishes in town. *134 Taunton Ave., tel. 508/385–3213. AE, MC, V. Moderate.*

HYANNIS **Baxter's Fish N' Chips.** On busy Lewis Bay, Baxter's serves possibly the best fried clams on the Cape, as well as other fried, baked, and broiled fresh fish and offerings from a summer raw bar. *Pleasant St., tel. 508/775–4490. MC, V. Moderate.*

Fazio's Trattoria. Drop in for excellent Italian fare—from soup to salad and pasta to pizza, the food is fresh and delicious—and the warm, cozy atmosphere, enhanced by Fazio's wood-burning brick oven. *586 Main St., tel. 508/771–7445. MC, V. Inexpensive.*

Up the Creek. This comfortable, casual spot offers a varied menu but specializes in seafood, including seafood strudel (pastry filled with lobster, shrimp, crab, cheese, and more) and excellent baked stuffed lobster. *36 Old Colony Rd., tel. 508/771–7866. AE, D, DC, MC, V. Inexpensive.*

MASHPEE **The Flume.** This clean, plain fish house, decorated only with a few Indian artifacts and crafts, offers a small menu of straightforward food, including outstanding chowder, fresh broiled fish, fried smelts and clams, and Indian pudding. *Lake Ave. (off Rte. 130), tel. 508/477–1456. MC, V. Inexpensive–Moderate.*

ORLEANS **Land Ho!** Decorated in a jumble of quarter boards and business signs, this landmark eatery with a lending rack of daily newspapers serves kale soup that has made *Gourmet* magazine, plus hearty sandwiches, grilled fish in summer, and very good chicken wings, chowder, and fish-and-chips. *Rte. 6A, tel. 508/255–5165. No reservations. MC, V. Inexpensive–Moderate.*

PROVINCETOWN **The Lobster Pot.** A wide selection of seafood (including two-pound-plus lobsters and full clambakes), award-winning chowder, and home-baked breads and desserts are the specialties at this family-operated, casual restaurant with a glass-walled dining room overlooking the water. *321 Commercial St., tel. 508/487–0842. AE, D, DC, MC, V. Moderate.*

The Moors. This unique restaurant, constructed of flotsam and jetsam found on Cape beaches and studded with nautical decor, specializes in seafood and Portuguese cuisine, such as kale, *chourico,* and linguiça soups; marinated swordfish steaks; and chicken with Madeira. *5 Bradford St. Ext., tel. 508/487–0840. AE, D, DC, MC, V. Moderate.*

SAGAMORE **The Bridge.** The Bridge specializes in Yankee pot roast, homemade pasta, and seafood dishes in a quiet setting by the Sagamore Bridge; a special heart-healthy menu is available. *Rte. 6A, tel. 508/888–8144. DC, MC, V. Inexpensive–Moderate.*

Sagamore Inn. Home-style Italian dishes like flawless eggplant Parmesan and rich chicken cacciatore, along with seafood specialties, are served in an old-Cape, family atmosphere. *Rte. 6A, tel. 508/888–9707. AE, MC, V. Inexpensive–Moderate.*

SANDWICH **Michael's at Sandy Neck.** Though the twin-lobster special ($10.95–$19.95) is the trademark of this relaxed restaurant, with a pubby dining room and a glassed-in porch, other seafood specialties include swordfish broiled, grilled, or blackened. *674 Rte. 6A, East Sandwich, tel. 508/362–4303. MC, V. Moderate.*

The Bee-Hive Tavern. Solid family dining in a cozy tavern is what the Bee-Hive is all about. The eclectic menu includes baked scrod, Cajun rib eye, lobster pie, tabbouli and hummus salads, and much more. *406 Rte. 6A, tel. 508/833–1184. MC, V. Inexpensive.*

YARMOUTH PORT **Jack's Outback.** This quirky place where customers get their own coffee serves good American home cooking, such as pot roast and mashed potatoes with gravy, superb soups, and simple but exceptional desserts. *161 Main St., tel. 508/362–6690. No credit cards. Inexpensive.*

SHOPPING

Crafts—from exquisite blown glass to earthy pottery and homespun country creations—are a specialty of this area, along with antiques and art. Shoppers can look for antique and new examples of scrimshaw—the art of etching finely detailed designs of sailing ships and sea creatures onto whalebone or teeth (today, a synthetic substitute).

SHOPPING DISTRICTS Provincetown is an important art center, boasting a number of internationally recognized artists. Wellfleet is a vibrant center for more local art and crafts. Route 6A from Sandwich to Brewster has many crafts, antiques, and antiquarian book shops; it also abounds in gift shops.

Hyannis's Main Street is the Cape's largest, including souvenir-type shops, ice-cream and candy stores, and miniature golf places. Chatham's Main Street is more genteel, with more upscale merchandise in art and crafts galleries and antiques and clothing stores.

MALLS AND OUTLETS The Cape Cod Mall (between Rtes. 132 and 28, Hyannis, tel. 508/771–0200) includes Woolworth's, Jordan Marsh, Sears, and Filene's among its 90 shops and a food court. Falmouth Mall (Rte. 28, Falmouth, tel. 508/540–8329) has Bradlees, Sears, T. J. Maxx, and 30 other shops. Cape Cod Factory Outlet Mall (Factory Outlet Rd., Exit 1 off Rte. 6, Sagamore, tel. 508/888–8417) has more than 20 outlets, including Corning/Revere, Carter's, Gitano, and Bass Shoe. The Factory Shoe Mart (Rte. 28, Dennis Port, tel. 508/398–6000; Rte. 28 at Deer Crossing, Mashpee, tel. 508/477–0017) carries all the brand names.

FLEA MARKETS AND FARM STANDS The Wellfleet Drive-In Theatre (Rte. 6, Eastham–Wellfleet line, tel. 508/349–2520) is the site of a giant flea market (weekends in spring; Wed., Thurs., and weekends July–fall). Fancy's Farm Stands (199 Main St., Orleans, tel. 508/255–1949) and The Cornfield (Rte. 28, West Chatham, tel. 508/945–1949; 2660 Main St., Brewster, tel. 508/896–8141) sell local and exotic produce, fresh-baked breads and pastries, and more.

OUTDOOR ACTIVITIES

BEACHES Swimming is possible from about mid-June sometimes into October at more than 150 ocean and freshwater beaches. Those on the bay are generally colder than Nantucket Sound beaches, on the south shore. Dune-backed ocean beaches on the National Seashore are cold and often have serious surf, but they are also the most beautiful; all have lifeguards, showers, and rest rooms. Old Silver Beach in North Falmouth has a sandbar that keeps it shallow at one end. Sandy Neck Beach in West Barnstable is a beautiful 6-mile barrier beach between the bay and the marshland.

BIKING The premier bike path is the easy-to-moderate 20-mile Cape Cod Rail Trail; between Dennis and Eastham, it passes salt marshes, cranberry bogs, ponds, and Nickerson State Park in Brewster, with 8 miles of its own trails through forest. On either side of the Cape Cod Canal is an easy, straight 6- to 8-mile trail overlooking the bridges and canal traffic. The Shining Sea bike path is an easy 3½-mile route between Falmouth and Woods

Hole that dips into woods as it skirts the coast. The Cape Cod National Seashore maintains three bike trails: a $1^3/_5$-miler through apple and locust groves to Coast Guard Beach in Eastham; an easy, 2-mile route amid dunes and marshes to Head of the Meadow Beach in Truro; and a $5^1/_4$-mile more strenuous loop in the Province Lands through dunes, woods, and marshes, with a picnic grove en route. For bike rentals, contact: Rail Trail Bike Rentals (Brewster, tel. 508/896–2361), Idle Times Bike Shop (Brewster, tel. 508/896–9242), or P & M Cycles (Buzzards Bay, near Cape Cod Canal, tel. 508/759–2830).

FISHING A license is needed to fish in the hundreds of freshwater ponds and is available at tackle shops, such as the Goose Hummock Shop (Rte. 6A, Orleans, tel. 508/255–0455) or Cape Cod Rod & Reel (210 Barnstable Rd., Hyannis, tel. 508/775–7543). There's good angling for blues, bass, and more along the canal; deep-sea fishing boats operate out of Hyannis, Falmouth, Provincetown, and elsewhere.

GOLF Over 45 courses dot the Cape and islands, including the championship layouts at New Seabury (Shore Dr., Mashpee, tel. 508/477–9110) and Ocean Edge (1 Villagers Rd., Rte. 6A, Brewster, tel. 508/896–5911).

HIKING/WALKING The Cape Cod National Seashore has nine self-guided trails (*see* Exploring, *above*). Lifecourse (Access and Old Bass River Rds., South Dennis) is a $1^1/_2$-mile jogging trail through woods with 20 exercise stations. Bike trails also make good walking trails, but watch your back!

ENTERTAINMENT

CONCERTS The Cape Cod Melody Tent (West Main St., Hyannis, tel. 508/775–9100) presents top names in summer concerts (country, jazz, rock) and comedy. Traditional band concerts are held in most towns throughout the summer; Chatham's are the most famous (Fridays at 8 PM), with dancing and sing-alongs.

DINNER SHOWS AND THEATER The top summer-stock venues are the Cape Playhouse (off Rte. 6A, Dennis, tel. 508/385–3911 or 508/385–3838) and the Falmouth Playhouse (off Rte. 151, North Falmouth, tel. 508/564–4546). The Barnstable Comedy Club (Main St., tel. 508/362–6333), contrary to its moniker, presents a wide range of music and drama.

Charleston
South Carolina

ate in the 20th century, Charleston, South Carolina, still resembles an 18th-century etching come to life—its low-profile skyline punctuated by the spires and steeples of nearly 200 churches. Parts of the historic district seem frozen in time: Block after block of old buildings have been restored for residential or commercial use. After three centuries of epidemics, earthquakes, fires, and floods, Charleston prevails and is today one of the nation's best-preserved historic cities.

Along the Battery (pronounced BAH-try in Charlestonese), on the point of the narrow peninsula bounded by the Ashley and Cooper rivers, handsome mansions surrounded by gardens face the harbor. Built with high ceilings and large rooms opening onto broad piazzas to catch sea breezes, their distinctive style is reflective of the West Indies. Before settling in the Carolinas in the late 17th century, many British colonists first went to Barbados and other Caribbean islands and learned to build houses suitable for that warm and humid climate.

Each year, from mid-March to mid-April, many private homes and gardens are opened to visitors. Then in late May to early June, the city's vibrant cultural life finds its greatest expression in the renowned Spoleto Festival USA and Piccolo Spoleto, when hundreds of local and international artists, musicians, and other performers fill the city's streets and buildings with sound and spectacle.

ESSENTIAL INFORMATION

WHEN TO GO In spring, riots of azaleas, daffodils, wisteria, and Carolina jessamine light the old city with an ethereal glow—Charleston's loveliest time. Summer days may be warm and humid, but even then, evening breezes make the temperature bearable, and brightly hued oleanders, cannas, and crape myrtle bloom in abundance. Autumn days are often clear and sparkling, and roses may

last into December. Expect chilly days and some rain—rarely snow—in winter. Then, too, many lodgings and restaurants offer attractively priced package plans.

BARGAINS The Citadel Corps of Cadets Dress Parade, held at the famed military college's Summerall Field every Friday at 3:45 PM, is open to the public. Also free is admission to the Citadel's Memorial Military Museum. Free concerts—a variety of jazz, classical, and folk music—are often held Sunday afternoon between 4 and 5 PM during the academic year in Hampton Park, located on Rutledge Avenue near the Citadel.

TOURIST OFFICES South Carolina Division of Tourism (Box 71, Columbia 29202, tel. 803/734–0235). Charleston Trident Convention and Visitors Bureau (Box 975, Charleston 29402, tel. 803/853–8000). You can pick up free maps and information at the Visitor Information Center (375 Meeting St., Charleston 29401, tel. 803/724–7474).

EMERGENCIES Fire, police, and rescue squad: Dial 911. Hospitals: Charleston Memorial Hospital (326 Calhoun St., tel. 803/577–0600) and Roper Hospital (316 Calhoun St., tel. 803/724–2000) have emergency rooms that are open all night.

ARRIVING AND DEPARTING

BY PLANE Charleston International Airport, in North Charleston, on I–26, 12 miles west of downtown Charleston, is served by Delta, United, and USAir. Taxi fare into town costs $12–$14.

BY CAR I–26 traverses the state from northwest to southeast and terminates at Charleston. North–south coastal route U.S. 17 passes through Charleston.

BY TRAIN Amtrak's (tel. 800/USA–RAIL) trains between New York and Florida stop at Charleston.

BY BUS Greyhound Lines (3610 Dorchester Rd., tel. 800/231–2222) connects Charleston with cities throughout the country.

GETTING AROUND

BY CAR A car is the most practical means of visiting outlying attractions. Within the compact historic district, it's advisable to park and explore on foot, by bicycle, or on a carriage tour.

BY BUS There's city-wide bus service (tel. 803/745–7928, fare 75¢) and the Downtown Area Shuttle (DASH; tel. 803/724–7368), trolley-style vehicles that provide fast service downtown and through the historic district on weekdays (fare 75¢; all-day pass, $1).

BY TAXI Cabs must be ordered by phone from Everready Cab Company (tel. 803/722–8383), Yellow Cab (tel. 803/577–6565), or Safety Cab (tel. 803/722–4066).

REST STOPS There are public rest rooms in the visitor center and in all museums.

GUIDED TOURS Nonstop harbor tours are offered aboard the *Charlestowne Princess* by Gray Line Water Tours (tel. 803/722–1112 or 800/344–4433). Fort Sumter Tours (tel. 803/722–1691) includes a stop at Fort Sumter in its harbor tour. Motorcoach tours are run by Gray Line (tel. 803/722–4444), Adventure Sightseeing (tel. 803/762–0088), Carolina Lowcountry Tours (tel. 803/797–1045 or 800/621–7996), and Doin' The Charleston Tours, Inc. (tel. 803/763–1233 or 800/627–4487). Carriage tours through the historic district are available from Charleston Carriage Company (tel. 803/577–0042), Old South Carriage Tours (tel. 803/723–9712), and Palmetto Carriage Works (tel. 803/723–8145). Historic Charleston Walking Tours (tel. 803/722–6460) and Charleston Strolls (tel. 803/766–2080) offer guided walking tours of the historic district. The Charleston Tea Party Walking Tour (tel. 803/577–5896) includes tea in a private garden. Unique Tours, Inc. (tel. 803/724–3421) offers 90-minute ghost tours of some of Charleston's most prominent haunted dwellings.

EXPLORING

If you're fascinated by history and architecture, you should plan at least three days for in-depth sightseeing of Charleston's house museums and churches, which are concentrated in the historic district. Nature lovers will want to save a day or so for exploring some of the city's outlying gardens.

For a good overview of the historic district, start at the Visitor Information Center (where you can park your car) to see *Forever Charleston,* a 24-minute slide and voice show of images and sounds of Charleston. *Tel. 803/724–7474. Open daily except Thanksgiving, Christmas and New Year's. Admission charged.*

Next, cross the street to visit **The Charleston Museum,** at the corner of John Street, the nation's oldest city museum, now housed in a $6 million contemporary complex. Founded in 1773, it's one of the South's major cultural repositories and is especially strong on South Carolina decorative arts. *360 Meeting St., tel. 803/722–2996. Open daily. Admission charged.*

You next come to the **Joseph Manigault House,** an outstanding example of Adam-style architecture. A National Historic Landmark, it was designed by Charleston architect Gabriel Manigault in 1803 and is noted for its carved wood mantels, elaborate plasterwork, and the curving cantilever staircase that graces the entrance hall. *350 Meeting St., tel. 803/722–2926. Open daily. Admission charged.*

You should now get your car from the visitor center and drive south along Meeting Street to explore the market area. En route, you can turn right on Hasell Street, where you'll spot **Congregation Beth Eloim,** the birthplace in 1824 of American Reform Judaism. It is the second-oldest synagogue in the United States and is considered one of the nation's finest examples of Greek Revival architecture. *90 Hasell St., tel. 803/723–1090. Open weekdays. Admission free.*

Follow King Street one block south to Market Street, where you can park in one of the area's garages. **Market Hall,** built in 1841 and modeled after the Temple of Nike in Athens, is the site of the **Confederate Museum.** Operated since 1898 by the Daughters of the Confederacy, it displays flags, uniforms, swords, and other memorabilia. *Temporarily located at 34 Pitt St., tel. 803/723–1541. Open weekends noon–5 PM. Admission charged.*

The Old City Market, between Market Hall and East Bay Street, is a series of low sheds that once housed colorful produce and fish markets. There are still vegetable and fruit vendors (who may protest vigorously if you attempt to photograph them), but there are now also restaurants and shops.

Omni Hotel at Charleston Place (130 Market St.), the city's only world-class hotel, is worth a visit for tea or Sunday brunch even if you're not staying there.

Gibbes Museum of Art, 1¹/₂ blocks south on Meeting Street, has notable collections of American art, including 18th- and 19th-century portraits of Carolinians. Don't miss the intricately detailed miniature rooms. *135 Meeting St., tel. 803/722–2706. Open daily except holidays. Admission charged.*

Circular Congregational Church, across the street from the Gibbes, is most unusual in design. Legend says its corners were rounded off so the devil would have no place to hide. *150 Meeting St., tel. 803/577–6400. Call for hours.*

Old Powder Magazine is around the corner on one of Charleston's few remaining cobblestone thoroughfares. Built in 1713 and used as a powder storehouse during the Revolutionary War, it's now a museum with costumes, furniture, armor, and other artifacts from 18th-century Charleston. *79 Cumberland St., tel. 803/722–3767. Open weekdays. Admission charged.*

St. Philip's Episcopal Church, about half a block south on Church Street, was established in 1670 as the Mother Church of the Province. The present building was constructed from 1835 to 1838. Its churchyard includes graves of statesman John C. Calhoun; DuBose Heyward, author of *Porgy*; and other notable South Carolinians. *146 Church St., tel. 803/722–7734. Call for hours.*

The Dock Street Theatre, across Queen Street, was built on the site of one of the nation's first playhouses. It combines the reconstructed early Georgian theater and the preserved Old Planter's Hotel (circa 1809). *135 Church St., tel. 803/723–5648. Open weekdays. Admission charged.*

The French Huguenot Church, across the street, is one of the nation's few remaining Huguenot churches. Services are conducted in a blend of French and English. *110 Church St., tel. 803/722–4385. Open weekdays. Donations accepted.*

The Four Corners of the Law, at the intersection of Meeting and Broad streets, has structures representing federal, state, city, and religious jurisdiction. The County Court House, U.S. Post Office and Federal Court, and City Hall (*see* Bargains, *above*) occupy three corners, and **St. Michael's Episcopal Church,** the fourth. Modeled after London's St. Martin's-in-the-Fields and completed in 1761, this is Charleston's oldest surviving church. *Broad and Meeting Sts., tel. 803/723–0603. Open Mon.–Sat.*

Walk east along Broad Street for one block, and turn south on Church Street. Near the end of the block, the **Heyward-Washington House,** built in 1772, was where George Washington stayed during his 1791 visit. It's notable for fine furnishings by such local craftsmen as cabinetmaker Thomas Elfe. *87 Church St., tel. 803/722–0354. Open daily. Admission charged.*

Walk south on Church Street to the end of the block, then west one block on Tradd Street and a half-block south on Meeting Street. **The Nathaniel Russell House,** built in 1808 and headquarters of The Historic Charleston Foundation, is one of the nation's finest Adam-style structures. Its interior is notable for ornate detailing, lavish period furnishings, and a "flying" staircase that spirals three stories with no apparent support. *51 Meeting St., tel. 803/723–1623. Open daily. Admission charged.*

After touring the historic district, drive 2 miles east on U.S. 17, over the Cooper River

Bridge, to Mount Pleasant. **Patriots Point Naval and Maritime Museum** is the world's largest facility of its kind. Berthed there are the aircraft carrier *Yorktown,* nuclear merchant ship *Savannah,* World War II submarine *Clamagore,* cutter *Ingham,* and destroyer *Laffey. Charleston Harbor, tel. 803/884–2727 or 800/327–5723. Open daily. Admission charged.*

Fort Sumter National Monument, on a manmade island in the harbor, was the site of the first shot fired in the Civil War. On April 12, 1861, Confederate forces at Fort Johnson opened fire on Sumter's Union troops, who surrendered after a 34-hour bombardment, leaving the fort in Confederate hands for nearly four years. National Park Service rangers conduct tours of the restored fort, which was a heap of rubble by the war's end. *Tel. 803/722–1691. Open daily. Admission free.*

West of the Ashley River via Rte. 171, 3 miles from town, is **Charles Towne Landing State Park** at the site of the original 1670 Charleston settlement. There's a reconstructed village and fortifications, and you can walk or bicycle through extensive English gardens, rent kayaks to explore the park's waterways, or take a tram tour. *1500 Old Towne Rd., tel. 803/556–4450. Open daily, except Dec. 24 and 25. Admission charged.*

Drive west of Charleston on the Ashley River Road (Rte. 61) to visit several historic mansions and gardens. **Drayton Hall,** 9 miles west of Charleston, was built between 1738 and 1742 and was owned by members of the Drayton family for seven generations. A National Historic Landmark, it is considered the nation's finest example of Georgian Palladian architecture. The only Ashley River plantation house to survive the Civil War intact, it has been left unfurnished to highlight its unusual ornamental details. *Ashley River Rd., tel. 803/766–0188. Open daily except holidays. Admission charged.*

At **Magnolia Plantation and Gardens,** a mile or so farther north, the informal gardens begun in 1686 have one of the continent's largest collections of azaleas and camellias. Tours of the manor house reflect plantation life. Nature lovers may canoe through a waterfowl refuge or walk or bicycle on wildlife trails in the garden's 500 acres. *Ashley River Rd., tel. 803/571–1266. Open daily. Admission charged.*

Middleton Place, 4 miles farther north, has the oldest landscaped gardens in the United States (they date from 1741). Much of the mansion was destroyed in the Civil War, but the restored south wing houses impressive collections of silver, furniture, and paintings. In the stableyard, a living outdoor museum, authentically costumed craftspeople demonstrate spinning, blacksmithing, and other plantation-era domestic skills. *Ashley River Rd., tel. 803/556–6020 or 800/782–3608. Open daily. Admission charged.*

Cypress Gardens, last but not least, lies about 24 miles north of Charleston via U.S. 52. On boat tours or waterside trails, you can explore swamp gardens vibrant with azalea, camellia, daffodil, wisteria, and dogwood blossoms. Peak season is usually late March into April. *U.S. 52, tel. 803/553–0515. Open daily except Thanksgiving and Christmas. Admission charged.*

THE NATURAL WORLD Francis Marion National Forest, about 40 miles north of Charleston via U.S. 52, comprises 250,000 acres of swamps, oak and pine trees, and little lakes thought to have been formed by meteors. It's an excellent spot for hiking, picnicking, camping, boating, and swimming. At the park's Rembert Dennis Wildlife Center (off U.S. 52 in Bonneau), deer, wild turkey, and striped bass are raised and studied.

HOTELS AND INNS

Rates tend to increase during the Spring Festival of Houses and Gardens and the Spoleto Festival USA, when reservations are essential. During Visitors' Appreciation Days, from mid-November to mid-February, discounts as high as 50% may apply. Lodgings in surrounding areas are usually cheaper than those on the peninsula. For a Courtesy Discount Card, write to the Charleston Trident Convention and Visitors Bureau (Box 975,

Charleston 29402, tel. 803/853–8000). Price categories for double occupancy, without 5% tax, are *Expensive,* $90–$120; *Moderate,* $51–$89; and *Inexpensive,* $50 and under.

EXPENSIVE **Battery Carriage House.** One of Charleston's earliest inns, this renovated 1845 mansion hosts 10 carriage-house units and overlooks the Battery and West Point Gardens. Rooms are handsomely furnished with period antiques, and evening turndown service is offered with chocolate and brandy. *20 S. Battery St., 29401, tel. 803/727–3100 or 800/775–5575. 10 rooms. Continental breakfast included. AE, D, DC, MC, V.*

Indigo Inn. All rooms here, elegantly furnished with 18th-century antiques and reproductions, focus on a picturesque interior courtyard, and there are eight slightly more expensive suites and rooms in nearby Jasmine House, a pre–Civil War Greek Revival building. *1 Maiden La., 29401, tel. 803/577–5900 or 800/845–7639. 40 rooms. Afternoon refreshments, Continental breakfast, concierge. AE, MC, V.*

The Meeting Street Inn. Rooms in this handsome 1870 house are furnished with reproduction four-poster beds, and all open onto a piazza. *173 Meeting St., 29401, tel. 803/723–1882 or 800/842–8022. 54 rooms. Whirlpool, lobby bar, suite for meetings. AE, DC, MC, V.*

Sheraton Charleston Hotel. Some of the spacious rooms and suites in this 13-story hotel outside the historic district overlook the Ashley River, and decor is highlighted by Queen Anne reproductions. *170 Lockwood Dr., 29403, tel. 803/723–3000 or 800/325–3535. 337 rooms. Dining room, cocktail lounge with dancing and live entertainment, pool, concierge, tennis courts, free parking. AE, D, DC, MC, V.*

Vendue Inn. Near the waterfront, this European-style inn in a renovated 1828 warehouse offers antiques-furnished public areas and guest rooms, along with deluxe suites in adjacent Vendue West, a restored 1800 house. Continental breakfast included. *19 Vendue Range, 29401, tel. 803/577–7970 or 800/845–7900. 34 rooms. Dining room, bar, concierge, parking. AE, D, MC, V.*

MODERATE **Comfort Inn Riverview.** This modern 7-story motor inn has some rooms overlooking the Ashley River. Continental breakfast included. *144 Bee St., 29401, tel. 803/577–2224 or 800/221–2222. 128 rooms, 2 with kitchenettes and whirlpools. Pool, fitness center, free parking. AE, D, DC, MC, V.*

Quality Inn Heart of Charleston. Spacious, cheerful rooms are decorated in the Charleston tradition, with 18th- and 19th-century reproductions. *125 Calhoun St., 29401, tel. 803/722–3391 or 800/228–5151. 126 rooms, some with balconies, 4 suites with wet bar. Restaurant, lounge, pool, coin laundry. AE, D, DC, MC, V.*

INEXPENSIVE-MODERATE **Days Inn Historic District.** This conveniently located economy inn is attractively furnished. *155 Meeting St., 29401, tel. 803/722–8411 or 800/325–2525. 124 rooms, 2 with refrigerators. Dining room, cocktail lounge, pool, garage. AE, D, DC, MC, V.*

Howard Johnson Riverfront. Overlooking a scenic stretch of the Ashley River, this inn near downtown is adjacent to the Citadel and has rooms with private balconies. Morning coffee is included. *250 Spring St., 29403, tel. 803/722–4000 or 800/654–2000. 152 rooms. Dining room, cocktail lounge, pool. AE, D, DC, MC. V.*

MOTELS

MODERATE **Best Western Inn** (1540 Savannah Hwy., 29407, tel. 803/571–6100 or 800/528–1234). 87 rooms; Continental breakfast, pool, wading pool. **Hampton Inn Riverview** (11 Ashley Pointe Dr., 29407, tel. 803/556– 5200 or 800/426–7866). 176 rooms, 3 with refrigerators; Continental breakfast, pool, tennis, golf, fishing, and marina. **Holiday Inn Riverview** (301 Savannah Hwy., 29407, tel. 803/556–7100 or 800/465–4329). 181 rooms with balconies; dining room, cocktail lounge, pool, exercise room, coin laundry. **Shem Creek Inn** (1401 Shrimp Boat La., 29464, tel. 803/881–1000 or 800/523–4951).

50 rooms with balconies; Continental breakfast, near beaches and downtown. **Quality Suites** (5525 N. Arco La., North Charleston 29418, tel. 803/747–7300 or 800/221–2222). 168 rooms, 13 with whirlpools; complimentary beverages, VCRs and microwaves, cocktail lounge, pool with gazebo, sauna, exercise room. **Town and Country Inn** (2008 Savannah Hwy., 29407, tel. 803/571–1000 or 800/334–6660). 130 rooms, 20 with kitchenettes; restaurant, piano bar, sports bar, indoor and outdoor pools, spa, sauna, fitness center with racquetball courts.

INEXPENSIVE **Airport Travelodge** (4620 Dorchester Rd., 29405, tel. 803/747–7500 or 800/255–3050). 104 rooms; Continental breakfast, small pool, coin laundry, VCR rentals. **Best Western Dorchester Motor Lodge** (I–26 and Dorchester Rd., 29405, tel. 803/747–0961 or 800/528–1234). 199 rooms; dining room, coffee shop, cocktail lounge, live entertainment, pool, coin laundry. **Best Western Naval Center** (2070 McMillan St., 29405, tel. 803/554–1600 or 800/528–1234). 97 rooms, some with whirlpools; outdoor pool, coin laundry. **Comfort Inn Airport** (5055 N. Arco La., North Charleston 29418, tel. 803/554–6485 or 800/221–2222). 122 rooms, 20 with whirlpools; pool, whirlpool, sauna, exercise room, coin laundry. **Cricket Inn** (7415 Northside Dr., North Charleston 29420, tel. 803/572–6677 or 800/872–1808). 121 rooms, 2 with kitchenettes; small pool. **Days Inn–Patriot's Point** (261 Hwy. No. 17 Bypass, Mount Pleasant 29464, tel. 803/881–1800 or 800/325–2525). 131 rooms; coffee shop, pool, pets accepted. **Econo-Lodge** (4725 Arco La., North Charleston, 29405, tel. 803/747–3672). 89 rooms; Continental breakfast, pool. **Hampton Inn** (4701 Arco La., North Charleston 29418, tel. 803/554–7154 or 800/426–7866). 125 rooms; Continental breakfast, pool, airport transportation. **La Quinta Motor Inn** (2499 La Quinta La., North Charleston 29418, tel. 803/797–8181 or 800/531–5900). 122 rooms; pool. **Masters Economy Inn** (6100 Rivers Ave., North Charleston 29418, tel. 803/744–3530 or 800/633–3434). 150 rooms, 26 with kitchenettes; pool, coin laundry.

DINING

Fresh seafood is abundant in and around Charleston, and there's Continental and American cuisine to please the most sophisticated palate. She-crab soup originated in the low country, and it's not to be missed. Neither are benne (sesame-seed) wafers, along with such coastal specialties as sautéed shrimp and grits. During peak times (mid-March–early June), reservations should be made for dinner. Price categories per person, not including 5% tax, service, and drinks, are *Moderate,* $20–$30, and *Inexpensive,* under $15.

MODERATE **Barbadoes Room.** Step through the Barbadoes's distinctive arches for an elegant dining experience. Seafood and low-country cuisine share the bill of fare in this large, airy, plant-filled enclave reminiscent of the Caribbean. *Mills House Hotel, Queen and Meeting Sts., tel. 803/577–2400. AE, DC, MC, V.*

Carolina's. Charleston's "Big City" bistro, this chic dining room is decorated in shades of black lacquer, white, and peach. You'll enjoy creative modern Carolina cuisine, including grilled seafood and beef. *10 Exchange St., tel. 803/724–3800. AE, MC, V.*

East Bay Trading Company. Coastal seafood, lamb, Carolina quail, and international specialties are showcased on three dramatic antiques-adorned levels around an atrium in this former warehouse. *161 E. Bay St., tel. 803/722–0722. AE, MC, V.*

82 Queen. The 82 Queen—occupying unique, pink stucco buildings that date from the 18th century—was recently voted the best restaurant in Charleston by locals; don't skip town without trying such low-country favorites as the first-rate crab cakes. *82 Queen St., tel. 803/723–7591. AE, MC, V.*

The Moultrie Tavern. Try early southern specialties at this converted 1833 brick warehouse filled with artifacts and art from the Civil War era. *18 Vendue Range, tel. 803/723–1862. AE, MC, V.*

Queen Street Seafood Inn. Feast on grouper fillet grilled with lemon butter; snapper Legare sautéed with capers, shallots, and freshly squeezed lemon juice; and other low-country specialties in intimate rooms decorated with Victorian furnishings. *68 Queen St., tel. 803/723–7700. AE, DC, MC, V.*

MODERATE-INEXPENSIVE **Shem Creek Bar & Grill.** This pleasant dockside spot is perennially popular for its oyster bar and wide variety of seafood entrées, including a steam pot big enough for two, with lobsters, clams, and oysters with melted lemon butter or hot cocktail sauce. *508 Mill St., Mount Pleasant, tel. 803/884–8102. AE, MC, V.*

INEXPENSIVE **Athens.** Baby squid in lemon, moussaka, pasticcio, spinach pie, and other delights rival those served in Greece's top tavernas, and the bouzouki music is straight from the *Plaka* in Athens. *325 Folly Rd., Cross Creek Shopping Center, James Island, tel. 803/795–0957. AE, MC, V.*

A.W. Shucks. The atmosphere at Shucks is friendly and casual—the perfect environment for lingering over fresh seafood or a plate of beef, chicken or pasta. *35 Market St., tel. 803/723–1151. AE, D, MC, V.*

California Dreaming. Crowds come to this high-volume eatery in a stone fort on the Ashley River for terrific views of the harbor and bountiful platters of barbecued chicken and the catch of the day. *1 Ashley Pointe Dr., tel. 803/766–1644. AE, MC, V.*

Colony House. Low-country specialties here include baked pompano and she-crab soup, presented with friendly service in the handsome ambience of a restored 1830 warehouse. (Some entrées are Moderate.) *35 Prioleau St., tel. 803/723–3424. AE, MC, V.*

Magnolias. In this 1828 warehouse with a circular bar and magnolia theme, innovative low-country, Creole, and southwestern food—mahimahi fillet with crabmeat, and cheese ravioli with seafood and dill—is served to discerning locals. *185 E. Bay St., tel. 803/577– 7771. AE, MC, V.*

SHOPPING

Visit the Old City Market at East Bay and Market streets for interesting, varied shopping. Next to the colorful produce market is the open-air flea market with crafts, antiques, and memorabilia. Here (and at stands along U.S. 17, near Mount Pleasant) women weave distinctive baskets of straw, sweet grass, and palmetto fronds. A portion of the Old City Market has been converted into a complex of specialty shops and restaurants. Other complexes are Rainbow Market (in two connected 150-year-old buildings), Market Square, and State Street Market. There are many antiques shops along King Street. Historic Charleston Reproductions (105 Broad St., tel. 803/723–8292) sells superb replicas of Charleston furniture and accessories, as does the Thomas Elfe Workshop (54 Queen St., tel. 803/722–2130).

OUTDOOR ACTIVITIES

BIKING The historic district is level and compact, ideal for biking, and many city parks have trails, as does Palmetto Islands County Park. You can rent bikes at The Bicycle Shop (tel. 803/722–8168) and Carolina Carriage Company (tel. 803/723–8687), which also rents tandems.

FISHING Fresh- and saltwater fishing is excellent along 90 miles of coastline. Surf fishing is permitted on many beaches, including Palmetto Islands County Park's.

GOLF Public courses include Charleston Municipal (tel. 803/795–6517), Patriots Point (tel. 803/881–0042), and Shadowmoss (tel. 803/556– 8251). The Charleston Trident Convention and Visitors Bureau has a list of area courses, including those at private resorts where the public may play when space permits.

SWIMMING People swim from April through October. Public beaches are at Beachwater Park on Kiawah Island; Sullivan's Island; Folly Beach County Park and Folly Beach, on Folly Island.

TENNIS At Farmfield Tennis Courts (tel. 803/724–7402) and Shadowmoss (tel. 803/556–8251), courts are open to the public.

WALKING AND JOGGING Walking is the locomotion of choice all over the Historic District. Jogging paths wind through Palmetto Islands County Park, and Hampton Park has a fitness trail.

ENTERTAINMENT

CONCERTS The Charleston Symphony Orchestra (tel. 803/723–9693) presents its Classics Concerts Series at Gaillard Municipal Auditorium (77 Calhoun St., tel. 803/577–4500).

DANCE The Charleston Ballet Theatre (tel. 803/723–7334) and the Charleston Civic Ballet (tel. 803/722–8779) perform at Gaillard Municipal Auditorium.

THEATER In residence in Charleston's historic Dock Theater (135 Church St.) is the theater company AMAZINGSTAGE (tel. 803/577–5967), presenting a variety of stage productions for all ages.

SPECTATOR SPORTS The Charleston Rainbows, the San Diego Padres' minor-league team, play at College Park Stadium (701 Rutledge Ave., tel. 803/724– 7241).

Chicago
Illinois

hicago has everything for city lovers: culture, commerce, historic buildings, public transportation, ethnic neighborhoods, chic boutiques—and grit and grime. Masterpieces of skyscraper architecture embrace the curving shore of Lake Michigan, creating one of the most spectacular skylines in the world. An elegant system of boulevards and parks—much of it the worse for urban blight—encircles the central city. Except for a few bullet holes in the masonry around the Biograph Theater (where John Dillinger was shot), few traces remain of the disreputable 1920s gangster period that made Chicago, Illinois, famous around the world; the Biograph itself is now run by the Cineplex Odeon chain.

Home to the blues and the Chicago Symphony, to storefront theaters and the Lyric Opera, to neighborhood murals and the Art Institute, Chicago has come a long way in shedding its rough-and-tumble image as "city of the big shoulders," immortalized in the writings of Theodore Dreiser, Upton Sinclair, and Carl Sandburg. The infamous stockyards have long been closed, the steel mills to the south lie largely idle, and Chicago has become, for better or worse, a hub of finance second only to New York. But Chicagoans remain friendly in the midwestern manner: helpful and generally lacking in pretense.

Long and thin (in many spots less than 10 miles wide), Chicago proper hugs the shore of Lake Michigan. Many of the major attractions are clustered within a mile of the lakefront, either in the Loop (defined by the tracks of the elevated train) or near the Loop, in the Near North Side.

ESSENTIAL INFORMATION

WHEN TO GO Chicago promises activities and attractions to keep any visitor busy at any time of year. Travelers whose principal concern is to have comfortable weather for touring the city may prefer spring or fall, when

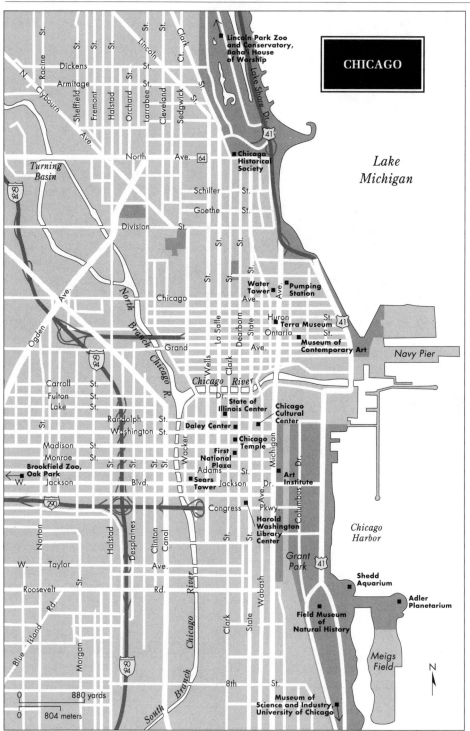

CHICAGO

Turning
Basin

Lake
Michigan

Lincoln Park Zoo
and Conservatory,
Baha'i House
of Worship

Dickens
Armitage
North   Ave.

Chicago
Historical
Society

Schiller   St.

Goethe   St.

Division   St.

Chicago

Water
Tower
Ave.

Pumping
Station

Huron   St.
Terra Museum
Ontario   St.

Museum of
Contemporary Art

Navy Pier

Grand

Ave.

Chicago River

State of
Illinois Center

Chicago
Cultural
Center

Carroll   St.
Fulton   St.
Lake   St.

Randolph   St.
Washington   St.

Daley Center

Chicago
Temple

First
National
Plaza

Madison   St.
Monroe   St.

Brookfield Zoo,
Oak Park
W.   Jackson   Blvd.

Adams   St.
Sears
Tower   Jackson   Dr.

Art
Institute

Congress   Pkwy.

Harold
Washington
Library
Center

Chicago
Harbor

Grant
Park

W.   Taylor

Roosevelt   Rd.

Shedd
Aquarium

Adler
Planetarium

Field Museum
of
Natural History

Meigs
Field

8th   St.

N

Museum of
Science and Industry,
University of Chicago

0   880 yards

0   804 meters

moderate temperatures can make it a pleasure to be out and about, and the city's cultural institutions are well into their seasons.

Summertime brings many opportunities for outdoor recreation. Yet the temperatures will climb to the 90s in hot spells, and the humidity can be uncomfortably high. In more temperate times, the presence of Lake Michigan has a moderating effect on the city's weather, keeping it several degrees cooler in summer, a bit warmer in winter.

Those winters can see very raw weather and occasionally the news-making blizzard, and temperatures in the teens (or even in the single or negative digits in December and January) are to be expected; wintertime visitors should come prepared for the cold. There are January sales to reward those who venture out, and many indoor venues let one look out on the cold in warm comfort.

BARGAINS Most museums offer free admission one day a week: the Art Institute and the Museum of Contemporary Art are free on Tuesdays; the Chicago Academy of Sciences and the Chicago Historical Society, Mondays; and the Field Museum of Natural History and the John G. Shedd Aquarium, Thursdays. The Oriental Institute is free every day.

The Reader (a free weekly newspaper available at many stores and restaurants) lists times and locations for the free choral programs, recitals, and other performances given at area churches and music schools. The University of Chicago Concert Office (tel. 312/702–8068), the American Conservatory of Music (tel. 312/263–4161), and Chicago Musical College of Roosevelt University (tel. 312/341–3780) also host free programs. The Chicago Cultural Center (78 E. Washington St., tel. 312/346–3278) has free concerts Wednesdays at 12:15 PM and various other noontime programs throughout the week.

Spiegel (1105 W. 35th St., tel. 312/254–0091) and Sears (5555 S. Archer Ave., tel. 312/284–3200) both operate warehouse stores on the city's South Side that sometimes offer fabulous bargains to sharp-eyed shoppers—but don't expect elegant surroundings or helpful salespeople. Lands' End (2241 N. Elston Ave., tel. 312/276–2232; 2317 N. Elston Ave., tel. 312/384–4710), the Wisconsin mail-order firm, has two outlet stores in Chicago.

TOURIST OFFICES The Chicago Office of Tourism (Historic Water Tower in the Park, 806 N. Michigan Ave., Chicago 60611, tel. 312/280–5740) maintains two walk-in centers, one at the Pumping Station (163 E. Pearson St.) and the other at the Chicago Cultural Center (Randolph St. at Michigan Ave.).

EMERGENCIES **Police, fire,** and **ambulance:** Dial 911. **Hospitals:** Northwestern Memorial Hospital (Superior St. at Fairbanks Ct., Near North, tel. 312/908–2000). Rush Presbyterian St. Luke's Medical Center (1753 W. Congress Pkwy., near the Loop, tel. 312/942–5000). **Pharmacies:** Walgreen's (757 N. Michigan Ave., tel. 312/664–8686) is open 24 hours.

ARRIVING AND DEPARTING

BY PLANE All major airlines serve O'Hare International Airport (tel. 312/686–2200), 20 miles northwest of downtown Chicago; Midway Airlines, Delta, Northwest, Southwest, and USAir serve smaller, less congested Midway Airport (tel. 312/767–0500), 7 miles from downtown on the southwest side.

Between the Airports and Hotels. Metered taxi service is available from both airports to Near North and downtown; expect to pay $28–$32 plus 15% tip for the 20- to 30-minute ride (which can stretch to more than an hour during rush hours) from O'Hare and $12–$15 plus tip for the 20- to 30-minute ride from Midway. Don't accept any offers of "limo service"; these services are unregulated and may cost you more than a licensed cab. Continental Airport Express (tel. 312/454–7799) operates minivans from both airports to major Near North and downtown hotels; one-way fares are $13 from O'Hare and $9.50 from Midway. The Chicago Transit Authority's rapid-transit station at O'Hare is in the underground concourse near terminal 2; the fare is $1.50. The first downtown stop is at Washington and Dearborn streets; from there you can take a taxi to your hotel or change to other rapid-transit lines. The CTA is best avoided late at night. A new rapid-transit line to Midway Airport was scheduled to open in mid-1993, with stops around the Loop elevated line. The stops closest to most downtown hotels are along Wabash Avenue at Randolph, Madison, and Adams streets.

BY CAR The main arteries through Chicago are I–90/94 (from the north and the south) and I–55 (from the southwest). Coming from the south, I–94 branches off I–80 south of the city and merges with I–90 to become the Dan Ryan Expressway. Coming from the north, I–90 merges with I–94 at Montrose Avenue, about 3 miles south of the city's northern border, to become the John F. Kennedy Expressway.

BY TRAIN Amtrak (tel. 800/USA–RAIL) offers service to Union Station (Jackson and Canal Sts., tel. 312/558–1075).

BY BUS Greyhound Lines (tel. 800/231–2222) has nationwide service to its main terminal (630 W. Harrison St.). Indian Trails (tel. 312/928–8606) also serves this terminal from Indiana and Michigan. This station is not within easy walking distance of anywhere you're likely to be staying, so be prepared to take a cab.

GETTING AROUND

Chicago's planners followed a grid pattern in laying out the city's streets. Madison Street is the baseline for streets and avenues that run north–south; Michigan Avenue (for example) is North Michigan Avenue above Madison Street, South Michigan Avenue below it. House numbers start at 1 at the baseline and climb in each direction, generally by 100 a block. Thus the Fine Arts building at 410 South Michigan Avenue is four blocks south of Madison Street. Each increment of 800 in any direction is about a mile, so it's easy to calculate how far you have to walk between locations. Even-numbered addresses are on the west side of the street, odd numbers on the east side.

For streets that run east–west, State Street is the baseline; 18th Street (for example) is East 18th Street east of State Street and West 18th Street west of State Street. House numbers start at 1 at the baseline and rise in each direction, east and west. Even-numbered addresses are on the north side of the street, odd numbers on the south side.

BY CAR It's best to leave your car behind for most city-based excursions and use Chicago's extensive network of buses and rapid transit. Street parking is difficult or impossible downtown and only a little better in the neighborhoods; "permit parking" has taken over some of the more affluent residential areas, making it illegal for nonresidents to park on side streets. Parking lots and garages charge $5.50–$15 a day.

A car is convenient if you plan to visit the outlying neighborhoods or suburbs. The following Interstate highways lead to the suburbs: I–94 for the North Shore and the south suburbs, I–90 for northwest, I–290 for western, and I–55 or I–57 for the southwest.

BY BUS, SUBWAY, AND EL TRAIN Buses travel all major arteries, both north–south and east–west, stopping only at posted bus stops (usually every other corner). The standard CTA fare is $1.50 for buses 6–9 AM and 3–6 PM (nonrush-hour bus fare is $1.25) and for mass-transit trains (known as the El); dollar bills are accepted. You can buy a roll of 10 tokens good for buses or the El for $12.50 at currency exchanges and Jewel and Dominick's supermarkets. A transfer costs 30¢, and you must buy it when you board the first bus or train. Bus and El information and maps are available by writing to the CTA (Merchandise Mart, 60654) or by calling the RTA Information Center (tel. 312/836–7000).

BY TAXI Chicago taxis are metered and charge $1.20 for the first $^1/_5$ of a mile, 20¢ for each $^1/_6$ of a mile thereafter, and 50¢ for each additional passenger between the ages of 12 and 65. Drivers expect a 15% tip. A short hop from the Near North to the Loop costs $4–$7, including tip. Keep in mind that city cabs can drop passengers off in the suburbs but can't pick them up there. The principal taxi companies are Yellow Cab Company and Checker Cab Company (both at tel. 312/829–4222),

American United Cab Company (tel. 312/248–7600), and Flash Cabs (tel. 312/561–1444).

REST STOPS North Michigan Avenue's three vertical malls have rest rooms: Water Tower Place (835 N. Michigan Ave.), Chicago Place (700 N. Michigan Ave.), and the 900 North Michigan Avenue building. Downtown you can find public rest rooms at the Harold Washington Library Center (State and Van Buren Sts.), Marshall Field (111 N. State St.), Carson Pirie Scott (1 S. State St.), and the Chicago Cultural Center (78 E. Washington St.). In Lincoln Park there are rest rooms at the zoo (2200 N. Cannon Dr.), the Chicago Historical Society (Clark St. and North Ave.), and North Avenue Beach.

GUIDED TOURS **Orientation:** Chicago Motor Coach Company (tel. 312/337–1446) operates double-decker tour buses that give one-hour narrated tours of Chicago landmarks ($7 adults, $5 senior citizens). Climb on at the Sears Tower (Jackson Blvd. at Wacker Dr.), Orchestra Hall (220 S. Michigan Ave.), the Field Museum (E. Lake Shore Dr. at Roosevelt Rd.) or the Water Tower (Michigan Ave. at Pearson St.). Wendella Sightseeing Boats (400 N. Michigan Ave., tel. 312/337–1446) ply the Chicago River and Lake Michigan May–September, leaving from the north side of the Michigan Avenue Bridge. The cost of the guided tour is $7–$11 adults, $5–$7 children. Mercury Skyline Cruises (tel. 312/332–1353), offering similar tours and prices, leave from the south side of the bridge.

Special-Interest: The Chicago Architecture Foundation gives walking tours of the Loop and several other historic neighborhoods. Tour times vary and prices are $5–$10 per person depending on the tour. For information, call the CAF Tour Center (224 S. Michigan Ave., tel. 312/922–8687). The Tour Center also has maps and self-guided tours, as well as architecture-related books and gifts.

EXPLORING

With careful planning, you can hit Chicago's high points in three or four days—but it would take weeks to exhaust all of the city's possibilities. Architecture buffs should be sure to tour the Loop, Hyde Park, and the suburb of Oak Park. Shoppers will want to stop in at Marshall Field & Co.'s State Street flagship store—past its prime but still one of the world's great department stores—and cruise the swanky shops on North Michigan Avenue. For a great view of the city's skyline, go to Navy Pier at the east end of Grand Street (600 E. Grand St.), or to the tree-lined promenade of Olive Park, which extends north into the lake at the same place.

The Art Institute has one of the world's most renowned collections of French Impressionism, as well as outstanding Medieval and Renaissance works and fine holdings in Asian art and photography. If you're interested in architecture, don't miss the reconstruction of the trading room from Louis Sullivan's Chicago Stock Exchange Building, demolished in the 1960s. *Michigan Ave. at Adams St., tel. 312/443–3600. Open daily. Admission charged Wed.–Mon., free Tues.*

Baha'i House of Worship (100 Linden Ave., Wilmette, tel. 708/273–3838), the national headquarters of the Baha'i faith, is an elegant, nine-sided building that incorporates a wealth of architectural styles and religious symbols. To get there, take Lake Shore Drive north to its end, then follow the signs for Sheridan Road. You'll cross the Chicago city limits and drive through Evanston to reach Wilmette.

Brookfield Zoo. The animals here inhabit natural settings, including a rain forest, a rocky seascape for seals and sea lions, and a marsh. The daily dolphin shows are perennial favorites. To reach the zoo, take I–290 (Dwight D. Eisenhower Expressway) west to First Avenue and follow the signs. *8400 W. 31st St., Brookfield, tel. 708/485–0263. Open daily. Admission charged Wed.–Mon., free Tues. (parking fee).*

Chicago Historical Society has permanent and changing exhibits on Chicago's past, plus a long-running exhibit on the roots of the Civil War. *Clark St. at North Ave., tel.*

312/642–4600. Open daily. Admission charged Tues.–Sun., free Mon.

Occupying the same peninsula just south of the Loop is **The Field Museum of Natural History,** with displays of dinosaur bones, minerals and gems, and Indian artifacts; the **Adler Planetarium,** with a sky show; and the **Shedd Aquarium,** which recently unveiled an "oceanarium" housing several whales. *Field Museum: Lake Shore Dr. at Roosevelt Rd., tel. 312/922–9410. Open daily. Admission charged. Planetarium: 1300 Lake Shore Dr., tel. 312/322–0304. Open daily. Admission free; admission charged for sky show. Aquarium: 1200 S. Lake Shore Dr., tel. 312/939–2426. Open daily. Admission charged.*

Lincoln Park Zoo and Conservatory offer the best fauna and flora to be found within the city limits. The zoo includes a "koala condo," a seal pool, a rookery, a new big-cat house, and a Farm-in-the-Zoo. The conservatory has permanent exhibits of many exotic plants as well as seasonal flower shows. Lincoln Park itself, which stretches between 1600 and 5600 North along the lakefront, has rolling lawns, beaches, statuary, tennis courts, and a golf course. *Zoo: 2200 N. Cannon Dr., tel. 312/294–4660. Conservatory: 2400 N. Stockton Dr., tel. 312/294–4770. Open daily. Admission free to both.*

The Museum of Contemporary Art, started by a group of art patrons who found the Art Institute unresponsive to modern work, concentrates on 20th-century art, principally after 1940. *237 E. Ontario St., tel. 312/280–5161. Open Tues.–Sun. Admission charged Wed.–Mon., free Tues.*

The Museum of Science and Industry is a massive structure dating from the 1893 World's Fair. Among the many exhibits are a 1,200-foot-long model of the Santa Fe Railroad, a German U-boat captured during World War II, a coal mine, and an Omnimax theater. Visit during the week if you can—the museum tends to be crowded on weekends. *57th St. at Lake Shore Dr., tel. 312/684–1414. Open daily. Admission charged.*

Oak Park, a suburb of Chicago, contains the largest collection of Wright-designed buildings in the world, including the Frank Lloyd Wright Home and Studio. Also in Oak Park is Wright's poured-concrete Unity Temple (875 Lake St., tel. 708/383–8873), built in 1905 for a Unitarian congregation on a budget. Take I–290 (Eisenhower Expressway) to Harlem Avenue. Turn right and drive north on Harlem to Chicago Avenue. Then turn right and drive three blocks to Forest Avenue. *Frank Lloyd Wright Home and Studio: 951 Chicago Ave., Oak Park, tel. 708/848–1500. Open daily. Admission charged.*

Outdoor sculptures by famous artists are scattered throughout the Loop. Look for the Picasso at the Daley Center (Washington and Dearborn Sts.), the Miro at the plaza of the Chicago Temple (77 W. Washington St.), Claes Oldenburg's giant baseball bat at 600 West Madison Street, a Chagall mosaic at First National Plaza (Monroe and Dearborn Sts.), a Dubuffet outside the State of Illinois Center (Randolph and Clark Sts.), and a Calder stabile at 230 South Dearborn Street. There's also a Calder mobile in the lobby of the Sears Tower (233 S. Wacker Dr.).

River North, bordered on the south by the Chicago River, on the north by Chicago Avenue, on the east by Clark Street, and on the west by Sedgwick Avenue, has more than 70 small art galleries offering all manner of specialties from furniture to fantasy. Galleries can be found at 750 North Orleans Street at Chicago Avenue, 301 West Superior Street at Franklin Street, and 311 West Superior Street at Orleans Street. Many galleries are closed on Sundays or Mondays. For current exhibits, pick up the *Chicago Gallery News* at a Tourist Information Center (*see* Tourist Offices, *above*). Most galleries have openings the first Friday evening of every month, and gallery-hopping is customary and free. Small shops and restaurants abound here as well.

Terra Museum contains Ambassador Daniel Terra's private collection of American art. The intimate galleries include pieces by Andrew Wyeth, Edward Hopper, John Singer Sargent, Winslow Homer, and Mary Cassatt.

666 N. Michigan Ave., tel. 312/664–3939. Open Tues.–Sun. Admission charged.

University of Chicago, located off the still-visible Midway of the 1893 Columbian Exposition in Hyde Park, is home to two museums: the David and Alfred Smart Museum of Art, with exhibits of Renaissance through modern art, and the Oriental Institute, which specializes in the ancient Near East. The Gothic campus is a pleasant place to stroll, and there are several excellent bookstores in the neighborhood, including Powell's (1501 E. 57th St., tel. 312/955–7780) for used books, 57th St. Books (1301 E. 57th St., tel. 312/684–1300), and the Seminary Cooperative Bookstore (5757 S. University Ave., tel. 312/752–4381). *Smart Museum: 5550 S. Greenwood Ave., tel. 312/702–0200. Open Tues.–Sun. Admission free. Oriental Institute: 1155 E. 58th St., tel. 312/702–9521. Open Tues.–Sun. Admission free.*

HOTELS AND INNS

Most travelers to Chicago will want to stay on the Near North Side or in the Loop, near many of the major cultural institutions, shopping areas, and architectural masterpieces. Accommodations are cheaper near O'Hare Airport, where there are lots of hotels and motels, but it's drab, and the trip into town can take up to an hour at peak traffic times or in bad weather. Most city hotels have special weekend rates; be sure to inquire when making reservations. Auto club or AARP members may also qualify for discounts. Loop hotels generally cost slightly less than those in the Near North, but the neighborhood can get a little creepy late at night. The streets are livelier on the Near North Side, and there's a better assortment of restaurants and night spots.

Chicago hosts some of the world's largest conventions; it's nearly impossible to get a hotel room at any price during one of these gargantuan gatherings, and bargain rates are suspended. Some hotels charge $5–$10 more per night from April to October. Price categories for double occupancy, without 12.4% tax and service charges, are *Expensive,* $150–

$200; *Moderate,* $100–$150; and *Inexpensive,* under $100.

LOOP **Blackstone.** The ornate lobby gives a clue to what this grand hotel once was; if it ever gets the renovation it sorely needs, the prices will skyrocket. For now, you get basic accommodations (there's no room service) in a great location. *636 S. Michigan Ave., 60605, tel. 312/427–4300 or 800/622–6330, fax 312/427–4300. 305 rooms, 25 suites. Restaurant, lounge, jazz club, access to health club, theater, valet parking. AE, D, DC, MC, V. Moderate.*

Congress. A recent renovation has spruced up the rooms at this large, turn-of-the-century hotel, which was apparently built in pieces, with some sections grand and distinctive and others more modern and characterless. The location, however, is excellent. *520 S. Michigan Ave., 60605, tel. 312/427–3800 or 800/635–1666, fax 312/427–4840. 818 rooms. 4 restaurants, 2 lounges with live entertainment, access to nearby health clubs. AE, DC, MC, V. Moderate.*

Essex Inn. This pleasantly decorated modern building just south of the "best" stretch of South Michigan Avenue is a good place for large groups. Although not glamorous, the hotel is nicely situated opposite Grant Park. *800 S. Michigan Ave., 60605, tel. 312/939–2800 or 800/621–6909, fax 312/939–1605. 255 rooms. Restaurant, lounge with live entertainment, outdoor heated pool, free shuttle bus to North Michigan Ave. AE, D, DC, MC, V. Inexpensive.*

Grant Park Hotel. Taken over and completely refurbished by Best Western, the Grant Park is near the museums at the south end of the park. *1100 S. Michigan Ave., 60605, tel. 312/922–2900 or 800/528–1234, fax 312/922–8812. 172 rooms. Restaurant, outdoor pool, exercise room and sauna, on-site parking for a fee. AE, D, DC, MC, V. Moderate.*

NEAR N./RIVER N./LINCOLN **Forum Hotel Chicago.** If you want to splurge, this refurbished '60s-vintage hotel is in a superb spot, midway between Michigan Avenue shopping and Loop cultural attractions. Some of the spacious rooms have excellent lake views, and for a nominal fee, guests have access to the lavish health club and 1920s rococo swimming pool of the luxury Hotel Inter-Continental next door. *525 N. Michigan Ave., 60611, tel. 312/944–0055 or 800/332–4246, fax 312/944–1320. 517 rooms, 6 suites. 2 restaurants, lounge, 24-hr room service, concierge. AE, D, DC, MC, V. Moderate–Expensive.*

Claridge Hotel. Intimate rather than bustling, this '30s-vintage hotel in the Gold Coast north of the Michigan Avenue shopping district was tastefully renovated several years ago. Four floors are designated for nonsmokers. *1244 N. Dearborn Pkwy., 60610, tel. 312/787–4980 or 800/245–1258, fax 312/266–0978. 173 rooms, 3 suites. Continental breakfast included, restaurant, bar, access to nearby health club, valet parking, concierge, limousine service. AE, D, DC, MC, V. Moderate.*

Comfort Inn of Lincoln Park. At the northern edge of Lincoln Park, this basic but comfortable establishment is removed from the Loop and the Near North Side but is convenient to the lakefront neighborhoods of Lincoln Park and Lakeview. *601 W. Diversey Pkwy., 60614, tel. 312/348–2810 or 800/787–0800, fax 312/348–1912. 74 rooms. Continental breakfast included, free parking. AE, D, DC, MC, V. Inexpensive.*

Inn of Chicago. An excellent location, simple but attractive rooms, and a 24-hour restaurant make the inn a very good value—except during conventions, when the rates increase. *162 E. Ohio St., 60611, tel. 312/787–3100 or 800/528–1234, fax 312/787–8236. 357 rooms, 26 suites. Restaurant, lounge, access to nearby health club, valet laundry, valet parking. AE, D, DC, MC, V. Moderate.*

Lenox House. The Lenox is composed of one-bedroom suites and living room–style "studio" suites with Murphy beds. The hotel does not have parking, but there are several city lots nearby. *616 N. Rush St., 60611, tel. 312/337–1000 or 800/445–3669, fax 312/337–7217. 325 suites. Restaurant, bar, wet-bar kitchens, concierge. AE, D, DC, MC, V. Moderate.*

Raphael. European-style multilingual service, tastefully furnished rooms with refrigerators, and a '30s-vintage building make the Raphael a very classy hotel at a reasonable price. *201 E. Delaware Pl., 60611, tel. 312/943–5000 or 800/821–5343, fax 312/943–9483. 172 rooms. Restaurant, lounge, health-club access, valet parking. AE, D, DC, MC, V. Moderate.*

Richmont. Comfortable but not luxurious, this renovated hotel matches good facilities with reasonable prices (weekend packages are an even better bargain). Be sure to dine in the hotel's delightful bistro, the Rue St. Clair. *162 E. Ontario St., 60611, tel. 312/787–3580 or 800/621–8055, fax 312/787–1299. 193 rooms, 26 suites. Continental breakfast included, restaurant (15% dinner discount for guests), bar with live jazz, access to nearby health club, valet service, valet parking for a fee. AE, D, DC, MC, V. Moderate.*

River North Hotel. This recently renovated, pleasant, modern hotel is one of the few in the River North gallery district, and it's a bit less expensive than comparably equipped hotels along the Michigan Avenue "main drag." *125 W. Ohio St., 60610, tel. 312/467–0800 or 800/727–0800, fax 312/467–1665. 148 rooms, 58 suites. Restaurant, lounge, indoor pool and health club, valet, concierge, free parking. AE, D, DC, MC, V. Moderate.*

DINING

Once a steak-and-potatoes town, in the last decade Chicago has blossomed into a food lover's haven. Steaks, ribs, Italian beef, and the ubiquitous Vienna Hot Dog have been augmented by many excellent French and Italian restaurants, plus a variety of more exotic cuisines from Middle Eastern to Thai and Vietnamese. Most of the establishments below are in the Near North, River North, and Loop areas, within walking distance of the major hotel districts, with a few out in the city's residential neighborhoods and ethnic enclaves.

Ethnic restaurants are everywhere in Chicago. Try Greektown (Halsted and Madison

Sts.), Chinatown (Wentworth Ave. and 23rd St.), and Little Italy (Taylor St. between Racine Ave. and Ashland Ave.). Chinese and Vietnamese restaurants can be found on Argyle Street between Broadway and Sheridan Road, Indian restaurants line Devon Avenue between 2200 West and 3000 West, and Thai, Japanese, Chinese, Korean, Jamaican, and Ethiopian restaurants fill Clark Street from Belmont Avenue to Addison Street.

Price categories per person not including 8.5% tax, service, and drinks, are *Expensive,* over $30; *Moderate,* $18–$30; and *Inexpensive,* under $18.

LOOP/GREEKTOWN/CHINATOWN **The Berghoff.** Traditional German food, lighter lunches, and house-label light and dark beer are the hallmarks of this Loop institution, whose cavernous, wood-paneled dining room serves a large business lunch crowd with dispatch. *17 W. Adams St., tel. 312/427–3170. AE, DC, MC, V. Closed Sun. Moderate.*

Courtyards of Plaka. This sophisticated Greektown restaurant offers standard as well as less familiar Greek dishes, plus whole sea bass, shellfish, and broiled pork chops. Live music and white tablecloths make it the most upscale spot in the area. *340 S. Halsted St., tel. 312/263–0767. AE, D, DC, MC, V. Moderate.*

Emperor's Choice. This sophisticated but comfortable restaurant demonstrates that Chinese seafood can go well beyond plates of shrimp and vegetables; the house specialties—octopus, squid, tuna, and shellfish cooked in a variety of ways—are fresh and expertly prepared. *2238 S. Wentworth Ave., tel. 312/225–8800. AE, D, MC, V. Moderate.*

New Rosebud Cafe. This popular restaurant in Little Italy specializes in good, old-fashioned southern Italian cooking, with one of the best red sauces in town, and exquisitely prepared pastas. Expect to wait, even with reservations. *1500 W. Taylor St., tel. 312/942–1117. AE, DC, MC, V. Closed Sat. lunch, Sun. Moderate.*

Three Happiness. Those in the know arrive at 9:30 AM in order to get a table when the doors open at 10, for the dim sum brunch. Lunch and dinner are available, too. *2130 S. Wentworth Ave., tel. 312/791–1229. AE, DC, MC, V. Inexpensive.*

NEAR N./RIVER N./LINCOLN **Eccentric.** Talkshow star Oprah Winfrey is a partner in this combination French café/Italian coffeehouse/English pub, and her horseradish mashed potatoes are not to be missed. Steaks and chops are excellent, too. *159 Erie St., tel. 312/787–8390. Reservations accepted for 6 or more. AE, D, DC, MC, V. No lunch weekends. Moderate–Expensive.*

Hatsuhana. The best sushi and sashimi in Chicago are supplemented by extensive and unusual daily specials, including steamed baby clams in sake and broiled king mackerel with soybean paste. *160 E. Ontario St., tel. 312/280–8287. Reservations advised. AE, DC, MC, V. Closed Sat. lunch, Sun., holidays. Moderate–Expensive.*

Blackhawk Lodge. Rustic, vacation-lodge decor sets this American regional restaurant apart. The hickory-smoke aromas from the kitchen are irresistible, as are the barbecued ribs. *41 E. Superior St., tel. 312/280–4080. Reservations accepted. AE, D, DC, MC, V. Moderate.*

Un Grand Cafe. This relaxed, attractive, Montmartre-style bistro uses fresh American produce to create such simple French dishes as cassoulet, onion soup, steak fries, and various fish dishes with vegetables. *2300 N. Lincoln Park W., tel. 312/348–8886. No reservations. AE, D, DC, MC, V. Closed lunch, Sun., holidays. Moderate.*

Frontera Grill. Authentic Mexican food that goes far beyond chips and salsa is served up at this casual café, along with such dishes as charbroiled catfish (Yucatán-style) and skewered tenderloin with *poblano* peppers, red onion, and bacon. Expect a crowd. *445 N. Clark St., tel. 312/661–1434. AE, D, DC, MC, V. Closed Sun. and Mon. Moderate.*

Scoozi! A big tomato hangs outside this huge, noisy, trendy place that serves up delicious country-style Italian dishes; try the osso buco (braised veal shanks in roasted vegetables). Be prepared for crowds. *410 W. Huron St., tel. 312/943–5900. AE, DC, MC, V. Moderate.*

Trattoria Convito. This small, casual spot near Michigan Avenue shopping has a restaurant upstairs and a take-out deli downstairs, both offering regional Italian dishes. *11 E. Chestnut St., tel. 312/943–2984. AE, MC, V. Moderate.*

Tucci Benucch. This cozy, Italian country kitchen in the Avenue Atrium serves hearty but healthy fare: a garlicky roasted chicken, a grilled eggplant sandwich, and thin-crust pizzas and pasta dishes with such unusual toppings as red peppers and smoked chicken. Dishes are prepared with olive oil instead of butter. *900 N. Michigan Ave., tel. 312/266–2500. AE, D, DC, MC, V. No reservations. Moderate.*

Ed Debevic's. Brave the crowds (or go at off hours) to savor the high-camp decor—and surprisingly good food—of this 1950s-style diner. *640 N. Wells St., tel. 312/664–1707. No credit cards. Inexpensive.*

Pizzeria Uno. Chicago deep-dish pizza got its start here; Uno offers the genuine article with a variety of toppings. For a shorter wait, try Pizzeria Due (same ownership and menu, different decor, and longer hours) one block away. *Uno: 29 E. Ohio St., tel. 312/321–1000; Due: 619 N. Wabash Ave., tel. 312/943–2400. AE, D, DC, MC, V. Inexpensive.*

NORTH **The Bangkok.** This comely and sophisticated spot presents unusual and varied renditions of Thai cuisine, offering both mild and spicy dishes, plus a weekend brunch buffet. *3542 N. Halsted St., tel. 312/327–2870. AE, DC, MC, V. Moderate.*

Pasteur. Steamy and often packed on weekends, this Vietnamese restaurant has an extensive menu; try the noodle salads and the do-it-yourself barbecued beef appetizer. *4759 N. Sheridan Rd., tel. 312/271–6673. AE, MC, V. Closed lunch, Mon. Moderate.*

Ann Sather. Expect a wait on weekend mornings at these cheery Swedish restaurants, where Chicagoans flock for omelets, Swedish pancakes, and renowned cinnamon rolls. Lunches and dinners feature hearty, uncomplicated home cooking. *5207 N. Clark St., tel. 312/271–6677; 929 W. Belmont Ave., tel. 312/348–2378. MC, V. Inexpensive.*

SHOPPING

SHOPPING DISTRICTS Chicago's two main shopping areas are North Michigan Avenue (between the Chicago River and Oak Street) and the Loop. Three "vertical malls" line Michigan Avenue, offering mid- to high-priced clothing, trinkets, and housewares. Chicago Place (700 N. Michigan Ave.) is anchored by Saks Fifth Avenue; the top level has a food court with a variety of quick dishes available. Water Tower Place (835 N. Michigan Ave.) has Lord & Taylor and a branch of Marshall Field & Co. The Avenue Atrium (900 N. Michigan Ave.) has Bloomingdale's and Henri Bendel. Both the Atrium and Water Tower Place have movie theaters. At the north end of Michigan Avenue, top designers have shops on Oak Street between Michigan Avenue and State Street. While in the Loop, also visit Carson Pirie Scott & Co. (1 S. State St.) and look for the ornate Louis Sullivan ironwork on the main entrance at State and Madison. The seventh floor of Marshall Field & Co.'s flagship store (111 N. State St.) has half a dozen restaurants serving everything from soup to hot entrées to ice cream. The Walnut Room is a traditional lunch stop for Chicago shoppers and the site of the store's giant tree at Christmas.

The North Pier complex (435 E. Illinois St.), on the lake just south of Navy Pier, is teeming with small, fascinating shops, including a seashell store, a hologram showroom, and a shop where T-shirts and jackets are custom-designed and embroidered.

SPECIALTY SHOPS **Gifts:** For souvenirs of Chicago, try the City of Chicago Store (435 E. Illinois St. in the North Pier complex, tel. 312/467–1111) or the Chicago Architecture Foundation Tour Center (224 S. Michigan

Ave., tel. 312/922–3432). You can easily please any chocolate lover with a box of Marshall Field's Frango mints, possibly the best of Chicago's edible souvenirs; pick them up at Water Tower Place (835 N. Michigan Ave.) or at the main store (111 N. State St.). **Books:** Even very esoteric books can be found at the flagship Kroch & Brentano (29 S. Wabash Ave., tel. 312/332–7500). **Housewares:** Visit the palatial Crate and Barrel (646 N. Michigan Ave., tel. 312/787–5900). **Records:** Look in at Rose Records (214 S. Wabash Ave., tel. 312/987–9044) or the Jazz Record Mart (11 W. Grand St., tel. 312/222–1467).

OUTDOOR ACTIVITIES

BEACHES Public beaches and promenades line much of the lakefront. The most popular beaches are Oak Street Beach and North Avenue Beach. South of Oak Street Beach is a concrete promenade with a swimming area, popular for lap swimming, that has lifeguards from Memorial Day through Labor Day.

JOGGING/WALKING/BIKING A 19-mile jogging, walking, and bicycle path with mileage markers stretches along the lakefront through Lincoln and Grant parks. Enter at Oak Street Beach (across from the Drake Hotel), at Grand Avenue underneath Lake Shore Drive, or by heading through Grant Park on Monroe Street or Jackson Boulevard until you reach the lakefront. It's populated in the early morning and late afternoon (especially if you head north from the Loop), but beware after dark and in the more desolate section south of McCormick Place. Walkers and runners should always be on the lookout for speeding cyclists. Bicycles can be rented at Fullerton Avenue near the exit from Lake Shore Drive, and from Turin Bicycles in the North Pier complex (tel. 312/923–0100) or Village Cycle Center (1337 N. Wells St., tel. 312/751–2488). For more information on biking in Chicago, contact the Chicagoland Bicycle Federation (Box 64396, Chicago 60664, tel. 312/427–3325).

TENNIS Public courts can be rented at the Daley Bicentennial Plaza (Grant Park, 337 E. Randolph Dr., tel. 312/294–4790). The 12 hard-surface, lighted courts are open April–October. Call the day before you want to play to reserve a court. They fill up fast for early morning, late afternoon, and weekends but are easier to get midday.

ENTERTAINMENT

For listings of the city's theater, music, comedy, and other nightlife events, check the Friday section of the *Chicago Tribune,* the Weekend section of the *Sun-Times,* the second section of *The Reader* (the free weekly paper), or the monthly *Chicago* magazine. Visitors looking for "Rush Street," Chicago's legendary nightlife and music scene, will be disappointed to find that it has moved to Division Street and is much diminished.

THEATER Theater lovers will find a wealth of large and small acting companies doing everything from splashy Broadway musicals to avant-garde performance art. Most Chicago theaters are in residential neighborhoods north of the Loop; some well-known off-Loop theater groups include Steppenwolf, Remains Theater, Wisdom Bridge, the Body Politic, and Pegasus Players. Behind the Art Institute, the venerable Goodman Theater (200 S. Columbus Dr., tel. 312/443–3800) mounts consistently popular and interesting productions of classics and new plays. The Auditorium Theater (50 E. Congress Pkwy., tel. 312/559–2900) mounts touring productions of hit Broadway musicals. The Court Theater (5535 S. Ellis Ave., tel. 312/753–4472) in Hyde Park performs Shakespeare and modern classics, with mixed results. Candlelight Dinner Playhouse (5620 S. Harlem Ave., Summit, tel. 708/496–3000) matches mediocre food with outstanding productions of Broadway musicals. The dinner/theater package is a good deal, or you can go just for the show. For information about half-price tickets, call Hot Tix (108 N. State St., tel. 312/977–1755).

MUSIC **Classical:** Orchestra Hall (220 S. Michigan Ave., tel. 312/435–6666) hosts concerts by both the Chicago Symphony and a host of individual performers and smaller groups.

Opera: The Lyric Opera (20 N. Wacker Dr., tel. 312/822–0770) has name stars at name prices, and tickets are hard to come by.

Jazz: The Jazz Showcase (Blackstone Hotel, 636 S. Michigan Ave., tel. 312/427–4300) is good for serious listening, nationally known acts, and an unusual no-smoking policy; the Green Mill (4802 N. Broadway, tel. 312/878–5552) is a perfect re-creation of a '20s club in seedy Uptown—go early on weekends if you want a seat; the Gold Star Sardine Bar (680 N. Lake Shore Dr., tel. 312/664–4215) packs them in as its name implies; and Pops for Champagne (2934 N. Sheffield Ave., tel. 312/472–1000) is a large, elegant room that offers a champagne bar in addition to the music.

Blues: Blue Chicago (937 State St., tel. 312/642–6261), Buddy Guy's Legends (754 S. Wabash Ave., tel. 312/427–0333), and B.L.U.E.S. (2519 N. Halsted St., tel. 312/528–1012) offer live blues performances.

DANCE Two professional dance troupes worth watching are the Hubbard St. Dance Company (tel. 312/663–0853) and the Joseph Holmes Dance Theater (1935 S. Halsted St., tel. 312/942–0065).

COMEDY Second City (1616 N. Wells St., tel. 312/337–3992) has launched the careers of some of the great comics of the past 30 years, including Mike Nichols, Elaine May, Dan Aykroyd, John Belushi, and Bill Murray, but its recent track record is spotty—check current reviews before you go. Also try Improvisations (504 N. Wells St., tel. 312/782–6387) and Zanies (1548 N. Wells St., tel. 312/337–4027).

FILM The Fine Arts Theaters (410 S. Michigan Ave., tel. 312/939–3700) show first-run foreign and "art" films; the Art Institute Film Center (Columbus Dr. at Jackson Blvd., tel. 312/443–3737) has special showings and series; and the Music Box Theater (3733 N. Southport Ave., tel. 312/871–6604), a lovingly restored '20s movie palace with twinkling stars on the ceiling, shows classics, animation, and offbeat first-run movies.

SPECTATOR SPORTS The Black Hawks play hockey October–April and the Bulls play basketball November–May at Chicago Stadium (1800 W. Madison St., tel. 312/733–5300). The Bears play football at Soldier Field (425 E. McFetridge Dr., tel. 312/663–5100) August–January. April–October, the Cubs play at Wrigley Field (1060 W. Addison St., tel. 312/404–2827) and the White Sox play at Comiskey Park (333 W. 35th St., tel. 312/924–1000). The Cubs play most of their games during the day; starting time is usually 1:20 PM.

Crater Lake National Park
Oregon

ixty-eight hundred years ago, Mt. Mazama, then one of the highest peaks in Oregon, decapitated itself in an eruption 42 times the magnitude of the 1980 eruption of its northern neighbor, Mt. Saint Helens. Forty-two-and-a-half cubic *miles* of rock was pulverized into fragments and sent screaming into the sky; some of the building-size debris landed as far away as present-day Saskatchewan. Incandescent lava and boiling mud, moving on superheated gas, carbonized surrounding forests; Indian camps as far as 70 miles away were buried beneath a rain of hot ash, pumice, and rock. The mountain collapsed inward on itself, leaving a smoking void where its graceful summit once had been.

Rain and snowmelt eventually filled this caldera, creating a lake of such guileless purity that even today sunlight penetrates to a depth of 400 feet. This mountain, enclosing a bowl filled with water of intense blue, is now Ore-

gon's most famous tourist attraction, Crater Lake National Park.

A remote place, Crater Lake lies 143 miles from the nearest major city, Eugene. Comprising only 183,224 acres (among the smallest national parks in the West), Crater Lake Park is sometimes derided as having little to recommend it other than its breathtaking lake—at 1,932 feet, the deepest in the United States. But if Crater Lake lacks the three-ring grandeur of Yellowstone or Yosemite, it also lacks the crowds. Only 500,000 visitors annually disturb the peace at Crater Lake, compared with the millions that throng other "brand-name" national parks each year.

The lack of crowds has less to do with a dearth of activities than with the fact that Crater Lake remains an undiscovered gem among national parks. The lake and its eerie, volcano-tortured environs merit more than a passing glance; the grandeur of this place puts many in a mood as reflective as the lake

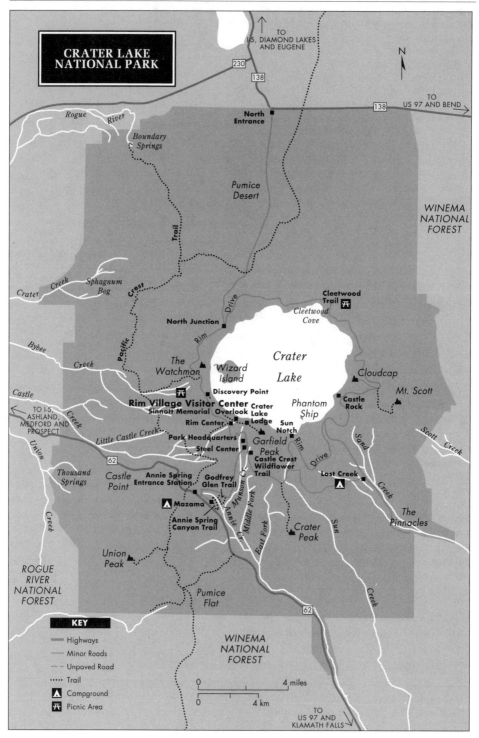

CRATER LAKE
NATIONAL PARK

TO
I-5, DIAMOND LAKES
AND EUGENE

230

138

N

TO
US 97 AND BEND

138

North
Entrance

Rogue   River

Boundary
Springs

Pumice
Desert

WINEMA
NATIONAL
FOREST

Trail

Crater   Creek

Sphagnum
Bog

Crest

Cleetwood
Trail

Cleetwood
Cove

Pacific

Rim   Drive

North Junction

Bybee

Creek

The
Watchman

Wizard
Island

Crater
Lake

Cloudcap

Mt. Scott

Castle

TO I-5,
ASHLAND,
MEDFORD AND
PROSPECT

Rim Village Visitor Center
Sinnott Memorial
Rim Center
Park Headquarters
Steel Center

Little Castle Creek

Crater
Lake
Lodge

Discovery Point

Overlook

Garfield
Peak

Castle Crest
Wildflower
Trail

Phantom
Ship

Castle
Rock

Sun
Notch

Scott   Creek

Rim   Drive

Lost Creek

Union

Creek

Thousand
Springs

Castle
Point

62

Annie Spring
Entrance Station

Godfrey
Glen Trail

Mazama

Annie Spring
Canyon Trail

Annie Munson Cr
Middle Fork
East Fork

Crater
Peak

Sun   Creek

The
Pinnacles

ROGUE
RIVER
NATIONAL
FOREST

Union
Peak

Pumice
Flat

62

Creek

KEY

Highways
Minor Roads
Unpaved Road
Trail
Campground
Picnic Area

WINEMA
NATIONAL
FOREST

0   4 miles
0   4 km

TO
US 97 AND
KLAMATH FALLS

itself. Here is one of the great showcases for Nature the Builder, who from cataclysm has created something to awe generations.

ESSENTIAL INFORMATION

WHEN TO GO The peak visitor months at the park are July and August, but keep in mind that when you're above 7,000 feet in the Cascades, summer is a relative thing—midsummer snowstorms on the rim of Crater Lake are not uncommon. Although surrounding lower valleys often reach 110° during the summer, the park's high elevation usually keeps temperatures at a breezy 75°–80°, even during the hottest months.

Mid-September is the ideal time to visit Crater Lake: The days are still warm and clear, but the crowds thin considerably. The only caveat is that at this elevation, on any given night the temperature can fall below freezing—even after a day with temperatures in the 70s.

Snow is the lake's main source of moisture, with the vast majority falling from November to late May. Except for Mt. Rainier, no other national park receives as much annual snowfall as Crater Lake. (A year without at least 25 feet of snow at Rim Village is considered a drought, and drifts of up to 50 feet are not uncommon.)

FESTIVALS AND SEASONAL EVENTS **2nd Sat. in Aug.:** Rim Run is a high-altitude road race along Rim Drive. As many as 500 runners compete in the 5-K, 10-K, and marathon-length events. The run is Crater Lake's only special event of note, and both lodging and restaurant space are at a premium during this week.

BARGAINS For those who can handle the steep, 2-mile round-trip hike to the dock, the two-hour boat tour of Crater Lake is spectacular and well worth the $10 cost.

The 360° panorama of Rim Drive provides priceless photographic opportunities found nowhere else in the world.

TOURIST OFFICES Ashland Chamber of Commerce and Visitor Center (110 E. Main St., Ashland 97520, tel. 503/482–3486). Roseburg Visitor Information Center (410 S.E. Spruce St., Roseburg 97470, tel. 503/672–2648). Crater Lake National Park (Box 7, Crater Lake 97604, tel. 503/594–2211).

EMERGENCIES **Police, fire,** and **ambulance:** Dial 911. **Doctors:** Rogue Valley Medical Center (2825 Barnett Rd., Medford, tel. 503/773–6281) is closest to the park's year-round access point. **Dentists:** Workinger Dental Group (832 Crater Lake Ave., Medford, tel. 503/772–3411) accepts emergency patients without appointments or will refer.

ARRIVING AND DEPARTING

BY PLANE The closest airport of any size is Jackson County Airport (Medford, tel. 503/772–8068), 64 miles southwest of the park in Medford, with daily service from United and Horizon airlines. There is no public transportation to Crater Lake.

BY CAR I–5, Oregon's main north–south route, lies about 60 miles west of the park boundary. State Routes 62 and 138 connect Crater Lake with I–5 to the south and north, respectively. The drive from Medford (which skirts Rogue River for more than 40 miles) takes about two hours via Rte. 62. Roseburg is about 2¹/₂ hours to the west of Crater Lake on Rte. 138, which goes through the beautiful Umpqua National Forest. The park is about 250 miles from Portland—drive time about six hours.

BY BUS Greyhound Lines (tel. 800/231–2222) makes stops in Roseburg, Chemult, Bend, Klamath Falls, Medford, and Grants Pass. No public transportation is available to the park from any of these locations.

BY TRAIN Amtrak (tel. 800/USA–RAIL) stops in Klamath Falls. Car rentals are available here, but there is no public transportation to the park.

GETTING AROUND

BY CAR A car, abetted by a pair of reliable hiking shoes, is the best way to get around within the park. The 33-mile Rim Drive encircles the lake, providing access to more than a dozen viewpoints that are generally less than a mile off the road.

REST STOPS Public rest rooms with flush toilets are available at Steel Information Center, at Mazama Campground near the south entrance, and at Rim Village on the south side of the lake. The four designated picnic areas on Rim Drive (at the Watchman, Cleetwood Cove, and Skell Head) all have chemical toilets.

EXPLORING

Crater Lake National Park encompasses more than 400 square miles of high alpine meadows, bare pumice plains, deep canyons, snowy peaks, and, of course, the geological rarity for which the park is named—a crater-bound lake. You can easily tour the park in a day, though two to three days will make for a richer, more relaxing experience. Admission to the park is $5 if you visit by car or $3 if you walk in.

Ranger-led talks explain the origin of Crater Lake. During the summer, the talks take place at the Sinnott Memorial Overlook in Rim Village. In the overlook, a scale model of the lake adds to your understanding of the tectonic forces at work even today. The park rangers giving the 10- to 15-minute presentations are well prepared and welcome questions. An 18-minute video providing an overview of the park is shown every half-hour at Steel Information Center. The video has some very good footage, but the scope of the lake does not fit well on the small screen. Unless you hit the park on one of its snowy or foggy days, a trip to the rim gives you a much better sense of things.

The Watchman, an 8,035-foot-high precipice complete with a lookout tower, gives one of the most impressive views of the lake. After a 0.7-mile hike (short but rather steep), you can look down 2,000 feet into the lagoon of Wizard Island. The trail to the Watchman leaves Rim Drive near Lightning Springs, just clockwise around the lake from Rim Village.

The 33-mile-long **Rim Drive** affords views from every possible angle. A nonstop drive, without pauses for sightseeing, will take more than an hour because of the road's meanderings. Frequent stops for viewpoints or short hikes easily make this a half-day trip. Virtually all daylight hours are good for the journey; you might want to travel clockwise so that you reach the east side of the lake as the sun is going down over the western rim. All along Rim Drive are scenic turnouts and picnic areas.

The Boat Tour of the lake offers the only opportunity to get a firsthand look at the surface of the lake, since private boats are not permitted to sail here. Ninety-five percent of the people who visit Crater Lake never actually stick their finger in the lake itself, primarily because it lies at the bottom of a steep mile-long trail. But the opportunity to cruise this unique lake is not to be missed.

The boat tours transport you past Wizard Island, the ghostly Phantom Ship, along lichen-stained cliffs towering nearly 2,000 feet overhead and into hidden coves, where the cobalt-blue depths shade gradually to the clean, rocky bottom of the lake, visible 50 feet, 100 feet, even 200 feet down. Bring your camera—the tour provides ample opportunities for picture taking.

You can get off the boat at **Wizard Island** and spend the day hiking, fishing, picnicking, and, for the truly intrepid, swimming in the incredibly clear but cold (!) 45° water—and then hop the last launch back at about 6:30 PM. Run by a park concessionaire, the tours employ specially built launches that carry about 60 passengers on a two-hour circuit. Depending upon the weather and how well the boats have weathered the winter, boat tours usually commence by late June and cease in mid-September. *Tel. 503/594–2211. 1st of 9 daily tours leaves from Cleetwood Cove dock on the lake's north side at 10 AM; last departs at 4:30 PM. Admission charged.*

$10 for adults and $5.50 for children under 11.

Cloudcap Lookout, clockwise around the lake, is another must-see. From this higher vantage point, Wizard Island and all the postcard views of the lake are quite distant, and the view is more expansive.

The Pinnacles is a spooky area of strangely beautiful volcanic spires, accessible via a 7-mile-long spur road leaving Rim Drive near Kerr Notch. The Pinnacles are not unlike the sculpted sandstone monoliths of Utah's Bryce Canyon National Park. Castle Creek Canyon, on the park's southwest side, also has spires, some 100 feet high. The road dead-ends at The Pinnacles, so the weary sightseer must double back, seeing the same things twice.

The Annie Spring Canyon Trail, which takes off from Mazama campground, is a sturdy jaunt, but still easy compared to the rim hikes. The 2-mile loop threads through Annie Creek Canyon, giving views of the narrow cleft, scarred by volcanism and blooming with lichens. Watch for water ouzels—sprightly diving birds with cheerful songs—which wander along the bottom of nearby Annie Creek looking for their meals.

Castle Crest Wildflower Trail wanders for about a mile along the upper reaches of Munson Creek near Steel Information Center. The creekside walk is easy going, and in July the wildflowers are in full fragrant force.

Godfrey Glen Trail, farther down the Munson Valley, loops through a suspended valley for about 2 miles. Deer are frequently seen here, and the flowers are also plentiful.

THE NATURAL WORLD The glittering lake and its stunning surroundings are, of course, the park's main natural attractions. But don't overlook the evidence of Mt. Mazama's violence: charred stumps and logs protruding from vast beds of pumice; frozen rivers of lava; and the eerie Pinnacles, a lunar landscape of hollow spires of ash and pumice, fused by escaping jets of white-hot gas.

Nature has healed herself here, as she always does. Sixty-eight hundred years after the fact, the slopes of Mt. Mazama are covered with old-growth forests and delicate alpine meadows; black bear, deer, bobcat, foxes, marmot, and elk call Crater Lake home. In its shadowed depths swim prodigious trout, some 3 feet in length.

Within the lake itself are other geologic features of note. Wizard Island, a near-perfect 700-foot-high cinder cone, is a volcano within a volcano. Near the southeast portion of the lake is the Phantom Ship, a tattered, eerie island of basalt that, in certain lights, resembles an early 20th-century battleship.

HOTELS AND INNS

Accommodations are extremely limited in or near the park; in fact, there are fewer than 150 motel units of any kind within a 25-mile radius of Crater Lake. The good news is that prices are low, especially during the winter. Still, camping is probably the most congenial option available, so you may want to consider bringing your camping gear or RV.

If it's luxury you crave, the Medford/Ashland area (about 70 miles southwest of Crater Lake via Rte. 62) has the Pacific Northwest's best concentration of upscale bed-and-breakfast inns, with a sumptuous network of restaurants and shops to serve them. Contact the Ashland Chamber of Commerce and Visitor Center (110 E. Main St., Ashland 97520, tel. 503/482–3486) or the Ashland Bed and Breakfast Reservation Network (tel. 503/482–2337) for information and reservations.

Price categories for double occupancy, without 9% tax, are *Expensive,* $70–$110; *Moderate,* $50–$70; and *Inexpensive,* under $50.

CRATER LAKE NATIONAL PARK Crater Lake Lodge. This historic old lodge, perched on the rim of the caldera, was nearly destroyed by the park's savage winters. Now, renovated from the foundation up, it is scheduled to reopen in the summer of 1995. Its 75 guest rooms, freshly decorated in a sophisticated but authentically rustic style, are a welcome oasis of comfort in the park itself. Nearly half the rooms have lake views. *Box 7, Crater Lake 97604, tel. 503/594–2211. 75 units with bath. Restaurant. MC, V. Moderate–Expensive.*

Mazama Village. The only other lodging within the park is this 80-unit motel complex located near Highway 62. Built in low-slung, four-story buildings meant to weather the winter, the accommodations are basic, with few frills. *Box 128, Crater Lake 97604, tel. 503/594–2511. 80 units. MC, V. Moderate.*

DIAMOND LAKE **Diamond Lake Resort.** Located on a mountain lake 25 miles northwest of Crater Lake, this large resort has 50 modern, plain motel rooms and 40 simple, rustic cabins. *Diamond Lake 97731-9708, tel. 503/793–3333. 90 units with bath. 3 restaurants, lounge, fishing, boat rentals. MC, V. Moderate.*

PROSPECT **Prospect Historical Hotel & Motel.** This lovely old roadhouse hotel, built in 1889 and looking like a set from an old John Ford movie, was thoroughly reopened in 1990 after a long hiatus. Presently there are eight smallish (but comfortable) rooms in the main hotel and 15 new motel rooms out back that are larger and better for families. By car you're 34 miles from the entrance to Crater Lake. *391 Millcreek, Prospect 97536, tel. 503/560–3664, fax 503/560–3825. Restaurant, lounge, cable TV. MC, V. Moderate.*

Union Creek Resort. The '30s-vintage lodge and adjacent cabins are listed on the National Register of Historic Places. Cabins range from very small sleeping cabins to creekside A-frames with decks; the nine heavy-timbered lodge rooms are more colorful, but they're cramped and sometimes noisy. *Prospect 97965, tel. 503/560–3565. 13 cabins, all with private bath, 9 lodge rooms, all with shared bath. Restaurant. MC, V. Inexpensive–Moderate.*

CAMPGROUNDS

Crater Lake National Park has two camping areas—the large (198-site) Mazama Campground and the more remote, smaller (16-site) Lost Creek Campground. Reservations are not accepted, but spots are usually available on a daily basis. During the peak months of July and August, it's a good idea to arrive before noon in order to secure a spot. The maximum stay at both campgrounds is 14 days. There are another 900 National Forest campsites available within an hour's drive of the park.

Lost Creek Campground. In order to keep the atmosphere more primitive, RVs are not allowed here. The road to Mazama is steep enough—a 3,000-foot gain from Union Creek to Steel Information Center—and if you drive to Lost Creek you can add another 10 miles of narrow curves. This tiny but spectacular campground on the east flank of the park has two advantages over Mazama: It's less crowded, and it's on the road to The Pinnacles, an eerily beautiful region of weird volcanic spires. *Box 7, Crater Lake 97604, tel. 503/594–2211. 16 tent sites ($6), flush chemical toilets and running water only. No reservations.*

Mazama Campground. This well-maintained and scenic campground, located conveniently near the park's main (Rte. 62) entrance, has some popular sites overlooking lush Annie Creek Canyon. The road in is steep and winding, particularly for RVs, but the high Cascades views and proximity to both the lake and the Annie Creek Trail make the drive worthwhile. *Box 7, Crater Lake 97604, tel. 503/594–2211. 198 RV and tent sites, no hookups ($10), showers, bathroom, picnic tables, laundry facilities, barbecue areas and camper store. No reservations.*

DINING

If you can't survive without morning espresso and duck à l'orange, Crater Lake may not be the National Park for you. The park is so isolated that few other dining options exist nearby, and the park itself offers only fast food as an alternative to the picnic basket. The Medford/Ashland area, about 80 miles south of the park on Rte. 62, has southern Oregon's broadest array of dining options. Price categories per person, not including tax, service, and drinks, are *Expensive*, $15–$25; *Moderate*, $8–$15; and *Inexpensive*, under $8.

CRATER LAKE NATIONAL PARK **Wizard Pizza.** This park institution is known for its fresh-baked pizza and fried chicken. As an added bonus, they'll deliver to the nearby campgrounds. *Rim Village, tel. 503/594–2211. MC, V. Closed Sept.–May. Inexpensive.*

Lao Rock Cafeteria. This barnlike cafeteria, where diners eat family style at long tables, features hot dishes and simple sandwiches. *Rim Village, tel. 503/594–2211. MC, V. Inexpensive.*

The Watchman. More sophisticated than the other dining options within the park (at least until the dining room at the newly renovated Crater Lake Lodge opens in 1995), the full-service Watchman offers an array of steak and seafood choices. *Rim Village, tel. 503/594–2211. MC, V. Closed Sept.–May. Moderate.*

DIAMOND LAKE **The Cafe.** The resort's small, informal ground-floor café is best suited for hearty breakfasts and lunches. *Diamond Lake Resort, tel. 503/793–3333. MC, V. Inexpensive–Moderate.*

The Thielsen Room. Upstairs at Diamond Lake Resort is this rustic dining room serving up such specialties as prime rib and chicken cordon bleu. *Diamond Lake Resort, tel. 503/793–3333. MC, V. Inexpensive–Moderate.*

The South Shore Pizza Parlor. This workmanlike pizza parlor is on the south side of Diamond Lake. *Diamond Lake, tel. 503/793–3333. MC, V. Inexpensive.*

MEDFORD/ASHLAND **Chateaulin.** One of southern Oregon's most romantic restaurants occupies a brick-and-ivy storefront a block from the Shakespeare Festival center. The elegant, traditional French fare (and local wines) lure diners from as far away as Portland. *50 E. Main St., Ashland, tel. 503/482–2264. AE, DC, MC, V. Expensive.*

Chata. Locals rave about the food, the service, and the warm atmosphere at this Eastern European restaurant. Try the *piroshki* (meat-or vegetable-filled dumplings in a delicate sour-cream sauce) or the *co za bimba* ("What a party!" in Polish)—a thick T-bone steak sautéed with fresh mushrooms, so named because that's what someone in meat-scarce Poland might say if presented with such a feast. *1212 S. Pacific Hwy., Talent (just north of Ashland on Rte. 99), tel. 503/535–2575. MC, V. Moderate.*

Thai Pepper. This local favorite serves fiery and satisfying (if not scrupulously authentic) Thai food in a soothing creekside setting; although it's located above Ashland Creek, it feels like a small café in downtown Bangkok. *84 N. Main St., Ashland, tel. 503/482– 8058. MC, V. Moderate.*

PROSPECT **Beckies Cafe.** This local institution has been serving up toothsome home-cooked trout and succulent huckleberry pie to hungry locals for more than 60 years. *Rte. 62, Union Creek Resort, Prospect, tel. 503/560–3563. MC, V. Inexpensive.*

Prospect Hotel Restaurant. The dining room of this beautiful old hotel serves up hearty Mexican food (and margaritas by the liter) in surprisingly civilized surroundings. *391 Millcreek, Prospect, tel. 503/560–3664. MC, V. Inexpensive.*

SHOPPING

The only shopping within the park is at the Spartan Rim Village Gift Shop (tel. 503/594–2211). Historic Jacksonville, its artsy neighbor Ashland, and Medford all have their share of intriguing galleries, gift shops, flea markets, and food and wine stores. Jacksonville is especially noted for its western antiques shops.

ANTIQUES Ashland Antique Emporium (90 N. Pioneer, Ashland, tel. 503/482–9668) sells antiques and collectibles from this century. The Main Antique Mall (30 N. Riverside, Medford, tel. 503/779–9490) is the largest antiques emporium in southern Oregon, offering pieces from a variety of periods and styles. The Jacksonville Chamber of Commerce (185 N. Oregon St., Jacksonville, tel. 503/899–8118) has maps pinpointing shops in downtown Jacksonville.

OUTDOOR ACTIVITIES

BEACHES You're welcome to swim in Wizard Island's lagoon, even though it has no beach. But remember: Composed entirely of snowmelt, the water in Crater Lake is very cold—45°–55° year-round.

BIKING The 33-mile Rim Drive is popular for bicyclists, although no designated bicycle path exists, and the road is steep and narrow in places. No bike rentals are available in the park.

FISHING A state fishing license is not required, but access to the lake is limited; if you want to fish, try the area near the boat launch or take poles on the boat tour and cast from Wizard Island. Rainbow trout and kokanee salmon lurk in Crater Lake's aquamarine depths, some growing to monster lunker size. The problem is finding them—or, rather, because no organic bait is allowed, getting them to bite.

GOLF The nearest courses are in Medford, Klamath Falls, Oakridge, and Roseburg. The free guide "Oregon Golf Courses" is available at most information centers.

HIKING The Herculean, 2,500-mile Pacific Crest Trail passes just west of Crater Lake. For easier hikes, try the trails—ranging from short nature loops to rugged mountain tracks—that crisscross the 280-square-mile park. For more information, obtain a copy of the *Crater Lake Trail Guide,* available at the park information centers at Rim Village and at Steel Information Center.

RAFTING There are no rafting venues within the park, but the nearby Rogue River is a world-famous rafting spot. For information on companies that provide rafting opportunities, contact Oregon Guides and Packers (Box 10841, Eugene 97440, tel. 503/683–9552).

SKIING Equipment rentals are available at Rim Village (tel. 503/594–2511). Crater Lake has no maintained trails; most cross-country skiers follow a portion of Rim Drive as best they can. The road is plowed to Rim Village but may be closed temporarily due to severe storms. There is downhill skiing at Willamette Pass, 50 miles north of Crater Lake, and at Mt. Ashland, 85 miles southwest.

ENTERTAINMENT

During the summer, the Park Service offers free slide shows or short films at an outdoor amphitheater near Mazama Campground. The shows are well attended by overnight visitors; check park bulletin boards for dates, times, and meeting points.

More than 100,000 theater lovers converge on Ashland for the annual Oregon Shakespeare Festival (tel. 503/482–4331), which runs from February to October.

From late June through September, the Peter Britt Festival (tel. 503/773–6077) offers open-air concerts by a veritable who's who of nationally known jazz, bluegrass, folk, and classical music performers. The concerts are held in the historic gold-rush town of Jacksonville.

Denali National Park
Alaska

A 6-million-acre wilderness of taiga, tundra, and high mountain peaks, Denali National Park and Preserve is best known as home of the highest mountain on the North American continent, 20,320-foot Mt. McKinley (locals, in fact, still refer to the park as McKinley Park). Denali ("The High One") is the Native American word for the mountain, though to many Alaskans Mt. McKinley is simply "the mountain."

Climbers from around the world dream of conquering this peak, and hundreds attempt the mountain each spring. Climbing parties begin their ascent at the village of Talkeetna, south of the park near Mile 99 on the George Parks Highway (Hwy. 3), the main route to Denali. When you pass by on your way to the park—if you drive—you will find them gathering at the airstrip there, and you can sense some of the excitement of the challenge ahead.

For most of the half-million visitors who come here in a year, the Denali experience is considerably less strenuous, though no less an adventure. The protection that the national park provides brings grizzly bears, caribou, moose, and other wildlife close to a single 88-mile-long dirt road that runs into the heart of the park, from the entrance at Riley Creek to Wonder Lake. The chance to see these animals so near, and in such abundance, is one of the best reasons to make the long trip to Alaska.

To enhance viewing opportunities, Denali is closed to private vehicles, other than those with campground permits for sites inside the park. For most visitors, Denali is an 11-hour ride on an old school bus to see the mountain at the end of the road. If you tire of the ride, you can get out and walk, then catch another bus (they leave every half hour) in either direction.

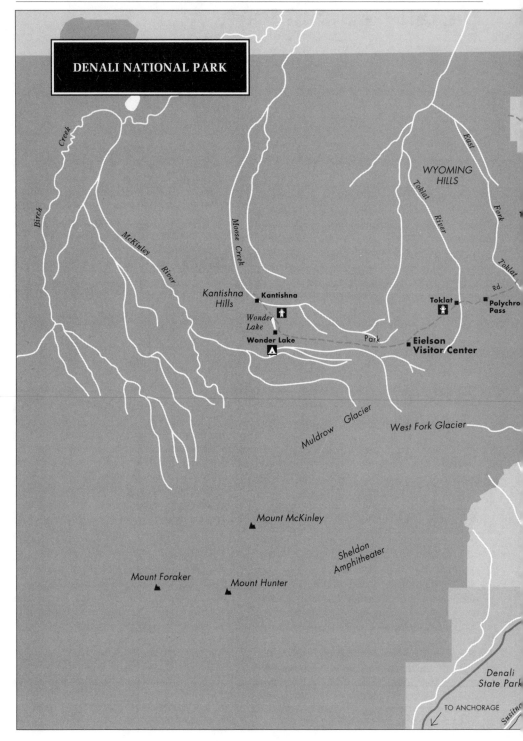

DENALI NATIONAL PARK

Birch Creek

McKinley River

Moose Creek

WYOMING HILLS

East Fork

Toklat River

Toklat

Kantishna Hills

Kantishna

Toklat

Toklat Rd.

Polychro Pass

Wonder Lake

Wonder Lake

Park

Eielson Visitor Center

Muldrow Glacier

West Fork Glacier

Mount McKinley

Sheldon Amphitheater

Mount Foraker

Mount Hunter

Denali State Park

TO ANCHORAGE

Susitna

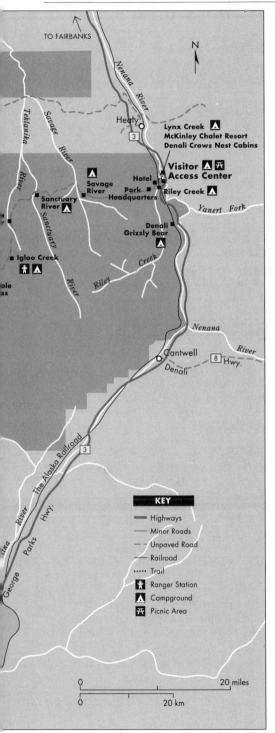

TO FAIRBANKS

N

Nenana River

Teklanika River

Savage River

Healy

3

Lynx Creek ▲
McKinley Chalet Resort
Denali Crows Nest Cabins

Visitor ▲ 🖼
Access Center

Savage
River ▲

Hotel

Sanctuary
River ▲

Park ■
Headquarters

Riley Creek ▲

Yanert Fork

Sanctuary River

Denali
Grizzly Bear ▲

Igloo Creek
🚹 ▲

Creek

Riley River

Nenana

Cantwell

River

8 Hwy.

Denali

The Alaska Railroad

3

George Parks Hwy.

KEY

━━ Highways
── Minor Roads
- - - Unpaved Road
── Railroad
⋯⋯ Trail
🚹 Ranger Station
▲ Campground
🖼 Picnic Area

0 ├──────────┤ 20 miles

0 ├──────────┤ 20 km

ESSENTIAL INFORMATION

WHEN TO GO Even though snow and 30° nights are always possible, and rain is likely, summer weather is the best of the year, with 65° daytime temperatures. And because snow closes the park road much of the rest of the year, summer is the primary visitor season; the July 4th weekend is especially crowded. At these times, a coupon for the free shuttle bus can be as rare and valuable as a gold nugget from the Kantishna Hills. Many Alaskans avoid the crunch by coming in late May or early September. But if you come in summer, you won't be disappointed. Even then, hikers can find solitude less than half a mile off the road. The third week in August, the mountain slopes in the park turn brilliant gold, red, and orange. Berries are in season, and the tundra smells like wine as the berries ferment on the bushes.

FESTIVALS AND SEASONAL EVENTS June 21–22: Summer Solstice is bigger than the Fourth of July, and Alaskans celebrate with all-night softball games, barbecues, and midnight foot races.

BARGAINS Ranger programs are free, night and day. Denali is renowned as a spot for outdoor photographers: Big mammals, big skies, and the biggest mountain in North America provide plenty of subject matter. As of the 1993 season, the Igloo Creek and Sanctuary River campgrounds within the park were free of charge because their wells had been shut down.

TOURIST OFFICES Alaska Division of Tourism (Box 110801, Juneau 99811, tel. 907/465–2010). Denali National Park and Preserve (Box 9, Denali National Park 99755, tel. 907/683–2686 for recorded information; 907/683–1266 in summer or 907/683–2294 in winter). Alaska Public Lands Information Center (605 W. 4th Ave., Anchorage 99501, tel. 907/271–2737).

EMERGENCIES For **police, fire,** and **ambulance:** Dial 911. **State troopers:** tel. 907/683–2232. Inside Denali, call 907/683–9100 or contact a ranger; note that there are no phones west of park headquarters. **Doctors:** Clinic services are available weekdays 9–5 at the

Healy Clinic (tel. 907/683–2211) in Healy, 13 miles north of the park entrance.

ARRIVING AND DEPARTING

BY PLANE There is no scheduled service to the park, but you can charter a flight from Anchorage and Fairbanks, the nearest major airports.

BY CAR The scenery between the park and Anchorage, 237 miles south, or Fairbanks, 121 miles north, is nearly as lovely as that in the park itself: wilderness country with broad views to the mountains. Access is via the George Parks Highway (Hwy. 3), a two-lane road with roadhouses or gas stations at 50-mile intervals. It takes about five hours to drive from Anchorage, three hours from Fairbanks. Streams that cross the road en route offer good fishing, and Byers Lake State Campground, 147 miles north of Anchorage, has picnic tables; just watch out for visiting black bears.

Rental RVs are available to those who want to drive to the park and camp; the average cost is $125–$150 a day for RVs that sleep four. Contact Murphy's RV (Box 202063, Anchorage 99520, tel. 907/276–0688); ABC Motorhome Rentals (2360 Commercial Dr., Anchorage 99501, tel. 907/279–2000); or Clippership Motorhome Rentals (5401 Old Seward Hwy., Anchorage 99518, tel. 907/562–7051).

BY TRAIN Traveling via the daily trains from Anchorage and Fairbanks is a good option since shuttle buses are generally the only private vehicles allowed deep into the park. The journey is just as scenic as coming by highway, if not more interesting: While the railroad parallels the road much of the way, trains also detour into more remote country, where homesteaders still flag down the local when they want to be picked up. Once at the park depot, which is inside the park entrance, most hotels will send someone to get you.

Express trains leave Fairbanks and Anchorage at 8:30 AM, arriving at 12:30 PM and 3:45 PM, respectively. Round-trip fare is $90 from Fairbanks, $170 from Anchorage. For the latest information, contact Alaska Railroad Passenger Services (Box 107500, Anchorage 99510, tel. 907/265–2494 or 800/544–0552; in Fairbanks, tel. 907/456–4155).

Private companies often hook plush touring cars to the regular train and even provide full restaurant service. Princess Tours' Midnight Sun Express (519 W. 4th Ave., Anchorage 99501, tel. 907/276–7711; 3045 Davis Rd., Fairbanks 99709, tel. 907/479–9660) and Gray Line of Alaska's McKinley Explorer (745 W. 4th Ave., Anchorage 99501, tel. 907/277–5581; 1980 S. Cushman Ave., Fairbanks 99701, tel. 907/456–7742) charge $228 round-trip from Anchorage and $112 round-trip from Fairbanks.

BY BUS You can also arrive by bus aboard Gray Line of Alaska (see By Train, above). Round-trip fare is about $130 from Anchorage and $80 from Fairbanks.

GETTING AROUND

BY CAR Private cars are allowed on the park road only up to the Savage River Bridge at Mile 14.8; those who are camping at Teklanika River may drive to the campground at Mile 29. Gasoline is available only at the park entrance.

BY BUS Most visitors to Denali ride the free park-service shuttle bus. These run frequently between the Visitor Access Center at the park entrance and Eielson Visitor Center (8 hours round-trip). From Eielson, buses travel to the end of the road at Wonder Lake (11 hours round-trip from the entrance).

To board, you need a bus coupon, which you can pick up at the Visitor Access Center. This simply reserves your seat for a given departure. Drivers will let you off just about anywhere on the road, so you can walk around for a while. You can then catch another bus later on (though on very busy days you may have to wait an hour or two for a bus with empty seats).

If you are camping at one of the campgrounds beyond the entrance, the coupon system doesn't apply.

REST STOPS Park shuttle-bus riders will find flush toilets at the Eielson Visitor Center at Mile 66 and Wonder Lake at Mile 85. The only other bathroom facilities found along the park road beyond the entrance area are at the Savage River campground (Mile 13).

GUIDED TOURS **By Plane.** Small-plane tours of the park, which last 70 minutes and depart from the park landing strip, are expensive but offer a magnificent panorama of the park you've traveled so far to experience. Reservations are advised and the fee is $135 per person; contact Denali Air (Box 82, Denali National Park 99755, tel. 907/683–2261).

By Helicopter. ERA Helicopters (6160 Airpark Dr., Anchorage 99502, tel. 907/683–2574 or 800/843–1947) operates 50-minute tours for $165 per person from its helipad 1/2 mile north of the park entrance.

By Bus. A privately run alternative to the park-service shuttle departs the Denali National Park Hotel (*see* Hotels and Inns, *below*) daily at 6 AM and 3 PM. The vehicles are more comfortable than the park-service school buses, and a boxed lunch is included in the price. Six- or seven-hour wilderness tours cost $45 for adults and $22 for children; three-hour natural-history tours cost $25 and $14, respectively. Another option is the bus to Kantishna Roadhouse (*see* Hotels and Inns, *below*), in the historic gold mining district at the end of the park road.

On Foot. Daily ranger-led walks and off-road hikes depart from the Eielson Visitor Center at Mile 66 on the park road. Registration is required at the Visitor Access Center for off-road programs.

EXPLORING

Denali is a true wilderness. Just half a mile off the park road, you can find yourself picking blueberries, alone with the scent of tundra, enjoying the special alertness that comes of knowing you may spot or be spotted by a bear. Rangers know where animals have been seen recently—the ones you want to photograph as well as the ones you want to avoid. So consult with them when you make your plans to find out about the many things worth disembarking from the bus to see. Note: Admission to the park costs $3 per person.

Horseshoe Lake is an oasis of calm 1 mile from the bustle of the train depot and Park Hotel—a perfect destination for an after-dinner stroll, when the lingering Arctic evening beckons you to stretch your legs after a long day in the bus. Little parka squirrels beg for tidbits along the shores.

Dog-sled demonstrations are held three times daily at kennels near park headquarters, Mile 3.4 on the park road. Sled dogs still figure in Alaskan life, both for work and recreation. In winter, adventurous travelers charter teams for travel into the park or as support for cross-country ski trips. Denali Dog Tours and Wilderness Freighters (Box 30, Denali National Park 99755, tel. 907/683–2664).

Igloo Mountain, at Mile 33, is home to many Dall sheep. You can see them with binoculars or a telephoto lens up on the rocky slopes.

Sable Pass, at Mile 38.3, is a critical wildlife habitat area set aside for grizzlies. You won't be allowed to hike here—or even to get off the bus if bears are present.

Polychrome Pass, at Mile 46, is a popular place to get off the park shuttle bus, take a rest stop, and enjoy the wide views of the Toklat River below. Caribou and wolves are occasionally spotted on the gravel bars.

Muldrow Glacier is one of several Alaska Range ice sheets that can be seen from the park road. It's only 1/2 mile from Mile 67.

Wonder Lake, at the end of the park road, is the classic spot from which to photograph Denali, if it's not blocked by clouds.

THE NATURAL WORLD The animals of Denali are the best reason to visit. Grizzlies are present throughout the park. The grizzly sows usually bear two cubs in their dens in midwinter; since these usually stay with the mother for two to three years, park visitors often see mother grizzlies with two yearlings in tow, feeding on vegetation along the road. Black bears are rarely seen within Denali, although they do inhabit the surrounding woodlands.

The Denali caribou herd has diminished in size over the years, from the tens of thousands that once lived here to around 2,200 animals. But visitors frequently spot these animals from the park road. Both sexes have large antlers and big, round hooves that provide good support on snow and tundra.

Moose are commonly seen as well, the antlers of the bulls reaching 70 inches across. Dall sheep roam the higher elevations and are commonly seen on slopes above the first 70 miles of the park road. They are bright white with large, curling horns on the males. Denali wolves are extremely wary, intelligent, and unusual to see—and if you spot one even in the distance, you should consider yourself lucky.

The ubiquitous song of the tundra, a falling "Three Blind Mice" tune, is the voice of the white crowned sparrow, common throughout Alaska. There are also golden eagles, loons, swans, geese, and ducks—159 species in all.

HOTELS AND INNS

While there is only one hotel inside the park entrance, there are several lodges in the Kantishna gold mining district that offer a true wilderness experience without sacrificing the modern comforts of hot showers and queen-size beds. These accommodations are very expensive, averaging $250 per person per night, and some lodges require a minimum two- or three-night stay. Other hotels, cabin complexes, and campgrounds are grouped north and south of the park entrance on the George Parks Highway. Unless otherwise noted, all properties are open in summer only. Advance reservations are absolutely essential.

Prices for double occupancy are *Expensive,* $100–$150; *Moderate,* $50–$100; and *Inexpensive,* under $50. Some properties include a 4% room tax in their rates.

INSIDE THE PARK **Camp Denali.** This cabin compound in the heart of the park has shared

bathrooms but no electricity. Many consider it the best place to stay in the park for its rustic charm and delicious home cooking. *Box 67, Denali National Park 99755, tel. and fax 907/683–2290. 17 cabins. Very Expensive.*

Denali National Park Hotel. Created in 1973 from a handful of modular buildings and a few Pullman cars, this hotel stands out for its convenience to the railroad station and shuttle buses rather than for its utilitarian exterior and accommodations. *Box 87, Denali National Park 99755, tel. 907/683–2215 or 907/276–7234. 100 rooms. Cafeteria, snack shop, auditorium. AE, D, MC, V. Expensive.*

The following wilderness lodges are in the Kantishna gold mining district at the very end of the 88-mile park road and are rated Very Expensive: **Kantishna Roadhouse** (Box 130, Denali National Park 99755, tel. 907/479–2436 or 800/942–7420, fax 907/479–2611); **North Face Lodge** (Box 67, Denali National Park 99755, tel. and fax 907/683–2290); and **Denali Backcountry Lodge** (Box 189, Denali National Park 99755, tel. 907/683–2594 or 800/841–0692, fax 907/683–1341).

NEAR THE PARK **McKinley Chalet Resort.** This large complex of log chalets on the George Parks Highway stands on a bluff above the Nenana River. Many rooms have river views in addition to the comfortable sitting areas, which are standard. The resort's popular "Alaska Cabin Nite" features a fish-and-rib feast accompanied by gold-rush-era skits. *On Hwy. 3, 1 mi north of park entrance. Box 87, Denali National Park 99755, tel. 907/683–2215 or 907/276–7234. 288 rooms. Restaurant, dinner theater, pool, hot tub, exercise room, box lunches on request. AE, D, MC, V. Expensive.*

Denali Crow's Nest Log Cabins. The simple, calico-curtained units in this complex, which climbs the hillside above the George Parks Highway, are especially pleasant on a sunny day, because each has a big deck with great views across the valley. *On Hwy. 3, 1 mi north of park entrance. Box 70, Denali National Park 99755, tel. 907/683–2723. 39 units. Restaurant, hot tubs. MC, V. Expensive.*

Denali Grizzly Bear Cabins and Campground. Owned and operated by an Alaskan family since 1958, the handful of cabins here include turn-of-the-century trappers' cabins dating from 1904. The tent cabins are the bargain of the area—only $23 a night for three people if you bring your own linens. *Located 6 mi south of park entrance on Hwy. 3. Box 7, Denali National Park 99755, tel. 907/683–2696. V. Inexpensive–Moderate.*

Denali Hostel. There are no age requirements to stay in dormitories here, and it's hard to beat the rates, especially since they include bus service to and from the park, offered several times daily. *Located 10 miles north of the park entrance, Box 801, Denali National Park 99755, tel. 907/683–1295. No credit cards. Inexpensive.*

CAMPGROUNDS

IN THE PARK There are seven campgrounds in the park ($12, no credit cards). Three campgrounds are open to private vehicles (Riley Creek, Savage River, and Teklanika), three are accessible only by shuttle bus and accommodate tents only (Sanctuary River, Igloo Creek, and Wonder Lake), and one is for backpackers (Morino, near Riley Creek). None have hookups, but three have bathrooms (Riley Creek, Savage River, and Wonder Lake). As of press time, wells at Igloo Creek and Sanctuary River were out of service, and there was no charge for these campgrounds. Showers and supplies (including food and propane) are available only near the park entrance.

All sites are assigned on a first-come, first-served basis. To secure a site, apply at the Visitor Access Center at the park entrance; you will be assigned to what's available. If there's nothing when you arrive, you will have to wait. In the meantime, you will be glad to have reserved a site in advance for one or two nights at a private campground outside the park. However, when you make your arrangements for your first night in the park, you can also request sites for up to 14 days—at the same campground or at others.

If you want to camp in the backcountry, you'll need a permit. Apply at the Visitor Access Center.

OUTSIDE THE PARK **Denali Grizzly Bear Cabins and Campground.** This wooded compound on the Nenana River is 6 miles south of the park entrance. *On Hwy. 3, Box 7, Denali National Park 99755, tel. 907/683–2696. 10 sites with hookups ($21), 49 sites without hookups ($15). Showers, bathrooms, dump station, picnic tables. Reservations advised. V.*

Lynx Creek. Located 1¹/₂ miles north of the park entrance, this ranks as one of the best bets among full-service campgrounds, and the Nenana River flows alongside. *On Hwy. 3, Box 118, Denali National Park 99755, tel. 907/683–2548. 12 sites with electrical hookups ($20), 13 sites without hookups ($15). Showers, bathrooms, dump station, picnic tables. No reservations accepted. MC, V.*

DINING

One drawback of a road trip in Alaska or the Yukon is the dearth of good food along the way. The Denali area is no exception. Hotels and roadhouses here generally serve pretty good hamburgers, but menus are heavy on fried foods, and there's not a local specialty in sight. That said, there are a few bright spots near the park. And nobody dresses up, so you can come as you are.

Price categories per person, not including service or drinks, are *Moderate,* $20–$40, and *Inexpensive,* under $20. All restaurants listed here are open in summer only.

Alaska Cabin Nite. This family-style dinner and show features nearly two hours of gold-rush-era skits and a feast of salmon and halibut (with surprisingly good barbecued ribs for those who want them). At $26, it's one of the best buys in the park. *McKinley Chalet Resort, Hwy. 3, 1 mi north of park entrance, tel. 907/683–2215. Reservations advised. AE, D, MC, V. Moderate.*

Lynx Creek Pizza & Pub. This popular spot with a busy jukebox doesn't look like much, but the friendly spirit at the common tables, and the vegetarian and lean reindeer sausage pizzas, will make you glad you came. *Hwy. 3, 1 mi north of park entrance, tel. 907/683–2548. No reservations. No credit cards. Inexpensive.*

OUTDOOR ACTIVITIES

BIKING The park road is open to bikes all the way to Wonder Lake. The Denali Princess Lodge (tel. 907/683–2282) has mountain bikes to rent.

BOATING Narrated trips down the Nenana River aboard covered, heated tour boats lead to an operating prospector's camp. Tours last $3^1/2$ hours and cost $75; contact Denali Wildlife Safaris (tel. 907/768–2660).

FISHING You'll find grayling in clear mountain streams and lake trout in Wonder Lake—but little in other waters, which are milky with ground-up rock that fish can't tolerate. You'll need a state license ($15 for 3 days).

HIKING The real wilderness experience in Denali is reserved for those who get off the buses and walk. With the exception of areas that have been closed as critical wildlife habitats, you can hike anywhere in the park, picking your own route across the open tundra or on river bars as the spirit moves you—providing you're skilled with topographic maps. But you don't have to possess the backcountry skills required for such activities to enjoy the park. All marked trails begin near the park entrance. Among them is the Taiga Loop Trail, an easy, 1.3-mile walk through dense spruce forest and past the rushing creek waters; access is from the Denali National Park Hotel. The Mt. Healy Overlook trail, a four- to five-hour round-trip, also begins at the park hotel and gains 1,700 feet in $2^1/2$ miles. This is hard going, but within most visitors' abilities if they take it slow—and worth the effort for the outstanding views it gives of the Nenana River below and of Mt. McKinley far beyond. Carry water.

HORSEBACK RIDING Wolf Point Ranch (tel. 907/768–2620) offers guided horseback riding just south of the park in Cantwell. Denali Wilderness Lodge (tel. 907/683–1287 or 800/541–9779), 30 miles east of the park, offers daily fly-in packages that include horseback riding at this former bush camp, homestead, and hunting lodge first settled after the turn of the century. Horseback riding is not permitted inside the park, except for guests of Kantishna Roadhouse (*see* Hotels and Inns, *above*).

PHOTOGRAPHY Denali is one of America's premier outdoor photography locations. The shot of a moose wading in Wonder Lake, water cascading from its antlers, is a classic. Necessary equipment includes a telephoto lens (to get visually close to potentially dangerous animals), a polarizing filter (to cut through haze) or 81-series amber warming filter (to balance cool light from overcast skies), and a tripod. Bring plenty of film—long summer days mean plenty of photo opportunities.

WHITE-WATER RAFTING Officially designated as Class IV water, the nearby Nenana River narrows through canyons and churns in white-water rapids. The trip is scary, cold, wet, thrilling, and not prohibitively expensive; you don't have to have any special abilities, just plenty of nerve. Sedate scenic floats, available elsewhere on the river, have greater appeal for the faint of heart. The outfitter provides rain gear and required shuttle service. Denali Raft Adventures (Denali National Park 99755, tel. 907/683–2234). McKinley Raft Tours (Box 138, Denali National Park 99755, tel. 907/683–2392).

ENTERTAINMENT

Apart from Alaska Cabin Nite at the McKinley Chalet Resort (*see* Dining, *above*), the big evening activities here are ranger programs held around campfires at Riley Creek, Savage River, Teklanika, and Wonder Lake campgrounds, and in the auditorium of the Park Hotel. Check the bulletin boards for exact times and topics.

Disney World and the Orlando Area
Florida

 rlando, a high-profile city of fast growth in central Florida, is the number one tourist destination in the United States, attracting more than 13 million visitors annually. Most of these visitors come to enjoy the whimsical pleasures of Walt Disney World, a lush, clean resort of 27,400 acres that is twice the size of Manhattan. When most people imagine Disney World, they usually think of the Magic Kingdom, which encompasses only 98 acres, but in actuality there is much more. In addition to two other theme parks—Epcot and Disney–MGM Studios—some 2,500 acres are occupied by hotels and villa complexes, each with its own theme and each equipped with recreational facilities.

From the gardens full of birds and butterflies, bamboo thickets, and topiary statues, to the lakes thrumming with motorboats and the shops brimming over with treasures and trinkets, every detail is as highly polished as the best Disney film. You can relax, stop fighting the battles of the real world, and let yourself be seduced by the pleasantness of it all. As you take a heart-stopping ride through Magic Kingdom's Space Mountain galaxy, or in Epcot Center, inspect the rose gardens in the shadow of the Canadian pavilion, or gasp at the laser pyrotechnics of the IllumiNations fireworks, the pleasure of the moment is enough.

If you find that you and Mickey Mouse need a short vacation from each other, you'll find much to do in the Orlando area; many of the attractions outside Disney World can be equally enjoyable (including Universal Studios Florida and Sea World) and sometimes less crowded and less expensive. The city itself has retained its charming parklike atmosphere, with homes near spring-fed lakes and the smell of orange blossoms and citrus trees in the air.

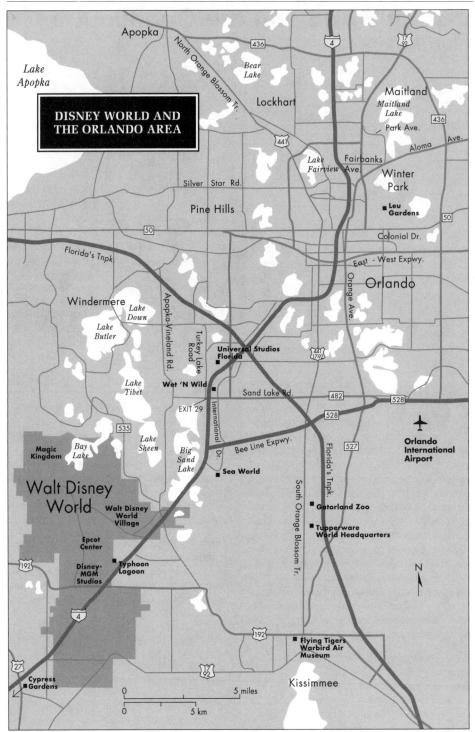

DISNEY WORLD AND
THE ORLANDO AREA

ESSENTIAL INFORMATION

WHEN TO GO December, January, and February offer the best weather, when the humidity disappears and the daily temperature averages in the low 70s. It can get quite cool when the sun goes down. Count on hot and humid weather from April through October, with a daily shower usually late in the afternoon. Average daily maximum temperatures are in the 80s in April and October and in the 90s from May to September.

The most crowded time of the year to visit is from Christmas through New Year's Day. The parks are also packed around Easter. Memorial Day weekend is not only crowded, but temperatures can be quite high. Other inadvisable times to visit are from mid-June through mid-August, Thanksgiving weekend, the week of Washington's Birthday in mid-February, and the weeks of college spring break in late March. The rest of the year is generally hassle-free, particularly from early September until just before Thanksgiving. The best time of all is from just after the Thanksgiving weekend until the beginning of the Christmas holidays. Another excellent time is from early January through the first week of February. If you come here during summer, late August is best.

FESTIVALS AND SPECIAL EVENTS **New Year's Day:** Florida Citrus Bowl Football Classic matches two national college football powers. **Early Feb.:** Walt Disney World Village Wine Festival includes the participation of 60 U.S. wineries. **Mar. 20–22:** Winter Park Sidewalk Art Festival draws art enthusiasts to chic Park Avenue. **Mid-Oct.:** Disney World Classic is played at golf courses at Lake Buena Vista. **Mid-Nov.:** Light Up Orlando is a street party downtown with live entertainment.

BARGAINS For no admission charge, visit Spaceport USA (Kennedy Space Center, about 50 miles east of Orlando, tel. 407/452–2121; open daily), with a Museum of Space History and an Astronauts Memorial. For $3 ($1 for children), Leu Botanical Gardens (1730 N. Forest Ave., Orlando, tel. 407/246–2620; open daily) offers 57 acres of fragrant flora—including rose gardens and a floral

clock—and plentiful sitting areas. The Belz Factory Outlet Mall (5401 W. Oakridge Rd. at the north end of International Dr., tel. 407/352–9600) has more than 160 outlet stores. Several Orlando-area restaurants have reduced-priced menus before 6 PM.

TOURIST OFFICES Walt Disney World (Box 10040, Lake Buena Vista 32830, tel. 407/824–4321). For Disney World information and brochures, go to any Disney theme park ticket window or call 407/824–4321 daily 8 AM–9 PM. Orlando Visitor Information Center (8445 International Dr. in the Mercado Mediterranean Village, tel. 407/363–5800).

EMERGENCIES **Police, fire,** and **ambulance:** Dial 911. **Hospitals:** Orlando Regional Medical Center/Sand Lake Hospital (9400 Turkey Lake Rd., tel. 407/351–8500). **Doctors:** Family Treatment Center (6001 Vineland Rd., 1 block west of Kirkman Rd., tel. 407/351–6682). Buena Vista Walk-In Medical Center (adjacent to the Walt Disney World Village entrance on Rte. 535, tel. 407/828–3434). **Pharmacies:** Eckerd Drugs (908 Lee Rd., Orlando, tel. 407/644–6908) and Walgreens (4578 S. Kirkman Rd., Orlando, tel. 407/293–8389) have 24-hour pharmacies.

ARRIVING AND DEPARTING

BY PLANE Served by several major U.S. airlines, Orlando International Airport (tel. 407/825–2001), located on the southeast edge of town, is only minutes from the main attractions. Disney World and Universal Studios information booths are at the airport; tickets and maps are available to save you time from standing in line at the parks.

Between the Airport and Hotels. If you're driving a rental car from the airport and your lodging is on International Drive or around Disney World, take the Beeline Expressway (Rte. 528) west. The Beeline also hooks up with I–4 if you need to head into downtown Orlando. Several shuttle and limousine services at the airport offer regularly scheduled service to and from all major hotels (about $13 adults, $8 for children): Mears Transportation Group (tel. 407/423–5566), Town &

Country Limo (tel. 407/828–3035), and First Class Transportation (tel. 407/862–2277). Taxis are the quickest way to travel from the airport. They cost about $35 plus tip from the airport to hotels on U.S. 192 or around Disney World; about $25 plus tip to International Drive hotels.

BY CAR I–4 and Florida's turnpike are the main thoroughfares into Orlando.

BY BUS Greyhound Lines (tel. 800/231–2222) has a west-side terminal at 555 North Magruder Avenue.

BY TRAIN Amtrak (tel. 800/USA–RAIL) has stops in Winter Park (150 Morse Blvd.), in Orlando (1400 Sligh Blvd.), and, 20 minutes later, in Kissimmee (416 Pleasant St.).

GETTING AROUND

WALT DISNEY WORLD By Bus. If you're staying at Disney World, the best way to get around is by bus; rarely will you have to wait more than 20 minutes for one. On-site hotels have schedules. Disney World also has a monorail and a water-based transportation system. Transportation is free for those staying at a Walt Disney World Village hotel and for those with a three-park ticket. Otherwise, a ticket for unlimited transportation costs $2.50 a day.

ORLANDO By Car. The most important artery in the Orlando area is I–4, which ties everything together. On this road, remember that when the signs say east you are often going north, and when the signs say west, you are often going south. International Drive (Exits 28, 29, and 30B from I–4), another main road, has several major hotels, restaurants, attractions, and shopping centers. The other major highway, U.S. 192, also known as Irlo Bronson Memorial Highway, cuts across I–4 at Exits 25A and 25B. This highway goes through the Kissimmee area and crosses Walt Disney World property, taking you to the Magic Kingdom's main entrance.

By Taxi. Taxi fares start at $2.45 and cost $1.40 for each additional mile. Call Yellow

Cab Co. (tel. 407/699–9999) or Town and Country Cab (tel. 407/828–3035).

By Bus. Tri-County Transit Authority (tel. 407/841–8240) public buses are an inexpensive way (75¢) to get around Orlando.

REST STOPS All the major attractions provide maps that clearly mark rest rooms. The major shopping areas and malls also offer clean rest rooms. Public bathrooms in the downtown Orlando area are ample. The Church Street Station Exchange, with shops and restaurants, offers public rest rooms. A public rest room and concession area is available at Lake Eola, near the band shell. Lake Ivanhoe Park (off I–4 at Orange Ave. and Midway Dr.) offers a public rest area.

GUIDED TOURS Walt Disney World: For information on guided tours of the Magic Kingdom ($5 adults; $3.50 children, plus admission), inquire at the City Hall information desk, Magic Kingdom, or at the guided tour booth at the Epcot entrance plaza (tel. 407/824–4321). Tours include some of the rides and pavilions. **Boat:** Scenic Boat Tours (312 Morse Blvd., Winter Park, tel. 407/644–4056) offers relaxing cruises past large lakeside homes and Rollins College ($5.50 adults; $2.75 children).

EXPLORING

Walt Disney World. A visit to Disney World is not particularly cheap; a ticket ($36.95 adults; $29.55 children under 10) allows a single day's admission to one of the three main theme parks: Disney-MGM Studios Theme Park, Epcot, and the Magic Kingdom. For more than three days, you can purchase the All Three Parks Passport, with admission to all the parks and free transportation. Passports are available for four to six days and can save a lot of money and may be advisable even if you're only staying two days. Disney World is open daily, with longer hours in the summer and during holidays; call 407/824–4321 for information on admission prices (there are 16 categories) and hours. The best time to be at the parks is first thing in the morning (until 11) and in the evening.

Disney-MGM Studios Theme Park. This park transports visitors behind the scenes and in front of the cameras at a working movie and television studio reminiscent of '30s and '40s Hollywood. The park can be seen in one day. Begin with **The Great Movie Ride,** as it often opens before the other attractions do. Then visit **The Magic of Disney Animation** because lines get long and most of the artists leave by 5 PM. The **Backstage Studio Tour** takes you on a tram ride through the back lot, and then guided walking tours explain the creation of special effects. The best attractions are **Star Tours,** a breathtaking simulated ride into space (which isn't recommended for those who are prone to motion sickness or have back problems, heart conditions, and other physical limitations) and **Epic Stunt Spectacular,** in which performers, with the help of audience volunteers, re-create action scenes from the movie *Raiders of the Lost Ark.* Other attractions include **The Monster Sound Show,** a humorous lesson on sound effects; and **Jim Henson's Muppet Vision 3D,** which combines a 3-D movie with live action and Audio-Animatronics. New in 1994 will be The Twilight Zone Tower of Terror, a 13-story thrill ride.

Epcot Center. This park was designed more for thoughtful adults (and curious children) than for a thrill-seeking crowd; for many adults, it is the most enjoyable part of Disney World. Although Epcot stands for Experimental Prototype Community of Tomorrow, the park is filled with attractions that more often explain past and present. Epcot is divided almost equally into two distinct areas, **Future World** and **World Showcase.** To minimize your time in lines, go left through Communicore East and see as many attractions as you can before the crowd catches up to you. Then leave Future World and work your way clockwise around the 40-acre lagoon in World Showcase. Dinner and early evening hours are the less crowded times in either section.

In Future World, many of the attractions involve rides. One of the most popular places to visit is **Wonders of Life,** with Cranium Commandos, a delightful stage and film presentation about the brain of a teenage boy, **The Making of Me,** a movie on reproduction, pregnancy, and birth; and **Body Wars,** a simulated ride through the body's immune system. Other impressive attractions are **Universe of Energy,** which teaches you about the origins of energy and takes you to a world of dinosaurs; **Journey into Imagination,** a combination 3-D rock video, family fun ride, and hands-on play area, and **The Land,** with a boat ride through a greenhouse of the future. The World Showcase features pavilions devoted to the native food, entertainment, and wares of 11 countries. Among the highlights are **Mexico,** devoted to the country's major tourist spots and involving a boat ride; **Norway,** with a ride back in time in a small Viking vessel; and **China,** with a fascinating film that reveals the country's glorious landscapes. The **American Adventure** is a 30-minute Audio-Animatronics show, hosted by figures representing Benjamin Franklin and Mark Twain.

Magic Kingdom. When people think of Disney World, it's this park that sparks their imagination. Town Square's City Hall has an information desk. There are 45 major attractions in seven imaginary lands spread across 98 acres, but most of the rides are geared for younger children. The young at heart may enjoy the **WDW Railroad,** a 14-minute ride around the park's perimeter; **Pirates of the Caribbean,** a visit to pirate strongholds, in Adventureland; **Haunted Mansion** in Liberty Square; and **20,000 Leagues Under the Sea,** which takes you through a lagoon via a Nautilus submarine. Lines are shortest in the evening.

Typhoon Lagoon joins its sister water park **River Country** on the Disney property. It is a lushly landscaped, 50-acre aquatic entertainment complex at Walt Disney World with a saltwater pool containing a coral reef and Caribbean sea creatures, including baby sharks. *Tel. 407/560–4073. Open daily. Admission: $21.73 adults, $17.49 children under 10.*

ORLANDO AREA **Cypress Gardens.** Central Florida's oldest continuously running attraction, the Gardens contain some 8,000 varieties of perennial plants and flowers. A popular waterskiing show features high-speed stunts along Lake Eloise. You can also attend shows with alligators and birds and an ice-skating performance. *From Disney World take I–4 west to the U.S. 27S exit; follow signs to Winter Haven; at Waverly, turn right on Rte. 540 to the Gardens. Tel. 813/324–2111, 800/237– 4826, or 800/282–2123 in FL. Open daily. Admission: $24.30 adults, $17.40 children 3–9.*

Flying Tigers Warbird Air Museum. This former aircraft restoration facility is now a museum of World War II planes with souvenirs, models, and memorabilia. *231 Hoagland Blvd., Kissimmee, tel. 407/933–1942. Open daily. Admission: $6 adults, $5 senior citizens, $5 children, children under 5 free.*

Gatorland Zoo. This unusual attraction houses more than 400 alligators and 40 crocodiles swimming in a lake. The zoo contains other reptiles, in addition to monkeys, farm animals, and even a tapir. *14501 S. Orange Blossom Trail, Kissimmee, tel. 407/855–5496. Open daily. Admission: $11.61 adults, $8.43 children 3–11.*

Sea World of Florida. This aquatic park can be seen in one day. The star is Shamu, the killer whale who performs in a tank containing 5 million gallons of water. Other top attractions include **Clyde and Seamore 1,000 BC,** starring otters and walruses, and **Terrors of the Deep,** which takes you through the middle of a shark tank. The complex also includes petting and feeding pools, a dolphin and whale show, a 400-foot revolving observation tower, and a nightly Polynesian luau dinner show. New attractions include **The Thrill Ride Mission to Bermuda Triangle, Manatees the Last Generation,** and **Shamu's Happy Harbor.** *7007 Sea World Dr., Orlando, tel. 407/351–3600, 800/327–2424, or 800/432–1178 in FL. Open daily. Admission: $32.95 adults, $28.00 senior citizens 55 yrs. or older, $28.95 children 3–9; parking $4.*

Ripley's Believe It or Not Museum. There's antiques, oddities, miniatures, disasters and more in the Orlando version of this worldwide exhibition museum. *8201 International Dr., Orlando, tel. 407/363–4418 Open daily. Admission: $8.95.*

Universal Studios Florida. The largest motion picture and television studio outside of Hollywood makes learning fun with movie-theme attractions and more than 40 restaurants and shops. A walking tour takes you to more than 50 locations created for films. The main big rides include **Earthquake—The Big One, E.T.'s Adventure, King Kong Kongfrontation,** and **Jaws. Back to the Future** takes you on an amusing simulated ride through various time periods. The most fun attraction may be **The Funtastic World of Hanna-Barbera,** featuring Yogi Bear and the Flintstones. A show is always in production at the **Nickelodeon Production Center.** *Get off I–4 at Exit 29 and follow signs or take Exit 30B and go north on Kirkman Rd., 1000 Universal Studios Plaza, Orlando, tel. 407/363–8000. Open daily. Admission: $37.10 adults, $29.68 children 3–9, children under 3 free.*

Wet 'n Wild. At this popular aquatic park you can swim, slide, and play water sports with plenty of lifeguards on duty. *6200 International Dr., Orlando, tel. 407/351–3200. Open mid-Feb.–Dec., daily. Admission: $21.15 adults, $17.97 children 3–9, children under 3 free.*

HOTELS AND INNS

With more than 80,000 hotel rooms, Orlando leads the country in accommodations. You won't have trouble finding an inexpensive room (with prices even lower during the off-season, Sept.–mid-Dec.), but don't expect much more than a color TV and a pool. You'll be surprised at the number and quality of amenities if you spend a few extra dollars.

If you're planning a vacation centered around Disney World, you'll need to choose between convenience and cost. Although Disney World has few moderately priced lodgings, staying here means you won't need to drive; transportation within Disney World is free, quick, and efficient. You can leave the parks when they get crowded, return to your hotel for a nap or a swim, and head back to the parks in the evening when things are quieter. You can also make advance reservations at Epcot restaurants and save on entrance fees. Motels outside of Disney World, however, are usually less expensive, and many of them offer inexpensive shuttles to the parks. Price categories for double occupancy, excluding 9% tax, are *Expensive,* over $125; *Moderate,* $75–$125; and *Inexpensive,* under $75.

DISNEY-OWNED HOTELS These hotels may be booked through the Walt Disney World Central Reservations Office (Box 10100, Suite 300, Lake Buena Vista 32830, tel. 407/W–DISNEY). Reservations should be made several months in advance, and for the best rooms, during high season, a year in advance. You should also check with Delta Airlines (tel. 800/221–1212), which has many rooms allotted to its travel packages. Several hotels and attractions offer discounts of up to 40% from September to mid-December. For land packages, including admission tickets, car rentals, and hotels, contact Walt Disney Travel Company (1675 Buena Vista Dr., Lake Buena Vista 32830, tel. 407/828–3255). Land/air packages can be booked through Disney Reservation Service (tel. 800/828–0228). The newest Disney hotel, the sports-themed All-Star Resort, is scheduled to open in the summer of 1994. The best bargains among the Disney-owned hotels are:

Disney's Village Resort. This is a good value if you plan to share accommodations with another couple or a larger group; a one-bedroom villa with a study, for instance, has a fully equipped kitchen and sleeps five. *39 1-bedroom and 151 2-bedroom villas, 316 Club Suites, 60 3-bedroom villas, 4 Grand Vista Suites. Dining area, 5 pools, biking, 3 tennis courts. AE, MC, V. Expensive.*

Fort Wilderness. Campers stay amid 730 acres of woodland and streams along Bay Lake at the northern edge of Disney World. You can choose between a campsite with electrical outlets and a picnic table or a trailer home with a kitchen, full bath, color TV, telephone, and daily housekeeping. *407 trailers; 785 campsites. 2 pools, 2 tennis courts,* *biking and jogging paths, fishing, marina, horseback riding. AE, MC, V. Trailers: Expensive; campsites: Inexpensive.*

Caribbean Beach Resort. This cheerful, tropical-themed property has five two-story buildings on a 42-acre lake with access to foot and bike paths for exercise. *2,112 rooms. Counter-service restaurants, shops, pools, baby-sitting, marina. AE, MC, V. Moderate.*

Dixie Landings Resort. Connected to Port Orleans Resort by winding paths, the newest of the lower-priced Disney resorts has four plantation structures surrounded by formal gardens. *2,048 rooms. 2 dining areas, shops, 3 pools. AE, MC, V. Moderate.*

Port Orleans Resort. With cobblestone streets, courtyards, and intricate railings, this hotel reminds you of the French Quarter in New Orleans. *1,008 rooms. 2 dining areas, shops, 3 pools, playground, arcades. AE, MC, V. Moderate.*

HOTEL PLAZA This area on Disney property consists of seven independently owned hotels that offer free transportation, use of the golf and tennis facilities, and advance Epcot restaurant reservations. The following hotels offer good deals for the price:

Buena Vista Palace. This newly opened, upscale property features comfortable all-suite accommodations. *Hotel Plaza Blvd., Lake Buena Vista 32830, tel. 407/827–2727 or 800/327–2990. 1,028 suites. 9 restaurants and lounges, 3 pools, health club, game room, summer kid's program. AE, DC, MC, V. Moderate–Expensive.*

Grosvenor Resort. This attractive hotel, renovated in British Colonial style, has brightly decorated rooms and recreational facilities geared toward the active life. *1850 Hotel Plaza Blvd., Lake Buena Vista 32830, tel. 407/828–4444 or 800/624–4109. 629 rooms. 2 pools, 2 tennis courts. AE, DC, MC, V. Moderate.*

Off Disney property, the two main roadways flanking the parks—International Drive to the north and U.S. 192 to the south—have numerous affordable accommodations.

INTERNATIONAL DRIVE **Orlando Heritage Inn.** If you're looking for charm, try this Victorian-style inn, complete with reproduction turn-of-the-century furnishings, French windows and brass lamps, and genuine 19th-century antiques. *9861 International Dr., Orlando 32819, tel. 407/352–0008 or 800/447–1890. 150 rooms. Pool, shuttle. AE, D, MC, V. Moderate.*

Embassy Suites. This all-suite hotel has a southern flavor with hanging lamps, ceiling fans, tropical gardens, and complimentary breakfasts. *8978 International Dr., Orlando 32819, tel. 407/352–1400 or 800/433–7275. 245 suites. Pool, whirlpool, sauna, room refrigerators and microwaves. AE, DC, MC, V. Moderate.*

Radisson Inn & Aquatic Center. The best rooms face the pool at this large, modern hotel with outstanding athletic facilities, including an Olympic-size pool. *8444 International Dr., Orlando 33819, tel. 407/345–0505 or 800/333–3333. 300 rooms. 2 pools, Nautilus center, tennis, racquetball, handball, jogging, aerobics classes, access to golf country club. AE, DC, MC, V. Moderate.*

Days Inn East of Universal Studios. This is the best bargain next to Universal Studios Florida, with clean rooms and an on-site, 24-hour restaurant. *5827 Caravan Ct., Orlando 32819, tel. 407/351–3800. 262 rooms. Pool, restaurant, in-room safes. AE, D, MC, V. Inexpensive.*

Days Inn Orlando Lakeside. The motel fronts busy Sand Lake Road, just off I–4 and International Drive, but the other side is on tranquil Spring Lake, providing ample recreation. *7335 Sand Lake Rd., Orlando 32819, tel. 407/351–1900 or 800/777–DAYS. 690 rooms. 3 pools, beach, shuttle service. AE, D, MC, V. Inexpensive.*

Gateway Inn. This property offers helpful service, affordable rooms, and a free shuttle to major attractions. *7050 Kirkman Rd., Orlando 32819, tel. 407/351–2000, 800/327–3808, or 800/432–1179 in FL; fax 407/363–1835. 354 rooms. Restaurant, 2 pools,* playground, pets allowed. AE, D, MC, V. Inexpensive.

U.S. 192 **The Residence Inn.** This property facing a lake consists of a row of four-unit town houses with full kitchens, private entrances, and complimentary Continental breakfast and grocery-shopping service. *4786 W. Irlo Bronson Memorial Hwy., Kissimmee 34746, tel. 407/396–2056, 800/468–3027, or 800/648–7408 in FL. 160 units. Pool, water sports, fishing, picnic area. AE, DC, MC, V. Moderate–Expensive.*

Radisson Inn Maingate. Right near Disney World's main entrance, this sleek, modern building has cheerful rooms and large bathrooms. *7501 W. Irlo Bronson Memorial Hwy., Kissimmee 34746, tel. 407/396–1400 or 800/333–3333. 580 rooms. Restaurant, deli, pool with whirlpool and bar, game room, 2 tennis courts, jogging trail. AE, DC, MC, V. Moderate.*

Ramada Resort Maingate at the Parkway. The hotel offers large rooms and lushly landscaped grounds. *2900 Parkway Blvd., Kissimmee 34746, tel. 407/396–7000, 800/634–4774, or 800/272–6232. 716 rooms. Restaurants, deli, shops, swimming pool, 3 tennis courts, jogging. AE, DC, MC, V. Moderate.*

Sheraton Lakeside Inn. This 25-acre lakeside complex consists of 15 two-story buildings that offer many recreational activities, including free paddleboats. *7711 W. Irlo Bronson Memorial Hwy., Kissimmee 34746, tel. 407/239–7919 or 800/848–0801. 653 rooms. 3 pools, 2 children's pools, 4 tennis courts, miniature golf, game rooms, playground. AE, DC, MC, V. Moderate.*

Wilson World. Rooms are larger than those in most U.S. 192 motels, and there's a sandy beach and a lake in the back of the property. *7491 W. Irlo Bronson Memorial Hwy., Kissimmee 34746, tel. 407/396–6000 or 800/669–6753. 443 rooms. Restaurant, live entertainment, 2 pools. AE, D, MC, V. Moderate.*

HoJo Inn Main Gate East. Clean, courteous, and convenient to sights, this simple motel is for people who don't demand many extras other than a color TV and a heated pool. *6051 W. Irlo Bronson Memorial Hwy., Kissimmee 34746, tel. 407/396–1748 or 800/288–HOST. 367 rooms. Pool, game room. AE, D, MC, V. Inexpensive.*

MOTELS

MODERATE **Clarion Plaza Hotel** (9700 International Dr., Orlando 32819, tel. 407/352–9700 or 800/366–9700). 810 rooms; 2 restaurants, pool. **Comfort Inn at Lake Buena Vista** (8442 Palm Pkwy., Lake Buena Vista 32830, tel. 407/239–7300 or 800/999–7300). 640 rooms; 2 restaurants, 2 pools, shuttle. **Courtyard by Marriott Airport** (7155 Frontage Rd., Orlando 32812, tel. 407/240–7200). 149 rooms; pool, airport bus. **Holiday Inn Lake Buena Vista** (Rte. 535, Lake Buena Vista 32830, tel. 407/239–4500 or 800/HOLIDAY). 507 rooms; pool, shuttle. **Travelodge Maingate West** (7785 W. Irlo Bronson Memorial Hwy., Kissimmee 34746, tel. 407/396–1828 or 800/322–3056). 199 rooms; restaurant, pool, shuttle.

INEXPENSIVE **Cedar Lakeside** (4960 W. Irlo Bronson Memorial Hwy., Kissimmee 34741, tel. 407/396–1376 or 800/327–0072). 200 rooms; beach, pool, whirlpool, some kitchenettes. **Quality Inn International** (7600 International Dr., Orlando 32819, tel. 407/351–1600 or 800/825–7600). 728 rooms; restaurant, pets allowed. **Quality Inn Plaza** (9000 International Dr., Orlando 32819, tel. 407/345–8585 or 800/999–8585). 1,020 rooms; 3 pools.

DINING

When you visit central Florida, do as the locals do: Put on casual cotton clothes and find a place serving fresh seafood dishes, such as stone crabs, Apalachicola oysters, Florida lobsters, conch chowder, or pompano (a mild white fish). In recent years, a number of small, good ethnic restaurants have opened in the area. Many restaurants will accommodate special diets if given advance notice, and visitors should have no problem finding pastas, fresh vegetables, and low-fat entrées on local menus. Because the area caters to numerous cost-conscious tourists, many restaurants offer early-bird specials before 6 PM. Price categories per person, excluding 6% tax, service, and drinks, are *Moderate,* $20–$30, and *Inexpensive,* under $20.

WALT DISNEY WORLD Two good, inexpensive choices in the Magic Kingdom are **Pinocchio's Village House** in Fantasyland and **Tomorrowland Terrace** in Tomorrowland. Both large restaurants are only a tad better than a fast-food joint, but they offer some healthful choices, such as salads, soups, and turkey burgers.

Disney-MGM Studios Theme Park has two affordable places to eat:

50's Prime Time Cafe. Club sandwiches, turkey burgers, and mashed potatoes are served on Fiesta Ware or old-time TV dinner trays as old TV shows are telecast around the restaurant. Disney-owned hotel guests can make reservations one to two days in advance (tel. 407/828–4000), or make reservations as soon as you enter the park. *AE, MC, V. Moderate.*

Commisary. This counter-service restaurant features low-fat foods, such as marinated chicken-breast sandwiches served with cucumber salad or fresh fruit or stir-fried chicken and vegetables with rice and nuts. *AE, MC, V. Inexpensive.*

World Showcase in Epcot Center offers some of the finest dining in the entire Orlando area. The top-of-the-line places, such as those in the French, Italian, and Japanese pavilions, can be pricey; you can often save money by having lunch here and grabbing dinner elsewhere. Guests at a Disney-owned hotel or at Hotel Plaza can make reservations the day before (tel. 407/828–4000). Other visitors will need to go to Epcot when it opens and go straight to a WorldKey computer to make reservations.

Biergarten. Visitors dine on hearty German fare at long communal tables and are served by waitresses in typical Bavarian garb while an oompah band plays. *AE, MC, V. Moderate.*

Marrakesh. Try the national dish of Morocco, couscous, served with garden vegetables, as belly dancers and a three-piece Moroccan band set the mood. *AE, MC, V. Moderate.*

Mitsukoshi. At the Japanese pavilion, you can sample meat and fish cooked on a grill or try tempura shrimp at the Tempura Kiku dining room, with a great view of the lagoon. *AE, MC, V. Moderate.*

Restaurant Akershus. Norway's tradition of seafood and cold-meat dishes is highlighted at the Norway pavilion restaurant's *koldtbord,* or Norwegian buffet. *AE, MC, V. Moderate.*

Rose and Crown. This friendly British offering, on the lagoon, serves simple pub fare such as fish-and-chips. *AE, MC, V. Moderate.*

San Angel Inn. This lush tropical restaurant serves unusual Mexican specialties. *AE, MC, V. Moderate.*

ORLANDO AREA **Basil's.** Come here for quickly prepared innovative American cuisine, including chicken and seafood entrées, and admire the artful desserts. *1009 W. Irlo Bronson Memorial Hwy., Kissimmee, tel. 407/846–1116. AE, MC, V. Moderate.*

Beeline Diner. A '50s diner in the Peabody Hotel, open 24 hours, offers old tunes on the jukebox and salads, sandwiches, and griddle foods. *9801 International Dr., Orlando, tel. 407/352–4000. AE, DC, MC, V. Moderate.*

Darbar. At this lavishly decorated Indian restaurant, your best bet is the tandoori dinner for two, with lamb and chicken. There's also a good selection of curries and pilafs. *7600 Dr. Phillips Blvd., The Marketplace shopping center, Orlando, tel. 407/345–8128. AE, DC, MC, V. Moderate.*

Le Coq au Vin. The atmosphere here is mobile-home-modern, but the traditional French cuisine is first-class and fairly priced. House specialties include fresh rainbow trout, roast Long Island duck with green peppercorns, and homemade chicken-liver pâté. *4800 S. Orange Ave., Orlando, tel. 407/851–6980. AE, DC, MC, V. Moderate.*

Ming Court. This elegant Chinese restaurant overlooking a pond and floating gardens serves excellent jumbo shrimp in lobster sauce; also try the grilled chicken stuffed with nuts. *9188 International Dr., Orlando, tel. 407/351–9988. AE, DC, MC, V. Moderate.*

Ran-Getsu. A creative menu distinguishes this Japanese restaurant, complete with carp-filled pond and decorative gardens, and even a staple like sukiyaki is special. *8400 International Dr., Orlando, tel. 407/345–0044. AE, DC, MC, V. Moderate.*

Border Cantina. This pink-walled Tex-Mex on trendy Park Avenue serves scrumptious chicken fajitas. *329 S. Park Ave., Winter Park, tel. 407/740–7227. AE, MC, V. Inexpensive.*

Donato's Italian Market. Large, friendly, and informal, this place has better-than-average pizza, vegetable calzone, and large salads. *5159 International Dr., tel. 407/363–5959. AE, MC, V. Inexpensive.*

Rolando's. Cuban cuisine is a Florida staple, and the drive away from tourist-oriented areas is worth it to try Rolando's excellent, spicy black-bean soup and chicken with yellow rice. *870 Sermoran Blvd., Casselberry, tel. 407/767–9677. MC, V. Inexpensive.*

Phoenician. Inexperienced with Middle Eastern food? The best bet is to order a tableful of appetizers (*meza*) and sample as many as possible. Otherwise try the hummus, baba ghanouj, or the *lebneh* dishes. *7600 Dr. Phillips Blvd. in The Marketplace, Orlando, tel. 407/345-1001. AE, MC, V. Inexpensive.*

Pizzeria Uno. It's a chain, but when the pizza tastes this good, you can't hold that against it. *5 Church St., Orlando, tel. 407/839–1800. AE, MC, V. Inexpensive.*

SHOPPING

WALT DISNEY WORLD **Disney-MGM:** Sid Cahuenga's One-of-a-Kind at the main entrance carries movie posters, autographed pictures, and original costumes once worn by film stars. Animation Gallery, at the end of the Animation Tour, sells original Disney animation cels, books, and more. **Epcot:** You can do one-stop souvenir shopping at Future World's Centorium in Communicore East. **Magic Kingdom:** Monogrammed mouse ears can be found at The Chapeau on Main Street or at The Mad Hatter in Fantasyland, which is usually less crowded. The Frontier Trading Post sells western-style gifts.

MALLS Altamonte Mall is ¹/₂ mile east of I–4 on Rte. 436 (451 Altamonte Ave., Altamonte Springs, tel. 407/830–4400). Florida Mall is 4¹/₂ miles east of I–4 and International Dr. (8001 S. Orange Blossom Trail, Orlando, tel. 407/851–6255).

SHOPPING VILLAGES Church Street Exchange (Church Street Station, 129 W. Church St., tel. 407/422–2434) is a Victorian-theme "festival marketplace" filled with more than 50 specialty shops. Disney Village Market Place (Lake Buena Vista, tel. 407/282–3058) features Mickey's Character Shop, the world's largest Disney merchandise store, and shops selling art, fashions, and crafts. The Marketplace (7600 Dr. Phillips Blvd., Orlando, tel. 407/345–8668) has a pharmacy, post office, and one-hour film processor. Mercado Mediterranean Village (8445 International Dr., tel. 407/345–9337) houses more than 50 gift shops and an international food court. Old Town (5770 Irlo Bronson Memorial Hwy., Kissimmee, tel. 407/396–4888), east of I–4, has 70 shops, an Elvis Presley museum, an antique carousel, and an ice-cream parlor. Park Avenue in Winter Park is an upscale shopping district with restaurants, bookshops, galleries, and boutiques.

OUTDOOR ACTIVITIES

BEACHES The closest beaches are those at Cocoa Beach about 30 minutes away; about 100 miles of sandy beaches are accessible to the public between Ormond Beach and Sebastian Inlet. Canaveral National Seashore (tel. 407/867–2805), just east of New Smyrna Beach on Rte. A1A, is a 57,000-acre park that is home to more than 250 kinds of birds and animals. A self-guided hiking trail leads to the top of an Indian shell midden at Turtle Mound, where picnic tables are available.

Free brochures and maps are available at the Visitor Center on Rte. A1A.

BIKING The most scenic bike riding in Orlando is on Disney World property, along roads that take you past forests, lakes, golf courses, and Disney's wooded resort villas and campgrounds. Bikes are available for rent at Caribbean Beach Resort (tel. 407/934–3400), Fort Wilderness Bike Barn (tel. 407/824–2742), and Walt Disney World Village Villa Center (tel. 407/827–1100).

FISHING Fort Wilderness Campground (tel. 407/824–2900) in Disney World is the starting point for fishing trips, with a boat, equipment, and a guide for up to five anglers.

GOLF Golfpac (417 Whooping Loop, Altamonte Springs, tel. 407/260–2288) packages golf vacations and prearranges tee times at more than 30 courses around Orlando. Walt Disney World's three championship courses—the site of a PGA tournament in the fall—are among the busiest and most expensive in the region. At public courses, you pay for what you get. Outside Disney World, try Hunter's Creek Golf Course (14401 Sports Club Way, tel. 407/240–4653) and Metro West Country Club (2100 S. Hiawassee Rd., tel. 407/297–0052).

HORSEBACK RIDING Grand Cypress Equestrian Center (tel. 407/239–4608) offers private lessons, with novice and advanced trails. Fort Wilderness Campground Resort (tel. 407/824–2832) in Disney World offers tame trail rides through backwoods and along lakesides.

TENNIS At Walt Disney World, courts are free for guests, but you must make reservations, except at Fort Wilderness. You'll find courts at Disney Inn (tel. 407/824–1469), the Village Clubhouse (tel. 407/828–3741), Fort Wilderness Campground (tel. 407/824–3578), Contemporary Resort (tel. 407/824–3578), Grand Floridian (tel. 407/824–2438), Yacht and Beach Club (tel. 407/934–7000), and Swan (tel. 407/934–3000), and Dolphin (tel. 407/934–4000). Also try Orange Lake Country Club (8505 west U.S. 192, Kissimmee, tel. 407/239–2255) and Orlando Tennis

Center (649 W. Livingston St., tel. 407/246–2162).

WALKING/JOGGING Walt Disney World has several scenic walking and jogging trails. Pick up trail maps at any Disney resort. Fort Wilderness (tel. 407/824–2900) has a 2.3-mile course with fresh air and woods, and Caribbean Beach Resort has a ¼-mile trail. Park Avenue in Winter Park is a mile-walk of shops, museums, and restaurants, and there's an hour-long walk around Lake Eola in downtown Orlando.

WATER SPORTS At Walt Disney World, marinas at Caribbean Beach Resort, Contemporary Resort, Fort Wilderness, Polynesian Village, Grand Floridian, Disney's Yacht and Beach Club, and Disney World Shopping Village rent sunfish, catamarans, motor-powered pontoon boats, pedal boats, and tiny two-passenger water sprites. Polynesian Village marina and Fort Wilderness rent canoes. For waterskiing reservations, call 407/824–1000. Orange Lake Water Sports (8505 W. U.S. Hwy. 192, Kissimmee, tel. 407/239–4444) has waterskiing, jet-skiing, and parasailing on a private lake next to Disney World.

ENTERTAINMENT

WALT DISNEY WORLD Evening entertainment includes Broadway at the Top (Contemporary Resort, tel. 407/W–DISNEY), the Polynesian Revue (Polynesian Village Resort, tel. 407/W–DISNEY), Hoop-Dee-Doo Revue (Fort Wilderness Resort, tel. 407/W–DISNEY) with a western mess-hall setting; and Pleasure Island (tel. 407/934–7781), an entertainment complex with nightclubs, restaurants, shopping, 10 movie theaters, and fireworks. Don't miss Epcot's grand finale, IllumiNations, a brilliant laser and fireworks show held every night before the park closes along the shores of the lagoon.

Pleasure Island. Six clubs with everything from hot rock and cool country to crazed comedy and astounding adventure. Fireworks every night. *Tel. 407/824–4321. Admission: $14.79.*

ORLANDO AREA **Church Street Station** (129 W. Church St., Orlando, tel. 407/422–2434; admission charged) is a very popular downtown entertainment complex, with old-fashioned saloons, turn-of-the-century memorabilia, dance halls, dining rooms, and shopping arcades.

Theater: Carr Performing Arts Centre (401 Livingston St., Orlando, tel. 407/849–2020) presents performances of ballet, modern dance, classical music, opera, and theater.

Dinner Shows: Arabian Nights (6225 W. Irlo Bronson Memorial Hwy., Kissimmee, tel. 407/239–9223 or 800/553–6116) has performing horses. Fort Liberty (5260 W. Irlo Bronson Memorial Hwy., Kissimmee, tel. 407/351–5151 or 800/883–8181) is a Wild West act. King Henry's Feast (8984 International Dr., Orlando, tel. 407/351–5151 or 800/883–8181) is a 16th-century celebration. Mark Two (3376 Edgewater Dr., Orlando, tel. 407/843–6275 or 800/726–6275) is a dinner theater producing live Broadway shows. Mardi Gras (8445 International Dr., Orlando, tel. 407/351–5151 or 800/883–8181) is a New Orleans–style cabaret.

Spectator Sports: Orlando Magic play basketball October–April at the Orlando Arena (1 Magic Place, Orlando, tel. 407/839–3900). During spring training in March, you can watch baseball's Houston Astros at Osceola County Stadium (Kissimmee, tel. 407/933–5500), and the Kansas City Royals play at Baseball City (less than 30 minutes from Disney World, at the intersection of I–4 and U.S. 27, tel. 813/424– 2424).

Everglades National Park
Florida

he Everglades are 4.3 million acres of subtropical, watery wilderness that fan out from Lake Okeechobee, covering much of the lower half of the Florida Peninsula. Floridians like to call the area the Glades; in the 1940s, pioneering conservationist Marjory Stoneman Douglas described it as the "river of grass"—a vast, shallow river that seeps ever southward until it merges with the Gulf of Mexico to the west and Florida Bay to the south.

Rather than the dark, gloomy swamp that visitors sometimes expect, the Glades is a place of wide horizons, seemingly endless plains covered with tall saw grass and dotted with islands of hardwood trees called hammocks, mangroves filled with nesting birds, marshes sprinkled with blooming wildflowers, and sloughs teeming with fish and other wildlife. The park features wildlife rarely seen in the United States, such as the crocodile, wood stork, bald eagle, and manatee.

Mangroves and marine habitats can be found along the Gulf Coast in the western section of the park (in the Ten Thousand Islands region), as well as in Flamingo and Key Largo.

To preserve this ecosystem, the southwestern corner of the Everglades was designated a national park in 1947; it is now America's third-largest park, and its only subtropical one. A wetland of international importance, it has since been named an International Biosphere Reserve and a World Heritage Site. Everglades is also the most endangered park in the national park system, its fragile environment besieged by agricultural and industrial activities and encroaching urban development. In August 1992, Hurricane Andrew plowed through the Glades, leaving a wide path of devastation not only in the park but in its eastern gateway towns, Homestead and Florida City, as well. At press time, most of the park's damaged facilities had been repaired; the Long Pine Key trails, Chekika

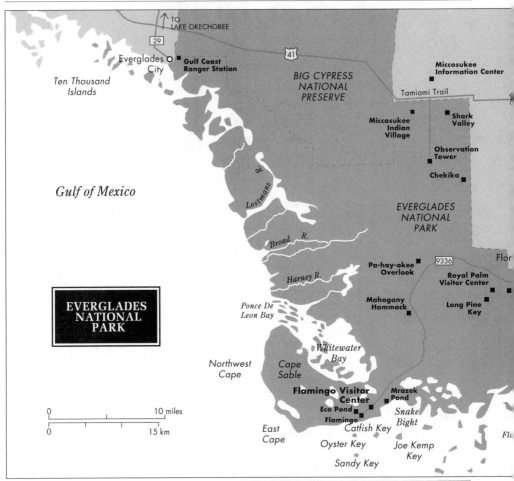

Campground, and the Pahayokee Overlook were set to reopen in winter 1993.

Today, people come to Everglades National Park from all over the world. A marked inland Wilderness Waterway trail for canoes and boats twists 99 miles through marine and estuarine areas. Shorter aquatic trails offer opportunities to explore the backcountry. A canopy-covered tram turtles its way along a 15-mile road through an ecologically rich area. Mid-December through Easter, visitors can enjoy a plethora of ranger-guided activities, including lectures and boat tours.

ESSENTIAL INFORMATION

WHEN TO GO Winter is the best time to visit the Everglades; both temperatures and mosquito activity are moderate, and low water levels make the trails drier. In spring, the weather turns increasingly hot and dry. After Easter, fewer visitors come, tours and facilities are less crowded, and the less expensive off-season rates are in effect at most nearby accommodations, but migratory birds depart and wildlife becomes less evident. June through early October brings intense sun, temperatures in the high 80s and 90s, high humidity, swarms of mosquitoes, and daily torrents of rain—a blessing for the park, but hardly bearable for the visitor. In mid-November, the weather cools, rains cease, water

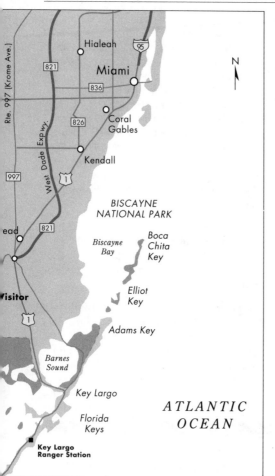

bearer and accompanying passengers to free park entry and a 50% discount off campground fees and car parking fees. Passports are issued at the parks with proof of age.

TOURIST OFFICES Greater Homestead–Florida City Chamber of Commerce (550 U.S. 1, Homestead 33030, tel. 305/247–2332). Tropical Everglades Visitors Association (160 U.S. 1, Florida City 33034, tel. 305/245–9180 or 800/388–9669). Everglades National Park (Box 279, Homestead 33030, tel. 305/242–7700). Everglades Area Chamber of Commerce (U.S. 41 and Rte. 29, Box 130, Everglades City 33929, tel. 813/695–3941).

EMERGENCIES **Police, fire,** and **ambulance:** Dial 911. In Everglades National Park (tel. 305/242–7700, or the Gulf Coast Ranger Station, tel. 813/695–3311), the rangers perform police, fire, and emergency medical functions; look for rangers at park visitor centers and information stations or phone the park switchboard. **Hospitals:** South Miami Hospital of Homestead (160 N.W. 13th St., Homestead, tel. 305/248–3232) has 24-hour emergency room services. **Doctors:** Physician Referral Service (tel. 305/248–DOCS). For the Gulf Coast Everglades area, Naples Community Hospital (350 7th St. N, Naples, tel. 813/262–3131) provides emergency services.

ARRIVING AND DEPARTING

BY PLANE Miami International Airport (MIA) (tel. 305/876–7000) is the closest commercial airport to Everglades National Park, 34 miles from Homestead and 83 miles from the Flamingo Resort in the park.

Between the Airport and Hotels. By Van: Eleven-passenger air-conditioned vans operate 24 hours a day on demand between MIA and Homestead. The shuttle leaves from the Super Shuttle booth (tel. 305/871–2000) outside most luggage areas on the lower level. The cost is $33–$37 for the first person, and $6 for each additional person traveling together, depending on the destination.

By Bus: Metrobus (tel. 305/638–6700 for schedule) runs on Rte. 1A from MIA to Homestead during peak weekday hours (6:30–9 AM

levels fall, the ground begins to dry out, and the mosquitoes subside. Wildlife moves toward the sloughs that retain water all year, and flocks of migratory birds and tourists swoop down from the north.

BARGAINS From mid-December through Easter, Everglades National Park offers free daily programs. Park rangers lead hikes, bicycle and bird-watching tours, and canoe trips (from Flamingo and the Gulf Coast). Rangers also host slide shows, workshops, and lectures on everything from endangered species to medicinal plants.

Everglades National Park's Golden Age Passport is free to all U.S. citizens or permanent residents over the age of 62 and entitles the and 4–6:30 PM). Greyhound Lines (tel. 800/231–2222) makes three trips daily from its depot (4111 N.W. 27th St., Miami, tel. 305/871–1810), stopping at the Homestead Bus Station (5 N.E. 3rd Rd., tel. 305/247–2040). To connect with one of Greyhound's buses, you can take an ARTS (Airport Region Taxi Service) cab from MIA to the depot for about $5.

By Taxi: Taxis are available at the airport. To return to MIA from the Homestead–Florida City area, reserve a cab through Kendall Taxi (tel. 305/388–8888).

BY CAR From the north, the main highways to Homestead/Florida City are U.S. 1, the Homestead Extension of the Florida turnpike, and Krome Avenue (Rte. 997/Old U.S. 27).

From Homestead to Everglades National Park's Main Visitor Center (11 mi) or Flamingo (49 mi), take U.S. 1 or Krome Avenue south to Florida City and turn right (west) onto Rte. 9336. To reach the park's western gateway at Everglades City, take U.S. 41 (the Tamiami Trail) west from Miami (80 mi). To reach the south end of Everglades National Park in the Florida Keys, take U.S. 1 south from Homestead. It's 27 miles to the Key Largo Ranger Station, located between mile markers 98 and 99 on the Overseas Highway.

GETTING AROUND

You can walk, drive, or cycle the length of the park's main road, Rte. 9336, but you might want to drive this 38-mile stretch and save your walking legs for exploring the numerous marked trails leading off from the highway. At Flamingo you can hike or bike on several trails or view the backcountry by boat (the only way to explore the mangrove islands and estuaries of the Gulf Coast is by boat).

REST STOPS All of the park's visitor centers—Main Visitor Center, Royal Palm, Flamingo, Shark Valley, and Gulf Coast—have rest rooms.

GUIDED TOURS Concession-operated boat tours are available at Flamingo and Everglades City; concession-operated tram tours

are offered at Flamingo and Shark Valley. TW Recreational Services offers several boat tours at Flamingo (tel. 305/253–2241 from Miami or 813/695–3101 from the Gulf Coast; reservations recommended). Most popular are the Pelican Backcountry Cruise (2 hours; $11 adults, $5 children) and the Bald Eagle Florida Bay Cruise (90 minutes; $8 adults, $4 children). TW Recreational Services also operates a two-hour Wilderness Tram Tour along Snake Bight Trail—shaded by lush, tropical vegetation with horizon-wide views of the coastal prairie ($12; available Dec.–Mar. only).

TRF Concessions operates the popular two-hour tram tour at Shark Valley (tel. 305/221–8455; $7.30 adults, $3.65 children); reservations are recommended December–March.

Everglades National Park Boat Tours (tel. 813/695–2591 or 800/445–7724 in FL) offers several cruises from the Gulf Coast Visitor Center in Everglades City. Particularly popular is the Ten Thousand Islands Tour, where you might see manatee and nesting osprey (1 hour/45 min.; $10.60 adults, $5.30 children).

EXPLORING

Everglades National Park is open daily. Admission is $5 per car (good for seven days), free to U.S. citizens over age 62 and Golden Access Passport holders.

Everglades National Park's main road, Rte. 9336, begins at the Main Visitor Center and winds for 38 miles, ending in Flamingo. Leading off from the main road are more than a dozen marked walking trails. A slew of free ranger-conducted walking tours—such as "Slough Slogs," where you can get your feet wet and experience the real Everglades—and canoe trips are offered from mid-December through Easter.

Begin your tour of Everglades National Park at the **Main Visitor Center** (park headquarters), where you will find limited interpretive materials available in a temporary facility that replaces the center that was damaged by

Hurricane Andrew. The new visitor center is scheduled to open in the fall of 1995. *11 mi west of Homestead on Rte. 9336, tel. 305/242–7700. Open daily. Admission free.*

As you head deeper into the Glades, notice the prairies of 10-foot-high saw grass (an ancient sedge) bordering the road to the **Royal Palm Visitor Center.** Here you will find the ¹/₂-mile **Anhinga Trail,** one of the best wildlife-viewing trails in the United States. The trail is a combination of pavement and boardwalk that cuts through the Taylor Slough—a marshy river that's home to alligators, turtles, marsh rabbits, anhingas, herons, fish, and purple gallinules. Another ¹/₂-mile trail, the **Gumbo Limbo,** also originates here. This one winds through a junglelike grove of tropical trees, orchids, and ferns. Each trail takes about 30 minutes to complete. The Visitor Center has a small bookshop, vending machines, and a museum exhibiting the park's ecosystems. *Tel. 305/242–7700. Open daily. Admission free.*

Back on Rte. 9336, you'll come to **Long Pine Key,** a 7-mile network of trails running through a pine forest, which was largely destroyed by Hurricane Andrew. Check with park headquarters concerning the status of the Key trails. Continue until you get to the **Pahayokee Overlook.** Midway along this ¹/₄-mile boardwalk trail is an observation tower overlooking a sea of grasses punctuated by tree islands called hammocks—a panorama that gave the Glades its name. Vultures, blackbirds, hawks, snakes, and the occasional alligator can be seen along this trail.

From here, the road turns south to **Mahogany Hammock,** a damp, dark jungle of massive mahogany trees and rare paurotis palms. A ¹/₂-mile, elevated boardwalk trail with railways and benches along the way circles through the hammock.

Bird-watchers will want to stop at **Mrazek Pond,** just off the main road before coming to Flamingo, and **Eco Pond,** between the Flamingo Visitor Center and the Flamingo campgrounds. Wood storks, ibis, egrets, and herons are just some of the birds that spend the winter here.

The road ends at **Flamingo,** where, at sunset, you can watch hundreds of wading birds head out to roost on the protected mangrove islands of Florida Bay. With campgrounds, a motel, restaurant, marina and store, boat tours, and several canoe and hiking trails, Flamingo is an excellent base for exploring the southwestern Glades, along with the winding, mangrove-lined rivers, channels, and keys of Florida Bay. At the visitor center look for the Flamingo restaurant and lounge, a gift shop, and the Buttonwood Patio Bar. *Tel. 305/242–7700 (Park Service), tel. 305/253–2241 (Flamingo Lodge). Visitor center open daily. Admission free.*

From the Tamiami Trail (U.S. 41), a separate park entrance leads you to **Shark Valley,** where you can stroll the ¹/₂-mile Bobcat Trail (a boardwalk) through the saw-grass prairie or travel a 15-mile road that loops through a shallow waterway called the Shark River Slough. You can hike, bicycle, or take a two-hour tram tour around this loop road, spotting alligators, otters, snakes, turtles, snail kites, and numerous birds along the way. An observation tower midway along the loop provides a spectacular view of the "river of grass." The visitor center has displays and books available, and there are vending machines. *Park Information, tel. 305/221–8776; tram reservations, tel. 305/221–8455. Open daily. Admission charged.*

West along the Tamiami Trail, near Shark Valley, the **Miccosukee Indian Village** is run as a tourist attraction—it even has its own museum. You can watch Indian families cook and make clothes, dolls, beadwork, and baskets. You'll also see an alligator-wrestling demonstration. For a separate fee, airboat rides, which visit a typical Glades hammock-style Miccosukee campsite, are available. You can obtain information on the tribe's history and special events at the Information Center (¹/₄ mile east of the village, next to the restaurant). *Tamiami Trail, 25 mi west of Miami, tel. 305/223–8380. Open daily. Admission charged.*

Continuing west on Tamiami Trail, you'll drive through part of the **Big Cypress Na-**

tional Preserve, with its wet prairies, marshes, and stands of Spanish-moss-draped cypress trees. Watch for alligators sunning themselves on the banks of the canal that parallels the road.

To reach the western entrance to Everglades National Park, turn left (south) from Tamiami Trail onto Route 29, drive 3 miles through Everglades City to the **Gulf Coast Ranger Station.** The visitor center offers exhibits, information, gifts, snacks, and the required free permits for backcountry camping. This is also the place to arrange a boat tour to the Ten Thousand Islands region of the park, or to rent canoes for exploring the backcountry waterways (see Guided Tours, above; Canoeing, below). *Gulf Coast Ranger Station, Rte. 29, Everglades City 33929, tel. 813/695–3311. Open Daily. Admission free.*

HOTELS AND INNS

If you plan to spend a lot of time in the Everglades, stay either in Everglades National Park itself or 11 miles away in Homestead–Florida City, where there are a number of reasonably priced motels. If you plan to spend only a day in the Everglades, you may prefer to stay in the Greater Miami or Greater Fort Lauderdale areas. Hotel and motel accommodations are also available on the Gulf Coast in Everglades City and Naples. All of the accommodations listed below are convenient to Everglades National Park.

Price categories for double occupancy, excluding 6% tax, are *Moderate*, $85–$95, and *Inexpensive*, $50–$85.

MODERATE **Port of the Islands Resort & Marina.** A Spanish Mission–style hotel is the focal point of this resort 12 miles from the park's Gulf Coast Ranger Station. Accommodations are luxurious but reasonably priced, and amenities include boat rentals, cruises, and even a 3,500-foot private airstrip. *25000 Tamiami Trail E., Naples 33961, tel. 813/394–3101 or 800/237–4173, fax 813/394-4335. 154 rooms, 23 with kitchenettes, 5 suites. Restaurant, lounge, 2 heated pools, fitness room, tennis courts, nature trail, boat and bike ren-*

tals, 137-slip marina and marina store, airstrip, 99 full-hookup RV sites. AE, DC, MC, V.

INEXPENSIVE **Days Inn.** Completely renovated since Hurricane Andrew, this motel offers rooms with plush emerald green carpets, floral-print spreads, and rich-looking wood furnishings. One-third of the rooms are no-smoking, and a senior-citizen discount is offered. *51 S. Homestead Blvd. (U.S. 1), Homestead 33033, tel. 305/245–1260 or 800/247–5152, fax 305/247–0939. 100 rooms. Restaurant, lounge, outdoor heated pool, guest laundry. AE, D, DC, MC, V.*

Flamingo Lodge Marina & Outpost Resort. This rustic, low-rise wilderness resort—the only lodging inside the park—is for serious nature lovers. The lodge has basic, well-kept rooms facing Florida Bay, an amiable staff, and raccoons that roam about the pool enclosure at night; the cottages are in a wooded area on the perimeter of a coastal prairie. If you plan to stay in winter, reserve well in advance. Some services are available only seasonally. *Box 428, Flamingo 33090, tel. 305/253–2241 or 813/695–3101 from Gulf Coast. 102 motel rooms, 24 kitchenette cottages, 1 8-person suite. Restaurant, lounge, screened outdoor pool, 50-slip marina, marina store with snack bar, coin laundry. AE, DC, MC, V.*

Hampton Inn. This quiet, two-story motel, which opened in 1990 and was remodeled after Hurricane Andrew, offers complimentary Continental breakfast and an entire floor of no-smoking rooms. *124 E. Palm Dr., Florida City 33034, tel. 305/247–8833 or 800/426–7866, fax 305/247–8833. 122 rooms. Continental breakfast included, pool, free local phone calls. AE, D, DC, MC, V.*

Holiday Inn Express. In this low-rise chain motel, completely remodeled since Hurricane Andrew, rooms have colorful tropical decor with rattan-style furniture. Several rooms, including the new suites, overlook the new landscaped pool and adjoining Tiki Bar. *990 N. Homestead Blvd. (U.S. 1), Homestead 33030, tel. 305/247–7020 or 800/HOLIDAY. 139 rooms, 10 king suites. Outdoor pool,* *poolside Tiki bar, breakfast room. AE, D, DC, MC, V.*

CAMPGROUNDS

The three campgrounds in Everglades National Park—Chekika, Flamingo, and Long Pine Key—are primitive, with no water or electricity. RVs are permitted, but there are no hookups. Modern comfort stations, with picnic tables, grills, tent and trailer pads, rest rooms, drinking water, and sanitary dump stations for sewage are available. However, Chekika and Long Pine Key were heavily damaged by Hurricane Andrew and, at press time, were not scheduled to reopen until early 1994; check with park headquarters (tel. 305/242–7700) for the latest details. Either way, camping here is on a first-come, first-served basis, so arrive early to get a good site, especially in winter. Between December 1 and March 31, the maximum stay is 14 days.

Near the western entrance to Everglades National Park, the Port of the Islands Resort & Marina, south of Naples, offers 99 full-hookup RV sites (*see* Hotels and Inns, *above*). RV campgrounds are also available in Homestead and Florida City.

Chekika. This area was added to the park in 1991, and the campsite here offers central rest rooms, hot and cold showers, and picnic tables. Sites cost $8 in winter (they're free in summer), and there's a $3 vehicle entrance fee. *Chekika Campground, Everglades National Park, SW 237th Ave. and 160th St., tel. 305/251–0371. No hookups. Register at campground.*

Flamingo. This camping area offers cold-water showers, drinking water, rest rooms, and a sewage dump station. Limited groceries and camping supplies can be purchased at the Flamingo Marina Store. *Everglades National Park, Box 279, Homestead 33030 (38 mi from Main visitor center), tel. 305/242–7700. 235 drive-in sites, 60 walk-in sites; no hookups ($8 per night for drive-in sites in winter, free in summer; $4 per night for walk-ins in winter and summer). Register at campground.*

Long Pine Key. Long Pine Key has no camp store, so all supplies must be obtained in Homestead. *Everglades National Park, Box 279, Homestead 33030 (6 mi from Main Visitor Center), tel. 305/242–7700. No hookups. $8 in winter; free in summer. Register at campground.*

Everglades National Park Backcountry Sites. Deep within the park there are 48 designated campsites—2 accessible by land, the rest by water only. Most are beach or forest sites, but 14 are chickee sites (raised wooden platforms with thatched roofs). All have chemical toilets. Obtain free camping permits from the rangers at Flamingo or the Gulf Coast station. Permits are issued for a specific site; capacity and length of stay are limited. Call ahead for information and daily updates. *Flamingo Ranger Station, Backcountry Reservations Office, Box 279, Homestead 33034, tel. 305/253–2241, ext. 182 or 813/695–3101, ext. 182. Gulf Coast Ranger Station, Rte. 29, Everglades City 33929, tel. 813/695–3311. Sites available on first-come, first-served basis.*

Southern Comfort RV Resort. Ten miles from Everglades National Park, this RV-only campground, completely renovated since Hurricane Andrew, offers full hookups, a beautiful pool, a barbecue area with Tiki bar, and a recreation pavilion. *345 E. Palm Drive, Florida City 33034, tel. 305/248–6909, fax 305/242–1345. 200 RV sites, hookups ($28 daily; $150 weekly); comfort stations with showers, laundry, store. Reservations accepted. MC, V.*

DINING

Florida is filled with restaurants, and there are good places to eat within a short drive of all the park entrances. While you can find every type of cuisine from Chinese to Italian to Mexican, local specialties include dolphin (known as mahimahi); grouper; yellowtail snapper; stone-crab claws; and swordfish, prepared a number of different ways; conch soup and fritters; and fried alligator.

The list below is a selection of independent restaurants on the Tamiami Trail, in the Homestead/Florida City area, at Flamingo, and in the Everglades City area. Many of these establishments will pack picnic fare for you to take to the park, and several will prepare your catch with all the trimmings if you fillet it. You can also find fast-food establishments with carryout service on the Tamiami Trail and in Homestead/Florida City. Price categories per person, not including 6% tax, service, and drinks, are *Moderate*, $15–$25, and *Inexpensive*, under $15.

EVERGLADES CITY **The Oyster House.** A local favorite, this rustic, nautically decorated seafood restaurant serves up heaping plates of Blue Crab fingers, fresh Chokoloskee Bay oysters, and the ever-substantial Everglades Platter (fried gator, frogs' legs, catfish, deviled crab). A variety of Florida wines is offered, and your catch will be prepared to order. *Rte. 29 (across from Gulf Coast Ranger Station), tel. 813/695–2073 or 813/695–3423. Reservations accepted. Closed Thanksgiving and Christmas. MC, V. Inexpensive.*

FLAMINGO **Flamingo Restaurant.** The only restaurant in Everglades National Park, Flamingo offers excellent seafood and breathtaking views of Florida Bay from the picture windows of its three-tier dining room. Specialties include fried marlin and pork loin roasted Cuban style with garlic and lime. Picnic boxes are available. Between April and mid-October there is buffet service only. *Flamingo Visitor Center, Everglades National Park, tel. 305/253–2241 or 813/695–3101 from the Gulf Coast. Reservations advised. AE, DC, MC, V. Moderate.*

FLORIDA CITY **Richard Accursio's Capri Restaurant.** A popular Italian restaurant since 1958, the Capri is known for its family atmosphere, good food, and varied menu, serving everything from pizza to conch chowder. *935 Krome Ave., tel. 305/247–1544. Reservations advised. AE, MC, V. Closed Sun. Inexpensive.*

HOMESTEAD **Chez Jean Claude (JC's Place).** The garish pink-and-purple facade of this refurbished 1931 "hurricane-proof" house (it lost only two roof shingles to Hurricane Andrew) does not prepare you for the intimate, understated dining rooms, with their white linen tablecloths and fresh flowers. Homemade stews are among the French-country specialties. *1235 N. Krome Ave., tel. 305/248–4671. Reservations accepted. Open for dinner only. Closed Mon. and Aug.–mid-Sept. AE, MC, V. Moderate.*

Mutineer Restaurant. Specializing in Florida seafood, this stylish roadside restaurant, complete with an indoor/outdoor fish pond, offers bilevel dining, a nautical ambience, and the lively Wharf Lounge. Among the Mutineer's fresh seafood dishes, a standout is snapper Oscar, topped with crabmeat and asparagus. *11 S.E. 1st Ave., tel. 305/245–3377. Reservations accepted. AE, D, DC, MC, V. Moderate.*

Tiffany's. Traditional American breakfasts and lunches are served up in this family-run restaurant designed to resemble a pioneer Miami house, with a warm, tearoom atmosphere. Try the hot crabmeat au gratin and the homemade carrot cake. *22 N.E. 15th St., tel. 305/246–0022. Open for breakfast and lunch only. Reservations accepted. AE, MC, V. Inexpensive.*

TAMIAMI TRAIL **Miccosukee Restaurant.** Eye-catching murals and waitresses in vibrant woven skirts prepare the way for some traditional Miccosukee Indian recipes, among them pumpkin bread, fried catfish, and Indian fry bread (slabs of dough deep-fried in peanut oil). *On Tamiami Trail near Shark Valley entrance to Everglades National Park, tel. 305/223–8380, ext. 332. AE, DC, MC, V. Inexpensive.*

OUTDOOR ACTIVITIES

BIKING Bicycle rentals are available at Flamingo Lodge Marina & Outpost Resort (TW Recreational Services, tel. 305/253–2241 or 813/695–3101; $2.50 per hour, $12 all day). Ask the rangers for "Foot and Canoe Trails of the Flamingo Area," a leaflet that also lists bike trails. Inquire about water levels and insect conditions before you set out.

The concession at Shark Valley (tel. 305/221–8455) rents bikes for $2 per hour. You may ride along the Loop Road, a 15-mile round-trip. Yield right-of-way to trams.

CANOEING The subtropical wilderness of southern Florida is a mecca for flat-water paddlers. There are six well-marked canoe trails in the Flamingo area, including the southern end of the 99-mile Wilderness Waterway from Flamingo to Everglades City. Bring your own canoe cushions, and be sure to get the required free permit from the rangers at Flamingo or the Gulf Coast station if you plan to camp overnight. You can rent canoes at Everglades National Park Boat Tours (Gulf Coast Ranger Station, Everglades City, tel. 813/695–2591 or 800/445–7724 in FL; $20 full day, $15 half-day), North America Canoe Tours at Glades Haven (800 S.E. Copeland Ave., Everglades City, tel. 813/695–4666; $20 first day, $18 per day thereafter), and Flamingo Lodge Marina & Outpost Resort (Ever-glades National Park, Flamingo, tel. 305/253–2241; $25 full day, $20 half-day).

FISHING The inland and coastal waters of the Everglades are popular for both saltwater and freshwater fishing. There are largemouth bass in freshwater ponds, while snapper, red-fish, and trout can be caught in Florida Bay. The mangrove shallows of the Ten Thousand Islands yield tarpon and snook. Freshwater and saltwater fishing require separate Florida fishing licenses. Check at a park visitor center for specific fishing regulations and closed areas. Boats can be rented at Flamingo Lodge Marina & Outpost Resort (Everglades National Park, Flamingo, tel. 305/253–2241). Everglades City has boat rentals, chartered fishing trips, and fishing guides in abundance. For U.S. Coast Guard licensed fishing guides try Fishing on the Edge (tel. 813/695–2322) or Capt. Clint Butler (tel. 813/695–4103).

Gettysburg
Pennsylvania

Cannons and monuments lining the roadside signal to visitors that they have arrived in historic Gettysburg, Pennsylvania, site of perhaps the most famous battle of the Civil War (or War Between the States, depending on the side of the Mason-Dixon line from which you come). Here, for three days in July of 1863, Union and Confederate forces faced off in a bloody conflict that left some 51,000 casualties. The resulting Confederate defeat is regarded by many historians as the turning point of the war. Consecrating a national military cemetery on the site the following November, President Lincoln delivered a two-minute speech—the Gettysburg Address—that has gone down in history.

Covering over 5,000 acres, the Gettysburg National Military Park contains more than 40 miles of scenic avenues winding around the landmarks of the battle. The National Cemetery in particular is a well-shaded spot for a lovely summer stroll. The tourist district at the southern end of town offers several museums and shops, and the historic downtown area contains more than 100 buildings restored to their original Civil War charm. In all, more than 1,000 markers and monuments commemorate the battle. Those who want to skip from the Civil War era to the mid–20th century can visit the home of former president Dwight D. Eisenhower, which is right next to the park. The orchards of Adams County, just north of town, are especially beautiful to drive through in May.

A visit to Gettysburg is easily combined with a trip to the Pennsylvania Dutch country (*see* the Pennsylvania Dutch Country chapter).

ESSENTIAL INFORMATION

WHEN TO GO Summer months and weekends can be quite crowded at this popular destination. Crowds begin thinning out after Labor Day, but weekends are still busy through November, and the action picks up

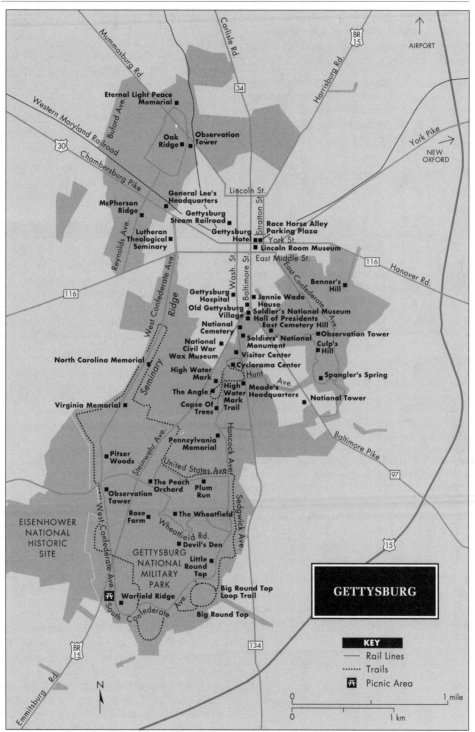

Eternal Light Peace Memorial

Oak Ridge

Observation Tower

General Lee's Headquarters

McPherson Ridge

Gettysburg Steam Railroad

Lutheran Theological Seminary

Gettysburg Hotel

Race Horse Alley Parking Plaza

York St.

Lincoln Room Museum

East Middle St.

Benner's Hill

Gettysburg Hospital

Jennie Wade House

Old Gettysburg Village

Soldier's National Museum

Hall of Presidents

National Cemetery

East Cemetery Hill

National Civil War Wax Museum

Soldiers' National Monument

Observation Tower

Culp's Hill

North Carolina Memorial

Visitor Center

High Water Mark

Cyclorama Center

The Angle

High Water Mark Trail

Meade's Headquarters

Spangler's Spring

Virginia Memorial

Copse Of Trees

National Tower

Pennsylvania Memorial

Pitzer Woods

United States Ave.

The Peach Orchard

Plum Run

Observation Tower

Rose Farm

The Wheatfield

EISENHOWER NATIONAL HISTORIC SITE

Devil's Den

GETTYSBURG NATIONAL MILITARY PARK

Little Round Top

Warfield Ridge

Big Round Top Loop Trail

Big Round Top

GETTYSBURG

KEY
— Rail Lines
...... Trails
🏕 Picnic Area

0   1 mile

0   1 km

AIRPORT

NEW OXFORD

N

again beginning on Easter Sunday. The best hotel rates are November through March, but if you visit then, be aware that some museums close during the winter months.

In August, the maximum temperature averages about 90°, with punishing humidity. January and February are cold, with an average high of 30°. Spring and fall months bring changeable weather, with many warm days but brisk, cool nights.

FESTIVALS AND SPECIAL EVENTS **Late June–early July:** Gettysburg Civil War Heritage Days commemorates the Battle of Gettysburg with living history encampments, band concerts, and battle reenactments. **Early Oct.:** National Apple Harvest Festival is an old-time festival featuring apple products, live country music, arts and crafts, antique autos, steam engines, orchard tours, pony rides, and homemade foods. **Mid-Nov.:** Remembrance Day, the anniversary of Lincoln's Gettysburg Address, includes a parade and wreath-laying ceremony.

BARGAINS The Gettysburg area's chief attraction—the battlefield park itself—charges no admission fee, and the park service offers a wide variety of free walks and lectures that are not widely advertised, so be sure to ask at the visitor center for topics and schedules.

TOURIST OFFICES Gettysburg Travel Council (35 Carlisle St., Gettysburg 17325, tel. 717/334–6274, fax 717/334–1166); Gettysburg-Adams County Area Chamber of Commerce (30 York St., Gettysburg 17325, tel. 717/334–8151); Gettysburg Tour Center (778 Baltimore St., Gettysburg 17325, tel. 717/334–6296).

EMERGENCIES Dial 717/334–8101 for **police, fire,** and **ambulance.** You can also call the **state police** (tel. 717/334–8111). **Hospitals:** Gettysburg Hospital (147 Gettys St., tel. 717/334–2121 or for 24-hour emergency services 717/337–HELP). **Doctors:** Physician referral service (tel. 717/334–4646).

ARRIVING AND DEPARTING

BY PLANE The closest major airport is the Harrisburg International Airport (tel. 717/948–3900), served by American, Continental, Delta, Northwest, United, and USAir airlines. Pick up the Pennsylvania Turnpike (I–76) from the airport and head west to Rte. 15, which leads about 40 miles south to Gettysburg.

BY CAR Gettysburg's major east/west corridor is Rte. 30, and from the north or south, Rte. 15.

GETTING AROUND

BY CAR A car is the most practical means of touring the Gettysburg area, although the best way to explore the downtown area is on foot. Parking in the downtown area can sometimes be a problem; the Race Horse Alley Parking Plaza off Stratton Street, behind the Gettysburg Hotel, offers covered, lighted parking.

BY TROLLEY Gettysburg's downtown area is served by a trolley. The fare is 50¢, paid to the trolley driver.

REST STOPS There are rest rooms conveniently located at the visitor center and throughout the battlefield. Rest rooms in the downtown area can be found at the Adams County Library and Adams County Courthouse, both on Baltimore Street.

GUIDED TOURS Auto tour maps can be picked up at the Visitor Center; auto tour tapes, which can be bought or rented at the numerous tour centers, re-create the historic three-day battle with sound effects as you drive through the battlefield at your own pace.

Gettysburg Battlefield Bus Tours (tel. 717/334–6296) offers narrated 23-mile bus tours of the battlegrounds; Eisenhower Farm Tour (tel. 717/334–1124) visits the president's homestead; Gettysburg Railroad Steam Train (tel. 717/334–6932) is a 16- or 50-mile narrated steam-train ride through the countryside; the Association of Battlefield Guides (tel. 717/334–1124) arranges for licensed guides to drive you through the battlefield in your car.

EXPLORING

The Gettysburg National Military Park surrounds the town of Gettysburg, and at times the two are indistinguishable. Entering town from the south, you'll discover stone walls, rolling farmlands, and stately homes that were used as hospitals during the famous battle. Many of the oak trees along the roadway have stood for more than 150 years.

Gettysburg National Military Park. There are several trails for walking around the park (*see* Hiking/Walking, *below*), or you can stop at the Visitor Center (Emmitsburg Rd., tel. 717/334–1124) to pick up an auto tour map, which outlines an 18-mile driving tour to 16 marked historic sites, tracing the three-day battle in chronological order. The center also offers the Electric Map presentation (admission charged, sit on the south side for the best view of the action), and across the parking lot is the **Cyclorama Center,** with its 360° canvas depicting the battle (tel. 717/334–1124; admission charged). Highlights of the auto tour include the **Eternal Peace Light Memorial;** the view from the ridge at **Little Round Top;** the **Wheatfield,** site of a particularly bloody skirmish; the **Pennsylvania Memorial,** marking the site where Union artillery held the line on Cemetery Ridge; **Culp's Hill** (an optional 5-mile loop), with its observation tower and short walking trail; **High Water Mark,** site of the battle's climax, when some 7,000 Union soldiers repulsed the 12,000 Confederate soldiers of Pickett's Charge; and the **National Cemetery,** where President Lincoln delivered the Gettysburg Address on November 19, 1863.

Eisenhower National Historic Site. Adjacent to the park to the west is the Georgian-style farmhouse used as a retirement home by President Dwight D. Eisenhower. Shuttle buses take tours to the site from an information center on the lower level of the visitor center of the park (*see above*). Tel. 717/334–

1124. Closed early Jan.–early Feb. Admission charged.

National Civil War Wax Museum. Just west of the National Cemetery, this audiovisual presentation brings to life some 200 Civil War figures in 30 scenes, as well as a reenactment of the Battle of Gettysburg and an animated figure of Lincoln giving the Gettysburg Address. *Bus. Rte. 15, tel. 717/334–6245. Admission charged. Open Mar. 1–weekend after Thanksgiving, daily; Dec.–Feb., weekends only.*

Hall of Presidents and First Ladies. To the north of the cemetery is a gallery displaying wax reproductions of the presidents "narrating" the story of America. *789 Baltimore St., tel. 717/334–5717. Open Mar.–Nov. Admission charged.*

Jennie Wade House. Directly north of the Hall of Presidents, you can walk through the carefully restored brick home of Jennie Wade, the only civilian to be killed in the battle of Gettysburg. *Baltimore St., tel. 717/334–4100. Open Mar.–Nov. Admission charged.*

Other worthwhile attractions surrounding the battlefield include **Soldier's National Museum** (777 Baltimore St., tel. 717/334–4890; open Mar.–Nov.; admission charged) with its miniature dioramas of the Civil War's 10 major battles, and the **National Tower** (999 Baltimore Pike, tel. 717/334–6754; admission charged) for 360° views from a perch 307 feet above the battlefield.

Lincoln Square. The heart of Gettysburg's historic downtown area is Lincoln Square, which you can reach by following Baltimore Street north of the park to York Street. On the south side of the square, the **Lincoln Room Museum** (tel. 717/334–8188; open Mar.–Nov.; admission charged) houses the bedroom where the president finalized his famous address. On the north side of the square, the recently restored **Gettysburg Hotel** (tel. 717/337–2000 or 800/528–1234) was known as the vacation White House during the Eisenhower administration and hosted a number of other historic figures. Look for the Civil War–era cannonball still embedded in the redbrick building across the street.

Go west on York Street, which turns into Chambersburg Pike and takes you to **General Lee's Headquarters.** Used by Gen. Lee and his staff on the eve of July 1, 1863, this building houses one of the finest collections of Civil War relics. *Rte. 30W, tel. 717/334–3141. Open Mar.–Nov. Admission free.*

HOTELS AND INNS

Bed-and-breakfasts with unique Civil War charm have joined the family-oriented motels throughout the Gettysburg area. Price categories for double occupancy, without sales tax, are *Expensive,* $85–$100; *Moderate,* $65–$85; and *Inexpensive,* under $65.

EXPENSIVE **Best Western Gettysburg Hotel 1797.** Built before the Civil War, this venerable stucco hotel with green-striped awnings was reconstructed from a burned-out shell and reopened in 1991. It's a cut above the motels and B&Bs that predominate in the area. *1 Lincoln Sq., 17325, tel. 717/337–2000 or 800/528–1234. 83 rooms. Suites have whirlpool tubs and fireplaces; covered parking. AE, D, DC, MC, V.*

MODERATE **The Brierfield Bed and Breakfast.** Conveniently located near the major attractions, this restored 1878 house offers homey comfort, including well-furnished guest rooms and shady porches. *240 Baltimore St., 17325, tel. 717/334–8725. 3 rooms. Full breakfast included. No credit cards.*

Farnsworth House Inn. This Civil War–period B&B is an elegant Victorian house complete with actual bullet holes from the battle. Its restaurant (*see* Dining, *below*) serves authentic Civil War–era specialties. *401 Baltimore St., 17325, tel. 717/334–8838. 4 rooms. Full breakfast in garden included, restaurant. AE, D, MC, V.*

Hickory Bridge Farm. Set on a working 100-acre farm in the rolling orchard country of western Adams County, guests stay either in the pre-Revolutionary farmhouse or in one of two cottages. Found on the grounds are a small covered bridge, a trout stream, and a herd of Black Angus cattle. *96 Hickory Bridge Rd. (between Rte. 116 and U.S. 30, 8 mi west of Gettysburg), Oritanna 17353, tel. 717/642–5261. 6 rooms. Full breakfast included, restaurant. MC, V.*

The Little House Guest House. Originally a two-story Victorian carriage house, this small home-away-from-home with exposed brick walls and wooden beams includes a living room, an upstairs bedroom, and a kitchen. It can comfortably accommodate up to four people. *Rear 20 N. Washington St., 17325, tel. 717/334–3940. No credit cards.*

The Tannery Bed & Breakfast. Located in a residential area near major attractions, this Gothic-style Victorian home, built by a Civil War veteran in 1868, has shady porches and several common rooms where guests can relax. *449 Baltimore St., 17325, tel. 717/334–2454. 5 rooms with bath. Continental breakfast included, off-street parking. MC, V.*

INEXPENSIVE **Hosteling International–Gettysburg.** Offering Spartan dormitory-style lodging in bunk beds, this Civil War–era former hospital downtown gives an exceptional value; families or couples can opt for private accommodations. *27 Chambersburg St., 17325, tel. 717/334–1020. 60 beds. Kitchen, library, rooftop patio, common room. No credit cards.*

Blue Sky Motel. This family-owned motel 5 miles north of Lincoln Square is on a main road, but the landscaping creates a quiet country atmosphere. Guest rooms are paneled in knotty pine. Rates include complimentary morning coffee. *2585 Biglerville Rd., 17325, tel. 717/677–7736 or 800/745–8194. 16 rooms, 1 efficiency. Pool, picnic area. MC, V.*

MOTELS

EXPENSIVE **Holiday Inn** (516 Baltimore St., 17325, tel. 717/334–6211 or 800/HOLIDAY, fax 717/334–7183). 100 rooms; restaurant, pool, whirlpool baths. **Ramada Inn** (2634 Emmitsburg Rd., 17325, tel. 717/334–8121 or 800/776–8349). 203 rooms; restaurant, lounge, pool with 3 Jacuzzis, saunas, fitness center, tennis, racquetball, chip and putt golf, exercise course.

MODERATE **Comfort Inn** (871 York Rd., 17325, tel. 717/337–2400 or 800/228–5151). 81 rooms; indoor pool, whirlpool. **Days Inn** (865 York Rd., 17325, tel. 717/334–0030). 113 rooms; indoor pool, whirlpool. **Holiday Inn Express** (869 York Rd., 17325, tel. 717/337–1400 or 800/HOLIDAY). 51 rooms; indoor pool, whirlpool. **Quality Inn Gettysburg Motor Lodge** (380 Steinwehr Ave., 17325, tel. 717/334–1103 or 800/228-5151). 105 rooms; pool, fitness center, whirlpool, sauna, putting green, lounge.

INEXPENSIVE **Howard Johnson's Lodge** (301 Steinwehr Ave., 17325, tel. 717/334–1188). 77 rooms; pool, lounge, parking. **Perfect Rest Motel** (2450 Emmitsburg Rd., tel. 717/334–1345). 25 rooms. **Quality Inn—Larsons** (Rte. 30W, 17325, tel. 717/334–3141). 41 rooms; pool, putting green.

DINING

The predominant Pennsylvania Dutch ancestry in the area is reflected on dinner menus in such dishes as chicken and dumplings or *Snitz un Knepp* (a pie made with dried apples). Restaurants serve fresh locally grown fruits and vegetables, and menus feature items "cooked from scratch."

Price categories per person, not including 6% tax, service, and drinks, are *Moderate,* $15–$25, and *Inexpensive,* under $15.

MODERATE **Blue Parrot Bistro.** This cozy bar/restaurant near Lincoln Square offers an informal, intimate atmosphere, with a dinner menu including heart-healthy pastas. You can grab a quick lunch of soup or a deli combo from the counter bar. *35 Chambersburg St., tel. 717/337–3739. MC, V.*

Dobbin House Tavern. Built in 1776, this beautifully restored building in the tourist district features light, low-calorie, and charbroiled fare, and dinners by candlelight. *89 Steinwehr Ave., tel. 717/334–2100. AE, MC, V.*

Farnsworth House Inn. The menu at this restored inn (*see* Hotels and Inns, *above*) harks back to such Civil War–era dishes as game pie, peanut soup, and spoon bread. The partially covered outdoor garden, surrounded by ivy and sculptures and serenaded by the sounds of a waterfall, is a peaceful spot in which to relax after a day of touring the battlefield. *401 Baltimore St., tel. 717/334–8838. AE, D, MC, V.*

JD's Pub and Restaurant. Located on Lincoln Square, this lively pub-like restaurant offers a variety of pasta and seafood dishes, plus a full range of salads. *21 Lincoln Sq., tel. 717/334–7100. AE, MC, V.*

Hotel Gettysburg 1897. The dining room in this Lincoln Square hotel is among the most elegant spots in town. The house honors former president Eisenhower and his first lady with a prime rib special in their name—the Ike or Mamie cut (the Eisenhowers were frequent dinner guests here). *985 Baltimore St., tel. 717/334–9227. AE, MC, V.*

INEXPENSIVE **Hoss's Steak and Sea House.** The decor is rustic and the atmosphere family-oriented at this newly opened restaurant. Upon entering, diners order beef, chicken, ham, or seafood by number from a picture board and are then escorted to a table. Dinners include all-you-can-eat salad and dessert bar with homemade soups and warm breads. *1140 York Rd. (U.S. 30), tel. 717/337–2961. AE, D, MC, V.*

Dutch Cupboard Deli Delight. In the heart of the tourist district, this deli offers old-fashioned Dutch cooking, featuring soups, salads, and deli sandwiches. *523 Baltimore St., tel. 717/334–6227. MC, V.*

Lincoln Diner. You'll find the locals at this old-fashioned diner one block from Lincoln Square. Open 24 hours, it features fast service and Italian and Greek cooking. *32 Carlisle St., tel. 717/334–3900. No credit cards.*

Food for Thought Cafe. A favorite of the crowd from nearby Gettysburg College, this health-conscious eatery offers a coffee-shop atmosphere where you can linger as long as you like and order from a menu that includes Create-Your-Own Pita Sandwiches and organic side dishes. *48 Baltimore St., tel. 717/337–2211. No credit cards.*

Sunny Ray Family Restaurant. This restaurant, located on Rte. 30W, prepares food the old-fashioned way, including homemade soup and real mashed potatoes. There's a large salad bar and lighter menu selections as well. *90 Buford Ave., tel. 717/334–4816. No credit cards.*

Shoney's. Earth tones, rows of booths, and a glass atrium create a light, airy feeling in this '90s-style diner. The salad bar features homemade soups; the menu offers selections for children and specials for senior citizens. *Bus. Rte. 15 (adjacent to the National Civil War Wax Museum), tel. 717/334–7618. AE, D, MC, V.*

SHOPPING

Gettysburg has numerous shops that feature handmade crafts and furniture, antiques, gifts, Civil War memorabilia, and books. Tourist shops sell T-shirts, postcards, and other less expensive keepsakes; homemade quilts and furniture, handcrafted by the local Amish community, can be found south of town. Stop at one of the many roadside markets north of Gettysburg, such as Sandoes Market, An Apple A Day, or Hollabaugh Brothers, for fresh fruits and vegetables at bargain prices.

SHOPPING DISTRICTS Downtown, along the streets radiating from Lincoln Square, you'll discover unique stores offering clothing, crafts, books, art, and hard-to-find items. In the tourist district, virtually every other shop along Steinwehr Avenue sells bullets and relics excavated from the battlefield. At Old Gettysburg Village (777 Baltimore St.), you'll find quaint shops, including a fudge kitchen, doll shop, general store, and military art store.

SPECIALTY STORES Antiques: Mel's Antiques and Collectibles (rear of 103 Carlisle St., tel. 717/334–9387; open Fri.–Sun only) has many bargains. Arrow Horse International Market and Antiques (51 Chambersburg St., tel. 717/337–2899) sells gifts, antiques, and baskets as well as vegetarian foods, fresh-baked breads, international groceries, and coffee beans. You may also want to drive to New Oxford Borough, 10 miles east of Gettysburg on Rte. 30, which has numerous antiques shops.

Gifts: Codori's Bavarian Gift and Christmas Shop (19 Barlow St., tel. 717/334–5019) offers German and Scandinavian gifts, music boxes, nutcrackers, nativities, and Hummel figures. Irish Brigade Gift Shop (504 Baltimore St., tel. 717/337–2519) has a complete line of Irish jewelry, crystal, sweaters, linens, and china as well as Civil War–related items. The Country Curiosity Store (89 Steinwehr Ave. at the Dobbin House Tavern, tel. 717/334–2100) is a charming shop selling quilts, candles, bric-a-brac, and rebel flags. Gettysburg's largest gift shop may be found in the National Civil War Wax Museum (Bus. Rte. 15, tel. 717/334–6245).

War Memorabilia: The Horse Soldier (777 Baltimore St., tel. 717/334–0347) sells original military Americana, including guns, swords, documents, and photographs. For a vast selection of Civil War memorabilia, visit Farnsworth Military Impressions (401 Baltimore St., tel. 334–8838).

OUTDOOR ACTIVITIES

BIKING Marked bicycle routes offer a great way to discover the battlefield at your own pace. Bike rentals can be found at Artillery Ridge Campground (610 Taneytown Rd., tel. 717/334–1288).

HIKING/WALKING A number of trails can be found on the Gettysburg Battlefield, including: the High Water Mark Trail (1 mile, begins at the Cyclorama Center); the Big Round Top Loop Trail (1 mile); and paths winding through the enormous rocks, caves, and crevices that hid Confederate sharpshooters in Devil's Den. For a longer hike, inquire about the 9-mile Billy Yank Trail or the 3½-mile Johnny Reb Trail. For a more contemplative experience, plan an early morning or evening walk through the National Cemetery, near the spot where Abraham Lincoln delivered the Gettysburg Address. Few others will be present at this time of day, leaving you alone with the ghosts of the past.

HORSEBACK RIDING For trail riding across the battlefield, contact Hickory Hollow Farm (219 Crooked Creek Rd., tel. 717/334–0349) or National Riding Stables (610 Taneytown Rd., tel. 717/334–1288).

SKIING Skiing during the winter months can be found at Ski Liberty (8 miles from Gettysburg on Rte. 116, Carroll Valley, tel. 717/642–8282).

Grand Canyon National Park
Arizona

Neither words nor photographs can adequately describe the Grand Canyon; it must be seen up close and in person. More than 80 million years ago, a great wrenching of the earth pushed the land in the region up into a domed tableland. Ever since, the mighty Colorado River has chewed at this Colorado plateau, carving it away to create a geologic profile of the Earth's history and revealing, at the bottom of the canyon, the oldest exposed rock on the planet. Above the twisting line of river rise wildly carved stone buttes, whose colors change with the time of day. The view you see at midmorning is repainted by the setting sun. Standing for the first time at the canyon's edge is an experience that is never forgotten.

This vast and beautiful scar on the surface of our planet is 277 miles long, 17 miles across at the widest spot, and nearly 6,000 feet below the rim at its deepest point. Grand Canyon National Park encompasses the great gorge itself and vast areas of scenic countryside along the North and South rims. The South Rim, 81 miles from Flagstaff on U.S. 180, is more accessible, has more services and amenities, and is more crowded. The North Rim, 210 miles from Flagstaff through lonely but scenic country, is set in lush forest where you can get away by yourself only a few yards from motels and campgrounds.

ESSENTIAL INFORMATION

WHEN TO GO You can visit the South Rim anytime of year. Because it's at 7,000 feet, the summer offers warm days, with short but sometimes frequent afternoon thundershowers, and crisp evenings. Temperatures in spring and fall generally stay above 32° and often climb into the 70s, and in winter range from around 20° to near 50°. Snow further enhances the beauty of the canyon, and the roads are kept open. The North Rim, parts of it above 8,000 feet, is officially open from

May 16 to October 21, but unexpected snow can change those dates. For information on weather, call 602/638–7888.

Nearly 4 million people visit the canyon each year; almost 90% of them head for the South Rim, and summer crowds there are enormous. You must make summer reservations months in advance. If you visit in spring, fall, or winter, the crowds will have thinned out and prices, in some cases, will be lower. For our purposes, the "summer season" covers the months of June, July, and August. "Colder months" refers to the rest of the year.

BARGAINS At the Grand Canyon even the dining and lodging are reasonably priced. The entrance fee is $4; a car is $10 regardless of the number of passengers. When the gate-keepers are off duty (roughly 6 PM–7 AM), you may enter free. Among the daily free activities are lectures on the canyon's history, geology, plants and wildlife, and ancient inhabitants. These daily programs are listed in a free newspaper, *The Grand Canyon Guide,* available at visitor centers and at lodgings and stores, which has an area map showing shuttle-bus routes and rest rooms. In summer at the South Rim, a free shuttle bus takes visitors along the West Rim and to other stops in and near Grand Canyon Village. Visitors may also browse through the public areas and exhibits at the historic El Tovar Hotel and Bright Angel Lodge. Of course, scenery, the main attraction at the canyon, is always free.

TOURIST OFFICES Grand Canyon National Park (Box 129, Grand Canyon, AZ 86023, tel. 602/638–7888). Grand Canyon Park Lodges–South Rim (Box 699, Grand Canyon, AZ 86023, tel. 602/638–2401), for information on lodging and all other tour and recreational information inside the park. Grand Canyon Lodge–North Rim (Box 400, Cedar City, UT 84720, tel. 801/586–7686).

EMERGENCIES For **police, fire,** or **ambulance** dial 911 (from any motel or hotel room in Grand Canyon National Park, dial 9–911). **Clinics:** Grand Canyon Clinic, Grand Canyon Village (South Rim), has medical (tel. 602/638– 2551) and dental (tel. 602/638–2395) services. The North Rim Clinic at Grand Canyon Lodge has a nurse practitioner (tel. 602/638–2611). **Road Services:** the Fred Harvey Garage at Grand Canyon Village (tel. 602/638–2225) and the Chevron Station on the North Rim access road (tel. 602/638–2611, ext. 290) have road service.

ARRIVING AND DEPARTING

BY PLANE Sky Harbor International Airport in Phoenix (tel. 602/273–3300), served by all major airlines, has the best connections to Grand Canyon. From there and also from Flagstaff's Pulliam Airport (tel. 602/774–1422) and Las Vegas, Nevada's, McCarran International Airport (tel. 702/261–5743), connecting flights leave for Grand Canyon Airport (tel. 602/638–2446) on the South Rim. Transportation by van to the village of Tusayan, 6 miles south of the park, and to Grand Canyon Village on the South Rim, is provided by the Tusayan/Grand Canyon Shuttle (tel. 602/638–2475). The trip to Tusayan lodges is free; to Grand Canyon Village the fare for adults is $5 one-way, $8 round-trip. A 24-hour taxi service (tel. 602/638–2822) is available; the 15-minute trip costs $5 per person.

The Trans Canyon shuttle van (tel. 602/638–2820) makes the 235-mile trip to the North Rim from Grand Canyon Village daily ($60 one-way, $100 round-trip). You can also rent a car at the Grand Canyon Airport from Budget (tel. 800/527–0700) or Dollar Rent-A-Car (tel. 602/638–2625).

BY CAR Your best access to the Grand Canyon (South Rim) is from Flagstaff (on I–40), via U.S. 180 (81 miles) or U.S. 89 north, then west on Route 64 (107 miles). The longer route is more scenic. If you are driving on I–40 from the west, the most direct route is via Route 64 from Williams (58 miles). To reach the North Rim, drive north from Flagstaff on U.S. 89 to Bitter Springs, then take U.S. 89A to Route 67 and turn south to the North Rim (210 miles).

BY TRAIN Amtrak (tel. 800/USA–RAIL) has daily service to Flagstaff and, April through October, from there to Williams by bus. From

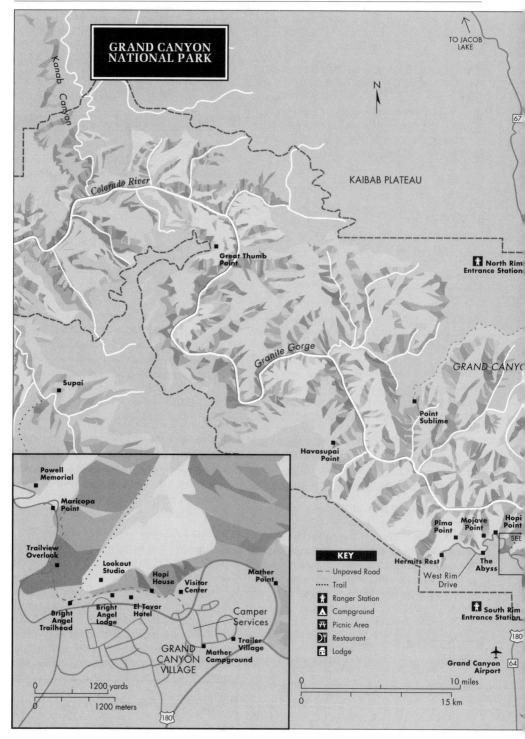

GRAND CANYON
NATIONAL PARK

N

TO JACOB
LAKE

67

Kanab Canyon

Colorado River

KAIBAB PLATEAU

Great Thumb
Point

Granite Gorge

North Rim
Entrance Station

Supai

Point
Sublime

GRAND CANYO

Havasupai
Point

Powell
Memorial

Maricopa
Point

Trailview
Overlook

Lookout
Studio

Hopi
House

Visitor
Center

Mather
Point

Pima
Point

Mojave
Point

Hopi
Point

SEE

Bright
Angel
Trailhead

Bright
Angel
Lodge

El Tovar
Hotel

Camper
Services

Hermits Rest

The
Abyss

West Rim
Drive

GRAND
CANYON
VILLAGE

Mather
Campground

Trailer
Village

South Rim
Entrance Station

180

KEY

Unpaved Road
Trail
Ranger Station
Campground
Picnic Area
Restaurant
Lodge

Grand Canyon
Airport

64

0   1200 yards

0   1200 meters

180

0   10 miles

0   15 km

Flagstaff, bus connections can be made to Grand Canyon Village and Tusayan through Nava-Hopi Tours (tel. 602/774–5003 or 800/892–8687). From Williams, you can continue by train on the historic Grand Canyon Railway (518 E. Bill Williams Ave., Williams 86046, tel. 602/635–4000 or 800/843–8724), whose turn-of-the-century steam engines make one round-trip a day from Williams. The trip takes $2^1/_4$ hours each way.

BY BUS Greyhound Lines (tel. 800/231–2222) serves Flagstaff and Williams.

GETTING AROUND

ON FOOT Once you reach the Grand Canyon, you don't need a car. At Grand Canyon Village many scenic viewing points, museums, hotels, and restaurants are within easy walking distance, and visitors can also catch a free shuttle bus (in summer) or a taxi, or sign up for bus tours. At the North Rim, viewing points and other attractions are within walking distance of Grand Canyon Lodge.

BY CAR AND RV Because of the scenic drives in and around the National Park, having your own car or RV is a convenience. At the South Rim in summer, when lodging space is tight, an RV would be an advantage. The free parking lots are large. The route to the remote North Rim is never congested.

BY BUS AND TAXI Scenic bus tours and shuttles (some free in summer) and local taxi services (tel. 602/638–2475 or 602/638–2822) provide adequate local transportation in Grand Canyon Village, nearby Tusayan, and at the North Rim (see Guided Tours, below).

REST STOPS There are bathrooms throughout the National Park at the Visitor Center, lodgings, museums, and many viewing points. Nava-Hopi Tours buses have rest rooms.

GUIDED TOURS There's plenty to choose from among the Grand Canyon's guided tours by raft, air, bus, and mule. The raft trips are relatively expensive and must be booked well in advance (see Outdoor Activities, below). Plane and helicopter rides over the canyon from the South Rim (cost: $50–$75 per person) are offered by Air Grand Canyon (tel. 602/638– 2618) and Kenai Helicopters (tel. 602/638–2764), among others.

The Fred Harvey Transportation Company in Grand Canyon Village (tel. 602/638–2631) offers motorcoach trips along the South Rim and as far away as Monument Valley. Its Desert View Tour (4 hours, 25 miles; $17 adults, $8.50 children) stops at Yaki Point and at Grandview Point; Moran Point, where landscape artist Thomas Moran painted; the Tusayan Ruin and Museum, to learn about the early Anasazi culture; and at the Desert View and Watchtower (tel. 602/638–2736), the South Rim's highest elevation, where there's a gift shop, general store, trading post, and service station. At the North Rim, minibus tours to Cape Royal and Point Imperial can be booked at Grand Canyon Lodge (tel. 602/635–4000). Nava-Hopi Tours (tel. 602/774–5003), in Flagstaff, runs a daily guided tour to the South Rim and East Rim that takes in the Old Cameron Trading Post, Yavapai and Mather points, and the IMAX film at Tusayan.

You can take mule rides into the canyon from the North Rim and South Rim, but you must be taller than 4'7", weigh less than 200 pounds, speak English, and not be pregnant. A typical two-hour ride costs about $25, an all-day trip $70 (lunch included). Overnight trips to Phantom Ranch at the bottom of the canyon run about $260 ($463 for two), including one night's lodging and meals. Write as early as possible to the Reservations Dept. (Box 699, Grand Canyon 86023, tel. 602/638–2401) for South Rim rides, and Grand Canyon Trail Rides (Box 128, Tropic, UT 84776, tel. 602/638–2292 or 801/679–8665 in winter) for the North Rim.

EXPLORING

We suggest two tours to cover the main points of interest on both the South Rim and North Rim (the South Rim tour is in two parts; the first is taken on foot, the second—to the so-called West Rim—by car or bus). Unless otherwise noted, points on the tours are open daily and admission is free.

SOUTH RIM TOUR **Mather Point** offers your first look into the awesome gulf—you have an extraordinary view of the inner gorge and numerous buttes that rise out of the chasm. **The Visitor Center** (tel. 602/638–7888) provides a comprehensive orientation to the Grand Canyon, information, natural-history exhibits, short movies and slide programs, and a bookstore. Park rangers are on duty to answer questions and help plan excursions. **The Yavapai Museum** (tel. 602/638–7888), less than a mile northeast of the visitor center, has exhibits tracing the long geologic history of the canyon; the polarized picture windows provide excellent views into the depths of the gorge and signboards identify the features of the panorama. Buy booklets (25¢ each) here for a self-guided tour west along the rim, starting at the museum. **The Village Nature Trail** is a paved, level, and easy route along the canyon edge, with marvelous views. Highlights along the 2½-mile walk include **Hopi House** (tel. 602/638–2631), a multistory building that duplicates a Hopi Indian pueblo and is one of the best-stocked gift shops in the area, and **El Tovar Hotel** (tel. 602/638–2401), an imposing log-and-stone structure built in 1905 and considered one of the finest hotels in the national park system; you can browse through the rustic lobby and people-watch. Eventually you'll reach Bright Angel Trailhead, the start of a well-maintained track that leads to the floor of the canyon. From the trailhead, you can walk directly back east past the mule barn to **Bright Angel Lodge,** another of the canyon's historic hotels. It has a dining room (full meals, light lunches) and a soda fountain and is a good spot for resting after your walk.

You can tour the **West Rim** during most of the year by car, and in summer take the free shuttle bus from the vicinity of Bright Angel Lodge. **Trailview Overlook** offers a good view of Bright Angel Trail as it loops its way down to the inner gorge. **Maricopa Point** offers a clear view of the Colorado River. The large granite **Powell Memorial** is dedicated to the early canyon explorer John Wesley Powell. **Hopi Point** looks out over the Colorado River where it is 350 feet wide, and **Mojave Point** reveals three sets of white-water rapids. At

The Abyss, a sheer canyon wall drops 3,000 feet to the Tonto Plateau. At **Pima Point,** you'll see a clear view of the Tonto Trail, which winds more than 70 miles through the canyon. **Hermits Rest,** named for Louis Boucher, a 19th-century prospector who lived in the canyon, sells refreshments and has the only rest rooms on the West Rim.

NORTH RIM TOUR You approach the North Rim of the Grand Canyon through the Arizona Strip, the land between the canyon and the Utah border, ending with a magnificent 45-mile drive south on Route 67, along the 9,000-foot-high Kaibab Plateau. Most visitors immediately go to the historic **Grand Canyon Lodge** (tel. 801/586–7686 or 602/638–2611), which has a huge lounge area with hardwood floors, high, beamed ceilings, and wide windows that give a superb view of the canyon. There is also a spacious viewing deck outside. The short trail to **Bright Angel Point** starts on the grounds of the hotel and proceeds along a crest of rock that juts out into the canyon. The ¹/₂-mile round-trip is exciting because of the sheer drop on each side of the trail. Afterward, you can lunch in the rustic stone-and-log dining room of the lodge, then browse through the nearby curio shop or take a leisurely walk down **Transept Trail,** which starts near the lodge's east patio.

To reach Point Imperial and Cape Royal, two of the North Rim's most popular viewing points, drive north from Grand Canyon Lodge, bear right at the signposted fork, and continue for 11 miles. **Point Imperial,** at 8,803 feet, the highest point on either rim, reveals not only the canyon but thousands of square miles of surrounding countryside. Return west to a signed junction and turn left to **Cape Royal,** which is 15 miles south on the paved road. From here you can see **Angel's Window,** a giant eroded hole through the projecting ridge of Cape Royal. Near the parking area there's a wonderfully scenic spot for a picnic, with rest rooms. The nearby **Cliff Springs Trail** is an easy 1-mile walk through a heavily forested ravine to another impressive view of the canyon.

THE NATURAL WORLD The South Rim, at about 7,000 feet, is forested primarily by ponderosa pine, piñon pine, and Utah juniper. Shrubs include cliff rose, mountain mahogany, and fern-bush. The Kaibab Plateau on the North Rim is thickly forested with ponderosa pine, spruce, fir, and quaking aspen. Two animal species are unique to the area: the Kaibab squirrel, with its white tail and tufted ears, is found only on the North Rim, and the pink rattlesnake is found at lower elevations down in the canyon. Mule deer are frequently seen in the park as they cross the roads (so drive carefully). Coyotes are seldom seen but often heard as they howl and yip at night, and you might see hawks and ravens riding the updrafts over the canyon.

HOTELS AND INNS

Try to make summer reservations as early as possible, particularly within the park. If you can't get rooms near the canyon, you might find vacancies in Flagstaff or Williams, on the Navajo Reservation at the Cameron Trading Post (U.S. 89, tel. 602/679–2231), or in Tuba City at the Tuba Motel (U.S. 160, tel. 602/283–4545). Price categories for double occupancy, excluding 5¹/₂% tax, are *Expensive,* $85–$200; *Moderate,* $50–$85; and *Inexpensive,* under $50.

SOUTH RIM **El Tovar Hotel.** Built in 1905 of native stone and pine logs in the style of a European hunting lodge, this is regarded as one of the finest national park hotels; reservations are a must. *Box 699, Grand Canyon 86023, tel. 602/638–2401, fax 602/638–9247. 78 rooms and suites. Dining room, lounge, gift shop, air-conditioning. AE, D, DC, MC, V. Expensive.*

Best Western Grand Canyon Squire. The rooms are Standard American Roadside in design and decor, without the charm of the older lodges in Grand Canyon Village, but there are some nice amenities. *Tusayan 86023, tel. 602/638–2681 or 800/528–1234, fax 602/638–2782. 150 units. Dining room, coffee shop, gift shop, heated pool, indoor whirlpool, air-conditioning, tennis courts. AE, D, DC, MC, V. Moderate–Expensive.*

Bright Angel Lodge. This rustic hostelry built in 1935 sits within a few yards of the canyon rim, with rooms in the main lodge or in quaint cabins. *Box 699, Grand Canyon 86023, tel. 602/638–2401, fax 602/638–9247. 90 units. Dining room, steak house, lounge, gift shop. AE, D, DC, MC, V. Moderate–Expensive.*

Phantom Ranch. At the bottom of the Grand Canyon, accessible only to hikers or mule riders, the ranch has four 10-bed dormitories and 12 stone-and-timber cabins. *Box 699, Grand Canyon 86023, tel. 602/638– 2401, fax 602/638–9247. Meals available. AE, D, DC, MC, V. Inexpensive–Moderate.*

Quality Inn. This is a clean, comfortable motel—with typically bland motel architecture and decor—located 1 mile south of the park's south entrance. *Tusayan 86023, tel. 602/638–2673. 185 units. Dining room, coffee shop, gift shop, heated pool, air-conditioning. AE, D, DC, MC, V. Inexpensive–Moderate.*

NORTH RIM **Grand Canyon Lodge.** This rugged, spacious lodge, a few yards from the rim at Bright Angel Point, opened in 1937. The main building has massive limestone walls and timbered ceilings. The accommodations are in rustic cabins (five with views) and motel units scattered among the pines. *TW Services, Box 400, Cedar City, UT 84721, tel. 801/586–7686, fax 801/586–3157. 161 cabins and 40 motel units. Dining room, cafeteria, lounge, gift shop. AE, DC, MC, V. Inexpensive–Moderate.*

Kaibab Lodge. This group of rustic cabins (and two Mongolian yurts that sleep 10, dormitory style, at $15 each), 18 miles north of the canyon rim, has a gas station and is open in winter (mid-Dec.–Mar.) for cross-country skiing and hikes. *Rte. 64, Box 30, Fredonia 86022, tel. 602/638–2389, 602/526–0924, or 800/525–0924, fax 602/527–9398. 25 units and 20 yurt spaces. Dining room, country store, gift shop, TV in lodge, no phones. MC, V. Inexpensive–Moderate.*

MOTELS

These rustic but clean, no-frills lodgings on U.S. 89A, 45 to 80 miles from the North Rim,

range from Indian-style rock-and-mortar buildings to frame cabins.

INEXPENSIVE-MODERATE **Cliff Dwellers Lodge** (Marble Canyon 86036, tel. 602/355– 2228). 20 rooms; restaurant, general store. **Jacob Lake Inn** (Jacob Lake 86022, tel. 602/643–7232). 35 rooms; restaurant, lunch counter, general store, gift shop. **Lees Ferry Lodge** (Lees Ferry 86036, tel. 602/355– 2231). 8 rooms, double cabin; restaurant, gift shop, tackle shop. **Marble Canyon Lodge** (Marble Canyon 86036, tel. 602/355–2225 or 602/355–2227). 51 rooms; restaurant, general store, coin laundry.

CAMPGROUNDS

All campgrounds here are attractively located, most of them in heavy pine forests—and they're very popular, particularly at the South Rim. If you can't get reservations, try the Kaibab National Forest, which is open to "at-large" camping. Inside the park, camping is permitted only in designated areas, and a permit is required for camping within the canyon. Write to Backcountry Reservation Office (Box 129, Grand Canyon 86023, tel. 602/638–7888) well in advance. Remember that *everything* that goes into the canyon must be packed out, even cigarette butts and used toilet paper. Gasoline and groceries are available at Grand Canyon Village, Desert View, and on the North Rim.

SOUTH RIM **Desert View Campground.** This National Park Service (NPS) campground is 25 miles from South Rim in an area generally referred to as East Rim. Still, it has a magnificent view of the canyon from the Watchtower Lookout, plus a grocery store, service station, and trading post. *Tel. 602/638–7888. 50 RV and tent sites, no hookups ($8); flush toilets. No reservations. Open May–Oct. No credit cards.*

Grand Canyon Camper Village. This commercial campground 1 mile south of the National Park entrance on U.S. 180 is generally rated among the best in the South Rim area. *Tel. 602/638–2887. 200 RV sites with full hookups ($20), water and electricity ($18), 60* tent sites ($13); flush toilets, coin-op showers, grills and picnic tables. Reservations accepted. Open all year. No credit cards.

Mather Campground. This popular NPS South Rim location is heavily booked in summer, so make reservations as early as possible. *Tel. 602/638–7888. 319 RV and tent sites, no hookups ($10); water, flush toilets, coin-op showers, laundry, dump station, grills, picnic tables. Reservations through Mistix, tel. 800/365–2267. Open all year. MC, V.*

Trailer Village. This Fred Harvey park, near the visitor center on the South Rim, is convenient for RVs, but make reservations well in advance. *Tel. 602/638–2401, fax 602/638–9247. 80 RV sites with full hookups ($17); flush toilets, showers, laundry and grocery store nearby. Open year-round. MC, V.*

NORTH RIM **Demotte Campground.** This attractive National Forest Service site is in an area of tall pines, 20 miles north of the North Rim. *Tel. 602/643–7395. 22 RV and tent sites, no hookups ($8); pit latrines, barbecue grills, picnic tables. No reservations. Open May–Oct. No credit cards.*

Jacob Lake Campground. This is another Forest Service campground in the secluded pine country of the Kaibab Plateau about 40 miles north of the North Rim. *Tel. 602/643–7395. 53 RV and tent sites, no hookups ($10); pit latrines, grills, picnic tables. No reservations. Open May–Oct. MC, V.*

North Rim Campground. In a heavy grove of pines near a general store 1 mile north of Grand Canyon Lodge, this is the only designated campground inside the park at the North Rim. *82 RV and tent sites, no hookups ($10); water, flush toilets, showers and laundry, nearby dump station, grills, picnic tables. Reservations through Mistix, tel. 800/365–2267. Open May–Oct. MC, V.*

DINING

Throughout Grand Canyon country, restaurants cater to tourists on the move, and most places serve standard American fare, prepared quickly and offered at reasonable prices. The most serious dining is in the El Tovar Hotel, but expect to pay more than $30 per person. Budget diners should head for the cafeterias. Price categories per person, excluding 5% tax, service, and drinks, are *Moderate,* $15–$25, and *Inexpensive,* under $15.

SOUTH RIM **Bright Angel Restaurant.** This is an informal but respectable place for breakfast, lunch, or dinner in the memorable Bright Angel Lodge. Try the breast of chicken almondine or the prime rib. *At the rim in Grand Canyon Village, tel. 602/638–2401. AE, D, DC, MC, V. Moderate.*

Fred Harvey Cafeterias. There are three decent, perhaps predictable, cafeterias with wide selections at **Maswik Lodge** and **Yavapai Lodge** (tel. 602/638–2401) in Grand Canyon Village and at **Desert View Trading Post** (Rte. 64, tel. 602/638–2360). *AE, D, DC, MC, V. Inexpensive.*

The Steak House. This is the place for a warm western atmosphere, right down to the checkered tablecloths. Steaks and chicken are prepared over an open wood grill; salmon garnished with local vegetables is another favorite. *Tusayan, tel. 602/638–2780. AE, MC, V. Inexpensive.*

NORTH RIM **Grand Canyon Lodge Dining Room.** The huge, high-ceilinged dining room serves decently prepared entrées, including grilled rainbow trout, shrimp tempura, and a vegetable lasagna. *Grand Canyon Lodge, tel. 801/586–7686 or 602/638–2611. AE, D, DC, MC, V. Moderate.*

Grand Canyon Lodge Cafeteria. Dining choices are limited on the North Rim; this is your best bet for a meal tailored to budget and appetite, with a wide selection. *Grand Canyon Lodge, tel. 801/586–7686 or 602/638–2611. AE, D, DC, MC, V. Inexpensive.*

Vermilion Cliffs Restaurant. If you make the long drive up U.S. 89 to the North Rim, you'll need at least one food stop, and this is probably the best along the route. It has rock walls, a rustic interior, and surprisingly good American fare. *At Lees Ferry Lodge off U.S.*

89A near Marble Canyon Bridge, tel. 602/355–2231. MC, V. Inexpensive.

SHOPPING

At the South Rim, nearly every lodging and retail store carries Indian artifacts, Grand Canyon souvenirs, and some casual clothing. Most of the Indian jewelry, rugs, baskets, and pottery are authentic, but several outlets deserve special mention: Desert View Trading Post on Route 64 (tel. 602/638–2360), El Tovar Gift Shop in the hotel (tel. 602/638–2631), and Cameron Trading Post, 1 mile north of the junction of Route 64 and U.S. 89 (tel. 602/679–2231). Babbitt's General Store (tel. 602/638–2262), a good stop for all types of necessities, has branches in Grand Canyon Village, Tusayan, and Desert View.

OUTDOOR ACTIVITIES

BIKING The park has miles of scenic paved roads and dirt roads, but bicycles are not permitted on any of the walking trails. You must bring your own bike; there are no rentals at Grand Canyon.

HIKING From leisurely walks on well-defined paths to arduous treks into the canyon and from one rim to the other, rangers can provide you with maps and information.

HORSEBACK RIDING/MULE RIDES On the South Rim, gentle horses can be rented April through November from Apache Stables at the Moqui Lodge in Tusayan (tel. 602/638–2891) for a variety of guided rides (at about $15 an hour, less for longer rides). There are guided mule rides from the North or South Rim (*see* Guided Tours, *above*).

RAFTING White-water raft trips through Grand Canyon can be the adventure of a lifetime. Summer reservations must be made as much as a year in advance. More than 25 companies offer multiday raft trips, among them Canyoneers, Inc. (tel. 602/526–0924), Diamond River Adventures (tel. 602/645–8866), and Expeditions, Inc. (tel. 602/774–8176). Smooth-water, one-day float trips—about $75 per person—are run by Fred Harvey Transportation Company (tel. 602/638–2401) and Del Webb Wilderness River Adventures (tel. 602/645–3279).

ENTERTAINMENT

Be sure to see *Grand Canyon, Hidden Secrets* at the IMAX theater in Tusayan—it's a truly dazzling introduction to the Grand Canyon (tel. 602/638–2203; shows daily every half hour 8:30 AM–8:30 PM; $7 adults, $4 children). There are cocktail lounges at El Tovar (piano), Bright Angel Lodge (live entertainment), Maswik Lodge (sports bar), Yavapai Lodge (dancing), Moqui Lodge (live entertainment), and Grand Canyon Lodge on the North Rim.

Grand Teton National Park
Wyoming

Few Rocky Mountain vistas are more impressive than the jagged Teton Range in northwestern Wyoming. Guarding the Jackson Hole Highway (U.S. 89) like brawny, behemoth sentinels, these mountains have served as a backdrop to mountain men, cattle barons, conservationists, Hollywood cowboys, and political summit meetings. The Indians call them Teewinot—"many pinnacles." Nineteenth-century French trappers called them Les Trois Tetons—"the three breasts." The most prominent Tetons rise north of Moose Junction: 11,901-foot Nez Perce, 12,804-foot Middle Teton, 13,770-foot Grand Teton, 12,928-foot Mt. Owen, and 12,325-foot Teewinot Mountain, south to north. Beneath the Tetons stretches the 8- to 15-mile-wide by 40-mile-long valley, called Jackson Hole since the early 1800s. Through Jackson Hole, the Snake River winds in braided channels for 27 miles. Between the Snake and the Tetons lie a string of sparkling lakes: Phelps, Taggart, Jenny, Leigh, and Jackson.

Lacking the geysers, roadside wildlife, and summer traffic jams of its northern neighbor, Yellowstone National Park, Grand Teton draws a hardier sort of wilderness enthusiast: This is prime hiking, climbing, and rafting country. Still, civility abounds. You can forgo the rough outdoor life for a gentle walk around Jenny Lake, or an evening drink facing the Tetons on the Jackson Lake Lodge veranda, or a night of whooping it up in a saloon in the nearby town of Jackson.

ESSENTIAL INFORMATION

WHEN TO GO The park's July average daily maximum temperature is 81°, with an average minimum of 41°. Locals say there are three seasons: July, August, and winter. Though that's an exaggeration, snow is possible year-round. A spring of mild days and cold nights extends into June, when average

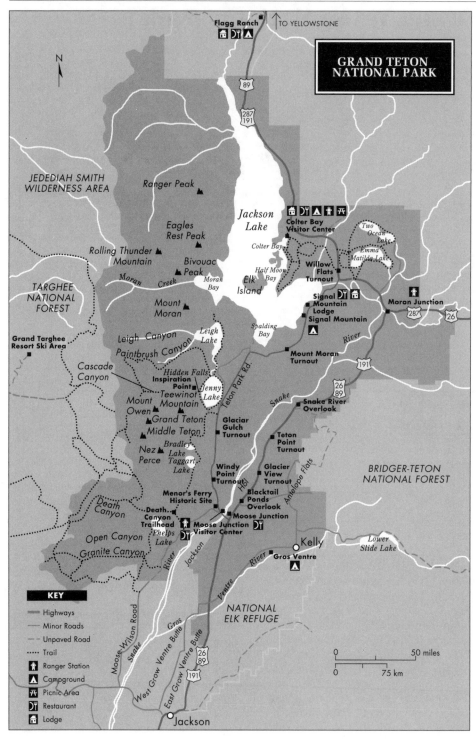

highs and lows are 71° and 37°. Snow begins regularly in October, when average highs and lows are 57° and 24°. January average maximum and minimum temperatures are 25° and 2°. The park averages 49 inches of snow in January, while July and August are generally dry.

Grand Teton's crowds are smaller than Yellowstone's year-round, and they are genuinely sparse in winter, when park lodgings close. While most of Teton Park Road closes to wheeled vehicles, U.S. 89 along the park's eastern edge stays open, providing good access to cross-country ski trails and frozen Jackson Lake, which is open to snowmobiles. In April, most of Teton Park Road opens to bicyclists and foot travelers only.

BARGAINS Free ranger-led activities usually originate at Moose and Colter Bay visitor centers. They include guided walks, naturalist tours, photography workshops, and campfire programs. In Jackson, Bubba's Bar-B-Que (515 W. Broadway, tel. 307/733-2288) serves a weighty chicken and turkey barbecue lunch platter for $4.25 and an all-you-can-eat salad bar for $3.95. Some otherwise expensive lodgings offer shoulder-season (Apr.–May and mid-Oct.–late Nov.) specials.

TOURIST OFFICES Superintendent, Grand Teton National Park (Drawer 170, Moose 83012, tel. 307/733-2880). Moose Visitor Center (same address as above, tel. 307/733-2880). Colter Bay Visitor Center (same address as above, tel. 307/543-2467). Park lodging, dining, and tours: Grand Teton Lodge Company (Box 240, Moran 83013, tel. 307/543-2811). Jackson Hole Chamber of Commerce (Box E, Jackson 83001, tel. 307/733-3316). Jackson Hole Visitors Council (Box 982, Dept. 41, Jackson Hole 83001, tel. 800/782-0011, ext. 41). Wyoming Division of Tourism (I-25 at College Dr., Cheyenne 82002, tel. 307/777-7777 or 800/225-5996).

EMERGENCIES Police: Dial Park Dispatch (tel. 307/733-2880 or 307/543-2851) or Teton County Sheriff's Office (tel. 307/733-2331). Doctors: Grand Teton Medical Clinic (near Chevron Station, Jackson Lake Lodge,

tel. 307/543-2514; June–mid-Sept. Walk-in clinic: Emerge+A+Care (Powderhorn Mall, West Broadway, Jackson, tel. 307/733-8002).

ARRIVING AND DEPARTING

BY PLANE Jackson Hole Airport (tel. 307/733-7682), 8 miles north of town off U.S. 89, receives daily flights connecting through Denver and Salt Lake City. Some lodgings provide free airport shuttle service. One-way taxi fare from the airport to Jackson is around $12. Taxi companies include Buckboard Cab (tel. 307/733-1112) and Dollary (tel. 307/733-0935).

BY CAR The Jackson Hole Highway (U.S. 26–89–191) is open all year from Jackson to Moran Junction, east over Togwotee Pass (U.S. 26–287) and north to Flagg Ranch, 2 miles south of Yellowstone Park's south entrance (closed in winter).

BY BUS Greyhound Lines (tel. 800/231-2222) has daily service to West Yellowstone and Rock Springs from Salt Lake City. There is no direct bus service to Jackson Hole.

GETTING AROUND

BY BUS Grand Teton Lodge Company (tel. 307/543-2811) runs buses June through mid-September from the Town Square in Jackson to Jackson Lake Lodge twice daily, with airport and Jenny Lake Loop stops upon request. There are also shuttle buses between Jackson Lake Lodge and Colter Bay (June–mid-Sept.). Jackson's START bus line runs regularly from the Town Square to Teton Village (late May-mid-Sept., early Dec.–early Apr.).

BY CAR Starting at Moose Junction, Teton Park Road skirts the foot of the Tetons for 20 miles to Jackson Lake Junction (closed from early December through early May between Cottonwood Creek and Signal Mountain Lodge). There is a short cut from Teton Village into the park, the Moose-Wilson Road, which turns to gravel for a few miles before joining Teton Park Road at Moose Visitor Center (road closed early December through early May due to snow, and always closed to trucks, trailers, and RVs). The Jackson Hole Highway (U.S. 26–89–191) is longer than Teton Park Road but faster. Its scenic parking areas are Blacktail Ponds, Glacier View, Teton Point, and Snake River Overlook. Another series of scenic parking areas extends past Jackson Lake Junction, overlooking Jackson Lake. Scenic parking areas on Teton Park Road are Windy Point, Glacier Gulch, and Mount Moran turnouts; Moose and Colter Bay visitor centers; and Jackson Lake, Jenny Lake, and Signal Mountain lodges.

REST STOPS Both visitor centers and all three park lodges have public rest rooms. Dornan's Corner at Moose Junction and Flagg Ranch just north of the park also have rest rooms.

GUIDED TOURS **Bus and Jeep:** Grayline Tours departs Dirty Jack's Theatre (140 N. Cache St., Jackson, tel. 307/733–4325) for a daily trip to the park. The Teton Village Tram (tel. 307/733–2292) provides a scenic overview of Jackson Hole. Wild West Jeep Tours (Jackson, tel. 307/733–9036) will take you through Grand Teton backcountry June through early September. Access Tours (Box 2985, Jackson, WY 83001, tel. 307/733–6664 or 800/929–4811) caters to the physically disabled, offering multiday park tours. **Walking:** Jackson Hole Museum (tel. 307/733–2414) tours historic Jackson on foot (June–early Sept.). In the park, rangers at Moose and Colter Bay visitor centers lead guided walks both easy and strenuous—be sure to inquire.

EXPLORING

Admission to Grand Teton Park ($10 per vehicle or $4 per person on foot or bike) also buys entry into Yellowstone Park for up to one week. National Park Service Golden Age and Golden Access Passports give free entry to persons over 62 and to blind or disabled persons. The following covers major highlights from Jackson, northward.

National Elk Refuge is home to the nation's largest elk herd. The best time to view the majestic animals is winter, when U.S. Fish and Wildlife Service sleigh rides (fee charged) take visitors close to nearly 9,000

elk. The refuge road leaving from Jackson's north end is paved for a few miles and open to visitors in summer. *USFWS, Box C, Jackson 83001, tel. 307/733–9212. Refuge Headquarters, Broadway St., 1 mi east of Jackson Town Sq. Open weekdays.*

Moose Junction Visitor Center has ranger naturalists and carries publications. Just north of the visitor center, the 1/2-mile Menor's Ferry Historical Trail goes past turn-of-the-century Snake River cabins and displays on Jackson Hole pioneer life. *Tel. 307/733–2880. Open daily, except Christmas. Admission free.*

Snake and Gros Ventre Rivers, in the park's southeast, are traverse rolling plains and river flats that attract bison, antelope, and moose. From Jackson Hole Highway, take the Antelope Flats Road at Gros Ventre toward Kelly to the paved Teton National Forest access road, which winds along the Gros Ventre River. Return to Antelope Flats Road along the Gros Ventre to rejoin Jackson Hole Highway. Halfway between Moose and Moran junctions, the Snake River Overlook surveys a sweeping bend of the Snake, with a wayside exhibit identifying Teton peaks in the background. Two miles beyond, the Cunningham Cabin Trail is an easy walk to an 1890 homestead.

Jenny Lake. Take the one-way road heading south from North Jenny Lake Junction, 12 miles north of Moose. Just before you rejoin the Park Road at South Jenny Lake Junction, you'll see Jenny Lake, a favorite hiking area. The 6.6-mile Jenny Lake trail skirts the shoreline, with Teton Range views from the east shore. Cascade Canyon, the park's most popular trail, follows Jenny Lake's south shore and climbs for a gentle 1/2-mile to Hidden Falls. A strenuous 1/2 mile farther leads you to Inspiration Point and views of Jenny and Jackson lakes. The now-difficult trail continues into Cascade Canyon itself for some of the park's best Teton Range close-ups. A shuttle boat crosses Jenny Lake regularly from the marina on the east shore, eliminating 2 miles of the hike each way. *Ranger station, horseback rides (fee charged). Teton Boating Co.*

offers scenic cruises and lake shuttle (fees charged), tel. 307/733–2703. Open June–late Sept., daily.

Jackson Lake. South of Jackson Lake Junction along Teton Park Road, Mt. Moran Turnout affords your first view of the northern Tetons. Just past the junction, Willow Flats Turnout completes that view: From south to north, you'll see 12,605-foot Mt. Moran, 10,825-foot Bivouac Peak, 10,908-foot Rolling Thunder Mountain, 11,258-foot Eagles Rest Peak, and 11,355-foot Ranger Peak. Also south of Jackson Lake Junction, Signal Mountain Road climbs 800 feet in 5 miles for a sweeping view of the entire 40-mile Teton Range and Jackson Hole. Visit Jackson Lake Lodge's 1920s rustic lobby, with comfortable old leather chairs and floor-to-ceiling windows overlooking the northern Tetons. From the lodge, take the Lunchtree Hill Trail, an easy 1/2 mile to the top of a rise overlooking Willow Flats and the northern Tetons. *Signal Mountain Lodge (tel. 307/543–2831) has a store, gas station, and marina. Open late May–mid-Sept. Jackson Lake Lodge (tel. 307/543–2811) has stores, gas station, horseback rides. Open June–mid-Sept.*

Colter Bay is the hub of park activities on Jackson Lake. One-and-a-half-hour cruises depart its marina all day: You'll see close-ups of glaciers, waterfalls, and the wild western shore of Jackson Lake (fee charged). Take the easy 3-mile circular trail from Colter Bay Visitor Center through pine forest and open meadows past Heron Pond and Swan Lake, a favorite habitat of great blue herons, moose, and beavers. Even gentler is the 1.8-mile self-guiding Colter Bay Nature Trail along the forest edge. *Visitor Center: tel. 307/543–2467. Open early May–late Sept., daily. Service station, marina, tackle shop, store, boat and horseback rides.*

THE NATURAL WORLD Over 50 types of wild-flowers bloom in the park's glacial canyons in July and August—a list of these, as well as a list of the park's nearly 300 bird species, is available at Moose and Colter Bay visitor centers. Great blue herons and ospreys nest at Oxbow Bend—stop at the turnout with binoculars. White pelicans and bald eagles also fish in this prime bird habitat's shallow water. Look for hawks and falcons along Antelope Flats Road. Oxbow Bend and Willow Flats turnouts are good places for observing moose, beavers, and otters. In summer, elks and big-ear mule deer haunt forest edges along Teton Park Road at sunrise and sunset.

HOTELS AND INNS

Grand Teton National Park doesn't have Yellowstone Park's variety of inexpensive lodgings. A larger choice of lower-priced properties can be found in nearby Jackson and Teton Village ski resort (open in summer), 12 miles north of Jackson on the Moose-Wilson road (*see also* Yellowstone Park chapter). Rates at Teton Village—but not in Jackson—are often $10–$40 higher during the winter ski season. You can reserve some rooms through Jackson Hole Central Reservations (Box 510, Teton Village 83025, tel. 307/733–4005 or 800/443–6931). Price categories for double occupancy, excluding 6% tax, are *Moderate*, $50–$85, and *Inexpensive*, under $50.

MODERATE **Best Western Inn at Jackson Hole.** Lodgepole pine beds and oak furniture lift this Teton Village inn far above the general run of chain motels. *Box 328, Teton Village 83025, tel. 307/733–2311 or 800/842–7666, fax 307/733–0844. 83 units. 3 restaurants, pool, 3 Jacuzzis, coin laundry, valet service, kitchens, fireplaces, room service. AE, D, DC, MC, V.*

Colter Bay Village Cabins. The log accommodations, some of them remodeled settlers' cabins, are situated on a terraced drive overlooking Jackson Lake. *Colter Bay Village, Grand Teton Lodge Co., Box 240, Moran 83013, tel. 307/543–2855, 307/543–2811 for same-day reservations, fax 307/543–2869. 209 cabins. Restaurant, coin laundry, airport shuttle. AE, DC, MC, V.*

Cowboy Village Resort. These log cabins on a quiet side street just south of downtown Jackson have porches, barbecue grills, and picnic tables. *Flat Creek Rd. off W. Broadway,*

Box 1747, Jackson 83001, tel. 307/733–3121 or 800/962–4988, fax 307/733–9638. 57 cabins. Kitchens. AE, D, MC, V.

Flagg Ranch Village. This sprawling year-round resort lies on the Snake River, 4 miles north of Grand Teton and 2 miles south of Yellowstone. The cabins are well equipped and ideal for families. John D. Rockefeller Memorial Pkwy., Box 187, Moran 83013, tel. 307/733–8761 or 800/443–2311, fax 307/543–2356. 54 rooms, 6 cabins. Restaurant, grocery store, coin laundry, fireplaces. MC, V.

Grand Targhee Resort. On the back (west) side of the Tetons, this popular ski center is also a summer resort featuring hiking trails, horseback rides, and other outdoor activities. The spacious rooms lack character, but some have fine mountain views. 12 mi east of Driggs, ID off U.S. 33. Box SKI, Alta 83422, tel. 307/353–2304 or 800/443–8146, fax 307/353–8148. 63 units. Restaurant, pool, coin laundry. AE, MC, V.

Signal Mt. Lodge. The log cabins here have pine beds, wicker chairs, and old-fashioned lamps. Four-unit chalets have modern furnishing with kitchens. All are situated on Jackson Lake, with views of Mt. Moran from the Aspen restaurant and a back deck. Grand Teton National Park, Box 50, Moran 83013, tel. 307/543–2831 or 307/733–5470, fax 307/543–2569. 79 cabins and rooms (some in moderate range). Restaurant, kitchens, and fireplaces. AE, D, MC, V.

Sojourner Inn. This is Teton Village's major hotel, though rooms aren't as inviting as those at the Best Western (all have mountain views, however). Box 348, Teton Village 83025, tel. 307/733–3657 or 800/445–4655, fax 307/733–9543. 100 rooms. Restaurant, pool, sauna, valet and room service. AE, D, DC, MC, V.

Teton View Bed & Breakfast. Between Jackson and Teton Village, this B&B has rooms with mountain views, queen-size beds, and flannel sheets; homemade pastries and breads are served. 2136 Coyote Loop, Box

652, Wilson 83014, tel. 307/733–7954. 3 rooms. Laundry room. MC, V.

Togwotee Mt. Lodge. Seventeen miles from the eastern park entrance on U.S. 26/287, this big, family-oriented log lodge with a central fireside room offers horseback rides, snowmobile rentals, and other outdoor services. Box 91-J, Moran 83013, tel. 307/543–2847 or 800/543–2847. 34 rooms. Restaurant, sauna, laundry room, room service, airport shuttle. AE, D, V.

INEXPENSIVE **Camp Creek Inn.** This lodging consists of newly remodeled A-frames with knotty pine interiors, 16 miles south of Jackson in Hoback Canyon. U.S. 89, Star Rte. Box 45-B, Jackson 83001, tel. 307/733–3099 or 800/228–8460, fax 307/733–3195. 9 cabins. Restaurant, bar. MC, V.

Colter Bay Tent Cabins. Rooms have canvas walls and sheet-metal ceilings on wood frames with bare-minimum furnishings and shared bathrooms, but the price and location are unbeatable. Colter Bay Village, Grand Teton Lodge Co., Box 240, Moran 83013, tel. 307/543–2855, 307/543–2811 for same-day reservations, fax 307/543–2869. 72 cabins. Restaurant, airport shuttle. AE, DC, MC, V.

The Hostel. A favorite of families and skiers, this modest, cozy Teton Village lodging, open year-round, features four twin beds (two in a bunk) per room and a lounge with a huge stone fireplace. Box 546, Teton Village 83025, tel. 307/733–3415, fax 307/739–1142. 60 rooms. Laundry and game rooms, no room phones or TVs. MC, V.

MOTELS

Note: all addresses are Jackson 83001.

MODERATE **Best Western Executive Inn** (325 W. Pearl St., Box 1101, tel. 307/733–4340 or 800/528–1234). 137 rooms; pool, valet, and room service. **Days Inn** (1280 W. Broadway, tel. 307/739–9010 or 800/325–2525). 78 rooms. **Forty-Niner Motel** (330 W. Pearl St., Box 575, tel. 307/733–7550 or 800/451–2980). 114 rooms; restaurant, valet and room service. **Parkway Inn Best Western** (Box 494, tel. 307/733–3143). 51 rooms; pool, fitness center, valet service. **Pony Express Motel** (Box 972, tel. 307/733–2658 or 800/526–2658). 41 rooms; pool. **Virginian Lodge** (750 W. Broadway, Box 1052, tel. 307/733–2792 or 800/262–4999). 150 rooms; restaurant, pool, kitchenettes, valet service.

■INEXPENSIVE■ Hoback Motel (U.S. 89 South of Jackson, Star Rte., Box 23, tel. 307/733–5129). 18 rooms. **Motel 6** (1370 W. Broadway, tel. 307/733–1620). 155 rooms; pool. **Snow King Lodge Motel** (400 E. Snow King Ave., Box 1053, tel. 307/733–3480). 18 rooms; kitchenettes. **Teton Gables Motel** (Junction of Rtes. 191–189–22, Box 1038, tel. 307/733–3723). 36 rooms; restaurant.

CAMPGROUNDS

The National Park Service operates five park campgrounds, each charging $8 per night on a first-come, first-served basis. No reservations are accepted; campsites fill up in July and August. Park Service campsites don't provide hookups, unlike the concessioner-operated Colter Bay RV Trailer Village and Flagg Ranch Village.

Colter Bay is busy, noisy, and fills by noon, but it's close to many activities and services. *1¹/₂ mi off U.S. 89–287, near cabins. Grand Teton National Park, Box 170, Moose 83012, tel. 307/733–2880. 310 combination sites. No hookups. Showers, bathrooms, LP gas available, picnic tables and barbecue areas. No reservations or credit cards.*

Colter Bay Trailer Village, near Colter Bay Marina, is a large, often crowded RV-only park close to boat rentals, scenic cruises, horseback rides, a store, and a visitor center. *Grand Teton Lodge Co., Box 240, Moran 83013, tel. 307/733–2811. 112 RV sites. Hookups, showers, bathrooms, LP gas available. Reservations advised. MC, V.*

Flagg Ranch Campground lies within a bustling tourist complex 4 miles north of Teton Park on U.S. 89–287. *Box 187, Moran 83013, tel. 307/733–8761 or 800/443–2311. 100 RV sites, 75 tent sites. Hookups, showers, bathrooms, LP gas available, laundry, picnic ta-*

bles and barbecue areas. Reservations accepted. MC, V.

Gros Ventre is as pristine as Colter Bay is cluttered, in an isolated area frequented by moose along the Gros Ventre River; it usually doesn't fill until nightfall. *2 mi southwest of Kelly on Gros Ventre Rd., Grand Teton National Park, Box 170, Moose 83012, tel. 307/733–2880. 360 sites. No hookups. Bathrooms, picnic tables and barbecue areas. No reservations or credit cards.*

Jenny Lake is a quiet, small, lakeside campground for tents only, close to the Jenny Lake trailhead; this area is extremely popular and fills by 8 AM in July and August. *On Teton Park Rd., 8 mi north of Moose. Grand Teton National Park, Box 170, Moose 83012, tel. 307/733–2880. 49 tent sites. No hookups. Bathrooms, picnic tables and barbecue areas. No reservations or credit cards.*

DINING

Several innovative area restaurants combine native game, birds, and fish (especially quail and trout) with Old World ingredients and New Age health consciousness. An alpine spaetzle-and-sausages tradition remains, but it has been enhanced over the past decade by many new poultry and pasta dishes. Whole-grain breakfasts and soups are crowding out eggs and burgers, too. Price categories per person, excluding 5% tax, service, and drinks, are *Moderate,* $15–$25, and *Inexpensive,* under $15.

■MODERATE■ The Cadillac Grille. As slick as it gets in Jackson, this art deco–style restaurant does nouvelle-cuisine presentations of buffalo, venison, and other native game and fish. *Cache St. on Town Sq., Jackson, tel. 307/733–3279. AE, DC, MC, V.*

Gouloff's. Across the street from the Jackson Hole Racquet Club outside town, this small, locally popular restaurant offers entrées of venison and game birds, among other specialties. *Teton Village Rd., Jackson, tel. 307/733–1886. AE, MC, V.*

Jackson Lake Lodge Mural Room. Wildlife and landscape paintings in this cavernous restaurant compete with striking Teton views from its grand picture windows. Large summertime crowds flock to the Mural Room for fresh beef and game, and a small selection of heart-wise entrées. *Jackson Lake Lodge, tel. 307/543–2811. AE, DC, MC, V.*

Off Broadway. Just off the main tourist prowl with a sunny deck in back, this smoke-free and health-conscious eatery has an extensive pasta and seafood selection. *30 King St., Jackson, tel. 307/733–9777. MC, V.*

Sweetwater Restaurant. Sweetwater's is a crowded local favorite for its Greek appetizers, seafoods, and vegetable dishes. Recent expansions at this downtown, log-cabin eatery include two additional log-walled dining rooms and a pleasant outdoor deck. *Corner of King and Pearl Sts., Jackson, tel. 307/733–3553. AE, MC, V.*

INEXPENSIVE **Bubba's Bar-B-Que.** Not your average beef 'n' beans joint, this local landmark features wooden booths, antique signs, and tributes to western gunmen, plus huge turkey and chicken barbecue platters. *515 W. Broadway, Jackson, tel. 307/733–2288. AE, MC, V.*

The Bunnery. Whole-grain breads, pancakes, waffles, and muffins are served in a bustling nook called the Hole-in-the-Wall Mall. *130 N. Cache St., Jackson, tel. 307/733–5474. AE, V.*

Dynamic Health Restaurant and Juice Bar. Grain burgers, hummus, spinach-tofu lasagna, and other creative lunches are found in a small restaurant that doubles as a health-products store. *130 W. Broadway, Jackson, tel. 307/733–5418. MC, V.*

Jackson Lake Lodge Pioneer Room. Nothing fancy here, just hearty soups and sandwiches served at long counters by friendly waiters and waitresses. *Jackson Lake Lodge, tel. 307/543–2811. AE, DC, MC, V.*

Bar J Chuckwagon Suppers. Besides an all-you-can eat meal of barbecued beef, potatoes, beans, biscuits, cake, and a drink, the Bar J offers a first-class western show most nights featuring the Bar J Wranglers. *Teton Village Road, 1 mi from Wilson, tel. 307/733–3370. Reservations recommended. AE, MC, V.*

Jedediah's House of Sourdough. Mountain-man memorabilia surround diners, who enjoy sourdough and whole-grain pancakes, waffles, and biscuits—not to mention buffalo burgers—at this laid-back, log-cabin breakfast and lunch spot. *1 block east of Town Sq., E. Broadway, Jackson, tel. 307/733–5671. AE, MC, V.*

SHOPPING

JACKSON Cache Creek Square, located on the corner of Cache Street and Broadway across from Town Square, includes Teton Traditions (western gifts, tel. 307/733–4100), The Hole Works (Indian and cowboy crafts, tel. 307/733–7000), and Jack Dennis Outdoor Shop (outdoor clothing and cowboy boots, tel. 307/733–6838). Chet's Way next door includes Warbonnet Indian Arts (on-premises Navajo weaving, tel. 307/733–6158). Across the Town Square's northwest corner is Gaslight Alley (corner Cache and Deloney Sts.), home to Buckskin Mercantile (western wear, tel. 307/733–3699), The Shirt Smuggler (souvenir clothing, tel. 307/733–9037), and Valley Bookstore (western subjects, guide books, tel. 307/733–4533). Wyoming Outfitters (corner of Center St. and Broadway, tel. 307/733–3877) is another major western-wear retailer. Jackson also has an outstanding selection of photograph and art galleries.

GRAND TETON NATIONAL PARK Jackson Lake Lodge Apparel and Gift Shops (in the lodge, tel. 307/543–2811) sells fine western wear and Indian crafts. Signal Mountain Lodge Gift Shop and Moosle Beach Club Store (in the lodge, tel. 307/543–2831) sell Indian crafts and outdoor clothing.

OUTDOOR ACTIVITIES

BIKING The RKO Road 4 miles north of Moose provides an easy four-hour mountain ride along the Snake River. A bike lane allows northbound bike traffic along the one-way Jenny Lake Loop Road for a one-hour ride. A four-hour, moderate ride on paved road goes from Gros Ventre Junction to Slide Lake. For bike rentals and repairs try Teton Cyclery (175 N. Glenwood St., Jackson, tel. 307/733–4386) or Mountain Bike Outfitters (at Dornan's Corners, Moose Junction, tel. 307/733–3314).

CROSS-COUNTRY SKIING In Grand Teton Park, ski the gentle 6-mile Flagg Canyon Trail at Flagg Ranch Village, heading north toward Yellowstone along a cliff above the Snake River. The 3-mile Swan Lake–Heron Pond Loop near Colter Bay Visitor Center is gentler still. The 9-mile Jenny Lake Trail is mostly level. The 4-mile Taggart Lake–Beaver Creek Loop south of Jenny Lake offers easy to moderately difficult trails. Rossignol Nordic Ski Center at Teton Village rents skis and also offers 25 kilometers of trails (Box 290, Teton Village 83025, tel. 307/733–2292).

FISHING Native cutthroat, rainbow, brook, and lake trout are all caught in Teton Park waters. Unlike Yellowstone, the park requires a Wyoming fishing license (fee charged). Jenny and Leigh lakes are open all year, Jackson Lake is open January 1–September 30 and November 1–December 31, and Snake River is open April 1–October 31. Only the park's northern half allows live bait.

HIKING (Note: all distances/times are round-trip, except where noted.) The park has 200 miles of hiking trails (*see* Exploring, *above,* for popular short hikes). A spur off Jenny Lake Road leads to String Lake, where the 7.4-mile, four-hour Bearpaw Lake Trail borders Leigh Lake and provides close-ups of Mt. Moran. The 11-mile, seven-hour moderate Granite Canyon Trail starts with a ride up the Teton Village Tram (fee charged) and then down through alpine meadows and sagebrush. A popular 8.8-mile, four-hour easy hike leaves Colter Bay Trailhead to follow the shore of Hermitage Point on Jackson Lake.

RAFTING The Snake River between Moran Junction and Moose is extremely popular with beginners' tour groups, drawn by its scenery and lack of white water. Float companies charge $10–$30 for 5- or 10-mile scenic trips. Try Osprey Float Trips (Triangle X Ranch, Moose, tel. 307/773–5500) and Solitude Float Trips (Moose, tel. 307/733–2871).

Hot Springs and the Ozarks
Arkansas

Midway between the Appalachians and the Great Plains lie the velvety hills of Arkansas, a land of simple pleasures where crooked highways wind their way through peaceful mountain towns. One such settlement is Hot Springs, which grew up almost a century ago around a series of geothermal springs whose waters were said to be medicinal. Casino gambling flourished during the town's heyday in the 1910s and '20s, drawing the likes of Al Capone, Andrew Carnegie, Jack Dempsey, and Babe Ruth. Although there is no more gambling (except at the Oaklawn Park Thoroughbred racecourse), bathers still come by the thousands each year to the spas around Hot Springs National Park, the country's smallest national park property (4,900 acres).

Besides the thermal waters, the hottest attraction these days is a self-guided car tour of locations associated with President Bill Clinton, who moved to Hot Springs from Hope, Arkansas, when he was seven years old. Other nearby attractions include Lake Hamilton, 15 minutes from downtown Hot Springs, and the Ouachita National Forest, the largest in the South. The unique lifestyle of the Ozark Mountains is well preserved today at the Ozark Folk Center near Mountain View. Musicians saw their fiddles, cloggers dance, and craftsmen show their skills and sell their wares.

In the Victorian and hilly burg of Eureka Springs, the bed-and-breakfast capital of the region, you'll find scores of gingerbread houses tucked away on shady back streets and an unrivaled concentration of artists, whose galleries and shops line serpentine Spring Street.

ESSENTIAL INFORMATION

WHEN TO GO Temperatures average in the 40s in winter and around 80° at the height of summer. The fall foliage attracts droves of

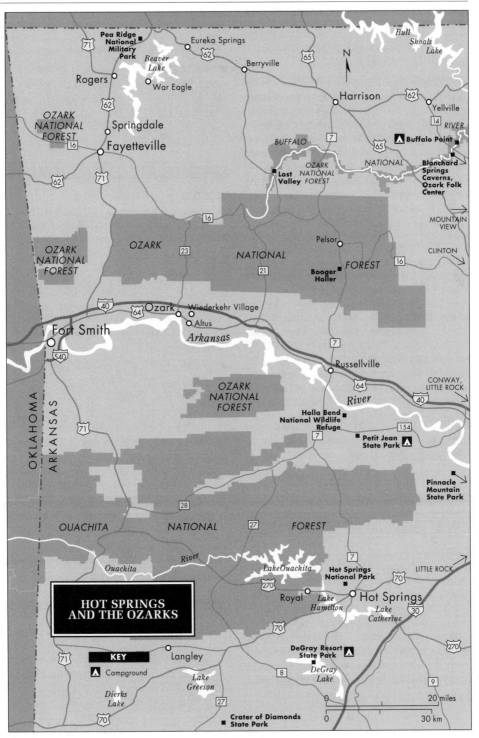

HOT SPRINGS
AND THE OZARKS

KEY

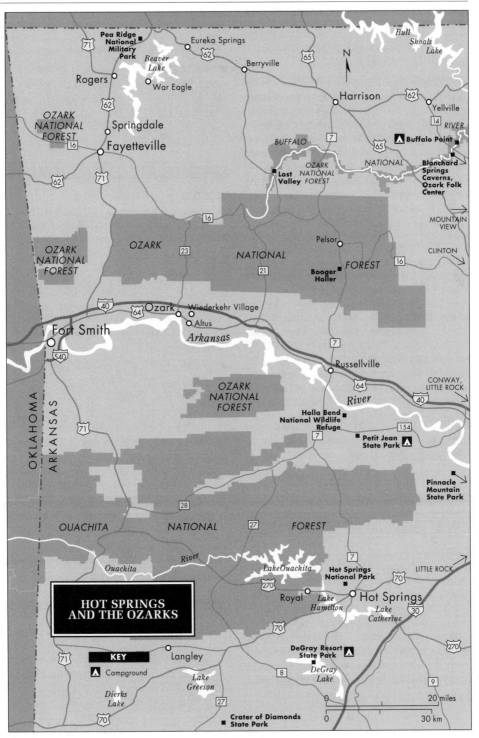 Campground

visitors, which drives up rates, especially in Eureka Springs. The busiest time in Hot Springs is racing season (late Jan.–Apr.), when hotel rates jump noticeably.

■**BARGAINS** The Hot Spring Visitors Center distributes books of discount coupons that are valid at local attractions and eateries. Eureka Springs's historic hotels—the Basin Park, Grand Central, New Orleans, Crescent, and Palace—offer "secret season" rates from early November into April, when doubles average less than $50 and go as low as $29. At the stately Arlington Hotel (*see* Hotels and Inns, *below*), a full breakfast and room that sleeps four costs $55 during the off- season.

■**TOURIST OFFICES** The Arkansas Department of Tourism (1 Capitol Mall, Little Rock 72201, tel. 800/NATURAL). The Hot Springs Visitors Center (600 Central Ave., Hot Springs National Park 71901, tel. 501/623–1433), or write to Hot Springs Convention & Visitors Bureau (134 Convention Blvd., Hot Springs National Park 71901, tel. 800/SPA–CITY). The Eureka Springs Chamber of Commerce visitor information center (near the junction of U.S. 62 and Main St., Box 551, Eureka Springs 72632, tel. 800/6–EUREKA).

■**EMERGENCIES** Dial 911 to reach the **police, fire brigade,** or an **ambulance. Hospitals:** St. Joseph's Regional Health Center (300 Werner Dr., Hot Springs, tel. 501/622–1000); Eureka Springs Hospital (24 Norris St., Eureka, tel. 501/253–7400).

ARRIVING AND DEPARTING

■**BY PLANE** Most air traffic in and out of Arkansas is through Little Rock Regional Airport-Adams Field, served by Delta (tel. 800/221–1212), American (tel. 800/433–7300), Southwest (tel. 800/531–5601), Northwest (tel. 800/225–2525), TWA (tel. 800/892–2746), and USAir (tel. 800/428–4322). Airport Shuttle (tel. 800/643–1505) provides daily shuttle service between the airport and Hot Springs for $18 per person.

■**BY CAR** Two major interstate highways cross Arkansas. I–40 runs east and west; I–30 runs diagonally northeast to southwest. From

the north, U.S. 65 is the fastest way into the state and is a scenic drive; U.S. 71 and U.S. 65 lead in from Louisiana.

■**BY TRAIN AND BUS** Amtrak (tel. 800/USA–RAIL) has frequent service to Little Rock via Dallas and St. Louis. Greyhound Lines (tel. 800/231–2222), which serves North Little Rock from major U.S. cities, has two buses daily between Little Rock and Hot Springs.

GETTING AROUND

■**BY CAR** A car is essential for visiting Hot Springs and the Ozarks, although Bathhouse Row in Hot Springs and Eureka Springs's central district can be explored on foot.

■**BY BUS AND TROLLEY** Motorized trolleys travel the streets of Hot Springs; individual rides cost 50¢, daily passes, $2. A good way to travel around Eureka Springs, especially on crowded weekends, is via the open-air buses that stop at every motel ($2.50 all day; $1 per ride).

■**REST STOPS** Tourist information centers with rest rooms are conveniently situated on most highways entering the state. Public rest stops are uncommon, but proprietors of roadside shops and cafés usually don't mind if travelers ask to use their facilities.

■**GUIDED TOURS** One of the best ways to see Hot Springs is with the White & Yellow Ducks Land & Lakes Tours (tel. 501/623–1111), in World War II amphibious vehicles that ply local waterways and streets on two-hour trips that cost $8.50. National Park rangers conduct guided thermal tours daily, starting at the Fordyce Bathhouse Visitors Center on Bathhouse Row.

EXPLORING

Outdoors people and those who like to drive could spend weeks exploring the Ozark and Ouachita Mountains around Hot Springs. Camping, hiking, and fishing opportunities abound, and the mountain vistas are one step beyond impressive. For walkers, diners, and music lovers, Hot Springs makes a good base; arts lovers will be smitten by Eureka Springs;

and the Ozark Folk Center at Mountain View offers everyone an easy overview of mountain culture. Our suggested itinerary starts in Hot Springs, then travels north on scenic Rte. 7 (with a few side trips) to Eureka Springs, 196 miles north, and finally east along the Buffalo River to Mountain View.

Hot Springs. The central Hot Springs attraction is Bathhouse Row, within the National Park, so named for the old spas lined up along Central Avenue, two of which are open to the public. The recently renovated 70-year-old **Fordyce Bathhouse Visitor Center** (tel. 501/623–1433) gives an interesting look back at local history along the row. For a quick steam, soak, or massage, make a beeline for the **Buckstaff Bathhouse** (tel. 501/623–2308; $11.50 for thermal treatments, $11.50 for 20-minute massage), which operates every day but Sunday. Above the bathhouses and the historic district is the Grand Promenade, a 1/4-mile walk along a shady hillside. Several trails branch off from there to climb Hot Springs Mountain, for example, the Peak Trail, which takes an hour or more coming and going. An alternative is motoring up to an overlook, but for an even better view, take the elevator 216 feet up **Hot Springs Mountain Tower** (admission: $4.25) at the summit.

Crater of Diamonds State Park, about an hour southwest of Hot Springs, is the only diamond mine in the world open to the public. Visitors roam 40 acres that are frequently plowed to turn up fresh stones; old buildings from mining days are still on the grounds. *Off Rte. 301, Murfreesboro, tel. 501/285–3113. Open daily. Admission charged.*

Scenic Highway 7, famous for its vistas, leads north from Hot Springs toward Eureka Springs, crossing the Arkansas River at Russellville and climbing into the Ozarks. A few miles south of Russellville, turn east on Route 154 to visit **Petit Jean Mountain.** Begin at the park's visitor center or at Mather Lodge, built of stone and logs in the 1930s (*see* Hotels and Inns, *below*). A free brochure directs you on a driving tour to 16 highlights. A 3 1/2-mile hike on Seven Hollows Trail takes you through wooded glades and an eerie place

called Turtle Rocks. A good Boy Scout trail approaches 90-foot Cedar Falls along the bluffs, and Cedar Falls Trail starts at Mather Lodge and wanders all the way up the canyon (2.2 miles, 2 hours). In Rock House Cave, an ancient bluffside shelter, Indian pictographs can be discerned. *Off Rte. 154 south of Russellville, tel. 501/727–5441. Admission free.*

Booger Holler, on Route 7, 20 miles north of Russellville, is a big store where you can get crafts and Arkansas-smoked hams. Another repository of local culture is **Hankins General Store** in the tiny burg of Pelsor, where hound dogs sleep on porches and old geezers in overalls doze in rocking chairs. For a hiking diversion, take Route 16 east 6 miles to **Pedestal Rocks.** The hike (an hour) goes down a gradually sloping path through a thick forest, emerging at the edge of tablelike formations that hang above the valley below. The view and the solitude make it a classic picnic spot. Back on Route 7, continue north to Harrison, then take U.S. 65 west to U.S. 62 to Eureka Springs.

Eureka Springs, once an enclave of 1960s counterculture, today draws visitors for its notable Victorian charms and its vibrant arts community. A free map and guide, distributed at all Eureka Springs galleries, highlights Spring Street, a crooked lane with a striking Old World look and feel, and its neighborhood, with scores of shops selling everything from books to regional pottery and quilts. There are plenty of restaurants in the area, and four convenient historic hotels. You can spend a day walking around the Spring Street historic district and then by car follow the signs of the "Historic Route" to see some pretty Victorian neighborhoods and an interesting church.

Pea Ridge National Military Park is one of the most quietly beautiful and stirring places in the Ozarks. The site of the Civil War battle that saved Missouri for the Union in 1862, it's worth a half-day side trip from Eureka Springs. Steeped in violent history, today it is a windswept expanse of prairies and woodland. A well-crafted car tour leads visitors from site to site, through waving green seas of tall grass, past old cannons and split-rail fences. There's a visitor center, picnic tables, a beautiful overlook, the Elkhorn Tavern, and several trails. *Off Rte. 62, tel. 501/451–8122. Open daily. Admission charged.*

The Buffalo National River, best known for canoeing, flows through a bluff-lined valley in a National Reservation extending west from Route 7 about 70 miles east toward Mountain View; you can rent canoes in Jasper. The area south of Yellville is one place to spend half a day, and Buffalo Point, a campground and picnic spot off Route 14, is a good place to start. There are trails for hikes of varying difficulty, cabins, and a ranger station. Take Route 14 farther south to **Rush,** an old ghost town (the turnoff is marked). The surrounding Buffalo Mining District, 1,300 acres on the National Register of Historic Places, has a network of trails that meander past old homesteads and mine shafts (the ranger station has maps).

Mountain View, nearly 60 miles east of Route 7, in the heart of the Ozarks, has managed to retain much of the musical charm of the hills; local musicians gather to play daily at about noon on the town square. At the Ozark Folk Center State Park at the edge of town, where craftsmen toil at such traditional tasks as blacksmithing, mandolin construction, and candle making, you can catch an evening concert and even stay overnight (*see* Hotels and Inns, *below*). *Tel. 501/269–3871. Open late Mar.–early Nov. Admission charged.*

In nearby **Blanchard Springs Caverns,** take an elevator 476 feet deep into the limestone heart of a mountain, where two magnificent subterranean trails wind their way through a series of dank chambers. Both trails follow a paved sidewalk most of the way and are not especially difficult; the shorter trail, Dripstone (.7 miles), is handicapped accessible. Farther into the park is one of the prettiest camping and picnicking sites in the state, a pair of frigid but popular swimming holes, and wide lawns and trails. *Blanchard Spring Caverns: 9 mi north of Mountain View via Rtes. 9 and 14, tel. 501/757–2211. Open Apr.–Oct., daily. Closed Mon., Tues., and holidays Nov.–Mar. Admission charged.*

THE NATURAL WORLD Arkansas's nickname—the Natural State—is an apt one. Holla Bend National Wildlife Refuge on the Arkansas River near Russellville is a stop for migratory waterfowl and the winter home of bald eagles (binoculars are helpful). At Petit Jean State Park, birders can watch for 130 species. At Pinnacle Mountain State Park on Route 10 near Maumelle, rangers lead spring wildflower forays and autumn-foliage walks. Dogwood decorates the mountainsides from late March into mid-April; a little-known but beautiful dogwood drive is Route 16 between Pelsor and tiny Witts Spring.

HOTELS AND INNS

Arkansas has reasonably priced lodging for every taste. Rooms are most in demand in October; rates drop dramatically November–March. Price categories for double occupancy, without 9% tax, are *Moderate,* $50–$85, and *Inexpensive,* under $50.

EUREKA SPRINGS **Grand Central Hotel.** The Grand Central was built in 1883, making it the oldest hotel in Eureka Springs. After a 40-year hiatus, this Victorian masterpiece has been reopened and completely renovated; every suite is decorated with Victoriana and antiques. *37 N. Main St., tel. 501/253–6756. 14 suites. AE, D, MC, V. Expensive.*

Heart of the Hills Inn. A night in this 1883 house in the historic district is a night among antiques; one room also has a Jacuzzi. You can take the trolley from downtown and be dropped off within spittin' distance. *5 Summit St., Eureka Springs 72632, tel. 501/253–7468. 4 rooms. Full breakfast included, off-street parking. MC, V. Moderate.*

Palace Hotel and Bath House. A former brothel and spa within a short walk of the shopping district, this hotel has rooms that border on the luxurious and a basement spa with whirlpools and massage. *135 Spring St., Eureka Springs 72632, tel. 501/253–7474. 8 suites. Off-street parking. MC, V. Moderate.*

Elmwood House. Although this downtown inn has been standing for 104 years and today shows signs of age, it is serviceable and clean, has a strong sense of history, and good on-site parking. *110 Spring St., Eureka Springs 72632, tel. 501/253–7227. 6 suites, 2 with bath. No credit cards. Inexpensive.*

HOT SPRINGS **Spillway Resort and Marina.** About 15 minutes from town, these secluded cabins with wide porches are in a tranquil lakeside compound. *Rte. 227, Box 321, Mountain Pine 71956, tel. 800/525–2516. 6 cabins. D, MC, V. Moderate.*

Vintage Comfort Bed & Breakfast Inn. The restored Queen Anne house is within walking distance of Bathhouse Row and downtown. *303 Quapaw Ave., Hot Springs National Park 71901, tel. 501/623–3258. 4 rooms. Full breakfast. MC, V. Moderate.*

Wildwood 1884. This grand Victorian mansion—built in 1884 and listed on the National Register of Historic Places—is home to Hot Springs's newest bed-and-breakfast inn, opened in June 1993. Antiques and period decor mesh nicely with modern, squeaky-clean facilities. *808 Park Ave., tel. 501/624–4267. 8 rooms. Full breakfast included. AE, D, MC, V. Moderate.*

The Williams House Bed and Breakfast Inn. This 100-year-old Victorian brick and brownstone near Bathhouse Row shopping is well furnished and is run by a friendly hostess. *420 Quapaw Ave., Hot Springs National Park 71901, tel. 501/624–4275. 6 rooms. MC, V. Inexpensive–Moderate.*

De Gray Lakeview Cottages. These rustic but adequate cabins are close to Hot Springs and next to a public golf course and lake. *Rte. 3, Box 450, Bismark 71929, tel. 501/865–3389. 6 cottages. No credit cards. Inexpensive.*

MOUNTAIN VIEW **Commercial Hotel.** This old, comfortable inn with a bakery right on the town's musical square attracts fiddlers and banjo players to its porch daily. *Corner of Peabody and Washington Sts., Box 72, Mountain View 72560, tel. 501/269–4383. 8 rooms. AE, D, MC, V. Inexpensive.*

Ozark Folk Center. This center of culture and entertainment, roughly 2 miles outside Mountain View, has a large, quaint lodge with a rough-hewn quality about it. *Box 500, Mountain View 72560, tel. 800/264–3655. 60 rooms with bath. Restaurant. AE, D, MC, V. Inexpensive.*

PETIT JEAN **Mather Lodge.** This simple but cozy lodge atop Petit Jean Mountain, for years an attractive retreat, has wonderful views and 31 modern cabins. *Rte. 3, Box 340, Morrilton 72110, tel. 800/628–7936. 24 rooms. Restaurant. AE, MC, V. Inexpensive.*

MOTELS

MODERATE **Best Western Eureka Inn** (1 Van Buren St., Eureka Springs 72632, tel. 501/253–9551). 85 rooms; pool, restaurant, racquetball, game room. **Inn of the Ozarks** (Hwy. 62. West, Eureka Springs 72632, tel. 800/528–1234). 122 rooms; pool, tennis court. **Avanelle Motor Lodge** (1204 Central Ave., Hot Springs 71901, tel. 501/321–1332). 65 rooms; restaurant, pool. **Ramada Inn** (218 Park Ave., Hot Springs 71901, tel. 800/272–6232). 191 rooms; restaurant, live entertainment, gift shop, pool, exercise room.

INEXPENSIVE **Downtowner Motor Inn & Spa** (135 Central Ave., Hot Springs 71901, tel. 800/251–1962). 150 rooms; restaurant, bathhouse, pool. **Ozarka Lodge** (Hwy. 23S and Hwy. 62E, Eureka Springs 72632, tel. 800/321–8992). 44 rooms; pool. **Swiss Village Inn** (Rte. 1 at Hwy. 62E, Eureka Springs 72632, tel. 800/447–6525). 55 rooms; pool, restaurant. **Traveler's Inn** (Rte. 1, Hwy. 62E, Eureka Springs 72632, tel. 800/643–5566). 60 rooms; restaurant, pool.

CAMPGROUNDS

The U.S. Forest Service campground in the park next to **Blanchard Springs Caverns** is one of the best. Hot showers are within a short walk of most campsites, and deer in the narrow valley are a common sight around twilight. *Tel. 501/757–2213 or 800/283–2267. 32 tent sites ($8); no RV hookups. Showers, bathrooms, dump station, picnic tables and bar-*

becue areas. *Phone reservations only, 10 days in advance.*

At **Petit Jean State Park** at Russellville, the campsites are divided into four areas, each with its own bathhouse. The park has "rent-a-camp" kits for the unequipped (available Apr.–Oct.). *Tel. 501/727–5441. 127 campsites ($12). Water and electric hookups, showers, bathrooms, dump station, picnic tables and barbecue areas. Reservations by phone.*

Hot Springs National Park's single campground, in scenic Gulpha Gorge, is 2 miles from downtown. *Off Rte. 70B, tel. 501/624–3383. 45 tent and RV campsites ($7). No hookups. Water, toilets, dump station, picnic tables and barbecue areas. No reservations.*

DeGray Resort State Park, 20 miles south of Hot Springs on Rte. 7 on a 14,000-acre lake, has a 96-room lodge, a marina with boat rentals, a public golf course, swimming, water-skiing, and hiking. *Rte. 3, Box 490, Bismarck 71929, tel. 501/865–4501. 113 tent and RV sites ($12–$19). Hookups, showers, bathrooms, dump station, picnic tables and barbecue areas. Phone reservations.*

Fourteen first-come, first-served campgrounds surround the **Buffalo National River,** all free and relatively primitive except sites at Tyler Bend ($7) and those with electrical hookups at Buffalo Point ($5–$10). *Box 1173, Harrison 72601, tel. 501/741–5443.*

DINING

Although traditional pork barbecue is widespread, most barbecue restaurants now serve chicken as well. Cajun and Creole food can be found, and country cooking is common: chicken or beef served with vegetables, gravy and corn bread, often with fruit cobbler for dessert. Price categories per person not including 5% tax, service, and drinks, are *Moderate,* $15–$25, and *Inexpensive,* under $15.

EUREKA SPRINGS **Cafe Armagost.** A roadside restaurant-in-a-house where the tables are close together but the service is fast and the menu is full of good soups and salads, wonderful chicken dishes, and tasty seafood.

52 Kingshighway, tel. 501/253–8075. Open for dinner only. AE, D, MC, V. Moderate.

Devito's Restaurant. Situated in the middle of shops and galleries is this excellent Italian café, where fresh fish and homemade pastas compliment a modest selection of imported wines. *5 Center St., tel. 501/253–6807. Closed Wed. AE, MC, V. Moderate.*

Victorian Sampler. Duck out of the historic district's shopping traffic, and grab a quiet table at this charming Victorian home; the homespun house specialties run the gamut from chicken and veggies to pork ribs and corn bread. *33 Prospect Dr., tel. 501/253–8374. MC, V. Moderate.*

Bubba's. A hole-in-the-wall where smoky barbecue is the specialty, though zesty pork and lean chicken sandwiches are also served. *U.S. 62, tel. 501/253–7706. No credit cards. Inexpensive.*

HOT SPRINGS **Arlington Hotel.** The Continental menu is good, but the restaurant is best known for its hearty and healthy Sunday brunch. *Corner of Central and Fountain Sts., tel. 501/623–7771. AE, DC, MC, V. Inexpensive–Moderate.*

Mrs. Miller's. A Hot Springs institution, Mrs. Miller serves up some of the state's finest home-cooked cuisine, everything from fried quail to chicken pot pie. This is the perfect stop if you're headed to Lake Hamilton. *4723 Central Ave., tel. 501/525–8861. MC, V. Inexpensive–Moderate.*

Cafe New Orleans. This restaurant across from the old Arlington Hotel is run by a group of friends from New Orleans who truly know their Creole and Cajun cooking. *210 Central Ave., tel. 501/624–3200. MC, V. Inexpensive.*

La Hacienda. A Mexican-American family serves authentic Mexican food (with the spices toned down for the American clientele) that's an especially good bargain at lunchtime. *4716 Central Ave., tel. 501/525–8203. MC, V. Inexpensive.*

Magee's Café. This former auction house (1871) right across from Bathhouse Row is a good place to unwind with a pastry and a cup of coffee. It's the sort of place where poets and folk musicians like to mingle. *362 Central Ave., tel. 501/623–4091. AE, MC, V. Inexpensive.*

McLard's. There are many barbecue joints in Hot Springs, but local aficionados claim McLard's is the best. Long lines and somewhat surly service seem to be inevitable parts of the McLard experience. *505 Albert Pike, tel. 501/624–9586. Closed Sun. and Mon. No credit cards. Inexpensive.*

SHOPPING

Factory Outlet Hot Springs Stores, on Rte. 7, 3 miles south of the Hot Springs racetrack, is a popular discount store. On Spring Street in Eureka Springs, good deals and good quality can be found on pottery, quilts, soaps, candles, and scrimshaw. Mountain Valley Spring Company (150 Central Ave., Hot Springs, tel. 800/643–1501) bottles and sells the fabled water from the national park. Bring your own container and collect the thermal for free at the two Thermal Water Jug Fountains at the end of Bathhouse Row. To buy Ouachita Mountain quartz crystals, try Ron Coleman's Rocks-R-Gems (tel. 501/624–7280), on Highway 70 just before Hot Springs.

OUTDOOR ACTIVITIES

CANOEING The Buffalo National River is at its best in early summer. Canoes can be rented from Buffalo Camping and Canoeing (Gilbert, tel. 501/439– 2888) and at half a dozen shops in Mt. Ida on Highway 27. The state tourism department distributes a floater's guide to Arkansas.

FISHING Area lakes harbor largemouth and smallmouth bass, bream, and catfish. There are trout streams in the Ozark National Forest not far from Eureka Springs. For a fishing

guide, contact the Arkansas Game and Fish Commission (2 Natural Resources Dr., Little Rock 72205, tel. 501/223–6300).

GOLF Several courses are noted in the guide put out by the state's tourism department (tel. 800/NATURAL). DeGray Resort State Park near Hot Springs has an 18-hole public course.

HIKING Arkansas has backcountry trails galore, a good many of them concentrated around the Buffalo National River, and in the Ouachita and Ozark national forests.

HORSEBACK RIDING Mountain-trail rides, hayrides, and lunch and dinner rides can be arranged at Castleberry Stables outside Hot Springs (tel. 501/623–6609 or 501/623–9939).

WATER SPORTS Swimming is good at Buffalo Point on the Buffalo River, south of Yellville on Rte. 14. Boats can be rented for waterskiing on Lake Hamilton, Lake Ouachita, and DeGray Lake.

ENTERTAINMENT

CONCERTS The Ozark Folk Center at Mountain View has nightly mountain music April–October, with special Sunday night gospel concerts (tel. 800/243–3655). In Hot Springs, the Music Mountain Jamboree (tel. 501/767–3841) features country and bluegrass.

MUSEUMS At the Mid-America Museum (tel. 501/767–3461; admission charged) in Hot Springs, science comes to life in big exhibits such as the tornado chamber, lifelike dinosaurs, and a laser show.

HORSE RACING Oaklawn Park (tel. 501/623–4411) at Hot Springs has pari-mutuel betting on horse races from late January or early February (schedule varies) through most of April.

Las Vegas
Nevada

as Vegas used to be a fantasy-land for adults that existed for one reason: gambling. Yes, there were museums and galleries here, but the truth was that virtually everybody came to win or lose money. With gambling becoming legalized around the country, the city is struggling against time to turn Vegas into a Disney-like family destination, with a vacation's worth of fun things for kids to see and do, but for now, Vegas is still the country's premier gambling town. As you stroll or drive along Las Vegas Boulevard, you're constantly reminded of this. There are no supermarkets, post offices, movie theaters, or other familiar businesses of everyday life on the famous Strip; it's a place where you can buy a hamburger, get married, and lay a bet. In town, you can stop in a a 7-Eleven or a supermarket at any hour and find people playing slots across the aisle from the Cheerios and Froot Loops.

A drive through town will show you an extraordinary collection of neon sculpture and flashing lights, especially on Fremont Street downtown. To the east, 25 minutes away, are both Hoover Dam, one of the greatest man-made wonders, and Lake Mead, one of the largest "artificial" lakes in the world. Drive only a few minutes from the neon Strip and you'll discover a southwestern landscape of red rock, Joshua trees, and yucca. Zion, Bryce, Death Valley, and other natural wonders are only a few hours away.

ESSENTIAL INFORMATION

WHEN TO GO Las Vegas, the largest city in Nevada, is 2,162 feet above sea level, but the desert still defines the climate: bone-dry and hot in the summer, sunny and pleasant in spring and fall, cool and sometimes downright cold in winter. The weather is best from October through March, with highs in the 60s and a low of 35°. In summer, the fierce desert

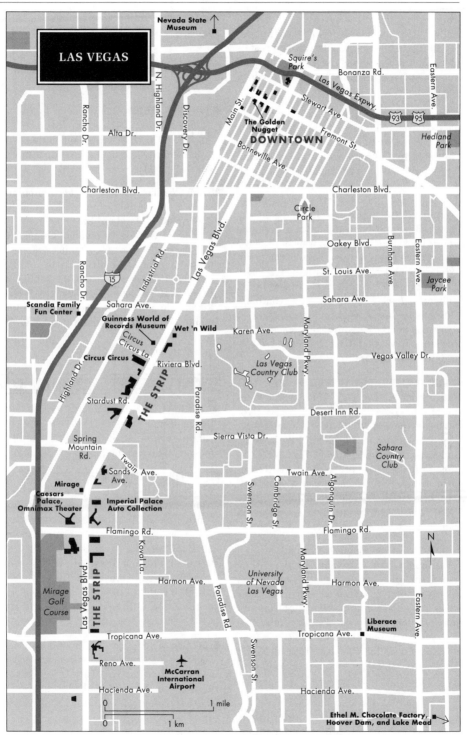

LAS VEGAS

Nevada State Museum

Squire's Park

Bonanza Rd.

Las Vegas Expwy.

Stewart Ave.

The Golden Nugget

DOWNTOWN

Fremont St.

Bonneville Ave.

N. Highland Dr.

Discovery Dr.

Main St.

Eastern Ave.

93 95

Hedland Park

Rancho Dr.

Alta Dr.

Charleston Blvd.

Charleston Blvd.

Circle Park

Las Vegas Blvd.

Oakey Blvd.

Burnham Ave.

Eastern Ave.

St. Louis Ave.

Jaycee Park

Industrial Rd.

15

Rancho Dr.

Sahara Ave.

Sahara Ave.

Scandia Family Fun Center

Guinness World of Records Museum

Wet 'n Wild

Karen Ave.

Maryland Pkwy.

Vegas Valley Dr.

Circus Circus La.

Circus Circus

Riviera Blvd.

Las Vegas Country Club

Highland Dr.

Stardust Rd.

THE STRIP

Paradise Rd.

Desert Inn Rd.

Sierra Vista Dr.

Sahara Country Club

Spring Mountain Rd.

Twain Ave.

Sands Ave.

Twain Ave.

Swenson St.

Cambridge St.

Algonquin Dr.

Mirage

Caesars Palace, Omnimax Theater

Imperial Palace Auto Collection

Flamingo Rd.

Flamingo Rd.

N

Mirage Golf Course

Las Vegas Blvd

THE STRIP

Koval La.

Harmon Ave.

University of Nevada Las Vegas

Maryland Pkwy.

Harmon Ave.

Eastern Ave.

Paradise Rd.

Tropicana Ave.

Tropicana Ave.

Liberace Museum

Reno Ave.

McCarran International Airport

Swenson St.

Hacienda Ave.

Hacienda Ave.

0   1 mile

0   1 km

Ethel M. Chocolate Factory, Hoover Dam, and Lake Mead

sun pushes the mercury to 110° (this so-called "dry heat" is relatively free of humidity and quite tolerable). When the sun is at its fiercest, Las Vegas lives indoors, in the hotel rooms, showrooms, and the casinos, where everything is air-conditioned.

There is neither a peak nor an off-peak season in Las Vegas. The only true slow period is right before Christmas, when quiet descends on the Strip and hotel rooms are abundant. Spring and fall tend to be busy times, as do holiday weekends year-round; New Year's Eve and Valentine's Day (when thousands of people fill the wedding chapels) and the Super Bowl (when the hordes crowd the sports books) are the busiest weekends of the year. Conventions frequently pack the town, so check your travel dates with the Las Vegas Convention & Visitors Authority (*see* Tourist Offices, *below*). Hotel room rates routinely fluctuate with a vengeance. Sunday through Thursday are the bargain nights (except during large conventions), while Friday and Saturday get top dollar.

FESTIVALS AND SEASONAL EVENTS May 1–5: The Senior Classic Golf Tournament takes place at the Desert Inn (3145 Las Vegas Blvd. S, 89109, tel. 702/733–4444). **May 18–27:** Helldorado Days recall the Wild West with a rodeo, contests, and parades. **Dec. 6–14:** National Finals Rodeo brings finalists to compete at the Thomas and Mack Center (tel. 702/731–2115). **Dec. 31:** The biggest New Year's Eve Party in the West is celebrated downtown on Fremont Street.

BARGAINS Hotel rooms, food, drink, and entertainment cost a fraction of what they would in other cities, simply because the highly profitable casinos subsidize the other costs. Las Vegas is renowned for its cheap and ample buffets (breakfast $3–$4, dinner $6–$7); you can eat breakfast for as little as 99¢, a steak dinner for $2, and drink alcoholic beverages for free in many casinos as long as you're playing the tables.

Lounges provide free live music all over town (at most you don't even have to drink). Circus acts, exploding volcanoes, and people-watching are other good entertainment bargains.

To tour the Strip inexpensively, take the local bus or shuttle, which creep through the brightly lit district for $1.

TOURIST OFFICES Las Vegas Chamber of Commerce (711 E. Desert Inn Rd., 89109, tel. 702/735–1616). Las Vegas Convention & Visitors Authority (3150 Paradise Rd., 89109, tel. 702/737–2011).

EMERGENCIES **Police, fire** and **ambulance:** Dial 911. **Hospitals:** Humana Hospital Sunrise (3186 S. Maryland Pkwy., tel. 702/731–8000) and University Medical Center (1800 W. Charleston Blvd., tel. 702/383–2000). **Doctors:** Physicians Medical Center (3121 S. Maryland Pkwy., tel. 702/732–0600). **Dentists:** Paradise Dental Center (2221 Paradise Rd. at Sahara Ave., tel. 702/735–8189). **Pharmacies:** White Cross Drugs (Commercial Center, 953 E. Sahara, tel. 702/735–1733) is open late at night.

ARRIVING AND DEPARTING

BY PLANE Thanks to renovation, McCarran International Airport (tel. 702/261–5743), slightly southeast of the city, is one of the most attractive and efficient in the nation.

BETWEEN THE AIRPORT AND DOWNTOWN Surprisingly, the least expensive mode of transportation from the airport to town is limousine. Bell Trans (tel. 702/739–7990) operates a limo shuttle service that costs $3.25 per person to the Strip hotels, $4.50 to the downtown ones. You will also find taxis lined up, mostly Yellow, Checker, and Star (tel. 702/873–2000). The cab ride to the Strip will cost $10–$15, and $15–$18 to downtown.

BY CAR The major highways leading to Vegas are I–15, running east from Los Angeles and west from Salt Lake City, U.S. 93 running north from Arizona, and U.S. 95 running south from Reno. If you take U.S. 93, you will drive across the top of the mighty Hoover Dam en route.

BY TRAIN Amtrak (tel. 800/USA–RAIL) passes through Las Vegas. The depot is in back of the Plaza Hotel (1 N. Main St., tel. 702/385–6896)—you disembark right into a casino.

GETTING AROUND

BY CAR Las Vegas is an easy city to drive in because it is so compact. Las Vegas Boulevard runs north and south, a 3¹/₂-mile section of it known as the Strip. Here the major hotel-casinos are found, one right after the other. Every hotel has free self-parking, or have a valet do it for a customary $1–$2 tip.

BY BUS Citizen Area Transit (CAT, tel. 702/228–7433) and Las Vegas Transit (tel. 702/384–3540) run Strip buses from the Hacienda Hotel at the southern end of the Strip to the downtown area. The buses stop at the major hotels, and the fare is $1.

BY TAXI Desert Cab (tel. 702/736–1702) and Yellow, Checker, and Star Cabs (tel. 702/873–2000) are the major cab companies in Las Vegas. It should not be necessary to call for one from major hotels, as they wait outside. This is not the case in less trafficked neighborhoods. The fare is $2.20 for the first fraction of a mile, 20¢ for each additional ¹/₇ of a mile. For more than three passengers, there is a surcharge of 20¢ a mile.

REST STOPS There are no public rest stops in Las Vegas. Hotels, restaurants, and gas stations provide convenient alternatives.

GUIDED TOURS Gray Line (1550 S. Industrial Rd., tel. 702/384–1234 or 800/634–6579) offers sightseeing tours of the city and its environs. Large luxury coaches do city tours (Ethel M's chocolate factory, Nevada State Museum, and such celebrity homes as Siegfried and Roy and Wayne Newton), as well as trips outside the city to Red Rock Canyon and Old Nevada, and Hoover Dam and Lake Mead.

EXPLORING

THE CITY There are really two Las Vegases: the older downtown section of the city, and the fabled Strip, where the glitzy new hotels are clustered.

Downtown is where it all began for Las Vegas, back in 1905, when the San Pedro, Los Angeles, and Salt Lake Railroad founded it as a division point. Downtown still retains some of its old-time honky-tonk character. It's also the place for budget gambling and ultrabargain food. Of the dozen or so hotels lining Fremont Street, the Golden Nugget (129 Fremont St., tel. 702/385–7111) stands out from the neon crowd, redone in white marble and gold.

The **Strip** starts 2 miles south of downtown, at the Sahara, and keeps running south for another 3¹/₂ miles. This legendary area is home to 30 or so hotels. The famous names—The Mirage, Caesars Palace, Bally's, Stardust, Sands, Flamingo—evoke images of beautiful people, mobster types, and high rollers, all throwing $100 chips around a crap table. Though no longer exclusively a playground for the rich, the Strip is still a fantasyland. Hotels worth a special visit are **Caesars Palace** (3750 Las Vegas Blvd. S, tel. 702/731–7110), with its theatrical re-creation of ancient Rome, and the **Mirage** (3400 Las Vegas Blvd. S, tel. 702/791–7111), which features an erupting volcano, a dolphin pool out back, and a glassed-in grotto for white tigers. If you are traveling with children, a stop at **Circus Circus** (2880 Las Vegas Blvd. S, tel. 702/734–0411) is a must. Here, a carnival midway looms over the casino, and trapeze artists somersault in the air above the gamblers' heads.

Ethel M. Chocolate Factory is Willy Wonka come to life. Stop here to watch the candy being made on your way to the Hoover Dam. *2 Cactus Dr., Henderson, tel. 702/433–2500. Open daily. Admission charged.*

Exhibits and film footage re-create record-setting events in sports, science, and entertainment at the **Guinness World of Records**

Museum. *2780 Las Vegas Blvd. S, tel. 702/792–3766. Open daily. Admission charged.*

Hoover Dam is considered one of the seven man-made wonders of the world. The dam rises 727 feet high (the equivalent of a 70-story building) and is 660 feet thick (greater than the length of two football fields). It was completed in 1935 for two purposes: flood control and the generation of electricity. Construction of the dam required 4.4 million cubic yards of concrete—enough to build a two-lane highway from San Francisco to New York. *On U.S. 93, 25 mi southeast of Las Vegas just outside of Boulder City, tel. 702/293–8367. Open daily. Admission charged for the dam tour.*

Two hundred antique cars are housed at **Imperial Palace Auto Collection,** including a historic Mercedes that once belonged to Adolf Hitler. *In Imperial Palace Hotel, 3850 Las Vegas Blvd. S, tel. 702/731–3311. Open daily. Admission charged (but coupons for free entry are distributed outside the hotel).*

Created by the construction of Hoover Dam, **Lake Mead** is the largest man-made body of water in the Western Hemisphere. Its surface covers 229 square miles, and the irregular shoreline extends 550 miles for boating, swimming, or fishing. *On U.S. 93, beginning at Hoover Dam and extending northeast, tel. 702/293–8906 (Lake Mead Visitor Center). Open daily. Admission free.*

Liberace Museum displays the master showman's pianos, flashy costumes, and extravagant automobiles. *1775 E. Tropicana Ave., tel. 702/798–5595. Open daily. Admission charged.*

Regional history is the theme indoors at the **Nevada State Museum,** while lakeside exhibits feature native plants and animals. *In Lorenzi Park, 700 Twin Lakes Dr., tel. 702/486–5205. Open daily. Admission charged.*

Omnimax Theater's 70mm films with wraparound sound focus on such stomach-hurtling subjects as rocket launches and white-water rafting. *In Caesars Palace, 3570 Las Vegas Blvd. S, tel. 702/731–7900. Open daily with shows on the hour. Admission charged.*

Scandia Family Fun Center, an outdoor game center, has batting cages and three miniature golf courses. *2900 Sirius Ave., tel. 702/364–0070. Open Mon.–Sat. Admission free, but there's a fee to play the games.*

Wet 'n Wild, a 26-acre water park, has pools, slides, every conceivable water ride. *2600 Las Vegas Blvd. S, tel. 702/737–3819. Open mid-Apr.–Sept., daily. Admission charged.*

THE NATURAL WORLD Nature enthusiasts will want to take excursions from Las Vegas into the Southwest desert. The nearest site of interest is Red Rock Canyon, 15 miles due west of the city. Here the rocks glow reddest and are strikingly lovely at sunrise or sunset.

Farther out, 60 miles northeast of Las Vegas on I–15 is Valley of Fire State Park, so named for its flame-colored rock. Here, the red stone formations have been eroded into strange and wondrous shapes. Many have petroglyphs, a sort of graffiti-meets-stone-carvings, from Anasazi Indians who lived in the valley 2,000 years ago.

HOTELS AND INNS

As a rule, downtown Las Vegas hotels tend to be less costly than those on the Strip, although some lack the amenities of swimming pools and tennis courts. Except for holiday weekends and peak convention periods, you should have no trouble finding a room. For hotel availability and recommendations, contact the Las Vegas Convention & Visitors Authority Hotel and Room Reservations (tel. 702/892–0777).

In Las Vegas, almost every hotel houses a casino. Gambling, after all, is the hotels' reason for being. Therefore the facility is not listed separately.

Price categories for double occupancy, excluding 8% room tax, are *Moderate,* $50–$85, and *Inexpensive,* under $50.

THE STRIP **Bally's.** This huge, spread-out affair is more like a self-contained city than a hotel. The casino is the most cavernous in town. *3645 Las Vegas Blvd. S, 89109, tel. 702/739–4111 or 800/634–3434. 2,832 rooms. 5 restaurants, 2 showrooms, pool, tennis courts, shopping mall, AE, DC, MC, V. Moderate.*

Flamingo Hilton. A sense of history lingers in this first of the luxury palaces, opened in 1946 and later refurbished by the Hilton group. The Flamingo is currently the second-largest hotel in town, which makes it third-largest in the world. *3555 Las Vegas Blvd. S, 89109, tel. 702/733–3111 or 800/732–2111; fax 702/733–3499. 3,530 rooms. 6 restaurants, showroom, 2 pools, tennis courts. AE, D, DC, MC, V. Moderate.*

Riviera. This sprawling 39-year-old hotel-casino has four showrooms and a 125,000-square-foot casino, the largest in the world. *2901 Las Vegas Blvd. S, 89109, tel. 702/734–5110 or 800/634–3420; fax 702/731–3265. 2,200 rooms. 5 restaurants, 4 showrooms, pool, tennis courts. AE, D, DC, MC, V. Moderate.*

Stardust. A new 1,000-room tower, a spectacular neon facade and sign, and nearly 40 years on the Strip make this one of the landmark Las Vegas hotel properties. *3000 Las Vegas Blvd. S, 89101, tel. 702/732–6111 or 800/634–6757. 2,500 rooms. 4 restaurants, pool, tennis courts. AE, D, DC, MC, V. Moderate.*

Tropicana. Near the airport, the beautifully appointed grounds feature waterfalls and an immense swimming pool, where you can play swim-up blackjack. *3801 Las Vegas Blvd. S, 89109, tel. 702/739–2222 or 800/468–9494, fax 702/739–2323. 1,900 rooms. 5 restaurants, showroom, 2 pools, AE, D, DC, MC, V. Moderate.*

Circus Circus. The first hotel in town to cater to families, this carnival-style place is ideal for the kids but a bit of a madhouse for grown-ups. *2880 Las Vegas Blvd. S, 89109, tel. 702/734–0410 or 800/634–3450. 2,793 rooms.*

4 restaurants, 3 pools, RV park, midway with circus acts. AE, DC, MC, V. Inexpensive.

Excalibur. Named for King Arthur's sword, Vegas's newest hotel, also the world's largest, is modeled after a medieval castle. *3850 Las Vegas Blvd. S, 89109, tel. 702/597–7777 or 800/937–7777. 4,032 rooms. 7 restaurants, swimming pool, village of shops. AE, D, DC, MC, V. Inexpensive.*

Hacienda. The southernmost hotel on the Strip, the Hacienda is refreshingly low-key as things go in Las Vegas, with a lushly landscaped pool area and one of the oldest wedding chapels in town. *3950 Las Vegas Blvd. S, 89109, tel. 702/739–8911 or 800/634–6713. 840 rooms. 3 restaurants, showroom, pool, tennis courts, RV park. AE, D, DC, MC, V. Inexpensive.*

DOWNTOWN **Jackie Gaughan's Plaza.** You're an elevator's ride away from Amtrak at this hotel, built on the site of the old Union Pacific depot. The Plaza is also the scene of the fireworks on New Year's Eve. *1 S. Main St., 89109, tel. 702/386–2110 or 800/634–6575, fax 702/382–8281. 1,034 rooms. Restaurant with a view overlooking downtown. AE, D, DC, MC, V. Moderate.*

Four Queens. The casino claims the world's largest slot machine; to keep an eye on your valuables rather than on the mammoth slot machine, the guest towers have 24-hour security, and the rooms are large and comfortable. *202 Fremont St., 89109, tel. 702/385–4011 or 800/634–6045. 720 rooms. 2 restaurants. AE, D, DC, MC, V. Moderate.*

El Cortez. The southwest corner of this hotel is the oldest original casino wing in the country, and the rooms in the newer tower are all minisuites. *600 E. Fremont St., tel. 702/385–5200 or 800/634–6703. 315 rooms. 2 restaurants. AE, D, DC, MC, V. Inexpensive.*

MOTELS

MODERATE **Courtyard by Marriott** (3275 Paradise Rd., 89109, tel. 702/791–3600). 149 rooms; restaurant, pool, spa. **Rodeway Inn**

(3786 Las Vegas Blvd. S, 89109, tel. 702/736–1434). 97 rooms; pool.

INEXPENSIVE **Center Strip** (3688 Las Vegas Blvd. S, 89109, tel. 702/739–6066). 92 rooms with refrigerators and VCRs. **La Quinta** (3782 Las Vegas Blvd. S, 89109, tel. 702/739–7457). 114 rooms; pool.

DINING

You can eat very well for very little money in Las Vegas. The hotels keep food prices down to attract—and to keep—patrons inside near the slots and tables. The buffets are incredibly inexpensive and bountiful, and the coffee shops often advertise rock-bottom prices for steaks, prime rib, and lobster. Snack bars have food priced so cheaply, you wonder why they don't just give it away. Many good restaurants are found beyond the hotel area, away from the sound of slot machines, where the locals know to go.

For the restaurants listed below, price categories per person, excluding 7% tax, services, or drinks, are *Moderate,* $15–$25, and *Inexpensive,* under $15.

MODERATE **Bootlegger.** Locals flock to this popular Italian restaurant for the excellent seafood dishes, notably the lobster diavolo. *5025 S. Eastern Ave., tel. 702/736–4939. AE, D, DC, MC, V.*

Cafe Michelle. Chicken and salads are the primary lure at this French sidewalk café, with outdoor umbrellas and red-and-white checked tablecloths. *1350 E. Flamingo St., tel. 702/735–8686. MC, V.*

Cathay House. Here you can enjoy a lovely view of the city while dining on spicy Szechuan cuisine. *5300 Spring Mountain, tel. 702/876–3838. AE, DC, MC, V.*

The Steak House. Fine aged steaks are cooked over an open-hearth grill in this quiet, wood-paneled restaurant. *In Circus Circus Hotel. 2880 Las Vegas Blvd. S, tel. 702/734–0410. AE, D, DC, MC, V.*

The Tillerman. Seafood is the favorite at this garden-setting spot, located 3 miles east of the Strip. Here the catch of the day is flown in fresh and served under an open skylight on hot desert nights. *2245 E. Flamingo St., tel. 702/731–4036. AE, D, DC, MC, V.*

INEXPENSIVE **Chicago Joe's.** The pastas at this unpretentious restaurant have a fan club of their own. *820 S. 4th St., tel. 702/382–5637. MC, V.*

Old Heidelberg. Despite its German name, this small, family-run nook near the Sahara Hotel features Continental fare such as veal calvados. *604 E. Sahara Ave., tel. 702/731–5310. MC, V.*

Dona Maria's. The enchilada-style tamales (best with the green sauce) and other Mexican dishes are the best in town. *1000 E. Charleston, tel. 702/786–6358. AE, MC, V.*

Silver Dragon. At this replica of a Peking palace, you'll find traditional Chinese food, sweet-and-sour dishes, and lemon fish. *1510 E. Flamingo St., tel. 702/737–1234. AE, MC, V.*

BUFFETS Las Vegas is famous for its lavish buffets. Nearly every hotel offers breakfast, lunch, and dinner buffets. **Circus Circus** (2880 Las Vegas Blvd. S, tel. 702/734–0411) is cheapest: at $3.99 for dinner, it's always mobbed with people getting what they paid for. The **Rio** (3770 W. Flamingo, tel. 702/252–7777) and **Palace Station** (2411 W. Sahara Blvd., tel. 702/367–2411) buffets are the best. On weekends, the better hotels serve more sumptuous buffets. The most elegant of these is the Sterling Champagne Brunch at **Bally's** (3645 Las Vegas Blvd. S, tel. 702/739–4111). It's expensive, but worth it.

SHOPPING

There are two main shopping areas for tourists on the Strip. Shops are in major hotels, such as Bally's or Caesars Palace, and the Fashion Show Mall (3200 Las Vegas Blvd. S, tel. 702/369–8382). These stores are expensive, feature designer labels, and are hardly for impulse purchases.

At the other extreme are the undeniably tacky souvenir shops, which sell T-shirts and the quintessential Las Vegas dice clock.

OUTDOOR ACTIVITIES

FISHING Fishing is available year-round on Lake Mead. Visitors may obtain a three-day permit from any of the marinas. The nearest one to Las Vegas is Lake Mead Marina (tel. 702/293–3484).

GOLF Golf is the favorite recreation of this sun-blessed city, and a number of courses are available. The best is found at the Desert Inn (3145 Las Vegas Blvd. S, tel. 702/733–4290), but it is open only to hotel guests. The Sahara Country Club (1911 E. Desert Inn Rd., tel. 702/796– 0016), and Angel Park (100 S. Rampart, tel. 702/254–4653) are open to the public.

SWIMMING Most hotels have swimming pools, but if you prefer the beach, try Boulder Beach on Lake Mead, next to Las Vegas Marina. The water gets tepid in summer but refreshes during other seasons.

TENNIS Many of the larger hotels have courts, open to both guests and visitors (*see* Hotels and Inns, *above*).

ENTERTAINMENT

Las Vegas, of course, means show biz, and the nightlife here is varied. You will find household-name superstars like Frank Sinatra and Bill Cosby, and big production shows—spectacularly staged musicals, performed by scantily clad show girls—interspersed with specialty acts. There are also smaller-scale revues and several magic acts.

The dinner show, once a Vegas institution, is vanishing from the scene. Only three hotels still have them: The **Tropicana** (3801 Las Vegas Blvd. S, showroom reservations tel.

702/739–2411), the **Flamingo Hilton** (3555 Las Vegas Blvd. S, tel. 702/733–3333), and the **Excalibur** (3850 Las Vegas Blvd. S, tel. 702/597–7600).

The rest provide two cocktails with the price of admission, and that price varies. The big stars command $40–$100 a seat; big productions average $25. The small revues run about $15.

There is no advance ticket purchasing for Vegas shows. To make a reservation, call the hotel the day of or the day before the show. Count on waiting in line at the showroom for about 30 minutes before you are seated, and to get a good seat in a crowded room, you must tip the maître d' $5–$20—depending on the performer and the number of people waiting. While tipping the maître d's is a questionable practice, it's the way things are done in Las Vegas.

SUPERSTARS Some of the hotels featuring big-name performers are **Bally's** (3645 Las Vegas Blvd. S, tel. 702/739–4567); **Caesars Palace** (3750 Las Vegas Blvd. S, tel. 702/731–7333); the **Desert Inn** (3145 Las Vegas Blvd. S, tel. 702/733–4444). Free tourist magazines in the hotel gift shops list which stars are in town and their performance schedules.

BIG PRODUCTION SHOWS "Jubilee" at Bally's (3645 Las Vegas Blvd. S, tel. 702/739–4567); "Folies Bergere" at Tropicana (3801 Las Vegas Blvd. S, tel. 702/739–2411), and "City Lites" at the Flamingo Hilton (3555 Las Vegas Blvd. S, tel. 702/733–3333) are some of the long-running hits.

SMALLER REVUES "La Cage" and "Crazy Girls" at the Riviera (2901 Las Vegas Blvd. S., tel. 702/734–5110), though less extravagant and less expensive than the major productions, are no less enjoyable and entertaining.

The Lincoln Trail
Illinois, Indiana, Kentucky

tretching from the rolling green hills of northern Kentucky to Indiana's Ohio Valley and to the wide-open prairies of southern and central Illinois, the Lincoln Trail conjures up images of log cabins, tiny farms surrounded by split-rail fences, and prairie air scented with wood smoke. Exaggerations? Not really, for you don't have to walk too far from your car to find all of these on the historic Lincoln Trail.

Abraham Lincoln's presence is still felt along the strip of middle America now known as the Lincoln Trail; dozens of spots along the trail, countless historical markers, and three national historic sites pay homage to Lincoln's memory. The Abraham Lincoln Birthplace National Historic Site, near Hodgenville, Kentucky, enshrines in a large granite memorial the tiny log cabin where Lincoln was born. Remote southern Indiana's Lincoln Boyhood National Memorial marks the farm where Lincoln labored for 14 diffi-

cult years. And in Springfield, Illinois, where Lincoln practiced law for 24 years, the Lincoln Home National Historic Site preserves the only home he ever owned, and the place where he received word of his election to the presidency in 1860.

Much of the region cut by the Lincoln Trail is rural, dotted with small towns and neat, orderly farms. Even Springfield, the Illinois prairie capital known as Mr. Lincoln's Hometown, is surrounded by seemingly endless cornfields. You won't find much glitter along the Lincoln Trail: Except for Springfield, which bustles when the legislature is in session, the pace is slow and life is fairly sedate.

ESSENTIAL INFORMATION

WHEN TO GO July and August are the trail's hottest months, when maximum temperatures often reach the upper 80s or higher, with high humidity. Winters see modest snowfall and average temperatures in the upper 20s,

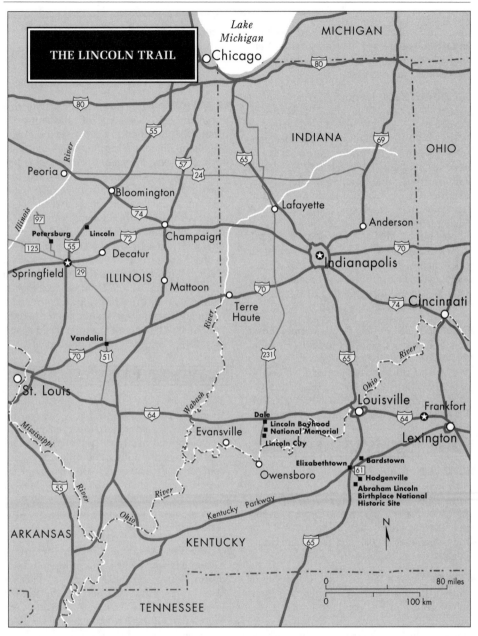

although freezing rain often occurs. Although the summer (June, July, and Aug.) is peak season, the region is perhaps loveliest in autumn, when the crowds thin out, the heat and humidity are lower (and temperatures remain mild into late Oct.), and the land is ablaze with color.

FESTIVALS AND SEASONAL EVENTS Mid-Feb.: Lincoln's Birthday is celebrated with musical programs, speakers, and other events at

Hodgenville, Kentucky; Lincoln City, Indiana; and Springfield, Illinois; **2nd weekend in Oct.:** Lincoln Days, in Hodgenville, Kentucky, features rail-splitting contests, Lincoln look-alikes, and a parade.

TOURIST OFFICES Kentucky Department of Travel Development (Capital Plaza Tower, Frankfort, KY 40601, tel. 502/564–4930 or 800/255–TRIP). Indiana Tourism Development Division (1 N. Capitol, Suite 700, Indianapolis, IN 46204-2288, tel. 317/232–8860). Illinois Tourist Information Center (310 S. Michigan Ave., Chicago, IL 60604, tel. 312/793–2094). Louisville Convention & Visitors Bureau (400 S. 1st St., Louisville, KY 40202, tel. 606/584–2121 or 800/626–5646). Abraham Lincoln Tourism Bureau (601 Pekin St., Lincoln, IL 62656, tel. 217/732–8687). Springfield Convention & Visitors Bureau (109 N. 7th St., Springfield, IL 62701, tel. 217/789–2360 or 800/545–7300).

EMERGENCIES Police, fire, and **ambulance:** Dial 911. **Doctors:** Hardin Memorial Hospital (N. Dixie Ave., Elizabethtown, KY, tel. 502/765–1640). St. Joseph's Hospital (Leland Heights, Huntingburg, IN, tel. 812/683–9111). Memorial Medical Center (800 N. Rutledge St., Springfield, IL, tel. 217/788–3030).

ARRIVING AND DEPARTING

BY PLANE Standiford Field Airport (tel. 502/368–6524), 5 miles south of downtown Louisville, Kentucky, has scheduled daily flights by major U.S. carriers. Capital Airport (tel. 217/788–1060), 5 miles north of downtown Springfield, Illinois, is served by regional carriers.

BY CAR A car is the most practical means of touring the Lincoln Trail. I–65 intersects Kentucky from north to south and passes near Hodgenville's Lincoln attractions. For travelers heading to Indiana's Lincoln Boyhood National Memorial, I–64 crosses southern Indiana from east to west. In Illinois, I–55 passes through Springfield, and I–74 and I–70 lead to other Lincoln sites.

BY BUS Greyhound Lines (tel. 800/231–2222) serves the region's major hubs, but service to the historic sites and smaller towns on the Lincoln Trail is sporadic.

BY TRAIN Amtrak (tel. 800/USA–RAIL) makes regular stops in Springfield and Lincoln, Illinois.

REST STOPS There are rest stops with rest rooms on I–65, just south of Elizabethtown, Kentucky. The park's visitor center at the Abraham Lincoln Birthplace National Historic Site, near Hodgenville, Kentucky, has rest rooms. In Indiana, rest stops on I–64, just west of Exit 57, near Dale, have rest rooms and tourist information about the entire state, and both the Lincoln Boyhood National Memorial and the adjacent Lincoln State Park offer rest rooms. In Illinois, a rest stop on I–64 at the Indiana border has rest rooms. The Vandalia Tourist Information Center, at the junction of U.S. 51 and I–74, has rest rooms. In Springfield, the Abraham Lincoln Home National Historic Site Visitor Center (426 S. 7th St.) and the Capitol Complex Visitor Center (425 S. College St.) have rest rooms.

EXPLORING

You can cover the Lincoln Trail in a week to 10 days. From the beginning of the trail in Hodgenville, Kentucky, to Lincoln City, Indiana, is approximately 135 miles via I–65 and I–64. It's about another 250 miles from Lincoln City to Springfield, Illinois, via I–64 west to U.S. 51, then north to Rte. 29. Most of Springfield's Lincoln-oriented sites are clustered in the city's center, within easy walking distance of one another.

KENTUCKY **Abraham Lincoln Birthplace National Historic Site** contains Lincoln's traditional birth cabin, enshrined in a large neoclassical memorial designed by John Russell Pope. The National Park Service Visitor Center offers a short film about Lincoln's Kentucky years and displays period artifacts, including the Lincoln family Bible. *2995 Lincoln Farm Rd., Hodgenville, tel. 502/358–3874. Open daily. Admission free.*

The Lincoln Museum, in downtown Hodgenville, has artifacts, paintings, and artwork pertaining to Lincoln's Kentucky years and

12 life-size dioramas of scenes from the life of America's 16th president. *66 Public Sq., Hodgenville, tel. 502/358–3163. Open daily. Admission charged.*

Lincoln's Boyhood Home, 7 miles northeast of Hodgenville on Knob Creek, is a reconstructed cabin on the site where Lincoln lived from 1811 to 1816. A small museum adjacent to the cabin displays period antiques and artifacts. *U.S. 31E, tel. 502/549–3741. Open Apr.– Nov., daily. Admission charged.*

INDIANA **Lincoln Boyhood National Memorial** marks the site of the Lincoln family farmstead from 1816 to 1830. Operated by the National Park Service, the visitor center museum has original Lincoln artifacts, photographs, paintings, sculpture, and a film about Lincoln's Indiana years. A walking trail leads to Lincoln's mother's grave, and the Trail of 12 Stones contains stones from significant spots in Lincoln's life. *5 mi south of I–64 Exit 57, then 2 mi east on Rte. 162, Lincoln City, tel. 812/937–4541. Open daily. Living History Farm open mid-Apr.–Oct., daily. Admission charged.*

Lincoln State Park has a church built by Lincoln's father and a small cemetery where his sister, Sarah, is buried. The park has hiking trails and offers boating, fishing, and camping. The drama *Young Abe Lincoln* (*see* Entertainment, *below*) is presented here in the summer. *Rte. 162, Lincoln City, tel. 812/937–4710. Open daily. Admission charged.*

ILLINOIS **Vandalia Statehouse State Historic Site** was Illinois's capitol from 1834 until 1839. The Federal-style building where Lincoln served in the legislature has been restored and now holds state offices, legislator's chambers, and courtrooms with Lincoln-era furnishings. *315 W. Gallatin St., Vandalia, tel. 618/283–1161. Open Mar.–Nov., daily. Admission free.*

Lincoln Home National Historic Site preserves the home where Lincoln and his wife lived from 1844 to 1861 and is the showpiece of the restored historic area. Restored and refurbished by the National Park Service, the home contains some original furnishings. Tickets are required for guided tours and are obtained at the visitor center. *426 S. 7th St., Springfield, tel. 217/789–2357. Open daily. Admission free.*

Lincoln Depot Museum, two blocks east, is where Lincoln left Springfield in 1861 to assume the presidency. His impromptu farewell address ranks among his most eloquent speeches. The depot has restored waiting rooms and shows a film depicting his farewell to Springfield and the events that took place on his journey to Washington. *10th and Monroe Sts., Springfield, tel. 217/544–8695 or 217/788–1356. Open Apr.–Aug., daily. Admission free.*

Lincoln-Herndon Law Offices State Historic Site, three blocks west and one block north of the depot, contains offices Lincoln shared with his law partner, William Herndon. From 1843 to 1852, the building held the only Federal Court in Illinois. *209 S. 6th St., Springfield, tel. 217/785–7289. Open daily. Donations accepted.*

Old State Capitol State Historic Site, across the street, is where Lincoln made his famous "House Divided" speech and argued more than 300 cases before the state supreme court. President Lincoln's body lay in state here in 1865. The magnificently restored building, with former state offices and legislative chambers, displays an actual draft of the Gettysburg Address written by Lincoln. *6th and Adams Sts., Springfield, tel. 217/785–7960. Open daily. Donations accepted.*

Lincoln's Tomb State Historic Site, 2 miles north of the Old Capitol, holds the remains of Lincoln, his wife, and three of their four children. Designed by Larkin Mead, this soaring edifice dominates a 12-acre plot and houses an impressive collection of Civil War and Lincoln statuary. At 7 PM each Tuesday from June through August, the 114th Infantry Regiment performs impressive drills in authentic Civil War uniforms. *Oak Ridge Cemetery, Springfield, tel. 217/782–2717. Open daily. Admission free.*

Lincoln's New Salem State Historic Site, 20 miles northwest of Springfield, is the restored prairie village of New Salem, where Lincoln lived from 1831 to 1837. The village museum displays New Salem artifacts, and costumed interpreters give demonstrations of weaving, candle making, and other 1830s skills. *2 mi south of Petersburg on Rte. 97, tel. 217/632–4000. Open daily. Admission free.*

Lincoln, 31 miles northeast of Springfield via I-55, is the only town named for Abraham Lincoln during his lifetime. Lincoln christened his namesake with watermelon juice on August 27, 1853; a historical marker at the Amtrak station marks the spot.

Postville Courthouse State Historic Site is a replica of the courthouse where the circuit-riding Lincoln practiced law during sessions from 1840 to 1847. The building has a small courtroom with period furnishings and photographs. *914 5th St., Lincoln, tel. 217/732–8930. Open Fri. and Sat. Admission free.*

Lincoln College Museum, in McKinstry Memorial Library, houses some 2,000 Lincoln artifacts, including items from Lincoln's Springfield home and the White House to Lincoln's assassination. In the library's presidential museum are documents bearing the signatures of all the U.S. presidents. *300 Keokuk St., Lincoln, tel. 217/732–3155. Open Feb.–mid-Dec., daily. Admission free.*

HOTELS AND INNS

Family-oriented motels remain the mainstay along the Lincoln Trail, although bed-and-breakfast accommodations are growing in popularity. Contact Kentucky Homes Bed & Breakfast (1431 St. James Ct., Louisville 40208, tel. 502/635–7341) for a brochure listing more than 100 B&Bs throughout Kentucky and southern Indiana, and for a free copy of *A Guide to Illinois Bed & Breakfasts & Country Inns,* contact the Illinois Bed & Breakfast Association (Box 96, Elash, IL 62028). Rates for lodging places tend to be lower before Memorial Day and after Labor Day. Price categories for double occupancy, without sales tax (6% in Kentucky, 5% in Indiana, and 6.25% in Illinois), are *Expensive,* over $85; *Moderate,* $50–$85; and *Inexpensive,* under $50.

KENTUCKY **Best Western Cardinal Inn.** This modern motel with large rooms is a 20-minute drive from Hodgenville's Lincoln attractions. *642 E. Dixie Hwy., Elizabethtown 42701, tel. 502/765–6139 or 800/528–1234. 67 rooms. Restaurant adjacent, pool, coin laundry, playground. AE, D, MC, V. Inexpensive.*

Lincoln Memorial Motel. Set on part of the original Lincoln farm, adjacent to the Lincoln Birthplace National Historic Site, this motel is convenient to Hodgenville's Lincoln attractions. *U.S. Hwy. 31E and Kentucky Rte. 61, Hodgenville 42748, tel. 502/358–3197. 16 rooms. Pool, wading pool. AE, MC, V. Inexpensive.*

INDIANA **Stone's Budget Host Motel.** This no-frills motel in a small-town atmosphere is only 3 miles from the Lincoln Boyhood National Memorial. *410 S. Washington St., Dale 47523, tel. 812/937–4448. 23 rooms. Restaurant. AE, D, DC, MC, V. Inexpensive.*

ILLINOIS **Springfield Renaissance Hotel.** Elegant public areas; large, comfortable rooms; attentive service; and a convenient downtown location make this hotel a good choice if you want to splurge. *701 E. Adams St., Springfield 62701, tel. 217/544–8079 or 800/228–9898. 320 rooms. Restaurant, cocktail lounge, entertainment, indoor pool, saunas, whirlpool, fitness center, valet service. AE, D, MC, V. Expensive.*

Corrine's Bed & Breakfast Inn. This 1883 Queen Anne home six blocks from the Lincoln Home is now a bed-and-breakfast with beautifully appointed rooms and attentive service. *1001 S. 6th St., Springfield 62701, tel. 217/527–1400. 4 rooms (2 with private and 2 with shared bath). Fireplace in public dining room, sun porch. AE, D, MC, V. Moderate–Expensive.*

MOTELS

INEXPENSIVE–MODERATE **Kentucky: Days Inn** (I–65 N., Elizabethtown 42701, tel. 502/769–5522 or 800/325–2525). 122 rooms; restaurant adjacent, pool, playground. **Howard Johnson** (708 Dixie Hwy., Elizabethtown 42701, tel. 502/765–2185). 80 rooms; restaurant, pool, coin laundry.

Indiana: Best Western Dutchman Inn (U.S. 231 and 22nd St., Huntingburg 47542, tel. 812/683–2334 or 800/528–1234). 95 rooms; restaurant, pool. **Holiday Inn** (U.S. 231 S, Jasper 47546, tel. 812/482–5555 or 800/HOLIDAY). 200 rooms; restaurant, indoor pool, sauna, whirlpool.

Illinois: Best Inns of America (500 N. 1st St., Springfield 62702, tel. 217/522–1100). 91 rooms; Continental breakfast included, outdoor pool. **Crossroads Motel** (1305 W. Woodlawn Rd., Lincoln 62656, tel. 217/735–5571). 30 rooms; outdoor pool, playground. **Drury Inn** (3180 S. Dirksen Pkwy., Exit 94 off I–55, Springfield 62703, tel. 217/529–3900). 118 rooms; indoor pool, whirlpool, minisuites. **Vandalia Travelodge** (1500 N. 6th St., Vandalia 62471, tel. 618/283–2363). 48 rooms; outdoor pool, playground.

DINING

The Lincoln Trail offers a selection of foods ranging from biscuits and gravy to Continental cuisine. Lean cuts of meat, fish, and poultry are available. A guide to healthful dining in Springfield, Illinois, prepared by the Illinois affiliate of the American Heart Association and the Capitol District Dietetic Association, is available from the Springfield Convention & Visitors Bureau (109 N. 7th St., Springfield 62701, tel. 217/789–2360 or 800/545–7300).

Price categories per person, excluding tax (6% in Kentucky, 5% in Indiana, and 6.25% in Illinois), service, and drinks, are *Expensive,* over $20; *Moderate,* $10–$20; and *Inexpensive,* under $10.

KENTUCKY **Stone Hearth Restaurant.** This is an informal, family-oriented eatery that yet attains a certain elegance with its white-cloth dinner tables spread around the restaurant's namesake—a cozy stone hearth. The menu is long and typically all-inclusive: Pick from many grilled chicken and beef dishes or a heaping plate of pasta. *1001 N. Mulberry St., Elizabethtown, tel. 502/765–4898. AE, DC, MC, V. Moderate.*

INDIANA **Stone's Budget Host Motel.** Don't be misled simply because this family-style restaurant is located inside a motel; the dining room is packed many nights, and the food, southern Indiana home cooking, is first-rate. *410 S. Washington St., Dale, tel. 812/937–4448. AE, D, DC, MC, V. Inexpensive.*

ILLINOIS **Bauers.** In a converted historic building near the state capitol, Bauers serves broiled lean steaks, Continental cuisine, and a variety of fresh seafood served in several cozy dining rooms. *620 S. 1st St., Springfield, tel. 217/789–4311. AE, D, DC, MC, V. Moderate–Expensive.*

Jim's Steakhouse. Broiled steaks, fresh seafood, and succulent cuts of thick prime rib are featured at this popular supper club just south of downtown. *2242 S. 6th St., Springfield, tel. 217/522–2111. AE, MC, V. Moderate–Expensive.*

Chesapeake Seafood House. A long list of seafood and beef dishes satisfy hungry Springfielders at the popular Chesapeake, located in a prim, finely restored 1850s residence. *3045 Clear Lake Ave., Springfield, tel. 217/522–5220. AE, D, DC, MC, V. Inexpensive–Moderate.*

Guzzardo's Italian Villa. Hearty helpings of American and Italian dishes—from lean steaks and salads to seafood and pasta—have made Guzzardo's a hot spot in Lincoln. *509 Pulaski St., Lincoln, tel. 217/832–6370. AE, MC, V. Inexpensive–Moderate.*

Feed Store. Amid Springfield's Lincoln attractions, the Feed Store serves up soups, salads, and light sandwiches in a family-style setting that's often packed. *516 E. Adams St., Springfield, tel. 217/528–3355. No credit cards. Inexpensive.*

Norb Andy's. This pleasantly dark downtown café offers fish, poultry, and the much-imitated horseshoe sandwich—a hot open-face blend of meat and Cheddar cheese topped with shoestring potatoes. Wednesday to Saturday you can sip coffee while groovin' to a live jazz band. Low-sodium and butterless dishes are available. *518 E. Capitol St., Springfield, tel. 217/523–7777. AE, DC, MC, V. Inexpensive.*

OUTDOOR ACTIVITIES

HIKING In Indiana, Lincoln State Park (Rte. 162, Lincoln City, IN, tel. 812/937–4710) and the Harrison-Crawford Wyandotte Complex (7240 Old Forest Rd., Corydon, IN, tel. 812/738–8232) offer several miles of hiking trails. In Springfield, Illinois, Lincoln Memorial Garden (2301 E. Lake Shore Dr., tel. 217/529–1111), Lincoln Park (1601 N. 5th St., tel. 217/522–5431), Adams Wildlife Sanctuary (2315 E. Clear Lake, tel. 217/544–5781), and Riverside Park (4105 Sand Hill Rd., tel. 217/789–2353) have easy hiking trails; contact the Springfield Convention & Visitors Bureau (109 N. 7th St., Springfield, 62701, tel. 217/789–2360 or 800/545–7300) for additional information. Also in Illinois, New Salem State Park (2 mi south of Petersburg on Rte. 97, tel. 217/632–7952) and Sangchris Lake State Park have several miles of hiking trails.

ENTERTAINMENT

CONCERTS Lincoln Jamboree (U.S. 31 and Rte. 61S, Hodgenville, KY, tel. 502/358–3545) presents country-music concerts on Saturday nights. The Springfield Symphony Orchestra and Illinois Chamber Orchestra of Sangamon State University give concerts at Sangamon State University Auditorium (tel. 217/786–6160) from early fall through late spring. Springfield Muni Opera (2501 Wabash Ave., Springfield, IL, tel. 217/793–6656) presents lavish Broadway-style productions in a theater under the stars in summer.

DANCE Springfield Ballet Company (tel. 217/544–1967) performs at Sangamon State University Auditorium.

THEATER The musical dramas *Big River* or *Young Abe Lincoln* is presented in an outdoor amphitheater at Lincoln State Park, nightly except Mondays, from mid-June to late August (Box 7-21, Lincoln City, IN, tel. 812/937–4493 or 800/284–4223). The Springfield Theatre Center (101 E. Lawrence, Springfield, IL, tel. 217/523–0878) hosts a wide variety of productions from September through June. Broadway productions and drama are offered at Sangamon State University Auditorium (tel. 217/786–6160) throughout the year. The Great American People Show (Box 401, Petersburg, IL, tel. 217/632–7755) presents *Your Obedient Servant, A. Lincoln* in an outdoor amphitheater at Lincoln's New Salem Historic Site from mid-June to mid-August.

SPECTATOR SPORTS The Springfield Cardinals, a St. Louis Cardinals class-A baseball team, play at Lanphier Ball Park (1351 N. Grand Ave. E, Springfield, IL, tel. 217/525–6570) from April through August.

Los Angeles
California

hose from purportedly more sophisticated cities note what Los Angeles, California, lacks. Others from more provincial towns raise an eyebrow at what it has. Regardless of the varying opinions about Los Angeles, the city attracts people from all over—and lots of them (in 1992 alone the city hosted more than 25 million overnight visitors). Indeed, you cannot do Los Angeles in a day or a week or even two. This second-largest city in America holds too many choices between its canyons and its coast to be exhausted in one trip; you will be exhausted first.

We cannot predict what *your* Los Angeles will be like. You can laze on a beach, soak up some of the world's greatest art collections, or tour the movie studios and stars' homes. You can window-shop along the luxurious Rodeo Drive in Beverly Hills or browse for hipper novelties on boutique-lined Melrose Avenue. The possibilities are endless.

So, relax. *Everybody's* a tourist in Los Angeles. Even the stars are star-struck (as evidenced by the celebrities watching other celebrities at Spago, Wolfgang Puck's world-renowned restaurant). Los Angeles is a city of ephemerals, of transience, and above all, of illusion. Nothing there is quite real, and that's the reality of it all. There's an air of anything-can-happen—and it often does.

Ask anyone here about the quality of life in Los Angeles. Even the homeless, of which there are too many, make their way to the coast to escape less hospitable climates. It's not perfect, but whether you love it or hate it, Los Angeles is an overwhelming spectacle in the best sense.

ESSENTIAL INFORMATION

WHEN TO GO Almost anytime of year is the right time to go to Los Angeles; the climate is mild and pleasant year-round, rarely dipping lower than 60° during the day. There's no

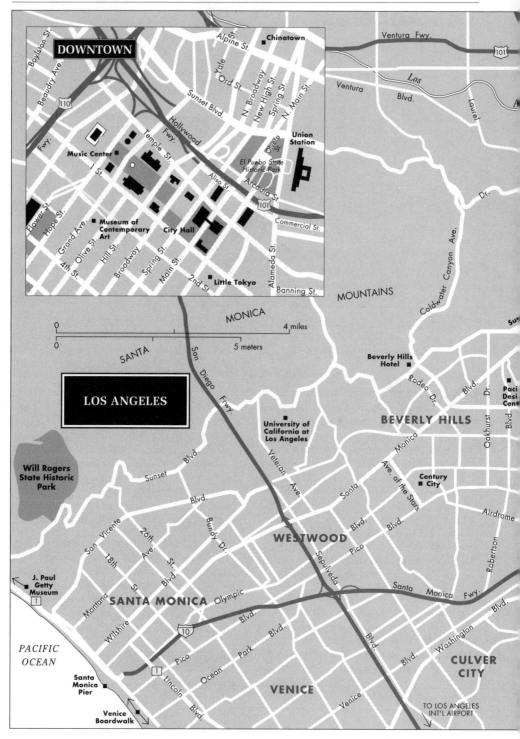

DOWNTOWN

Boylston St.
Beaudry Ave.
110 Fwy.
Alpine St.
Ord St.
Yale
N. Broadway
New High St.
Spring St.
N. Main St.
Sunset Blvd.
Chinatown
Ventura Fwy.
101
Ventura
Los
Blvd.
Laurel
Hollywood Fwy.
Temple St.
Music Center
1 St.
Flower St.
Hope St.
Grand Ave.
Olive St.
Hill St.
Broadway
Spring St.
Main St.
4th St.
Museum of Contemporary Art
City Hall
2nd St.
Little Tokyo
Diego St.
El Puebo State Historic Park
Union Station
Aliso St.
Arcadia St.
Commercial St.
101
Alameda St.
Banning St.

MONICA
SANTA
MOUNTAINS
Coldwater Canyon Ave.
Dr.

0 _____ 4 miles
0 _____ 5 meters

San Diego Frwy.
Beverly Hills Hotel
Rodeo Dr.
Blvd.
Dr.
Oakhurst
Blvd.
Paci Desi Cent

LOS ANGELES

Will Rogers State Historic Park
University of California at Los Angeles
Sunset
Blvd.
Blvd.
Veteran Ave.
Santa
Monica
BEVERLY HILLS
Ave. of the Stars
Century City
Airdrome
Robertson

San Vicente
26th Ave.
18th St.
Bundy Dr.
St.
Blvd.
WESTWOOD
Sepulveda
Santa
Blvd.
Pico
Santa Monica Fwy.
Blvd.

J. Paul Getty Museum
1
Montana
SANTA MONICA
Wilshire
Olympic
Blvd.
Blvd.
Blvd.
Blvd.
Washington
Blvd.
CULVER CITY

PACIFIC OCEAN
Santa Monica Pier
10
Pico
Ocean
Park
Blvd.
1
Lincoln Blvd.
VENICE
Venice
Blvd.
TO LOS ANGELES INT'L AIRPORT

Venice Boardwalk

official tourist season in L.A.— it's busy all year—but crowds swell around such big events as the Rose Bowl and the Academy Awards and during school holidays. Hotel bargains occasionally become available during the summer, when Los Angeles smog can be at its worst. The rainy season usually runs from November through March, with the heaviest downpours usually coming in January. Summers are virtually rainless.

BARGAINS Los Angeles's street action is free and a great way to gain insight into what makes this metropolis tick. Explore West Hollywood's Melrose Avenue, a thoroughfare of flashing neon, Technicolor hairdos, and up-to-the-minute trends, and Venice Boardwalk, the bohemian corner of Los Angeles, packed with jugglers, acrobatic roller skaters, sweaty muscle builders, leftover hippies, and a parade of bikinis. Melrose activity starts about noon every day, and Venice is especially hopping on weekends, particularly after lunch.

Admission to many Los Angeles museums is free: California Museum of Science and Industry (tel. 213/744–7400) and Califiornia Afro-American Museum (tel. 213/744–7432), both in Exposition Park; J. Paul Getty Museum in Malibu (tel. 310/458–2003); Los Angeles Maritime Museum (tel. 310/548–7618); Cabrillo Marine Museum (310/548–7562); Travel Town Museum (tel. 213/662–5874) in Griffith Park; and the Hollywood Bowl Museum (tel. 213/850-2058) in Hollywood. The Los Angeles Municipal Art Gallery (213/485–4581) at Barnsdale Park in Hollywood charges $1 for admission, but their Junior Art Center is free. Mann's Chinese Theater and the Hollywood Walk of Fame also cost nothing to explore, but be sure to visit during daylight, since this section of Hollywood is seedier than one might imagine.

Free tickets are available for many television show tapings. You can find out a month in advance of your visit what's scheduled to tape on a specific date by sending a stamped, self-addressed envelope to Audiences Unlimited, 100 Universal City Plaza, Building 152, Universal City, CA 91608; for information call 818/506–0067. You can also stop by and pick up tickets in person at the Audiences Unlimited information center (Fox Plaza, 5746 Sunset Blvd., Hollywood). Each network's studio also has a ticket booth, but tickets are handed out on a first-come basis so plan on going to pick up tickets first thing in the morning; or phone ahead to check availability: ABC (4151 Prospect Ave., Los Angeles, tel. 310/557–7777), CBS (7800 Beverly Blvd., Los Angeles, tel. 213/852–2458), NBC (3000 W. Alameda Ave., Burbank, tel. 818/840–3537), Fox (5746 Sunset Blvd., Hollywood, tel. 213/462–7111). Tickets are also given out in front of Mann's Chinese Theater, during the Universal Studios Tour, and by the Greater Los Angeles Visitors Bureau.

TOURIST OFFICES Los Angeles Convention and Visitors Bureau (633 W. 5th St., Los Angeles, CA 90071, tel. 213/624–7300).

EMERGENCIES **Police, fire,** and **ambulance:** Dial 911. **Hospitals:** Hollywood Presbyterian (Vermont Ave. at Fountain Ave., tel. 213/913–4896) and Cedars-Sinai (Beverly Blvd. at San Vicente Blvd., tel. 310/855–6517) have 24-hour emergency rooms. **Doctors:** Physician Referral Service (tel. 213/483–6122). **Dentists:** L.A. Dental Society (tel. 213/380–7669). **Pharmacies:** Horton and Converse (6625 Van Nuys Blvd., tel. 213/873–1556) in Van Nuys and Horton and Converse (11600 Wilshire Blvd., tel. 310/478–0801) in West L.A. are open until 2 AM.

ARRIVING AND DEPARTING

BY PLANE Los Angeles International Airport, LAX (tel. 310/646–5252), lies about 22 miles from downtown L.A., slightly less from Beverly Hills, a bit more from Hollywood.

BETWEEN THE AIRPORT AND DOWNTOWN By **Bus.** RTD, Rapid Transit District, (tel. 213/626–4455) buses run every few minutes. It takes 58 minutes to get from LAX to downtown hotels, and the fare is $1.10.

By Taxi. L.A. Taxi (tel. 213/627–7000) and Independent (tel. 213/385–8294) cabs, available curbside, take about 25 minutes to downtown hotels. The fare is about $24.

By Shuttle. Super Shuttle (tel. 310/417–8988) is available by calling on the courtesy phone at the baggage claim. It takes 30–40 minutes to get from LAX to downtown hotels, and the fare is $12. Rates to other areas vary. Other shuttle services include Best Shuttle (tel. 310/670–7080), Prime Time Shuttle (tel. 310/558–1606), and Shuttle One (tel. 310/670–6666).

By Car. Los Angeles can be reached via I–5 from the north and south, or from the north coast via U.S. 101. From the east, take I–10.

From LAX, take Century Boulevard to I–405: south to Long Beach, Newport Beach, and San Diego; north to I–10E to downtown, Century City, and Hollywood. For Hollywood, take I–10 downtown, to I–110 north to U.S. 101 north to Hollywood.

If it's rush hour and the freeways are jammed, an alternate route is Sepulveda Boulevard, running parallel to I–405. Follow Sepulveda north from LAX for about 2 miles. Turn right at Wilshire Boulevard, thus skirting Century City, and cut through Beverly Hills on your way downtown, or travel 1/2 mile farther on Sepulveda to Sunset Boulevard and turn right, which will take you through Bel Air and Beverly Hills to Hollywood.

By Train. Amtrak (tel. 800/USA–RAIL) serves Los Angeles's famed Union Station, one of the nation's last grand railroad stations.

By Bus. Greyhound Lines (tel. 800/231–2222) has many drop-off stations throughout the greater Los Angeles area.

GETTING AROUND

BY CAR You'll save money if you plan your car rental (a must in this town) well in advance of your trip. Because Los Angeles is so spread out, it's impossible to negotiate without a car. The fastest way to get around town is to use the freeway system. The best map source is the "Thomas Guide to Los Angeles," available in bookstores and supermarkets.

BY BUS The city's southern California RTD (tel. 213/626–4455) is cheap ($1.10 per ride, 25¢ for a transfer), but getting from one place to another can often take a long time because buses travel surface streets instead of freeways. If you're staying on the west side of the city, Santa Monica's Big Blue Bus Line (tel. 310/451–5444) is clean and convenient.

BY TRAIN AND METRO Train service in Los Angeles has improved, but it is still limited. The Metro Blue Line (tel. 213/972–6000) is a light-rail train that runs between downtown's Union Station and Long Beach, and the fare is $1.10. The Metro Red Line (tel. 213/972–6000) is a subterranean train, still under construction, but one line is operational between downtown and MacArthur Park. The fare is 25¢. Metrolink (tel. 800/621–7828) connects downtown with four outlying areas: Moorpark, San Bernardino, Santa Clarita, and Riverside. The round-trip fares range from $10 to $14 depending on your destination.

BY TAXI Avoid taxis if you can—cab rides are prohibitively expensive and not very reliable. If you must take a cab, don't expect to hail one on the street. Radio-dispatched cab companies include L.A. Taxi (tel. 213/627–7000) and L.A. Checker Cab (tel. 213/481–1234). Expect to pay a minimum of $12 for even the shortest distance.

REST STOPS Public rest rooms can be found in Griffith Park in Hollywood, MacArthur Park (6th and Alvarado St.), Roxbury Park (471 S. Roxbury Dr., Beverly Hills), and along the coast at state beaches. Also, look for public rest rooms in such large shopping centers as The Beverly Center (8500 Beverly Blvd., West Hollywood), Arco Plaza (505 S. Flower St., downtown), and Century City Shopping Center (10250 Santa Monica Blvd., Century City).

GUIDED TOURS **Orientation Tours:** Gray Line (6541 Hollywood Blvd., Hollywood, CA 90028, tel. 213/856–5900), one of the country's best-known tour companies, picks up passengers from more than 140 hotels to tour Disneyland, Universal Studios, Catalina Island, and other area attractions. L.A. Tours and Sightseeing (6333 W. 3rd St., Farmer's Market, Los Angeles, CA 90036, tel. 213/937–3361) covers places of interest in various parts of the city. **Special-Interest Tours:** Grave Line Tours (Box 931694, Hollywood 90093, tel. 213/469–3127 for information or 213/469–4149 for reservations) digs up the dirt on notorious suicides and visits the scenes of various murders, scandals, and other crimes via a luxuriously renovated hearse.

EXPLORING

In a city whose residents think nothing of a 40-mile commute to work, visitors have their work cut out for them. Be prepared to put miles on your rental car.

The Beverly Hills Hotel (9641 Sunset Blvd., Beverly Hills, tel. 310/276–2251), also known as the Pink Palace, has Spanish Colonial Revival architecture and a soft pastel exterior that belies the excitement inside. It's here that Hollywood moguls make deals in the Polo Lounge and many stars keep bungalows as second homes. Unfortunately, the hotel is currently closed for renovations and is not expected to reopen until early 1995.

L.A.'s **Chinatown** runs a pale second to San Francisco's Chinatown, but it still offers visitors an authentic slice of life, beyond the tourist hokum. The neighborhood, near downtown, is bordered by Yale, Bernard, Alameda, and Ord streets, and the main street is North Broadway, where, every February, giant dragons snake down the center of the pavement during Chinese New Year celebrations.

Farmer's Market is a popular stop on L.A. city tours, thanks to tour-bus operators and its easygoing, all-year-outdoor setting. When it first opened in 1934, the market sold farm-direct produce at bargain prices. These days, the produce is still tantalizing but definitely high priced. No longer farm-direct, the stands offer out-of-season peppers and tiny seedless champagne grapes from Chile at top prices. In addition, there are dozens of cooked-food stalls offering Cajun gumbos, Mexican enchiladas, and frozen yogurt. *6333 W. 3rd St., tel 213/933–9211. Open daily. Admission free.*

George C. Page Museum of La Brea Discoveries is situated at the tar pits, half underground and with an encompassing bas-relief that depicts life in the Pleistocene era. The museum has a collection of more than 1 million Ice Age fossils. A tar contraption shows visitors just how hard it would be to free oneself from the sticky mess. *5801 Wilshire Blvd., tel. 213/936–2230. Open Tues.–Sun. Admission charged, except second Tues. of each month.*

The **Hollywood Bowl** has hosted summer evening concerts since 1922. The shell accommodates 17,000 spectators, in boxes— where local society matrons serve up fancy al fresco preconcert meals for their friends—or cement bleachers in the rear. Some prefer the back row for its romantic appeal. The official season begins in early July and runs through mid-September. *2301 N. Highland Ave., tel. 213/850–2000. Admission charged.*

Hollywood and Vine was once considered the heart of Hollywood. The mere mention of the intersection inspired thoughts of starlets and movie moguls passing by. These days, though, it's far from the action, with the only stars being those on the sidewalk. The corner has become little more than a place for visitors to get their bearings.

The **Hollywood Sign,** with its 50-foot-high letters, is visible for miles, even on the smoggiest days. To find it, look to the Hollywood Hills that line the northern border of town. It is high on Mount Lee, north of Beachwood Canyon, which is approximately 1 mile east of Hollywood and Vine. The sign was erected in 1923 as a promotional scheme for a real estate development called Hollywoodland. (The sign originally read "Hollywoodland"; "land" was taken down in 1949.)

The **J. Paul Getty Museum,** a re-creation of a 1st-century Roman villa, contains one of the country's finest collections of Greek and Roman antiquities as well as a few items of uncertain provenance. The main level houses sculpture, mosaics, and vases. Of particular interest are the 4th-century Attic stelae (funerary monuments) and the Greek and Roman portraits. On the upper level, richly brocaded walls set off paintings and furniture. All major schools of Western art from the late 13th to the late 19th century are represented in the collection, with an emphasis on Renaissance and Baroque art. Parking reservations are required at the Getty and there is no way to visit without using the parking lot, unless you are dropped off or take a tour bus. *17985 Pacific Coast Hwy., Malibu, tel. 310/458–2003. Open Tues.–Sun. Admission free.*

Little Tokyo, bound by First, San Pedro, Third, and Los Angeles streets just east of downtown, is the original ethnic neighborhood for Los Angeles's Japanese community. Nisei Week (*Nisei* is the name for second-generation Japanese) is celebrated here every August with traditional drums, obon dancing, a carnival, and a parade.

The Los Angeles County Museum of Art, the largest museum complex in Los Angeles, has put the city on the map, artwise. Look over the Picassos and Rembrandts in the Ahmanson Gallery and stop by the Robert O. Anderson Building if you're interested in Japanese scroll paintings and screens. Mimes and itinerant musicians practice their art outside the museum on warm weekends. *5905 Wilshire Blvd., tel. 213/857–6111. Open Tues.–Sun. Admission charged.*

Mann's Chinese Theater (6925 Hollywood Blvd., tel. 213/464–8111) has finally stuck as the new name for "Grauman's Chinese." The theater opened in 1927 with the premiere of Cecil B. de Mille's *King of Kings.* The architecture is a fantasy of Chinese pagodas and temples only Hollywood could create. Although you'll have to buy a movie ticket to appreciate its interior trappings, the famous courtyard is open for browsing. Stop by to see the handprints and footprints of some 160 celebrities, past and present.

Melrose Avenue is for you if you're entertained by postpunks and other people with spiked hairdos wearing just about the most outlandish ensembles imaginable. Would-be rock stars and weekend punkers hang out and provide a colorful show for ordinary folk. The busiest stretch, with dozens of one-of-a-kind boutiques and small, chic restaurants, is between Fairfax and La Brea avenues.

The Museum of Contemporary Art houses a permanent collection of international modern art from 1940 to the present. Included are works by Mark Rothko, Franz Kline, and Susan Rothenberg. The red sandstone building was designed by one of Japan's renowned architects, Arata Isozaki. *250 S. Grand Ave., tel. 213/626–6222. Open Tues.–Sun. Admission charged, except Thurs. after 5 PM.*

The Music Center has been Los Angeles's cultural center since it opened in 1969. Until 1990, the Dorothy Chandler Pavilion (the largest of three theaters on the premises) was the site of the Academy Awards. The round building in the center is the Mark Taper Forum, a cozy, 750-seat theater offering experimental theater, often the prelude to a Broadway run. At the north end, the Ahmanson is the venue for many musical comedies. *135 N. Grand Ave., tel. 213/972– 7211. Call for tour times. Admission free.*

The Pacific Design Center, dubbed the Blue Whale, is an all-blue glass building designed by Cesar Pelli in 1975. The center houses showrooms filled with the most tempting furnishings, wallpapers, and accessories. In 1989, the center added a second building by Pelli, this one clad in green glass. The showrooms were originally geared exclusively to the interior design trade and discouraged casual browsers, but the building is now open to and welcomes the general public. *8687 Melrose Ave., West Hollywood, tel. 310/657– 0800. Closed weekends.*

Many shops along **Rodeo Drive** in Beverly Hills between Santa Monica and Wilshire boulevards may be familiar to you because they carry the name of their famous designer/owners, such as Ralph Lauren, Armani, Ferragamo and Gucci. These are very expensive boutiques, but fortunately, browsing is free (and fun). Several nearby restaurants have outside patios where you can sit and sip a drink while watching the fashionable shoppers stroll by.

Santa Monica Pier is located at the foot of Colorado Avenue and is easily accessible to beach goers as well as drive-around visitors. Cafés, gift shops, a psychic adviser, bumper cars, and arcades line the truncated pier, which was severely damaged in a storm in the mid-1980s. The 46-horse carousel, built in 1922, has seen action in many movie and television shows, most notably the Paul Newman/Robert Redford film *The Sting. Tel. 310/394–7554. Closed Mon. Fee charged for riding carousel.*

Sunset Strip was famous in the '50s, as in "77 Sunset Strip," but it was popular even in the 1930s, when such nightclubs as Ciro's and Mocambo were in their heyday. Drive this windy, hilly stretch of L.A. once to enjoy the hustle and bustle, the vanity boards (huge billboards touting new movies, new records, new stars), and the dazzling shops. At Horn Street, Tower Records (a behemoth of a record store) is open until midnight during the week and 1 AM on Fridays and Saturdays. The world-famous Spago restaurant is also nearby, tucked half a block up the hill on Horn Street.

Union Station (800 N. Alameda St., tel. 800/872–7245), directly east of Olvera Street across Alameda, is one of those quintessentially California buildings that seemed to define Los Angeles to movie goers around the country in the 1940s. Built in 1939, its Spanish Mission style is a subtle combination of Streamline Moderne and Moorish. The majestic scale of the waiting room is definitely worth a walk over.

Universal Studios Tour offers the chance to see what happens behind the movie camera at the world's largest motion picture and TV studio. This well-run tour includes an entertaining tram ride throughout the studio grounds that lets you catch a glimpse of King Kong and Jaws, and allows you to live the special effects of the films *Earthquake* and *Backdraft*. There is also a wide selection of complementary live-action shows, including a Wild West Stunt Show and a "Miami Vice" special-effects show. *100 Universal Plaza, Universal City, tel. 818/508–9600. Open daily. Admission charged.*

Venice Boardwalk, beginning at Washington Street and running north, is the liveliest waterfront walkway in Los Angeles, a colorful mishmash of street life. Bikini-clad roller skaters attract crowds to their impromptu demonstrations, and locals parade their unusual breeds of dogs along the walkway. A local bodybuilding club works out on the adjacent beach, and strollers stop to ogle the pecs of these weight lifters. Venice Boardwalk is especially fun on the weekends.

A few hours at **Will Rogers State Historic Park** (1591 Will Rogers Ranch Rd., Pacific Palisades, tel. 310/454–8212) will help you understand why all of America fell in love with this cowboy/humorist in the 1920s and 1930s. The two-story ranch house on Rogers's 187-acre estate is a folksy blend of Navajo rugs and Mission-style furniture. Rogers was a polo fan, and in the 1930s his front-yard polo field attracted such friends as Douglas Fairbanks for weekend games. The tradition continues with polo games year-round on Saturday afternoons and Sunday mornings, weather and field conditions permitting. There is a $5 entrance fee to the park, but once you're inside everything is free.

HOTELS AND INNS

You can find almost any kind of accommodation in Los Angeles, everything from a simple motel that allows you to park right in front of your room to a posh hotel like the Beverly Hills, where an attendant will whisk you off to your own private bungalow. Because L.A. is so spread out—it's actually a series of suburbs connected by freeways—it's a good idea to select a hotel not only for its ambience, amenities, and price but also for a location that is convenient to where you plan to spend most of your time. Price categories for double occupancy, without 14% tax, are *Expensive,* over $90; *Moderate,* $50–$90; and *Inexpensive,* under $50.

AIRPORT AREA **Crown Sterling Suites Hotel.** Formerly Embassy Suites, this Spanish Mission–style all-suites hotel features an indoor pool and Capistrano Restaurant, serving fish and pasta specialties. *1440 E. Imperial Ave., El Segundo 90245, tel. 310/640–3600 or 800/433–4600, fax 310/322–0954. 350 units. Restaurant, pool, refrigerators in rooms, underground parking, free airport transportation. AE, DC, MC, V. Moderate–Expensive.*

Red Lion Inn. This Spanish American–style hotel is just 3 miles north of LAX near Marina del Rey. The Culver's Club lounge offers lively entertainment and dancing. *6161 Centinela Ave., Culver City 90203, tel. 310/649–1776 or 800/547–8010, fax 310/ 649–4411. 371 rooms. Restaurant, lounge, pool, sauna, health club, free parking. AE, DC, MC, V. Moderate–Expensive.*

Airport Park View Hotel. This contemporary three-story hotel located across from Hollywood Park, near the Forum, and close by the 405 freeway, offers convenient if nondescript lodgings that were completely renovated in 1992. *3900 Century Blvd., Inglewood 90303, tel. 310/677–8899 or 800/793–PARK, fax 310/677-6900. 178 rooms. Coffee shop, pool, free parking, free cable movies, meeting and banquet facilities. AE, DC, MC, V. Inexpensive.*

BEVERLY HILLS **Beverly House Hotel.** This is a small, elegantly furnished, European-style bed-and-breakfast hotel. Even though it's near busy areas of L.A. (Century City and Beverly Hills shopping), this hotel is quiet and actually quaint. *140 S. Lasky Dr., Beverly Hills 90212, tel. 310/271–2145 or 800/432–5444, fax 310/276–8431. 50 rooms. Continental breakfast included, laundry service available, free parking. AE, DC, MC, V. Moderate–Expensive.*

DOWNTOWN **Inn Towne.** This three-story hotel, with large beige-and-white rooms, is near the convention center and a block from the famous 24-hour Pantry restaurant. *925 S. Figueroa St., 90015, tel. 213/628–2222, fax 213/687–0566. 170 rooms. Restaurant, lounge, pool, room service, free parking. AE, DC, MC, V. Moderate.*

Figueroa Hotel. This hotel has managed to keep its charming Spanish style intact as it enters its second half-century. *939 S. Figueroa St., 90015, tel. 213/627–8971, 800/421–9092, fax 213/689–0305. 285 rooms. Restaurant, coffee shop, lounge, pool, Jacuzzi, airport service, free parking. AE, DC, MC, V. Moderate.*

Holiday Inn L.A. Downtown. This standard Holiday Inn is near the Museum of Contemporary Art and Dodger Stadium. Pets are allowed. *750 Garland Ave., 90017, tel. 213/628–5242 or 800/628–5240, fax 213/628–1201. 204 rooms. Restaurant, lounge, pool, free parking. AE, DC, MC, V. Expensive.*

Comfort Inn. This hotel, centrally located between downtown and Hollywood near the Wilshire commercial district, has modern-style rooms with color TVs. *3400 3rd St., 90020, tel. 213/385–0061 or 800/266–0061, fax 213/385–8517. 120 rooms. Coffee shop, pool, free parking. AE, DC, MC, V. Inexpensive.*

HOLLYWOOD **Hollywood Holiday Inn.** You can't miss this hotel, one of Hollywood's tallest, and centrally located to all of Hollywood's major attractions. *1755 N. Highland Ave., 90028, tel. 213/462–7181, fax 213/466–9072. 470 rooms. Restaurant, coffee shop, pool, coin laundry, parking. AE, DC, MC, V. Expensive.*

Sunset Dunes Motel. Across the street from two TV stations, this hotel is popular with studio folk. *5625 Sunset Blvd., 90028, tel. 213/467–5171, fax 213/469–1962. 54 rooms. Restaurant, lounge, free parking. AE, DC, MC, V. Moderate.*

SOUTH BAY **Barnaby's Hotel.** This charming hotel, with spacious European-style guest rooms, is only 2½ miles south of LAX and only minutes from the beach. The hotel provides free shuttle service to the airport and to nearby shops and restaurants. *3501 Sepulveda Blvd., Manhattan Beach 90266, tel. 310/545–8466 or 800/552–5285, fax 310/545–8621. 128 rooms. Restaurant, pub, lounge, pool, Jacuzzi, botanical gardens. AE, DC, MC, V. Expensive.*

VENICE **Marina Pacific Hotel & Suites.** Facing the Pacific and one of the world's most vibrant boardwalks, this Spanish-style property, with rooms decorated in pink, is nestled among art galleries, shops, and elegant, offbeat restaurants. *1697 Pacific Ave., Venice 90291, tel. 310/452–1111 or 800/421–8151, fax 310/452–5479. 92 rooms. Restaurant, parking, coin laundry. AE, DC, MC, V. Moderate–Expensive.*

SAN FERNANDO VALLEY **Safari Inn.** Often used for location filming, this hotel offers high standard services, an Italian restaurant, and is close to Universal Studios and NBC. *1911 W. Olive Ave., Burbank 91506, tel. 818/845–8586 or 800/782–4343, fax 818/845–0054. 104 rooms. Restaurant, cocktail lounge, pool, Jacuzzi, free parking. AE, DC, MC, V. Moderate.*

SANTA MONICA **Holiday Inn Santa Monica Pier.** Convenient to beaches, shopping, restaurants, and of course the Santa Monica Pier, this inn features standard Holiday Inn rooms and amenities. *120 Colorado Ave., 90401, tel. 310/451–0676 or 800/947–9175, fax 310/393–7145. 132 rooms. Restaurant, lounge, pool, coin laundry, gift shop, meeting and banquet rooms, valet parking. AE, DC, MC, V. Expensive.*

Carmel Hotel. This charming 1920s hotel, one block from the beach and across the street from Santa Monica's Third Street Promenade (*see* Shopping, *below*), features electric ceiling fans for a tropical feel. *201 Broadway, 90401, tel. 310/451–2469 or 800/445–8695, fax 310/393–4180. 110 rooms. Restaurant, free overnight parking. AE, DC, MC, V. Moderate.*

Palm Motel. This quiet, unceremonious hotel has old-fashioned rooms. Guests are offered coffee, tea, and cookies at breakfast. *2020 14th St., 90405, tel. 310/452–3822. 26 rooms. Coin laundry, free parking. MC, V. Inexpensive.*

WEST LOS ANGELES **Century Wilshire Hotel.** Most units in this European-style hotel near the UCLA campus are suites featuring kitchenettes, tiled baths, and homey, English-style, pastel decor. *10776 Wilshire Blvd., 90024, tel. 310/474-4506 or 800/421-7223, fax 310/474-2535. 100 rooms. Continental breakfast included, heated pool, free parking. AE, DC, MC, V. Moderate.*

Century City Inn. This comfortable, small hotel has rooms with VCRs, refrigerators, microwaves, coffeemakers, and complimentary gourmet coffees and teas. Baths boast whirlpool jets and phones. *10330 W. Olympic Blvd., 90064, tel. 310/553-1000 or 800/553-1005, fax 310/277-1633. 45 rooms. Continental breakfast included, parking, laundry service, free video library. AE, DC, MC, V. Expensive.*

DINING

Once this city was known only for its chopped Cobb salad, Green Goddess dressing, drive-in hamburger stands, and outdoor barbecues; but today Los Angeles is home to some of the best French and Italian restaurants in the United States, as well as a plethora of places featuring international cuisines. Many new, good dining establishments open in this town every week, creating stiff competition among restaurants—thus making L.A. one of the world's least expensive big cities in which to eat. To save on meals, try the pricier restaurants at lunchtime. Locals tend to dine early, between 7:30 and 9 PM. Make reservations whenever possible.

Price categories per person, not including 8.25% tax, service, and drinks, are *Moderate,* $15–$25, and *Inexpensive,* under $15.

BEVERLY HILLS **The Grill on the Alley.** This wood-paneled and brass-trimmed New York–style steak house offers basic American fare. *9560 Dayton Way, tel. 310/276-0615. AE, MC, V. Moderate.*

California Pizza Kitchen. Unusual gourmet pizza is dished up in a contemporary setting with fast counter service and a few sidewalk tables. *207 S. Beverly Dr., tel. 310/275-1101. AE, MC, V. Inexpensive–Moderate.*

Ed Debevic's. A return to the '50s is the theme of this fun-loving diner. *134 N. La Cienega Blvd., tel. 310/659-1952. AE, MC, V. Inexpensive.*

DOWNTOWN AND ENVIRONS **Engine Co. #28.** The ground floor of this National Historic Site building was refurbished and refitted to become a very polished, "uptown" dowtown bar and grill, and it's been crowded from day one. The reason? All-American food carefully prepared and served with obvious pride. Don't miss the corn chowder and "Firehouse" chili. *655 S. Figueroa St., tel 213/624-6966. Reservations recommended. No weekend lunch. AE, MC, V. Moderate.*

The Original Pantry. A tradition since 1924, especially for breakfast, this 24-hour dining spot serves up such down-home fare as ribs and chicken in a modest setting reminiscent of an old-fashioned diner. *877 S. Figueroa St., downtown, tel. 213/972-9279. No credit cards. Moderate.*

May Flower Restaurant. This luncheon spot in Chinatown features Cantonese cuisine, including a knock-out rice porridge. *800 Yale St., downtown, tel. 213/626-7113. No credit cards. Inexpensive.*

Song Hay Inn. This casual Chinese restaurant tucked inside an unobtrusive shopping center offers the best wonton soup in the city. *2720 Griffith Park Blvd., tel. 213/662-0978. MC, V. Inexpensive.*

HOLLYWOOD/WEST HOLLYWOOD/MID-WILSHIRE

Angeli. This Italian cucina serving up fresh gourmet pizzas gets very busy—so make reservations. *7274 Melrose Ave., Hollywood, tel. 213/936-9086. AE, MC, V. Inexpensive.*

The Authentic Cafe. Great salads are the mainstay of the multinational menu at this very active but tiny "in" spot. *7605 Beverly Blvd., Los Angeles, tel. 213/939-4626. MC, V. Inexpensive.*

Canter's. This is the most authentic Jewish deli in the city, with great blintzes and chicken soup, and no-nonsense waitresses. *419 N. Fairfax Ave., mid-Wilshire, tel. 213/651-2030. Inexpensive.*

Chan Dara. This restaurant serves up Thai food at its best, including such dishes as satay and barbecued chicken, in a pleasant and friendly environment. *310 N. Larchmont Blvd., tel. 213/467–1052. AE, MC, V. Inexpensive.*

Barney's Beanery. A landmark in town, this lively and very hip hangout serves up heaping portions of all-American favorites. An adjoining bar is packed on weekends, when there are long waits for a game of pool on Barney's dining-room pool tables. *8447 Santa Monica Blvd., West Hollywood, tel. 213/654– 2287. AE, MC, V. Inexpensive.*

The Hard Rock Cafe. Hip and happening, this rock-and-roll-style restaurant is big on ambience (with lots of music memorabilia) but not so great with food—mostly burgers, heaping salads, and pastas. *8600 Beverly Blvd., Beverly Center, West Hollywood, tel. 310/276– 7605. AE, MC, V. Inexpensive.*

Johnny Rocket's. A new breed of the '50s diner stirs up action on Melrose. Come here for the atmosphere and the Harley-Davidson motorcycles parked outside. *7507 Melrose Ave., West Hollywood, tel. 213/651–3361. No credit cards. Inexpensive.*

THE WEST SIDE **Beaurivage.** If you're looking for a romantic, seaside restaurant that won't cost you an arm and a leg, come here for such Provençal favorites as mussel soup and roast duckling Mirabelle. *26025 Pacific Coast Hwy., tel. 310/456–5733. AE, DC, MC, V. Moderate.*

Orleans. Such Cajun cuisine as jambalaya, gumbo, and terrific blackened fish and prime rib are served up in this spacious restaurant. *11705 National Blvd., West Los Angeles, tel. 310/479– 4187. AE, MC, V. Moderate.*

Rose Cafe. Sink back into a '60s setting, big with the beach crowd and great for breakfast. *220 Rose Ave., Venice, tel. 310/399–0711. MC, V. Inexpensive.*

The Sidewalk Cafe. With a great view of Venice Boardwalk at its most active, this is a restaurant where the scenery never gets boring even if the simple fare is a bit mundane. *1401 Ocean Front Walk, Venice, tel. 310/399– 5547. AE, MC, V. Inexpensive.*

SHOPPING

MAJOR SHOPPING DISTRICTS **Downtown.** Although downtown Los Angeles has many enclaves to explore, the bargain hunter should head straight for the Cooper Building (860 S. Los Angeles St., tel. 213/622–1139). Six floors of small shops, mostly selling women's fashions, offer 50%–70% discounts off retail prices. Grab a free map in the lobby and see as many of the 50 shops as you can handle. Nearby are myriad discount outlets selling everything from shoes to suits to linens. The stores are open Monday through Saturday 9:30–5:30, Sunday 11–5.

Melrose Avenue. West Hollywood, especially Melrose Avenue, is great for vintage styles in clothing and furnishings. The 1¹/₂ miles of intriguing, one-of-a-kind shops and bistros stretch from La Brea to a few blocks west of Crescent Heights; it is definitely one of Los Angeles's hottest shopping areas. Shops include Betsey Johnson (7311 Melrose Ave., tel. 213/931–4490), offering the designer's vivid, hip women's fashions; Wound and Wound (7374 Melrose Ave., tel. 213/653– 6703), displaying an impressive collection of wind-up toys that make great inexpensive gifts; Wacko (7416 Melrose Ave., tel. 213/651–3811), a wild space crammed with all manner of inflatable toys, cards, and other semi-useless items that make good Los Angeles keepsakes; and Wild Blue (7220 Melrose Ave., tel. 213/939–8434), a fine shop/gallery with fair prices on functional and wearable art.

Westwood. Westwood Village, near the UCLA campus, is a young and lively area for shopping. The atmosphere in Westwood is invigorating, especially during summer evenings, when there's a movie line around every corner, all kinds of people strolling the streets, and cars cruising along to take in the scene. Morgan and Company (1131 Glendon Ave., tel. 310/208–3377) is recommended for fine jewelry, and The Wilger Company (10924 Weyburn Ave., tel. 310/208–4321) offers fine men's clothing.

The Beverly Center and Environs. Mall shopping is so important in Los Angeles that it is actually a sociological phenomenon. The Beverly Center (8500 Beverly Blvd., Los Angeles, 90048, tel. 310/854–0071), bound by Beverly Boulevard, La Cienega Boulevard, San Vicente Boulevard, and Third Street, covers more than 7 acres and contains some 200 stores, including the Eddie Bauer Home Collection (tel. 310/289–9809) for home furnishings and furniture, By Oliver (tel. 310/652–9485) for fashionable women's clothes, and two stores called Traffic for contemporary clothing for men (tel. 310/659–4313) and women (tel. 310/659–3438). Since it opened in the spring of 1982, the mall has catered to an upscale market. Still, sales abound, as do opportunities for people-watching.

Venturing outside the confines of the Beverly Center will unearth some other interesting shops, the most tempting of which is Freehand (8413 W. 3rd St., tel. 213/655–2607), a gallerylike venue featuring American crafts, clothing, and jewelry, mostly by California artists. A helpful sales staff will work with any budget to come up with just the right gift.

Century City. Century City Shopping Center & Marketplace (10250 Santa Monica, Blvd. 90067, tel. 310/277–3898) sits among gleaming steel office buildings. Here, in the center of a thriving business atmosphere, is a city kind of mall—open-air. Besides the Broadway and Bullocks, both department stores, you'll find trendy boutiques with clothes, jewelry, and gifts. Stop by the Pottery Barn (tel. 310/552–0170) for contemporary furnishings at comfortable prices.

Santa Monica. In this seaside section of town you'll come across Montana Avenue, a stretch of a dozen blocks that has become L.A.'s version of New York City's Columbus Avenue. Shops on Montana Avenue include A.B.S. Clothing (1533 Montana Ave., tel. 310/393–8770), selling contemporary sportswear designed in Los Angeles, and Brenda Himmel (1126 Montana Ave., tel. 310/395–2437), offering fine stationery and gifts. The stretch of Main Street leading from Santa Monica to Venice (Pico Blvd. to Rose Ave.) makes for a pleasant walk, with a collection of quite good restaurants, unusual shops and galleries, and an ever-present ocean breeze.

Santa Monica's newest shopping area is the renovated **Third Street Promenade,** which is closed off to vehicles between Broadway and Wilshire. It's a great place to stroll and browse through some uniquely California shops like Urban Outfitters (1440 3rd St. Promenade, tel. 310/394–1404) for casual clothes and novelties, or Z Gallerie (1426 3rd St. Promenade, tel. 310/394–4685) for home furnishings and poster art.

Beverly Hills. Last but in no way least (in terms of high prices, that is), is Beverly Hills, the most famous section of town. Rodeo Drive is often compared with such renowned streets as 5th Avenue in New York and the Via Condotti in Rome. Along the several blocks between Wilshire and Santa Monica boulevards, you'll find an abundance of big-name retailers—but don't explore Beverly Hills without looking around the streets that surround illustrious Rodeo Drive. There are plenty of treasures to be found on those other thoroughfares as well.

On Rodeo Drive, Cartier (370 N. Rodeo Dr., tel. 310/275–4272) offers all manner of gifts and jewelry bearing the double-C logo, and Hammacher-Schlemmer (309 N. Rodeo Dr., tel. 310/859–7255) is a fabulous place for unearthing those hard-to-find presents for adults that never grew up. Off Rodeo Drive, Ann Taylor (357 N. Camden Dr., tel. 310/858–7840) is the flagship shop of this chain of women's clothing stores, offering the epitome of the young executive look, and a good selection of casual clothing and Joan & David shoes as well.

DEPARTMENT STORES The Broadway (The Beverly Center, 8500 Beverly Blvd., tel. 310/854–7200) offers moderately priced cosmetics, housewares, and clothing for men, women, and children. Bullocks (Citicorp Plaza, 925 W. 8th St., downtown, tel. 213/624–9494) is more upscale than the Broadway, carrying an extensive collection of clothing for everyone as well as housewares and cosmetics. Stores are throughout Southern California, with the flagship store being at The Beverly Center (8500 Beverly Blvd., tel. 310/854–6655). I. Magnin (Wilshire District, 3050 Wilshire Blvd., tel. 213/382–6161) is a large store with many designer labels for men and women and a good handbag and luggage department. Robinson's-May (9900 Wilshire Blvd., Beverly Hills, tel. 310/275–5464) is the merger of two old Los Angeles department stores, the first being high-end and the later selling modestly priced clothing and furniture. Now as one store they claim to offer a little and the best of both. Nordstrom (Westside Pavilion, 10830 W. Pico Blvd., West Los Angeles, tel. 310/470–6155) is a Seattle-based department store known for its customer service and the soothing piano music played in each store, as well as for its wide selection of upscale clothing.

OUTDOOR ACTIVITIES

BIKING Wide bike lanes exist for a 5-mile stretch along San Vicente Boulevard in Santa Monica/Brentwood, and there are paths along the beach from Temescal Canyon to Redondo Beach. In Griffith Park, you can circle the perimeter from Riverside Drive and Los Feliz Boulevard, along the golf course, and north to Burbank in the San Fernando Valley. For rentals, try Woody's (3159 Los Feliz Blvd., tel. 213/661–6665) near Griffith Park, and Spokes and Stuff (20½ Washington Blvd., Venice, tel. 310/306–3332).

FISHING The nearest freshwater fishing is in the San Bernardino Mountains at Lake Arrowhead and Big Bear Lake, about a two-hour drive from downtown. For fishing information in the area, call 714/866–5796. Saltwater fishing is available off piers in Malibu, Santa Monica, and Redondo Beach. For deep-sea fishing, rent space on a boat from Redondo Sport Fishing Company (233 N. Harbor Dr., tel. 310/372–2111). Prices are $19 for half a day, $28 for ³/₄ of a day, and $47 for a full day. Pole rental is $7. A fishing license for one day is $6.30.

GOLF City courses are economical places to tee off. Try Rancho Park Golf Course (10460 W. Pico Blvd., West Los Angeles, tel. 310/838–7561) or in Griffith Park at Harding Golf Course and Wilson Golf Course (tel. 213/663–2555) and Roosevelt Course (tel. 213/665–2011).

HIKING For a nice 2-mile hike, check out the picturesque Hollywood Reservoir in the Hollywood Hills, reached by Beechwood Canyon. Griffith Park boasts some 53 miles of hiking trails. Call the Sierra Club (3345 Wilshire Blvd., Suite 508, Los Angeles, 90010, tel. 213/387–4287) and participate in their guided hikes through the massive park. Or, walk the boardwalk in Venice.

HORSEBACK RIDING Bar "S" Stables (1850 Riverside Dr., Glendale, tel. 818/242–8443) rents horses for $13 per hour, and Sunset Stables (at the end of Beechwood Dr. in Hollywood, tel. 213/469–5450) provides horses for a Sunset Ride through the park at dusk ending at a Mexican restaurant in Burbank (cost: $30, not including food).

SKIING Ski season in this part of the country is from November through April, if the snow lasts. The best nearby skiing is Big Bear at Snow Summit (tel. 714/866–4621). A day lift ticket costs $38.75.

SWIMMING Griffith Park (3401 Riverside Dr., tel. 213/665–5188) has a public pool open during the summer and is usually crowded with lots of children. West Hollywood Park (647 N. San Vicente Blvd., tel. 310/652–3063) also has a public pool. The beach communities offer ocean swimming, but expect very cold water nearly year-round and avoid winter swims—there are no lifeguards on duty at that time.

TENNIS Griffith Park has courts at Vermont Canyon (2715 N. Vermont, Los Angeles, tel. 213/664–3521), nestled in the Los Feliz Hills near Roosevelt Golf Course and evening-lit courts at Riverside Drive and Los Feliz Boulevard (3401 Riverside Dr., Los Angeles, tel. 213/661– 5318). There's a small court fee only in the evenings and on weekends; they're free other times. Call for reservations if you want to play after 4 PM. Farther west, Plummer Park (7377 Santa Monica Blvd., West Hollywood, tel. 213/876–1725) has free tennis courts Monday through Friday and a small court fee on weekends.

ENTERTAINMENT

For the most complete listing of weekly events, get the current issue of *Los Angeles* or *California* magazines. The "Calendar" section of the *Los Angeles Times* also offers a wide survey of Los Angeles arts events, as do the more irreverent free publications, *L.A. Weekly* and *L.A. Reader.*

Most tickets can be purchased by phone (with a credit card) from Ticketmaster (tel. 213/480–3232), Good Time Tickets (tel. 213/464–7383), and Murray's Tickets (tel. 213/234–0123).

BALLET AND DANCE The American Ballet Theater performs at the Shrine Auditorium (665 W. Jefferson Blvd., tel. 213/749–5123) in March, and visiting companies dance at UCLA Center for the Arts (405 N. Hilgard Ave., tel. 310/825–2101).

CONCERTS The Los Angeles Philharmonic plays the Music Center (135 N. Grand Ave., tel. 213/972–7211) October–April; during the summer they perform at the Hollywood Bowl (2301 N. Highland Ave., tel. 213/850–2000). For country-and-western music, try the Palomino Club (6907 Lankershim Blvd., North Hollywood, tel. 818/764–4010). Admission starts at $3 and goes up depending on who's playing.

DINNER SHOWS El Cid (4212 W. Sunset Blvd., tel. 213/668–0318) in Hollywood is a 16th-century-style Spanish tavern featuring Flamenco. It's open Wednesday through Sunday.

FILM The Vista Theater (4473 Sunset Dr., tel. 213/660–6639) shows good double bills. The Royal Theatre (11523 Santa Monica Blvd., West Los Angeles, tel. 310/477–5581) and the Rialto (1023 S. Fair Oaks Ave., South Pasadena, tel. 818/799–9567) show contemporary art films. If you just want to catch Hollywood's latest blockbuster, call 213/777–FILM to find the theater nearest you.

THEATER The John Anson Ford Amphitheater (2580 Cahuenga Blvd., tel. 213/974–1343), in the Hollywood Hills, is best known for its Summer Nights series, which includes music, dance, theater, and opera. The Wilshire Theater (8440 Wilshire Blvd., tel. 213/468–4716) is a renovated, 1,900-seat house with an art deco–style interior. Musicals from Broadway are the usual fare. The James A. Doolittle (1615 N. Vine St., tel. 213/972–7211) mounts new plays, dramas, comedies, and musicals and offers a few preview nights for each show at discounted prices. Another less expensive alternative are equity-waiver theaters, where big-name stars are known to exercise their craft for the love of it. Check area newspapers for these listings.

SPECTATOR SPORTS The L.A. Dodgers play baseball at Dodger Stadium (1000 Elysian Park Ave., tel. 213/224–1500) April through September. The L.A. Lakers shoot hoops at Great Western Forum (3900 Manchester Ave., Inglewood, tel. 310/419–3182) November through April. You can watch the L.A. Raiders (tel. 310/322–5901) play football at the L.A. Coliseum (3911 Figueroa St., tel. 213/748–6131) or the L.A. Rams kick off at the Anaheim Stadium (2000 S. Gene Autry Way, tel. 714/254–3000) August through December. L.A. Kings (tel. 310/419–3160) face off in hockey games at the Great Western Forum September through March. L.A. Strings (tel. 310/419–3257) presents tennis matches at the Great Western Forum July through August.

The Maine Coast

he coast of Maine conjures up images of stern gray rocks, crashing surf, austere spruce-fringed bays, and horizons broken by distant blue islands. You certainly don't have to hunt very hard to find all of these, but Maine's coast also contains many other—and very different—images.

South of the rapidly gentrifying town of Portland, you'll find long stretches of hard-packed white-sand beach bordered by nearly unbroken ranks of beach cottages, motels, and oceanfront restaurants. Kennebunkport, now world famous because of its presidential summer resident, is a classic old New England port town of stately white clapboard houses, velvety green lawns, and rambling Victorian summer "cottages."

Just north of Portland you'll come upon still another Maine coast scene: the shopping mecca of Freeport, where some 3.5 million shoppers a year descend on L.L. Bean and the 85 upscale outlets that have grown up in its shadow.

The quick changes continue as you move "downeast": There is Boothbay Harbor, one of the yachting capitals of New England and the perfect place to jump on a cruise boat; Camden, the premier town on Penobscot Bay and the headquarters of the East Coast's largest windjammer fleet; and finally Mount Desert Island, where you'll find the highest mountain on the East Coast, the nation's second most popular national park, and some of the most glorious scenery anywhere in the world.

And so it goes. If you search long enough, you can find just about anything on Maine's immense coastline—except warm water. The icy water temperature takes some getting used to, but true devotees wouldn't want it any other way.

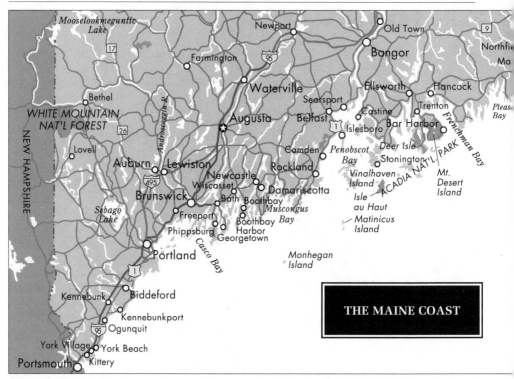

THE MAINE COAST

ESSENTIAL INFORMATION

WHEN TO GO In July, the hottest month of the year, maximum temperature averages 76°. Mainers will tell you that fog is their air-conditioning: It does keep things cool in the summer, but it can also obstruct views and make sailing impossible. The ocean moderates winter's chill (January's average high temperature is 31°F), but the damp can make you *feel* the cold bitterly.

Although July and August are peak season, Maine is at its best after Labor Day: Rates drop, crowds thin out, foggy days are less common, and mosquitoes vanish. Leaves begin turning in late September, and temperatures usually remain mild into October. Spring in Maine tends to be rather damp and chilly.

FESTIVALS AND SEASONAL EVENTS **Early Aug.:** Maine Lobster Festival, Rockland, is a public feast held on the first weekend of the month (tel. 207/596–0376). The Maine Festival, the state's premier arts fair, brings together musicians, artists, and craftspeople at venues along the coast (tel. 207/772–9012).

BARGAINS Lobsters, as one might expect, are far cheaper in Maine than just about anywhere else in the country, particularly if you buy them direct from a lobsterman or lobstering cooperative.

Factory outlets, concentrated in Kittery, Wells, Freeport, and Ellsworth, and sprinkled along Coastal Rte. 1, are your best bet for bargain sportswear, shoes, and housewares.

TOURIST OFFICES Maine Publicity Bureau (Box 2300, Hallowell 04347, tel. 207/582–9300 or 800/533–9595). Acadia National Park (Box 177, Bar Harbor 04609, tel. 207/288–3338). Bar Harbor Chamber of Commerce (Box BC, Cottage St., Bar Harbor 04609, tel. 207/288–3393 or 800/288–5103). Boothbay Harbor Region Chamber of Commerce (Box 356, Boothbay Harbor 04538, tel. 207/633–2353). Freeport Merchants Association (Box

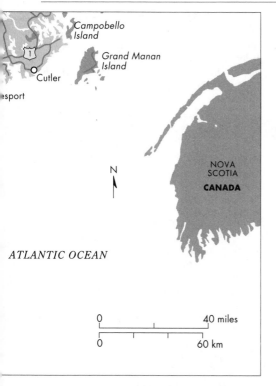

Campobello Island

Grand Manan Island

Cutler

sport

N

NOVA SCOTIA

CANADA

ATLANTIC OCEAN

0   40 miles

0   60 km

BY CAR AND BUS I–95 is the fastest route to and through Maine from coastal New Hampshire and points south, but it turns inland at Brunswick. Scenic Rte. 1 parallels the coast from Kittery to Machias.

GETTING AROUND

BY CAR AND BUS The most practical means of touring the coast is by car. *Maine Map and Guide,* available free from the Maine publicity bureau, is useful. Greyhound Lines (tel. 800/231–2222) and Vermont Transit (tel. 207/772–6587) connect towns in southwestern Maine with cities in New England.

REST STOPS Both the Kittery Information Center (located off northbound I–95) and the Yarmouth Information Center (located off I–95 at exit 17) have rest rooms as well as extensive tourist information about the entire state. You can exit from here onto coastal Rte. 1. On Rte. 1, midway between Wiscasset and Newcastle, is one of the state's prettiest rest stops overlooking Sherman Lake, with rest rooms. On the approach to Acadia National Park, just south of Trenton, there is an information area with rest rooms on Thompson Island on Rte. 3.

GUIDED TOURS Beckman Reception Services (587 Washington St., Canton, MA 02021, tel. 617/821–5900 or 800/343–4323) runs a clambake group tour to the Bar Harbor area and other general-interest tours.

Special-Interest: Golden Age Festival (5501 New Jersey Ave., Wildwood Crest, NJ 08260, tel. 609/522–6316 or 800/257–8920) offers a four-night bus tour geared to senior citizens, with outlet shopping, a Boothbay Harbor boat cruise, and stops at Pemaquid Point, Mount Battie, and Acadia National Park.

452, Freeport 04032, tel. 207/865–1212). Kennebunkport Chamber of Commerce (Cooper's Corner, Rtes. 9 and 35, Kennebunkport 04046, tel. 207/967–0857). Greater Portland Chamber of Commerce (145 Middle St., Portland 04101, tel. 207/772-2811).

EMERGENCIES **Maine State Police** (Augusta, tel. 800/452–4664; Gray, tel. 800/482–0737; Houlton, tel. 800/924–2261; Orono, tel. 800/432–7381). **Doctors:** Kennebunk Walk-In Clinic (Rte. 1N, tel. 207/985–6027). Penobscot Bay Medical Center (Rte. 1, Rockland, tel. 207/596–8000).

ARRIVING AND DEPARTING

BY PLANE Maine's major airports are Portland International Jetport (tel. 207/774–7301) and Bangor International Airport (tel. 207/947–384); each has scheduled daily flights by major U.S. carriers. Bar Harbor Airport (tel. 207/947–0384), 8 miles northwest of the city, is served by Continental Express and Northeast Express Regional.

EXPLORING

Those interested in history and architecture should stop at York, Kennebunkport, Portland, and Castine—a comfortable three- or four-day trip. Nature enthusiasts will want to bypass the crowded southern coast and visit one of the outer islands before hitting the trails of Acadia National Park.

The Yorks, a cluster of villages along coastal Rte. 1A (just east of Rte. 1), contain the **York Village Historic District,** where a number of 18th- and 19th-century buildings have been restored and maintained by the Old York Historical Society. Stop at the Jefferds Tavern to buy admission tickets for all buildings. *Rte. 1A, tel. 207/363–4974. Open mid-June–Sept., Tues.–Sat. Admission charged.*

Ogunquit, due north of York on Rte. 1, is a resort town with a good stretch of sand beach. Perkins Cove, a neck of land connected to the mainland by a pedestrian drawbridge, is a picturesque jumble of sea-beaten fish houses restored as shops and restaurants. You can walk from here to the Marginal Way, a mile-long footpath that hugs the shore.

Kennebunkport, reached by making a right turn off Rte. 1 onto Rte. 9 at Cozy Corners, is a town to stroll through. Don't miss Dock Square, the busy town center, with its shops and galleries, and the grand ship captains' homes along Maine, Pearl, and Green streets. Drive up Ocean Avenue past Victorian seaside mansions to Cape Arundel (you'll glimpse the entrance to former president Bush's house on the ocean side).

Portland, Maine's largest city, can be reached by taking Exit 6A off I–95 onto Rte. 295 and then taking Exit 5 onto Congress Street, which runs the length of the city. Just off this street, the distinguished **Portland Museum of Art** has a strong collection of seascapes by such masters as Winslow Homer, John Marin, and Andrew Wyeth. *7 Congress Sq., tel. 207/775–6148. Open Tues.–Sun. Admission charged.*

Portland's **Old Port Exchange** is a bustling waterside district of late-19th-century brick warehouses tastefully renovated with shops, galleries, and restaurants. Wander down Exchange, Union, and Fore streets, and end up at Custom House Wharf off Commercial Street.

Freeport, on Rte. 1, 15 miles northeast of Portland, is the home of **L. L. Bean** (Rte. 1, tel.

800/341–4341) along with dozens of outlets selling designer clothes, shoes, housewares, and toys at marked-down prices. **Bath,** 19 miles north on Rte. 1, has been known for shipbuilding since 1607. The town's **Maine Maritime Museum** offers nautical exhibits, including ship models, journals, photographs, artifacts, and the 142-foot Grand Banks fishing schooner *Sherman Zwicker.* There's also an apprentice shop where you can watch boatbuilders at work. Boat trips on the Kennebec River are also arranged. *243 Washington St., Bath, tel. 207/443–1316. Admission charged.*

Boothbay, due south of postcard-perfect Wiscasset on Rte. 27, is home of the **Boothbay Railway Village,** where you can ride 1$\frac{1}{2}$ miles on a narrow-gauge steam train through a re-creation of a turn-of-the-century New England village. *Rte. 27, Boothbay, tel. 207/633–4727. Open mid-June–mid-Oct., daily. Admission charged.*

Boothbay Harbor, a couple miles south on Rte. 27, is a town to wander through. Park at the waterfront, stroll along Commercial and Wharf streets, and leave time for a harbor cruise. Return to Rte. 1 and continue northeast through Newcastle and Rockland.

Camden, 8 miles north of Rockland on Rte. 1, is the famous resort town "where the mountains meet the sea"—the mountains being the Camden Hills (a 6,000-acre state park), the sea being scenic Penobscot Bay. The hike up to the summit of Mount Battie in Camden Hills State Park is mildly strenuous. From Camden, continue north and east on Rte. 1 through Searsport (the antiques capital of Maine).

Acadia National Park, which attracts more than 4 million visitors a year, offers 34,000 acres of woods and mountains, lakes and shore, footpaths for hiking, carriage paths for biking or cross-country skiing. Stop at the visitor center at Hulls Cove and then pick up the Park Loop Road. Good day hikes include the Great Head Loop, a 1$\frac{1}{2}$-mile trail from Sand Beach around a rocky promontory above the sea; the 3-mile loop trail around mountain-ringed Jordan Pond in the center of the park; and the 2¹/₂-mile hike up Penobscot and Sargent mountains from Jordan Pond.

THE NATURAL WORLD Wildlife on the coast includes harbor seals, guillemots, common eiders, loons, and the occasional peregrine falcon and bald eagle, as well as ubiquitous herring gulls, cormorants, and black-backed gulls. Puffins nest on Matinicus Rock, off the outer island of Matinicus, which is itself a marvelous place for bird-watching (as are Monhegan Island and Damariscove Island Preserve). Reid State Park is an ideal place to take in the variety of Maine's coastal habitats, from salt marsh to sand dune.

HOTELS AND INNS

Bed-and-breakfasts and Victorian inns have joined the family-oriented motels of Ogunquit, Boothbay Harbor, Bar Harbor, and the Camden region. Kennebunkport has the greatest variety of accommodations on the south coast, although prices tend to run high. You'll find better value in towns a bit off the track, such as Bath and Brunswick. Price categories for double occupancy, excluding 7% tax, are *Expensive*, $80–$100; *Moderate*, $60–$80; and *Inexpensive*, under $60.

BAR HARBOR **Wonder View Motor Lodge.** The views of Frenchman Bay and the location opposite the Bluenose ferry terminal distinguish this motel located outside of Bar Harbor. *Rte. 3, Box 25, 04609, tel. 207/288–3358 or 800/341–1553. 82 rooms with bath. Dining room, pool. AE, MC, V. Inexpensive–Expensive.*

BATH AREA **Fairhaven Inn.** The circa 1790 cedar-shingled house offers airy guest rooms furnished with handmade quilts and four-poster beds, along with lavish breakfasts (included). *RR 2, Box 85, North Bath 04530, tel. 207/443–4391. 7 rooms, 5 with private bath. Hiking and cross-country ski trails. AE, MC, V. Inexpensive–Moderate.*

BELFAST **Londonderry Inn.** This restored 1803 farmhouse, just a mile from Belfast, offers spotless, cheery, country-style rooms with views of fields and full country breakfasts. *Star Rte. 80, Box 3, 04915, tel. 207/338–*

3988. 5 rooms, with shared bath. MC, V. Inexpensive.

BOOTHBAY HARBOR **Brown Brothers Wharf.** All the rooms have private balconies on the water in this centrally located motel, and fishermen can tumble out of bed and onto a charter boat. *Atlantic Ave., 04538, tel. 207/633–5440. 70 rooms. Restaurant, lounge, docking facilities. AE, MC, V. Moderate–Expensive.*

The Pines. This motel offers more seclusion, just a mile from the center of town, more space, and far better value than the cluster of motels on and around the harbor. *Sunset Rd., Box 693, 04538, tel. 207/633–4555. 29 rooms with bath. Pool, playground, tennis court. MC, V. Moderate.*

CAMDEN **Windward House.** This bed-and-breakfast in a Greek Revival house at the edge of town is worth a splurge for the romantic furnishings, attentive hospitality, and gourmet breakfasts. *6 High St., 04843, tel. 207/236–9656. 7 rooms with bath, 1 suite. AE, MC, V. Expensive.*

Camden Main Stay. This intimate bed-and-breakfast is within walking distance of Camden's harbor and shops. The enthusiastic innkeepers will help plan your excursions along the coast. *22 High St. (U.S. Rte. 1), Camden, ME 04843, tel. 207/236–9636. 8 rooms, 3 with private bath. MC, V. Moderate–Expensive.*

KENNEBUNKPORT **Bufflehead Cove.** The friendly gray-shingled bed-and-breakfast affords country seclusion, dollhouse-pretty rooms, and hearty breakfasts just five minutes from Dock Square. *Box 499, 04046, tel. 207/967–3879. 3 rooms, 2 suites, all with bath. Private dock. AE, MC, V. Expensive.*

The Green Heron. Situated on Ocean Avenue, a longish walk from Dock Square, this simple, unpretentious inn provides its loyal clientele with rustic hospitality and sumptuous breakfasts included. *Box 2578, 04046, tel. 207/967–3315. 10 rooms and small cottage, all with bath. No credit cards. Moderate.*

PORTLAND Portland Regency Inn. The only major hotel in the heart of the Old Port Exchange, this property has spacious rooms and all the amenities of a big-city hotel at an affordable price. *20 Milk St., 04101, tel. 207/774–4200 or 800/727–3436. 95 rooms with bath, 8 suites. Restaurant, nightclub, health club. AE, D, DC, MC, V. Expensive.*

SOUTHWEST HARBOR The Moorings Inn. This collection of lodgings—an inn, cottages, and a motel—is located on a quiet section of Mount Desert Island, overlooking the only fjord on the East Coast. *Box 722, 04679, tel. 207/244–5523 or 207/244–3210. 9 rooms and 3 cottages, all with bath. Bicycles, canoes, outdoor gas grill. No credit cards. Inexpensive–Moderate.*

WELLS Wonderview Motor Village. The cottages (some with one bedroom and some with two) and motel units are set well back from the road, and screen porches overlook the salt marsh. *Box 326, Rte. 1, 04090, tel. 207/646–2304. 12 units. Playground, shuffleboard, picnic tables. MC, V. Inexpensive–Moderate.*

WISCASSET The Stacked Arms. This bed-and-breakfast, just a few miles outside of Wiscasset, has pretty grounds and spotless, homey bedrooms in a suburban setting. *RFD 2, Box 146, 04578, tel. 207/882–5436. 6 rooms, 1 with private bath. D, MC, V. Moderate.*

MOTELS

MODERATE Beechwood Motel (Rte. 9, Kennebunkport 04046, tel. 207/967–2483). 112 rooms; pool; tennis court. **Day's Inn Kittery/Portsmouth** (2 Gorges Rd.; Rte. 1 Bypass, Kittery 03904, 207/439–5555). 108 rooms; restaurant, lounge, pool. **Highbrook Motel** (94 Eden St., Bar Harbor 04609, tel. 207/288–3591 or 800/338–9688). 26 rooms. **Navigator Motor Inn** (520 Main St., Rockland 04841, tel. 207/594–2131). 82 rooms; restaurant, lounge. **Snow Hill Lodge** (Rte. 1, Box 550, Lincolnville Beach 04849, tel. 207/236–3452). 30 rooms.

INEXPENSIVE Admiral's Ocean Inn (Rte. 1, Box 99A, Belfast 04915, tel. 207/338–4260). 18 rooms and 2 suites; Continental breakfast included, pool, pets permitted. **Coastline Inn** (80 John Roberts Rd., South Portland 04106, tel. 207/772–3838). 55 rooms. **Gull Motel** (Box 811, Belfast 04915, tel. 207/338–4030). 14 rooms.

CAMPGROUNDS

The three campgrounds within Acadia National Park—Blackwoods and Seawall on Mount Desert Island and the Duck Harbor camping area on Isle au Haut—are extremely popular during the summer months. You can reserve ahead at Blackwoods for June 15–September 15 by contacting Mistix (Box 85705, San Diego, CA 92138, tel. 800/365–2267). Seawall accepts no reservations. You can reserve a lean-to site at Isle au Haut by mail only; write Acadia National Park (Box 177, Bar Harbor 04609) after April 1 for the application.

Blackwoods. Set in a dense grove of spruce and fir on the east side of the island, Blackwoods is the largest of the in-park campgrounds and the closest to the busy Park Loop Road. *Acadia National Park, Box 177, Bar Harbor 04609, tel. 207/288–3338. 310 RV and tent sites, no hookups, flush toilets, picnic tables and barbecue areas. Maximum stay 14 nights.*

Duck Harbor. Accessible only by mail boat, rugged and remote Isle au Haut offers camping at five Adirondack-style lean-tos in a spruce forest a few yards from the steep, rocky shore of Duck Harbor. *Acadia National Park, Box 177, Bar Harbor 04609, tel. 207/288–3338. 5 lean-tos, no tent or RV sites, no hookups, outhouses only, picnic tables and barbecue areas. Maximum stay 3 nights.*

Seawall. Located on the quieter west side of Mount Desert Island, Seawall is removed from the worst of summertime congestion. The dramatic Seawall rocky beach and picnic area are a short walk away, and you can drive easily to the town of Southwest Harbor. *Acadia National Park, Box 177, Bar Harbor*

04609, tel. 207/288–3338. 210 RV and tent sites, no hookups, flush toilets, picnic tables and barbecue areas. Maximum stay 14 nights.

DINING

Dining in Maine means lobster, and lobster can be found on the menus of a majority of Maine restaurants. Shrimp and crab are also caught in the cold waters off Maine, and they are often served in imaginative combinations with lobster, haddock, salmon, and swordfish. Price categories per person, excluding 6% tax, service, and drinks, are *Moderate,* $15–$25, and *Inexpensive,* under $15.

BAR HARBOR **Jordon Pond House.** Oversize popovers and tea are a tradition at this rustic restaurant in the park. The dinner menu features lobster stew and fisherman's stew. *Park Look Rd., tel. 207/276–3316. AE, D, MC, V. Moderate.*

BATH **Kristina's Restaurant and Bakery.** This old frame house is home to some of the finest baked goods on the coast as well as to New American cuisine dinners of fresh seafood and grilled meats. *160 Centre St., tel. 207/442–8577. D, MC, V. Inexpensive–Moderate.*

BOOTHBAY HARBOR **Andrew's Harborside.** The harbor view and outdoor deck overshadow the standard offerings of fried and broiled seafood at this family-oriented Boothbay eatery. *8 Bridge St., tel. 207/633–4074. AE, DC, MC, V. Moderate.*

BRUNSWICK **The Great Impasta.** The small, storefront Italian restaurant is popular for lunch, tea, or dinner. Try the seafood lasagna, or mix and match your favorite pasta and sauce to create a new dish. *42 Main St., tel. 207/729–5858. AE, MC, V. Inexpensive–Moderate.*

CAMDEN **Cappy's Chowder House.** Touristy, sometimes raucous, but always cheerful, Cappy's serves burgers, chowders, and seafood in a nautical setting jam-packed with couples, families, visitors, and locals. *Main St., tel. 207/236–2254. No reservations. MC, V. Open for 3 meals year-round. Moderate.*

FREEPORT **Harraseeket Lunch.** Escape Freeport's shopping frenzy at this no-frills lobster pound offering seafood baskets and lobster dinners, served indoors or out. *Main St., South Freeport, tel. 207/865–4888. No credit cards. Inexpensive.*

KENNEBUNKPORT **Windows on the Water.** This popular seafood restaurant overlooks Dock Square and Kennebunkport's lively working harbor. If you're in the mood to splurge, make reservations for "A Night on the Town": a five-course dinner for two, including wine and all gratuities, for $69. *Chase Hill Rd., tel. 207/967–3313. AE, D, DC, MC, V. Expensive.*

Mabel's Lobster Claw. George and Barbara Bush have been coming to this homey, family-style restaurant for years; you can dine on baked stuffed lobster, eggplant parmigiana, shrimp, and onion rings. *425 Ocean Ave., tel. 207/967–2562. No credit cards. Moderate.*

OGUNQUIT **Ogunquit Lobster Pond.** Select your lobster live, then dine under the trees or in the rustic dining room of the log cabin. *Rte. 1, tel. 207/646–2516. AE, MC, V. Moderate.*

PORTLAND **Street & Co.** At what may be Maine's best seafood restaurant, you enter through the kitchen—with all its wonderful aromas—and dine amid dried herbs and grocery staples. *33 Wharf St., tel. 207/775–0887. AE, MC, V. No lunch. Moderate–Expensive.*

Hu-Shang Exchange. When the urge for Chinese food strikes, come to this softly lit, soothing restaurant for both mild and spicy specialties such as lamb with ginger and scallions or moo shu shrimp. *29–33 Exchange St., tel. 207/773–0300. AE, MC, V. Moderate.*

Parker Reidy's. This lively and sometimes noisy restaurant in a former bank building in the Old Port serves seafood, teriyaki dishes, and sandwiches in a Victorian setting. *83 Exchange St., tel. 207/773–4731. AE, V. Moderate.*

WALDOBORO **Moody's Diner.** This big, bustling, roadside diner serves fresh-baked pies and home-cooked standards in a setting of neon, chrome, and linoleum. *Rte. 1, tel. 207/832–5362. No credit cards. Inexpensive.*

YORK HARBOR **Dockside Dining Room.** The airy, water-view dining room of this secluded inn right on York Harbor features seafood. *York Harbor off Rte. 3, tel. 207/363–2722. MC, V. Moderate.*

SHOPPING

FACTORY OUTLETS The success of L.L. Bean (Rte. 1, tel. 800/341–4341) has fostered the growth of a great retail marketplace in the Freeport area, with scores of factory outlets. Notable outlets in the area include Calvin Klein (48 West St., tel. 207/865–1772), the Patagonia Outlet (9 Bow St., tel. 207/865–0506), and Mikasa Store (31 Main St., tel. 207/865–9441). Kittery, Wells, and Ellsworth also have a concentration of outlets.

FLEA MARKETS AND ANTIQUES Searsport hosts a number of large flea markets throughout the summer months. The Montsweag Flea Market (Rte. 1, Woolwich) is open Wednesday and Friday through Sunday during summer, weekends only in spring and fall. Kennebunkport, Wells, and Searsport are the best places to go for antiques.

OUTDOOR ACTIVITIES

BEACHES Maine's ocean temperatures are slightly warmer south of Portland, but most people still find the water too cold for prolonged swimming. York, Ogunquit, Wells, Kennebunk Beach, and Old Orchard Beach have long sandy beaches open to the public.

BIKING The back roads around Kennebunkport, Camden, and Deer Isle are well-suited to biking, as are the carriage paths of Acadia National Park. Maine Publicity Bureau publishes a statewide list of bike rentals, and Maine Coast Cyclers (Camden, tel. 207/236–8608) can provide further information.

BOATING AND SAILING Motorboats and sailboats may be rented at most towns on the coast, including Kennebunkport, Boothbay Harbor, Rockland, Camden, and Bar Harbor. You can rent canoes or kayaks for trips in the Acadia region at Bar Harbor and Ellsworth. Organized boating excursions depart from Portland and Boothbay harbors.

FISHING Maine Department of Inland Fisheries and Wildlife (284 State St., Augusta 04333, tel. 207/289–2043) has the latest information on fishing regulations and seasons. Deep-sea fishing cruises operate out of Portland and Boothbay harbors.

HIKING Acadia National Park and Camden Hills State Park offer the most extensive trail systems (*see* Exploring, *above*). Also try the Beehive Trail off Acadia's Park Loop Road, the easy Ocean Trail that follows the dramatic coastline from Sand Beach to Otter Point, and the moderately steep Gorham Mountain Trail that skirts the Cadillac Cliffs.

Mammoth Cave National Park
Kentucky

Mammoth Cave National Park, in south-central Kentucky, has something you can't lay eyes on anywhere else on the planet: a hole in the ground with 330 miles of winding subterranean passages. It's a first-class natural wonder, as reliably awe-inspiring as that other famous hole in the ground, the Grand Canyon. (The second-longest cave on Earth, Optimisticeskaya, in the Ukraine, is barely a *quarter* as long as Mammoth.)

The cave's marvels range from 192-foot-high Mammoth Dome to 105-foot-deep Bottomless Pit; from a rugged climb called Mt. McKinley to a drifting voyage on the River Styx, 360 feet down, where eyeless fish swim; from a saltpeter mine abandoned after the War of 1812 to a tuberculosis hospital abandoned after an ill-advised experiment in 1843; from an unforgiving passage called Fat Man's Misery to a vaulting chamber known as—what else?—the Grand Canyon.

The cave itself is millions of years old—mummified remains of early Native Americans have been found in its depths. Its official history, however, only began in the 1790s, when, according to legend, a buckskin-clad hunter named Houchins discovered its entrance while tracking a wounded bear. But it was not until later in the 19th century that the cave became a popular tourist attraction. Stagecoaches and a railway brought the first visitors. Edmund Booth, a well-known actor, gave readings in the cave. And Jenny Lind, the Swedish nightingale, sang in one of its chambers.

As the cave gained fame, it inevitably became a bone of contention for real-estate entrepreneurs. Once it was discovered the public would pay to see the natural wonder, would-be owners offered competing tours of "the greatest cave that ever was," and for a time, a circus-hawker mentality prevailed. All that came to an end, however, in the 1940s, when Mammoth Cave was declared a national park.

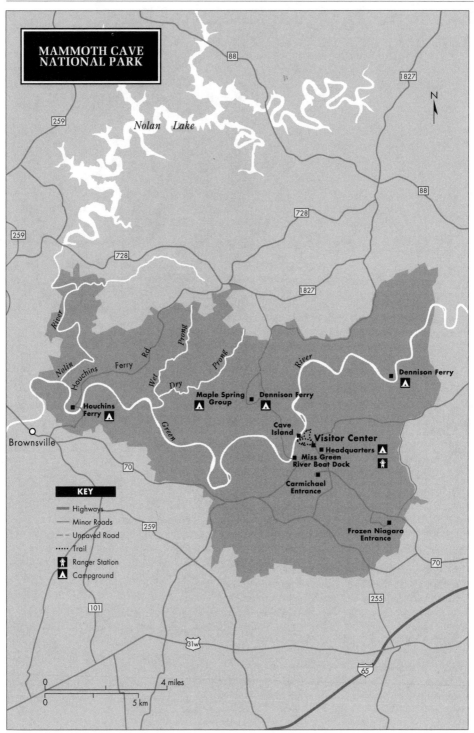

For the 50 years since, the park has been a refuge from the hectic and a place for discovery.

ESSENTIAL INFORMATION

WHEN TO GO Mid-March to mid-April is the best time to visit the park. Redbud and dogwood trees are in bloom, and springtime temperatures average 65°. Be aware, though, that temperatures can climb well into the 80s and dip down into the 30s. Five inches of rainfall are normal for this time of year, with occasional severe thunderstorms. Because the park is only moderately crowded in early spring, cave tours are not fully booked—though reservations are always advisable—and the hotels offer their off-season rates, at least until April 15.

Fall is also a glorious time in the park. The weather cools, the crowds thin out, and the trees are ablaze with color. If you're just interested in viewing the caves, winter is the time to do so (the tours are underbooked, and you have the guides to yourself), but organized park activities are sharply curtailed, and the area seems to sink into hibernation.

FESTIVALS AND SEASONAL EVENTS **Apr.:** Wildflower Month at Mammoth Cave National Park; daily nature walks, bus tours and special programs. **Weekend after Memorial Day:** Glasgow Highland Games at Barren River Lake State Resort Park (35 miles south on U.S. 31E); a gathering of Scottish clans with such sporting events as battle-axe throwing and tossing the Kyber. **Early Aug.:** Cave City Arts & Crafts Fair (9 miles east of the park on Hwy. 70); artisans from across the nation display and sell their wares. **Early Sept.:** Watermelon Festival, Tompkinsville (40 miles southeast on Hwy. 63); crafts, live entertainment, and ripe thumpers. **Last weekend in Oct.:** Hart County Tobacco Festival, Munfordville (15 miles northeast on I–65). **Mid-Dec.:** Christmas Sing in the Cave, with subterranean holiday music performed by a local choir.

BARGAINS At Campfire Circles at night, the rangers speak gratis about the region's plants and animals and the cave's distinctive history. For a leisurely stroll of an hour and a half, join the Wildflower Walks, offered free to acquaint visitors with the park's seasonal blossoms.

Take a ferry ride across Green River at the Green River or Houchins dock. Ferries operate daily, except under high-water conditions, at no charge. The park's extensive nature trails, of course, are there for the asking.

TOURIST OFFICES Mammoth Cave National Park (Park Office, Mammoth Cave 42259, tel. 502/758–2251). Edmonsen County Recreational Tourist & Convention Commission (Box 353, Brownsville 42210, tel. 502/597–2819). Cave City Tourist & Convention Commission (Cave City 42127, tel. 502/773–3131).

EMERGENCIES **Police:** Kentucky State Police (Bowling Green, tel. 502/782–2010). **Hospitals:** T. J. Samson Community Hospital (North Race St., Glasgow, tel. 502/651–4444); HCA Greenview Hospital (1801 Ashley Circle, Bowling Green, tel. 502/781–4330); Cavernar Memorial Hospital (Highway 31W, Horse Cave, tel. 502/786–2191). **Doctors:** The Medical Center at Bowling Green (Bowling Green, tel. 502/781–2150). **First aid within the Park:** weekdays, the Chief Ranger's Office (tel. 502/758–2251); weekends, the Chief Guide's Office (tel. 502/758–2321).

ARRIVING AND DEPARTING

BY PLANE Two major airports serve the area: Louisville's Standiford Field (tel. 502/367–4636) and Nashville International Airport (tel. 615/275–1675) in Tennessee. Each is about 90 miles from the park. You'll need to rent a car; both airports have Alamo, Avis, Budget, Dollar, Hertz, National, and Thrifty branches. From Standiford Field, drive west on I–264 to I–65 (5 miles from downtown Louisville), take I–65 south to Exit 53 at Cave City, then follow KY 70 west about 9 miles to the park. From Nashville, take I–65 north to Exit 48 at Park City, then follow KY 255 west about 8 miles to the park.

BY CAR Coming from either north or south, 1–65 provides the best access. From the north, take Exit 53 at Cave City to Route 70 west and drive 9 miles to the park's visitor center. From the south, take Exit 48 at Park City to Route 255 west and drive 8 miles to the visitor center. Cumberland Parkway runs through hardwood ridge country, a more scenic, less direct route.

BY BUS Greyhound Lines (tel. 800/231–2222) offers bus service to Cave City, 10 miles from Mammoth Cave National Park.

GETTING AROUND

BY CAR A car is the only viable method of transportation within the park.

REST STOPS Three rest areas on I–65 provide rest rooms and tourist information: one, north of Exit 53; a second, south of Exit 43; a third, north of Exit 28. The visitor center at the park also has rest rooms and a full array of maps and brochures.

GUIDED TOURS Guided tours of the cave depart daily from the visitor center. The Historic Tour (2 hours, 2 miles) takes you through the more famous passages, past mining operations from the War of 1812 and prehistoric artifacts. The Frozen Niagara (2 hours, 3/4 mile) displays spectacular rock formations that resemble a giant, multicolored waterfall. The Half-Day Tour (4 1/2 hours, 4 miles) invites the more ambitious to explore canyons and tubelike passages. During the summer, The Lantern Tour (3 hours, 3 miles) recreates the eeriness of the cave in days before electricity. Most tours are moderately strenuous and demand some climbing and stooping. Prices range from $4 to $6 for adults, $2 to $3 for children. Reservations are advised at all times and are a must in summer.

EXPLORING

It is possible to see the cave in half a day and be on your way. It is preferable, however, to linger in the park and explore the riches of "the surface world." Nature trails beckon the hiker; the most popular are listed here.

IN THE PARK **Cave Island Nature Trail.** This mile-long path begins at the cave mouth and winds through the woods past the River Styx Springs, named for its black-colored waters. En route, see limestone deposits shaped like jagged ice crystals.

Heritage Trail. This 3/4-mile path, not far from the visitor center, makes for a pleasant afternoon stroll. Along the way, see wildflowers, trees, and the Old Guides Cemetery, where the first cave explorers are buried. Stop at Sunset Point, a spectacular lookout, in time to watch the sun go down.

Ganter Cave. Within park boundaries, this less-traveled cave is open to exploring for qualified cavers. Requirements are stiff for safety reasons. Groups are limited to four to nine adults, with one experienced caver for every two novices. Approval is needed from the Chief Ranger's Office (tel. 502/758–2251).

Green River. Twenty-five miles of this river flow through the park, its waters a shaping force in the cave. You can cross the Green River by ferry for free (*see* Bargains, *above*) or take a paddle wheeler down it. From April through October, the *Miss Green River* makes several cruises daily. On the twilight cruise, you may spot deer on the shoreline under the gentle cover dusk provides. Tickets for the paddleboat may be purchased at the visitor center.

BEYOND THE PARK **The Blue Grass Country.** This picturesque part of Kentucky is a half-day's ride from Mammoth Cave. Take the scenic route: South on 1–65 to Cumberland Parkway, east on the Cumberland to I–75, then north on I–75 to Lexington. The route connects with several points of interest. South of I–75, near Middlesboro, is the Cumberland Gap, the historic gateway to the West, where early pioneers thrust their way through the mountains into Tennessee. If there happens to be a full moon, go to Cumberland Falls nearby. It's one of two places in the world where you can see a moonbow. That's a rainbow, formed by moonlight, striking a waterfall. Return to I–75 and take Exit 95 for Ft. Boonesborough State Park, where you'll find a replica of the fort where Daniel

Boone fought in the glory days. Take a look inside the cabins, too, where artisans are at work on 18th-century crafts, using period tools. Just north of Lexington on I–75, detour for the Kentucky Horse Park, which features an equestrian museum and many of the riding arts.

THE NATURAL WORLD   As this cluttered planet goes, Mammoth Park is still a fairly pristine place. If you get off the beaten path, it's possible to recapture a bit of the Kentucky that old Houchins, the cave's supposed discoverer, knew. Along the backcountry trails, you can spot red foxes, opossums, raccoon, and rabbits. A variety of birds will trill in startled protest when strangers invade their territory. Joppa Motor Trail, southwest of the visitor center, is an excellent place to catch a glimpse of wild turkeys and the region's white-tailed deer.

The 7 miles of forest trails, leading from the visitor center, contain some very old, unusually large sycamores, beeches, and tulip poplars. Along the far ridge, stands of oaks and hickories abound. The Big Woods, off Little Jordan Road, is considered virgin forest. Its trees loom up, darkly austere, impenetrable.

Wildflowers bloom throughout the park from April through September, 200 species in all. Spring brings trillium and the humble daisy; midsummer, the rarer orchid. In August, honeysuckle fills the air with its extravagant sweetness. And in September, the primrose dots the woods with color.

HOTELS AND INNS

The park boasts a single hotel, which rather resembles an inn. There are three other lodging options associated with the hotel. Spaced rectangularly around a parking lot, they have no eating facilities but are all within a five-block walk of the main hotel restaurant. Cabins, campsites, or motels in nearby towns are also available. Outside the park, Cave City has more motels than either Horse Cave or Park City. Prices for double occupancy, excluding 9% tax, are *Expensive*,

$50–$90; *Moderate*, $30–$50; and *Inexpensive*, under $30.

IN THE PARK   **Mammoth Cave Hotel.** This clean but simple two-story inn, within steps of the visitor center, offers the best lodging in the park. The rooms are pleasant and the restaurant serves generous, country-style breakfasts. *Mammoth Cave 42259, tel. 502/758–2225. 38 rooms. Free parking. AE, DC, MC, V. Expensive.*

Mammoth Cave Hotel Cottages. These one-room cottages furnished in Early American are a quarter-mile from the main hotel. They have air-conditioning and electric heat. *Mammoth Cave 42259, tel. 502/758–2225. 10 rooms. AE, DC, MC, V. Open Mar.–Nov. Moderate.*

Sunset Point Motor Lodge. Built like an old-fashioned motor lodge around an open court, Sunset Point offers generous-size rooms and is recommended for families and larger groups. *Reservations can be made through the Mammoth Cave Hotel Cottages, Mammoth Cave 42259, tel. 502/758–2225. 20 rooms. Free parking. AE, DC, MC, V. Expensive.*

Woodland Cottages. Also ¼ mile from the main hotel, these one-to-a-room New England–style cabins are for those who favor rustic lodgings: They're not in great shape, but they're cheap. *Mammoth Cave 42259, tel. 502/758–2225. 23 rooms. Free parking. Open May–Oct. AE, DC, MC, V. Inexpensive.*

MOTELS

MODERATE   **Best Western Kentucky Inn** (Box 356, Cave City 42127, tel. 502/773– 2321 or 800/528–1234). 51 rooms; pool, coin laundry. **Best Western–Mammoth Resort** (Park City 42160, tel. 502/749–4101). 93 rooms; restaurant, pool, tennis court. **Days Inn–Cave City** (Box 2009, Cave City 42127, tel. 502/773– 2151 or 800/325–2525). 110 rooms; pool, coin laundry. **Heritage Inn** (Box 2048, Cave City 42127, tel. 502/773–3121 or 800/264–1514). 116 rooms; pool. **Interstate Inn** (Box 397, Cave City 42127, tel. 502/773–3101, fax 502/773–6082). 140 rooms; pool. **Quality Inn**

(Box 547, Cave City 42127, tel. and fax 502/773–2181 or tel. 800/228–5151). 100 rooms; adjoining restaurant, pool.

INEXPENSIVE **Budget Host Inn** (Box 332, Horse Cave 42749, tel. 502/786–2165 or 800/888–CAVE). 80 rooms; coin laundry. **Cave Land Motel** (Box 242, Cave City 42127, tel. 502/773–2321). 14 rooms; pool. **Holiday Motel** (Hwy. 31W, Cave City 42127, tel. 502/773–2301). 25 rooms; pool. **Jolly's Motel** (Box 327, Cave City 42127, tel. 502/773–3118, fax 502/773–7151). 24 rooms; pool.

CAMPGROUNDS

There are four campgrounds within Mammoth Cave National Park that allow you to camp near your car. Twelve more backcountry sites are available to hikers on foot. All are in beautiful, natural settings. Like the park itself, the campgrounds are less crowded before Memorial Day and after Labor Day. Even in summer, however, they are run on a first-come, first-served basis. The exception, Maple Springs Campgrounds, which accommodates horses, requires reservations, which are made through the Chief Ranger's Office (tel. 502/758–2251). Backcountry sites require a permit, obtainable free at Headquarters Campground, near the visitor center (tel. 502/758–2212).

Dennison Ferry Campground. This secluded, quite primitive campground is on the east side of the park, 7 miles from the visitor center, and borders Green River. *Mammoth Cave National Park, Mammoth Cave 42259, tel. 502/758–2212. 4 tent sites, 1 chemical toilet, picnic tables and barbecue areas. No reservations.*

Headquarters Campground. Located ¼ mile from the visitor center, Headquarters is larger and less rugged than the rest. *Mammoth Cave National Park, Mammoth Cave 42259, tel. 502/758–2212. 111 tent sites, RV parking, showers, bathrooms, LP gas available, picnic tables and barbecue areas. No reservations. No credit cards.*

Houchins Ferry Campground. Your car is the only reminder of civilization at this small campsite, 14 miles from headquarters, on the west side of the park. *Mammoth Cave National Park, Mammoth Cave 42259, tel. 502/758–2212. 12 tent sites, 2 chemical toilets, picnic tables and barbecue areas. No reservations.*

Maple Springs Campground. Because of the hitching posts, which lend an Old West flavor, these campgrounds, north of Green River, are the park's most popular. *Mammoth Cave National Park, Mammoth Cave 42259, tel. 502/758–2212. 6 tent sites, chemical toilets, picnic tables and barbecue areas, parking for horse trailers. Reservations required. No credit cards.*

DINING

Friendly southern restaurants dominate the area. Those on low-cholesterol or special diets may have a problem finding restaurants to accommodate their needs. Most tourists are forced to rely on the fast-food chains, such as Wendy's and McDonald's, which are scattered throughout nearby towns. The restaurants listed below, however, feature regional specialties.

The restaurants here fall into the *Inexpensive* category: Price per person, excluding 6% tax, service, and drinks, is under $15.

INSIDE THE PARK **Mammoth Cave Hotel Restaurant.** This pleasant, busy restaurant at the inn features southern fare, such as country ham, and generous, country-style breakfasts. *Mammoth Cave, tel. 502/758–2225. AE, DC, MC, V.*

NEAR THE PARK **Bolton's Landing.** Distinctive Kentucky fare, such as catfish fried in corn meal, and the Hot Brown sandwich—turkey and chicken topped with cheese, tomatoes, and bacon, baked to perfection and served open-faced. *U.S. 31-E, Glasgow, tel. 502/651–8008. AE, DC, MC, V. Closed Sun.*

Hickory Villa Restaurant. Tourists and locals come here for the barbecued beef and chicken, slathered with a sauce the place says is made from a 100-year-old recipe. *Rtes. 70* *and 90, Cave City, tel. 502/773–3033. AE, DC, MC, V.*

Watermill Restaurant. Casual country food in casual country surroundings. Southern fried chicken is the house specialty. There's also an all-you-can-eat buffet. *Hwy. 70 west of Cave City, tel. 502/773–3186. AE, DC, MC, V.*

OUTDOOR ACTIVITIES

BIKING A gentle-grade, mile-long bike trail runs from Headquarters Campground to Carmichael Entrance Road, skirting the edge of a bluff and passing through shaded woodlands. No bicycles are for rent in the park, however, so visitors must bring their own.

BOATING Almost 30 miles of the Green and Nolin rivers are open to boaters and canoers in the park. Unfortunately, there are no boats for rent, so visitors must provide their own crafts. The most popular boat trip launches at Dennison Ferry Campground and floats down the Green River to Houchins Ferry. The trip, which takes about six hours, carries guests past scenic woodlands and dramatic bluffs. No launch fees or permits are required for boating. However, you do need a Coast Guard–approved life preserver for each person on board.

FISHING Fishing is available year-round on both the Green and Nolin rivers. Within the park, you don't need a fishing license, but all other Kentucky state regulations apply. Check at the visitor center for specifics. If you drop a line in the water, you are likely to catch musky, bass, white perch, or catfish.

HIKING Ten hiking trails, covering about 70 miles, are open within the park's boundaries. Trails range in length from under 1 to 10 miles and are graded easy to strenuous, according to hills and inclines. Ask for trail maps at the visitor center.

HORSEBACK RIDING Jesse James Riding Stables (Rte. 70W, Cave City 42127, tel. 502/773–2560) offers half-day guided rides through the park's backcountry for $25 per person. You can also rent horses by the half hour for trail rides on the 300 acres of property adjoining the stables.

ENTERTAINMENT

THEATER Horse Cave Theater (Main St., Horse Cave, tel. 502/786–2177) produces five plays from June through November, performed by professional players. Green River Amphitheater (Brownsville, tel. 502/597–3818) offers *The Death of Floyd Collins* from Memorial Day weekend through Labor Day.

MUSIC Mammoth Jamboree (Rte. 70, Cave City, tel. 502/773–3314) has live country bands and singers year-round on Friday and Saturday nights and on major holidays.

Memphis
Tennessee

The Great River—the Mississippi—shaped and defined Memphis's early character and still gives the city and its hinterland a distinctive way of life. Before Memphis was founded in 1819 by Andrew Jackson and named by him for that other Memphis, on the Nile, an Indian river culture flourished here from the 11th to the 15th century. Although a Deep South city, there are no antebellum mansions or definitive reminders of the Old South here. The city found real prosperity only in the late 19th century, when cotton and lumber barons built their imposing Victorian mansions.

In a trend somewhat unusual for southern cities, a flurry of adaptive-use projects has brought a rush of residents back to the heart of the city. Two former hotels, both on the National Register of Historic Places, have been converted into luxury apartments, and rehabilitated cotton warehouses loverlooking the Mississippi are now condominiums.

Memphis, the youngest major city along the lower Mississippi, took time out to listen and invent the blues and was slow to get caught up in the Sun Belt's boom. But today, still making music, it stands tall on its high bluffs, facing the river with a burgeoning skyline. Memphis capitalizes on its location with a unique entertainment park on an island in midriver. And downtown, for years down-at-heel, has come alive with new civic improvements, including the Main Street Trolley, the Pyramid arena, and the National Civil Rights Museum.

Elsewhere downtown, Storied Beale Street bustles with clubs and restaurants as it did in its heyday, when W. C. Handy first trumpeted his blue notes in PeeWee's Saloon.

One young man, influenced by the blues, went on to become the king of rock-and-roll, and today crowds flock to Elvis Presley's Graceland, one of Tennessee's major showplaces.

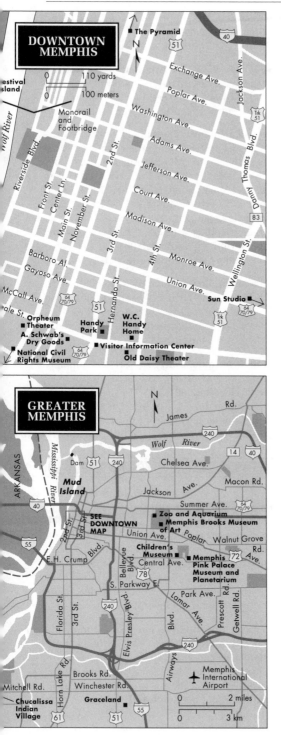

DOWNTOWN MEMPHIS

GREATER MEMPHIS

WHEN TO GO Spring and autumn are the ideal times for visiting Memphis. Many people come during the month-long **Memphis in May International Festival,** when the summer's heat and humidity have not yet set in. Winters are generally mild, although snow and ice storms do sometimes occur.

FESTIVALS AND SEASONAL EVENTS **Jan. 8:** Elvis Presley's Birthday Tribute. **Apr.:** Dr. Martin Luther King, Jr. Memorial March. **May:** Memphis in May International Festival: food and musical, cultural, and sports events. **June:** Carnival Memphis (formerly Cotton Carnival): exhibits, music, and family activities. **July:** Mid-South Music and Heritage Festival: food, music, children's activities and cultural exhibits and demonstrations. **Aug.:** Elvis International Tribute Week: music, Graceland tours and graveside, candlelight vigil. **Sept.:** Mid-South Fair: agricultural exhibits, rides, food, games, contests, concerts, a midway, and a rodeo. **Oct.:** National Blues Music Awards "The Handys."

BARGAINS There's no admission charge at the Beale Street Substation Police Museum (159 Beale St., tel. 901/528–2370); the Crystal Shrine Grotto (Memorial Park Cemetery, 5668 Poplar Ave., tel. 901/767–8930), a dramatic natural cavern with rock-crystal carvings; Coors Brewery (5151 E. Raines Rd., tel. 901/375–2100); or the Agricenter International, an aquaculture and farm complex (7777 Walnut Grove Rd., tel. 901/757–7777). The Memphis Botanic Garden (750 Cherry Road, tel. 901/685–1566) is free on Tuesday after 12:30 PM. The Memphis Pink Palace Museum and Planetarium (3050 Central Ave., tel. 901/320–6320) offers free admission to museum exhibits Thursday 5–8 PM, and the zoo is free on Monday 3:30–5 PM.

TOURIST OFFICES Tennessee Department of Tourist Development (Room T, Box 23170, Nashville 37202, tel. 615/741–7994). Memphis Convention and Visitors Bureau (47 Union Ave., Memphis 38103, tel. 901/543–5300). The Visitor Information Center (340 Beale St., Memphis 38103, tel. 901/543–5333).

EMERGENCIES Dial 911 for **police, fire,** or **ambulance. Hospitals** with 24-hour emergency service include Baptist Memorial Hospital (889 Madison Ave., tel. 901/227–2727) and Methodist Hospital Central (1265 Union Ave., tel. 901/726–7000).

ARRIVING AND DEPARTING

BY PLANE Memphis International Airport, 9½ miles south of downtown, is served by American, Delta, Northwest, TWA, United, and USAir. City Wide Cab (tel. 901/324–4202) operates taxi service to downtown hotels (fares average $16).

BY CAR From Memphis, I–55 leads north to St. Louis and south to Jackson, Mississippi; I–40 runs east to Nashville and Knoxville; I–240 loops around the city.

BY TRAIN AND BUS Amtrak (tel. 800/USA–RAIL) serves Memphis with the City of New Orleans between New Orleans and Chicago. Southeastern Greyhound Lines (203 Union Ave., tel. 901/523–7676) connects Memphis with cities and towns throughout the country.

GETTING AROUND

BY CAR Memphis attractions are spread out, so you'll need a car, though in some downtown areas you can park and walk from one to another.

BY BUS Memphis Area Transit Authority buses (tel. 901/274–6282; fare $1) cover the city and immediate suburbs. There's short-hop service (35¢) on designated buses between Front, Third, and Exchange streets daily from 9 to 3. The Trolley II (35¢) shuttles between downtown and the Medical Center. MATA Showboat buses resembling riverboats connect attractions, restaurants, hotels, and stores daily except holidays.

BY TAXI Companies include Yellow Cab (tel. 901/577–7700) and City Wide Cab (tel. 901/324–4202). Taxi fare is $2.35 for the first mile, $1.10 for every additional mile.

REST STOPS Cossitt Library (Front and Monroe Sts.) and A. Schwab's Dry Goods Store (163 Beale St.) have public rest rooms.

GUIDED TOURS Orientation: Both Cottonland Tours (tel. 901/774–5248) and Gray Line (tel. 901/948–8687) conduct three-hour tours to downtown highlights and Graceland.

Special-Interest: Cottonland Tours has excursions focused on gardens and galleries, Graceland, the Mississippi, shopping, and Southland Greyhound Park. Gray Line offers Elvis Memorial, nightlife, and Mud Island tours. Blues City Tours (tel. 901/522–9229) runs Graceland, Mud Island, and Beale Street tours, riverboat rides, and dinner and show tours. Heritage Tours (tel. 901/527–3427) explores the black-culture sites.

Excursion Boats: Memphis Queen Line (tel. 901/527–5694) runs 1½-hour sightseeing cruises March–December. It also offers dinner and moonlight cruises with entertainment by the area's top bands.

Carriage Tours: Bluff City Carriage Company (tel. 901/521–9462) and Carriage Tours of Memphis (tel. 901/527–7542) have horse-drawn carriage rides through downtown, highlighting locales from the 1993 film *The Firm,* which was shot primarily in Memphis.

EXPLORING

You should plan to explore Memphis in segments, beginning with the central city and branching outward (not all attractions listed below are located on the map). The city is laid out in a grid system. Madison Avenue divides north from south; Main Street separates east from west (Main is called Main Street Mall on the North side; its South side dead-ends in E. H. Crump Boulevard).

The **Visitor Information Center** on Beale Street is a good place to start a walking tour. Here you can pick up free maps and brochures and park free. On leaving the center, turn left and walk a few steps to the **W. C. Handy Memphis Home and Museum,** which displays photographs, sheet music, and other memorabilia of the Father of the Blues. *352*

Beale St., tel. 901/527–2583. Open Tues.– Sun. Admission charged.

From the home, turn right and walk west past Handy Park, between Third and Hernando streets, to admire a statue of W. C. Handy clutching his famed trumpet. Continue west through the **Beale Street Historic District.**

A. Schwab's Dry Goods Store (163 Beale St., tel. 901/523–9782) is an old-fashioned, 118-year-old dry-goods store where Elvis purchased some of his glitzy threads. You'll find every thing from top hats and tambourines to women's dresses up to size 60 and men's trousers up to size 74. And everybody gets a free souvenir. Walk two blocks west, board the trolley at Main and Beale, and travel south to Calhoun. Walk two blocks east.

The **National Civil Rights Museum** opened in 1991 at the historic Lorraine Motel, where Dr. Martin Luther King, Jr., was assassinated. The museum features exhibits and interactive displays tracing the history of the American Civil Rights movement. *450 Mulberry St., tel. 901/521–9699. Closed Tues. Admission charged.*

From the museum take the trolley to the north end of Main Street and walk one block west to **The Pyramid,** a $65 million entertainment and sports arena honoring Memphis's Egyptian heritage, opened in 1991. A massive stone statue of Rameses guards the 32-story structure, which seats 22,000. Seasonal tours are offered. *1 Auction Ave., tel. 901/521–9675.*

Take the footbridge or monorail from 125 Front Street to **Mud Island,** a 52-acre river park situated a few blocks south of The Pyramid. In the park there's a five-block-long scale model of the river that replicates its every twist, turn, and sandbar from Cairo, Illinois, to New Orleans. There are shops, restaurants, a swimming pool and beach, an amphitheater for big-name entertainment, and the World War II B-17 bomber *Memphis Belle. Tel. 901/576–7241. Closed Mon. Admission charged.*

From Mud Island you'll want to retrieve your car and drive east from downtown for 1 mile, along Union Avenue. **Sun Studio,** at Union and Marshall, is the birthplace of rock-and-roll. Sam Phillips opened it in 1950 and recorded such acts as Elvis Presley, Jerry Lee Lewis, B. B. King, Howlin' Wolf, Muddy Waters, Carl Perkins, and Roy Orbison. The studio is open daily for continuous, 30-minute tours, and it still operates as a studio by night. *706 Union Ave., tel. 901/735–3670. Admission charged.*

Drive north to Poplar Avenue and head east toward Overton Park, where you can visit the **Memphis Zoological Gardens and Aquarium,** one of the South's most notable zoos. It houses more than 400 species on 70 wooded acres. As part of a $22 million expansion, a new Cat Country exhibition opened in 1993, and a Primate World and Children's Village are slated for completion by late 1994. There's also a 10,000-gallon aquarium, a large reptile house, and an African veld setting for larger creatures. *2000 Galloway Dr., Overton Park, tel. 901/726–4787. Open daily. Admission charged (free Mon. 3:30–5 PM).*

Memphis Brooks Museum of Art has collections spanning eight centuries, including Italian Renaissance works; English portraits; Impressionist and American modernist paintings; and a large display of Doughty Bird figurines. *Overton Park, tel. 901/722–3500. Closed Mon. Donations.*

Southeast of the park is the newly renovated **Memphis Pink Palace Museum and Planetarium,** next to the 1920s pink marble mansion built by Clarence Saunders, founder of the Piggly Wiggly supermarket chain. A 165-seat planetarium and changing exhibits on natural and cultural history include a hand-carved miniature three-ring circus, full-scale replica of America's first self-service grocery store, and a life-size triceratops dinosaur that roars and stomps. *3050 Central Ave., tel. 901/320–6320. Open daily. Admission charged.*

The **Children's Museum of Memphis** is a short drive west of the Pink Palace. An interactive museum for children and their families, the museum offers a child-size version of a working city, including a real fire engine and police motorcyle. *2525 Central Ave., tel. 901/458–2678. Closed Mon. Admission charged.*

Graceland, 12 miles southeast of town via the I–55 south, is Memphis's most-visited attraction. A guided tour of the colonial-style mansion once owned by Elvis Presley reveals the spoils of stardom—from his gold-covered piano to his glittering show costumes—and a circuit of the grounds leads to his tomb. *3675 Elvis Presley Blvd., tel. 901/332–3322 or 800/238–2000 outside TN. Open daily. Admission charged.*

Chucalissa Indian Village, 10 miles southwest of downtown, preserves traces of the simple river culture that existed from A.D. 1000 to 1500. Ongoing archaeological excavations of the reconstructed site are conducted by Memphis State University. In the C. H. Nash Museum at the village, you'll see prehistoric tools, pottery, and weapons, plus a free slide presentation. Near the museum, Choctaw Indians skillfully fashion jewelry, weapons, and pottery, all of which are for sale. *1987 Indian Village Dr., tel. 901/785–3160. Open daily. Admission charged.*

HOTELS AND INNS

Memphis hotels and motor inns are especially busy in May and June and in mid-August, on the anniversary of Elvis's death. Bed-and-Breakfast in Memphis (Box 41621, 38174–1621, tel. 901/726–5902) arranges accommodations in a wide range of private lodgings. Price categories for double occupancy, without 13¼% tax, are *Expensive,* $70–$125; *Moderate,* $50–$70; and *Inexpensive,* under $50.

EXPENSIVE **The French Quarter Suite Hotel.** All the one-bedroom suites in this charming New Orleans–style inn have living rooms and whirlpool tubs, and some have balconies. *2144 Madison Ave., 38104, tel. 901/728–4000. 104 suites. Dining room, lounge with entertainment, pool, health club. AE, D, DC, MC, V.*

Holiday Inn Crowne Plaza. This sleek 18-story hotel, adjacent to the Convention Center, offers a concierge floor and ample reading areas and lighting in its spacious rooms. *250 N. Main St., 38103, tel. 901/527–7300 or 800/465–4329. 406 rooms. Restaurant, lobby piano lounge, indoor pool, health club, sauna. AE, D, DC, MC, V.*

Memphis Airport Hotel and Conference Center. Guest rooms rise around a five-story, plant-filled atrium, and some suites have kitchenettes. *2240 Democrat Rd., 38132, tel. 901/332–1130 or 800/654–4191. 380 rooms. Restaurant, nightclub, indoor and outdoor pools, 2 fitness centers, 2 tennis courts, jogging track. AE, D, DC, MC, V.*

MODERATE **Hampton Inn Airport.** Spacious, well-lighted rooms in this contemporary inn have Scandinavian-style teak furnishings, though a convenient location close to the airport is the real draw. *2979 Millbranch Rd., 38116, tel. 901/396–2200 or 800/426–7866. 128 rooms. Pool. AE, D, DC, MC, V.*

Econo Lodge. All rooms in this standard two-story chain inn have private patios. *3280 Elvis Presley Blvd., 38116, tel. 901/345–1425 or 800/446–6900. 122 rooms. Restaurant, pool, wading pool, playground. AE, D, DC, MC, V.*

Lowenstein-Long House. If you're into Victoriana, you may want to opt for this landmark mansion on an acre of lawn; rooms are spacious, with high ceilings and large baths. *217 N. Waldran St., 38105, tel. 901/527–7174. 8 rooms. Kitchen, laundry. No credit cards.*

INEXPENSIVE **Days Inn Memphis Airport.** This completely renovated motor inn near Graceland has light, well-maintained, spacious rooms. *1533 E. Brooks Rd., 38116, tel. 901/345–2470 or 800/325–2525. 242 rooms. Dining room, lounge with entertainment, heated pool. AE, DC, MC, V.*

La Quinta Motor Inn–Medical Center. This two-story inn near the medical center and midtown attractions has spacious, well-maintained but visually plain rooms. *42 S.*

Camilla St., 38104, tel. 901/526–1050 or 800/531–5900. 130 rooms. Pool. AE, D, DC, MC, V.

MOTELS

MODERATE **Best Western Riverbluff Inn** (340 W. Illinois Ave., 38106, tel. 901/948–9005 or 800/345–2604). 99 rooms; restaurant, lounge, pool, coin laundry. **Days Inn Downtown** (164 Union Ave., 38103, tel. 901/527–4100 or 800/325–2525). 106 rooms; restaurant, coffee shop, lounge. **Holiday Inn–Overton Square** (1837 Union Ave., 38104, tel. 901/278–4100 or 800/465–4329). 175 rooms; dining room, lounge, pool, parking garage. **Sheraton Airport Memphis** (2411 Winchester Rd., 38116, tel. 901/332–2370 or 800/365–2370). 211 rooms; dining room, lounge, heated pool, exercise room, lighted tennis courts.

INEXPENSIVE **Day's Hotel** (3222 Airways Blvd., 38116, tel. 901/332–3800 or 800/668–4200). 123 rooms; dining room, lounge, pool, sauna, coin laundry. **Hampton Inn–Medical Center** (1180 Union Ave., 38104, tel. 901/276–1175 or 800/426–7866). 126 rooms; Continental breakfast. **Quality Inn Airport South** (2949 Airways Blvd., 38116, tel. 901/345–1250 or 800/221–2222). 140 rooms; lounge, pool, playground.

DINING

Memphis, the "pork barbecue capital of the universe," also offers Cajun and Creole, French, Italian, Greek, Mexican, and Asian food. But many restaurants now serve heart-healthy and vegetarian dishes, and you can order grilled or poached seafood or other entrées without sauce. Price categories per person, not including 8¼% tax, service, and drinks, are *Moderate,* $15–$25, and *Inexpensive,* under $15.

MODERATE **Captain Bilbo's River Restaurant.** This rustic riverfront warehouse, one of Memphis's busiest eateries, offers simple, consistently well-prepared entrées like shrimp in brown butter and flounder stuffed with shrimp and crabmeat. *263 Wagner Pl., tel. 901/526–1966. AE, MC, V.*

Paulette's. This cordial country-inn dining room specializes in filet mignon, grilled seafood and poultry, and homemade soups. If you enjoy decadent dessert crepes, Paulette's is a must. *Overton Sq., 2110 Madison Ave., tel. 901/726–5128. AE, DC, MC, V.*

Salsa. Fresh tortilla chips and tangy salsa, plus enchiladas and other Mexican specialties are popular choices at this lively Southwestern-style cantina. *6150 Poplar, tel. 901/683–6325. AE, DC, MC, V.*

Marenas. A different Mediterranean cuisine is featured each month at this unique midtown restaurant; one month it may be French, another Egyptian or North African. *1545 Overton Park, tel. 901/278–9774. AE, DC, MC, V.*

INEXPENSIVE **Huey's.** This friendly neighborhood bar and restaurant is a Memphis institution. Patrons have voted "Huey Burgers" the best in town for eight years running. *1927 Madison Ave., tel. 901/726–9767; 2858 Hickory Hill, tel. 901/374–4373. AE, MC, V.*

Charlie Vergos' Rendezvous. In a back-alley basement crammed with memorabilia and bric-a-brac, this popular establishment serves what many experts swear are the choicest barbecued ribs and pork-loin plates in the world. *General Washburn Alley at 52 S. Second St., tel. 901/523–2746. AE, MC, V.*

Automatic Slim's Tonga Club. Southwestern cuisine with a Caribbean twist is the hallmark of this trendy downtown eatery. Jamaican jerk chicken or tomato-basil soup and vegetarian black beans are dinner favorites; for dessert try the taco-shaped cookie stuffed with creamy custard and berries. *83 2nd St., tel. 901/525–7948. AE, MC, V.*

Cafe Roux. Don't fret if Louisiana isn't on your itinerary: Spicy Cajun and Creole dishes are what put chef Michael Cahhal's Cafe Roux on the culinary map. Outstanding entrées include the rich Acadian catfish, thick jambalaya, fried oyster po'boys, and beignets. *7209 Winchester Ave., tel. 901/755–7689; 94*

S. Front St., tel. 901/525–7689. AE, DC, MC, V.

Corky's. Arguably Memphis's most popular barbecue restaurant, Corky's draws huge crowds who routinely endure hour-long waits for smoke-flavored, slow-cooked pork or beef ribs (wet or dry). Less filling are the juicy pork sandwiches topped with coleslaw. *5259 Poplar Ave., tel. 901/685–9744. AE, DC, MC, V.*

The Little Tea Shop. Since 1918, this homey restaurant has attracted luncheon crowds for its first-rate southern cooking. Traditional favorites include shrimp Arnaud and lace cornbread with creamed chicken. *69 Monroe Ave., tel. 901/525–6000. No credit cards.*

The Spaghetti Warehouse. Pasta, salads, and a hearty minestrone draw crowds to this whimsically renovated downtown warehouse. Kids should enjoy eating in a restored trolley car in the center of the dining room. *40 W. Huling Ave., tel. 901/521–0907. DC, MC, V.*

SHOPPING

With four suburban branches, Goldsmith's (tel. 901/766–2200) is Memphis's major department store, but you'll find a wider selection in the Beale Street Historic District, which is crammed cheek-to-jowl with galleries and souvenir stores. Hickory Ridge Mall (tel. 901/795–8844) in suburban, southeast Shelby County, is one of the city's nicest malls, with dozens of department stores, boutiques, a cineplex, food court and indoor children's carousel. Six shops at Graceland sell every possible kind of Elvis memorabilia. Twenty miles east of downtown Memphis, the Belz Factory Outlet Mall (3536 Canada Road, Exit 20 off I–40 in Lakeland, tel.

901/386–3180) is a direct factory outlet with bargains galore in its 50 stores.

OUTDOOR ACTIVITIES

HIKING There are trails at Shelby Farms Plough Recreation Area (tel. 901/572–4278), Lichterman Nature Center (5992 Quince Rd., tel. 901/767–7322), and at T. O. Fuller State Park next to Chucalissa Indian Village (tel. 901/543–7581).

TENNIS The Memphis Park Commission (tel. 901/325–5759) operates several facilities that offer tennis lessons and golf.

ENTERTAINMENT

Among the offerings at the Orpheum Theatre (tel. 901/525–3000 for tickets) are classical, rock music, and comedy performances, Broadway road shows, and ballet. The Memphis Symphony Orchestra performs at Vincent de Frank Music Hall, Cook Convention Center (tel. 901/324–3627). At Playhouse on the Square (tel. 901/725–0776) there's repertory theater year-round. The Memphis International Cultural Series stages world-class art and historical exhibitions each summer at the Memphis Cook Convention Center (One Convention Plaza, tel. 901/576–1231 or 800/755–8777; admission charged). Treasures of gold, textiles, and mummies from pre-Incan Peru are planned for exhibit in 1994.

For live blues and dancing, try Captain Bilbo's River Restaurant (263 Wagner Pl., tel. 901/526–1966) or Rum Boogie Cafe (182 Beale St., tel. 901/528–0150); the Omni New Daisy Theatre stages blues, jazz, and rock concerts (330 Beale St., tel. 901/525–8981). For the best in live blues, check out B. B. King's Blues Club (143 Beale St., tel. 901/527–5464).

Miami
Florida

What they say about Miami is true. This city *is* different. Once a sleepy southern resort town, Miami today is a burgeoning giant of international commerce as well as a place to find serious relaxation on sunny, sandy, stylish beaches. Like most big cities, Miami inspires the first-time visitor with all sorts of hopes and dreams, be it early retirement or life as a dedicated beach bum.

More than 45% of Greater Miami's population is Hispanic—the majority from Cuba. Downtown, staid-suited lawyers and bankers share the sidewalks with immigrant fruit vendors hawking their wares from pushcarts. European youths with backpacks stroll the streets. Would-be actresses and models sip espresso from sidewalk cafés. Pushing your way through downtown streets you hear Spanish, Chinese, Creole, French, Yiddish, Hebrew, Portuguese, and even a little English now and then—a veritable babble of tongues that contributes to the city's exotic international flavor. Although your first stop in Miami may be the beach, don't miss the opportunity to sample the ethnic bars and restaurants of neighborhoods like Little Havana or Little Haiti.

As a big city, Miami has its share of crime, violence, and drug trafficking—but not the pervasive lawlessness portrayed on made-for-TV movies and reruns of "Miami Vice." The flourishing drug culture certainly has fueled get-rich-quick lifestyles, but you probably won't find Miami's seamy underside unless you go looking for it.

Instead, what you will find is a city that does indeed move to a different rhythm (one that sounds decidedly like a salsa beat). The so-called capital of Latin America, Miami is a sprawling metropolis where cultural diversity adds a certain spice to carefree days in the sun.

MIAMI BEACH

Bass Museum of Art

South Beach Art Deco District

Fisher Island

Virginia Key

GREATER MIAMI

Bill Baggs Cape Florida State Recreation Area

0 _____ 5 miles

0 _____ 5 km

One final note: Although Hurricaine Andrew devastated much of South Miami in 1992, the storm did little damage to those parts of town that tourists visit most.

ESSENTIAL INFORMATION

WHEN TO GO The best months for guaranteed sun and hot weather are November, April, and May. Between December and March, average daytime temperatures range from 60° to 80°.

Winter is Miami's unabashed tourist season; rates are highest as winter-weary northerners descend on Greater Miami. School holidays are especially hectic, when college students and families compete for restaurant reservations, parking spaces, and spots on the beach. It often rains in January, however, and cold fronts occasionally arrive, bringing with them chilly days and near-freezing nights. Fortunately, these blasts of cool weather pass quickly.

Room rates are lowest in summer, when many hotels offer budget-priced package deals. Crowds thin noticeably in summer, but that's because the season is very hot, always humid, and often wet.

FESTIVALS AND SEASONAL EVENTS Mid-Jan.: Art Deco Weekend spotlights Miami Beach's historic district with an Art Deco street fair featuring crafts, food, and live entertainment (tel. 305/672–2014). **Mid-Feb.:** Coconut Grove Art Festival is the state's largest (tel. 305/447–0401). **Early Mar.:** Carnival Miami is a celebration staged by the Little Havana Kiwanis Club (tel. 305/644–8888). **First weekend in June:** Miami-Bahamas Goombay Festival in Miami's Coconut Grove celebrates the city's Bahamian heritage (tel. 305/443–7928).

BARGAINS Performing Arts for Community and Education (PACE) (Box 40, Miami 33168–0040, tel. 305/681–1470) and the University of Miami School of Music (tel. 305/284–6477) at the Coral Gables campus offer free concerts.

There are 28 national, state, and county parks in the Greater Miami area. Most are free to the public or charge only a minimal entrance fee. For a list of these parks, contact the Greater Miami Convention and Visitors Bureau (*see* Tourist Offices, *below*).

TOURIST OFFICES Greater Miami Convention and Visitors Bureau (701 Brickell Ave., Suite 2700, Miami 33131, tel. 305/539–3000 or 800/283–2707) has a satellite tourist center at Miami International Airport. Greater Miami Chamber of Commerce (1601 Biscayne Blvd., Miami 33132, tel. 305/350–7700).

EMERGENCIES **Police, fire,** and **ambulance:** Dial 911. The following **hospitals** have 24-hour emergency rooms: Mount Sinai Medical Center (4300 Alton Rd., Miami Beach, tel. 305/674–2121); University of Miami/Jackson Memorial Medical Center (1611 N.W. 12th Ave., Miami, tel. 305/325– 7429; emergency room, tel. 305/585–2708; interpreter service, tel. 305/585–6316), which has Greater Miami's only trauma center; and Baptist Hospital of Miami (8900 N. Kendall Dr., Miami, tel. 305/596–6556). **Pharmacies:** Eckerd Drugs (825 Miami Gardens Dr., N.E. at 185th St., North Miami Beach, tel. 305/932–5740; 9031 S.W. 107th Ave., Miami, tel. 305/274–6776) and Walgreen's (5731 Bird Rd., Miami, tel. 305/666–0757).

ARRIVING AND DEPARTING

BY PLANE Miami International Airport (MIA) (tel. 305/876–7000) is 8 miles west of downtown Miami.

Between the Airport and Center City. For taxi service from the airport to hotels in the airport area, ask a uniformed county taxi dispatcher to call an Airport Region Taxi Service (ARTS) cab for you. These special blue cabs offer a short-haul flat fare in two zones: An inner-city ride is $6; an outer-city fare is $8. Maps are posted in cab windows. A regular taxi from MIA to the Port of Miami costs about $15.

SuperShuttle vans operate 24 hours a day and shuttle between MIA and all destinations in Dade or Broward counties, the Port of Miami,

and even Palm Beach or the Lower Keys. It's best to make reservations 24 hours in advance. *Tel. 305/764–1700 from Broward, 305/871–2000 from Dade, or 800/SHUTTLE nationwide. Lower rate for 2nd passenger in same party.*

BY CAR The main highways into Greater Miami from the north are Florida's turnpike (toll) and I–95. From the northwest, take I–75 or U.S. 27 into Miami. From the Everglades to the west, use the Tamiami Trail (U.S. 41). From the south, use U.S. 1 and the Homestead Extension of Florida's turnpike.

BY TRAIN Amtrak (tel. 800/USA–RAIL) runs twice daily between Miami and New York City.

BY BUS Greyhound Lines (tel. 800/231–2222) buses stop at five bus terminals in Greater Miami.

GETTING AROUND

Miami is laid out on a grid with four quadrants—northeast, northwest, southeast, and southwest—which meet at Miami Avenue and Flagler Street. Miami Avenue separates east from west, while Flagler Street separates north from south. *Avenues* and *courts* run north–south; *streets, terraces,* and *ways* run east–west. And *roads* run diagonally from northwest to southeast.

Many named streets also bear numbers. For example, Le Jeune Road is also N.W. and S.W. 42nd Avenue. Also, Hialeah has its own grid, with Palm Avenue separating east from west and Hialeah Drive separating north from south. Your best bet is to use a good street map. If you can, learn how to ask and understand simple directions in Spanish; in some areas you may have to search for someone to answer you in English.

BY TRAIN Metrorail runs from downtown Miami north to Hialeah and south along U.S. 1 to Dadeland. Trains run every 7½ minutes during peak hours, 15–20 minutes other times. Trains are only crowded during rush hours. Operating hours are weekdays 6 AM–midnight, weekends 6:30 AM–6:30 PM, and until midnight for such special events as the Orange Bowl parade (fare: $1.25). At the TRI-RAIL station you can transfer to the commuter train and ride to the West Palm Beach Airport. This system will also take you to several stations where you can board an Amtrak train. Information for this system is available by calling 800/TRI–RAIL.

You can switch to Metromover/Peoplemover, a separate inner-city mass-transit system, at Government Center Station. This system circles the heart of the city on twin elevated loops, linking major hotels, office buildings, and shopping areas. Its hours of operation are weekdays 6:30 AM–midnight, weekends 8:30 AM–midnight, and sometimes later for special events (fare: 25¢).

BY BUS Metrobus stops are marked by blue-and-green signs with a bus logo and route information. The $1.25 fare must be paid in exact change. The frequency of service varies widely. Obtain specific schedule information in advance for the routes you want to ride by calling 305/638–6700.

BY TAXI There are some 2,000 taxicabs in Dade County. Fares are $1.10 for the first $1/7$ mile, 25¢ for each additional $1/7$ mile, and 25¢ for each 48 seconds of waiting time. There's no additional charge for extra passengers, luggage, or road and bridge tolls. Some drivers will take advantage of visitors, taking them the long way around to their destination; ask at your hotel or restaurant how long the cab ride should take and the best route to get there. Taxi companies with dispatch service include Central Taxicab Service (tel. 305/534–0694), Miami-Dade Yellow Cab (tel. 305/633–0503), and Speedy Cab (tel. 305/861–9999).

BY CAR You'll need a car to visit many Miami attractions and points of interest listed in this chapter, but some are accessible via public transportation. Parking downtown is inconvenient and expensive if you park in a private lot, so if you're staying outside the downtown area, leave your car at your hotel or at an outlying Metrorail station and take the train downtown.

REST STOPS Florida's shopping malls are air-conditioned, immaculate, and filled with benches, tables, rest rooms, and a selection of places to eat.

EXPLORING

From a distance, you see downtown Miami's future—a 21st-century skyline already stroking the clouds with sleek fingers of steel and glass. By day, this icon of commerce and technology sparkles in the strong subtropical sun; at night, it basks in the man-made glow of floodlights.

To see only the downtown area would be to miss the best of Greater Miami. So take time to visit several neighborhoods, sample the ethnic foods, and experience Miami's diverse subcultures.

Art Deco District is the only district in the United States in which all structures date from the early 20th century. More than 800 buildings in this mile-square area are listed on the National Register of Historic Places. *Art Deco* is the term given to the modern architecture that emerged in the late '20s and '30s. Its forms are eclectic, abstracted from nature (especially birds, butterflies, and flowers); from ancient Aztec, Mayan, Babylonian, Chaldean, Egyptian, and Hebrew designs; and from the streamlined, aerodynamic, and geometric shapes that flourished in the post-Depression building boom of the late '30s and early '40s. Sherbet-colored buildings with neon signs, rounded corners, vertical columns, fluted eaves, and Mediterranean arches can be found all along this inner ear–shaped district that lies on the east side of South Beach, bordered by the ocean, Lenox Court, and 6th and 23rd streets.

Bass Museum of Art houses a diverse collection of European art, including *The Holy Family,* a painting by Peter Paul Rubens; *The Tournament,* a 16th-century Flemish tapestry; and works by Albrecht Dürer and Henri de Toulouse-Lautrec. Park behind the museum and walk around to the entrance past massive tropical baobab trees. *2121 Park*

Ave., Miami Beach, tel. 305/673–7530. Open Tues.–Sun. Admission charged.

Bayfront Park, located on Biscayne Boulevard in downtown Miami, has a band shell where various musicians and artists perform throughout the year. From the park there's a wonderful view of the bay. Another park attraction is **Bayside,** an inviting cluster of shops and restaurants.

Coconut Grove, the Greenwich Village of South Florida, is one of the oldest neighborhoods in Miami, dating back to the late 1800s. The Grove, as locals call it, offers a blend of the bohemian and the chic. Early settlers include Bahamian blacks, "conchs" from Key West, and New England intellectuals. Artists, writers, and scientists then established winter homes here. By the end of World War I, the colony was so successful that more people listed in Who's Who gave addresses in Coconut Grove than anywhere else.

Hippies thronged to the Grove in the 1960s, followed by transplanted intellectuals, jet-setters, writers, artisans, and Yuppies—all seeking a laid-back lifestyle in a warm climate. To this day, Coconut Grove reflects its pioneers' eclectic origins—posh estates exist side by side with rustic cottages, modest frame homes, and starkly modern dwellings. The tone has become increasingly upscale, mellow, and sophisticated, boasting galleries, boutiques, and elegant restaurants, not to mention the bars and sidewalk cafés where the literati hang out.

Stroll along the redbrick pavement of the Main Highway and browse in the various shops. Stop in for a matinee at the Coconut Grove Playhouse or take an evening rickshaw ride—a Grove experience that's more fun than any taxi.

Coconut Grove Farmers Market takes place each Saturday in a vacant lot on Margaret Street, one block west of McDonald Avenue (S.W. 32nd Ave.). Vendors set up outdoor stands offering homegrown tropical fruits and vegetables (including organic produce), honey, seafoods, macrobiotic foods, and ethnic fare from the Caribbean, the Middle East,

and Southeast Asia. Also for sale are plants, handicrafts, candles, jewelry, and handmade clothing. A masseur plies his trade, musicians play, and Hare Krishnas chant.

Coral Castle is said to have taken Edward Leedskalnin 20 years to carve from 1,000 tons of coral as a tribute to his fiancée, who jilted him just hours before their wedding. The castle is an engineering marvel: the nine-ton gate swings open at a light touch, there are solar-heated bathtubs, and even a coral "telescope" aimed at the North Star. *28655 S. Dixie Hwy., Homestead area, tel. 305/248–6344. Open daily. Admission charged.*

Coral Gables, the first fully planned community in the United States, was designed and developed by George Merrick, who chose an Old World Spanish Mediterranean theme. Today, this community is marked by broad boulevards, Spanish plazas and fountains, imposing entrance gates, huge banyan trees, and miles of waterways weaving through its residential areas. Merrick, who began selling lots in 1921, named most of the streets for Spanish explorers, cities, and provinces. Street names are at ground level beside each intersection on whitewashed concrete cornerstones. Merrick's home, **Coral Gables House** (located in the heart of Coral Way, one of the most beautiful residential areas in Miami) was built in 1907 and is open to the public as a museum. Upscale boutiques, art galleries, and restaurants can be found along the stretch of Coral Way from Douglas Road (37th Ave.) to Le Jeune Road (42nd Ave.), called Miracle Mile. Notable structures along this bit include **Coral Gables City Hall** (405 Biltmore Way, tel. 305/446–6800) and **Venetian Pool** (2701 DeSoto Blvd., tel. 305/460–5356), a unique municipal swimming lagoon adorned with caves, cascading waterfalls, and arched bridges.

Fairchild Tropical Garden consists of 83 acres—the largest botanical garden in the continental United States. There's also a rare plant house, a rain forest, and a sunken garden. Tram tours leave on the hour from 10 AM until 4 PM. *10901 Old Cutler Rd., Coral Ga-*

bles, tel. 305/667–1651. Open daily. Admission charged.

Historical Museum of Southern Florida, in the Metro-Dade Cultural Center, houses hands-on displays and exhibits that interpret the South Florida experience through the ages. Displays are based on early Tequesta and Seminole Indian tribes, pirates, boom and bust years, and sunken ships. The Museum Tour concentrates on the exhibits, which cover 10,000 years of Miami's history and include a 15-minute slide show. The Curator's Cabinet Tour combines the Museum Tour with a look behind the scenes at departments visitors seldom see, including a research center with 500,000 photographs and the museum's cataloging and conservation departments. 101 W. Flagler St., Downtown Miami, tel. 305/375–1492. Open daily. Admission charged.

Little Haiti is a 200-block area on Miami's northeast side that has become home to 60,000 of the 150,000 Haitians who have settled in Greater Miami. Center your exploring around the two-block area from Miami Avenue to N.E. 2nd Avenue, where local merchants have painted their stores in the pastel and brilliant hues of the Caribbean. Storefront restaurants serve up such Creole specialties as fried goat, while local clubs pulse to the music of compas (a cross between salsa and merengue). Stop at **Baptiste Bakery** (7488 N.E. 2nd Ave.) for Haitian breads and cakes made with coconut and other tropical ingredients.

Little Havana was formed 30 years ago, when the tidal wave of Cubans fleeing the Castro regime flooded an older neighborhood just west of downtown Miami. Today, with a half-million Cubans widely dispersed throughout Greater Miami, Little Havana remains a magnet for Cubans and Anglos alike who wish to experience traditional Cuban culture— from the Spanish/Mediterranean–style architecture to the strong Cubano coffee. Here the Spanish language is king, with many residents and shopkeepers speaking almost no English. If you don't speak Spanish, point and smile to communicate. A stroll down

Calle Ocho (also known as S.W. 8th St.) will take you through the heart of Little Havana.

If your time is limited, explore the colorful three-block stretch from S.W. 14th Avenue to S.W. 11th Avenue. Old men in guayaberas, or pleated jackets, play dominoes at Domino Park on 14th Avenue while vendors hawk exotic fruits along the streets. At the northwestern edge of Little Havana, at Flagler Street and 17th Avenue, is **Plaza de la Cubanidad,** where redbrick sidewalks surround a water sculpture and a monument to Cuban patriots.

Lowe Art Museum has a permanent collection of 8,000 works, including Renaissance and Baroque art, American paintings, Latin American art, and Navajo and Pueblo Indian textiles and baskets. The museum also hosts traveling exhibitions. 1301 Stanford Dr., Coral Gables, tel. 305/284–3535 for recorded information or 305/284–3536 for museum office. Open Tues.–Sun. Admission charged.

Matheson Hammock Park, Dade County's oldest and most scenic park, offers both walking and bike trails as well as lake fishing. The park's most popular feature, however, is a bathing beach, where the tide flushes a saltwater "atoll" pool through four gates. 9610 Old Cutler Rd., Coral Gables, tel. 305/666–6979. Open daily. Pool lifeguards on duty in winter: 8:30 AM–6 PM; summer: 7:30 AM–7 PM. Small fee for parking.

Metro Zoo was devastated by Hurricane Andrew but has since undergone restoration and is still the place to find koala bears, rare white Bengal tigers, and Pygmy hippos, among other animals, roaming free on islands surrounded by moats. This 290-acre, "cageless" zoo also has "Wings of Asia," a 1½-acre aviary, where hundreds of exotic birds from Southeast Asia fly through a rain forest beneath a protective net enclosure. The zoo has 3 miles of walkways, a monorail with four stations, and an open-air amphitheater for concerts. 12400 S.W. 152nd St., South Dade, tel. 305/251–0400. Open daily. Admission charged.

Miami Beach and Miami are separate cities. Miami Beach, a string of 17 islands in Biscayne Bay, is often considered America's Riviera, luring refugees to its warm sunshine, sandy beaches, and graceful palms. Since 1912, when millionaire promoter Carl Graham Fisher began pouring a hefty portion of his fortune into developing this necklace of sandy islands, Miami Beach has experienced successive waves of boom and bust. While thriving in the early '20s and the years just after World War II, Miami Beach also suffered the devastating 1926 hurricane, the Great Depression, travel restrictions during World War II, and an invasion of criminals released from Cuba during the 1980 Mariel boat lift. Today, a renaissance is under way. A multimillion-dollar "sandlift" has restored the beach, while a scenic boardwalk entices strollers, joggers, and people-watchers. The area between 25th and 87th streets is still the hub of Miami's tourism, with legendary high-rise hotels and gleaming condominiums lining the wide swath of beach.

Miami Museum of Science and Space Transit Planetarium, with more than 150 hands-on sound, gravity, and electricity exhibits, is a haven for children and adults alike. A wildlife center houses native Florida snakes, turtles and tortoises, birds of prey, and large wading birds. Multimedia astronomy and laser shows are featured in the planetarium. *3280 S. Miami Ave., Miami, tel. 305/854–4247 or 305/854–2222 for planetarium show times and prices. Open daily. Admission charged.*

Miami Seaquarium houses Lolita, a killer whale. Her main competition are the sea lion and dolphin shows, which take place three times a day. You can also touch the tide-pool inhabitants, feed sea lions and stingrays, watch the divers hand-feed the reef fish and moray eels, and admire sharks, manatees, and the tropical-reef fish in the 235,000-gallon aquarium. *4400 Rickenbacker Causeway, Key Biscayne area, tel. 305/361–5705. Open daily. Admission charged.*

Monkey Jungle celebrates a reversal of roles—the human beings are "caged," while the monkeys roam wild. Enjoy the antics of the more than 500 monkeys representing 35 species, including orangutans from Borneo and Sumatra, golden lion tamarins from Brazil, and lemurs from Madagascar. Monkey shows begin at 10 AM and run every 45 minutes. *14805 S.W. 216 St., South Dade, tel. 305/235–1611. Open daily. Admission charged.*

Parrot Jungle & Gardens has more than 1,100 exotic birds—including colorful macaws, parrots, and cockatoos—that fly free, eat from your hand, and even pose for photographs. To get the birds' attention, you'll need seeds, which can be purchased from old-fashioned gumball machines. Attend a trained-bird show and watch baby birds in training. The "jungle" is a natural subtropical hammock of flowering trees and plants surrounding a sinkhole. Stroll among orchids, ferns, bald cypress trees, and massive live oaks. Also see the cactus garden and Flamingo Lake, with a breeding population of 75 Caribbean flamingos. Opened in 1936, Parrot Jungle is one of Greater Miami's oldest and most popular tourist attractions. *11000 S.W. 57th Ave., Miami, tel. 305/666–7834. Open daily. Admission charged.*

South Beach, known fondly as Sobe, is a vibrant neighborhood full of pastel-colored hotels and trendy outdoor cafés. An exciting revival has transformed this once downtrodden area into the SoHo of the South, an artsy place of entertainment and culture. Sip an espresso at a café and watch the parade of artists, models, backpackers, and young couples stroll by. So many TV commercials, shows, and movies are filmed here that you may recognize a number of buildings or even get to watch a scene being filmed. Reggae and calypso music concerts can be heard at Lumus Park on the beach. Small boutiques with new-wave clothing, frozen yogurt stores, art galleries, and antiques shops have popped up along Ocean Drive and Washington Avenue. Whether you visit during the day or stop by for an evening meal or walk, this area is hopping with people hoping to see and be seen. Bounded by the ocean, South Beach runs from Government Cut (the southernmost point of Miami Beach) north to Dade Boulevard and 23rd Street.

South Miami was a pioneer farming community that grew into a suburb. South Miami still retains its small-town charm. If you have a car, take a self-guided tour along Sunset Drive, an officially designated "historic and scenic road" that leads to and through downtown South Miami. Slow down at the northwest corner of Sunset Drive and Red Road (57th Ave.) to take a gander at the mural on a pink building in which an alligator seems ready to devour a horrified man. This trompe l'oeil fantasy, *South Florida Cascade,* by illusionary artist Richard Haas, highlights the main entrance to **The Bakery Centre** (5701 Sunset Dr., South Miami, tel. 305/662–4155), a commercial center and small shopping mall.

Virginia Key and Key Biscayne are Greater Miami's playground islands, separated from dense, urban Miami Beach by Government Cut and the Port of Miami. Parks occupy much of both keys, providing facilities for golf, tennis, softball, picnicking, and basking on the beach. Also on the Keys are several marinas, an assortment of water-oriented tourist attractions, and the laid-back village where Richard Nixon set up his presidential vacation compound.

Vizcaya Museum and Gardens, an Italian palazzo perched on the shore of Biscayne Bay, was the brainchild and winter home of Chicago industrialist James Deering. He designed his estate in Italian Renaissance style, with acres of elaborate, formal gardens and fountains that are unrivaled outside of Europe. The house contains 34 rooms of 15th- through 19th-century antique furniture, paintings, and sculptures in Renaissance, Baroque, Rococo, and Neoclassic styles. Guided Tours are available. *3251 S. Miami Ave., Miami, tel. 305/579–2813 or 305/579–2808. Open daily except Christmas. Admission charged.*

Weeks Air Museum is undergoing renovations and may be back in operation after January of 1994; the gift shop, however, remains open and currently explores the history of aviation with displays of a World War I–vintage Sopwith Camel (of Snoopy fame), a B-17 Flying Fortress bomber, and P-51 Mustangs from World War II. *14710 S.W. 128th St., South Dade, tel. 305/233–5197. Open daily. Admission charged.*

HOTELS AND INNS

Over the years, everything from small inns to glittering high-rise condominiums and chain motels to luxurious resorts have sprung up to meet the diverse needs of Miami's stream of visitors. High-season rates start shortly before Thanksgiving and stay in effect until after spring break. Off-season rates can be a real bargain, with the best values available just after Easter until Memorial Day. The categories below are based on the high-season price—off-peak rates can be a full 25%–40% lower. Price categories for double occupancy, without 8%–12% tax, are *Moderate,* $90–$120, and *Inexpensive,* $50–$90.

COCONUT GROVE **Doubletree Hotel at Coconut Grove.** Since a thorough renovation in 1988, this casually elegant high rise with bay views matches large, airy rooms—most with balconies—with modern furnishings and excellent guest facilities. *2649 S. Bayshore Dr., 33133, tel. 305/858–2500 or 800/222–TREE. 190 rooms, including 32 no-smoking rooms. Restaurant, piano bar, pool, 2 tennis courts, sun deck. AE, DC, MC, V. Moderate.*

CORAL GABLES **Hotel Place St. Michel.** Art Nouveau chandeliers, hand-loomed rugs, and antiques imported from England, Scotland, and France are hallmarks of this intimate, historic, low-rise inn situated in the heart of downtown Coral Gables. *162 Alcazar Ave., 33134, tel. 305/444–1666 or 800/247–8526. 28 rooms. Continental breakfast included, restaurant, lounge, snack shop. AE, DC, MC, V. Moderate.*

DOWNTOWN MIAMI **Best Western/PLM Marina Park Hotel.** Owned by a French chain, this hotel boasts tropically furnished rooms and an unbeatable location, just across the street from the Bayside Marketplace shopping and entertainment plaza. The best views are from east rooms overlooking the Port of Miami. *340 Biscayne Blvd., 33132, tel. 305/371–4400 or 800/528–1234. 200 rooms. Restaurant, bar, pool. AE, DC, MC, V. Inexpensive.*

Hotel Occidental Parc. This elegant high-rise hotel is right on the Miami River. *100 S.E. 4th St., 33131, tel. 305/374–5100 or 800/521–5100. 87 suites, 44 rooms. Restaurant, lounge, pool, room safes, minibars. AE, DC, MC, V.*

Hyatt Regency Hotel. This plush 24-story hotel adjoins the James L. Knight International Center and is within walking distance of downtown Miami. It's also within sight of the Peoplemover station, which will take you to the Metro Rail. The best views of the bay are from east-facing rooms. *400 S.E. 2nd Ave. 33131, tel 305/358–1234. 615 rooms. 43 no-smoking rooms. 17 rooms handicapped accessible. 2 restaurants, bar, pool, meeting rooms. AE, DC, MC, V. Moderate.*

Miami River Inn. This striking historic inn (the oldest continuously operating inn south of St. Augustine) is a 10-minute walk across the 1st Street Bridge to the heart of downtown. Second- and third-story rooms have stunning views of the city; avoid the tiny rooms in building D. *118 S.W. South River Dr., 33130, tel. 305/325–0045. 40 rooms. Continental breakfast included, pool, Jacuzzi. AE, MC, V. Inexpensive.*

MIAMI BEACH **Bay Harbor Inn.** Down-home hospitality is offered by this family-owned and -operated inn set along Indian Creek in Bay Harbor Islands. The mood is elegant but relaxed, and antiques decorate the airy rooms. *9660 E. Bay Harbor Dr., Bay Harbor Islands 33154, tel. 305/868–4141. 35 rooms. Continental breakfast included. 2 restaurants, lounge, pool. AE, DC, MC, V. Moderate.*

Beekman Hotel. Located seaside and just two blocks south of Bal Harbour Shoppes, this high-rise hotel offers studios, one- and two-bedroom units, with full kitchens and balconies. *9499 Collins Ave., Surfside 33154, tel. 305/861–4801 or 800/237–9367. 125 apartments. Snack bar/café, pool, beach. AE, MC, V. Moderate.*

Quality Inn Shawnee Miami Beach Resort. This high-rise resort is smack on the beach in the revitalized heart of Miami Beach. Despite its chain affiliation, the modern rooms are spacious and well appointed. *4343 Collins Ave., 33140, tel. 305/532–3311 or 800/221–2222. 475 rooms, including 10 no-smoking. 2 restaurants, coffee shop, snack bar, 2 lounges, pool, beauty salon, gift shop. AE, D, DC, MC, V. Moderate.*

Art Deco Hotels. This trio of restored, low-rise hotels—the **Hotel Cardozo** (1939), **Hotel Carlyle** (1941), and **Hotel Leslie** (1937)—are brazenly bathed in Art Deco pinks, whites, and grays. The rooms in all three are small but reasonably priced; the best face seaward. *1244 Ocean Dr., Miami Beach 33139, tel. 305/534–2135 or 800/338–9076. 168 rooms. Restaurants, bars with live entertainment in the Carlyle and Cardozo. AE, DC, MC, V. Inexpensive.*

NORTH DADE **Holiday Inn–North Miami-Golden Glades.** Location is the main draw here—it's only 2 miles from the beach, Calder Race Course, and Joe Robbie Stadium, and just a skip away from the highway. *148 N.W. 167th St., Miami 33169, tel. 305/949–1441 or 800/HOLIDAY. 163 rooms, including 18 no-smoking rooms. Restaurant, lounge, pool. AE, DC, MC, V. Moderate.*

MOTELS

MODERATE **Best Western Miami Airport Inn** (1550 N.W. Le Jeune Rd., 33126, tel. 305/871–2345). 190 rooms; restaurant, lounge, pool. **Courtyard by Marriott–Miami West** (3929 N.W. 79th Ave., 33166, tel. 305/477–8118 or 800/321–2211). 133 rooms; restaurant, lounge, pool, whirlpool, fitness center, coin laundry.

INEXPENSIVE **Budgetel Inn** (3501 N.W. Le Jeune Rd., 33142, tel. 305/871–1777 or 800/428–3438). 152 rooms; Continental breakfast included, pool, coin laundry. **Days Inn** (3401 N.W. Le Jeune Rd., 33142, tel. 305/871–4221 or 800/325–2525). 155 rooms; restaurant, pool. **Days Inn–Oceanside** (4299 Collins Ave., 33140, tel. 305/673–1513 or

800/356–3017). 133 rooms; restaurant, lounge, pool, coin laundry. **Hampton Inn** (2500 Brickell Ave., 33129, tel. 305/854–2070 or 800/HAMPTON). 69 rooms; Continental breakfast included, pool. **Quality Inn–Airport** (2373 N.W. Le Jeune Rd., 33142, tel. 305/871–3230 or 800/666–0668). 160 rooms; restaurant, pool.

DINING

You can eat your way around the world in Greater Miami, enjoying just about every kind of cuisine imaginable in upscale bistros or at sidewalk stands. The waters off South Florida's coastline are rich in mahimahi, snapper, pompano, grouper, yellowfin tuna, and swordfish. Stone crabs and conch are two other local delicacies. Tropical fruits grow well here, and you'll find sauces made from papayas, mangoes, avocados, guavas, and coconuts.

One of Miami's best bargains is the "early bird dinner," where, for a fixed price—usually under $15—you get a full meal, which includes soup or salad, a choice of entrées with vegetables and potato, dessert, and a soft drink. Almost all restaurants offer an early-bird; the only catch is that you usually have to be seated before 6:30 PM. Call ahead to ask whether this special is offered and by what time you must be seated. And make reservations—the early-bird dinner is very popular and often very crowded.

Except where noted, casual neat clothing is acceptable at the restaurants listed below. Price categories per person, not including 6% tax, service, and drinks, are *Moderate,* $15–$25, and *Inexpensive,* under $15.

DOWNTOWN MIAMI **East Coast Fisheries.** This family-run restaurant features fresh seafood caught by its own 38-boat fleet in the Keys. From tables along the second-floor balcony, watch the cooks grill your dinner in the open kitchen below. *360 W. Flagler St., tel. 305/373–5515. AE, MC, V. Moderate.*

Las Tapas. Ordering different *tapas*—"little dishes" in Spanish—allows you to create your own smorgasbord of tastes in a single meal. Tapas to try include *la tostada* (smoked salmon and capers on melba toast) and *pincho de pollo a la plancha* (grilled chicken marinated in brandy); you can also order standard-size Spanish entrées. *Bayside Marketplace, 401 Biscayne Blvd., tel. 305/372–2737. AE, DC, MC, V. Moderate.*

Granny Feelgood's. "Granny" is a shrewd gentleman named Irving Field, who caters to health-conscious lawyers, office workers, and backpackers with such specials as spinach fettuccine, grilled tofu, and grilled chicken salads. *190 S.E. 1st Ave., tel. 305/358–6233. No smoking. AE, MC, V. Closed Sun. Inexpensive.*

LITTLE HAVANA **Acapulco.** Authentic Mexican food is the specialty at this popular but intimate adobe restaurant. Homemade chips and chunky guacamole prepare the way for such entrées as *carnitas asada* (grilled pork in lemon and butter), *mole poblano* (chicken in chocolate sauce), and combination platters of tacos, burritos, and enchiladas. *727 N.W. Unity Blvd. (N.W. 27th Ave.), tel. 305/642–6961. AE, DC, MC, V. Moderate.*

Islas Canarias. Dishes from the Canary Islands and Cuba—from ham hocks with boiled potatoes to palomilla steak and fried plantains—are featured at this gathering place for Cuban poets, pop-music stars, and media personalities. *285 N.W. Unity Blvd. (N.W. 27th Ave.), tel. 305/649–0440. No credit cards. Inexpensive.*

MIAMI BEACH **Pineapples.** Art deco pink brightens this health-food restaurant where specialties include lasagna filled with tofu and mushrooms, and large salads brimming with sprouts. *530 Arthur Godfrey Rd., tel. 305/532–9731. No smoking. AE, MC, V. Moderate.*

The News Cafe. Beach views plus a clientele that likes to schmooze have made the News Cafe the hippest joint on Ocean Drive. Stop in for a drink or a light meal—anything from bagels to chocolate fondue. *800 Ocean Dr., tel. 305/538–6397. AE, DC, MC, V. Inexpensive.*

SOUTH MIAMI **New Chinatown.** The 200-seat dining room at New Chinatown, located southwest of Coral Gables, offers bright and busy family dining. The vast menu—drawn from Cantonese, Mandarin, Szechuan, and Teppan regional choices—features more than 60 meatless entrées. *5958 S. Dixie Hwy., tel. 305/662–5649. AE, MC, V. Moderate.*

SOUTHWEST MIAMI **Mykonos.** Only a few Greek travel posters offset the spartan atmosphere of this family-operated restaurant near Coconut Grove. The menu, though, is first-rate: It includes marinated lamb and chicken dishes, calamari and octopus sautéed in wine and onions, and sumptuous Greek salads brimming with feta cheese and olives. *1201 Coral Way, tel. 305/856–3140. AE. Inexpensive.*

WEST DADE **Shula's.** Coach Don Shula led the Miami Dolphins in their perfect 1972 season, and his cedar-shingled restaurant on the grounds of Miami Lakes is crammed with the appropriate memorabilia (including an autographed playbook from former president Nixon). The menu ranges from black Angus beef to prime rib and fish—all of which seems an afterthought in season when the topic of conversation is (unabashedly) football. *15400 N.W. 77th Ave., tel. 305/822–2325. Reservations advised. AE, DC, MC, V. Moderate.*

SHOPPING

Greater Miami has more than a dozen major shopping malls, an international free zone, and hundreds of miles of commercial streets lined with shopping centers and storefronts. Major department stores abound, with most malls boasting at least three.

SHOPPING DISTRICTS Many garment manufacturers sell their products in the more than 30 factory outlets and discount fashion stores in the Miami Fashion District, located east of I–95, along 5th Avenue from 25th to 29th streets.

The **Miami Free Zone** (MFZ) (5 minutes west of Miami International Airport off the Dolphin Expwy. [Rte. 836], 2305 N.W. 107th Ave., tel. 305/591–4300) is an international wholesale trade center with products from 75 countries, including clothing, computers, cosmetics, liquor, and perfumes. You can buy goods duty-free for export or pay duty on goods you intend to keep here in the United States.

Bayside Marketplace (401 Biscayne Blvd., tel. 305/577–3344) is for people-watching as well as shopping. There's always a medley of cheerful street performers at this large waterfront mall/entertainment plaza. Be sure to stop in at the Pier 5 Market, which showcases artisans and inventors. The mall adjoins a 145-slip marina, where you can see luxurious yachts moored and ride in an authentic 36-foot-long Venetian gondola.

FLEA MARKETS South Florida's largest flea market, The New Opalocka/Hialeah Flea Market (12705 Le Jeune Rd., tel. 305/688–8080) showcases more than 1200 vendors and 10 different restaurants.

OUTDOOR ACTIVITIES

BEACHES Miami Beach is famous for its broad sandy expanse, which extends 10 miles from Haulover Cut to Government Cut. A wide boardwalk, which is popular with strollers and joggers, can be found between 21st and 46th streets. All the city beaches are free, and during the winter and summer lifeguards are on duty every day (except at Bal Harbour and Surfside beaches).

BIKING Dade County has about 100 miles of off-road bicycling trails. Bike rentals can be found at Dade Cycle (3216 Grand Ave., Coconut Grove, tel. 305/444–5997).

BOATING AND SAILING Bayside Marketplace (tel. 305/888–3002) offers catamaran cruises on Biscayne Bay. Easy Sailing (Dinner Key Marina, Coconut Grove, tel. 305/858–4001) rents 19- to 127-foot boats by the hour or for the whole day. It also offers motorboat and sailing lessons, scuba certification courses, and deep-sea fishing.

FISHING Florida's waters abound with mahimahi, pompano, snapper, grouper, yellowfin tuna, and swordfish. Half- and full-day fishing charters are available with Bayside Cruises (Bayside Marketplace, tel. 305/888–3002), Chuck Smith Charters (Bayside Marketplace, tel. 305/378–2332), Kelley Fishing Fleet (Haulover Marina, Miami Beach, tel. 305/945–3801), and Miami Water Transit & Charter (Eden Roc Yacht & Charter Center, Miami Beach, tel. 305/751–2126).

GOLF Florida is famous for its excellent and popular golf courses; following are some in the Miami area. The Doral Hotel Golf Club's Blue course is a stop on the PGA Tour. Open to the public, par 72, total holes 99, greens fees (4400 N.W. 87th Ave., Miami, tel. 305/592– 2000). The Turnberry Isle Country Club courses feature double greens reminiscent of St. Andrews, Scotland, and other special design features. Open to hotel guests and club members only, par 72, total holes 36, greens fees, tee times two days in advance (199th St., and Biscayne Blvd., North Miami Beach, tel. 305/932–6200). The Miami Lakes Golf Club features large greens and elevated tees. Open to the public, par 72, total holes 36, greens fees (N.W. 154th St., Miami Lakes, tel. 305/821–1150). The Key Biscayne Golf Club (also known as The Links at Key Biscayne) is rated highly among U.S. public courses. Open to the public, par 72, total holes 18, greens fees (3500 Crandon Blvd., Key Biscayne, tel. 305/361–9139).

SNORKELING AND SCUBA DIVING Diving enthusiasts will be pleasantly surprised by the wide range of both natural and artificial reefs available in the Greater Miami area. Biscayne National Park (Canal Dr., east of Homestead, tel. 305/247–2400) R.J. Diving Ventures (Sunset Harbour Marina, Miami Beach, tel. 305/940–1182) and V & P Diving Ventures (Miami Beach, tel. 305/448–2905) both offer snorkeling and diving excursions, instruction, and equipment rental.

TENNIS Greater Miami has 11 public tennis centers. All of them charge nonresidents an hourly fee. Many local high schools have tennis courts that can be used for free if they are unoccupied and it's after school hours. Courts can be rented in Coral Gables at the Biltmore Tennis Center (1150 Anastasia Ave.,

Coral Gables, tel. 305/460–5360); in Miami Beach at the Flamingo Park Tennis Center (1100 12th St., Miami Beach, tel. 305/673–7761); and in Metro-Dade at the International Tennis Center (7300 Crandon Blvd., Key Biscayne, tel. 305/361–8633).

WALKING The **Historical Museum of Southern Florida** (101 W. Flagler St., Miami, tel. 305/375–1492) conducts a series of tours throughout the Greater Miami area. The Miami Design Preservation League (661 Washington Ave., tel. 305/672–2014) offers a 90-minute tour of the Art Deco District on Saturday mornings at 10:30 AM. Also available is the League's *Art Deco District Guide,* with six detailed walking and driving tours of the Art Deco District. Paul George, a history professor at Florida Atlantic University and the University of Miami, and a former president of the Florida Historical Society, leads 3½-hour walking tours of Coconut Grove, Coral Gables, Little Havana, Miami's old city cemetery, the Miami Beach Art Deco District, and Southside. His "Explore Miami's History" tour takes place on Saturdays from 9 AM to 1 PM. For reservations, call 305/858–6021.

ENTERTAINMENT

During the busy winter season, Miami's calendar is jammed with cultural events, gallery exhibits, concerts, lectures, and dance and theater performances. *The Miami Herald* publishes information on the performing arts every Friday in the Weekend Section. Other good sources are *Miami Today,* a free weekly newspaper available each Thursday; *New Times,* another free weekly paper; and the *Greater Miami Calendar of Events* (for a free copy, call 305/375–4634).

CONCERTS Greater Miami moves to many beats. The New World Symphony (541 Lincoln Rd., tel. 305/673–3330; box office tel. 305/673–3331) is an advanced training orchestra for gifted young musicians. From October through May, the Philharmonic Orchestra of Florida (174 E. Flagler St., tel. 305/945–5180) performs classical music and pop concerts. The Concert Association of Greater Miami (555 Hank Meyer Blvd., tel.

305/532–3491) presents a series of classical artists, while chamber concerts by internationally known guest ensembles are offered by the Friends of Chamber Music (44 W. Flagler St., tel. 305/372–2975).

DANCE Edward Villella's Miami City Ballet (905 Lincoln Rd., Miami Beach, tel. 305/532–7713) performs modern jazz and ballet from September through March. The earthy qualities of the flamenco can be seen in the refreshing choreography of the Spanish dance company, Ballet Flamenco La Rosa (tel. 305/672–0552). Classical ballet is performed by the Miami Repertoire Ballet (tel. 305/251–5822).

COMEDY CLUBS Laugh away your evenings at Uncle Funny's Comedy Club (Holiday Inn-Calder, 21485 N.W. 27th Ave., tel. 305/624–7266), Improv Comedy Club and Restaurant (Cocowalk mall, 3014 Grand Ave., tel. 305/441–8200). Improvisational comedy theater takes place every weekend at Mental Floss (3138 Commodore Plaza, Coconut Grove, tel. 305/448–1011).

OPERA The Greater Miami Opera (1200 Coral Way, tel. 305/854–7890) is a 50-year-old world-class opera company. Its International Series stars opera luminaries. You'll save money if you ask for tickets for its National Series, which uses the same sets and chorus but features rising young singers in the principal roles.

THEATER National touring productions of hit broadway shows can be seen at the Jackie Gleason Theater of the Performing Arts (1700 Washington Ave., Miami Beach, tel. 305/673–7311). Other venues include the Actor's Playhouse (8851 S.W. 107 Ave., tel. 305/595–0010), Gusman Center for the Performing Arts (174 E. Flagler St., tel. 305/372–0925), the innovative Coconut Grove Playhouse (3500 Main Hwy., tel. 305/442–2662), and the Minorca Playhouse (232 Minorca Ave., Coral Gables, tel. 305/446–1116), home to the Florida Shakespeare Festival.

SPECTATOR SPORTS Daily listings of local sports events can be found in the sports section of *The Miami Herald*. Miami's NBA team, the Miami Heat (tel. 305/577–HEAT), can be seen at the Miami Arena. Football fans can watch the Miami Dolphins play at Joe Robbie Stadium (2269 N.W. 199th St., tel. 305/620–2578) or the University of Miami Hurricanes play at the Orange Bowl (1400 N.W. 4th St., tel. 305/643–7100). Baseball followers can catch Florida's expansion team, the Marlins, who play at Joe Robbie Stadium. Tickets can be purchased at the stadium box office or over the phone from Ticketmaster (tel. 305/350–5050).

Minneapolis and St. Paul
Minnesota

innesota's Minneapolis and St. Paul are known as the Twin Cities, but they are hardly identical. St. Paul has been described as the last of the Eastern cities, with its Victorian and Art Deco architecture, the domes of the State Capitol and St. Paul Cathedral, and the tooting steamboats on its 29 miles of Mississippi riverfront. Minneapolis is brasher and busier, with several new downtown skyscrapers, a contemporary sculpture garden, and a revitalized Warehouse District with appealing shops, galleries, and restaurants.

Sibling rivalry has rewarded the 2.2 million people of the area with an envious metropolitan lifestyle. Both communities enjoy world-class orchestras, art museums, and a vibrant theater community that offers everything from Kabuki to Neil Simon. In both cities, residents have access to climate-controlled skyway systems, allowing them to drive downtown, park, and go about their daily business without once setting foot outdoors—a blessing during the long winters. Sports fans also fare well here, thanks to the local professional basketball, baseball, and football teams.

The jewel of the Twin Cities is a lake system that enhances the residential areas and provides the foundation for parks filled with jogging and biking trails, beaches, and public docks. Minneapolis alone has 22 lakes. Although commonly associated with the rich heritage of its Irish, German, and Scandinavian pioneers, the area offers a cultural diversity these days that extends from its first Native American citizens to its most recent Southeast Asian settlers.

ESSENTIAL INFORMATION

WHEN TO GO Spring and fall are usually the gentlest seasons, with warm days and mild nights. Average maximum temperatures in April and May range between 56° and 68°, while average minimum temperatures fall between 36° and 48°. With its beautiful foliage, fall has become an especially popular time for tourists. Fall average maximum temperatures range from 59° to 72° and average minimum temperatures fall between 41° and 52°.

July and August can be humid, with temperatures usually at least in the mid-80s and several days that near 100°. Summer mosquitoes can also be a nuisance. Winter visitors will find daily temperatures that average in the teens, but these can dip below 0° with wind-chill factored in. With an average snowfall of 42 inches, January, February, and March are the best times for cross-country skiing.

FESTIVALS AND SEASONAL EVENTS **Late Jan.– early Feb.:** St. Paul Winter Carnival features ice sculptures and entertainment. **Early June:** Taste of Minnesota is four days of feasting, plus a big Fourth of July fireworks display on the State Capitol lawn. **Mid-July–Aug.:** Summerfest features Viennese waltzes, food fairs, and music at Minneapolis's Peavey outdoor plaza. **Late Aug.:** The Minnesota State Fair is held in St. Paul. Contact local tourist offices for information on events (*see* Tourist Offices, *below*).

BARGAINS You can ride an old street car near Lake Harriet in Minneapolis for only 75¢. Every six weeks, the Minneapolis Warehouse District hosts a free "gallery crawl," with show openings and refreshments (contact New North Artscape, tel. 612/337–5198). Many of the theater events offer senior-citizen discounts and lower prices for tickets sold shortly before curtain time. The Mississippi Mile public parkway on the downtown Minneapolis riverbanks has walking and biking trails, picnic spots, and a hotline for free events (tel. 612/342–1231).

TOURIST OFFICES The St. Paul Convention and Visitors Bureau (101 Norwest Center, 55 E. 5th St., St. Paul 55101, tel. 612/297–6985 or 800/627–6101) has a main information booth at Saint Paul Center (445 Minnesota St., tel. 612/223–5409). The Minneapolis Convention and Visitors Association (1219 Marquette Ave. S, Minneapolis 55403, tel. 612/348–4313 or 800/445–7412) and the

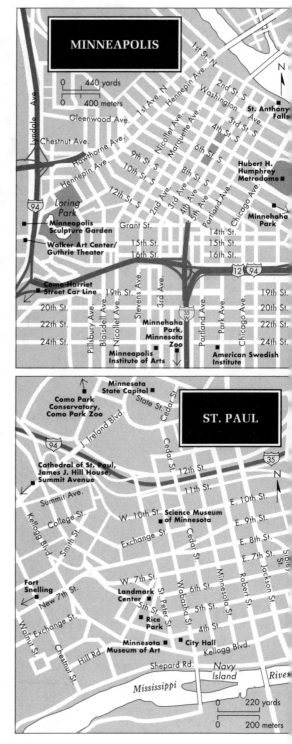

Minnesota Office of Tourism (375 Jackson St., 250 Skyway Level, St. Paul 55101, tel. 612/296–5029 or 800/657–3700) are also helpful.

EMERGENCIES Police, fire, and **ambulance:** Dial 911. **Hospitals:** Hennepin County Medical Center (701 Park Ave. S, downtown Minneapolis, tel. 612/347–3131). **Doctors:** Referral Service (tel. 612/291–1209). Road-condition information (tel. 612/296–3076).

ARRIVING AND DEPARTING

BY PLANE The Minneapolis–St. Paul International Airport (tel. 612/726–5555) lies south of the cities on Rte. 5, 8 miles from downtown St. Paul and 10 miles from downtown Minneapolis. The Metropolitan Transit Commission (tel. 612/827–7733) provides buses between the airport and both cities. Fares during weekday peak hours are $1.35; fares during weekday nonpeak hours and during the weekends are $1.10. Taxis to and from the airport take about 20 minutes from both downtown St. Paul (about $13) and downtown Minneapolis (up to $18).

To drive from the airport, take West 7th Street or Shepard Road to downtown St. Paul; for downtown Minneapolis, take Route 5 east to Route 55 north, or Route 5 west to I–35W north. Major car-rental companies are located near the baggage-claim area.

BY TRAIN The Twin Cities Amtrak depot in St. Paul (730 Transfer Rd., tel. 800/USA–RAIL) serves both cities.

BY BUS Greyhound Lines (tel. 800/231–2222) serves both cities at St. Paul Greyhound terminal (7th St. at St. Peter St., tel. 612/222–0509) and Minneapolis Greyhound terminal (29 N. 9th St, tel. 612/371–3320).

BY CAR I–94 runs east–west through downtown Minneapolis and St. Paul and converges with I–35 (I–35E into St. Paul and I–35W into Minneapolis), a north–south artery.

GETTING AROUND

Minneapolis is spread out. You can explore downtown on foot, but for the city's far-flung sights you'll need to drive or take a bus or a cab. Downtown St. Paul and its major sights are easily explored on foot; only a few sights require a car or bus.

BY CAR In Minneapolis, Hennepin Avenue crosses the Mississippi to divide the north and south ends of town and becomes a main downtown thoroughfare. Another major artery is Lyndale Avenue, running south from the river. In St. Paul, Summit and Grand avenues run parallel with I–94; both end at the river.

BY BUS The Metropolitan Transit Commission (MTC, tel. 612/827–7733) runs buses in both cities. Fares are $1.10 during peak hours, 85¢ during nonpeak hours. Exact fare or tokens are required. The MTC runs two transit stores (719 Marquette St., in downtown Minneapolis; 101 E. 5th St., on the skyway level, in downtown St. Paul), where you can pick up schedules and buy tokens.

BY TAXI Taxis must be ordered by phone or hired at cabstands. Fares start at $1.75 and $1.30 for each mile. In Minneapolis, try Blue and White (tel. 612/333–3331) and Yellow (tel. 612/824–4444). In St. Paul, contact Yellow (tel. 612/222–4433) and City Wide (tel. 612/292–1616). Town Taxi (tel. 612/331–8294) serves both cities and all suburbs.

REST STOPS Public rest rooms are available at community centers in parks in both cities. Saint Paul Center and Town Square Park (Minnesota St.) in downtown St. Paul also have public rest rooms.

GUIDED TOURS Most tours are active between Memorial Day and Labor Day. Gray Line (tel. 612/591–0999), Airport Express (tel. 612/827–7777), and Metro Connections (tel. 612/333–8687) have tours of both cities. Mississippi River tours are provided by the Padelford Packet Boat Co. (tel. 612/227–1100) aboard the *Anson Northrup* and *Josiah Snelling*, modern stern-wheelers modeled after 19th-century Mississippi riverboats.

Cruises on Minneapolis's Lake Harriet are offered aboard the stern-wheeler *Queen of the Lakes* (tel. 612/348–4825 or 612/348–2248).

EXPLORING

MINNEAPOLIS Downtown Minneapolis is easily walkable in any season. If the weather turns truly bitter, the skyway system connects hundreds of shops and restaurants. Following are the main attractions in or just south of downtown.

Minneapolis Institute of Arts. More than 80,000 works from every age and culture are on display here, with exhibits of photography, sculpture, paintings, drawings, and prints; free tours daily. *2400 3rd Ave. S, tel. 612/870–3131. Open Tues.–Sun., except major holidays. Admission free.*

St. Anthony Falls, on the edge of downtown, are harnessed by dams and bypassed by the Upper St. Anthony Lock, which allows river traffic to reach the city. An observation deck and a small visitor center have good views of lock operations and exhibits on the Mississippi. *Foot of Portland Ave., tel. 612/333–5336. Observation deck open Apr.–Oct., daily. Admission free.*

Walker Art Center. This outstanding contemporary art museum features a strong permanent collection of paintings, sculpture, prints, and photography. The center offers cultural programs regularly and adjoins the country's largest regional theater, The Guthrie (*see* Entertainment, below). Across from the center is the Minneapolis Sculpture Garden, the largest urban sculpture garden in the nation, with 40 fanciful creations in tree-lined plazas. The garden is linked to Loring Park and downtown Minneapolis by a footbridge. *Center: Hennepin Ave. and Vineland Pl., tel. 612/375–7600. Open Tues.–Sun., except major holidays. Admission charged, senior citizens free. Garden open daily. Admission free.*

Outside downtown, **Minnehaha Park,** on the Mississippi near the airport, is home to the charming Minnehaha Falls. The Minnehaha Parkway, which follows Minnehaha Creek, offers 15 miles of jogging, biking, and roller-skating trails to Lake Harriet. *From downtown, drive on I–35W south to Rte. 62 east and then get on Rte. 55; or take Bus 7A, 7B, or 7C. Open daily. Admission free.*

OUTSIDE MINNEAPOLIS **Minnesota Zoo.** This delightful zoo contains more than 1,700 animals and more than 2,000 plant varieties; it features six trail systems, a beaver exhibit, a koala lodge, a bird show, and camel rides. *13000 Zoo Blvd., Apple Valley, tel. 612/431–9200 or 612/432–9000. From downtown drive on I–35E south to Cedar Ave. and follow zoo signs, or take Bus 57. Open daily. Admission charged.*

ST. PAUL Visitors can easily explore downtown on foot, either on the streets or in the skyway system (bounded by Kellogg Blvd. at the river, and 8th, Wacouta, and St. Peter Sts.). Buses can take you from downtown up the hill to the State Capitol, St. Paul Cathedral, and the shops on Grand Avenue. The following highlights are arranged from north to south around downtown St. Paul.

City Hall. This 1931, 20-story building is known for its Art Deco interior, its 85-foot-long Memorial Hall, and the onyx *Indian God of Peace,* standing 36 feet high and weighing 60 tons. *4th St. between St. Peter and Wabasha Sts., tel. 612/298–4012. Open weekdays. Admission free.*

Rice Park. West of the museum is St. Paul's oldest urban park, only one block square. The park is a favorite with locals, who eat lunch here in warm weather. Each winter, the city's Winter Carnival ice-carving contest is held here.

Landmark Center. This towering old federal courts building of Romanesque Revival design faces Rice Park. It features a skylighted six-story indoor courtyard with stained-glass skylights and a marble-tiled cortile. *75 W. 5th St., tel. 612/292–3225. Free guided tours, tel. 612/292–3230. Open daily. Admission free.*

Science Museum of Minnesota. This science-technology center and natural-history museum has exhibits emphasizing hands-on participation—making it very popular with children. *30 E. 10th St., tel. 612/221–9488. Open daily. Admission charged.*

Minnesota State Capitol. This noble 1905 structure contains more than 25 varieties of marble, sandstone, limestone, and granite, and its 223-foot-high dome is the world's largest unsupported marble dome. *75 Constitution Ave., tel. 612/297–3521. Open daily. Free guided tours daily.*

WEST OF DOWNTOWN **St. Paul Cathedral.** Styled after St. Peter's in Rome, this Classical Renaissance granite domed church, completed in 1915, seats 3,000 and has stunning stained-glass windows. *239 Selby Ave., at Summit Ave., tel. 612/228–1766. Open daily. Admission free.*

Summit Avenue. This 5-mile stretch of stately homes and mansions, from the cathedral to the Mississippi, is the nation's longest expanse of intact residential Victorian architecture. F. Scott Fitzgerald lived at 599 Summit Avenue in 1918 when he wrote *This Side of Paradise;* the Governor's Mansion is at 1006 Summit Avenue. You can visit the **James J. Hill House,** an elaborate 1891 mansion that belonged to the former railroad magnate. *240 Summit Ave., tel. 612/297–2555. Open Wed.–Sat. Admission charged.*

Como Park. This urban playground is home to a lake, the Como Park Conservatory (tel. 612/489–1740), the Como Park Zoo (tel. 612/488– 5572), picnic areas, walking trails, and tennis and swimming facilities. *By car, take I–94 to Snelling Ave., north to Midway Pkwy., then east to the park. Open daily. Admission free.*

HOTELS AND INNS

Where you want to stay may well depend on whether or not you have a car. Accommodations are cheaper outside the metropolitan area, but downtown locations offer closer proximity to the main sights. When you go also determines where you want to stay— some hotels are attached to downtown shopping and entertainment centers by skyways to avoid the icy winters. Bargains can some-

times be found by staying at bed-and-breakfasts in the cities. For information on B&Bs, contact the Minnesota Office of Tourism (tel. 612/296–5029 or 800/657–3700). Price categories for double occupancy, excluding 6% tax, are *Moderate,* $50–$90, and *Inexpensive,* under $50.

MINNEAPOLIS **Best Western Normandy Inn.** This homey little hotel tucked between skyscrapers is no more than a 10-minute walk from the Metrodome, Convention Center, and Orchestra Hall. *405 S. 8th St., 55404, tel. 612/370–1400 or 800/372–3131. 357 rooms. 2 restaurants, piano bar, free van transport downtown. AE, D, DC, MC, V. Moderate.*

Best Western Regency Plaza Hotel. The most attractive feature here is the busy downtown address—next door to the new Target Center and a block away from shopping and entertainment. *41 N. 10th St., 55403, tel. 800/423– 4100. 186 rooms, 7 suites. Restaurant, pool, free downtown shuttle bus. AE, D, DC, MC, V. Moderate.*

Holiday Inn Metrodome. A 10-minute bus ride from downtown, this showy hotel is located in the heart of a theater and entertainment district and near both the Metrodome and the University of Minnesota. *1500 Washington Ave. S, 55454, tel. 612/333–4646 or 800/465–4329. 265 rooms, 22 suites. Free transportation by appointment. AE, D, DC, MC, V. Moderate.*

ST. PAUL **Days Inn Civic Center.** This clean, no-nonsense downtown lodging is usually filled with folks who are attending activities across the street at the St. Paul Civic Center. *175 W. 7th St., 55102, tel. 612/292–8929 or 800/635–4766. 200 rooms, 3 suites. 24-hr restaurant. AE, D, DC, MC, V. Moderate.*

Excell Inn of St. Paul. This three-story hotel is near the Sun Ray Shopping Center on the eastern side of St. Paul, off I–94 and White Bear Avenue. *1739 Old Hudson Rd., 55106, tel. 612/771–5566 or 800/356–8013. 101 rooms, some designated no-smoking. Senior-citizen discount for those 55 and older. AE, DC, MC, V. Moderate.*

Sunwood Inn Bandana Square. Near I–94, this reliable hotel is connected by skyway to Bandana Square, a popular shopping center. *1010 West Bandana Blvd., 55108, tel. 612/647–1637. 103 rooms, 6 suites. Pool, whirlpool, sauna. AE, DC, MC, V. Moderate.*

MOTELS

The following are in the *Inexpensive* price category:

MINNEAPOLIS **Burnsville Super 8** (1101 Burnsville Pkwy., Burnsville 55337, tel. 612/894–3400 or 800/800–8000). 67 rooms; Continental breakfast included. **Days Inn University** (2407 University Ave. SE, 55414, tel. 612/623–3999 or 800/325–2525). 130 rooms; Continental breakfast included. **Prime Rate Motel** (12850 W. Frontage Rd., Burnsville 55337, tel. 612/894–8554 or 800/358–8554). 98 rooms; Continental breakfast included, pool.

ST. PAUL **Comfort Inn Roseville** (2715 Long Lake Rd., Roseville 55113, tel. 612/636–5800 or 800/221–2222). 118 rooms; Continental breakfast included, no-smoking rooms. **Days Inn Roseville** (2550 Cleveland Ave. N, Roseville 55113, tel. 612/636–6730 or 800/325–2525). 115 rooms; Continental breakfast included, no-smoking rooms. **Motel 6** (2300 Cleveland Ave. N, Roseville 55113, tel. 612/639–3988). 113 rooms.

DINING

The Twin Cities have a growing number of northern Italian and Southeast Asian eateries. You'll also find many comfortable neighborhood spots, known either for ethnic specialties or pleasant home cooking that seems to qualify as American cuisine these days: salads, pasta, burgers, and homemade pies. Most of the listings below will accommodate health-conscious diets if given advance notice. On many local menus, vegetarian entrées and fresh salads are offered. Price categories per person, excluding 6% tax, service, and drinks, are *Moderate,* $8–$12, and *Inexpensive,* under $8.

MINNEAPOLIS **Black Forest Inn.** Families, students, and artists all love the hearty German cuisine—try the schnitzel with potato pancakes and applesauce—and the varied selection of beers on tap and in bottles. In summer, be sure to request a table in the grape arbor. *1 E. 26th St., tel. 612/872–0812. AE, DC, MC, V. Moderate.*

Chez Bananas. This offbeat storefront café in the chic Warehouse District balances savory Caribbean food with some oddball decorations: vinyl bats, inflatable palm trees, and windup toys. *129 N. 4th St., tel. 612/340–0032. D, DC, MC, V. Moderate.*

Chez Paul. For the feel of a French café without spending too many francs, stick to this elegant restaurant's more casual bistro and pastry shop. *1400 Nicollet Ave. S, tel. 612/870–4212. AE, D, MC, V. Moderate.*

Loring Cafe. The Loring offers a terrific view of handsome Loring Park, vaguely bohemian decor, and a menu that includes manicotti with lamb and Chinese chicken salad with sesame–ginger dressing. *1624 Harmon Pl., tel 612/332–1617. AE, MC, V. No lunch weekends, no dinner Mon. Moderate.*

It's Greek to Me. Small and unpretentious, this bustling café serves some of the best Greek food in town. *626 W. Lake St., tel. 612/825–9922. No credit cards. Inexpensive.*

Pam Sherman's Bakery and Café. People-watchers and shoppers alike stop for lunch or a piece of irresistible chocolate cake at this bakery and deli in the trendy uptown district. *2914 Hennepin Ave. S, tel. 612/823–7269. No credit cards. Inexpensive.*

ST. PAUL **Dixie's Bar & Smokehouse.** This casual spot in the heart of the Grand Avenue retail district serves up an eclectic mix of southern cuisines, mixing Cajun, Creole, and Tex-Mex styles. *695 Grand Ave., tel. 612/222–7345. AE, D, MC, V. Moderate.*

Khyber Pass Café. An enthusiastic Afghani family serves their sometimes spicy native cuisine—including lamb and chicken dishes simmered with garlic or coriander chutney—in a sleepy St. Paul neighborhood. *1399 St.*

Clair Ave., tel. 612/698–5403. MC, V. Moderate.

Cafe Latte. Furiously popular with the post-theater crowd, this eclectic cafeteria is almost always jammed with devotees hungering for homemade soups, first-rate salads, stews, scones, chocolate desserts, and espresso drinks. *850 Grand Ave., tel. 612/224–5687. AE. Inexpensive.*

Gladstone Café. Enjoy homemade muffins and soups at this popular cafeteria on the main floor of the historic Landmark Center. *75 W. 5th St., 612/227–4704. No credit cards. Inexpensive.*

Mickey's Diner. Listed on the National Register of Historic Places, this streamlined 1930s downtown diner dishes up great breakfasts and burgers. *36 W. 7th St., tel. 612/222–5633. No credit cards. Inexpensive.*

Old City Café. The only kosher restaurant in the Twin Cities, this tiny café is also one of the area's few vegetarian restaurants, featuring Middle Eastern dishes and potato knishes. *1571 Grand Ave., tel. 612/699–5347. No credit cards. Inexpensive.*

Russian Tea House. The Tea House is a simple café that offers home-cooked Russian specialties, including a great piroshki—mild ground beef and rice baked inside a chewy, leavened roll. *1758 University Ave. W, tel. 612/646–4144. No credit cards. Inexpensive.*

SHOPPING

Museum shops often offer the best Minnesota-made wares. Try the shops at Walker Art Center in Minneapolis and Landmark Center, and the Science Museum in downtown St. Paul (*see* Exploring, *above*). Byerly's (3777 Park Center Blvd., St. Louis Park, tel. 612/929–2100), one of the most popular stores in the area, is a grandiose grocery with chandeliers, carpeted aisles, and gold-plated bird cages.

MAJOR SHOPPING DISTRICTS **Minneapolis:** Nicollet Mall, a mile-long pedestrian mall in the center of downtown, has skywalks connecting many of the shops and restaurants. This mall has Dayton's flagship department store, where downtown shoppers can pick up everything from groceries to Oriental rugs. The store offers several restaurants and snack bars. South of the city is **Southdale** (66th St. and France Ave., Edina, tel. 612/925–7885), with three department stores and 180 shops.

St. Paul: Saint Paul Center (Minnesota World Trade Center, bounded by Minnesota, Wabasha, 6th, and 8th Sts.) has major department stores and specialty shops. **Victoria Crossing:** Victoria Crossing (Grand Ave. and Victoria St.) is a collection of small shops, specialty bookstores, and restaurants. It provides an anchor for the dozens of shops that span Grand Avenue about 1 mile south of I–94.

OUTDOOR ACTIVITIES

For information on outdoor activities in the area, contact the Outdoor Recreation Information Center (tel. 612/296–6699), the Minneapolis Parks and Recreation Board (tel. 612/348–2226), and the St. Paul Parks and Recreation Board (tel. 612/292–7400).

BEACHES In Minneapolis, sun worshipers have a choice of beaches at 22 lakes; the beaches at Lake Calhoun and Lake Harriet are popular with locals. In suburban St. Paul, Square Lake and Lake Phalen beaches are often visited; Lake Phalen has a changing house and snack bar.

BIKING/JOGGING Minneapolis offers 36 miles of bike paths, including the parkways of Minnehaha Creek, Lake Calhoun, and Lake of the Isles. Joggers and bicyclists have separate marked paths, so be sure to stay on the correct side. St. Paul offers 37 miles of biking and jogging trails; favorite paths include Summit Avenue and Mississippi Boulevard.

CROSS-COUNTRY SKIING In Minneapolis you can cross-country ski in Minnehaha Park and on several golf courses. In St. Paul, Como Park and Phalen Park are favorites for this sport.

GOLF **Minneapolis:** Hiawatha Golf Course (4553 Longfellow Ave. S., tel. 612/724–7715);

Theodore Worth Golf Course (Glenwood Pkwy. and Plymouth Ave., tel. 612/522–4584). **St. Paul:** Phalen Park (1615 Phalen Dr., tel. 612/778–0424); Highland Park (1403 Montreal Ave., tel. 612/699–3650); and Como Park (1431 N. Lexington Pkwy., tel. 612/488–9673).

TENNIS Public courts can be found in Kenwood and Loring parks in Minneapolis and in Como and Phalen parks in St. Paul.

ENTERTAINMENT

For arts-events calendars, check the monthly *Mpls.–St. Paul;* the weekly *Twin Cities Reader* and *City Pages;* and the daily newspapers, the *St. Paul Pioneer Press* and the Minneapolis-based *Star Tribune.*

DANCE The Northrop Dance Series (tel. 612/624–2345) is a major showcase for dance in the region. The Hennepin Center for the Arts (tel. 612/332–4478) is home to several dance companies.

THEATER The Guthrie Theater (tel. 612/377–2224 or 800/848–4912) is the area's major theater, featuring avant-garde and the classic plays. The West Bank Theater District near the University of Minnesota has the highest concentration of theaters in Minneapolis. The Chanhassen Dinner Theatres (tel. 612/934–1525) has four theaters under one roof.

MUSIC The Minnesota Orchestra performs in Orchestra Hall (tel. 612/371–5656). The Orpheum Theater (tel. 612/339–7007) is a Hennepin Avenue mainstay that offers popular concerts. The St. Paul Chamber Orchestra (tel. 612/224–4222) features more than 85 concerts each year at the Ordway Music Theater (tel. 612/282–3000), which also hosts jazz, pop, dance theater, and mime performances.

SPECTATOR SPORTS The Minnesota Twins (tel. 612/375–1116) play baseball April through September, and the Minnesota Vikings (tel. 612/333–8828) play football August through December at Hubert H. Humphrey Metrodome (900 S. 5th St., Minneapolis). The Minnesota Timberwolves (tel. 612/337–3865) play basketball November through April at Target Center (600 1st Ave. N at 6th St.). Hockey fans can see the Minnesota North Stars (tel. 612/853–9300) September through April at Met Center (Cedar Ave., Bloomington).

Mount Rushmore, the Black Hills, and the Badlands

South Dakota

 ature provides a fitting backdrop for the widely recognized Mount Rushmore National Memorial in western South Dakota, where the faces of former presidents Washington, Roosevelt, Jefferson, and Lincoln are carved into granite cliffs, surrounded by the Black Hills' pine-covered mountains, icy trout streams, and secluded valleys. Work on this huge memorial to democracy began in 1927 under the supervision of artist Gutzon Borglum, who employed jackhammers and dynamite to coax the presidents' images from the stone. As the crown jewel of the Black Hills' tourism industry, Mount Rushmore National Memorial hosts 2 million visitors each year. While the memorial and the facilities immediately surrounding it can become quite crowded during the busy summer season, visitors who are seeking serenity can easily retreat to the wilder seclusion of the Black Hills' backcountry or visit during the off-season.

Just a two-hour drive east, 244,000-acre Badlands National Park offers a sharp contrast in environment. The lush, pine-tree-blanketed high country of the Black Hills is a far cry from this stark, almost lunar landscape marked by sheer cliffs and buttes. Formed over the aeons by sedimentary rock deposits from the Black Hills and by ash from the volcanoes at Yellowstone Park, the eerie Badlands are home to fossils from an extinct menagerie of saber-toothed cats, giant pigs, and other unusual creatures. Once the stomping grounds of Indians and grizzled mountain men, the Badlands now offer easy driving, scenic overlooks, well-marked hiking trails, and a chance to safely experience the most desolate terrain of the Great Plains.

ESSENTIAL INFORMATION

WHEN TO GO The peak tourist season falls between Memorial Day and Labor Day, when daytime temperatures around Mount Rush-

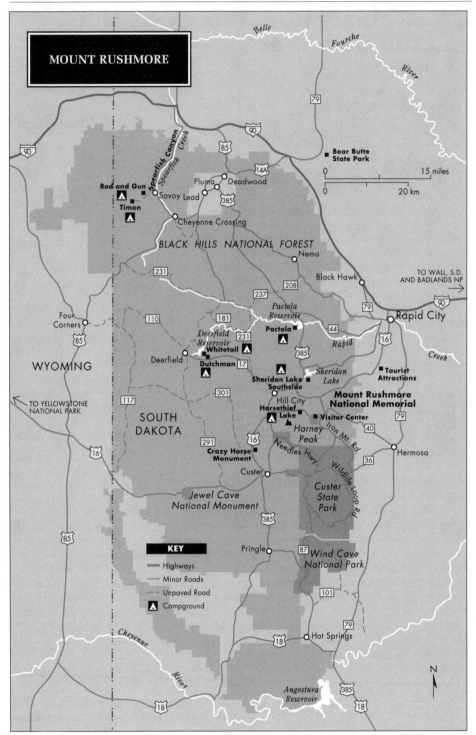

more hover in the 80s and are even higher in the Badlands. The biggest crowds arrive in early August for the Sturgis Motorcycle Classic, when thousands of bikers roar through the Black Hills on Harley-Davidsons. The sunny, warm days often linger long into the fall, though temperatures begin to dip considerably at night. Winters are very cold (with temperatures dropping into the teens), but at least during the off-season (October through May) hotel rates are often reduced by more than half.

FESTIVALS AND SEASONAL EVENTS **Easter:** A nondenominational Easter sunrise service takes place on the main view terrace at the visitor center. **June–Aug.:** Throughout summer, bands and choruses from across the country perform free concerts at the Mount Rushmore amphitheater. Contact the visitor center (tel. 605/574–2523) for a schedule of related events. **July 4:** Independence Day is always a big event at Mount Rushmore. For a schedule of events, contact the visitor center (tel. 605/574–2523).

BARGAINS All the activities and programs at Mount Rushmore National Memorial are free. In Rapid City, follow Main Street to Jackson Boulevard and turn left to reach Canyon Lake (tel. 605/394–4175). The city park there has canals and hundreds of acres of manicured grass and trees. Farther west down Jackson Boulevard is the Cleghorn Springs Fish Hatchery (tel. 605/394–2397). Several varieties of trouts are spawned here by the thousands, and visitors can inspect the facilities free of charge. For a close look at some of the fossils unearthed in the Badlands, take a walk through the Museum of Geology at South Dakota School of Mines and Technology. *501 E. St. Joseph St., tel. 605/394–2467. Open daily. Admission free.*

TOURIST OFFICES South Dakota Department of Tourism (Capital Lake Plaza, Pierre 57501; tel. 605/773–3301, 800/843–1930, or 800/952–2217 in SD). Rapid City Convention and Visitors Bureau (Box 747, 444 Mt. Rushmore Rd. N, Rapid City 57709, tel. 605/343–1744). Mount Rushmore National Memorial (Box 268, Keystone 57751, tel. 605/574–2523). Badlands National Park (Box 6, Interior 57750, tel. 605/433–5361). Black Hills National Forest Supervisor's Office (RR 2, Box 200, Custer 57730, tel. 605/673–2251).

EMERGENCIES **Police:** Dial 911 or 605/394–2151. **Hospitals:** Rapid City Regional Hospital (353 Fairmont Blvd., tel. 605/341–1000). If an emergency should occur while you are in one of the parks, contact one of the patrolling park rangers or head for the nearest visitor center, where a medical-emergency team is located.

ARRIVING AND DEPARTING

BY PLANE Rapid City Regional Airport (tel. 605/394–4195), with several major carriers and daily flights, is the only commercial airport in the area.

BY CAR I–90 is the most direct route to the Badlands and the Black Hills. To reach Badlands National Park from I–90, take Exit 110 at Wall, or Exit 131 at Cactus Flat. To get to Mount Rushmore from I–90, take Exit 57 in Rapid City.

GETTING AROUND

BY CAR A car is the easiest way to get to Mount Rushmore, the Black Hills, and the Badlands. A free road map can be obtained from the South Dakota Department of Tourism, and more detailed maps are available at each park's visitors bureau (*see* Tourist Offices, *above*).

BY BUS The Jackrabbit Lines bus station (333 6th St., tel. 605/348–3300) in downtown Rapid City serves two regional bus lines, Jackrabbit and Powder River, both of which make connections with Greyhound Lines elsewhere.

REST STOPS Comfort stations with rest rooms are located along I–90 at Wasta between Rapid City and Badlands National Park. There are also rest rooms in the park headquarters at Mount Rushmore National Memorial and Badlands National Park. Every national forest campground has pit toilets.

GUIDED TOURS **Orientation:** Gray Line of the Black Hills (1600 E. St. Patrick St., Rapid City 57701, tel. 605/342–4461 or 800/456–4461) offers a variety of bus tours to Mount Rushmore, Black Hills National Forest, Custer State Park, and Crazy Horse Monument, all ranging in price from $12 to $30. Stagecoach West (Box 264, Rapid City 57709, tel. 605/343–3113) and Golden Circle Tours (40 5th St. N., Custer 57730, tel. 605/673–4349) offer similar tours in the same price range. Golden Circle Tours also offers a $25 tour to more remote spots in the Black Hills, including visits to abandoned gold mines, a picnic lunch, and a stop at Spring Creek, where guests can pan for gold and garnets.

Special-Interest: Gray Line of the Black Hills runs a tour to the Black Hills Passion Play in Spearfish every Tuesday, Thursday, and Sunday from June through August. The bus trip and a ticket to this reenactment of the last days of Christ costs $22. Gray Line also has a "Wild West Evening" tour to Deadwood, where gambling is the big draw. Golden Circle can tailor their mountain bike tour to the ability of the participants. Bikes, helmets, and a picnic lunch are included, and a shuttle van joins the group at various points to pick up tired bikers.

EXPLORING

Mount Rushmore National Memorial, to the southwest of Rapid City, and Badlands National Park, to the southeast, are only a two-hour drive from each other. Travelers with a time restriction can see both in one day, but in order to really appreciate the natural beauty of the area, visitors should set aside at least three or four days to make a few side trips into the wilderness. All the activities in the park are free of charge.

MOUNT RUSHMORE NATIONAL MEMORIAL Because of ongoing construction near the memorial, which is located 25 miles southwest of Rapid City on Route 16, visitors find it more convenient to leave their campers and RVs parked in campgrounds or elsewhere. It will be easier to find parking at Mount Rushmore with a smaller vehicle. Otherwise, the Mount Rushmore National Memorial can be explored on foot in just an hour or so (try to visit during the morning, when the lighting is most dramatic, or at sunset in order to see the nightly lighting ceremony). Visitors to the memorial can also stroll down the Avenue of Flags to the visitor center, where there's a video outlining Mount Rushmore's complete history. The view of the memorial from the visitor-center terrace is terrific.

Located below the huge carvings is the amphitheater, where a variety of concerts are held during the summer. The nightly lighting ceremony during summer features a patriotic presentation by one of the park rangers and a short film about the memorial before the faces are lit up. The time of the ceremony varies with the sunset, but it is usually at 9 PM during the summer. In winter the monument is lighted without much pomp shortly after dark, usually about 6 PM. *Box 268, Keystone 57751, tel. 605/574–2523. Admission free.*

Iron Mountain Road (Rte. 16A), a scenic drive that connects Mount Rushmore with Custer State Park in the south, was specially designed for sightseeing. As you follow the winding road through mountain passes and over old wooden bridges, notice how tunnels along the route provide glimpses of Mount Rushmore in the distance.

Custer State Park in the southern hills is home to an abundance of coyotes, eagles, antelope, mule deer, and over 1,400 buffalo. The park's Wildlife Loop Road takes about an hour to drive, and you'll spot plenty of buffalo grazing on the side of the road as you pass—these impressive beasts are dangerous, so don't get too close if you stop to take pictures.

Spearfish Canyon, found at the extreme northern end of the Black Hills Forest, is most spectacular in early October, when the aspen and birch trees lining its limestone cliffs erupt into brilliant yellows and oranges.

Commercial tourist attractions along Mount Rushmore Road to Mount Rushmore National Memorial include **Bear Country U.S.A.** (Rte. 16, Rapid City, tel. 605/343–2290), **Reptile**

Gardens (Hwy. 16, Rapid City, tel. 605/342–5873), and **Marine Life Aquarium** (Rte. 16, Rapid City, tel. 605/343–7400). All of them charge admission fees of about $3.50 for children and $7.50 for adults, and only the aquarium remains open in the winter.

The Crazy Horse Monument, which when completed will show a 563-foot-high stone sculpture of an American Indian sitting on a horse, is located between Custer and Hill City. Continuously worked on since 1947, this monument to Native Americans is not part of the national park system, but rather, is a private family endeavor funded by admission fees. *Rte. 89, tel. 605/673–4681. Open daily. Admission charged ($5 per person or $12 per car).*

Jewel Cave National Monument and **Wind Cave National Park,** about 20 miles from one another in the southern hills, are, respectively, the second- and third-longest caves in the country. If you plan on taking a tour through one or both of the caves, be sure to bring a jacket to guard against the chilly underground temperatures. *Hot Springs 57747, tel. 605/673–2288 (Jewel Cave) or 605/745–4600 (Wind Cave). Parks open daily; caves open for tours May–Sept. Admission: entrance to parks free; cave tours $2–$8 adults, $1–$2.50 children and senior citizens.*

THE BADLANDS By following U.S. 240 through Badlands National Park and stopping at the 13 scenic overlooks along this highway, you can get a good idea of what the park is like. But for a better understanding of the Badlands, leave the car behind to take a few short hikes around Cedar Pass and in the 64,000-acre Sage Creek Wilderness Area. Entrance into the park costs $3 per car.

Cedar Pass Visitor Center on the eastern side of the Badlands National Park has exhibits on Badlands geology, wildlife, and early inhabitants. Brochures and maps detailing the area are available, and park rangers are on hand to answer questions. *U.S. 240, Box 6, Interior 57750, tel. 605/433–5361. Open daily.*

Hiking trails around the Cedar Pass Visitor Center give visitors a good opportunity to stretch their legs and get a close look at the Badlands. The trails range in length from 1/4 to 5 1/2 miles, and all are well marked. Notch Trail is a somewhat difficult hike, while Castle Trail is fairly easy but lengthy; the short Fossil Exhibit Trail features fossils displayed under glass. Information about each trail is available in the Cedar Pass Visitor Center.

Sage Creek Rim Road begins just south of the western Pinnacles entrance in Badlands National Park. The road skirts the north side of the Sage Creek Wilderness Area and runs southeast toward Cedar Pass through the Roberts Prairie Dog Town. Thirteen scenic overlooks along the way provide fine views of the Badlands' unique rock formations.

HOTELS AND INNS

Hotel rates are highest during summer but are often reduced by half or more after the peak season. The best values are found far from I–90, the main tourist route into the Black Hills. Good deals for motels in mountain surroundings can also be found in the smaller towns of Hill City, Custer, and Hot Springs, and in the outlying areas. Be sure to make your reservations well in advance, since motels are often booked solid during the summer. No campgrounds or hotels are available at Mount Rushmore National Memorial, so most visitors to the memorial stay in Rapid City, Hill City, or in motels and campgrounds along the route. Visitors to the Badlands National Park can find lodging in the Cedar Pass Lodge located inside the park, or in the nearby towns of Wall and Kadoka. Price categories for double occupancy during high season, excluding taxes, are *Expensive,* over $70; *Moderate,* $50–$70; and *Inexpensive,* under $50.

NEAR MOUNT RUSHMORE NATIONAL MEMORIAL

Hotel Alex Johnson. This luxurious landmark hotel, with 11 stories of alpine woodwork and Indian artistry, is the most famous hotel in Rapid City: No wonder it's hosted five U.S. presidents. *523 6th St., Rapid City 57701, tel. 605/342–1210 or 800/888–ALEX. 120 rooms. Health club, sauna, steam* showers, room service. AE, D, DC, MC, V. Expensive.

Edelweiss Mountain Lodging. The homey guest houses and cabins here—many of them former private homes—are comfortably settled among ponderosa pines on a gravel road 3 miles off Highway 385. Each cabin is unique; large groups might like the Waite cabin, which has four bedrooms and a pool table. HC33, Box 3128, Rapid City 57702, tel. 605/574-2430. 18 guest houses. MC, V. Moderate–Expensive.

Bel Air Inn. Located on the busiest strip in Rapid City, the Bel Air Inn is convenient to all the sights but is often noisy and lacking the charm of more secluded Black Hills lodgings. 2101 Mt. Rushmore Rd., Rapid City 57701, tel. 605/343-5126 or 800/456-5055. 30 rooms. Pool, cable TV. AE, D, DC, MC, V. Moderate.

Castle Inn. Found on a centrally located but rather noisy street, this well-kept motel is typical of the moderately priced accommodations available in Rapid City. 15 E. North St., Rapid City 57701, tel. 605/348-4120 or 800/658-5464. 20 rooms. Heated pool, cable TV. AE, D, DC MC, V. Moderate.

Lewis Park Cabins and Motel. Located on a back street in Hill City, these 1930s cabins offer small-town living tucked away among mountain ridges and aspen trees. Each unit is furnished and equipped with a full kitchen. The handful of motel-style rooms lack the charm of the cabins. 110 Park Ave., Box 382, Hill City 57745, tel. 605/574-2565. 4 cabins, 5 rooms. D, MC, V. Inexpensive.

Spring Creek Inn. Found in the pine-covered mountains near Hill City on Highway 16-385, the knotty-pine guest rooms here are one of the best lodging deals in the Black Hills. In summer, croquet games are set up on the grassy lawn, and fishermen angle for trout in nearby Spring Creek. HCR 87, Box 55, Hill City 57745, tel. 605/574-2591. 14 rooms, 1 cottage, 3 chalets, and 3 vacation homes. D, MC, V. Inexpensive.

NEAR BADLANDS NATIONAL PARK **Plains Hotel.** This modern family motel near I–90 and downtown Wall is convenient for visitors to Badlands National Park. 912 Glen St., Box 393, Wall 57790, tel. 605/279-2145 or 800/528-1234. 74 rooms. Pool, cable TV. AE, D, DC, MC, V. Moderate.

Cedar Pass Lodge. Guests can gaze out at the buttes of Badlands National Park from these ideally located cabins near the park's visitor center. Built in the 1930s, the clean, carpeted cabins were remodeled in 1987, but the knotty-pine walls remain. Box 5, Interior 57750, tel. 605/433-5460. 24 cabins. Restaurant nearby. AE, D, DC, MC, V. Inexpensive.

CAMPGROUNDS

Camping facilities abound both in and around the Black Hills and the Badlands, and while most provide water, showers, electricity, and sewage disposal, some have even more elaborate facilities. For a listing of all campgrounds, complete with maps and full descriptions, request a copy of the South Dakota Campground Guide from the South Dakota Department of Tourism (see Tourist Offices, above). The two national park campgrounds in the Badlands accept campers on a first-come, first-served basis, while reservations for the various Black Hills National Forest campgrounds (tel. 800/283-2267) can be made by calling well in advance of your arrival date. All the national forest campgrounds are scheduled to open on May 15. However, many will have only limited service (no rest rooms or water) until Memorial Day weekend. Many campgrounds close on September 30.

THE BLACK HILLS **Dutchman Campground.** At an elevation of 6,100 feet, this is one of the coolest spots in the Black Hills, where campers can escape from the summer heat even in July. Water is available at its 45 campsites. Cost: $7.50. 45 sites, tent or RV; pit toilets, picnic tables.

Horsethief Lake Campground. This is the closest public campground to Mount Rushmore National Memorial, and, as a result, it is always the most crowded. Located 1 mile west of Mount Rushmore off Highway 244, the campground offers easy access to the Norbeck Wildlife Preserve and Centennial Trail. There are 36 campsites and drinking water. *Cost: $12–$14. 36 sites, tent or RV; chemical toilet, picnic tables.*

Pactola Campground. This large campground has 80 campsites near Pactola Lake. The beautiful lakefront offers boating, fishing, and a beach. *Cost: $10–$12. 80 sites, tent or RV. Chemical and pit toilets, hot showers, concession store, laundry.*

Rod and Gun Campground and Timon Campground. Both of these small campgrounds offer secluded camping along Little Spearfish Creek not far from Roughlock Falls. Each has seven campsites and water. *Cost: $7. 7 sites, tent or RV, pit toilet.*

Sheridan Lake Southside Campground. Twelve of the campsites at this large facility are near a beach, boat ramp, and the Centennial Trail. The best spots are closest to Sheridan Lake. Drinking water is available. *Cost: $10–$12. 129 sites, tent or RV, shower at beach area, pit toilet, picnic tables.*

Whitetail Campground. This campground above Deerfield Lake offers solitude and good fishing. Water is available at 17 campsites. *Cost: $7.50 17 sites, tent or RV, pit toilet.*

THE BADLANDS **Cedar Pass Campground.** Located close to the Cedar Pass Visitor's Center, this campground has very little in the way of facilities, though water is provided (except in the winter). *Cost: $7. 110 sites. Flush toilets, picnic tables, electricity in wash house, no reservations.*

Sage Creek Primitive Campground. The key word here is *primitive*. Located just south of the Sage Creek Rim Road in the Badlands Sage Creek Wilderness Area, this campground is for those who really like to rough it. This facility has no water. *Pit toilets, picnic tables.*

DINING

Most restaurants in the Badlands and Mount Rushmore are found in the towns outside the parks, and visitors should be aware that many establishments close for the winter. Those who are adventurous will want to try the local specialty—buffalo—found on the menus of several regional restaurants (raised on a number of western South Dakota ranches, buffalo meat tastes similar to beef but contains less fat and cholesterol). Price categories per person, not including tax, service, or drinks, are *Moderate*, $6–$11, and *Inexpensive*, under $6.

INSIDE THE PARKS **Cedar Pass Lodge Restaurant.** Native American crafts decorate this small family restaurant—the park's only full-service eatery—in Badlands National Park, next to the Ben Rifel/Cedar Pass Visitor Center. The menu features tacos and quarter-pound buffalo burgers. *Cedar Pass, tel. 605/433–5460. AE, D, DC, MC, V. Inexpensive.*

NEAR THE PARKS **Casa Del Rey.** The Americanized Mexican food served here is mild enough for almost any gringo's taste. Tortilla chips and salsa pave the way for chili rellenos, chimichangas, and burritos. *1902 Mt. Rushmore Rd., tel. 605/348–5679. AE, MC, V. Moderate.*

The Great Wall Chinese Restaurant. For years this has remained one of the most popular restaurants in Rapid City, and you may encounter a short wait before sitting down to one of their low-fat Chinese meals. Take-out is available. *315 E. North St., Rapid City, tel. 605/348–1060. MC, V. Moderate.*

Hunan Chinese Restaurant. Another popular Rapid City spot where low-fat Chinese dishes lure large crowds of locals. *1720 Mt. Rushmore Rd., Rapid City, tel. 605/341–3888. AE, MC, V. Moderate.*

The Saigon Restaurant. Spicy, authentic Vietnamese and Chinese food is served in this family-run hole-in-the-wall. It may not look like much, but it's the food that really counts: spicy shrimp with red sauce and onions, chicken with broccoli, and numerous ginger-inspired dishes. *221 E. North St., Rapid City, tel. 605/348–8523. No credit cards. Moderate.*

Alpine Inn. Opera music and stained-glass windows enhance the elegant, European atmosphere at the popular Alpine Inn, located in the quiet logging town of Hill City. Lunch includes sandwiches and light entrées; the only dinner entrée is steak, succulent 6- or 9-ounce cuts that are so reasonably priced people come from miles around and don't seem to mind a short wait. *Harney Peak Hotel, Main St., Hill City, tel. 605/574–2749. No credit cards. Inexpensive–Moderate.*

SHOPPING

GIFTS AND CRAFTS For Sioux Indian pottery, go to Sioux Pottery Crafts (2209 Hwy. 79S, Rapid City, tel. 605/341–3657). Indian art is available at the gift shop in the Sioux Indian Museum (1002 St. Joseph St., Rapid City, tel. 605/348–0557).

OUTDOOR ACTIVITIES

BEACHES There are two small beaches along Sheridan Lake in the Black Hills, and Angostura Reservoir near Hot Springs is rimmed with miles of white sand. Both lakes have rest rooms, picnic tables, and barbecues, and Angostura also has a snack bar. Neither lake has lifeguards on duty.

BIKING The best biking in the Black Hills area is on the 5-mile-long, concrete bike path that runs along Rapid Creek in Rapid City. Bikes can be rented from Everybody's Bookstore (515 6th St., tel. 605/341–3224) in Rapid City or The Gold Strike (40 N. 5th St., tel. 605/673–4349) in Custer.

FISHING Spearfish Creek and Rapid Creek are both popular spots to angle for wild brown trout. Deerfield, Sheridan, Pactola, and Stockade lakes are also good for fishing, as is small, scenic Horsethief Lake near Mount Rushmore.

GOLF Black Hills golf courses that can be used for a daily fee include Belle Fourche Country Club (S. Hwy. 85, Belle Fourche, tel. 605/892–3472), Edgemont Golf and Racquet Club (south of Edgemont, tel. 605/662–5100), Executive Golf Course (along Rapid Creek in Rapid City, tel. 605/394–4124), Hart Ranch Resort (between Rapid City and Mount Rushmore, tel. 605/341–5703), Meadowbrook Golf Course (3625 Jackson Blvd., Rapid City, tel. 605/394–4191), Rocky Knolls Golf Course (Hwy. 16 west of Custer, tel. 605/673–4481), and Tomahawk Country Club (Hwy. 385 south of Deadwood, tel. 605/578–9979).

HIKING Dozens of trails, ranging from 100 yards to more than 100 miles, snake through the thick ponderosa pines and Black Hills spruce of the Norbeck Wildlife Preserve and the Black Elk Wilderness southwest of Mount Rushmore. A Sierra Club hiking map of the Norbeck Wildlife Preserve can be purchased from the Sierra Club (Box 1624, Rapid City 57709, tel. 605/348–1351) for $2.50.

HORSEBACK RIDING The western-horse pack trips offered in Badlands National Park and the Black Hills by Gunsel Horse Adventures (Box 1575, Rapid City 57709, tel. 605/343–7608) include 6- and 10-day pack trips on scenic trails through the pine forests and mountain meadows around Custer State Park and Mount Rushmore.

SKIING Two resorts in the northern hills that have downhill skiing are Terry Peak Ski Area (tel. 605/584–2165) and Deer Mountain Ski Area (tel. 605/584–3230). Two of the most popular cross-country ski trails in the Black Hills are Eagle Cliff near O'Neil Pass and Big Hill near Spearfish. Equipment rental costs $10 per day and is available at Ski Cross Country (701 3rd St., Spearfish, tel. 605/642–3851) and Deer Mountain Ski Area (near Lead, S.D., tel. 605/584–2165).

SNOWMOBILING More than 300 miles of groomed snowmobile trails link the Black Hills in South Dakota and Wyoming. The most extensive trails with the best snow run through the northern Hills. Free snowmobile maps are available from the South Dakota Department of Tourism (*see* Tourist Offices, *above*).

Nashville
Tennessee

The sprawling city of Nashville (population about 1 million) extends over eight counties in the middle Tennessee heartland, a pocket of rolling Cumberland Mountain foothills and bluegrass meadows that's one of the state's richest farming areas. Its impressive skyline, dotted with high-rise office towers, is a vivid reminder that it has been a long time indeed since Christmas Day 1779, when James Robertson and a small, shivering party of pioneers began to build a fortress and palisades on the Cumberland River's west bank.

Designated the state capital in 1843, the city began a steady growth that has accelerated mightily in the past decade. A banking and insurance hub, it is also a leading printing center for religious material. Heralded as the world's Country Music Capital and birthplace of the "Nashville Sound," it also proudly calls itself the Athens of the South. Far from developing a case of civic schizophrenia at such contrasting roles, Nashville has made both labels fit, becoming one of the middle South's liveliest and most vibrant cities in the process. Its role as a cultural leader is enhanced by its impressive performing-arts center and the many colleges, universities, and technical schools located here, most notably Vanderbilt University.

As every fan knows, it was Nashville's Grand Ole Opry that launched the amazing country-music boom when it began as radio station WSM's "Barn Dance" in 1925. The Opry performs in a sleek $15 million Opry House now, still as gleeful and down-home informal as in the early days.

ESSENTIAL INFORMATION

WHEN TO GO Nashville has a temperate climate year-round. Spring and autumn are the most pleasant times of year. The summer months, especially July and August, can be very hot and humid. Winters are not usually severe, but January and early February can

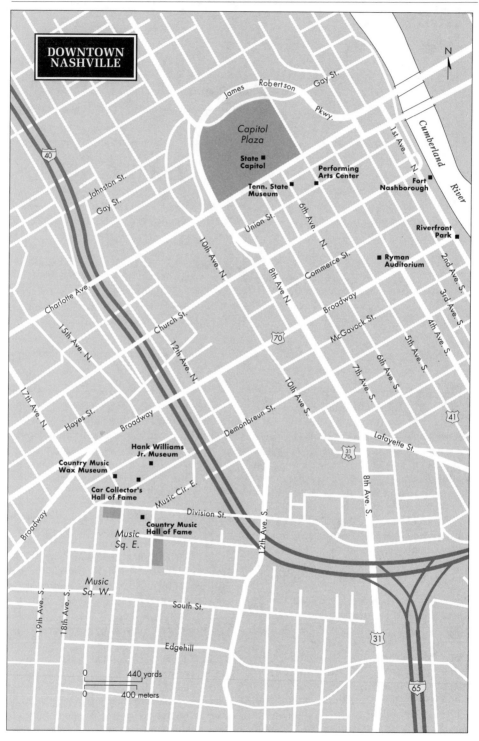

DOWNTOWN NASHVILLE

James Robertson Gay St.

Pkwy.

Cumberland River

Capitol Plaza

State Capitol

Performing Arts Center

1st Ave. N.

Fort Nashborough

Tenn. State Museum

Johnston St.

Gay St.

Union St.

6th Ave. N.

Riverfront Park

Ryman Auditorium

2nd Ave. S.

10th Ave. N.

Commerce St.

3rd Ave. S.

Charlotte Ave.

Church St.

8th Ave. N

Broadway

McGavock St.

4th Ave. S.

5th Ave. S.

15th Ave. N.

12th Ave. N.

70

7th Ave. S.

6th Ave. S.

41

17th Ave. N.

Hayes St.

Broadway

Demonbreun St.

10th Ave. S.

Lafayette St.

31
70s

8th Ave. S.

Hank Williams Jr. Museum

Country Music Wax Museum

Car Collector's Hall of Fame

Music Cir. E.

Division St.

12th Ave. S.

Broadway

Music Sq. E.

Country Music Hall of Fame

19th Ave. S.

18th Ave. S.

Music Sq. W.

South St.

31

Edgehill

0   440 yards
0   400 meters

65

produce bone-rattling cold and enough snow to shut down the city. The primary tourist season runs from April through October.

BARGAINS Tapings of several TNN (The Nashville Network) television shows are open to visitors. Admission is free to "Crook & Chase," taped at 7 PM Tuesday–Friday at Jim Owens Productions (1525 Mc Gavock St., tel. 615/889–6611; reservations required). Admission is also free to the Tennessee State Museum, Tennessee State Capitol, and Fort Nashborough. Many of the city's college art galleries can be visited without charge, and Vanderbilt often presents free concerts and plays. The parks department puts on free summer concerts and outdoor arts shows, notably the band-shell events and festivals in Centennial Park. For more information, call 615/259–6399.

TOURIST OFFICES Tennessee Department of Tourist Development (Room T, Box 23170, Nashville 37202, tel. 615/741–2158). Nashville Area Chamber of Commerce (161 4th Ave. N, Nashville 37202, tel. 615/259–4700). Tourist Information Center (103 Main St., at Interstate Dr., Nashville 37202, tel. 615/259–4747).

EMERGENCIES **Police, fire,** and **ambulance:** Dial 911. **Hospitals:** Centrally located Baptist Hospital (2000 Church St., tel. 615/329–5555) and Vanderbilt University Medical Center (1211 22nd Ave. S, tel. 615/322–7311) have emergency rooms that are open all night. **Pharmacies:** Walgreens has four Nashville-area stores that are open 24 hours (517 Donelson Pike, tel. 615/883–5108; 5412 Charlotte Ave., tel. 615/298–5594; 2622 Gallatin Road, tel. 615/226–7591; 15580 Old Hickory Blvd., tel. 615/333–2722).

ARRIVING AND DEPARTING

BY PLANE Nashville International Airport, approximately 8 miles from downtown, is served by American, Delta, Eastern, United, and USAir. Taxis are available at the terminal's ground level; the fare to downtown Nashville averages $13–$17.

BY CAR From Nashville, I–65 leads north into Kentucky and south into Alabama, and I–24 leads northwest into Kentucky and Illinois and southeast into Georgia. I–40 traverses the state east–west, connecting Nashville with Memphis and Knoxville.

BY TRAIN Amtrak does not serve the Nashville area.

BY BUS Greyhound (8th Ave. S and McGavock St., tel. 800/231–2222) connects Nashville with cities and towns throughout the United States.

GETTING AROUND

BY CAR Attractions are scattered, so you'll need a car. In some instances, you can park and walk from one attraction to another. Pick up a Tennessee map from a state welcome center or the Tourist Information Center; it's helpful for exploring Nashville's hinterland.

BY BUS Metropolitan Transit Authority (MTA) buses (tel. 615/242–4433) serve the entire county; fares are $1.15 ($1.25 for transfers) and $1.45 for express buses. For disabled persons, a wheelchair-lift van is available for downtown transport (tel. 615/351–RIDE). The Nashville Trolley Company (tel. 615/242–4433) also offers rides in the downtown area every 10 minutes (fares vary).

BY TAXI Companies include Checker Cab (tel. 615/256—7000), Nashville Cab (tel. 615/242–7070), and Yellow Cab (tel. 615/256–0101). Telephone for service.

REST STOPS There are free public rest rooms at the State Capitol and the Tennessee State Museum.

GUIDED TOURS Tours that may include drives past stars' homes and visits to the Grand Ole Opry, Music Row, and historic structures are offered by American Sightseeing (tel. 615/256–1200 or 800/826–6456), Gray Line (tel. 615/883–5555 or 800/251–1864), and Grand Ole Opry Tours (tel. 615/889–9490). Country & Western Round-Up Tours (tel. 615/883–5555) offers a daily Twitty City/Johnny Cash Special motorcoach tour. Johnny Walker Tours (tel. 615/834–8585 or 800/722–1524) has an evening Music Village Nightlife Tour, which includes a barbecue buffet dinner and top-name country entertainment. Belle Carol Riverboat Company (tel. 615/244–3430 or 800/342–2355) runs Cumberland River sightseeing, luncheon, and dinner cruises that leave from the Riverfront Park dock. Opryland USA (tel. 615/889–6611) has daytime and dinner cruises aboard the *General Jackson.*

EXPLORING

You should plan to explore Nashville in segments. It helps to remember that the river bisects the central city; numbered avenues are west of and parallel to the river, numbered streets east of and parallel to it. Start in **Riverfront Park** and walk one block northwest on First Avenue.

Fort Nashborough, high on limestone bluffs overlooking the river, is the site of the Nashville founders' first 1779 log fort. In a carefully re-created fort and blockhouses, costumed interpreters depict late-18th-century frontier life. *170 1st Ave. N, tel. 615/255–8192. Open Tues.–Sat. Admission charged.*

Walk three short blocks north on 1st Avenue and three blocks west on Charlotte Avenue to the **Tennessee State Museum** in the lower level of the **James K. Polk Cultural Center.** Among the displays are a log cabin, an exhibit on Indian life, and a demonstration of early printing techniques; you'll also see Davy Crockett's powder horn and rifle, Andrew Jackson's inaugural top hat, and Sam Houston's guitar. *505 Deaderick St., tel. 615/741–2692. Open daily. Admission free.*

Walk west along Charlotte Avenue to Capitol Plaza. The **Tennessee State Capitol** (1859) so impressed its architect, William Strickland, that he asked to be buried within its walls. On the grounds, among statues of Tennessee heroes, President James K. Polk and his wife are buried . *Capitol Plaza and Charlotte Ave., tel. 615/741–0830. Open daily. Admission free.*

Walk two blocks east on Charlotte Avenue and four blocks south on 5th Avenue. **The Ryman Auditorium and Museum,** "Mother Church" of country music, is now on the National Register of Historic Places. It was home for the WSM Grand Ole Opry from 1943 to 1974. *116 Opry Pl. (5th Ave. N), tel. 615/254–1445. Open daily. Admission charged.*

Now, continuing the tour by car, take the Demonbreun Exit off I–40 to Music Row. **The Country Music Hall of Fame and Museum** displays such icons as Elvis Presley's "solid gold Cadillac," along with priceless costumes, instruments, films, and photos. Other exhibits cover Johnny Cash and the Grand Ole Opry, and a tour of the legendary RCA Studio B is included. *4 Music Sq. E, tel. 615/256–1639. Open daily. Admission charged.*

The Hank Williams Jr. Museum, 1/2 block east along Demonbreun Street, displays family memorabilia of Hank Sr. and Jr. Exhibits include many of their stage costumes and guitars, along with Hank Sr.'s '52 and Hank Jr.'s '57 Cadillac. *1524 Demonbreun St., tel. 615/242–8313. Open daily. Admission charged.*

Car Collectors Hall of Fame, a few doors away, displays another of Elvis's Cadillacs, Webb Pierce's "silver dollar car," and 50 other flashy vehicles with country connections. *1534 Demonbreun St., tel. 615/255–6804. Open daily. Admission charged.*

At **The Country Music Wax Museum and Mall,** on the same block, more than 60 figures, dressed in original stage costumes, display the entertainers' own musical instruments. *118 16th Ave. S, tel. 615/256–2490. Open daily. Admission charged.*

Opryland USA, an attraction-filled show park 15 minutes from downtown, is a must-see. "The Grand Ole Opry" now performs here each weekend in the world's largest broadcast studio (it seats 4,424). There are nearly two dozen rides, more than a dozen live shows, crafts demonstrations, restaurants, and special events. Here, too, the **Roy**

Acuff Musical Collection and Museum (tel. 615/889–6700; admission free) contains memorabilia of the "king of country music," and **Minnie Pearl's Museum** (admission free) provides a nostalgic tour of her life. *2802 Opryland Dr., tel. 615/889–6700. Open late Mar.–Oct., daily. Admission charged.*

Music Valley Wax Museum of the Stars, just north of Opryland USA, contains more life-size figures of country stars. Outside, in the **Sidewalk of the Stars,** are their footprints, handprints, and signatures. *2515 McGavock Pike, tel. 615/883–3612. Open daily. Admission charged.*

To get a feeling for Nashville's history and culture, begin in Centennial Park. The renovated **Parthenon** is a replica of the Athenian original, right down to the Elgin Marbles. It contains a huge new statue of Athena and also houses an art gallery with changing exhibits. *West End Ave., Centennial Park, tel. 615/862–8431. Open Tues.–Sat. Admission charged.*

From Centennial Park, head west on West End Avenue and follow the signs for **Belle Meade Mansion,** a stunning Greek Revival house, the centerpiece of a 5,300-acre estate that was one of the nation's top Thoroughbred breeding farms. A Victorian carriage museum continues the equine theme. *110 Leake Ave., tel. 615/356–0501. Open daily. Admission charged.*

Take Harding Road east, turn right on Belle Meade Boulevard, and look for signs to Tennessee Botanical Gardens. **Cheekwood,** formerly the Cheek family mansion, is now a fine-arts center exhibiting 19th- and 20th-century American art and sculpture. The surrounding 55 acres of the **Tennessee Botanical Gardens** display herbs, roses, irises, daffodils, and wildflowers, and, with greenhouse, streams, and pools, is a delightful spot for a picnic. *Forrest Park Dr., adjacent to Percy Warner Park and Golf Course, tel. 615/356–8000. Open daily. Admission charged.*

From here, drive east on Harding Place/Battery Lane, taking I–65 south to the first of two Harding Place exits. **Travellers' Rest** is the restored clapboard home of John Overton, law partner and mentor of Andrew Jackson. The house, decorated with period furnishings, grew from a 1799 4-room cottage to a 12-room mansion with Federal and Greek Revival additions. *636 Farrell Pkwy., tel. 615/832–2962. Open daily. Admission charged.*

Northeast of Travellers' Rest (via Harding Place and Donelson Pike) is a most impressive landmark. **The Hermitage,** which Andrew Jackson built for his beloved wife, Rachel, on 600 acres of gently rolling farmland, reflects Old Hickory's life and times in such detail it seems he has just stepped out for a moment. It is furnished with many original family pieces, and the Jacksons are buried on the grounds. The huge new **Andrew Jackson Center** contains many Jackson artifacts, Rachel's Garden Cafe, and a museum store. A 16-minute film, *Old Hickory,* is shown in its auditorium. *4580 Rachel's La., Hermitage, tel. 615/889–2941. Open daily. Inclusive admission charged.*

THE NATURAL WORLD In the surrounding "Heartland," a bucolic enclave where meandering streams wind amid fields, orchards, and green pastures framed by white fences, many state parks (tel. 615/532–0001 or 800/421–6683) and other natural areas offer opportunities to hike or bicycle in dense hardwood forests, and to fish, swim, or go boating. Cedars of Lebanon State Park preserves the Southeast's largest remaining red cedar forest.

HOTELS AND INNS

Catering to budget-conscious tourists as well as corporate travelers, Nashville has a wide selection of accommodations. Some establishments increase rates slightly during the peak summer travel season. Price categories for double occupancy, without 11.75% tax, are *Expensive,* $80–$100; *Moderate,* $50–$80; and *Inexpensive,* $50 and under.

EXPENSIVE **Courtyard by Marriott–Airport.** This handsome, low-rise motor inn with a gardenlike courtyard offers some amenities you'd expect in higher-priced hotels: spacious rooms, king-size beds, and hot-water dispensers for coffee. *2508 Elm Hill Pike, 37214, tel. 615/883–9500 or 800/321–2211. 145 rooms. Restaurant, lounge, indoor pool, sauna, whirlpool, exercise room. AE, DC, MC, V.*

Holiday Inn–Briley Parkway. There's one of the popular Holidome Indoor Recreation Centers right inside the inn, so you can enjoy sports activities in any season. *2200 Elm Hill Pike at Briley Pkwy., 37210, tel. 615/883–9770 or 800/465–4329. 385 rooms. Restaurant, lounge with live entertainment, sauna, whirlpool, coin laundry, game room, table tennis, pool tables, putting green. AE, DC, MC, V.*

Ramada Inn Across from Opryland. This well-maintained, low-rise, contemporary motor inn has well-lighted, spacious rooms and is a short drive from Opryland. *2401 Music Valley Dr., 37214, tel. 615/889–0800 or 800/272–6232. 308 rooms. Dining room, lounge with live entertainment, heated indoor pool, sauna, whirlpool. AE, DC, MC, V.*

Holiday Inn–Vanderbilt. Adjacent to the Vanderbilt University campus, this attractive high rise is centrally located, with some of the city's finest restaurants nearby. *2613 West End Ave., 37203, tel. 615/326–8034 or 800/465–4329. 300 rooms. Dining room, lounge with live entertainment, heated pool, exercise room, coin laundry. AE, DC, MC, V.*

MODERATE **Comfort Inn–Hermitage.** Near the Hermitage, this low-rise inn offers first-rate accommodations, some with water beds or whirlpool baths. *5768 Old Hickory Blvd., 37076, tel. 615/889–5060 or 800/228–5150. 106 rooms. Indoor and outdoor pools, sauna. AE, DC, MC, V.*

Hampton Inn–Vanderbilt. Near the Vanderbilt University campus, this contemporary inn has colorful, spacious rooms, with some no-smoking units. *1919 West End Ave., 37203, tel. 615/329–1144 or 800/426–7866. 163 rooms. Free Continental breakfast, pool. AE, DC, MC, V.*

La Quinta Motor Inn–MetroCenter. The rooms here are especially spacious and bright, and some have full-length mirrors and recliners. *2001 Metro Center Blvd., 37228, tel. 615/259–2130 or 800/531–5900. 121 rooms. Pool. AE, D, DC, MC, V.*

Wilson Inn. Three miles from Opryland, this five-story hotel is new, clean, and convenient. Many rooms have kitchens, and coffee and doughnuts are served in the spacious lobby. *600 Ermac Dr., 37210, tel. 615/889–4466 or 800/333–9457. 110 rooms. Facilities: pool. AE, D, DC, MC, V.*

MOTELS

MODERATE **Best Western–Metro Inn** (99 Spring St., 37207, tel. 615/259–9160 or 800/528–1234). 148 rooms; restaurant, pool, coin laundry. Some rooms *Inexpensive.* **Days Inn–Downtown Convention Center** (711 Union St., 37219, tel. 615/242–4311 or 800/325–2525). 100 rooms; deli, convenience market, free parking. **Drury Inn Airport** (837 Briley Pkwy., 37217, tel. 615/361–6999 or 800/325–8300). 148 rooms; breakfast included, pool. **Econo Lodge–Downtown** (303 Interstate Dr., 37213, tel. 615/244–6690 or 800/446–6900). 126 rooms; restaurant, lounge, heated indoor pool, whirlpool. **Econo Lodge–Opryland** (2460 Music Valley Dr., 37214, tel. 615/889–0090 or 800/446–6900). 86 rooms; pool. **Family Inns of America-Nashville** (3430 Percy Priest Dr., 37214, tel. 615/889–5090, 800/251–9752, or 800/332–9909 in TN). 57 rooms, 6 efficiencies; heated pool. **Holiday Inn–North** (230 W. Trinity La., 37207, tel. 615/226–0111 or 800/465–4329). 389 rooms; restaurant, cocktail lounge, 2 pools, exercise room, coin laundry, playground. Some rooms *Inexpensive.* **Quality Inn Hall of Fame Hotel** (1407 Division St., 37203, tel. 615/242–1631 or 800/221–2222). 102 rooms; restaurant, lounge with entertainment, pool. **Ramada Inn–Downtown** (840 James Robertson Pkwy., 37203, tel. 615/244–6130 or 800/272–6232). 180 rooms; restaurant, lounge, pool, coin laundry, garage. **Shoney's Inn of Nashville** (1521 Demonbreun St., 37203, tel. 615/255–9977 or 800/222–2222). 147 rooms; pool.

INEXPENSIVE Budgetel Inn (531 Donelson Pike, 37214, tel. 615/885–3100 or 800/428–3438). 150 rooms; pool, coin laundry. **Budgetel Inn–Nashville West** (5612 Lenox Ave., 37209, tel. 615/353–0700 or 800/428–3438). 110 rooms; pool. **Budget Host Inn** (10 Interstate Dr., 37213, tel. 615/244–6050 or 800/234–6779). 128 rooms; restaurant, lounge, pool. **Comfort Inn–Southeast** (97 Wallace Rd., 37211, tel. 615/833–6860 or 800/221–2222). 127 rooms; pool. **Days Inn–Nashville Central** (211 N. 1st St., 37213, tel. 615/254–1551 or 800/325–2525). 180 rooms; restaurant, lounge, heated indoor pool, whirlpool, exercise room. **Days Inn–Trinity Lane** (1360 Brick Church Pike, 37207, tel. 615/226–4500 or 800/325–2525). 150 rooms; restaurant, pool, playground. **Interstate Inn** (300 Interstate Dr., 37213, tel. 615/242–9621 or 800/444–4401). 84 rooms; pool.

DINING

Nashville is full of unpretentious cafés where fried chicken, catfish and hush puppies, barbecue, and buttermilk biscuits reign supreme. But more and more Music City restaurants are offering lighter cuisine and vegetarian fare. You'll find increasingly imaginative dishes in American, Continental, Chinese, Thai, Japanese, and Middle Eastern restaurants. Price categories per person, not including 8.25% tax, service, and drinks, are *Moderate,* $15–$25, and *Inexpensive,* under $15.

MODERATE Midtown Cafe. A quiet, elegant but relaxed ambience greets diners at this centrally located café just a couple of quick blocks from famous Music Row and featuring excellent seafood entrées. Many feel the Midtown offers the city's finest Caesar salad, and don't miss out on a taste of the Lemon Artichoke soup. *102 19th Ave. S., tel. 615/320–7176. AE, MC, V, DC.*

Kobe Steaks. Traditional Japanese decor, with shoji screens and lacquer furniture, enhances the atmosphere of this popular restaurant, where you can sit around group tables to dine on seafood or steak, prepared right there on teppan grills. *210 25th Ave. N, tel. 615/327–9081. AE, D, DC, MC, V.*

Mario's Ristorante Italiano. Country-music stars and visiting celebrities come here to see and be seen and to dine on seafood, pasta, and such northern Italian dishes as veal *saltimbocca* in this elegant Nashville institution. *2005 Broadway, tel. 615/327–3232. AE, DC, MC, V.*

Sunset Grill. Pasta, veal, lamb and seafood dishes top the menu at this midtown hot spot, where you're liable to see city business and political leaders rubbing shoulders with Nashville's biggest stars. *2001-A Belcourt Ave., tel. 615/386–3663. AE, DC, MC, V, D.*

106 Club. A white baby grand and a shiny, black-enamel-and-glass-brick bar set the tone in this intimate art deco dining room, where the cuisine is a mix of international favorites and such California nouvelle offerings as veal medallions with lichees. *106 Harding Pl., tel. 615/356–1300. AE, DC, MC, V.*

Peking Garden. Paper lanterns, paintings, and other traditional Chinese decor create the ideal setting for sampling a mind-boggling selection of regional Middle Kingdom food. *1923 Division St., tel. 615/327–2020. AE, MC, V.*

Morton's. The venerable Chicago steakhouse recently opened one of its eateries downtown in the shadow of the State Capitol. Huge steaks, salads and one-pound baked spuds are the specialties. *625 Church St., tel. 615/259–4558. AE, DC, MC, V.*

INEXPENSIVE Houston's. Great burgers, salads, and delectable prime rib keep this West End Avenue restaurant hopping at noon and at night. Well worth the wait for a table, you can't go wrong with their baked-potato soup and house salad. *3000 West End Ave., tel. 615/269–3481. AE, MC, V.*

Elliston Place Soda Shop. Generations of Vanderbilt students have eaten the sandwiches, plate lunches, and breakfasts at the 1950s-style booths and old-fashioned soda fountain of this landmark. *2111 Elliston Pl., tel. 615/327–1090. No credit cards.*

Faison's. Veal, poultry, seafood, and pasta attract a younger, stylish crowd to this attractively renovated bungalow bistro. *2000 Belcourt Ave., tel. 615/298–2112. AE, DC, MC, V.*

Loveless Cafe. An institution as renowned as the Opry and the Parthenon, this laid-back establishment 20 miles southwest of downtown attracts hordes of city folks for downhome cooking. *Rte. 5, Hwy. 100, tel. 615/646–9700. No credit cards.*

Old Spaghetti Factory. Diners enjoy heaping portions of pasta, spaghetti, and veal in a converted 1890s warehouse decked with Victorian artifacts. *160 2nd Ave. N, tel. 615/254–9010. No credit cards.*

Satsuma Tea Room. Dining at this welcoming little downtown retreat is a reminder of meals at Grandma's house, and the fresh vegetables, soups, meats, home-baked breads, and desserts are all first-rate. It's a Nashville lunch-hour institution. *417 Union St., tel. 615/256–0760. No credit cards.*

SHOPPING

Nashville's best shopping is located in its suburban malls, most notably The Mall at Green Hills (2126 Abbott Martin Rd., tel. 615/298–5478), Hickory Hollow Mall (5252 Hickory Hollow Pkwy, tel. 615/731–4500), The Bellvue Center (7620 Hwy. 70 S., tel. 615/646–8690), and CoolSprings Galleria (1800 Galleria Blvd., tel. 615/771–2128). Church Street Centre (625 Church St., tel. 615/254–4260) is the major downtown shopping area.

ANTIQUES Murfreesboro, about 15 miles outside town, calls itself the Antique Center of the South. Pick up a free shopping guide at Cannonsburgh Pioneer Village (tel. 615/890–0355), a living museum of 19th-century life in the South.

COUNTRY- AND-WESTERN WEAR Stores geared to the latest look in country clothing include Boot Country (2412 Music Valley Dr., tel. 615/883–2661), Loretta Lynn's Western Stores (120 16th Ave. S, tel. 615/889–5582), and Nashville Cowboy (118 16th Ave. S, tel. 615/242–9497; 1516 Demonbreun St., tel. 615/256–2429).

RECORDS AND TAPES Fans can find good selections at Tower Records (2400 West End Ave., 615/327–3722); Ernest Tubb Record Shops (2412 Music Valley Dr., tel. 615/889–2474; 417 Broadway, tel. 615/255–7503); and for used records, tapes, and CDs, try The Great Escape (1925 Broadway, tel. 615/327–0646; 139 Gallatin Rd. N, Madison, tel. 615/865–8052).

OUTDOOR ACTIVITIES

BOATING AND FISHING Boats can be rented at J. Percy Priest Lake, 11 miles east of Nashville off I–40, and Old Hickory Reservoir, 15 miles northeast of Nashville via U.S. 31 E.

GOLF Among courses open to the public year-round are Harpeth Hills (tel. 615/373–8202), Hermitage Golf Course (tel. 615/847–4001), and Rhodes Golf Course (tel. 615/242–2336). Hermitage is the site each April of the LPGA Sara Lee Classic.

HIKING There are extensive trails (and a nature preserve) in heavily wooded Percy Warner Park.

HORSEBACK RIDING You can go riding at Riverwood Recreation Plantation and Riding Academy (tel. 615/262–1794) and Ramblin' Breeze Ranch (tel. 615/876–1029).

ICE SKATING September through April, there's indoor skating at Sportsplex (tel. 615/862–8480) in Centennial Park.

JOGGING Favorite sites include Centennial Park, the Vanderbilt University track, J. Percy Priest Lake, and Percy Warner Park.

TENNIS There are several municipal tennis facilities, and Centennial Sportsplex Tennis Center (tel. 615/862–8490) has grass and clay courts plus indoor courts.

ENTERTAINMENT

CONCERTS Performances by the Nashville Symphony Orchestra and out-of-town artists are staged at Andrew Jackson Hall, part of the

Tennessee Performing Arts Center (TPAC, tel. 615/741–7975; call Ticketmaster, tel. 615/741–2787 or 800/333–4849, for all TPAC theaters). Chamber concerts take place at TPAC's James K. Polk Theater. Vanderbilt University stages music, dance, and drama productions (many free) at its Blair School of Music (tel. 615/322–7651).

NIGHTLIFE Not surprisingly, the "world's country music capital" offers down-home live entertainment at every turn. If you can attend only one event, try to make it the Grand Ole Opry; write ahead for tickets (2804 Opryland Dr., 37214) or call 615/889–3060. You may see tomorrow's stars performing at the Nashville Palace (2400 Music Valley Dr., tel. 615/885–1540), and the Stock Yard Bull Pen Lounge (901 2nd Ave. N, tel. 615/255–6464). Bluegrass fans head for the Station Inn (402 12th Ave., tel. 615/255–3307). The songwriter's mecca is The Bluebird Cafe (4104 Hillsboro Rd., tel. 615/383–1461).

THEATER TPAC's Andrew Jackson Hall (*see* Concerts, *above*) hosts touring Broadway shows and ballet; the James K. Polk Theater stages local performances; and there are numerous small theater companies. The Nashville Academy Theatre (tel. 615/254–9103) stages children's performances.

SPECTATOR SPORTS You can root for the AAA Nashville Sounds, an affiliate of the Chicago White Sox baseball team, from April through August at Herschel Greer Stadium (tel. 615/242–4371).

The Natchez Trace
Mississippi, Alabama, Tennessee

The Natchez Trace Parkway is what highways were meant to be—peaceful, lush, and lovely, and a testament to the history and mystery often associated with the American South. Meandering through pine forests and cypress swamps, past magnificent antebellum mansions surrounded by softly swaying oak trees, the Natchez Trace Parkway is redolent of romance, too.

The Trace, as it's called, is an uncrowded, unpretentious swath of two-lane highway that cuts through rural Mississippi and Alabama on its way to Tennessee. The Trace connects Natchez and Nashville, and in between, it follows age-old trails worn by Choctaw and Chickasaw Indians. Flower-filled in spring, verdant in summer, and crisply colorful in fall, the Trace has changed little over the years, thanks in part to the noticeable absence of heavy traffic, litter, billboards, and commercial vehicles (trucks are banned on the Trace).

The Natchez Trace, impeccably maintained by the National Park Service, spans 415 of its projected 445-mile course; until the remainder is completed, the temporary northern terminus is Leipers Fork, Tennessee. However, the majority of miles (313 to be exact) run diagonally from the northwest to the southeast corner of Mississippi, growing more rural and serene the farther south the highway goes.

ESSENTIAL INFORMATION

WHEN TO GO Traffic is rarely a problem, but summer on the Trace is always hot and humid; temperatures on the southern leg average 82° and peak in the 90s, while summer in Nashville sees temperatures hover in the low 80s. Winter on the Trace means chilly mornings and 50° afternoons. Spring and autumn are the most moderate seasons, and the most colorful, with temperatures for both in the mid-60s. Springtime also brings wild-

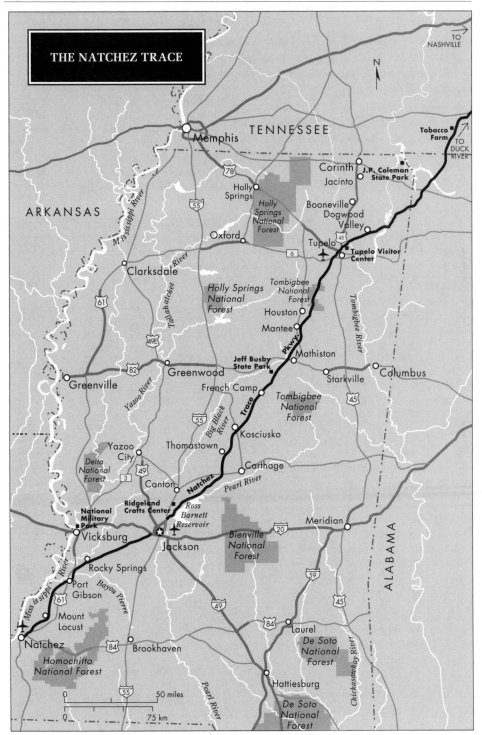

THE NATCHEZ TRACE

TO NASHVILLE

TENNESSEE

Memphis

Tobacco Farm
TO DUCK RIVER

ARKANSAS

Mississippi River

78

Holly Springs

Corinth
Jacinto

J.P. Coleman State Park

55

Holly Springs National Forest

Booneville
Dogwood Valley

Oxford

Tupelo

6

Tupelo Visitor Center

Clarksdale

Tallahatchee River

Holly Springs National Forest

Tombigbee National Forest

61

Houston

49E

Mantee

Tombigbee River

Pkwy

Mathiston

Jeff Busby State Park

Greenwood

82

French Camp

Trace

Starkville

Columbus

Greenville

Yazoo River

45

55

Big Black River

Kosciusko

Tombigbee National Forest

Thomastown

Yazoo City

49

Carthage

Natchez

Pearl River

3

Delta National Forest

Canton

Meridian

National Military Park

Ridgeland Crafts Center

Ross Barnett Reservoir

20

Vicksburg

Jackson

Bienville National Forest

59

Rocky Springs

Mississippi River

Port Gibson

61

Bayou Pierre

49

45

84

Mount Locust

Laurel

De Soto National Forest

Natchez

84

Brookhaven

Homochitto National Forest

Hattiesburg

Chickasawhay River

ALABAMA

0   50 miles

0   75 km

Pearl River

De Soto National Forest

flowers, which bloom in profusion along the highway: dogwood, redbud, wisteria, and honeysuckle are unforgettable in May. Autumn colors are equally vibrant, with reds, golds, and browns intermingling with the evergreens of pine and juniper.

BARGAINS The Tupelo Visitor Center offers a free film on the development of Natchez Trace, plus an excellent selection of books by southern writers. The Ridgeland Crafts Center outside Jackson (milepost 102.4, tel. 601/856–7546) is a dogtrot cabin filled with the reasonably priced work of members of the Craftsman's Guild of Mississippi. Grand Village of the Natchez Indians (400 Jefferson Davis Blvd., Natchez, tel. 601/446–6502) is a fun, no-admission roadside attraction, with an archaeological park and a museum.

TOURIST OFFICES Get the definitive free map of the route from the Natchez Trace Parkway Visitor Center (RR1, NT-143 [milepost 266], Tupelo, MS 38801, tel. 601/680–4025) or any of the other parkway rest stops. Metro Jackson Convention & Visitors Bureau (Box 1450 [1150 Lakeland Dr.], Jackson, MS 39215, tel. 601/960–1891 or 800/354–7695). Alabama Mountain Lakes Tourist Association (Box 1075, Mooresville, AL 35649, tel. 205/350–3500 or 800/648–5381). Natchez Convention & Visitors Bureau (Box 1485, Natchez, MS 39121, tel. 601/446–6345 or 800/647–6724). Nashville Visitor Information Center (161 4th Ave. N, Nashville, TN 37219, tel. 615/259–4700).

EMERGENCIES **Police, fire,** and **ambulance:** Dial 911 in Tupelo, Jackson, Nashville, Natchez, and Alabama. For help on the Natchez Trace, dial 0 and ask for the nearest Park Ranger. **Hospitals:** North Mississippi Regional Medical Center (830 S. Gloster St., Tupelo, tel. 601/841–3000), Mississippi Baptist Medical Center (1225 N. State St., Jackson, tel. 601/968–1776), Jefferson Davis Hospital (Sgt. Prentiss Dr., Natchez, tel. 601/442–2871), Vanderbilt University Medical Center (1211 22nd Ave. S, Nashville, tel. 615/322–7311).

ARRIVING AND DEPARTING

BY PLANE Delta, American, Continental Express, and Northwest airlines have nonstop daily flights to Jackson from Dallas, Atlanta, and New Orleans, and direct service from other major cities. The airport, Allen C. Thompson Field, is east of town off I–20. Tupelo Municipal Airport is served by Northwest Airlines and American Eagle. Nashville Metropolitan Airport, approximately 8 miles from downtown, is served by American, American Eagle, Comair, Delta, Northwest, Southwest, TWA, United, and USAir.

BY CAR Natchez, Mississippi, the southern beginning of the Natchez Trace, is served by U.S. 61. The Natchez Trace is incomplete at Jackson, connected through the city by I–55 and I–20. From the north, U.S. 78 and U.S. 45 lead to Tupelo. Nashville, Tennessee, about 35 miles north of the Trace, is served by I–65 and I–24 from the north and south, and by I–40 from the east and west.

BY TRAIN Amtrak (tel. 800/USA–RAIL) has frequent trains through Jackson from New Orleans and Chicago but does not serve the Nashville area.

BY BUS Buses from major cities to Nashville arrive at the Southeastern Greyhound Lines terminal (8th Ave. S and McGavock St., tel. 800/231–2222). Greyhound offers daily service to Tupelo, Corinth, Natchez, and Jackson.

GETTING AROUND

BY CAR A car is essential along the Natchez Trace Parkway, which is designed for independent travelers.

REST STOPS The National Park Service maintains almost 20 rest stops with rest room facilities along the parkway, all clearly marked on the Park Service map.

GUIDED TOURS Jackson Tour & Travel (tel. 601/981–8415 or 800/873–8572) organizes tours along the Trace, as well as to nearby New Orleans. Many companies in Nashville offer tours of the musical city; among them

Grand Old Opry Tours (tel. 615/889–9490) and Gray Line of Nashville (tel. 615/227–2270 or 800/251–1864). In Natchez, Pilgrimage Tours, Inc. (tel. 601/446–6631 or 800/647–6742) takes groups through 13 antebellum mansions (up to 30 during the spring and fall pilgrimage seasons), and sells separate admissions to individuals.

EXPLORING

The entire Natchez Trace Parkway could be driven in a very long day, but that's not the way to see it. Travelers who get the most out of the route take it little by little (minding the 50-mph speed limit), with frequent stops at the dozens of trails and historic sites. Four of the best stretches and the principal cities (from south to north) are noted below. Beyond the official parkway, Natchez and Jackson have enough historic diversions to make them destinations in themselves; Vicksburg and its Civil War history make it worth a half-day at least. Nashville, with its glitzy music scene, is just off the northern terminus (*see* the Nashville chapter).

Mount Locust to Rocky Springs (MP 15.5–54.8). At Mount Locust is a restored "stand," or inn, as it was in 1810, now a museum with interpretive programs. Coles Creek (MP 17.5) is a quiet picnic grounds, Owens Creek Waterfall (MP 52.4) has adjacent picnic tables, and the old town site of Rocky Springs (MP 54.8) can be reached by a short trail. En route, swing through the quiet town of Port Gibson, where grand historic mansions line the tree-canopied streets.

Ridgeland Crafts Center to French Camp (MP 102.4–180.7). The crafts center has exhibits, demonstrations, and goods for sale. Reservoir Overlook (MP 105.6) gives a bird's-eye view of the lake that parallels the route for 8 miles. Cypress Swamp (MP 122) has a 20-minute wetlands trail. The Upper Choctaw Boundary (MP 128.5) is an old border marked by a line of trees with a nearby 10-minute nature trail. In autumn, sorghum is made at French Camp (MP 180.7), a settlement founded in 1812.

Jeff Busby to Tupelo (MP 193.1–266). The Jeff Busby stop and its scenic overlook is a good place to rest and refuel. North from here, the original Trace leads into the forest (MP 221.4), and a marker (MP 243.3) points out where Hernando DeSoto camped during the winter of 1540–1541. At Bynum Mounds (MP 232.4), exhibits describe the local prehistoric people; Chickasaw Council House (MP 251.1) is a pretty place for a picnic, and at Tupelo, a national battlefield (MP 259.7) commemorates the battle of 1864.

Dogwood Valley to Tobacco Farm (MP 275.2–401.4). At Dogwood Valley, a 15-minute nature trail wanders through a stand of trees that flower in April. At Pharr Mounds (MP 286.7), a 90-acre burial ground, you can see eight 2,000-year-old mounds and exhibits on their construction and use; Tishomingo State Park (MP 302.8) is a good overnight spot for campers. At Freedom Hills Overlook (MP 317), as the Trace begins its 33-mile run across the northwest corner of Alabama, a quarter-mile trail leads to an 800-foot vantage point. A creekside trail at Rock Spring, Alabama (MP 330.2), wanders through a hilly forest, and at Old Trace Drive (MP 375.8), now in Tennessee, a road follows the original Trace for 2½ miles. Tobacco Farm (MP 401.4) has a curing barn and exhibits on the agriculture of the weed; a 2-mile unpaved side road follows the original route of the Trace to several scenic overlooks.

Natchez. This is a city out of time, its beautiful antebellum mansions spared the fiery fate of those in other southern towns, thanks to Natchez sympathies for the Union. Tours can be arranged through Pilgrimage Tour Headquarters. Historic Natchez-under-the-Hill—a former brothel district overlooking the Mississippi River—is a popular area for nightlife that includes dockside gambling.

Jackson. The soul of Mississippi's capital is preserved in its old downtown architecture and several museums. The Agriculture and Forestry Museum (1150 Lakeland Dr., tel. 601/354–6113; open daily, except Thanksgiving, Christmas, and New Year's; admission charged) is a working farm. The state's Old

Capitol Building is perched atop Capitol Green, with a view of the State Historical Museum (100 N. State St., tel. 601/359–1000; open daily, except holidays; admission charged). The Mississippi Arts Center has changing exhibits and an Impressions Gallery with interactive exhibits of electronic art (201 E. Pascagoula St., tel. 601/960–1515; open Tues.–Sun., except holidays; admission charged). The Eudora Welty Library is the biggest in Mississippi (300 N. State St., tel. 601/968–5811; open daily except holidays).

Vicksburg National Military Park. Adjacent to the historic river town of Vicksburg, this enormous park has a visitor center and a 16-mile drive past hundreds of memorials honoring the dead of both sides in the great siege of Vicksburg in 1863; one stop on the drive is at the USS *Cairo,* the first ironclad ever sunk by an electronic mine. *Clay St. (U.S. 80), 1 mi from I–20, Exit 4B, tel. 601/636–0583. Open daily, except Christmas. Admission charged.*

Tupelo. Elvis Presley was born in this city, and locals have seen fit to restore his boyhood home (off Old Hwy. 78, at 306 Elvis Presley Dr., tel. 601/841–1245; open Tues.–Sun., closed Thanksgiving and Christmas; admission charged). The Tupelo Museum has further Presley memorabilia as well as an old-time country store, a train depot, and an old Western Union office (off Rte. 6W, tel. 601/841–6438; open Tues.–Sun.; admission charged).

Nashville. Best known for its music, this Tennessee city is also a repository of southern culture (*see* the Nashville chapter).

THE NATURAL WORLD Dozens of well-marked nature trails, surprisingly unchanged by humans, offer something for hikers of every level. Wildflowers are brilliant in season along Sweetwater Branch trail (MP 363), a 20-minute walk along a fast-flowing stream. Occasional flooding along a 20-minute trail to Donavan Slough (MP 283.3) creates a botanically interesting plant variety. You can examine plants the Indians used in a short walk on the outskirts of Chickasaw Village (MP 261.8). At Cole Creek (MP 175.6) and at Cypress Swamp (MP 122) there are wetlands walks. At Bullen Creek (MP 18.4), a 15-minute trail wanders through a hardwood-pine forest.

HOTELS AND INNS

The Old South comes alive in historic lodging up and down the Natchez Trace, though some places—like the ones in Vicksburg—are a few miles off the parkway. Natchez is well endowed with accommodations, and Nashville has a large concentration of lodgings. Price categories for double occupancy, without room and tax (7% in Tennessee, 6% in Mississippi), are *Expensive,* $85–$100; *Moderate,* $50–$85; and *Inexpensive,* under $50.

NATCHEZ **Eola Hotel.** Nicely restored to its Roaring Twenties glory, this grand old hotel—it's listed on the National Register of Historic Places—has a tiny formal lobby and somewhat cramped rooms with antique reproduction furniture; the guest house across the street has bigger rooms with balconies. *110 N. Pearl St., 39120, tel. 601/445–6000 or 800/888–9140. 122 rooms. Restaurant. AE, DC, MC, V. Moderate.*

Monmouth. This massive and immaculate bed-and-breakfast inn, originally built in 1818, sits regally on 26 verdant acres. Rooms and suites in the Main and Carriage Houses, and in the garden cottages, feature period antiques and decor. *36 Melrose Ave., 39120, tel. 601/442–5852 or 800/828–4531. 19 rooms. Full breakfast included. AE, D, MC, V. Moderate–Expensive.*

VICKSBURG **Anchuca.** Visitors have rooms in the slave quarters or in the turn-of-the-century guest cottage of this oak-shaded antebellum mansion. *1010 1st East St., 39180, tel. 601/636–4931 or 800/262–4822. 9 rooms. Pool, hot tub. Breakfast and house tour included. AE, MC, V. Moderate–Expensive.*

Duff Green Mansion. This 1856 house, which was used as a Civil War hospital, is generously decorated with antiques, including half-tester beds. *1114 1st East St., 39180, tel. 601/638–6662. 7 rooms, 1 suite. Pool, court-*

yard, gazebo. Breakfast and house tour included. AE, MC, V. Moderate–Expensive.

JACKSON **Edison Walthall Hotel.** Distinguished by its decor, which seems like a restoration, this hotel is outfitted with marble floors, shiny brass, and a comfortable, old-fashioned bar. *225 E. Capitol St., 39201, tel. 601/948–6161 or 800/932–6161. 208 rooms. Heated pool, whirlpool, airport transportation, fitness center, copiers. AE, D, DC, MC, V. Moderate–Expensive.*

DUCK RIVER **The McEwen Farm Log Cabin Bed and Breakfast.** This farm near the northern end of the parkway has two comfortable cabins and a restored train station that has been turned into a two-bedroom lodge. *Box 97, Bratton La., TN 38454, tel. 615/583–2378. 4 rooms. MC, V. Expensive.*

NASHVILLE **Monthaven Bed & Breakfast.** This 1840 Greek Revival mansion on a farm just outside Nashville shows many Victorian elements and has a log cabin for guests. *1154 W. Main St., Hendersonville 37075, tel. 615/824–6319. 2 rooms, 1 cabin. Restaurant, pool. AE, D, DC, MC, V. Moderate.*

MOTELS

MODERATE **Executive Inn Tupelo** (1011 N. Gloster, Tupelo 38801, tel. 601/841–2222). 119 rooms; indoor pool, whirlpool, sauna, cable TV. **Holiday Inn–Downtown Jackson** (200 E. Amite St., Jackson 39201, tel. 601/969–5100 or 800/HOLIDAY). 358 rooms; restaurant, lounge, pool. **Nashville La Quinta Motor Inn** (2001 Metrocenter Blvd., Nashville 37227, tel. 615/259–2130 or 800/531–5900). 21 rooms; pool, cable TV. **Ramada Hilltop Natchez** (130 John R. Junkin Dr., Natchez 39120, tel. 601/446–6311 or 800/272–6232). 62 rooms; restaurant, lounge. **Ramada Renaissance Hotel–Jackson** (1001 Count Line Rd., Jackson 39211, tel. 601/957–2800 or 800/272–6232). 300 rooms; airport transportation, restaurant, live entertainment, lobby bar, gift shop, barbershop.

INEXPENSIVE **Comfort Inn–Vicksburg** (I–20 Frontage Road S, 39180, tel. 601/634–8607 or 800/228–5150). 50 rooms; exercise room, whirlpool, sauna. **Nashville Comfort Inn Hermitage** (5768 Old Hickory Blvd., 37076, tel. 615/889–5060 or 800/228–5150). 100 rooms, 7 suites; pool. **Tupelo Trace Inn** (3400 W. Main St., 38801, tel. 601/842–5555). 165 rooms; pool, playground, airport transportation.

CAMPGROUNDS

All three of the National Park Service campgrounds are open on a first-come, first-served basis and are rarely crowded. There are no hookups, no showers, and no fees. Each campground has central rest rooms with basins and flush toilets; each campsite has a picnic table and grill. For information, contact the superintendent, Natchez Trace Park Service (RR 1, NT143, Tupelo, 38801, tel. 601/842–1572).

J. P. Coleman State Park on Pickwick Lake in northernmost Mississippi has wooded campsites and rough-hewn cabins, many on the lake. Facilities include rowboat rentals, a pool, miniature golf, and waterskiing. It is 45 minutes off the parkway, but worth the drive. *Rte. 5, Box 504, Iuka 38852 (13 mi north of Iuka off U.S. 25), tel. 601/423–6515. 47 RV sites with full and partial hookups ($11), 16 tent sites ($6), and 10 cabins ($40–$48); showers, flush toilets, picnic tables and grills. Reservations required for cabins. MC, V.*

Tishomingo State Park is off the parkway in the Appalachian foothills—rare terrain in Mississippi. It has a primitive camping area, RV sites, six rustic cabins, a 13-mile nature trail through a scenic canyon, and canoe float trips. *Box 880, Tishomingo 38838 (3 mi north of Dennis off U.S. 25), tel. 601/438–6914. 62 RV sites with partial hookups ($10), tent sites ($6), six cabins ($38–$43); showers, bathrooms, picnic tables and barbecue areas. Reservations required for cabins. MC, V.*

DINING

Though most places along the Trace still reflect a bias for southern and Creole food, grilled entrées are replacing deep-fried offerings. Price categories per person, not including tax (8% in Mississippi, 7.75% in Tennessee), service, and drinks, are *Moderate,* $15–$25, and *Inexpensive,* under $15.

NATCHEZ **Natchez Landing.** Tables on the porch have a view of the Mississippi and the riverboat landing below the street, a bustling 19th-century hangout for gamblers and prostitutes. Grilled catfish is a specialty, the salads are good, and the barbecue respectable. *11 Silver St., Natchez-Under-the-Hill, tel. 601/442–6639. AE, MC, V. Inexpensive–Moderate.*

City Banc Cafe & Grill. Recently opened inside an old bank building in downtown Natchez, the City Banc balances its new marble floors and columns with hearty southern favorites and lighter nouveau entrées such as grilled lemon chicken and seafood pasta. *409 Franklin St., tel. 601/445–4946. AE, DC, MC, V. Moderate.*

Scrooge's. This old storefront has a saloon atmosphere downstairs and quieter dining upstairs. It serves beans and rice, mesquite-grilled chicken, and a number of seafood dishes. *315 Main St., tel. 601/446–9922. Closed Sun. AE, MC, V. Inexpensive.*

VICKSBURG **Tuminello's.** Vicksburg locals have enjoyed fresh seafood, steaks, and veal at Tuminello's since 1899, when this family-run business first opened. Almost a hundred years later, dinner at Tuminello's remains a popular tradition. *500 Speed St., tel. 601/634–0507. AE, DC, MC, V. Inexpensive–Moderate.*

JACKSON **Gridley's.** The city's barbecue spot of choice, with well-seasoned chicken as well as ribs, this café specializes in fast service and is open for breakfast on Saturday, serving plate-size pancakes for $1. *1428 Old Square Rd., tel. 601/362–8600. AE, MC, V. Inexpensive.*

Hal and Mal's Restaurant and Oyster Bar. This old warehouse, renovated with neon, 1930s memorabilia, and an eclectic mix of antiques, is the place for grilled fresh fish and grilled chicken. *200 Commerce St., tel. 601/948–0888. MC, V. Inexpensive.*

Ralph & Kacoo's. This is authentic Cajun, no doubt about it. Ralph and Kacoo started in south Louisiana, and they've since introduced Jackson to crawfish étouffée and blackened catfish the way it was meant to be—down-home Louisiana style. *100 Dyess Rd. at I–55, tel. 601/957–0702. AE, MC, V. Moderate.*

The Mayflower. A 1930s-style diner with black-and-white tiled floors, straight-back booths, and Formica-topped counters, this restaurant is known for its Greek salads and fresh fish sautéed in lemon butter. *123 W. Capitol St., tel. 601/355–4122. No credit cards. Inexpensive.*

NASHVILLE **Cakewalk Restaurant.** A popular spot with the Vanderbilt University crowd, this café's eclectic menu embraces healthy California and Southwest cuisine and regional favorites. *3001 West End Ave., tel. 615/320–7778. Dinner reservations recommended. DC, MC, V. Inexpensive.*

Jimmy Kelly's. This Nashville favorite has served great steaks and seafood for more than 50 years; nowadays it serves from a restored Victorian mansion. *217 Louise Ave., tel. 615/329–4349. Dinner only. AE, MC, V. Inexpensive–Moderate.*

SHOPPING

GIFTS AND CRAFTS Good deals on regional souvenirs can be had at the Old Country Store (U.S. 61, tel. 601/437–3661), a repository of local culture since 1890.

FLEA MARKETS AND ANTIQUES The Nashville Flea Market at the fairgrounds is on the fourth Saturday of every month (tel. 615/383–7636). And try the Smorgasbord Antique Mall (4144-B Lebanon Rd., tel. 615/883–5789). Jackson has C. W. Fewel III & Co. (840 N. State St., tel. 601/355–5375) and Bobbie King's (Woodland Hills Shopping Center, tel. 601/362–9803).

OUTDOOR ACTIVITIES

BOATING, FISHING, WATER SPORTS Elvis Presley Lake and Campground on the outskirts of Tupelo (tel. 601/841–1304), at Tishomingo State Park and J. P. Coleman State Park.

GOLF In Jackson, Lefleur's Bluff State Park (tel. 601/987–3998). Near Nashville, Hermitage Golf Course (tel. 615/847–4001) and Harpeth Hills (615/373–8202).

TENNIS In Jackson, Tennis Center South (2827 Oak Forest Dr., off McDowell Rd., tel. 601/960–1712) and Parham Bridges Park (5055 Old Canton Rd., tel. 601/956–1105). In Natchez, Duncan Park (Duncan St. at Auburn Ave). In Nashville, Centennial Sportsplex Tennis Center (tel. 615/872–8490).

ENTERTAINMENT

There's always something doing in Natchez, and even more so now that dockside gambling has arrived. The replica paddle wheeler *Lady Luck* (tel. 601/445–0605) is permanently docked at Natchez-under-the-Hill, on the Mississippi River, and offers Las Vegas–style gambling 24 hours a day, plus food and spirits. There is no admission charge.

In Jackson, The Dock (Main Harbor Marina at Ross Barnett Reservoir, tel. 601/856–7765) is especially popular on Sundays. Poet's (1855 Lakeland Dr., tel. 601/982–9711) has a nightly jazz trio (*see* the Nashville chapter).

New Orleans
Louisiana

For most visitors, New Orleans means Mardi Gras, the French Quarter, electrifying jazz, and great food. New Orleans is both an old-fashioned town with 10 historic districts and a major world city with a thriving port and an insouciant, fun-loving soul that bedevils progressives bent on jerking it into the 20th century.

Its party-town reputation is well founded—local folks eagerly celebrate anything at the drop of a hat. Mardi Gras is the biggest bash in all North America, and 6 million annual visitors is the city's version of having a few friends in. Carnival season officially starts on Twelfth Night, January 6, and builds up to its frenzied culmination on "Fat Tuesday," the day before the beginning of Lent.

To experience this fun-filled city, you must go beyond the usual tourist attractions to linger in a corner grocery store, sip a cold drink in a local joint, or chat with a stoop-sit-ter. Orleanians love their city. They treasure tradition, bask in the sultry semitropical climate, and look at life with a laid-back attitude that makes New Orleans seem a close cousin to her Caribbean neighbors.

ESSENTIAL INFORMATION

WHEN TO GO In June, July, and August, when it can stay above 95° for weeks, merely mustering the energy to lift a mint julep may cause malaise. Happily, virtually everything is air-conditioned. June through November is hurricane season, when torrential rains and high winds can hit. During the mild winters (around 47° to 60°) high humidity puts a chill in the air. The best time to visit is early spring, when days are pleasant, nights are coolish, and the city blossoms with flowers and festivals.

If you want to peacefully savor the city's considerable charms, avoid arriving the last weekend in April—the beginning of the 10-

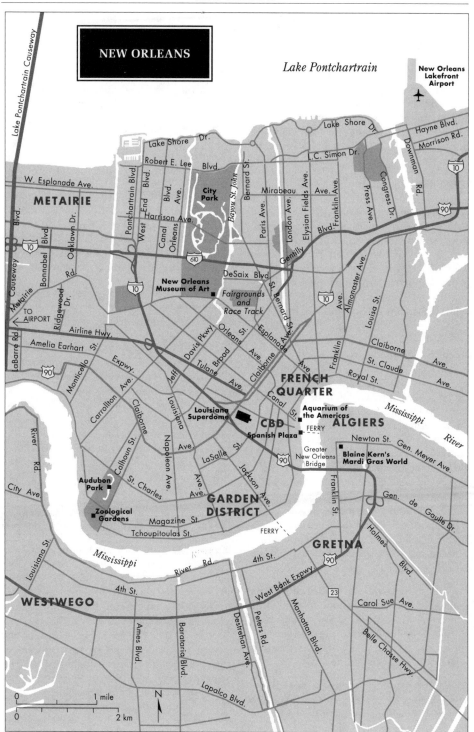

day Jazz Fest, when several thousand musicians and aficionados flock into town. And during Mardi Gras (Feb. or Mar.), about a million people jam the French Quarter and the Central Business District (CBD) to see the "greatest free show on earth." In summer, many hotels offer discount rates, and during the month-long Creole Christmas, which can be snow white or white hot, you can find attractive "Papa Noel" packages with low rates.

BARGAINS The ancient art of street theater is practiced in exuberant New Orleans style in Jackson Square and Woldenberg Riverfront Park. In the early 1990s, long-suffering neighbors around Jackson Square managed to get the loudest of the jazz bands banished to Woldenberg Riverfront Park, but Jackson Square abounds with tap dancers, bongo players, unicyclists, clowns, and fire-eaters who vie for attention (and loose change). New Orleans street musicians, incidentally the best in the busker business, are out in full force in all but the worst weather in the Square, the Riverfront Park, and on Royal Street; performers range from a solo vocalist doing soulful spirituals to a 10-piece Dixieland band tearing up the patch. Free concerts are performed regularly in Dutch Alley at the French Market; schedules are available at the Dutch Alley kiosk. And for the price of a drink, you can hang out and hear great jazz in one of the open-air cafés of the French Market. Doors of Bourbon Street music clubs are flung wide, and you have but to lean against a lamppost and soak it in. Old-time jazz legends play nightly in funky Preservation Hall, where a mere $3 buys four hours of the best traditional jazz in the world.

For a leisurely 12-minute scenic ride, take the commuter ferry from the foot of Canal Street across the Mississippi to Algiers and back. Passage is free each way for pedestrians; motorists pay $1 per vehicle for the trip from Algiers to Canal Street.

Mardi Gras parades begin marching a full two weeks before the final day, so if you book well in advance (say, a year) for the weekend before the big Mardi Gras weekend, you can get a room at a reasonable rate and still see what all the shouting's about. The Germaine Wells Mardi Gras Museum on the second floor of Arnaud's Restaurant (813 Bienville St., tel. 504/523–5433), with its dazzling display of Carnival gowns and memorabilia, is free to the public.

Park rangers of the Jean Lafitte National Park Service (916–18 N. Peters St., tel. 504/589–2636) conduct daily free history tours of the French Quarter and the Garden District.

TOURIST OFFICES Greater New Orleans Tourist and Convention Commission (1520 Sugar Bowl Dr., New Orleans 70112, tel. 504/566–5011). The New Orleans Welcome Center (529 St. Ann St., Jackson Square, New Orleans 70116, tel. 504/566–5068).

EMERGENCIES Dial 911 for **police, fire,** and **ambulance. Hospitals** with 24-hour emergency rooms are Charity Hospital (1532 Tulane Ave., tel. 504/568–2311), the Tulane University Medical Center (220 Lasalle St., tel. 504/588–5711), Touro Infirmary (1401 Foucher St., tel. 504/897–8250). **Doctors:** Orleans Parish Medical Society (tel. 504/523–2474). **Dentists:** New Orleans Dental Association (tel. 504/834–6449). **Pharmacies:** Walgreens (900 Canal St., tel. 504/523–7201) remains open until 9 PM, Eckerd (3400 Canal St., tel. 504/488–6661) and K&B (3100 Gentilly Blvd., tel. 504/947–6611) are both open 24 hours.

ARRIVING AND DEPARTING

BY PLANE New Orleans International Airport (tel. 504/464–0831), 15 miles west of the city in Kenner, is served by all major airlines. Ground transportation to downtown hotels takes 20–40 minutes on the Airport Shuttle (tel. 504/522–3500 or 800/543–6332, fax 504/592–0549; $10) and in taxis ($21 for one or two passengers, $8 for each additional passenger); the Airport Express Bus (tel. 504/737–9611; $1.10) takes 45 minutes to an hour to reach Elk Place in the CBD.

BY CAR I–10 runs from Florida to California and passes directly through the city. Exit at

Poydras Street for the business district; for the French Quarter, take the Vieux Carre exit.

BY TRAIN AND BUS Union Passenger Terminal (1001 Loyola Ave., CBD, tel. 504/528–1610 or 800/USA–RAIL) is the terminal for Amtrak trains and Greyhound Lines (tel. 800/231–2222).

GETTING AROUND

ON FOOT The best way to see the French Quarter and the CBD is on a leisurely stroll. The Garden District is also walkable, but you'll need transportation to get there and to other parts of town.

BY CAR The narrow streets of the French Quarter were laid out for horse-drawn rigs, not horseless carriages; and several streets are pedestrian malls during the day. Traffic is maddening during special events, parking signs are indecipherable, and illegally parked cars are towed away fast. It's best to leave your car in a secured garage.

BY STREETCAR The St. Charles Streetcar ($1 exact change, 10¢ for transfers), the city's movable historic landmark, makes the picturesque 5-mile trek from the CBD to Carrollton Avenue around the clock through the Garden District and Uptown, past Audubon Park and Audubon Zoo. The Riverfront Streetcar ($1.25 exact change) connects Esplanade Avenue to the New Orleans Convention Center. The Regional Transit Authority staffs a 24-hour route-information line (tel. 504/569–2700).

BY BUS Fare on the interconnecting lines is $1, plus 10¢ for transfers. The Vieux Carre Shuttle ($1 exact change), which looks like a miniature trolley, scoots around the Quarter and to the foot of Canal Street. A free map available at the New Orleans Welcome Center shows bus and streetcar routes most used by tourists.

BY TAXI Cabs are metered at $1.70 minimum, plus $1 per mile and 50¢ for each additional passenger. Cabs can be hailed in the CBD and the French Quarter, but in other areas it's usually necessary to call one from

Yellow-Checker Cabs (tel. 504/525–3311), Liberty Bell Cabs (tel. 504/822–5974), or United Cabs (504/522–9771 or 800/323–3303), many of which take credit cards ($5 minimum).

REST STOPS There are clean public rest rooms in the Jackson Brewery and Millhouse in the French Quarter, on the third level of Canal Place, the fourth level of the World Trade Center, and each level of Riverwalk in the CBD, and in department stores and hotels. During Mardi Gras and the Jazz Fest, virtually all restaurants, bars, and guest houses post REST ROOMS FOR PATRONS ONLY signs. During those special events the city sets up portable toilets in the Quarter and the CBD, but there aren't nearly enough to accommodate the huge crowds of people.

GUIDED TOURS **Orientation:** Two-hour city tours by bus are conducted by Gray Line (tel. 504/587–0861) and New Orleans Tours (tel. 504/592–1991 or 800/543–6332). Tours by Isabelle (tel. 504/367–3963) offers three-hour city tours in 14-passenger vans. Gray Line and New Orleans Tours also have combination city tours and riverboat rides.

Special-Interest: The three above companies offer full-day bus tours of plantations, with a lunch stop. Tours of the swamps and Cajun Country are run by Gator Tours (tel. 504/484–6100), Gray Line, Tours by Isabelle, and Honey Island Swamp Tours (tel. 504/641–1769). New Orleans Tours does nighttime tours to popular jazz clubs. To visit New Orleans's famed "Cities of the Dead," contact Save Our Cemeteries (tel. 504/588–9357).

Boat Excursions: For dinner-plus-jazz riverboat cruises, contact the *Creole Queen* (tel. 504/524–0814 or 800/445–4109) or the *Natchez* (tel. 504/586–8777 or 800/233–BOAT).

Walking Tours: Daily walking tours of the Quarter that take in two museums (about 2$^{1/2}$ hours) are led by the Friends of the Cabildo (tel. 504/523–3939). Heritage Tours (tel. 504/949–9805) offers a general literary tour and walks focusing on William Faulkner or Tennessee Williams. Classic Tours (tel.

504/899–1862) covers art, antiques, architecture, and history; the Preservation Resource Center (tel. 504/581–7032) occasionally does guided architecture tours.

EXPLORING

The serpentine Father of Waters dictates directions here. The city radiates out from an 8-mile stretch between a loop of the Mississippi River and Lake Pontchartrain. Downtown, which includes the French Quarter and the CBD, is "downriver," the Garden District and Uptown are "upriver," and north and south are "lakeside" and "riverside." Free maps for self-guided walking and driving tours are available at the New Orleans Welcome Center. Seeing and doing everything in the Quarter can take days; allow time for an afternoon or evening riverboat cruise, a day trip to the bayous or plantation country, and at least a half day each to see the Garden District, the parks, and the zoo.

Aquarium of the Americas. The spectacular design of the riverfront aquarium offers viewers close-up encounters with more than 7,000 aquatic creatures from the Amazon River Basin, the Caribbean Reef, the Mississippi River, and the Gulf Coast. *Foot of Canal St., CBD, tel. 504/861–2537. Open daily. Admission charged.*

Audubon Park and Zoo. Splendidly landscaped by Frederick Law Olmsted, the 340-acre park includes an 18-hole golf course, riding stables, tennis courts, picnic and play areas, hiking and biking trails, and a 2-mile jogging path with 18 exercise stations. The world-class Audubon Zoo occupies 58 acres between the park and the river. Wooden walkways lead to the Louisiana Swamp Exhibit, the tropical bird house, the flamingo pond, the sea lions, and the white tiger. The Mombasa miniature tram circles through the African Savannah. A free shuttle van runs from the Audubon Park entrance on St. Charles Avenue to the zoo, but a 25-minute walk will take you there through Oak Alley, one of the most enchanting settings in New Orleans. *6500 Magazine St., tel. 504/861–2537. Open daily. Admission charged for zoo.*

Blaine Kern's Mardi Gras World. The largest float-builder in the world is in Algiers, an old residential district across the river from downtown. A tour here takes you through the warehouses, or dens, where the spectacular floats are constructed. Mardi Gras World provides a free shuttle that meets each incoming ferry in Algiers and transports visitors to the Blaine Kern attraction. *233 Newton St., tel. 504/361–7821. Open daily. Closed Mardi Gras Day. Admission charged.*

Central Business District. One of the city's most exciting areas, where Canal Street meets the river (the "foot of Canal Street"), the CBD is within walking distance of the French Quarter and most downtown hotels. The riverfront has been dramatically developed in recent years, and here you'll find the Aquarium of the Americas, Spanish Plaza, riverboat landings, and Riverwalk (*see* Shopping, *below*). The state legislature has approved a land-based casino for New Orleans (as well as gambling riverboats on the state's waterways), and the likely location will be the long-closed Rivergate Exhibition Center at the foot of Canal Street.

City Park. Among the attractions in the park's 1,500 acres of greenery and scenery are lagoons for fishing or canoeing beneath moss-draped live oaks; golf courses, tennis courts, baseball diamonds, paths for jogging, hiking, and biking; a children's amusement park with a turn-of-the-century carousel; botanical gardens; and the New Orleans Museum of Art.

French Quarter. The heart and soul of the city is the original French Creole colony, which covers an easily walkable square mile. Start in Jackson Square to watch the street entertainers and to explore its historic buildings: St. Louis Cathedral, and the Cabildo and Presbytère, part of the **Louisiana State Museum complex** (tel. 504/568–6968; open Tues.–Sun.; admission charged). Royal Street has fine antiques stores and art galleries, while funky Bourbon Street is famed for its bars and music clubs. An only-in-New Orleans attraction is the **Voodoo Museum** (724 Dumaine St., tel. 504/523–7685; open daily; admission charged). At the **Musée Conti Wax Museum**

(917 Conti St., tel. 504/525–2605; open daily except Mardi Gras Day; admission charged), lifelike figures in colorful tableaux depict the city's history. In museums like the **Gallier House** (1132 Royal St., tel. 504/523–6722; open daily; admission charged) and the **Hermann-Grima House** (820 St. Louis St., tel. 504/525–5661; open daily; admission charged), you can get a taste of elegant 19th-century Creole living.

Garden District. Take the St. Charles Streetcar to First Street to see some of America's most palatial private houses. Walk one block toward the river to Prytania Street, 1st, 3rd, and 4th streets (which cross Prytania Street), and along St. Charles Avenue.

Lake Pontchartrain. A favorite playground for Orleanians, the 40-mile-long lake is a fit place for fishing and boating (but not swimming). The world's longest causeway crosses it to the piney woods on the north shore. Along Lakeshore Drive there are picnic grounds and marinas.

New Orleans Museum of Art. A nationally recognized museum, NOMA has a large permanent collection of pre-Columbian, African, and local art, works by some European and American masters, and Fabergé eggs. In 1993, the museum completed a $23.5 million expansion and now includes 130,000 square feet of space in which to display its $200 million collection. *City Park, tel. 504/488–2631. Open Tues.–Sun. Admission charged.*

Spanish Plaza. Several sightseeing riverboats tie up at this broad, open plaza at the foot of Canal Street. The plaza is laid with colorful mosaic tiles, and its centerpiece is a splashy fountain that's lighted at night. It is the site of the city's annual Lundi Gras bash—a free and freewheeling *bal masqué* that ushers in the final 24 hours of Mardi Gras.

THE NATURAL WORLD On tours into the murky reaches of the bayous and swamps, you'll get a gander at 'gators, egrets, nutria, and such. You can go canoeing on your own or with a guide deep into the former hideouts of pirates in the Barataria Unit of the Jean Lafitte National Historical Park (tel. 504/589–2330), an area of beautiful coastal wetlands with about 8 miles of trails.

HOTELS AND INNS

New Orleans has a wide variety of accommodations, including high-rise hotels, antiques-filled antebellum houses, Creole cottages, old slave quarters, and familiar hotel chains. Price categories for double occupancy, excluding 11% tax, are *Expensive,* $100–$125; *Moderate,* $75–$100; and *Inexpensive,* under $75.

MODERATE-EXPENSIVE **Clarion Hotel.** Easily accessible off I–10 and about a 10-minute walk from the French Quarter, this large full-service high rise has average-size and unimaginatively decorated rooms, but the rates are good for the CBD. *1500 Canal St., CBD, 70112, tel. 504/522–4500 or 800/824–3359, fax 504/525–2644. 736 rooms, 23 suites with wet bars. Restaurant, 24-hour deli, pool, hot tub, exercise room, laundry, free shuttle to French Quarter, valet parking. AE, DC, MC, V.*

Cornstalk Hotel. Individually decorated rooms with four-poster and canopy beds, armoires, fireplaces, balconies, and galleries are among the attractions of this 1816 Victorian-style house in the Lower Quarter. *915 Royal St., French Quarter, 70116, tel. 504/523–1515. 14 rooms. Free Continental breakfast. AE, MC, V.*

Crowne Plaza. A glass-and-concrete high rise smack in the midst of the CBD, the Crowne Plaza is an upmarket Holiday Inn hotel. Public areas are spacious, with plenty of fresh flowers and greenery, and guest rooms are large and color-coordinated with good-quality spreads, drapery, and upholstery. *333 Poydras St., 70130, tel. 504/525–9444 or 800/522–6963, fax 504/568–9312. 437 rooms, 2 suites. 2 restaurants, lounge, health club, outdoor pool and Jacuzzi, valet parking. AE, D, DC, MC, V.*

Le Pavillon. In the heart of the CBD, this European-style hotel with smart awnings, magnificent chandeliers, and rooms with high ceilings and hand-carved furnishings attracts savvy Europeans who know a bargain when they find one. *833 Poydras St., CBD, 70140, tel. 504/581–3111 or 800/535–9095, fax 504/522–5543. 220 rooms, 8 suites. 2 restaurants, pool and sun deck, 2 no-smoking floors, valet laundry, parking. AE, DC, MC, V.*

MODERATE **Chateau Motor Hotel.** Near Jackson Square, a carriageway sweeps into the small courtyard of this balconied Creole house, which has a mix of 19th-century Louisiana antiques and contemporary or traditional furnishings. Continental breakfast is included in the rate. *1001 Chartres St., French Quarter, 70116, tel. 504/524–9636, fax 504/525–2989. 39 rooms, 6 suites. Restaurant, pool, valet parking. AE, DC, MC, V.*

Le Richelieu. One of the city's best bargains, the five renovated row houses that comprise this hotel near the French Market contain large, walk-in closets, brass ceiling fans, full-size ironing boards, and many rooms have mirrored walls and refrigerators and balconies. *1234 Chartres St., French Quarter, 70116, tel. 504/529–2492 or 800/535–9653, fax 504/524–8179. 69 rooms, 17 suites. Restaurant, pool, valet service, free parking. AE, DC, MC, V.*

Park View Guest House. Adjacent to Audubon Park, this 1884 Victorian mansion has brass beds, ceiling fans, splendid views in rooms facing the park, and a casual atmosphere. *7004 St. Charles Ave., Uptown, 70118, tel. 504/861–7564. 25 rooms, 10 with shared bath. Free Continental breakfast. AE, MC, V.*

Prytania Park Hotel. A half block from the St. Charles Streetcar line, this hotel complex with several balconied units comprises an 1834 town house, with exposed brick walls and period reproductions, and newer contemporary sections with lofts, refrigerators, and microwaves. *1525 Prytania St., Garden District, 70130, tel. 504/524–0427 or 800/862–1984, fax 504/522–2977. 62 rooms, 6 suites. Free Continental breakfast. AE, DC, MC, V.*

St. Charles Inn. This small, modern Uptown hotel offers good-size rooms with dressing areas (those on the front can be noisy), a

friendly staff, and the convenience of the adjacent Que Sera Restaurant. *3636 St. Charles Ave., Garden District, 70115, tel. 504/899–8888. 40 rooms. Free newspaper and Continental breakfast. AE, DC, MC, V.*

Terrell Guest House. In a somewhat seedy neighborhood that's being renovated, this 1858 mansion, with handsome double parlors and 19th-century antiques, has a room and a suite in the main house and other rooms in the carriage house and slave quarters facing a patio with a fountain. *1441 Magazine St., Lower Garden District, 70130, tel. 504/524–9859 or 800/878–9859. 8 rooms, 1 suite. Free Continental breakfast. AE, MC, V.*

INEXPENSIVE-MODERATE **Bon Maison Guest House.** On the quiet end of Bourbon Street, this 1840 town house has simply furnished rooms in renovated slave quarters off a courtyard and in large suites in the main house atop very steep, winding stairs. *835 Bourbon St., French Quarter, 70116, tel. 504/561–8498. 3 rooms, 2 suites. Kitchenettes. MC, V.*

Hotel Villa Convento. Near the Old Ursuline Convent in the Lower Quarter, this family-run hotel occupying a three-story, 1848 Creole town house festooned with ironwork has antique reproductions in individually decorated rooms and a patio area. *616 Ursulines St., French Quarter, 70116, tel. 504/522–1793, fax 504/524–1902. 25 rooms. Free Continental breakfast. AE, DC, MC, V.*

INEXPENSIVE **French Quarter Maisonettes.** From a quiet residential street a broad carriageway leads through heavy iron gates to a lovely courtyard around which budget travelers stay in two- and three-room functionally furnished units (no phones), and receive helpful advice on inexpensive dining and sightseeing. *1130 Chartres St., French Quarter, 70116, tel. 504/524–9918. 1 room, 7 suites. No credit cards. Closed July.*

Maison St. Charles. You wouldn't know by the lobby's gilded tables and Frederic Remington sculptures that this is a Quality Inn—one of the chain's top-of-the-line hotels, built around five spacious, flower-filled courtyards. *1319 St. Charles Ave., 70130, tel.*

504/522–0187 or 800/831–1783, fax 504/525–2218. 121 rooms, 11 suites; restaurant, outdoor pool, heated whirlpool, no-smoking rooms, valet parking. AE, MC, V.

St. Charles Guest House. The affable owners of this simple European-style pension, one block off St. Charles Avenue, offer rooms in four buildings (some are small, with shared baths and no air-conditioning), a guide to self-conducted tours, and occasionally a home-cooked crawfish boil or red-beans-and-rice meal. *1748 Prytania St., Garden District, 70130, tel. 504/523–6556. 22 rooms, 4 with shared bath. Common room, outdoor pool and sun deck. AE, MC, V.*

MOTELS

MODERATE **Days Inn Downtown** (1630 Canal St., 70112, tel. 504/586–0110 or 800/232–3297, fax 504/561–2253). 206 rooms, 8 suites; restaurant, pool, laundry, free parking. **Holiday Inn Downtown–Superdome** (330 Loyola Ave., 70112, tel. 504/581–1600 or 800/535–7830, fax 504/586–0833). 296 rooms, 4 suites; restaurant, pool, hydrospa, parking. **Holiday Inn & Holidome–New Orleans Airport** (2929 Williams Blvd., Kenner, 70062, tel. 504/567–5611 or 800/HOLIDAY, fax 504/469–4915). 302 rooms, 1 suite; restaurant, lounge, indoor pool, Jacuzzi, exercise room, laundry facilities, free parking.

DINING

New Orleans restaurants reflect 270 years of ethnic culinary overlap by the French, African, Spanish, American Indian, Caribbean, Italian, German, and Yugoslavian schools, joined in the 1980s by Asian chefs. The lines between south Louisiana's two mother cuisines—Creole and Cajun—have blurred, but simply put, Creole cuisine carries an urban gloss, epitomized by rich, creamy sauces, while Cajun food is more rough-hewn and rural. A few restaurants offer limited listings of foods lower in calories, cholesterol, and fat; bear in mind that seafood is king in these parts, and you can pass up the rich sauces. Call in advance for reservations and to find out what meals are served. Price categories per person, not including 9% tax, service, and drinks, are *Moderate*, $15–$25, and *Inexpensive*, under $15.

MODERATE **Alex Patout's.** The fixed-price menus are good values in this stylish restaurant, which spotlights deep-flavored gumbo, sautéed lemon fish with a roasted-pepper sauce, eggplant stuffed with crab and shrimp, and duck with oyster dressing. *221 Royal St., French Quarter, tel. 504/525–7788. Jacket advised for dinner. AE, DC, MC, V.*

Bayona. Although chef Susan Spicer's dinner menu tops the moderate price range, you can get a taste of her popular cuisine at lunch when prices drop to well within budget. For starters, ask for grilled shrimp with black-bean cake and coriander sauce. The grilled quail salad comes with mixed greens and tasty surprises of raspberries, strawberries, and hazelnuts. *430 Dauphine St., French Quarter, tel. 504/525–4455. Reservations recommended. Jackets preferred for dinner. AE, DC, MC, V.*

Bayou Ridge Café. This popular café recently moved from its longtime location in Mid-City to the fringes of the Quarter. A slew of salads are offered, including panéed eggplant served with sun-dried tomatoes and feta, and grilled scallops with grapefruit butter. Pasta primavera is made with light olive oil, and buttery couscous is topped with spicy Moroccan vegetables. *437 Esplanade Ave., Faubourg Marigny, tel. 504/949–9912. Closed Mon. and Tues. AE, DC, MC, V.*

Chez Helene. The inspiration for TV's late "Frank's Place," Chez Helene has checkered cloths, a jukebox, and homey fare, including fried chicken, red beans, mustard greens with ham, and outstanding corn muffins. It's not in the best neighborhood, so drive yourself or call a cab. *1540 N. Robertson St., Bywater, tel. 504/945–0444. AE, DC, MC, V.*

Delmonico's. About as near as you can get to dining in a Garden District mansion, Delmonico's has wallpapered rooms, botanical prints, and period furnishings. Vegetable soup and okra gumbo are excellent starters;

beef fillet in burgundy sauce, broiled red snapper, and broiled, stuffed shrimp make fine entrées. *1300 St. Charles Ave., Lower Garden District, tel. 504/525–4937. Reservations recommended. AE, DC, MC, V.*

G&E Courtyard Grill. This chic dining room and courtyard uses fresh, organically grown herbs on dishes like grilled trout stuffed with garlic and tarragon, grilled duck with a Thai barbecue sauce and marinated Japanese cucumbers, and roasted free-range chicken with sweet peppers, capers, rosemary, and lemon. *1113 Decatur St., French Quarter, tel. 504/528–9376. AE, MC, V. Closed Mon.*

Galatoire's. This 90-year-old French Creole bistro, with mirrored walls, glistening brass chandeliers, and white-clothed tables serves lumps of crabmeat atop buttery broiled pompano, spring lamb chops in béarnaise sauce, and seafood-stuffed eggplant. *209 Bourbon St., French Quarter, tel. 504/525–2021. No credit cards. Closed Mon.*

Ralph & Kacoo's. Freshness and consistency are the trademarks of this seafood restaurant, where you'll find huge crowds, a long wait, and a heart-healthy menu approved by a dietitian. *519 Toulouse St., French Quarter, tel. 504/522–5226; 601 Veterans Blvd., Metairie, tel. 504/831–3177. AE, MC, V.*

INEXPENSIVE **Alberto's.** A small, bohemian upstairs Italian eatery noted for unusually low prices for such standouts as cannelloni flavored with an herbed tomato-and-cream sauce and freshly made fettuccine. *609 Frenchmen St., Faubourg Marigny, tel. 504/949–5952. No credit cards. Closed Sun.*

Bozo's. Bare-top tables and plain wood paneling set the tone for this no-nonsense seafood house (a favorite with locals), which serves such basics as fresh catfish and shellfish, simply but deliciously cooked. *3117 21st St., Metairie, tel. 504/831–8666. No credit cards. Closed Sun.*

Casamento's. The small and immaculate family-run eatery, on the scene since 1918, serves dishes like oysters poached in seasoned milk, and impeccably fresh and greaseless fried shrimp, trout, and oysters. *4330 Magazine St., Uptown, tel. 504/895–9761. No credit cards. Closed Mon. and early June–late Aug.*

Kung's Dynasty. Crispy duck, fine double-cooked pork, tender and spicy eggplant in garlic sauce, and stir-fried oysters are among the offerings in a Garden District cottage done in traditional Chinese decor. *1912 St. Charles Ave., Lower Garden District, tel. 504/525–6669. AE, MC, V.*

The Praline Connection. A couple of blocks downriver of the French Quarter, this neat-as-a-pin and laid-back family restaurant has stewed chicken, collard greens, sweet potato pie, corn bread, and some of the lowest prices in town. *542 Frenchmen St., Faubourg Marigny, tel. 504/943–3934. AE, MC, V.*

Saddlery. A cheerful corner restaurant, the Saddlery serves the likes of chicken-fried steak and mashed potatoes, marvelous barbecued ribs, and mouth-watering home-baked pastries. If you're a vegetarian, ask the chef to whip up a platter of pasta mixed with fresh vegetables. But cholesterol concerns are likely to fly out the windows when you spy the pies. *240 Decatur St. (at Bienville St.), French Quarter, tel. 504/522–5172. AE, D, DC, MC, V.*

Shoney's Restaurant. An all-you-can eat breakfast buffet and a salad bar attract locals and tourists alike to the familiar chain, with its casual ambience and straightforward American food. *619 Decatur St., French Quarter, tel. 504/525–2039. AE, MC, V.*

SHOPPING

Among the city's unique souvenirs are pralines (thin, hardened sugar-and-pecan patties), Creole and Cajun spices, packaged-to-go seafood, and packaged mixes of local dishes. Regional cookbooks, Mardi Gras masks, posters, and memorabilia are hot tickets; so are jazz records and parasols.

The main shopping areas are the French Quarter and the Central Business District. Magazine Street has secondhand stores, antiques shops and galleries, and Royal Street has more of the same, but more upscale. Riverwalk (1 Poydras St., tel. 504/522–1555) features more than 200 nationally known and local shops, restaurants, and cafés. In the Quarter, the Jackson Brewery, Millhouse, and Marketplace (Jackson Square, tel. 504/586–8021) are restored historic buildings filled with specialty shops and eateries. The Community Flea Market (French Market at Gov. Nicholls St., tel. 504/566–7789) is open weekends. GHB Jazz Foundation (1204 Decatur St., tel. 504/525–0200) and Record Ron's (1129 Decatur St., tel. 504/524–9444) have new releases, oldies, and local music.

OUTDOOR ACTIVITIES

BIKING Bikers wheel around the French Quarter, City Park, and Audubon Park. Rentals are available at Bicycle Michael's (618 Frenchmen St., tel. 504/945–9505).

BOWLING Don Carter's All Star Lanes (3640 Williams Blvd., Kenner, tel. 504/443–5353) is open 24 hours. At Mid-City Bowling Lanes and Sports Palace (4133 Carrollton Ave., tel. 504/482–3133), the most rocking bowling alley in the South, bowlers dance and bowl to live music Friday nights, on Rock 'n' Bowl, as a glitter ball revolves above.

HIKING AND RUNNING The Barataria Unit of Jean Lafitte National Historical Park Service (about an hour's drive from New Orleans near Lafitte, tel. 504/589–2330 or 504/589–2636) has several trails that explore Louisiana's Delta Wetlands and important archaeological sites. Audubon Park has a 2-mile jogging path, with exercise stations, and the Mississippi River levee and City Park are also popular.

TENNIS Audubon Park has 10 courts (tel. 504/895–1042), located at the back off Tchoupitoulas Street. City Park has 39 lighted courts (Victory Ave., tel. 504/483–9383).

ENTERTAINMENT

The sound of music almost drowns out all other art forms in New Orleans. This isn't a big-ticket theater, ballet, or opera town, but it's the best place in the world to hear Dixieland and traditional jazz, R&B, Cajun, zydeco, honky-tonk, and rock and roll out of Bourbon Street's clubs and Uptown hangouts. The most complete daily music calendar is broadcast every two hours, beginning at 11:30 AM, on WWOZ, 90.7 FM. Also see *Lagniappe* (the Friday entertainment section of *The Times Picayune*) and *Gambit,* a free weekly newspaper.

MUSIC For Dixie and traditional jazz, head for Preservation Hall (726 St. Peter St., tel. 504/523–8939), Pete Fountain's in the Hilton Hotel (2 Poydras St., tel. 504/523–4374), Jelly Roll's, where Al Hirt and the Dukes of Dixieland play (501 Bourbon St., tel. 504/568–0501), and the Palm Court Jazz Cafe (1204 Decatur St., tel. 504/525–0200). R&B is usually the beat at Tipitina's (501 Napoleon Ave., tel. 504/895–8477) and Snug Harbor (626 Frenchmen St., tel. 504/949–0696). There's live Cajun music and dancing Sunday night at Tipitina's, Thursday night at the Maple Leaf Bar (8316 Oak St., tel. 504/866–5323), and nightly at Michaul's (701 Magazine St., tel. 504/522–5517) and Mulate's (201 Julia St., tel. 504/522–1492). Blues is the mood at the Absinthe Bar (400 Bourbon St., tel. 504/525–8108), Muddy Waters (8301 Oak St., tel. 504/866–7174), and funky Benny's Bar (938 Valence St., tel. 504/895–9405), and rock rules at Jimmy's (8200 Willow St., tel. 504/861–8200).

Newport
Rhode Island

Perched gloriously on the southern tip of Aquidneck Island and bounded on three sides by water, Newport, Rhode Island, is one of the great sailing cities of the world and the host to world-class jazz, blues, and classical music festivals.

Its first age of prosperity was in the late 1700s, when it was a major port city, on a par with Boston and New York. Many homes and shops built in that era still stand in the Point and Historic Hill sections of the city—tidy, compact areas of brick, clapboard, and narrow streets.

In the 19th century, Newport became a summer playground for the wealthiest families in America, who built monuments to themselves, their wealth, and the Gilded Age in America. Each new home constructed on Bellevue Avenue was grander than the one built just before it, until Cornelius Vanderbilt II attained the acme of extravagance with the luxurious Breakers.

Newport on a summer afternoon can be exasperating, its streets jammed with visitors and the traffic slowed by the procession of air-conditioned sightseeing buses. Yet the quality of Newport's arts festivals persuades many people to brave the crowds. And when the crowds and opulence become oppressive, one can always escape to the small but beautifully situated beaches in and around the city.

ESSENTIAL INFORMATION

WHEN TO GO Newport's weather usually remains pleasant well into November, with October temperatures averaging 69°. Winters do tend to be damp and chilly. Spring comes a bit later on the coast than inland, but by May, temperatures average 59°. Newport, like all of New England, is at its best in the fall, when the crowds of summer thin out considerably.

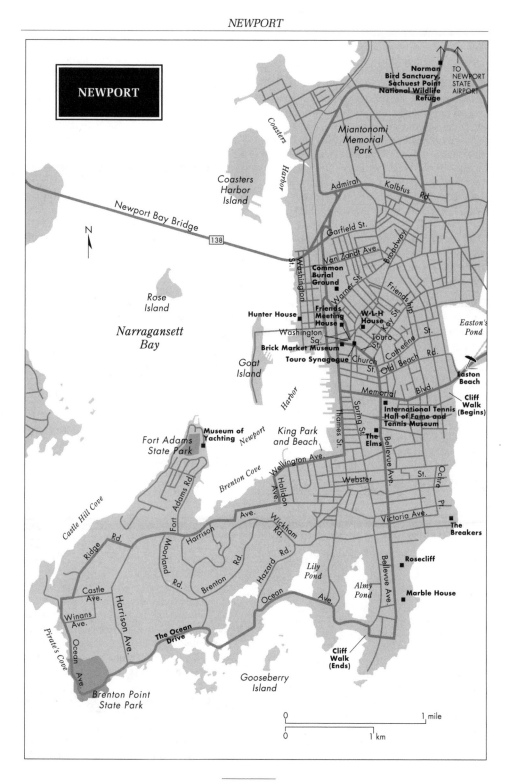

NEWPORT

Norman
Bird Sanctuary,
Sachuest Point
National Wildlife
Refuge

TO
NEWPORT
STATE
AIRPORT

Miantonomi
Memorial
Park

Coasters Harbor

Coasters
Harbor
Island

Newport Bay Bridge

Admiral

Kalbfus Rd.

138

Garfield St.

Van Zandt Ave.

Washington St.

Broadway

N

Common
Burial
Ground

Warner St.

Friendship

Rose
Island

Narragansett
Bay

Hunter House

Friends
Meeting
House

W-L-H
House

Key St.

St.

Easton's
Pond

Washington
Sq.

Touro
St.

Catherine

Brick Market Museum

Touro Synagogue

Church
St.

Old Beach Rd.

Easton
Beach

Goat
Island

Memorial

Blvd.

Cliff
Walk
(Begins)

Harbor

Spring St.

International Tennis
Hall of Fame and
Tennis Museum

Museum of
Yachting

Newport

King Park
and Beach

Thames St.

The
Elms

Bellevue Ave.

Fort Adams
State Park

Brenton Cove

Wellington Ave.

Halidon Ave.

Webster

St.

Ochre
Pl.

Castle Hill Cove

Fort Adams Rd.

Moorland Rd.

Harrison

Ave.

Wickham
Rd.

Victoria Ave.

The
Breakers

Ridge Rd.

Brenton

Rd.

Hazard Rd.

Lily
Pond

Bellevue Ave.

Rosecliff

Castle
Ave.

Ocean

Ave.

Almy
Pond

Marble House

Winans
Ave.

Harrison Ave.

The Ocean
Drive

Pirate's Cove

Ocean Ave.

Cliff
Walk
(Ends)

Brenton Point
State Park

Gooseberry
Island

0   1 mile

0   1 km

Rates at hotels are generally 30% lower from October through May.

FESTIVALS AND SEASONAL EVENTS **Mid-July:** **Newport Music Festival** brings together celebrated musicians for a two-week schedule of morning, afternoon, and evening concerts in Newport mansions (tel. 401/846–1133). **Lite Beer Hall of Fame Championship** and **Virginia Slims Hall of Fame Invitational** matches take place on grass courts at the International Tennis Hall of Fame at the Newport Casino (tel. 401/846–4567). **Early-Aug.:** **Newport Folk Festival** at Fort Adams State Park is the nation's premier folk festival (tel. 401/847–3709). **Mid-Aug.:** The **JVC Jazz Festival** brings renowned performers to Fort Adams State Park (tel. 401/847–3700).

TOURIST OFFICES **Newport County Convention and Visitors Bureau** and **Gateway Information Center** (23 America's Cup Ave., Newport 02840, tel. 401/849–8048 or 800/326–6030).

EMERGENCIES **Police:** tel. 911 or 401/847–1212. **Fire** and **ambulance:** tel. 911 or 401/846–2211. **Hospital:** Newport Hospital (Friendship St., tel. 401/846–6400). **Pharmacy:** Douglas Drug (7 E. Main Rd., Middletown, tel. 401/849–4600).

ARRIVING AND DEPARTING

BY PLANE The nearest airport to Newport is **Theodore Francis Green State Airport** (tel. 401/737–4000), with scheduled daily flights by six major U.S. airlines and additional service by regional carriers. The **Newport Shuttle** (tel. 401/846–2500) runs a frequent shuttle service ($13) between Theodore Francis Green Airport and the visitors bureau downtown, as well as the major hotels; some Newport hotels provide free airport shuttle service to guests.

BY CAR If you're coming from the south, exit I–95 at the town of Wyoming and follow Route 138 east across Rhode Island, across the Jamestown Bridge and Newport Bridge into Newport. If you're coming from the north, take Route 24 south to Route 114 or Route 138.

BY BUS **Bonanza Bus Lines** (tel. 401/846–1820) links Newport and Providence, where there are connections to New York, Boston, and other major northeastern cities.

BY FERRY Ferries leave Providence for Newport from the **India Street Pier** (tel. 203/442–7891).

GETTING AROUND

BY CAR A car can be a liability in summer, when traffic thickens on the city's narrow one-way streets. You can leave your car at the 350-car parking lot at the **Gateway Information Center** (23 America's Cup Ave.). Each of the Newport mansions has a parking lot.

BY BUS **Rhode Island Public Transit Authority** (tel. 401/847–0209) provides Newport area bus service.

REST STOPS The Gateway Information Center has public rest rooms; other convenient facilities are at the Seaman's Institute on Bowen's Wharf; the Harbor Center on Thames Street; and behind Burger King near the Mary Street Municipal Parking lot.

GUIDED TOURS Viking Bus Tours of Newport (Brick Market, tel. 401/847–6921) runs air-conditioned buses departing from the Gateway Information Center. Old Colony & Newport Railway (19 America's Cup Ave., tel. 401/624–6951) follows a 21-mile route along Narragansett Bay from Newport with a stop at Portsmouth's Green Animals Topiary Gardens. The round-trip takes a little over three hours. *The Spirit of Newport* (tel. 401/849–3575) gives one-hour minicruises of Newport Harbor and Narragansett Bay, departing from the Newport Harbor Hotel at 49 America's Cup Avenue every 90 minutes. For a small fee the Newport Historical Society (82 Touro St., tel. 401/846–0813) offers walking tours of historic Newport by fully trained guides, June 15 through September 30.

EXPLORING

To get a sense of how Newport has changed through the centuries, walk around Colonial Newport, the northwestern section of the city, with its narrow streets and historic houses and shops clustered around the harbor. You'll need a car or taxi (or bike!) to reach the Bellevue Avenue mansions in the southern section of the city.

Hunter House on Washington Street is a Colonial home (1748) with a carved pineapple over the doorway. Notice the elliptical arch in the central hall and, in the northeast parlor, the cherubs carved over the cupboard. *54 Washington St., tel. 401/847–1000. Open Apr.–Oct., daily. Admission charged.*

The Common Burial Ground, on Farewell Street, offers interesting examples of Colonial stone carving and a large section of pre- Revolution African-American graves.

Museum of Newport History at The Brick Market. On display in this fully restored 1760 building—which previously served as a market house, a theater, and town hall—is an engaging exhibit on Newport's history from 1636 to the present, including artifacts, furniture, and more. *Thames St. at Washington Sq., tel. 401/846–0813. Open year-round. Admission charged.*

The Wanton-Lyman-Hazard House, built about 1675, is Newport's oldest surviving residence. A site of the Stamp Act riot in 1765, the house is an excellent example of early architecture and is furnished with authentic period pieces. *17 Broadway, tel. 401/846–0813. Open June 15–Sept. 1, Thurs.– Sun. Admission charged.*

The Friends Meeting House, a short distance northwest of the Brick Market, was built in 1699, which makes it the oldest Quaker Meeting House in America. Note the wide-planked floors, simple benches, balcony, and medieval beam ceiling. *29 Farewell St., tel. 401/846–0813 (by appointment only). Open June–Aug., Mon.–Sat. Admission charged.*

Touro Synagogue is the oldest surviving synagogue in the United States, dedicated in 1763. Simple on the outside but elaborate within, it combines ornate Georgian decoration with requirements of the Jewish ritual. *85 Touro St., tel. 401/847–4794. Open late Apr.– early Sept., Sun.–Fri.; early Sept.–late Apr., Sun. and by appointment. Closed Sat. Calling in advance is recommended.*

The International Tennis Hall of Fame and the **Tennis Museum** are housed in the magnificent **Newport Casino,** a Stanford White building near the start of Bellevue Avenue. The museum features photographs and other tennis memorabilia. The first National Tennis Championships were held here in 1881. *Newport Casino, 194 Bellevue Ave., tel. 401/846– 4567. Open daily. Admission charged.*

To explore the grand mansions along Bellevue Avenue, it makes sense to drive (or ride a bicycle) from house to house, since the distances between them are considerable. You'll have plenty of walking to do inside the mansions and through the grounds. Six of the Newport mansions are maintained by the **Preservation Society of Newport County** (tel. 401/847–1000). A combination ticket—available at any of the properties—gives you a discount on individual admission prices. Each mansion provides a guided tour that lasts about one hour. Most are open daily from April to October.

Proceeding south along Bellevue Avenue, you can visit **The Elms,** with its handsome formal gardens; **Rosecliff,** modeled after the Grand Trianon at Versailles; and **Marble House,** with its grand Corinthian columns supporting an immense portico.

The Breakers, which you reach by turning left off Bellevue Avenue onto Victoria Avenue and continuing to Ochre Point Avenue, is a sumptuous, 70-room, limestone-sheathed palace. Among its marvels are a gold-ceilinged music room, rose alabaster pillars in the dining room, and a porch with a mosaic ceiling. *Ochre Point Ave., tel. 401/847–1000. Open Apr.–Oct., daily. Admission charged.*

The Museum of Yachting, at the end of the point in Fort Adams State Park, has galleries of pictures of yachts, mansions, and America's Cup races. *Ft. Adams, tel. 401/847–1018. Open mid-May–Oct., daily. Admission charged.*

THE NATURAL WORLD At the 450-acre **Norman Bird Sanctuary** (tel. 401/846–2577), about 2 miles east of the city of Newport on Third Beach Road, you can hike along ridges of "pudding stone," conglomerate rocks that were stretched by the pressure of the earth and then exposed by the action of the glaciers. Hanging Rock, the most scenic pudding-stone ridge, gives you a good view of the ocean. Other ridges in the sanctuary are dikes of lava that cooled before reaching the surface.

Norman Sanctuary and the adjoining **Sachuest Point National Wildlife Refuge** (tel. 401/847–5511) on Sachuest Point Road in Middletown are the best places for bird-watching. Spring and fall bring scores of songbird species, while snowy owls and sharp-shinned and red-tailed hawks may be seen in fall and winter.

HOTELS AND INNS

Newport lodgings can be expensive. Hotels in Newport range from Victorian bed-and-breakfasts with oak paneling, fireplaces, and marble-topped dressers to spanking-new hotels on the harbor. Few B&Bs are inside the mansion district, but several are located on its fringes. Rates are generally 30% lower off-season (Oct. through May). Price categories for double occupancy, excluding 12% tax, are *Expensive,* $85–$130; *Moderate,* $50–$85; and *Inexpensive,* under $50.

EXPENSIVE **Cliffside Inn.** Near Newport's Cliff Walk and downtown, this 1880 Victorian home on a quiet, tree-lined street offers a somewhat formal atmosphere with light and airy rooms, some with bay windows and fireplace. *2 Seaview Ave., 02840, tel. 401/847–1811. 12 rooms, each with private bath. Porch, eating area, hot breakfast included. AE, MC, V.*

Ivy Lodge. This large Victorian home with a wraparound porch, the only bed-and-breakfast in the mansions district, is a splurge, but worth it for the lavish appointments, including a 33-foot gothic paneled oak entry, a huge brick fireplace, and spacious rooms. *12 Clay St., 02840, tel. 401/849–6865. 8 rooms with private bath. Breakfast buffet included. AE, MC, V.*

Victorian Ladies. You'll find Victorian antiques and good soundproofing at this bed-and-breakfast, located on one of Newport's main thoroughfares and within walking distance of shops. *63 Memorial Blvd., 02840, tel. and fax 401/849–9960. 11 rooms with private bath. Air-conditioning, off-street parking. Breakfast included. MC, V.*

MODERATE-EXPENSIVE **Admiral Farragut Inn.** This pale yellow clapboard inn, in the center of Colonial Newport, features Shaker-style pencil-post beds and handmade spreads along with such modern amenities as telephones and air-conditioning. *31 Clarke St., 02840, tel. 401/848–8000 or 800/343–2863, fax 401/846–4289. 9 rooms with bath. Full breakfast included, sitting room, off-street parking. No children. AE, MC, V.*

Brinley Victorian Inn. Situated within walking distance of mansions and the harbor, this inn has two parlors, a library, a courtyard, and lots of Victorian lace and chintz. *23 Brinley St., 02840, tel. 401/849–7645. 17 rooms, 13 with bath. Continental breakfast included, off-street parking. MC, V.*

MODERATE **Bellevue House.** Located three blocks from the harbor, this small, homey inn, decorated on a nautical theme, occupies a building consisting of two floors of a Colonial home that were hoisted on top of a single-floor Victorian home. *14 Catherine St., 02840, tel. 401/847–1828. 8 rooms, 6 with bath. Off-street parking. No credit cards.*

Clover Hill. This turn-of-the-century house is a bit out of the center, but you'll find good value, full breakfast (included), and a welcome extended to children. *32 Cranston Ave., 02840, tel. 401/847–7094. 4 rooms, 2 with bath. No credit cards.*

Melville House. At this 1750 brown-shingled home you can experience the simple hospitality of Colonial decor (including some antiques) in the heart of Newport's Colonial district. *39 Clarke St., 02840, tel. 401/847–*

0640, fax 401/847–0956. 7 rooms, 5 with bath. Complimentary sherry and breakfast, bikes, off-street parking. AE, MC, V.

INEXPENSIVE-MODERATE **Commodore Perry Inn.** This property, with eight cozy rooms located above the Red Parrot restaurant, is a bargain for Colonial Newport, although it's not really an inn (it lacks a common room or dining area). *348 Thames St., 02840, tel. 401/848–8000 or 800/343–2863, fax 401/848–8006. 8 rooms with private bath. AE, MC, V.*

MOTELS

MODERATE **Best Western Mainstay** (151 Admiral Kalbfus Rd., 02840, tel. 401/849–9880 or 800/528–1234, fax 401/849–4391). 113 rooms; restaurant, pool. **Comfort Inn of Newport** (936 West Main Rd., Middletown 02840, tel. 401/846–7600 or 800/556–6464, fax 401/849–6919). 162 rooms; restaurant, pool, free shuttle to Newport. Seasonal only. **Harbor Base Pineapple Inn** (372 Coddington Hwy., 02840, tel. 401/847–2600, fax 401/847–5230). 48 rooms. **Motel 6** (249 J. T. Connell Hwy., 02840, tel. 401/848–0600). 79 rooms.

DINING

Traditional Rhode Island fare such as johnny-cakes (corn cakes cooked on a griddle) and quahogs (the native clam, pronounced KO-hog) served in soups and pies turn up on Newport menus. Italian and Portuguese immigrants serve their cuisine in friendly neighborhood restaurants. Newport restaurants tend to be rather casual and informal. Price categories per person, excluding 7% tax, service, and drinks, are *Moderate*, $15–$25, and *Inexpensive*, under $15.

MODERATE **Anthony's Seafood & Shore Dinner Hall.** Families flock to this large, light room with panoramic views of Newport Harbor to enjoy local seafood and lobster. *Lower Thames St. at Waites Wharf, tel. 401/848–5058. MC, V.*

Evelyn's Nanaquaket Drive-In. Fried seafood (available in low- cholesterol, salt-free preparations) is served outdoors at covered picnic tables overlooking Nanaquaket Pond or inside at Formica tables and booths. *2335 Main Rd., Tiverton, tel. 401/624–3100. No credit cards.*

The Lobster Pot. A glass wall affords a view of Narragansett Bay, and the menu features lobster, clam bakes, chicken, beef, and veal dishes. *119–21 Hope St., Bristol, tel. 401/253–9100. AE, MC, V.*

Muriel's Restaurant. Bring your own bottle of wine and enjoy award-winning seafood chowder at this local favorite. *58 Spring St., tel. 401/849-7780. MC, V.*

Salas'. Pastas, lobster, clams, and corn-on-the-cob are the principal fare at this lively, good-natured, waterfront dining spot. *341 Thames St., tel. 401/846–8772. AE, V.*

Ocean Coffee Roasters. This popular restaurant does a brisk business in Italian specialties as well as homemade muffins, sandwiches, and fresh-roasted coffee. *22 Washington Sq., tel. 401/846–6060. MC, V.*

INEXPENSIVE **Commons Inn.** The thick vinyl covering the booths looks like it's from the Eisenhower era, but this is a good, unassuming place for johnnycakes and quahog pie. *Little Compton Commons, tel. 401/635–4388. No credit cards.*

Franklin Spa. This neighborhood luncheonette is a good place for a quick sandwich or more substantial omelet or stew. *229 Spring St., tel. 401/847–3540. No credit cards.*

Gary's Handy Lunch. Local fishermen perch on chrome stools at the counter for homemade soups, sandwiches, and delicious coffee. *462 Thames St., tel. 401/847–9480. No credit cards. Closed for dinner.*

SHOPPING

Newport is not a city for bargain hunting. Its specialties include antiques, traditional clothing, and marine supplies. Many of Newport's arts and antiques shops can be found on Thames Street or near the waterfront. The Brick Market area—between Thames Street and America's Cup Avenue—has more than 50 shops.

SPECIALTY SHOPS Antiques. **Aardvark Antiques** (475 Thames St., tel. 401/849-7233) specializes in Architectural antiques, lawn ornaments, stained glass, and lighting fixtures. The **Old Fashion Shop** (38 Pelham St., tel. 401/847–2692) sells American furniture and accessories, including china, quilts, and glass.

Arts and Crafts. The Liberty Tree (104 Spring St., tel. 401/847–5925) has contemporary folk art, furniture, carvings, and paintings. **Thames Glass** (688 Thames St., tel. 401/846–0576) sells delicate and dramatic blown-glass gifts, hand-blown on the premises.

Flags. Ebenezer Flag Company (corner of Spring and Touro Sts., tel. 401/846–1891) offers a large selection of flags, banners, and wind socks.

Marine Items. JT's Ship Chandlery (364 Thames St., tel. 401/846-7256) is a major supplier of marine hardware, equipment, and clothing.

OUTDOOR ACTIVITIES

BEACHES Easton's Beach (Memorial Blvd.), also known as First Beach, is popular with families, teens, and visitors for its carousel and view of Cliff Walk. It has both changing rooms and food concessions. Second Beach, just east of Easton's Beach (Hanging Rock Rd., Middletown) is the largest and most attractive beach in Newport County, with changing rooms and food concessions. It tends to be a bit quieter than Easton's. Fort Adams State Park (Ocean Dr.), a very small beach with a picnic area and lifeguards during the summer, has beautiful views of Newport Harbor.

Scuba divers like the clear, deep water, but there are no changing rooms.

BIKING Bellevue Avenue, which is fairly flat, shaded, and studded with Newport's grandest mansions, makes a good and not too taxing bike route. **Ten Speed Spokes** (18 Elm St., tel. 401/847–5609) has bikes; **Fun Rentals of Newport** (1 Commercial Wharf, tel. 401/846–4374) has mopeds and more.

BOATING **Old Port Marine Services** (Sayer's Wharf, tel. 401/847–9109) offers harbor tours, yacht charters, and rides on a harbor ferry. **Sight Sailing of Newport** (Bowen's Wharf, tel. 401/849–3333) organizes two-hour sailing tours of Newport Harbor in a six-passenger sailboat and sailing instruction for beginners.

Long Wharf Charters (Long Wharf, Newport, tel. 849–2210) provides charter service for fishing and a variety of other excursions.

WALKING The 3-mile Cliff Walk begins at Easton's Beach and runs along Newport's cliffs, offering a breathtaking view of the Atlantic Ocean and many Newport mansions. This challenging walk is not recommended for the elderly or infirm.

ENTERTAINMENT

Coconuts Comedy Club (Doubletree Hotel on Goat Island, tel. 401/849–0077) hosts top comics from around the country between Wednesday and Saturday. **Clark Cooke House** (Bannister's Wharf, tel. 401/849–2900) has a piano bar upstairs, swing downstairs. **Viking Hotel** (1 Bellevue Ave., tel. 401/847–3300) offers mainstream jazz on Sunday afternoons in the summer.

Rhode Island Shakespeare Theater (St. George's School, Purgatory Rd., Newport, tel. 401/849–7892) performs classic and contemporary plays. The **Newport Jai-alai** (150 Admiral Kalbfus Rd., tel. 401/849–5000) season runs from May to mid-October.

New York City
New York

New York is the ultimate in big-city vacations with an undefinable aura that exists nowhere else. Its remarkable energy has something to do with being in the big league, where everybody's watching and keeping score. You can sit down in a restaurant, and at the next table you might spot a celebrity—perhaps Beverly Sills, Woody Allen, or Robert DeNiro. Even if you don't see someone you recognize, you always feel you just might.

Many people think of New York as expensive, unfriendly, and dirty, if not downright dangerous. New Yorkers frequently seem hurried and rude, but they will also often gladly come to your aid if you're lost—so don't hesitate to ask for directions. Crime and violence, seldom as random as rumor suggests, can be avoided. The littered sidewalks and slimy gutters that are so much a part of the city's identity coexist with some of the most glittering stores, restaurants, and night spots on earth. Expensive? Yes, as a rule. But inexpensive restaurants and modestly priced tickets are abundant. And much that you come here to experience won't cost you a thing.

New York is home to some of the world's great museums, a scintillating arts scene, superb shopping and restaurants, and some of the world's most stunning architecture: "New York" and "skyline" are virtually synonymous. Its attractions, such as the Statue of Liberty, Times Square, and the Empire State Building, though situated in Manhattan, belong to the world. Yet what truly sets it apart from several other world capitals is its varied population; the motley faces in its crowds reveal a global pedigree that you rarely encounter. This teeming spectacle, together with the city's vitality and culture, makes New York an essential destination for those who love to travel.

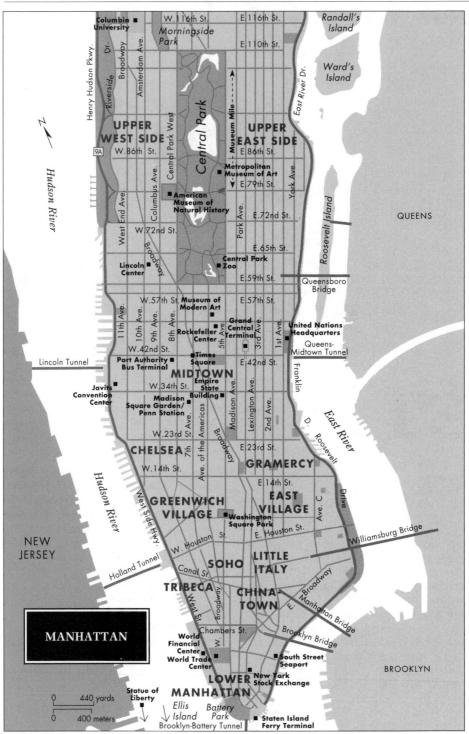

Columbia
University

W.116th St.   E.116th St.

Morningside
Park   E.110th St.

Randall's
Island

Ward's
Island

Henry Hudson Pkwy.

Riverside

Dr.

Broadway

Amsterdam Ave.

Hudson River

East River Dr.

UPPER
WEST SIDE

UPPER
EAST SIDE

QUEENS

Central Park

9A   W.86th St.   E.86th St.

Central Park West

Columbus Ave.

West End Ave.

Metropolitan
Museum of Art
E.79th St.

Roosevelt Island

American
Museum of
Natural History

Park Ave.

E.72nd St.

W.72nd St.

Broadway

E.65th St.

Lincoln
Center

Central Park
Zoo

E.59th St.

Queensboro
Bridge

W.57th St. Museum of
Modern Art   E.57th St.

11th Ave.

10th Ave.

9th Ave.

8th Ave.

Rockefeller
Center

5th Ave.

Grand
Central
Terminal

3rd Ave.

2nd Ave.

1st Ave.

United Nations
Headquarters

Queens-
Midtown Tunnel

Franklin

Lincoln Tunnel

W.42nd St.   E.42nd St.

Port Authority   Times
Bus Terminal   Square

MIDTOWN

Javits
Convention
Center

W.34th St.   Empire
State
Building

Madison
Square Garden/
Penn Station

Madison Ave.

Lexington Ave.

2nd Ave.

D.

Roosevelt

East River

W.23rd St.   E.23rd St.

CHELSEA

7th Ave.

Ave. of the Americas

Broadway

GRAMERCY

W.14th St.   E.14th St.

NEW
JERSEY

GREENWICH
VILLAGE

EAST
VILLAGE

Ave. C

Drive

Washington
Square Park

Hudson River

West Side Hwy.

W. Houston   St.   E. Houston St.

Williamsburg Bridge

Holland Tunnel

Canal St.

SOHO

LITTLE
ITALY

TRIBECA

W. St.

Broadway

CHINA-
TOWN

E.

Broadway

Manhattan Bridge

Chambers St.

World
Financial
Center
World Trade
Center

W.

Brooklyn Bridge

South Street
Seaport

BROOKLYN

New York
Stock Exchange

LOWER
MANHATTAN

Statue of
Liberty

Ellis
Island

Battery
Park

Staten Island
Ferry Terminal

Brooklyn-Battery Tunnel

0   440 yards

0   400 meters

MANHATTAN

ESSENTIAL INFORMATION

WHEN TO GO The most pleasant times to visit are usually fall, when cultural activities are in full swing and temperatures range from 50° to 70°, and spring, with plentiful rainfall and temperatures usually ranging from 40° to 70°. In winter, although there's an occasional bone-chilling day, temperatures don't usually drop below the 30s, and snow is hardly ever a problem. Summer is probably the most unpleasant time of year, with hot and humid days sometimes reaching the mid-90s; in August many Manhattanites vacate the island for summer escapes.

In late spring and summer, streets and parks are filled with ethnic parades, impromptu sidewalk concerts, and performances under the stars. With the exception of regular closing days and a few major holidays, the city's museums are open year-round.

FESTIVALS AND SEASONAL EVENTS **New Year's Eve:** New Year's kicks off with fireworks from all quarters and rowdy crowds in Times Square. **Late Jan.–Feb.:** Chinese New Year in Chinatown crackles with firecrackers while feasting celebrants crowd the restaurants. **Mar. 17:** St. Patrick's Day, one of dozens of ethnic processions down 5th Avenue, is a lively, often rowdy, bash. **Mid-Sept.:** The Feast of San Gennaro (tel. 212/226–9546) fills the streets of Little Italy. **Thanksgiving:** Macy's Thanksgiving Day Parade with giant balloons attracts huge crowds. **Late Nov.– early Jan.:** The Christmas season is particularly beautiful, with animated windows at Lord & Taylor and Saks Fifth Avenue, the New York City Ballet's *Nutcracker* performances (tel. 212/870–5500), and Radio City Music Hall's Christmas Spectacular (tel. 212/247–4777).

BARGAINS Several museums have pay-what-you-wish policies every day, including the Metropolitan Museum of Art, the American Museum of Natural History, the Museum of the City of New York (*see* Exploring, *below*), and the Museum of Television and Radio (25 W. 52nd St., tel. 212/621–6600); the same policy applies at the Museum of Modern Art and the Whitney Museum of Ameri-

can Art (*see* Exploring, *below*) on Thursday evenings. On Tuesday evenings, admission is free to several other museums on Museum Mile (*see* Exploring, *below*).

To save on theater tickets, pay half-price at the Theater Development Fund's TKTS booths in Duffy Square at 47th Street and Broadway or at 2 World Trade Center; music and dance events have a similar setup at the Bryant Park Music and Dance Half-Price Ticket Booth (42nd St. at 6th Ave., tel. 212/382–2323).

TOURIST OFFICE The **New York Convention and Visitors Bureau** (2 Columbus Cir., New York City 10019, tel. 212/397–8222).

EMERGENCIES **Police, fire,** or **ambulance:** Dial 911. **Hospitals:** St. Luke's-Roosevelt (9th Ave. at 58th St., tel. 212/523–6800) and St. Vincent's (7th Ave. at 12th St., tel. 212/790–7997) have emergency rooms with 24-hour service. **Doctors:** Doctors on Call (tel. 212/737–2333) makes house calls. **Dentists:** Emergency Dental Service (tel. 212/679–3966; 212/679–4172 after 8 PM) makes referrals. **Pharmacies:** In residential neighborhoods, many stay open until 11 PM; check the Yellow Pages in your hotel; Kaufman's (Lexington Ave. at 50th St., tel. 212/755–2266) is pricey but open 24 hours year-round.

ARRIVING AND DEPARTING

BY PLANE Virtually all major airlines serve La Guardia Airport and John F. Kennedy (JFK) International Airport, both located in the borough of Queens, or Newark International Airport in nearby New Jersey.

Between the Airports and Midtown Manhattan. Ground transportation by Carey Airport Express buses (tel. 718/632–0500) serves Grand Central Terminal and major hotels from La Guardia; the trip is 30–45 minutes and costs $8.50; from JFK it's about one hour and costs $11. Gray Line Air Shuttle Minibuses (tel. 212/757–6840; $12 from La Guardia, $15 from JFK) serves major hotels. Taxis are available at airport taxi stands (tel. 718/784–4343); they cost $25–$35 from La Guardia and $35–$45 from JFK, and even more if you hit a traffic jam, plus up to $2.50 in tolls. Buses from Newark take 30–45 minutes. Gray Line Air Shuttle Minibuses (tel. 212/757–6840; $17) serve major hotels, while the New Jersey Transit Airport Express (tel. 201/762– 5100; $7) operates to the Port Authority Bus Terminal, and Olympia Airport Express (tel. 212/964–6233; $7) goes to Grand Central Terminal. Taxis directly from the Newark airport cost $25–$35, considerably more with slow traffic, plus $3 in tolls.

BY CAR The Lincoln Tunnel (I–495), Holland Tunnel, and the George Washington Bridge (I–95) connect Manhattan with the New Jersey Turnpike system and points west. The Lincoln Tunnel is most convenient to midtown sites. From New England, take I–95 to the Bruckner Expressway (I–278), cross the Triborough Bridge and head south on FDR Drive. Tolls apply to all crossings.

BY TRAIN Amtrak (tel. 800/872–7245) operates lines on the Boston–Washington corridor and to Chicago and Montreal. Trains arrive at Penn Station (7th Ave. and 33rd St.).

BY BUS Greyhound Lines (tel. 800/231–2222) and other bus lines serve huge Port Authority Terminal (8th Ave. and 42nd St., tel. 212/564–8484 for carriers and schedules).

GETTING AROUND

ON FOOT Walking is the cheapest, often fastest, and usually the most interesting way to explore the city. Before you start out, keep a few simple rules in mind: Above 14th Street, city thoroughfares form a grid, with 5th Avenue dividing east from west. Numbered streets are straight lines running east to west; avenues—from 1st to 12th—run north to south. Below 14th Street, the situation is chaotic. Your stay will be simplified if you start out with a good map.

BY CAR Gridlocked traffic, cutthroat motorists, and scarce on-street parking make driving in Manhattan a nightmare. Travelers are advised to leave their cars at home. If you must drive to New York and plan to spend a few days, rent a car and drop it off in Man-

hattan; parking your own car in a lot will be very expensive.

BY SUBWAY New York's 24-hour, 230-mile subway system is usually the fastest way to get around and costs a good deal less than cabs. However, you'll need to remain cautious while using it. Tokens, required for entry and sold at each station, cost $1.25 (less for senior citizens except during rush hour). Buy several at once to cut token-booth waits. Subway maps, free from token booths, are also usually posted near booths and in each car. For route information, call 718/330–1234.

BY BUS Their slow pace makes buses great for sightseeing but infuriating when you're in a rush. They are generally safer than the subway. The fare, $1.25 per ride, must be paid by token or exact change (no bills or pennies); ask for a free transfer when boarding to change to an intersecting route. Service is around the clock but infrequent late at night. Routes and schedules are sometimes posted at key stops. For maps, stop at the Convention and Visitors Bureau (tel. 212/397–8222).

BY TAXI Taxis are usually easy to hail on the street or at hotels. A lighted center panel on top signals that the cab is available. Fare is $1.50 the first $1/5$ mile, 25¢ each $1/5$ of a mile thereafter, plus 50¢ for rides begun 8 PM to 6 AM. Drivers expect 15% tips. To avoid bad experiences, stick with yellow cabs, and know how to get where you're going and how much the trip should cost (ask at your hotel or restaurant).

REST STOPS The cleanest rest rooms tend to be in atriums of public spaces, or in department stores, hotels, and museums.

GUIDED TOURS The best way to get oriented is to circumnavigate Manhattan; the Circle Line (Pier 83, W. 42nd St., tel. 212/563–3200) provides three-hour cruises that reveal the city in its splendor. By bus, the basics are covered by Gray Line (tel. 212/397–2600) and Short Line (tel. 212/354–5122). Covering historic and other special-interest topics, guided walking tours offer fascinating looks at offbeat parts of New York. Sponsors include the

Municipal Art Society (tel. 212/935–3960 or 212/397–3809); Sidewalks of New York (tel. 212/517–0201); the Parks Department's Urban Park Rangers (tel. 212/427–4040); Penny Sightseeing (tel. 212/410–0080), whose walks focus on Harlem; and specialist guides Michael George (tel. 212/662–2597), Joyce Gold (tel. 212/242–4762), Arthur Marks (tel. 212/673–0477), and Peter Salwen (tel. 212/873–1944). Most walks take place on weekends and cost $5–$20 per participant.

EXPLORING

To see the city's best, focus on a few major sites; to cut down on time spent getting around, plan to take in close-together sites on the same days. Major destinations, all open year-round unless otherwise noted, include:

The American Museum of Natural History. With a collection of more than 36 million artifacts, this museum displays something for every interest, from dinosaur skeletons to animal-habitat dioramas to the 563-carat Star of India sapphire. *Central Park W at 77th St., Upper West Side, tel. 212/769–5100. Open daily. Donations requested.*

Central Park. This 843-acre triumph of landscape architecture gives New Yorkers a great green refuge from city concrete. For a 1¼-mile nibble of its flavor, enter at 77th Street and Central Park West, stroll southward along the lake curve east to the Esplanade, then turn south under its immense arching elms. Cross the road at the end of the Esplanade, still heading south, and leave the park at Central Park South. Note: Though crime is usually low here, stay away after dark and avoid deserted areas by day. The optimal times to visit are Saturday and Sunday afternoons, when every acre is teeming with a social microcosm of New Yorkers at play.

Chinatown. Home to half the city's 300,000 Chinese, this neighborhood is exotic to the core—especially narrow, twisting Mott Street, crowded with pedestrians at all hours and crammed with souvenir shops and good, inexpensive restaurants. Don't miss **Kam Man** (200 Canal St., tel. 212/571–0330), a supermarket whose stock ranges from fresh chicken feet to 100 kinds of noodles.

Ellis Island. Some 17 million men, women, and children were processed by this former federal immigration facility between 1892 and 1954. Now restored, it offers an evocative look at the first American experience of the ancestors of more than 40% of today's U.S. citizens. The boat trip to the island begins near Castle Clinton in Battery Park. *Tel. 212/363–3200. Open daily. Admission charged for boat trip; Immigration Museum, admission free.*

Empire State Building. King Kong's art-deco playground may no longer be the world's tallest skyscraper, but it's certainly one of the best-loved. There are two observation decks, and except in cloudy weather, the New York panorama is superb at either, both by day and by night. *5th Ave. at 34th St., Midtown, tel. 212/736–3100. Open daily. Admission charged.*

Greenwich Village. Originally a rural outpost, "the Village" has long been home to writers and artists. Despite high rents, its shabby one-of-a-kind shops, cafés, nonmainstream arts groups, and large student population still make it feel bohemian. Eat in one of its warm, cozy restaurants and take a stroll that beguiles at every turn; try **St. Luke's Place** (between Hudson St. and 7th Ave.) and **10th Street** (especially between 5th and 6th Aves.), and look in on charming **MacDougal Alley, Washington Mews,** and **Grove Court.**

Lower Manhattan. Long central to the city's wealth, this compact area mixes fine ornate old buildings with modern office towers fronted by masterpieces of modern sculpture. It's the center for New York's financial industry and the home of the **New York Stock Exchange** (20 Broad St., tel. 212/656–5168; free tours on weekdays only). The western edge of Lower Manhattan is anchored by the **World Trade Center,** with New York's two tallest buildings (tel. 212/435–7000 or 212/435–7397; Observation Deck admission charged). West of the World Trade Center, and across West Street and the West Side Highway, is the splendid **World Financial Center,**

whose soaring Winter Garden atrium offers handsome (if pricey) shops, a range of moderate-to-expensive restaurants, and free concerts (tel. 212/945–0505 for schedules). The World Financial Center is a part of Battery Park City, an ambitious commercial-residential development; its idyllic, Hudson River's–edge Esplanade is one of Manhattan's most refreshing corners. The eastern edge of Lower Manhattan is bordered by **South Street Seaport** (centered on Fulton St., between Water St. and the East River, tel. 212/669–9424), a complex that mixes a half-dozen small museum buildings (open daily; admission charged) showcasing the days of clipper ships with scores of shops.

The Metropolitan Museum of Art. The Western Hemisphere's largest art museum has a permanent international collection of some 3 million works, including the world's most comprehensive collection of American art, a collection of European work unequaled outside Europe, and world-renowned collections of ancient Greek, Roman, Asian, and Egyptian art. *5th Ave. at 82nd St., Upper East Side, tel. 212/535–7710. Open Tues.–Sun. Donations requested.*

Museum of Modern Art. A bright and airy six-story structure built around a secluded sculpture garden, this celebrated institution documents all the important movements of art since 1880. Its collection embraces not only painting and sculpture but photography, architecture, decorative arts, drawings, prints, illustrated books, and films. *11 W. 53rd St., Midtown, tel. 212/708–9400. Open Tues.– Sun. Admission charged.*

Museum Mile. Once known as Millionaire's Row, the stretch of 5th Avenue between 79th and 104th streets is home to many fine cultural institutions, often housed in the industrialists' gorgeous former mansions. Among them are the **Metropolitan Museum of Art** (*see above*); the **Guggenheim Museum,** in an assertive Frank Lloyd Wright rotunda (at 89th St., tel. 212/360–3500); the **Cooper-Hewitt Museum,** where Andrew Carnegie's grand but comfortable mansion shows off decorative arts (at 91st St., tel. 212/860–6898); the

International Center of Photography (at 94th St.; tel. 212/860–1777); and the memorabilia-packed **Museum of the City of New York** (at 103rd St., tel. 212/534–1672). The **Whitney Museum of American Art** (Madison Ave. at 75th St., tel. 212/570–3676) is nearby in a minimalist granite vault designed by Marcel Breuer. *Open Tues.–Sun. except Whitney Museum, open Wed.– Sun. Admission charged (free Tues. eve. except Metropolitan Museum and Museum of the City of New York; Whitney Museum free Thurs. eve).*

Rockefeller Center. This 22-acre complex of limestone buildings linked by shop-lined underground passageways is a city in its own right. **Radio City Music Hall** (6th Ave. at 50th St., tel. 212/247–4777) may be New York's most famous theater, and the central plaza's golden Prometheus statue is one of New York's most famous sights. The center's tallest tower, the 70-story GE Building (home of NBC-TV), has an information desk with tour brochures. Across 5th Avenue, between 51st and 52nd streets, don't miss grand **St. Patrick's Cathedral.** Rockefeller Center is located between 47th and 52nd streets, from 5th Avenue to 7th Avenue.

SoHo. Manhattan's postmodern chic pervades the still-gritty downtown streets of this former wasteland, now home to a distinctive mix of artists and Wall Streeters, lofts and galleries, and minimalist shops and restaurants. Gallery-lined West Broadway (parallel to and four blocks west of Broadway) is the main drag.

Staten Island Ferry. It's still the best deal in town: a half-hour ride across New York Harbor and back with great views of the Manhattan skyline and the Statue of Liberty for just 50¢. Hint: Pass up the new low-slung craft in favor of big old-timers with benches in the open air.

The Statue of Liberty. France's gift to America retains the power to impress. Arrive early to avoid a three-hour wait for the elevator to the viewing platform; from there, trek 12 stories up through the statue's body to the crown. Ferries depart near Castle Clinton, Battery

Park. *Tel. 212/363–3200. Open daily. Ferry: fare charged; statue: admission free.*

Times Square. At the intersection of Broadway, 7th Avenue, and 42nd Street, this is the heart of the Theater District, aswarm with pickpockets, porn fans, prostitutes, and destitutes. A good way to experience the lyricism of its squalor is to queue for half-price theater tickets at the TKTS booth (*see* Bargains, *above*), where you'll find affable crowds on line. Keep your eyes open: Ambitious redevelopment will soon make history of this scene.

United Nations Headquarters. On a lush 18 acres by the East River, this complex is comprised of the slablike 550-foot-high Secretariat Building, the domed General Assembly Building, and a delightful sculpture-dotted rose garden. Enter the **General Assembly Building** at the 47th Street door and take a tour or attend a session for free (tickets available in the lobby—first-come, first-served). *1st Ave. between 42nd and 48th Sts., Midtown, tel. 212/963–7713. Open daily. Tour admission charged.*

HOTELS AND INNS

Although most of New York's hotels are expensive, you can still book a clean, acceptable double room in several properties without wreaking havoc with your travel budget. Reputable discount booking firms such as Express Hotel Reservations (tel. 800/356–1123) offer 20%–30% savings; cheaper weekend rates are available at most Manhattan properties.

Bed-and-breakfast lodging may cost less and let you mingle with local residents; contact reservation services such as Bed and Breakfast Network of New York (130 Barrow St., 10014, tel. 212/645–8134), City Lights Bed and Breakfast, Ltd. (Box 20355, Cherokee Station, 10028, tel. 212/737–7049), New World Bed and Breakfast (150 5th Ave., Suite 711, 10011, tel. 212/675–5600 or 800/443–3800), and Urban Ventures (306 W. 38th St., 10018, tel. 212/594–5650).

Price categories for double occupancy, excluding 18¹/₄% tax plus $2 occupancy tax, are *Expensive,* $150–$210; *Moderate,* $100–$150; and *Inexpensive,* $75–$100.

MIDTOWN Algonquin. This genteel landmark's drawing-room atmosphere and burnished wood lobby have made it a favorite of literati; recent room renovations have retained Victorian-style furnishings while updating everything from phones to plumbing. *59 W. 44th St., 10036, tel. 212/840–6800 or 800/548–0345, fax 212/944–1419. 165 rooms. 2 restaurants, 2 lounges, free weekend parking. AE, D, DC, MC, V. Moderate–Expensive.*

Doral Inn. For its Lexington Avenue location, this hotel is a good value, with modestly decorated, cheerful rooms, and a fitness center that includes squash courts and a sauna. *541 Lexington Ave. (at 50th St.), 10022, tel. 212/755–1200 or 800/223–5823, fax 212/319–8344. 652 rooms. 2 restaurants, fitness center, self-service laundry. AE, DC, MC, V. Moderate–Expensive.*

Paramount. One of the city's best budget buys, the Paramount has trendy public areas, chic (if offbeat) furnishings in the smallish bedrooms, and baths with ultramodern touches like conical steel sinks. *235 W. 46th St., 10019, tel. 212/764–5500 or 800/225–7474, fax 212/354–5237. 610 rooms. 2 restaurants, 3 bars, take-out food shop, fitness center, playroom, VCRs in rooms. AE, D, DC, MC, V. Moderate–Expensive.*

Helmsley Middletowne. Although this low-key, residential-style money-saver has no restaurant or room service, it does offer oversize rooms or suites with homey traditional decor and pantries, plus a location near many restaurants. *148 E. 48th St., 10017, tel. 212/755–3000 or 800/221–4982, fax 212/832–0261. 190 rooms. AE, DC, MC, V. Moderate.*

Milford Plaza. Though rooms are small and the neighborhood can be seedy, this giant is conveniently located in the heart of the theater district; security appears to be tight in its bright public areas. *270 W. 45th St., 10036, tel. 212/869–3600 or 800/221–2690, fax*

212/944–8357. 1,300 rooms. 2 restaurants. AE, D, DC, MC, V. Moderate.

Wyndham. This genteel treasure opposite the posh Plaza Hotel offers some of Manhattan's most spacious quarters, furnished with fresh print bedspreads, comfortable chairs, and decorator wall coverings; suites, fitted with antiques, are only slightly pricier. The lobby is unusually secure, since a doorman controls access around the clock via an "in" buzzer. *42 W. 58th St., 10019, tel. 212/753–3500 or 800/257–1111, fax 212/754–5638. 201 rooms. Restaurant, lounge. AE, DC, MC, V. Moderate.*

Chatwal Inns. Small but attractive, immaculate, and gently priced rooms are offered at these five midtown properties: the Best Western Woodward (210 W. 55th St.), the President (234 W. 48th St.), the Quality Inn Midtown (157 W. 47th St.), the Chatwal Inn (132 W. 45th St.), the Aberdeen (17 W. 32nd St.), and the Hojo Inn (429 Park Ave. S, between 29th and 30th Sts.). *Tel. 800/826–4667. Restaurants and lounges, depending on the property. Continental breakfast included in some rates. AE, D, DC, MC, V. Inexpensive–Expensive.*

Days Hotel. This property features pleasant, upgraded rooms and reasonable daily garage rates, while the outdoor rooftop swimming pool makes this a good bet for families during the summer. *790 8th Ave. (at 48th St.), 10019, tel. 212/581–7000 or 800/325–2525, fax 212/974–0291. 366 rooms. Restaurant, lounge, pool. AE, D, DC, MC, V. Inexpensive–Moderate.*

Hotel Iroquois. Near the venerable Algonquin and the trendy Royalton, this unprepossessing establishment has a good location, presentable rooms, and a friendly staff, despite shabby hallways. *49 W. 44th St., 10036, tel. 212/840–3080 or 800/332–7220 outside NY, fax 212/398–1754. 135 rooms. AE, DC, MC, V. Inexpensive.*

Wellington Hotel. Small but clean and cheery rooms at reasonable prices attract budget-conscious Europeans to this large, old-fashioned property with a reassuringly bright lobby. *871 7th Ave. (at 55th St.), 10019, tel.*

212/247–3900 or 800/652–1212 outside NY, fax 212/581–1719. 700 rooms. Restaurant. AE, DC, MC, V. Inexpensive.

UPPER EAST SIDE **Pickwick Arms.** A well-lit, marble-clad lobby, friendly staff, and renovated rooms furnished in white bamboo make this an acceptable option in a neighborhood full of pleasant restaurants. *230 E. 51st St., 10022, tel. 212/355–0300 or 800/742–5945 outside NY, fax 212/755–5029. 385 rooms. AE, DC, MC, V. Inexpensive.*

UPPER WEST SIDE **Broadway American.** This small but stylish hotel is one of the city's true bargains. The least expensive rooms share baths, though most rooms come with private facilities. The decor is basic and modern; the neighborhood is bustling. *2178 Broadway, 10024, tel. 212/362–1100, fax 212/787–9521. 200 rooms. Restaurant. AE, DC, MC, V. Inexpensive.*

Excelsior. A great location across from the American Museum of Natural History, coupled with clean rooms, relatively new furnishings, and a helpful staff, make this a find. *45 W. 81st St., 10024, tel. 212/362–9200 or 800/368–4575, fax 212/721–2994. 160 rooms. Coffee shop, kitchenettes in suites. AE, DC, MC, V. Inexpensive.*

DINING

New York's restaurant scene is staggering not just for the number of restaurants—some 17,000 in all—but also for the variety of cuisines they celebrate and the quality of meals they serve.

Because the trend of customers' eating habits is generally toward lighter fare, a large number of dining spots now offer a selection of pastas as well as grilled or broiled fish and chicken dishes that can typically be ordered with sauce on the side.

Advance reservations are always a good idea. To save on meals, look into special all-inclusive prix-fixe menus, or visit at lunchtime or for weekend brunch, when you can still experience the kitchen's flair—but at lower prices. Price categories per person, excluding

8¼% tax, service, and drinks, are *Expensive,* over $30; *Moderate,* $20–$30; and *Inexpensive,* under $20.

SOUTH STREET SEAPORT **Sloppy Louie's.** Try this vintage fish house serving fresh-from-the-sea fare. It is one of the many good, moderately priced restaurants in this 19th-century historic district, which is also crammed with better-than-average fast-food spots. *92 South St., tel. 212/509-9694. AE, DC, MC, V. Inexpensive–Moderate.*

SOHO **Cupping Room Café.** In this mellow spot, exposed brick, a pot-bellied stove, and an antique bar set the scene for homey breakfasts and innovative American meals. *359 W. Broadway, tel. 212/925-2898. AE, DC, MC, V. Moderate.*

SoHo Kitchen. Soaring ceilings halo giant artwork at this chic hangout, and a well-groomed crowd congregates for good music, pasta and pizzas, and the stunning selection of 100 wines by the glass. *103 Greene St., tel. 212/925-1866. AE, DC, MC, V. Inexpensive.*

Spring Street Natural Restaurant. Hanging plants, huge windows, ceiling fans, and a colorful crowd make this a pleasant spot for light and vegetarian fare sparked with herbs and Asian flavorings. *62 Spring St., tel. 212/966-0290. AE, DC, MC, V. Inexpensive.*

CHINATOWN AND LITTLE ITALY **Benito's II.** This Little Italy charmer with exposed brick walls, a dark wood ceiling, and small tables offers substantial Italian fare that's often pungently laced with garlic. *163 Mulberry St., tel. 212/226-9012. No credit cards. Inexpensive–Moderate.*

Nice Restaurant. By day, this well-turned-out Chinese giant does well with the small dumplings known as dim sum that you pay for by the plateful; by night, try one of the larger entrées—such as soy-flavored squab and seasoned chicken. *35 E. Broadway, tel. 212/406-9510. AE. Inexpensive.*

Wong Kee. This clean, bright, uncluttered Chinese restaurant is on one of the busiest, most interesting streets in Chinatown. The "custard chicken" earns its name by being

exquisitely tender. *113 Mott St., tel. 212/226-9018. No credit cards. Inexpensive.*

EAST VILLAGE **Japonica.** Excellent sushi highlights a menu of out-of-the-ordinary Japanese fare at this modest but attractive favorite with decor that changes with the seasons. *100 University Pl., tel. 212/243-7752. AE. Inexpensive–Moderate.*

John's of 12th Street. In this vintage hole-in-the-wall, candles stuck in raffia-wrapped Chianti bottles throw flickering light on age-darkened walls, while companionable crowds of old and young gather for southern Italian fare. *302 E. 12th St., tel. 212/475-9531. No credit cards. Inexpensive.*

Passage to India. Sixth Street between 1st and 2nd avenues is packed wall-to-wall with Indian restaurants, and Passage to India is one of the best, serving delicious curries and 14 types of fresh-baked Indian breads. *308 E. 6th St., tel. 212/529-5770. AE, DC, MC, V. Inexpensive.*

WEST VILLAGE **Black Sheep.** The quintessential cozy little Village restaurant, this nook with exposed brick walls and rustic wood tables serves five-course prix-fixe dinners with Continental flair. Sunday brunches draw enthusiastic crowds. *344 W. 11th St., tel. 212/242-1010. AE (cash only at brunch). Moderate–Expensive.*

Jane Street Seafood Café. This fish house consistently delights with sea-fresh fare, sometimes grilled and sometimes sauced, always accompanied by crunchy, zingy coleslaw. *31 8th Ave., tel. 212/243-9237. AE, D, DC, MC, V. Moderate–Expensive.*

Provence. With its yellow walls and bouquets of dried flowers, this gutsy Provençal restaurant is as pleasant in winter as in summer, when tables sprout in its stone-fountained garden. *38 MacDougal St., tel. 212/475-7500. AE. Moderate–Expensive.*

Anglers & Writers Salon de Thé. At this charming tea room, it's hard to resist the delicious baked goods; the lively sandwiches, pastas, and antipasto platters are delicious, too. *420 Hudson St., tel. 212/ 675–0810. No credit cards. Inexpensive.*

GRAMERCY PARK AND UNION SQUARE **Union Square Café.** Light, innovative cooking that's never too far-out, a lively wine list, and well-mannered service make this smart, animated room a good value for the money. *21 E. 16th St., tel. 212/243–4020. Jacket and tie required. AE, DC, MC, V. Expensive.*

Friend of a Farmer. At this countrified charmer on quiet Irving Place, homey, rustic fare predominates—lively salads, apple butter-and-cheddar omelets, and sweets from the restaurant's own ovens. *77 Irving Pl., tel. 212/477–2188. No credit cards. Inexpensive.*

CHELSEA **Lola.** Boisterous and seductive, this chic, convivial room mixes the South with the Caribbean and a bit of France to great effect, particularly at Sunday's gospel brunches. *30 W. 22nd St., tel. 212/675–6700. Jacket and tie advised. AE. Moderate–Expensive.*

Twigs. This sleek little Italian café, all marble and brass, is a neighborhood standby for pastas and individual pizzas with well-blistered crusts and unusual toppings. *196 8th Ave., tel. 212/633–6735. AE, MC, V. Inexpensive.*

MIDTOWN EAST **Dock's.** This giant, high-ceilinged fish house is not only one of the neighborhood's better-looking eateries but also one of the city's best and least costly seafood specialists. *633 3rd Ave., tel. 212/986–8080. AE, DC, MC, V. Moderate–Expensive.*

Les Halles. Recalling the Gauloise smoky joints where Parisians once congregated for onion soup, this bistro purveys hearty French fare. *411 Park Ave. S, tel. 212/679–4111. AE, DC, MC, V. Moderate.*

Christine's. This diner with glass-topped cloths on crowded tables serves robust soups and other tasty Polish-American fare at extremely gentle prices. *344 Lexington Ave., tel. 212/953–1920. AE. Inexpensive.*

MIDTOWN WEST **Restaurant Row.** This Theater District landmark—46th Street between 8th and 9th avenues—is known for dining spots where the food is just fine and waiters know how to get you to the show on time. For basic pub fare at all hours and low prices, try the **Joe Allen** pub (326 W. 46th St., tel. 212/581–6464. MC, V. Inexpensive). For celebrity-watching, Italian food, and higher tabs, book at bright, casual **Orso** (322 W. 46th St., tel. 212/489–7212. MC, V. Moderate). For old-fashioned French food and a patronne who welcomes every diner, you want the refreshingly unchanged **Crêpe Suzette** (363 W. 46th St., tel. 212/581–9717. AE, DC, MC, V. Moderate).

Mickey Mantle's. Down-to-earth American fare takes second place here to the World Series footage on video monitors, the bartender who talks batting averages, and occasional appearances by the Bronx Bomber himself. *42 Central Park S, tel. 212/688–7777. AE, DC, MC, V. Moderate.*

Russian Samovar. Good grills and Russian specialties soothe theater folk in this snug, unprepossessing little dining room with long banquettes and well-spaced tables. *256 W. 52nd St., tel. 212/757–0168. AE, MC, V. Moderate.*

Bangkok Cuisine. Eighth Avenue in the 50s is full of Thai restaurants, and this one is among the best, with highly recommended steamed fish and crispy *mee krob* noodles on the menu. *885 8th Ave., tel. 212/581–6370. AE, MC, V. Inexpensive.*

Carnegie Deli. Delis are a colorful feature of the New York culinary scene, and this one, founded in 1934, serves sandwiches that are mile-high (no wonder there are usually lines outside). *854 7th Ave., tel. 212/757–2245. No credit cards. Inexpensive.*

La Bonne Soupe. Red-checked cloths cover wobbly tables at this pleasant old standby for light meals—and some of the tastiest soups in town. *48 W. 55th St., tel. 212/586–7650. AE, MC, V. Inexpensive.*

UPPER EAST SIDE **Pamir.** This tiny, dimly lit Afghan restaurant hung with rugs and shawls is aromatic with the spices of its cuisine, which crosses Indian and Middle Eastern fare. Try the kebabs and rice pilaws. *1437 2nd Ave., tel. 212/734–3791. MC, V. Moderate.*

Vašato. This folksy Czech spot with snowy tablecloths and yellow walls has served schnitzels to an affluent crowd since 1952, yet the welcome is as warm as ever. *339 E. 75th St., tel. 212/988–7166. AE, DC, MC, V. Moderate.*

Olio. With its simple decor, this boîte is not much to look at, but unusual Italian dishes such as lobster ravioli couple with gentle prices to create a standout. *788 Lexington Ave., tel. 212/308–3552. AE. Inexpensive.*

Serendipity 3. Movie goers and models, families and singles have made this ice-cream parlor-café-general store a longtime favorite for pastas, pizzas, sandwiches—and ice-cream sundaes worth a splurge. *225 E. 60th St., tel. 212/838–3531. AE, D, DC, MC, V. Inexpensive.*

LINCOLN CENTER/UPPER WEST SIDE **Café Luxembourg.** In this hip favorite, a sophisticated, good-natured staff offers brasserie standbys spiced with light nouvelle American ideas in a Paris bistro setting. *200 W. 70th St., tel. 212/873–7411. AE, DC, MC, V. Moderate–Expensive.*

Vince & Eddie's. Brick walls, a sprinkling of antiques, oilcloth-covered tables, and a fireplace set the mood for hearty French American fare. *70 W. 68th St., tel. 212/721–0068. AE, DC, MC, V. Moderate.*

Ollie's. The decor is basic, but regulars swear by the dumplings, noodles, and grilled shrimp at this crowded uptown Chinese dining spot. *2957 Broadway, tel. 212/932–3300. AE, MC, V. Inexpensive.*

Popover. This fun café guarded by troops of teddy bears delights one and all with huge, puffy popovers, soups, sandwiches, salads, and omelets—made with egg whites only, if you ask. *551 Amsterdam Ave., tel. 212/595–8555. AE, MC, V. Inexpensive.*

SHOPPING

New York shopping is theater, architecture, and people-watching rolled into one. Big stores and small ones, one-of-a-kinds and chains present an overwhelming array, from no-holds-barred bargains to the finest (and priciest) in the world.

MAJOR SHOPPING DISTRICTS New York's shops are collected in neighborhoods rather than malls. Hordes of New Yorkers turn out for genial browsing when the weather is fine.

South Street Seaport, downtown Manhattan's lively open-air museum and restaurant/retail complex, sprinkles one-of-a-kind boutiques amid upscale, nationally known chains.

The Lower East Side, once home to millions of Jewish immigrants, may look down-at-heels and unsavory. But as New Yorkers' bargain beat, it's a thriving retail center. Narrow, unprepossessing Orchard Street, its spine, is crammed with hole-in-the-wall clothing stores; Grand Street (off Orchard St., south of Delancey St.) is chockablock with linens, towels, and other items for the home. Shops close for the Jewish Sabbath on Friday afternoon and all day Saturday; on Sundays, uptowners appear in droves.

SoHo mixes major art galleries and fashionable clothing and housewares stores; despite high prices, it warrants a look. Landmarks include the gourmet food emporium Dean & DeLuca (Broadway at Prince St., tel. 212/431–1691). Many stores here close on Mondays.

Herald Square, where 34th Street and 6th Avenue intersect, is a bastion of reasonable prices. Giant Macy's (tel. 212/695–4400) department store is the linchpin. Immediately south, the new A&S Plaza atrium-mall makes for wonderful browsing with its spate of moderately priced stores.

Fifth and Madison avenues reveal Manhattan's most cosmopolitan facade. Along 5th Avenue from Central Park South to Rockefeller Center, you'll pass the famous F.A.O. Schwarz (at 58th St., tel. 212/644–9400) toy emporium and Bergdorf Goodman (at 58th St., tel. 212/753–7300). Moving south, there's Tiffany & Co. jewelers (at 57th St., tel. 212/755–8000), brass-and-marble Trump Tower (at 56th St.), Steuben glassware (at 55th St., tel. 212/752–1441), Cartier jewelers (at 52nd St., tel. 212/753–0111), and Saks Fifth Avenue (at 50th St., tel. 212/753–4000). Glittering as this all is, Madison Avenue from 57th Street to 86th Street is even more posh with its crowd of luxurious designer boutiques and superlative antiques stores-cum-museums.

Columbus Avenue, between 66th and 86th streets on the Upper West Side, has its own spate of glitzy shops—mostly modern in design, upscale but not top-of-the-line. Browsing is good any day, particularly since the shops are interspersed with moderately priced cafés and restaurants. If you're shopping for gifts for youngsters, don't miss Penny Whistle Toys (Columbus Ave. at 81st St., tel. 212/873–9090).

DEPARTMENT STORES Quality clothing is expensive everywhere, and the merchandise in New York's half-dozen department stores is no exception. What you can expect here is a much wider selection, particularly in the more up-to-the-minute styles and particularly at the higher price levels. Both Bloomingdale's (Lexington Ave. between 59th and 60th Sts., tel. 212/705–2000) and Macy's (Herald Sq., Broadway at 34th St., tel. 212/695–4400) are huge and easy to get lost in, but both have good markdowns.

If you want to see what's hot and trendy in men's and women's clothing and precious, one-of-a-kind gifts, visit Barneys New York (7th Ave. at 17th St., tel. 212/929–9000). Though markdowns are more than generous, some of the usual prices will make your head spin, despite the exquisite quality. The taste level is equally high at Bergdorf Goodman (5th Ave. at 57th St., tel. 212/753–7300) and at Saks Fifth Avenue (5th Ave. between 50th and 51st Sts., tel. 212/753–4000), embodying the spirit of service and style with which it opened in 1926. Particularly for classic women's clothing, Lord & Taylor (5th Ave.

between 38th and 39th Sts., tel. 212/391–3344) is hard to beat, and the store never overwhelms. Henri Bendel (712 5th Ave., at 56th St., tel. 212/247–1100) is stylish and sophisticated—with prices to match.

ANTIQUES Manhattan's antiques markets and shops offer everything from museum-quality wares to the wacky and eminently affordable. To see the former, browse along Madison Avenue north of 57th Street and 47th Street east of 5th Avenue. For the latter, stop at the Manhattan Art & Antiques Center (1050 2nd Ave., tel. 212/355–4400), with 100-plus dealers, and don't miss the weekend Annex Antiques Fair and Flea Market (6th Ave. at 26th St., tel. 212/243–5343).

SPECIALTY SHOPS Whether you fancy state-of-the-art cameras or architecture books, Manhattan has a specialist shop in the field. A few stand out.

Books: Gotham Book Mart (41 W. 47th St., tel. 212/719–4448) is an oasis for those who truly love to read. Whodunit-lovers love the Mysterious Bookshop (129 W. 56th St., tel. 212/765–0900). Try the Strand (828 Broadway, tel. 212/473–1452), Manhattan's biggest used-book store, for secondhand titles and discounted reviewers' copies.

Cameras and electronics: For price and selection, it's hard to do better than at 47th Street Photo (67 W. 47th St. and other locations, tel. 212/398–1410).

Menswear: Brooks Brothers (Madison Ave. at 44th St., tel. 212/682–8800) is America's temple of the traditional; you'll pay for all that hand-tailoring. For discounts on traditional as well as contemporary styles, try Moe Ginsburg (162 5th Ave., tel. 212/242–3482) and Syms (42 Trinity Pl., tel. 212/797–1199; cash only).

Records, tapes, and CDs: The best selections are at HMV (Broadway at 72nd St., tel. 212/721–5900; Lexington Ave. at 86th St., tel. 212/348–0800) and Tower (Broadway at 4th St., tel. 212/505–1500; Broadway at 66th St., tel. 212/799–2500; 3rd Ave. at 87th St., tel. 212/369–2500).

Women's clothing: Bargain mavens pilgrim to the flagship Loehmann's (236th and Broadway, tel. 718/543–6420), located in a safe enclave in the Bronx. They also visit S&W (165 W. 26th St., tel. 212/924–6656) for discounts, and Encore (1132 Madison Ave., tel. 212/879–2850), a resale shop where top-of-the-line designs go for secondhand prices.

OUTDOOR ACTIVITIES

BIKING Bikes are easily rented at bike stores such as AAA Bikes (in Central Park's Loeb Boathouse, near E. 74th St., tel. 212/861–4137), Metro Bicycles (1311 Lexington Ave. at 88th St., tel. 212/427–4450), and West Side Bikes (231 W. 96th St., tel. 212/663–7531).

TENNIS Fans jam the 24 public clay courts in Central Park (mid-park near 94th St., tel. 212/280–0205); since space is tight, call ahead to find out when it will be easiest to get a court.

WALKING/JOGGING Central Park is the favorite destination of the city's cyclists, joggers, race walkers, strollers, and roller skaters. For jogging and walking, prime circuits are the Reservoir (1.58 miles) and the park roads (up to 6 miles), which are closed to vehicular traffic 10 AM–3 PM and 7–10 PM weekdays, and from 7 PM Friday to 6 AM Monday on weekends. To run the Reservoir, enter on 5th Avenue at 90th Street. To join a group run, contact the New York Road Runners Club (9 E. 89th St., tel. 212/860–4455).

ENTERTAINMENT

Tickets are often modestly priced or available at half-price (*see* Bargains, *above*). To find out what's on, top sources are *The New York Times* (particularly Friday's "Weekend" and Sunday's "Arts & Leisure" sections), the *Village Voice* (particularly for the downtown scene), and *The New Yorker* and the Cue listings in *New York* magazine.

CONCERTS The New York Philharmonic's season runs from September through April at Avery Fisher Hall (tel. 212/875–5030) in Lincoln Center. There's always something on at Carnegie Hall (7th Ave. at 57th St., tel. 212/247–7800), whose acoustics are excellent even in the budget seats up high.

BALLET AND DANCE The New York City Ballet (tel. 212/870–5500) and American Ballet Theatre (tel. 212/362–6000) perform at Lincoln Center. Touring ballet and modern troupes often appear at City Center (131 W. 55th St., tel. 212/581–7907). Smaller groups perform at the Joyce Theater (8th Ave. at 19th St., tel. 212/242–0800) and the Dance Theater Workshop (219 W. 19th St., tel. 212/691–6500).

FILM The diversity of New York's film offerings—major releases, classics, foreign offerings, and independent flicks—will amaze you almost as much as the $7.50 ticket prices. For first-run film information, call the WPLJ/New York Magazine Movie Phone (tel. 212/777–FILM) from touch-tone phones. The Film Forum (209 W. Houston St., tel. 212/727–8110) offers small new films and revivals. For revivals, try the Gramercy Park (127 E. 23rd St., tel. 212/475–1600) or Theater 80 (80 St. Mark's Place, tel. 212/254–7400). In addition, there are programs at the American Museum of the Moving Image (35th Ave. at 36th St., Queens, tel. 718/784–0077), a major film museum, and at the Museum of Modern Art (11 W. 53rd St., tel. 212/708–9480), home of a world-renowned film archive.

THEATER Broadway is synonymous with New York theater, but even half-price tickets are pricey (*see* Bargains, *above*), so don't overlook Off- and Off-Off-Broadway shows, where tickets run $8–$35 per person. Downtown's Public Theater (425 Lafayette St., tel. 212/598–7150) is a landmark; its first-come, first-served Quiktix scheme cuts your cost further. Another good bet is the collection of small theaters known as Theatre Row, located on the downtown side of 42nd St. between 9th and 10th avenues; buy tickets at the joint box office, Ticket Central (416 W. 42nd St., tel. 212/279–4200).

OPERA The New York City Opera (tel. 212/870–5570; July–Nov.) is lively and relatively affordable, but if you love opera, you won't want to miss the Metropolitan Opera (tel. 212/362–6000; Sept.–Apr.), where every production is a lavish spectacle. To save at the Met, buy standing room (on sale Sunday for the coming week).

JAZZ AND CABARET Sunday jazz brunches are a lively and inexpensive way to hear hot sounds at such clubs as the Blue Note (131 W. 3rd St., tel. 212/475– 8592), which may well be the jazz capital of the world. Red Blazer Too (349 W. 46th St., tel. 212/262–3112) has '20s, Dixieland, and swing, and Sweet Basil (88 7th Ave. S, tel. 212/242–1785) ranges from swing to fusion. For cabaret, visit the venerable Oak Room at the Algonquin Hotel (59 W. 44th St., tel. 212/840–6800), or the Café Carlyle at the classy Carlyle Hotel (35 E. 76th St., tel. 212/744–1600).

SPECTATOR SPORTS Major-league baseball season stars the Yankees at Yankee Stadium (E. 161st St. at River Ave., the Bronx, tel. 718/293–6000) and the Mets at Shea Stadium (Flushing Meadows–Corona Park, Queens, tel. 718/587–8499). Both venues are easily accessible by subway. Madison Square Garden (tel. 212/465–6000), centrally located in midtown, hosts New York Rangers hockey action (Oct.–Apr.) and New York Knicks basketball (Nov.–Apr.).

Niagara Falls
New York and Ontario, Canada

Cynics have had their field day with Niagara Falls, calling it everything from "water on the rocks" to "the second major disappointment of American married life" (Oscar Wilde). Others have been more positive. Charles Dickens wrote: "I seemed to be lifted from the earth and to be looking into Heaven. Niagara was at once stamped upon my heart, an image of beauty, to remain there changeless and indelible." The falls were more dramatically immortalized by Hollywood in 1953, when Marilyn Monroe, as a steamy siren, lured her jealous husband down to the crashing cascades in the film classic *Niagara.*

Part of the longest unfortified border in the world, the falls are actually three cataracts: the American and Bridal Veil falls, in New York State, and the Horseshoe Falls in Ontario, Canada. There may be taller cataracts in Africa, South America, and even elsewhere in New York State, but in terms of sheer volume of water—more than 700,000 gallons per second in the summer—Niagara is unsurpassed in the world. The falls are responsible for the invention of alternating electric current, and they run one of the world's largest hydroelectric developments. And it really is all that water, on its way from four of the Great Lakes—Superior, Michigan, Huron, and Erie—to the fifth, Ontario, that makes Niagara the most famous and accessible waterfall in the world.

As with many other geographic features, Niagara's origins are glacial. More than 10,000 years before the first inscription "My Parents Visited Niagara Falls and All They Got Me Was This Lousy T-Shirt," the glaciers receded, diverting the waters of Lake Erie northward into Lake Ontario.

The malls, amusement parks, and tacky souvenir shops that surround the falls today attest to years as a major tourist attraction; on the New York side is America's oldest state

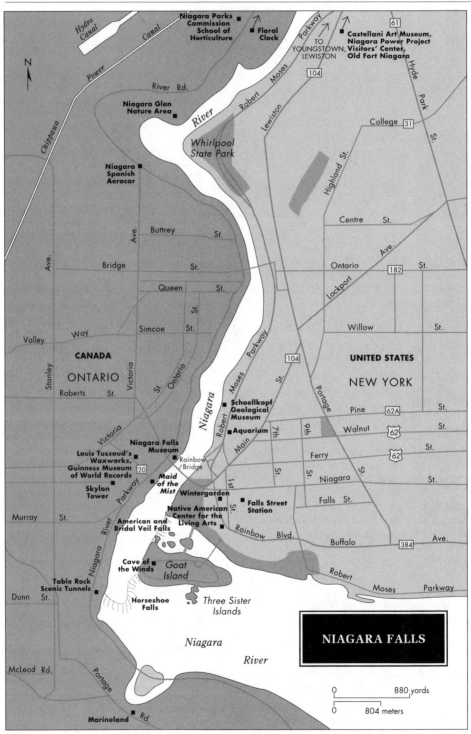

N

Hydro Canal

Power Canal

Niagara Parks Commission School of Horticulture

■ Floral Clock

Parkway

TO YOUNGSTOWN, LEWISTON

61

Castellani Art Museum, Niagara Power Project ■ Visitors' Center, Old Fort Niagara

Power

River Rd.

Moses

104

Hyde

Niagara Glen Nature Area ■

River

Robert

Lewiston

College 31

Park St.

Chippawa

Whirlpool State Park

Highland St.

Niagara Spanish Aerocar ■

Centre St.

Ave.

Buttrey St.

Ontario Ave. 182 St.

Bridge St.

Lockport

Queen St.

St.

Willow St.

Way

Simcoe St.

Parkway

104

Valley

CANADA

Moses

UNITED STATES

Stanley

ONTARIO

Victoria

St.

Ontario

Robert

Portage

NEW YORK

Roberts St.

Niagara

Schoellkopf Geological Museum

Pine St. 62A

Victoria

Aquarium ■

7th

9th

Walnut St.

Niagara Falls Museum ■

Main

62

Louis Tussaud's Waxworks, Guinness Museum of World Records

20

Rainbow Bridge

Ferry St.

62

Skylon Tower

Parkway

Maid of the Mist

Wintergarden

1st

St.

Niagara St.

Murray St.

River

Native American Center for the Living Arts ■

St.

Falls Street Station

Falls St.

American and Bridal Veil Falls

Rainbow Blvd.

Buffalo Ave. 384

Cave of the Winds

Goat Island

Robert

Table Rock Scenic Tunnels

Moses Parkway

Dunn St.

Horseshoe Falls

Three Sister Islands

Niagara

McLeod Rd.

Portage

River

Marineland ■ Rd.

NIAGARA FALLS

0   880 yards
0   804 meters

park. Despite the local tourist industry's unyielding and rather garish effort to accommodate hoards of visitors, the beauty of the falls remains undaunted.

ESSENTIAL INFORMATION

WHEN TO GO High season runs from Memorial Day through Labor Day, during which time most cultural activities take place and the falls boat rides are operating. Consequently, tourists abound and hotel prices are highest. Summer temperatures range from 75° to 85° with occasional light rainfall. The area near the falls is always misty, which in the summertime is rather refreshing. Very hot, humid days are infrequent.

Winter temperatures create ice-covered tree branches and rocks that reflect and sparkle. The railings and bridges can become almost crystalline.

FESTIVALS AND SPECIAL EVENTS Nov.–Jan.: From the Saturday after Thanksgiving to the Sunday after New Year's on the U.S. side and through mid-February on the Canadian side, the falls and surrounding area are aglow with various light shows for the spectacular Festival of Lights. Sophisticated indoor and outdoor light displays and entertainment take place in downtown Niagara. Even the brink of the falls is lit up.

BARGAINS If you plan to visit the majority of the Niagara Reservation State Park attractions, the Masterpass coupon book ($15 adults, $10 children) grants free admission to the six major New York State park attractions. Sold mid-May–October, the pass can be purchased at Niagara Reservation parking booths and Visitor Center, Grand Island Official Information Center, and designated locations in the Niagara Frontier State Parks.

The Niagara Parks Commission (tel. 416/356–2241) operates the People Mover buses in Niagara Falls, Ontario. The People Mover is a "loop" transportation system that allows tourists to get on and off all day at any of 12 stops along the Niagara Parkway. The cost is $3 for adults and $1.50 for children ages 6–12. Children under 6 ride free. Sightseers traveling by auto pay $8, which includes parking and a People Mover ticket for everyone in the car. People Mover buses operate mid-May–mid-October from 9 AM until 11 PM.

It is possible to be reimbursed for taxes on goods purchased in Canada, including hotel room charges totaling more than $100, so save your receipts. The provincial sales tax is 8% in Ontario, and the Government Service Tax (GST) is 7%. The cost of your room and goods purchased can be combined to reach the C$100 minimum.

Pick up your rebate forms at hotels or duty-free shops, or order them from Visitors Rebate Program (Revenue Canada, Customs and Excise, Visitors Rebate Program, Ottawa, Canada K1A 1J5, tel. 613/991–3346 or 800/66–VISIT from Canada). For the provincial and room tax form, contact the Retail Sales Branch (Ontario Provincial Treasury, 2300 Young St., 10th Floor, Toronto, Ontario, Canada M4P 1H6, tel. 416/487–1361). The process of getting reimbursed is rather long and complicated, but for those spending lots of Canadian dollars, it may be worth the trouble.

TOURIST OFFICES For information on the American side of the falls, contact: Niagara County Tourism (Niagara and Hawley Sts., Lockport, NY 14094, tel. 800/338–7890); Niagara Falls Tourism Information Center (4th and Niagara Sts., Niagara Falls, NY 14301, tel. 716/285–2400); the Niagara Falls Convention & Visitors Bureau (345 3rd St., Niagara Falls, NY 14303, tel. 800/421–5223 or 716/285–8711 for touch-tone 24-hr recorded message).

For information on the Canadian side of the falls, contact: Niagara Parks Commission (Box 150, Niagara Falls, Ontario, Canada L2E 6T2, tel. 416/356–2241 or 800/263–2558 for tour information); the Ontario Tourism Information Bureau (5355 Stanley Ave. at Highway 420, Niagara Falls, Ontario, Canada L2E 7C2, tel. 416/358–3221 or 800/668– 2746).

EMERGENCIES **Police, fire,** and **ambulance:** Dial 911. **Hospitals:** Niagara Falls Medical Center (621 10th St., Niagara Falls, NY, 14302, tel. 716/278–4000) and Mount St.

Mary's Hospital (5300 Lewiston Rd., Lewiston, NY 14092, tel. 716/297–4800). Greater Niagara General Hospital (5546 Portage Rd., Niagara Falls, Ontario, Canada, L2E 6X2, tel. 416/358– 0171).

ARRIVING AND DEPARTING

BY PLANE Greater Buffalo International Airport (tel. 716/632–3115) is the primary point of entry by air for Niagara Falls. Many charter tours, however, fly into Niagara Falls International Airport (tel. 716/297– 4494). Public buses operated by the Niagara Falls Metro Bus system (tel. 716/285–9319) run between the Buffalo and Niagara airports and downtown Niagara Falls. The bus ride to Niagara Falls from Buffalo International Airport requires a brief stopover in downtown Buffalo and costs about $2. Bus fare from Niagara International Airport costs $1.10. Taxi service to Niagara Falls costs approximately $30.

BY TRAIN On the American side, there's an Amtrak station just beyond downtown Niagara Falls, at the end of 27th Street off Lockport Rd., one block east of Hyde Park Blvd (tel. 716/285–4224; for reservations call 800/USA–RAIL). Taxi fare from the station to the falls is about $6. On the Canadian side, the Amtrak station (4267 Bridge Street, tel. 416/357–1644) is within walking distance of the falls in downtown Niagara Falls, Ontario.

BY BUS On the American side, the Greyhound Lines (tel. 800/231–2222) station is located at the Visitor Information Center next to the convention center at 4th and Niagara Streets. On the Canadian side, the station (4555 Erie Ave., tel. 416/354–4524) is a hub for the Canada Coach, Empire Trailway, Gray Coach, Greyhound, and Peter Pan bus lines.

BY CAR Access from the east and south is primarily via I–90, the New York State Thruway. The expressway spur, I–190, leads from 1–90 at Buffalo, across Grand Island to the Robert Moses Parkway into Niagara Falls. Approaches from the west are via a number of highways in Canada, including the Queen Elizabeth Way (QEW), with three bridges funneling traffic stateside.

GETTING AROUND

To avoid bridge traffic caused by Canadian shoppers invading the malls on weekends, travel to Canada in the morning and return home in the late afternoon or evening.

BY PUBLIC TRANSPORTATION AND VIEWMOBILE In Niagara Falls, New York, a Metro Bus system (tel. 716/285–9319) serves the Greater Niagara Falls area. Within downtown Niagara Falls, the cost is $1.10. The Niagara Reservation State Park operates the Viewmobile, a 40-minute guided trolley (train on wheels) ride that circles Goat Island (tel. 716/278–1770), making five stops. Visitors can get on and off all day for just $2.50.

In Niagara Falls, Ontario, the Niagara Transit bus system (tel. 416/356–1179) operates the Niagara Falls Shuttles. If purchased downtown or at the bus terminal, the shuttle cost is $3.50; the same ticket may be purchased along Lundy's Lane for $3. Either way, the ticket allows all-day transfers to and from various sites around downtown Niagara Falls, Ontario. The Niagara Parks Commission (tel. 416/356–2241) operates the People Mover buses (*see* Bargains, *above*).

ON FOOT All downtown Niagara Falls, New York, attractions are within a 10- to 15-minute walk. After exploring the American side you can even walk across the Rainbow Bridge into Canada. Most of the Canadian attractions, however, are a 20- to 30-minute walk; so for most visitors, riding the People Mover is preferable, after you've finished exploring Queen Victoria Park.

BY BICYCLE Bicycles are a very practical way to get around, and can be rented on the Canadian side at Cupolos (tel. 416/356–4850) on Ferry Street, near the corner of Stanley Avenue.

BY TAXI La Salle Dispatch Service (tel. 716/284–8833) is the most convenient taxi to the downtown Niagara Falls, New York, area. In Niagara Falls, Ontario, call Niagara Taxi (tel. 416/357–4000). A taxi ride from the Rainbow Bridge to the Floral Clock, 6 miles north, costs C$15–C$16.

The 5-0 Taxi Service (tel. 416/358–3232) also operates a specially equipped van for tourists traveling with wheelchairs.

GUIDED TOURS The Schoellkopf Geological Museum (tel. 716/278–1780) runs free guided geological walks on Goat Island; schedules are available by mail with a self-addressed, stamped envelope (Schoellkopf Geological Museum, Niagara Reservation, Box 1132, Niagara Falls, NY 14303–0132). The Niagara Glen Horticultural Department (tel. 416/358–8633), located 4 miles due north of the falls, runs free guided geological hikes down all the paths of the river to the bottom. Double Deck Tours (tel. 416/295–3051) offers a six-hour Niagara River Sightseeing package tour of the Canadian side. Tickets are available at the Table Rock House or in the Victoria Park Restaurant. Rainbow Helicopters, Inc. (tel. 716/284–2800) departs from the downtown heliport on the New York side of the falls for a 7-minute flight over the falls and Canada.

EXPLORING

Although the grandeur of the falls will undoubtedly be the highlight of your trip, the surrounding area is worth discovering. The Niagara River forms the Canadian–U.S. border; the land north of the falls on both sides of the river is comprised primarily of orchards and vineyards. Stateside is the historic community of Lewiston. Farther north, where the river opens into Lake Ontario, are the scenic villages of Youngstown on the U.S. side and Niagara-on-the-Lake on the Canadian side, each about a 20-minute drive from the falls. The latter is replete with many inns, restaurants, and shops, and is the site of the famous Shaw Festival (*see* Theater, *below*).

If the experience of the falls themselves isn't dramatic enough for you, you can always go to the movies. On the American side, the Visitor Center's Festival Theatre (tel. 716/278–1770) presents Niagara Wonders, a sensational view of the falls in a 70mm, 20-minute film, with six-channel digital sound. Shown Wednesday–Sunday 10 AM–6 PM, the price is $2 for adults, $1 for children 6–12. There's a special group rate of $1.50 per per-

son for parties of 10 or more. Across the border, Niagara Falls Ontario's IMAX Theatre and Daredevil Adventure (6170 Buchanan Ave., Niagara Falls, Ontario, tel. 416/374–IMAX) boasts the "biggest show in Niagara." Forty-five minutes long, *Niagara: Miracles, Myths, and Magic* shows the falls on Canada's largest movie screen, also with six-channel Dolby sound. Shows are on the hour, daily 11 AM–8 PM. In a separate exhibit is an interesting display of information and paraphernalia relating to attempts over the years by various daredevils to take the plunge over the falls. The price is C$7.50 for combined admission, C$6.50 for the IMAX show alone, and C$4.75 for the Daredevil Adventure alone.

THE AMERICAN SIDE **Goat Island.** This is the spot to begin your tour. Part of the state park, the island offers the closest possible views of the American falls and the upper rapids. There are excellent hiking and biking trails and some guided geological walks are offered. Hop on the Viewmobile sightseeing trains for an overview of each park attraction. The 40-minute tour includes a close-up view of the falls; Cave of the Winds, Schoellkopf Museum, Aquarium, and Three Sisters Island. *Goat Island, tel. 716/278–1700. Hours vary seasonally. Admission charged.*

Maid of the Mist. Theodore Roosevelt considered this ride "the only way to fully realize the Grandeur of the Great Falls of Niagara." It can be boarded on either the American or Canadian side. The captain expertly guides the boat past the base of the American and Bridal Veil falls and almost into the thunderous deluge of the Horseshoe Falls. *Niagara River at the base of the falls, tel. 716/284–8897. Open daily. Admission charged. Discount when using the Masterpass.*

Cave of the Winds. Get close to almost touching the falls by following wooden walkways to within 25 feet of the base. Thin, plastic yellow rain slickers are provided. *Trip starts on Goat Island, tel. 716/278–1730. Open mid-May–mid-Oct., daily. Admission charged.*

Native American Center for the Living Arts. Built in the shape of a turtle, the Iroquois symbol of the Earth, the center is just a couple hundred feet from the brink of the falls. It houses a museum and an art gallery focusing on Native American culture and art. Iroquois dance performances are held during the summer season; during the first week of May, the Center also hosts a powwow, a Native American festival of traditional dancing, arts and culture. If you need a break, there's a gift shop and restaurant on the premises. *25 Rainbow Blvd., tel. 716/284–2427. Closed Mon. Oct.–Apr. Admission charged.*

Schoellkopf Geological Museum. For insight into the interesting geological history of the falls, visit this museum in Niagara Reservation State Park. A geological garden and nature trail are on the grounds. *Take the first exit off the Robert Moses Parkway north of downtown, tel. 716/278–1780. Open Memorial Day–Labor Day, daily 9:30–7; Labor Day–Memorial Day, Thurs.–Sun. 10–5. Admission charged.*

The Aquarium of Niagara Falls. The world's first inland oceanarium, with over 2,000 aquatic creatures, has hourly dolphin, sea lion, and electric eel shows, an outdoor seal and sea lion pool, and interactive Great Lakes fish displays. *701 Whirlpool St., tel. 716/285–3575. Open daily. Admission charged.*

Niagara Power Project Visitors' Center. The hydroelectric power project has a video, displays, hands-on exhibits, and computer games explaining how water generates electricity and highlighting the importance and history of Niagara in this effort. *5777 Lewiston Rd., Lewiston, NY 14092, tel. 716/285–3211. Open daily. Admission free.*

The Castellani Art Museum. Located in the center of the Niagara University Campus, this 23,000-square-foot, $3½ million facility houses both rotating exhibitions and an impressive permanent collection of over 3,000 works of art, including impressive works by Roy Lichtenstein, Jasper Johns, Louise Nevelson, Cindy Sherman, Picasso prints and ceramics, and some pre-Columbian sculptures. Most were donated from the private collection of Armand J. Castellani, the museum's founder. Follow signs for the university north of the falls on Route 104. *Tel.*

716/286–8200. Open Wed.–Sat. 11–5, Sun. 1–5; other hours by appointment. Admission free.

Old Fort Niagara. This fort on the Historic trail in Youngstown has been occupied by the French, British, and Americans. The original stone buildings have been preserved in their pre-Revolutionary state. There are military reenactments May through October and crafts and archaeological digs throughout the year. *Take the Robert Moses Pkwy. north for 14 miles (about a 20-min ride) to Youngstown, tel. 716/745–7611. Open daily. Admission charged.*

THE CANADIAN SIDE Most bus and boat tours begin at Clifton Hill, and many of the better attractions are located near the falls and northeast of the Skylon Tower. Attractions beyond Clifton Hill are best visited by automobile.

Skylon Tower. Amusements, entertainment, and shops are in the tower, as well as an indoor/outdoor observation deck and a revolving restaurant. The view is particularly beautiful at night, when the falls are illuminated. *5200 Robinson St., tel. 416/356–2651. Open daily. Admission charged.*

Table Rock Scenic Tunnels. Raincoats are provided for the fish-eye view of the Canadian Horseshoe Falls and the Niagara River through three tunnels cut into the rock. Tours begin at the Table Rock House in Queen Victoria Park. *Tel. 416/358–3268. Open daily. Admission charged.*

Niagara Falls Museum. Located at the Rainbow Bridge, housed here is everything from schlock to quality—the Daredevil Hall of Fame, dinosaurs, and a collection of authentic Egyptian mummies. There are also Indian artifacts and zoological and geological exhibits. *5651 River Rd., tel. 416/356–2151. Open daily. Admission charged.*

Louis Tussaud's Waxworks. Life-size reproductions of the most famous and infamous people, from Bach and Cleopatra to Elvis and Prince Charles, are here in historically accurate costumes and settings. *4915 Clifton Hill,* *tel. 416/374–6601. Open daily. Admission charged.*

Guinness Museum of World Records. Contained here are hundreds of exhibits that made it into the famous record book. *4943 Clifton Hill, tel. 416/356–2299. Open daily. Admission charged.*

Marineland. The 4,500-seat aqua theater has a large troupe of performing sea lions, harbor seals and dolphins as well as two killer whales. The wildlife display includes a herd of buffalo, bears, and over 400 deer to be pet and fed. There are rides for all ages, including the world's largest steel roller coaster. *1 mi south of the falls, follow signs along the pkwy., tel. 416/356–2142. Open Apr.–Nov., daily. Admission charged.*

The Niagara Spanish Aerocar. This cable car transports you over the Niagara Gorge and back on an 1,800-foot-long cable. *River Rd., 2¹/₂ mi north of the falls, tel. 416/354–5711, 800/263–2558 for group tours. Open June–Labor Day, daily; off-season, when weather permits. Admission charged.*

The Niagara Glen. Free guided tours are given by a naturalist four times daily Thursday through Monday (between July and August) down a nature trail to the river's edge, where there are picnic tables. *Niagara River Pkwy., tel. 416/358–8633.*

The Niagara Parks Commission Botanical Gardens. Four miles north of the falls along the Niagara Parkway are 100 acres of lush gardens. All plants are labeled, so you can do a self-guided tour asking any questions of the gardeners, most of whom are students. *2564 Niagara River Pkwy., tel. 416/356–8554. Open daily. Admission free.*

The Floral Clock. Six miles north of the falls along River Road, the clock is one of the largest blooming clocks in the world, made up of nearly 15,000 plants. It keeps accurate time, and chimes ring every quarter hour. *14004 Niagara Parkway, tel. 416/357–2411.*

THE NATURAL WORLD From mid-March to the first two weeks in April almost every type of migratory bird in the Northeast—all types

of waterfowl, gulls, songbirds, even nesting bald eagles—can be spotted in the Niagara Falls area. Tanawanda Wildlife Management Area and Iroquois National Wildlife Refuge, about 45 minutes southeast of the falls, is one of the finest bird-watching sanctuaries in the country. *From Rte. 31 take Rte. 77 to the Refuge Headquarters on Casey Rd., tel. 716/948–5445. Open mid-Mar.–Apr., daily.*

HOTELS AND INNS

Hotels and motels in the Niagara Falls area fall primarily into two categories: major chains and lower-priced properties. For a unique experience, you may want to stay in a quaint bed-and-breakfast, but check prices beforehand. Those with fireplaces and complete amenities can cost as much as a luxury hotel. Rainbow Hospitality (466 Amherst St., Buffalo, NY 14207, tel. 716/874–8797) is a bed-and-breakfast reservation service that represents member B&Bs in Buffalo, Niagara Falls, and Canada. Niagara Region Bed-and-Breakfasts (4917 River Road, Niagara Falls, Ontario L2E 3G5, tel. 416/358–8988) represents over 30 member B&Bs in Niagara Falls, Canada. Many very good bed-and-breakfasts do not belong to these systems; for a complete listing, check with the convention and visitors bureaus in both New York and Ontario.

Price categories for double occupancy, excluding tax (5% in Ontario, 10% in New York State for bills under $100 and 15% for bills over $100), are *Expensive,* over $70; *Moderate,* $50–$70; and *Inexpensive,* under $50.

AMERICAN SIDE-EXPENSIVE Radisson Hotel–Niagara Falls. Just two blocks from the falls and connected to the Rainbow Factory Outlet Mall by an enclosed walkway, this newly renovated hotel is the largest in the area. Special honeymoon, second honeymoon, and Festival of Lights packages are available. *3rd and Old Falls Sts., 14303, tel. 716/285–3361 or 800/333–3333. 401 rooms. Restaurant, indoor heated pool. AE, DC, MC, V.*

MODERATE-EXPENSIVE Comfort Inn–The Pointe. This is the closest hotel to the falls, and many of the rooms enjoy a view of them.

It is attached to the Pointe Retail Complex, so the international eateries and gift shops found here are all added conveniences. *1 Prospect Pointe, 14303, tel. 716/284–6835 or 800/228–5150. 120 rooms. Restaurant, bar, comedy club, some rooms with Jacuzzis. AE, MC, V.*

Days Inn–Falls View. The marble in the lobby and the cathedral ceilings recall the '20s, when this was the only hotel in Niagara. It is spacious and moderately priced, and just steps away from the falls. *201 Rainbow Blvd., 14303, tel. 716/285–9321 or 800/325–2525. 200 rooms. Restaurant, lounge. AE, D, DC, MC, V.*

Inn at the Falls. Located 1,200 feet from the brink of the falls, the inn has views of both the falls and the downtown district and is conveniently attached to the Wintergarden atrium shopping mall. *240 Rainbow Blvd., 14303, tel. 716/282–1212 or 800/223–2557. 217 rooms. Restaurant, bar, banquet room, indoor pool, no-smoking rooms. AE, D, DC, MC, V.*

INEXPENSIVE-MODERATE **Budget Host Motel.** This motel is new and squeaky-clean, just four blocks from the falls. The rooms are spacious and tastefully decorated with bleached oak furniture. *219 4th St. at Rainbow Blvd., 14303, tel. 716/282–1734 or 800/333–2557. 114 rooms. Restaurant, souvenir shop, coin laundry, valet service. AE, D, DC, MC, V.*

Holiday. Located 3 miles east of the falls, the rooms are clean and comfortable but without telephones. *6650 Niagara Falls Blvd., tel. 716/283–8974. 17 rooms. Air-conditioning, cable TV, heated pool, picnic tables. AE, MC, V.*

INEXPENSIVE **Bel-Aire Motel.** Although 4½ miles from the falls, this small, clean motel is a terrific bargain. *9470 Niagara Falls Blvd., U.S. 62, tel. 716/297–2250. 25 rooms. Heated pool. AE, DC, MC, V.*

Coachman Motel. Just three blocks from the falls, the Coachman is one of the best values within walking distance. *523 3rd St., 14301.,*

tel. 716/285–2295. 19 rooms. Refrigerators. AE, D, DC, MC, V.

Plaza Court Motel. The Plaza Court is a good value, is attached to Plaza Court Campgrounds, and is close to the falls. There are no in-room telephones. *7680 Niagara Falls Blvd., 14304, tel. 716/283–2638. 10 rooms. Outdoor pool. AE, D, MC, V.*

Portage House. Located 7 miles north of the falls, the Portage House is at the entrance to ArtPark and is right in the heart of historic Lewiston. All 21 rooms have two double beds and are done in soft, muted tones. Free morning coffee is offered in the lobby. There are no phones in individual rooms. *280 Portage Rd., Lewiston 14092, tel. 716/754–8295. 21 rooms. AE, MC, V.*

CANADIAN SIDE-MODERATE **The Americana.** Set on 25 acres of grounds, this motel's new and extensive exercise facilities make it one of the nicer moderately priced motels on the strip. *8444 Lundy's La., Niagara Falls, Ont. L2H 1H4, tel. 416/356–8444. 120 rooms. Restaurant, lounge, coffee shop, indoor and outdoor pools, exercise room, sauna, basketball court, tennis court, squash court, picnic area. AE, D, DC, MC, V.*

INEXPENSIVE-MODERATE **Surfside Inn.** The Surfside's rooms are decorated in either French provincial, Italian provincial, or Chinese black-lacquered style. Rooms with water beds and Jacuzzis are available. There's a public beach across the street in King's Bridge Park. *3665 Macklem St., Niagara Falls, Ont. L2G 6C8, tel. 416/295–4354. 32 rooms; 8 suites. Closed Jan. and Feb. AE, MC, V.*

INEXPENSIVE **Alpine Motel.** Set back from the road, the Alpine is small, quiet, and has two rooms with two double beds for families. *7742 Lundy's La., Niagara Falls, Ont. L2H 1H4, tel. 416/356–7016. 10 rooms. Heated outdoor pool, refrigerators, patio, nearby golf. AE, MC, V.*

Detroit Motor Inn. Located 5 miles west of the falls at the city limits, this inn has reasonable rates and spacious grounds. *13030 Lundy's La. W, Niagara Falls, Ont. L2H 1H4,* *tel. 416/227–4747. 38 rooms with bath or shower. Dining room, lounge with pool tables, outdoor heated pool, miniature golf, barbecue facilities. AE, MC, V.*

Fiddler's Green. The Fiddler's has pleasantly decorated rooms and offers four efficiency units with refrigerator, stove, and cooking/dining utensils (for a small deposit). Also available are 12 mini efficiencies and two suites with whirlpools. *7720 Lundy's La., Niagara Falls, Ont. L2H 1H4, tel. 416/358–9833. 94 rooms. Indoor and outdoor pools. AE, MC, V.*

DINING

Scattered among the well-represented fast-food chains in Niagara are several respectable restaurants. The ethnic restaurants, particularly Italian, are very good. You can also find excellent Continental cuisine. All the restaurants listed will prepare special orders, when notified in advance, for those on reduced sodium, cholesterol, or calorie diets. Price categories per person, not including tax (7% in New York State, 15% in Ontario), service, and drinks, are *Moderate,* $15–$25, and *Inexpensive,* under $15. While the American dollar is worth about C$1.16, keep in mind that Canadian restaurants tend to be a little more expensive than their American counterparts. Casual dress is acceptable in the establishments listed, and reservations are not necessary.

AMERICAN SIDE—NIAGARA FALLS **Como.** The largest and one of the best Italian-American restaurants in Niagara Falls is known especially for its homemade pastas. The steak, Italian veal, and seafood dishes are also good. Every Friday a seafood special is served. *2220 Pine Ave., tel. 716/285–9341. AE, MC, V. Moderate.*

Fortunas. Owned by the same family that owns the Goose's Roost and Como, Fortunas has attracted area residents since 1945. The Italian home cooking includes all the old favorites in a warm, bustling environment. *827 29th St., tel. 716/282–2252. AE, MC, V. Closed Mon. and Tues. Moderate.*

Pete's Market House. This family restaurant serves hearty basics— steak, lobster, veal—in a warm, lively environment. The lines are long, the portions are huge, and the prices are pleasantly low. *1701 Pine Ave., tel. 716/282–7225. No credit cards. Moderate.*

Goose's Roost. Right by the bus terminal, the Roost specializes in Italian food, but the menu is extensive and varied. The casual mood belies the chandeliers and the mirrors on the ceilings. *343 4th St. at Niagara St., tel. 716/282–6255. AE, D, MC, V. Inexpensive.*

La Casa Cardenas. This casual and inexpensive Mexican restaurant is appropriately bustling and festive. The walls are bright red and covered with murals and Mexican trinkets. The menu also offers Californian selections, and any of the menu items can be ordered without meat. *921 Main St., tel. 716/282–0231. AE, D, MC, V. Inexpensive.*

LEWISTON **Apple Granny.** Right on the main strip in town and near ArtPark, Apple Granny's offers basic American fare—burgers and fries, steaks, and hearty meat-n-potato plates. After dinner you can hit the dance floor for some low-key, sedate dancing. *433 Center St., tel. 716/754–2028. AE, D, DC, MC, V. Inexpensive.*

CANADIAN SIDE **Casa D'oro.** The Italian menu combines the basics with more elaborate dishes in opulent surroundings. Specialties include pollo cacciatore, sole basilica (flavored with lime juice, paprika, and basil), and pasta primavera. The adjoining nightclub and bar has nightly dancing. *5875 Victoria Ave., tel. 416/356–5646. AE, DC, MC, V. Moderate.*

Embers Restaurant at Michael's Inn. The large, glass-enclosed open-hearth barbecue allows you to watch the chef prepare your meal. The menu specializes in Continental cuisine, with fresh fish daily. *5599 River Rd., tel. 416/354–2727. AE, DC, MC, V. Moderate.*

The Millery Dining Room. The Bistro prides itself on the variety and authenticity of its dishes. Dishes include prime rib, chicken, pasta, seafood, and salads. The cathedral ceilings, the fireplace, and the old wood tables make for a warm atmosphere. *Clarion Old Stone Inn, 5425 Robinson St., tel. 416/357–1234. AE, DC, MC, V. Moderate.*

Falls Manor Restaurant. This "country casual" spot serves a combination of British and American cuisine on big pine tables. In addition to meat dishes, you can have roast chicken or fish-and-chips. Try the seafood bisque and delicious roast chicken. *7104 Lundy's La., tel. 416/358–3211. AE, MC, V. Inexpensive.*

Table Rock Restaurant. Here at the brink of the falls, the spacious Table Rock Restaurant offers a spectacular view of the falls. The prices on the Continental menu are fixed by the Canadian government. *Just yards from Horseshoe Falls, tel. 416/354–3631. AE, D, MC, V. Inexpensive.*

Victoria Park Cafe and Dining Room. Right in the park is a comfortable indoor dining area and an outdoor terrace overlooking the Victoria Park gardens and the falls. The cafeteria offers soups, salads, pasta dishes, hot food, and sandwiches. The restaurant offers seasonal features and an early dinner special of prime rib. *Queen Victoria Park, 6345 Niagara Pkwy., tel. 416/356–2217. Closed Nov.–mid-May. AE, MC, V. Inexpensive.*

SHOPPING

Between 15 million and 18 million visitors come to Niagara Falls annually, and according to a recent survey, the second most popular activity—next to visiting the falls—is shopping. Niagara factory outlets offer up to 70% off retail prices on top-quality manufacturers' goods, including fine china and dinnerware, books, apparel, shoes, jewelry, and accessories. The outlets are easy to reach by foot or car and group tours are available. Rainbow Center Factory Outlet (302 Rainbow Blvd., Niagara Falls, NY 14303, tel. 716/285–9758 or 716/285–5525). This mall is a one-block walk from the falls. Factory Outlet Mall (1900 Military Rd, Niagara Falls, NY 14304, tel. 716/297–2022). Here are more than 90 stores just 7 miles from the falls. Book Warehouse (2420 Military Rd, Niagara Falls, NY 14304, tel. 716/297–3530). Located less than $1/4$ mile north of Factory Outlet Mall, they cut 50%–90% off the price of nearly 7,000 publishers' overruns.

ENTERTAINMENT

Call the Niagara Falls Convention and Visitors Bureau (tel. 716/285–8711) for a list of special events, activities, and performances.

ArtPark. The only U.S. state park devoted to the visual and performing arts, this 2,300-seat open-air amphitheater (with an additional 1,500 seats on the lawn) boasts first-quality opera, musicals, dance, and concerts. From late May to Labor Day free arts activities—demonstrations, participatory art workshops by artists, craftspeople, and performers—are held throughout the park. *Tel. 716/754–9001 in season, 716/745–3377 off-season. Call 800/659–7275 for Buffalo Philharmonic tickets.*

Shaw Festival. Held just 12 miles north of Niagara Falls, this world-renowned theater festival features the works of George Bernard Shaw and his contemporaries in three theaters. The festival runs from April to November and includes nine plays. Take the scenic Niagara Parkway and follow clearly marked signs for Niagara-on-the-Lake north of the falls. Once in town, the festival venues are easily found on the left. *Tel. 416/468–2172. Open Tues.–Sun. Admission charged.*

The Outer Banks
North Carolina

orth Carolina's Outer Banks comprise a series of barrier islands that curve 130 miles from the Virginia state line southward past Morehead City. For centuries a threat to shipping despite an extensive network of lighthouses and lifesaving stations, the area is called the Graveyard of the Atlantic. More than 400 years ago, a colony of English settlers on Roanoke Island disappeared without a trace. Their story is told annually in an outdoor drama, The Lost Colony, presented in the Waterside Theater. The coves and inlets of the islands offered seclusion to pirates, and the notorious Blackbeard lived and died here. For many years the Outer Banks remained isolated, home only to a few fishing families, whose descendants still speak with Elizabethan accents. Today, the islands, linked by bridges and ferries, are popular with visitors, who come in large numbers during the long summers mostly for the magnificent beaches. Crowds are reduced during the mild spring and fall. Much of the area is within the Cape Hatteras and Cape Lookout national seashores; the largest towns on the islands are Manteo, Kill Devil Hills (sites of the Wright brothers' flight), and Nags Head.

ESSENTIAL INFORMATION

WHEN TO GO Weather on the Outer Banks is relatively mild year-round, with an average temperature of 62°. In summer, when the mercury climbs as high as 87°, rates are at their peak, and ferry reservations are a must. August and September are the peak season for hurricanes and tropical storms, but authorities estimate that the probability of a hurricane striking the area is less than 15% per year. Spring and fall are breezy, balmy, and less crowded; many hotels and motels offer off-season rates September to May. On cooler winter days the thermometer can drop to the mid-30s or even below freezing. "Nor'easters" are common during the colder months of the year.

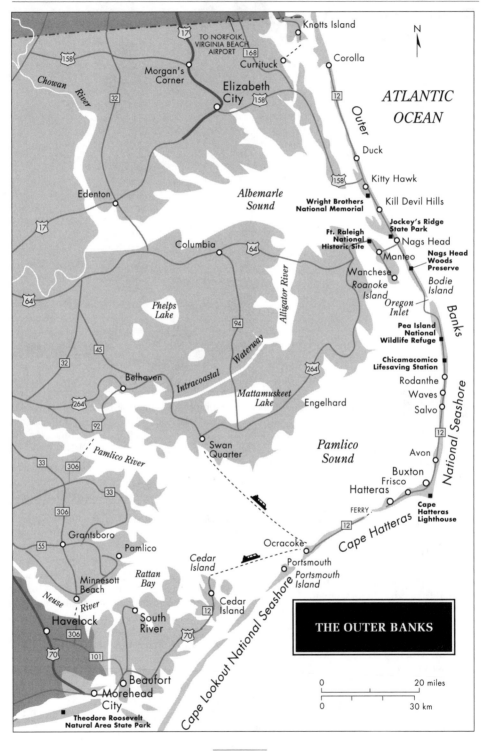

THE OUTER BANKS

BARGAINS Cape Hatteras National Seashore is the best bargain around. Not only are the beaches and scenery free, but there are festivals, lighthouses, and shipwrecks. Free activities in summer range from puppet shows to nature walks and campfire programs (tel. 919/473–2111). No admission is charged at Jockey's Ridge State Park, Nags Head Woods Preserve, Fort Raleigh, Pea Island National Wildlife Refuge, Chicamacomico Lifesaving Station, or Cape Hatteras Lighthouse.

TOURIST OFFICES Cape Hatteras National Seashore (Rte. 1, Box 675, Manteo 27954, tel. 919/473–2111). Dare County Tourist Bureau (Box 399, Manteo 27954, tel. 919/473–2138 or 800/446–6262). Division of Travel and Tourism (430 N. Salisbury St., Raleigh 27611, tel. 919/733–4171 or 800/VISITNC).

EMERGENCIES Dial 911 for **police, fire,** and **ambulance. The Outer Banks Medical Center** at Nags Head (tel. 919/441–7111) is open 24 hours a day.

ARRIVING AND DEPARTING

BY PLANE The closest commercial airport is the Norfolk (Virginia) International Airport, served by American, Continental, Delta, and USAir. Rental cars are available in the terminal.

BY CAR U.S. 158 links the Outer Banks with Norfolk and other places north. U.S. 64 and 264 are western routes. Toll ferries connect Ocracoke to Cedar Island and Swan Quarter on the mainland. There is a free ferry between Ocracoke and Hatteras Island.

BY TRAIN Amtrak (tel. 800/USA–RAIL) serves Newport News (Virginia) and, by Amtrak bus, Norfolk and Virginia Beach. You can rent cars in all three locations.

BY BUS Greyhound Lines (tel. 800/231–2222) serves Elizabeth City and Norfolk, Virginia.

BY BOAT Seagoing visitors traveling the Intracoastal Waterway may dock at Elizabeth City, Manteo, Belhaven, Beaufort, and other ports, where cars can be rented.

GETTING AROUND

BY CAR A car is the most practical way to get around on the Outer Banks. You can get detailed road maps that also list ferry schedules from the Dare County Tourist Bureau (*see* Tourist Offices, *above*). The main north–south road (U.S. 158/Rte. 12) has convenient mileposts (MP).

BY TAXI Beach Cabs (tel. 919/441–2500) offers 24-hour service. Island Limousine and Taxi (tel. 919/441–8803).

REST STOPS There are rest rooms and picnic shelters at Dare County Aycock Brown Welcome Center (U.S. 158 Bypass, MP 1.5) and at Jockey's Ridge State Park (MP 12). Dare County Tourist Bureau (U.S. 64 and Budleigh St., Manteo) and all the Cape Hatteras National Seashore's facilities have rest rooms. The ferry stops on Cedar Island, Ocracoke, and Hatteras have rest rooms that are open year-round.

GUIDED TOURS Kitty Hawk Aero Tours (tel. 919/441–4460) runs flights of about 45 minutes over the Outer Banks (Mar.–Labor Day, $19–$25 per person). Departures are from the First Flight Airstrip at the Wright Brothers National Memorial, or from Manteo.

EXPLORING

Bodie, Hatteras, and Ocracoke islands (from north to south) are linked to each other and to the mainland by bridges and ferries. You can drive the Outer Banks down U.S. 158/Rte. 12 in a day, but allow plenty of time in summer to wait for the ferries. For reservations, call 919/225–3551 for departures from Cedar Island; 919/928–3841 from Ocracoke; or 919/926–1111 from Swan Quarter. A "ghost fleet" map, available at the Wright Brothers National Memorial, is helpful in locating the sites of shipwrecks.

Wright Brothers National Memorial, a granite monument that resembles the tail of an airplane, sits atop a 90-foot dune as a tribute to Wilbur and Orville Wright, the two Ohio bicycle mechanics who took to the air on December 17, 1903. You can see a replica of

The Flyer, explore marked historic trails and exhibits, and hear an informative talk by a National Park Service ranger. *U.S. 158 Bypass, MP 8.5, Kill Devil Hills, tel. 919/441–7430. Open daily. Admission charged.*

Nags Head Woods Preserve, shielded from the salt-laden breezes by a ridge of high, ancient dunes, is a glorious 1,400-acre maritime forest. The preserve nurtures a diverse range of plant and animal species—including many that are not normally associated with the harsh environment of a barrier island. Tour this unique forest via several nature trails. *Off Rte. 158 at MP 9, Kill Devil Hills, tel. 919/441–2525. Open Tues., Thurs., and Sat. Admission free.*

Jockey's Ridge State Park, containing the tallest sand dune in the eastern United States, is a popular spot for hang gliding, kite flying, hiking, picnics, and photography. There is a 1¹/₂-mile self-guided nature trail with 14 stations and a natural-history museum, with guided tours on request. *U.S. 158 Bypass, MP 12, tel. 919/441–7132. Open daily. Admission free.*

The Elizabethan Gardens, created by the Garden Club of North Carolina in memory of Elizabeth I and the early colonists, has easy walking trails amid profuse period plantings and antique statuary. *Off U.S. 64/264 on the north end of Roanoke Island, tel. 919/473–3234. Open mid-Mar.–early Nov., daily. Admission charged.*

Fort Raleigh is a reconstruction of what is thought to be the first colonists' fort. An orientation film and guided tour explain its significance. The Thomas Hariot Nature Trail leads to an outlook on Roanoke Sound. *Off U.S. 64/264, Roanoke Island, tel. 919/473–2111. Open daily. Admission free.*

The Lost Colony, America's oldest outdoor drama, dating to 1937, reenacts the story of the Outer Banks' first colonists, who disappeared mysteriously in 1591. *Waterside Amphitheater, Roanoke Island, tel. 919/473–3414 or 800/488–5012. Mid-June–late Aug., Mon.–Sat. Backstage tours (see the play first). Admission charged for tours and play.*

North Carolina Aquarium. You can see hands-on and interactive exhibits, like the touch tank, and take behind-the-scenes tours and trips to coastal habitats. *Airport Rd., Roanoke Island, tel. 919/473–3493. Open daily. Donation requested.*

Elizabeth II State Historic Site. There's a little something for everyone here: a visitor center, museum, multimedia program, and a full-size floating replica of a 16th-century sailing ship, the *Elizabeth II.* You can also meet park workers portraying—in dress, speech, and attitude—haggard mariners and Elizabethan-era colonists. *Manteo water front, tel. 919/473–1144. Open Nov.–Mar., Tues.–Sun; Apr.–Oct., daily. Admission charged.*

Pea Island National Wildlife Refuge is a 6,000-acre haven for more than 265 species of birds, with observation platforms, dunes, marsh, beach, man-made habitats, and nature trails. *Rte. 12, between Oregon Inlet and Rodanthe, tel. 919/473–1131. Open Apr.– Nov., weekdays 8–4. Admission free.*

Chicamacomico Lifesaving Station, a few miles south of Pea Island, is a museum dedicated to the 24 lifesaving stations that once lined the Outer Banks. *Rte. 12, Rodanthe, tel. 919/473–2111 for scheduled openings and events. Admission free.*

Cape Hatteras Lighthouse, at 208 feet, is the tallest in America. Recent renovations allow visitors once again to climb the circular stairs to the top for fine views of the Atlantic. *The Visitor Center, Buxton, tel. 919/995–4474. Open daily. Admission free.*

Ocracoke Island, a small oasis of restaurants, motels, shops, and a visitor center (tel. 919/928–6711) has a quaint charm about it. The picturesque harbor, with the Ocracoke Lighthouse in the background, is where the pirate Blackbeard met his demise in 1718. Ferries make several trips a day from Ocracoke to Swan Quarter and Cedar Island on the mainland.

THE NATURAL WORLD Look for deer, rabbits, foxes, lizards, and various birds along the nature trail in Jockey's Ridge State Park. Walk through the rich environment of a maritime forest at the Nags Head Woods Preserve. The Pea Island National Wildlife Refuge is home to numerous species of wading, shore, and upland birds; large concentrations of snow geese winter there. You often see egrets, blue herons, and pelicans on the causeway connecting Bodie and Roanoke islands. Catch sight of a pod of porpoises working the surf while checking the beach for shells and interesting things. Wild ponies live near the Corolla Lighthouse, on Ocracoke Island, and on Shackleford Banks in the Cape Lookout National Seashore.

HOTELS AND INNS

Weathered beach cottages, condos, and motels line the beach at Nags Head and Kill Devil Hills. There are laid-back lodges and motels in Ocracoke, and motels and bed-and-breakfasts in Manteo and the Albemarle region. Hundreds of cottages and condos are available through local real-estate agencies; try Sun Realty (tel. 800/334–4745) or Resort Realty (tel. 800/458–3830). Camping information can be obtained from the National Park Service (tel. 919/473–2111). High-season price categories for double occupancy, without 8% tax, are *Moderate*, $60–$100, and *Inexpensive*, under $60.

MODERATE **The Berkeley Center Country Inn.** Secluded by trees on spacious, well-maintained grounds near the ferry dock, this former corporate retreat resembles a lifesaving station and is furnished with mixed antiques and reproductions. *Rte. 12, Box 220, Ocracoke 27960, tel. 919/928–5911. 10 rooms. Free Continental breakfast. Closed mid-Dec.–mid-Mar. No credit cards.*

The Figurehead Bed and Breakfast. Fly a kite, ride a bike, or relax in a beach chair at this weathered beach house on the Albemarle Sound, minutes from the ocean and several restaurants. *417 Helga St., Kill Devil Hills 27948, tel. 919/414–6929 or 800/221–6929. 3 rooms. Free bicycle use. Smoking limited. Continental breakfast. MC, V.*

The Island Inn and Dining Room. The inn's best rooms (in the third-floor Crow's Nest), with panoramic views, have been redone, and the dining room's island cuisine features wonderful crab cakes and hush puppies. *Rte. 12, Box 9, Ocracoke 27960, tel. 919/928–4351. 35 rooms. Heated outdoor pool. D, MC, V.*

Surf Side Motel. Every room at this peaceful oceanfront retreat has balconies and fine ocean views; one room even has a private whirlpool. If the pace is too relaxing, there are shops and restaurants nearby. *Box 400, Nags Head 27959, tel. 919/441–2105 or 800/552–SURF. 70 rooms, 6 efficiencies. Indoor/outdoor pools, golf privileges. AE, D, MC, V.*

INEXPENSIVE **C. W. Pugh's Bed & Breakfast.** Enjoy the comforts of a beautiful old beach house, surrounded by live oaks and the ocean, in the fishing village of Wanchese, on Roanoke Island. *Box 427, Wanchese 27981, tel. 919/473–5466. 2 rooms. Full breakfast. Open Mar.–Oct. AE, MC, V.*

Scarborough Inn. Heirloom beds and family antiques fill the simple rooms at the Scarborough, a quiet inn lined with wide porches and only minutes away from Manteo's attractions. *Box 1310, Manteo 27954, tel. 919/473–3979. 12 rooms, 4 in annex. Refrigerators, coffeemakers. AE, DC, MC, V.*

MOTELS

MODERATE **Castaways** (Box 557, Avon 27915, tel. 919/995–4444 or 800/845–6070). 68 rooms; restaurant, lounge, indoor pool, whirlpool. AE, MC, V. **Colony IV Motel** (Box 287, Kill Devil Hills 27948, tel. 919/441–5581 or 800/848–3728). 64 rooms, 12 efficiencies; room refrigerators, heated pool, whirlpool, laundry, game room, playground, miniature golf. AE, D, DC, MC, V. **Comfort Inn** (Rte. 12, Buxton 27920, tel. 919/995–6100 or 800/432–1441). 60 rooms; pool, room refrigerators. AE, D, DC, MC, V. **Days Inn** (Box 1096, Kitty Hawk 27949, tel. 919/261–4888 or 800/325–2525). 98 rooms; restaurant, pool. AE, D, DC, MC, V. **Elizabethan Inn** (Box 549, Manteo 27954, tel. 919/473–2102 or

800/346–2466). 100 rooms; restaurant, indoor/outdoor pools, health club, sauna, whirlpool, racquetball, picnic area, and room refrigerators. AE, D, DC, MC, V. **Sea Foam Motel** (7111 Virginia Dare Trail, Nags Head 27959, tel. 919/441–7320). 29 rooms, 18 efficiencies, 3 apartments/cottages; pool, room refrigerators, microwaves. Closed Dec.–Feb. AE, MC, V.

INEXPENSIVE Cape Hatteras Motel (Box 339T, Buxton 27920, tel. 919/995–5611). 5 rooms and 7 efficiencies; outdoor pool, tennis courts. AE, MC, V. **Edwards Motel & Cottages** (Box 262, Ocracoke 27960, tel. 919/928–4801). 5 rooms, 3 efficiencies, 2 cottages; picnic area, fish-cleaning tables. Closed Mid-Nov.–Easter. MC, V. **Hatteras Inn** (Rte. 12, Box 237, Hatteras 27943, tel. 919/986–2900). 17 rooms; bar. MC, V. **Owens Motel** (7115 Virginia Dare Trail, Nags Head 27959, tel. 919/441–6361). 25 rooms, 8 with kitchenettes; restaurant, pool, nearby fishing pier. Closed Dec.–Mar. AE, D, DC, MC, V. **Whalebone Motel** (Box 1119, Nags Head 27959, tel. 919/441–7423). 2 rooms, 16 efficiencies, 4 cottages; pets permitted. MC, V.

DINING

The Outer Banks has a wide variety of dining opportunities, from fast food to fancy. Fresh seafood is abundant and comes broiled, grilled, poached, battered and deep-fried, blackened, or sauced. Price categories per person, not including 5% tax, service, and drinks, are *Expensive*, $15–$25; *Moderate*, $8–$15; and *Inexpensive*, under $8.

EXPENSIVE Owens' Restaurant. Owens has been serving first-rate seafood—from fish-and-chips to grilled bass—for more than 40 years in an old Nags Head–style shingled cottage. *Rte. 12, MP 17, Nags Head, tel. 919/441–7309. Closed for lunch and Dec.–Mar. AE, D, DC, MC, V.*

The Sanderling Inn and Restaurant. Fresh ingredients and a deft hand are evident in the Continental and southern dishes served at Sanderling. The restaurant is housed in a restored lifesaving station and retains its soaring ceilings and natural wood wainscoting. *5 mi north of Duck on Rte. 12, tel. 919/261–4111. MC, V.*

MODERATE Clara's Seafood Grill. Grilled seafood and burgers are standard fare at this art deco–style eatery overlooking the Manteo waterfront. *Downtown Manteo, tel. 919/473–1727. , MC, V.*

Etheridge's Seafood Restaurant. The fish, lobster, bass, tuna or whatever's freshest—comes straight from local boats to the kitchen of this popular family-owned restaurant. *U.S. 158 Bypass, MP 9.5, Kill Devil Hills, tel. 919/441–2645. Closed Nov.–Feb. D, MC, V.*

Kelly's Restaurant and Tavern. Fresh fish is the theme at Kelly's, but it's the fresh-baked breads and desserts that lure small hordes of locals and visitors alike. *U.S. 158 Bypass, MP 10.5, tel. 919/441–4116. AE, MC, V.*

Lance's Seafood Bar & Market. It's hard to miss the hot pink building that houses Lance's; and while you're dining on steamed or raw seafood and putting the shells through the hole in the table, you can contemplate the restaurant's nostalgic fishing and hunting memorabilia. *U.S. 158 Bypass, MP 14, Nags Head, tel. 919/441–7501. MC, V.*

INEXPENSIVE The Dunes Restaurant. The early-bird (until 6 PM) and all-you-can-eat specials are worth the trip to this busy family-style restaurant, known for its large helpings of seafood, steak, and chicken. *U.S. 158 Bypass, MP 16.5., Nags Head, tel. 919/441–1600. D, MC, V.*

Sam & Omies. This stoically weathered restaurant will cook your (cleaned) fresh catch or serve you one of theirs. If fish makes you queasy, don't miss the Sam & Omies' hearty breakfasts. *7228 Virginia Dare Trail, tel. 919/441–7366. MC, V.*

Tides Restaurant. Whether you've come for breakfast or a seafood dinner, you'll likely rub elbows with locals rather than tourists at this casual eatery on Hatteras Island. *Rte. 12, Buxton, tel. 919/995–5988. MC, V.*

Waves Edge. Dine overlooking Pamlico Sound on mesquite-grilled seafood, beef, or chicken—specialties of the house at the open-air Waves Edge on Hatteras Island. *Rte. 12, Waves, tel. 919/987–2100. D, MC, V.*

SHOPPING

Antiques shops carry many nautical items, while numerous specialty shops cover all of the needs of the beach goer and souvenir hunter. Culture vultures can also pursue the work of local artists at a number of art galleries. Outlet shopping can be found at the **Soundings Factory Stores** at MP 16.5 and kites to fly on Jockey's Ridge at **Kitty Hawk Kites,** MP 13 (tel. 919/441–4124).

OUTDOOR ACTIVITIES

BEACHES The 70 miles of unspoiled beaches in Cape Hatteras National Seashore are ideal for all water activities, but you should swim only where there are lifeguard stations—Coquina Beach, Salvo, Cape Hatteras, Frisco, and Ocracoke; in commercial areas, lifeguards are stationed near motels and hotels. Beach volleyball is the game of choice for landlubbers. Surfers practice their trade along the length of the Banks, while divers concentrate on the wrecks. Fishing from the beach and piers is popular. Hanggliding lessons are available from **Kitty Hawk Kites** (*see* Shopping, *above*).

BICYCLING The pamphlet "Bicycling the Outer Banks of North Carolina" is available from the Dare County Tourist Bureau (*see* Tourist Offices, *above*). The best areas for the casual cyclist are Ocracoke and Manteo. Many hotels and inns have bicycles for their guests; rentals are available from Ocean Atlantic Rentals, Inc., at Beach Rd., MP 10, Nags Head (tel. 919/441–7823), Duck (tel. 919/261–4346), Corolla (tel. 919/453–2440), Waves (tel. 919/987–2492), and Avon (tel. 919/995–5868). Advanced reservations can be made by calling 800/635–9559.

BOATING AND SAILING There are 10 marinas along the Intracoastal—among them Pirate's Cove Yacht Club (tel. 919/473–3906) at Man-

teo, Oregon Inlet Fishing Center (tel. 919/441–6301), Hatteras Harbor Marina (tel. 919/986–2166), and the Park Service Docks (tel. 919/928–5111) in Ocracoke. Check with **Nags Head Watersports** (MP 17, tel. 919/480–2236) or **Kitty Hawk Sports** (MP 13, tel 919/441–6800) for all types of boat rentals and lessons. Sea kayaking and windsurfing on the sounds are very popular activities.

FISHING Blue and channel bass, sea mullet, trout, flounder, spot, croaker, tuna, dolphin, marlin, king mackerel, and billfish abound. Fall is the best time to fish from the eight ocean fishing piers between Kitty Hawk and Cape Hatteras—from certain bridges and causeways, and by surf-casting all along the beach. You can charter boats for Gulf Stream fishing trips from Hatteras Harbor Marina (tel. 800/676–4939), Oregon Inlet Fishing Center (tel. 800/272–5199), or the Pirate Cove Yacht Club (tel. 800/367–4728). Inland, there is good freshwater fishing for largemouth bass, white and yellow perch, and catfish. Freshwater licenses can be bought locally or from the North Carolina Division of Boating and Inland Fishing (tel. 919/733–3633).

HIKING/WALKING You can take a self-guided walking tour of Manteo, following the map available at **Manteo Booksellers** (105 Sir Walter St., tel. 919/473–1221), or hike for miles and miles on the uncrowded beaches and on marked trails in Jockey's Ridge State Park, Nags Head Woods Preserve, the Wright Brothers Memorial, and Fort Raleigh.

ENTERTAINMENT

DANCING Many of the night spots feature bands on weekends and certain mid-week nights. Check local newspapers for the latest attractions. The Big Band Preservation Society (tel. 800/334–3302 or 800/233–5929 in NC) holds nine dances from March through November at the Armada in Nags Head.

DINNER SHOWS Dine as the Elizabethans did at "Pastime with Goode Companie," a Renaissance dinner show at the Elizabethan Inn in Manteo. *Tel. 800/346–2466. Open mid-June–*

Labor Day., Tues.–Fri.; Labor Day.– late Oct., Wed. About $28 per adult.

SPECTATOR SPORTS The Dare County Tourist Bureau and Outer Banks Chamber of Commerce (*see* Tourist Offices, *above*) jointly publish a yearly (and free) **Vacation Guide** that lists all of the major events occurring in the Outer Banks.

Pennsylvania Dutch Country
Pennsylvania

he plain and fancy live side by side in Lancaster County, some 65 miles west of Philadelphia—an area more popularly known as Pennsylvania Dutch Country. Here horse-drawn buggies and horn-tooting cars vie for position on rural roads. The county is home to the nation's largest population of Plain people (Amish, Mennonite, and Brethren), descendants of German and Swiss immigrants who came to the area to escape persecution; they have thrived over the years while maintaining their own cuisine, language, and traditions. Tourists come here mainly to observe the Old Order Amish, who cling to a centuries-old way of life. These conservative people shun the amenities of modern civilization, such as electricity and cars, preferring to use kerosene or gas lamps, and to drive horse-drawn carriages. They also reject military service and Social Security benefits. Ironically, in turning their backs on the modern world, they have attracted its attention.

The Amish, however, are far from the only reason to visit this county. Along with the commercialism and the kitsch that have sprung up to cater to the tourist trade, you'll also discover much charm along the tranquil country lanes dotted with picture-perfect farms. You can also take a stroll past 18th-century buildings in lovely small towns; ride a bicycle, steam train, or horse-drawn buggy through the countryside; hike along the Susquehanna River; or sleep overnight in a caboose or a historic inn.

ESSENTIAL INFORMATION

WHEN TO GO "Changeable" best describes Lancaster's weather. Temperatures can range from 58° to 96° in summer and from 0° to 70° in winter. July just beats August as the hottest and most humid month, with temperatures ranging from an average high of 86° to an average low of 65°; December sees average highs of 40°, and lows of 24°. Snowfall has

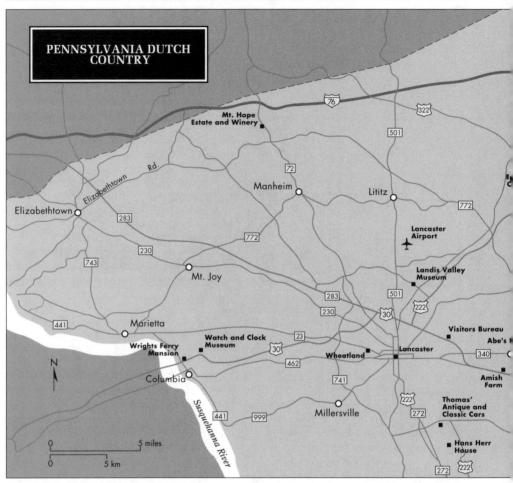

PENNSYLVANIA DUTCH COUNTRY

been very light in recent years, but the latest winter may have indicated a shift to frequent storms and heavy snows.

The region can be hectic, especially on summer weekends, when you'll find the main arteries, shops, and restaurants crowded with busloads of visitors. The same is true in October, when tourists come for the fall foliage. September, winter, and early spring are less crowded times, with good views of rolling farmland. Although many restaurants, shops, and farmers markets are closed on Sunday, commercial attractions remain open.

BARGAINS Festivals, quilt and farm equipment auctions, flea markets, and chicken-corn soup or ox-roast suppers are frequently staged to raise money for the volunteer fire company crews and attract large numbers of Amish people. The events offer good, cheap, home-cooked foods and inexpensive entertainment. The Pennsylvania Dutch Convention & Visitors Bureau publishes a calendar of these almost weekly events. The Visitors Bureau's (*see* Tourist Offices, *below*) "Free Map and Visitor's Guide" contains coupons with savings on dining, lodging, and admissions. Another free map with discount coupons comes from Amish Country Tours (*see* Guided Tours, *below*).

TOURIST OFFICES Pennsylvania Dutch Convention & Visitors Bureau (Dept. 2201, 501 Greenfield Rd., Lancaster 17601, tel. 717/299–8901 or 800/735–2629). Mennonite

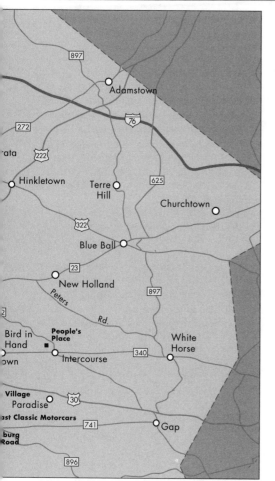

ARRIVING AND DEPARTING

BY PLANE Philadelphia International Airport (tel. 215/937–6937), 65 miles east of Lancaster, has scheduled daily flights by major carriers. Lancaster Municipal Airport (contact USAir Express at 717/948–5400) is 7 miles north of the city, and Harrisburg International Airport (tel. 717/948–3900) is 30 miles north of the city.

BY CAR From Philadelphia, take the Schuylkill Expressway (I–76) west to the Pennsylvania Turnpike. Lancaster County attractions are accessible from Exits 20, 21, and 22. From Exit 22, you can follow scenic Route 23 to Lancaster. You can also follow U.S. 30 west (Lancaster Pike) from Philadelphia to Lancaster County. Allow about 1¹/₂ hours for either route.

BY TRAIN Amtrak (tel. 800/USA–RAIL) has frequent train service (80 minutes) from Philadelphia's 30th Street Station to Lancaster's Amtrak station at 53 McGovern Ave.

BY BUS Capital Trailways (tel. 800/231–2222) has three runs daily from Philadelphia to the R&S Bus Terminal, 22 W. Clay St., Lancaster. The ride takes nearly 2¹/₂ hours, though at press time all service was temporarily discontinued; call for the latest details.

GETTING AROUND

BY CAR AND RV Because the area's attractions are spread out, a car is essential for touring. The main east–west arteries are U.S. 30 and Rte. 340; U.S. 222 is the main north–south route. You can pick up Rte. 772 where it intersects U.S. 30 near the town of Gap and follow it westward through towns like Intercourse and Mount Joy. Parking is plentiful and free at all attractions.

BY TAXI Yellow Cab (tel. 717/397–8108) is based in the city of Lancaster. The average crosstown fare is $5–$6. Lancaster County Taxi (tel. 717/626–8294) mainly serves the towns of Ephrata, Manheim, and Lititz and charges $1.30 for pickup plus $1.30 per mile.

Information Center (2209 Millstream Rd., Lancaster 17602, tel. 717/299–0954). Intercourse Information Center (3546 Old Philadelphia Pike, Intercourse 17534, tel. 717/768–3882). Susquehanna Heritage Tourist & Information Center (Box 510, Fifth & Linden Sts., 17512, tel. 717/684–5249 or 717/684–2199).

EMERGENCIES Police, fire, and **ambulance:** Dial 911. **Hospitals:** Community Hospital of Lancaster (1100 E. Orange St., tel. 717/397–3711). Lancaster General Hospital (555 N. Duke St., tel. 717/299–5511). St. Joseph's Hospital (250 College Ave., tel. 717/291–8211). **Doctors:** Lancaster City and County Medical Society (tel. 717/393–9588) gives referrals.

REST STOPS Public rest rooms can be found at the Pennsylvania Dutch Information Center, located at the Greenfield Road exit off U.S. 30; the Downtown Visitors Information Center, in the heart of Lancaster at S. Queen and Vine streets; the Mennonite Information Center, on Millstream Road off U.S. 30; and at the Rockvale Square Factory Outlet Village, at the intersection of U.S. 30 and Route 896.

GUIDED TOURS Amish Country Tours (Rte. 340, between Bird-in-Hand and Intercourse, tel. 717/768–7063 or 800/441–3505) has a variety of bus and minivan tours of the area, such as the popular Amish farmlands trip. Agencies providing private guides who accompany you in your car for about $20 at a two-hour minimum include Brunswick Tours (Lancaster, tel. 717/397–7541), Mennonite Information Center (Lancaster, tel. 717/299–0954), and Rutts Tours (Intercourse, tel. 717/768–8238). Abe's Buggy Rides (Rte. 340, ¹/₂ mi east of Rte. 896, no phone) and Ed's Buggy Rides (Rte. 896, 1¹/₂ mi south of U.S. 30, Strasburg, tel. 717/687–0360) offer horse-drawn carriage rides along scenic back roads. The Historic Lancaster Walking Tour (Downtown Visitors Center, tel. 717/392–1776) is a 90-minute stroll through this charming old city, conducted by guides in period costume.

EXPLORING

The People's Place, situated in Intercourse on Rte. 340 in eastern Lancaster County, provides an introduction to the Amish, Mennonite, and Hutterite peoples; a slide show features close-up shots of Amish life and sensitive narration. *Tel. 717/768–7171. Open Mon.–Sat. Admission charged.*

Intercourse (on Rte. 340) is a good starting point for exploring the country roads. Many Amish farms, distinguished by windmills and green blinds, are clustered in the area between Intercourse and **New Holland** (on Rte. 23). Drive along back roads, visit the roadside stands, and stop at the farms selling quilts, wooden toys, homemade root beer, or new potatoes.

The Amish Farm and House and **The Amish Village** both offer guided tours through an authentically furnished re-creation of an Amish home. At the Farm and House, a self-guided tour continues through cultivated fields, animal pens, and a museum. At the Village, an operating smokehouse, a blacksmith shop, and a one-room schoolhouse built by Amish craftsmen are open for inspection. *Amish House: U.S. 30, Lancaster, tel. 717/394–6185. Open daily. Admission charged. Amish Village: Rte. 896, Strasburg, tel. 717/687–8511. Open daily Apr.–Nov. Admission charged.*

Strasburg (reached by driving south from U.S. 30 or Rte. 340 on Rte. 896 and turning left on Rte. 741) is a town devoted to the railroad. The **Strasburg Rail Road** provides a scenic 9-mile round-trip excursion from Strasburg to Paradise on a rolling antique with a turn-of-the-century iron steam locomotive. Strasburg also has the **Railroad Museum of Pennsylvania,** housing colossal historic engines and railroad cars; the **Toy Train Museum,** displaying antique and 20th-century model trains; and the **Choo Choo Barn,** with a 1,700-square-foot exhibit of Lancaster County in miniature. *Rail Road: tel. 717/687–7522. Open Apr.–Nov., daily; Dec.–Mar. weekends, except 1st 2 weekends in Jan. Railroad Museum: tel. 717/687–8628. Open May–Oct., daily; Nov.–Apr., Tues.–Sun. Toy Train Museum: tel. 717/687–8976. Open May–Oct., daily; Apr. and Nov.–mid-Dec., weekends. Barn: tel. 717/687–7911. Open Apr.–Oct., daily; Nov. and Dec., weekends. Admission charged to all attractions.*

Pennsylvania Dutch Country is also classic car country. **Gast Classic Motorcars** (Rte. 896, Strasburg, tel. 717/687–9500; admission charged) displays more than 50 showpieces past and present. **Thomas' Antique & Classic Cars** (Rte. 222, Willow St., tel. 717/464–9264; admission charged) exhibits 20 more models, some for sale.

Lancaster, at the intersection of U.S. 30 and U.S. 222, is the nation's oldest inland city, dating from 1710. The best way to see its blocks of quaint row houses is on foot. The

Central Market at King and Queen streets is one of the oldest covered markets in the country (open Tues., Fri., and Sat.). Nearby, Old City Hall, reborn as the **Heritage Center Museum,** shows the works of Lancaster County artisans and craftsmen. *Tel. 717/299–6440. Open Tues.–Sat. Donation requested.*

Wheatland (1¹/₂ miles west of Lancaster) was the home of the only president from Pennsylvania—James Buchanan. The restored 1828 Federal mansion contains much of the 15th president's original furnishings. *1120 Marietta Ave. (Rte. 23), tel. 717/392–8721. Open Apr.–mid-Dec., daily, with guided tours. Admission charged.*

The Hans Herr House (reached by following U.S. 222 5 miles south from Lancaster and turning right onto Hans Herr Dr.), a former Mennonite meeting place, is a good example of medieval German architecture in North America and the oldest structure in the county, dating from 1719. *1849 Hans Herr Dr., Willow St., tel. 717/464–4438. Open Apr.– Dec., Mon.–Sat. Admission charged.*

Landis Valley Museum (2¹/₂ miles north of U.S. 30 on Oregon Pike or Rte. 272) is an outdoor museum devoted to Pennsylvania German rural life and folk culture before 1900. *2451 Kissel Hill Rd., tel. 717/569–0401. Open Tues.–Sun. Admission charged.*

Ephrata Cloister (10 miles north of the museum on Rte. 322), established in 1732, once housed a self-sufficient monastic community of German Pietists who lived an ascetic life of work, study, and prayer. Guides lead tours of three restored buildings; then visitors can tour the stable, print shop, and crafts shop by themselves. *Rte. 322 east of junction with Rte. 272, Ephrata, tel. 717/733–6600. Open daily. Admission charged.*

Lititz (west of Ephrata at the intersection of Rtes. 501 and 772) was founded by Moravians who settled here to do missionary work among the Indians. Its tree-shaded main street is lined with 18th-century cottages and specialty shops selling antiques, crafts, clothing, and gifts. Pick up a Historical Foundation walking-tour brochure at the **General Sutter**

Inn (Main St. and Rte. 501). You can eat lunch at the inn, a Victoriana lover's delight; twist a pretzel at the **Julius Sturgis Pretzel House** (219 E. Main St.), the nation's oldest pretzel bakery; and visit the museum of the **Wilbur Chocolate Company** (48 N. Broad St.).

HOTELS AND INNS

In Lancaster County, you can sleep under the stars at one of the many campgrounds or under a lace canopy at a historic country inn. There's a good selection of moderately priced motels that cater to families, many lining U.S. 30. The Pennsylvania Dutch Visitors Bureau (tel. 717/299–8901 or 800/735–2629) has free brochures listing bed-and-breakfasts and phones that will connect you directly with the hotel of your choice.

A number of families, many of them Mennonite, open their farmhouses to visitors and allow them to observe, and even participate in, day-to-day farm life. Accommodations are simple, comfortable, and inexpensive, ranging in price from $25 to $45. Make reservations weeks in advance; most farms are heavily booked during the summer. Some recommended farms include **Jonde Lane Farm** (1103 Auction Rd., Manheim 17545, tel. 717/665–4231), **Rocky Acre Farm** (1020 Pinkerton Rd., Mount Joy 17552, tel. 717/653–4449), and **Verdant View Farm** (429 Strasburg Rd., Paradise 17562, tel. 717/687– 7353). Contact the Pennsylvania Dutch Visitors Bureau (*see above*) or the Mennonite Information Center (tel. 717/299–0954) for more information about farm vacations.

Hotels charge peak rates from Memorial Day to Labor Day; you can expect about a 25% drop in spring and fall, and up to a 50% reduction in winter. Price categories for double occupancy, excluding 6% tax, are *Expensive,* $85–$100; *Moderate,* $65–$85; and *Inexpensive,* under $65.

BIRD-IN-HAND **Village Inn of Bird-in-Hand.** This Victorian-style country inn, updated with down-filled bedding and cable TV, offers a free two-hour tour of the area. *Box 253, 2695 Old Philadelphia Pike, 17505, tel.*

717/293–8369. 11 rooms, including 2 suites with Jacuzzis. Continental breakfast and evening snack included, access to pool and tennis courts. AE, D, MC, V. Moderate–Expensive.

CHURCHTOWN **Churchtown Inn.** A 1735 fieldstone mansion, between Morgantown and New Holland, is presided over by warm-spirited innkeepers who serve up a five-course breakfast (included). *2100 Main St. (Rte. 23), Navron 17555, tel. 215/445–7794. 8 rooms, carriage house. Children over 12 welcome. MC, V. Inexpensive–Expensive.*

EPHRATA **Inns at Doneckers.** Light, airy rooms and French country antiques distinguish the guest rooms in a collection of properties from the 18th century to the 1920s. *318–24 N. State St., 17522, tel. 717/738–9502. 40 rooms. Continental breakfast included. AE, D, DC, MC, V. Inexpensive–Expensive.*

LANCASTER **King's Cottage.** This elegant Spanish mansion has been transformed into a cozy B&B featuring antiques and a goldfish pond. Accommodations include full breakfast and afternoon tea. *1049 E. King St., 17602, tel. 717/397–1017 or 800/747–8717. 7 rooms. Children over 12 welcome. MC, V. Moderate–Expensive.*

Willow Valley Family Resort. A mom-and-pop operation that blossomed into a sprawling, stylish family resort, this Mennonite-owned property (there's no liquor served) offers the most personal attention and the best rates of the area's large resorts. *2416 Willow Street Pike, 17602, tel. 717/464–2711 or 800/444–1714, fax 717/464–4784. 353 rooms. 3 restaurants, 3 pools, lighted tennis courts, 9-hole golf course. AE, DC, MC, V. Expensive.*

LITITZ **General Sutter Inn.** The oldest continuously occupied inn in the state (circa 1764) is a Victoriana lover's dream reminiscent of Grandma's house. *14 E. Main St. (Corner of Rtes. 501 and 772), 17543, tel. 717/626–2115. 10 rooms, 2 suites. Dining room, coffee shop, tavern. AE, D, MC, V. Moderate–Expensive.*

Swiss Woods. Nestled on the edge of the woods overlooking Speedwell Forge Lake, this sublime Swiss-style chalet offers goose-down comforters and a hearty breakfast. *500 Blantz Rd., 17543, tel. 717/627–3358 or 800/594–8018. 6 rooms, 2 with Jacuzzis, 1 suite. Biking, fishing, hiking, canoeing. No smoking. D, MC, V. Moderate– Expensive.*

MOUNT JOY **Cameron Estate Inn.** This grand Federal mansion provides large guest rooms with canopy beds, Oriental rugs, and working fireplaces (in seven rooms), and a lovely porch overlooking the 15 wooded acres. *Donegal Springs Rd., 17552, tel. 717/653–1773. 18 rooms. Restaurant, Continental breakfast included, pool, tennis courts nearby. AE, DC, MC, V. Moderate–Expensive.*

STRASBURG **Strasburg Village Inn.** Outside, guests relax on the old-fashioned porch overlooking Main Street; inside the lure is elegant Williamsburg-style furnishings and canopy or four-poster beds. *1 W. Main St., 17579, tel. 717/687–0900 or 800/541–1055. 11 rooms. Full or Continental breakfast included. AE, D, MC, V. Moderate–Expensive.*

Historic Strasburg Inn. This sprawling, 58-acre Colonial-style property represents one of the best values in the heart of the Dutch Country. Rooms are modern and simple, but the restaurant and tavern recall 18th-century America. *Rte. 896 (Historic Dr.) 17579, tel. 717/687–7691 or 800/872–0201. 103 rooms. Restaurant, tavern, outdoor pool, bicycles, volleyball. AE, D, DC, MC, V. Moderate.*

MOTELS

MODERATE **Bird-in-Hand Family Inn** (Box 402, 2740 Old Philadelphia Pike, Bird-in-Hand 17505, tel. 717/768–8271 or 800/537–2535). 100 rooms; restaurant, pools, tennis courts. **Hilton Garden Inn** (101 Granite Run Dr., intersection of U.S. 30 and 272, Lancaster 17601, tel. 717/560–0880 or 800/HILTONS). 154 rooms; restaurant, pool, fitness center. **Olde Hickory Inn** (2363 Oregon Pike, Lancaster 17601, tel. 717/569–0477 or 800/255–6859). 83 rooms; restaurant, dinner theater, pool, health club, 9-hole golf course.

INEXPENSIVE **Red Caboose Motel** (Paradise La. off Rte. 741, Box 303, Strasburg 17579, tel. 717/687–6646). 40 rooms; restaurant, playground, buggy rides. **Smoketown Motor Lodge** (190 E. Brook Rd., Rte. 896, Smoketown 17576, tel. 717/397–6944). 10 rooms, Continental breakfast included. **Spruce Lane Motor Lodge** (2439 Old Philadelphia Pike, Box 241, Smoketown 17576, tel. 717/393–1991 or 800/446–4901). 12 rooms; Continental breakfast included, tennis courts, basketball.

CAMPGROUNDS

Camping is very popular in summer and fall months; book your stay several months in advance. The Lancaster County Visitors Bureau (tel. 717/299–8901 or 800/735–2629) lists about 30 campgrounds in their "Free Map & Visitor's Guide." Here are three of the best.

Mill Bridge Village and Campresort. Close to major attractions and attached to a restored 18th-century village, these campgrounds aren't too scenic, but they offer enjoyable summer activities, such as free buggy rides, concerts, and hayrides. *Box 86 (¹/₂ mi south of U.S. 30 on Ronks Rd.), Strasburg 17579, tel. 717/687–8181 or 800/645–2744. 113 RV and tent sites, showers, bathrooms, snack shop, fishing stream. AE, D, MC, V.*

Muddy Run Park. Lovely campgrounds with nature walks and bird-watching in the southern end of the county are set among 700 acres of woodland and rolling fields that surround a 100-acre lake. *172 Bethesda Church Rd. W, Holtwood 17532, tel. 717/284–4325. 163 trailer and tent sites, showers, bathrooms, LP gas available, charcoal grills, playground, general store, snack bar, boating, fishing. No credit cards.*

Spring Gulch Resort Campground. This glorious setting has shaded sites, cottages, a farmhouse, and a lodge to rent; there's swimming, miniature golf, tennis and volleyball courts, fishing, and other weekend activities. *475 Lynch Rd. (Rte. 897 between Rtes. 340 and 322), New Holland 17557, tel. 717/354–* *3100 or 800/255–5744. 400 RV and tent sites, showers, bathrooms, LP gas available. MC, V.*

DINING

The German-influenced Pennsylvania Dutch meals are hearty feasts prepared with local farm ingredients. To sample regional fare, try a family-style restaurant in the area. Diners may sit with up to a dozen people, and a set menu of food is placed on the table in bowls that are passed around. The dishes include fried chicken, grilled ham, roast beef, dried corn, buttered noodles, mashed potatoes, bread, pepper cabbage, desserts, and beverages.

Visitors on restricted or health-conscious diets may only want to sample one of these regional dinners, and even then, the menu may be too heavy. Luckily, Lancaster County also has smorgasbords, reasonably priced family restaurants, and a number of Continental and French restaurants in contemporary settings and quaint historic inns, where visitors will find it easier to eat according to specific needs. Price categories per person, excluding 6% tax, service, and drinks, are *Moderate*, $15–$25, and *Inexpensive*, under $15.

BIRD-IN-HAND **Bird-in-Hand Family Restaurant.** This casual, diner-style restaurant serves hearty, home-cooked regional favorites such as chicken-corn soup. No liquor is served. *2760 Old Philadelphia Pike, tel. 717/768–8266. Closed Sun. No credit cards. Inexpensive.*

EPHRATA **The Restaurant at Doneckers.** A light-fare menu of classic and country French cuisine (with heart-healthy choices) is served amid Colonial antiques in the Hearthside Café—a budget alternative to the much pricier formal menu. *333 N. State St., tel. 717/738–9501. AE, D, DC, MC, V. Moderate–Expensive.*

Nav Jiwan International Tea Room. This dining spot features a lunch menu representing a different ethnic cuisine each week; dinner is served on Friday nights only. *240 N. Read-*

ing Rd. (Rte. 272), tel. 717/738–1101. MC, V. Inexpensive.

INTERCOURSE **Stoltzfus Farm Restaurant.** Homemade Pennsylvania Dutch foods, including meats butchered right on the farm, are served family style in this small country farmhouse. *Rte. 772 (¹/₂ mi east of Rte. 340), tel. 717/768–8156. Closed Dec.–Mar. MC, V. Inexpensive.*

LANCASTER **Market Fare.** In this cozy dining room with big armchairs and fine art, an American menu of steaks, seafood, and veal is served with homemade soups and fresh-baked breads. A menu of lighter choices is available, as is a menu for children. A pasta menu is offered every Tuesday. *Market and Grant Sts. across from the Central Market, tel. 717/299–7090. AE, DC, MC, V. Moderate.*

MOUNT JOY **Bube's Brewery.** The only intact, pre-Prohibition U.S. brewery houses three first-rate restaurants (the brewery, however, no longer produces spirits): the casual Bottling Works for drinks and light meals; Alois's, in the adjacent Victorian hotel, for more formal six-course dinners; and The Catacombs, where steaks and seafood are served in aging cellars 43 feet belowground. *102 N. Market St., tel. 717/653–2056. Jackets required in Alois's and preferred in The Catacombs. AE, MC, V. Moderate.*

Groff's Farm. At this famous restored 1756 farmhouse with candlelight and fresh flowers, well-prepared Mennonite farm fare is served à la carte or family style to your private table. A new rooftop deck has added al fresco dining to the Groff's award-winning restaurant. *650 Pinkerton Rd., tel. 717/653–2048. D, DC, MC, V. Moderate.*

RONKS **Miller's Smorgasbord.** One of the few local restaurants open Sundays, Miller's is known for its lavish buffets, including a sensational breakfast spread and a good sampling of Pennsylvania Dutch foods. *2811 Lincoln Hwy. E, tel. 717/687–6621 or 800/669–3568. AE, MC, V. Moderate.*

SMOKETOWN **Good 'N Plenty.** An Amish farmhouse has been remodeled into a bus-tling, family-style restaurant seating more than 650 for festive dining on tasty, home-cooked foods. *Rte. 896 (¹/₂ mi off U.S. 30), tel. 717/394–7111. MC, V. Inexpensive.*

SHOPPING

SPECIALTY SHOPS The **Weathervane Shop** (Landis Valley Museum, 2451 Kissel Hill Rd., Lancaster, tel. 717/569–9312) carries handmade local crafts. For antique quilts, try **Pandora's** (Rte. 340, just east of U.S. 30, Lancaster, tel. 717/299–5305) or **Witmer Quilt Shop** (1070 W. Main St., New Holland, tel. 717/656–9526). **The Shops at Doneckers** (409 N. State St., Ephrata, tel. 717/738–9500) sell clothing and home furnishings in an 18-boutique complex. **The Artworks at Doneckers** is a marketplace of 40 artists' galleries and studios (100 N. State St., Ephrata, tel. 717/738–9503).

FACTORY OUTLETS A number of factory outlets line U.S. 30 near Rte. 896; at the intersection is **Rockvale Square Factory Outlet Village** (tel. 717/293–9595), the largest outlet center in Lancaster, with 95 stores and counting. The newest addition to outlet row is the designer **MillStream Factory Shops,** with 42 outlets including Ann Taylor and Brooks Brothers (tel. 717/392–7202).

ANTIQUES On Sundays, antiques hunters flock to the huge antiques malls (Renninger's, Barr's, Black Angus) located on Route 272 between Adamstown and Denver, 1 mile west of Pennsylvania Turnpike Exit 21.

FARMERS MARKETS The best ones are the **Central Market** in Lancaster (*see* Exploring, *above*), **Bird-in-Hand Farmers Market** (Rte. 340, Bird-in-Hand, tel. 717/393–9674), and the **Green Dragon Farmers Market and Auction** (N. State St., Ephrata, tel. 717/738–1117; open Fri.), a traditional agricultural market with livestock auctions, food stalls, and a flea market. The county's newest market may be found at **The Farmers Market at Doneckers** (100 N. State St., Ephrata, tel. 717/738–9555).

OUTDOOR ACTIVITIES

BIKING The gently rolling back roads are ideal for bicycling. The Pennsylvania Department of Transportation offers a free map of bike routes statewide (ask for publication No. 22) and more detailed maps by quadrant for $1.25. To order, call 717/787–5248 or 717/787–6746.

GOLF Lancaster Host Resort (U.S. 30, Lancaster, tel. 717/299–5500 or 800/233–0121) has 27 holes for regulation golf.

HIKING If you travel as far west in Lancaster County as Mount Joy, Marietta or Columbia, you should take the time to hike along the Susquehanna River. At Chickies County Park (Rte. 441 midway between Marietta and Columbia), a short path from the parking area leads to a bare rock outcropping with commanding views of the river as it snakes through the valley. Lake Aldred (tel. 717/284–2278) has 39 miles of hiking trails ranging from the mile-long Pequea Creek Nature Trail (for the novice) to the 15-mile-long section of the Conestoga Trail (for the more experienced). Susquehannock State Park (south of Rte. 372) and Muddy Run Recreation Park (Rte. 372 between Rte. 272 and the Susquehanna River) also have marked hiking trails.

Philadelphia
Pennsylvania

They no longer roll up the sidewalks at night in Philadelphia: An entertainment boom, a restaurant renaissance, and a cultural revival have helped transform the birthplace of the nation into a city of superlatives. It has the world's largest municipal park, one of the best public collections of art in the United States, the widest variety of urban architecture in America, and the highest concentration of institutions of higher learning in the country.

Philadelphia extends north, south, and west from downtown into more than 100 neighborhoods covering 130 square miles. Center City, the popular name for the museums, business and historic districts, radiates from City Hall. The Benjamin Franklin Parkway breaks the rigid grid pattern by leading diagonally out of downtown into Fairmount Park, which straddles the Schuylkill River and the Wissahickon Creek for 10 miles. If you stay at a downtown hotel, you can easily take in most of the city's major attractions on a two- or three-day visit.

ESSENTIAL INFORMATION

WHEN TO GO Although each of the four seasons brings distinct and pleasurable features to life in Philadelphia, late spring and early fall are the best times to visit. Like other northern American cities, Philadelphia can be uncomfortably hot and humid in the summer, with temperatures ranging from 62° to 85°F, and freezing cold in winter, when winter snowfalls average 21 inches and the temperature ranges from 26° to 49°F. In the fall and spring, the atmosphere as well as the climate are comfortable and welcoming, with temperatures ranging from 50° to 76°F.

FESTIVALS AND SEASONAL EVENTS **Jan. 1:** The Mummers Parade is an all-day event with 30,000 sequined and feathered paraders and musicians marching north up Broad Street to City Hall. **Mar.:** The Philadelphia Flower

Show is the nation's largest indoor flower show, featuring acres of landscapes, flowers, and other exhibits. **Apr.–May:** Philadelphia Open House is a two-week period during which selected private homes, gardens, and historic buildings open their doors to the public. **July:** Freedom Festival celebrates the nation's birth with several days of parades, hot-air-balloon races, ceremonies at Independence Hall, and a grand fireworks display. **Oct.:** Super Sunday turns the Benjamin Franklin Parkway into Philadelphia's biggest block party with food, entertainment, rides, and more than 400 exhibit booths. **Thanksgiving:** Thanksgiving Day Parade features thousands of marchers, floats, and local personalities. **Dec.:** Philadelphia reserves the whole month for Christmas festivities, including the Pennsylvania Ballet's heartwarming rendition of the *The Nutcracker* at Philadelphia's Academy of Music. Check the Philadelphia Convention and Visitors Center (*see* Tourist Offices, *below*) for information relating to these and other events.

BARGAINS Philadelphia's number one tourist attraction—Independence National Historical Park—is also its number one bargain. All the sites within the country's "most historic square mile" are free (tel. 215/597–8974). For a free fun ride and a great view, take the City Hall elevator up to the observation deck at the foot of William Penn's statue (tel. 215/686–1776). And in Fairmount Park, Boathouse Row consists of 11 architecturally varied 19th-century buildings, home to the 13 rowing clubs dubbed the "Schuylkill Navy." The view of the houses from the west side of the river is splendid—especially at night, when they're outlined with hundreds of small lights.

Tickets to hear the world-famous Philadelphia Orchestra at the Academy of Music can cost around $50, but you can hear concerts for free during the orchestra's summer season at the Mann Music Center (tel. 215/878–7707 or 215/567–0707).

The Philadelphia Museum of Art, one of the world's great museums, is free Sundays 10 AM–1 PM (tel. 215/763–8100). The Pennsylvania Academy of the Fine Arts is free on Saturdays 10 AM–1 PM (tel. 215/972–7600).

You can save on some theater tickets at UpStages, the ticket booth at the Visitors Center (tel. 215/636–1666).

For fresh, cheap eats and an experience in itself, wander around the Reading Terminal Market and sample from the more than 70 stalls, lunch counters, and restaurants (tel. 215/922–2317). You can get a taste of Philadelphia's most expensive restaurant, Le Bec-Fin (dinners cost $100), for under $10 at its downstairs bistro.

TOURIST OFFICES Philadelphia Visitors Center (16th St. and John F. Kennedy Blvd., 19102, tel. 215/636–1666 or 800/537–7676). Philadelphia Convention and Visitors Bureau (1515 Market St., Suite 2020, 19102, tel. 215/636–3300). National Park Service Visitor Center (3rd and Chestnut Sts., tel. 215/597–8974), for information about Independence National Historical Park.

EMERGENCIES **Police, fire,** and **ambulance:** Dial 911. **Hospitals:** Pennsylvania Hospital (8th and Spruce Sts., tel. 215/829–3358) is closest to the historic district; near City Hall is Hahnemann University Hospital (Broad and Vine Sts., tel. 215/448–7963). **Doctors:** For referrals, call the Philadelphia County Medical Society (tel. 215/563–5343). **Dentists:** For referrals, call the Philadelphia County Dental Society (tel. 215/925–6050). **Pharmacies:** The downtown pharmacy with the longest hours is Corson's Pharmacy (15th and Spruce Sts., tel. 215/735–1386); CVS Pharmacy (6501 Harbison Ave., tel. 215/333–4300) in the northeast section of the city is open 24 hours.

ARRIVING AND DEPARTING

BY PLANE Philadelphia International Airport (tel. 215/492–3181) is located in the southwestern part of the city, 8 miles from downtown.

BY TRAIN SEPTA's Airport Express train is an easy and relatively cheap way to travel between the airport and downtown. The

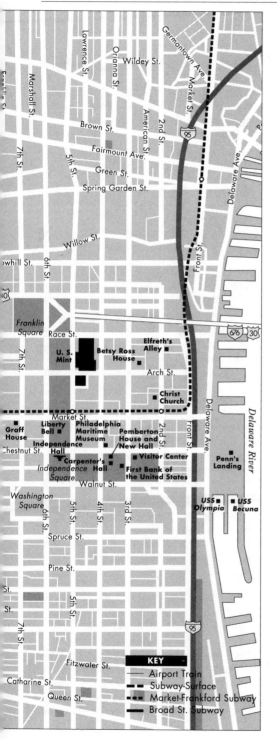

KEY
— Airport Train
--- Subway-Surface
▄▄▄ Market-Frankford Subway
— Broad St. Subway

downtown stops are 30th Street Station (30th and Market Sts.); Suburban Station (16th St. and John F. Kennedy Blvd.); and Market East Station (10th and Market Sts.). It runs every 30 minutes from 6:10 AM to 12:10 AM. The trip takes 25 minutes and costs $5 ($7 if you buy your ticket on the train).

BY BUS Greyhound Lines (tel. 800/231–2222) operates out of a new terminal at 10th and Filbert streets, just north of the Market Street East commuter rail station.

BY TAXI Taxis line up at every exit door of the terminals. The 20-minute trip into town will cost about $20, plus tip, varying slightly in heavier traffic. A few steps from the taxis are the "limos" (vans, not limousines). At about $8 per person, limos are cheaper, but service is less frequent and they stop only at certain hotels and downtown points.

GETTING AROUND

ON FOOT Foot power is the best way to see downtown Philadelphia. William Penn laid out his original city—today's compact 2-square-mile downtown—in a simple grid pattern with numbered streets starting with Front Street near the Delaware River and running west to 26th Street near the Schuylkill River. City Hall at Broad (14th St.) and Market streets is thought of as the center of town. Divide your sightseeing between the historic district and the riverfront on the east, and the museum/Parkway area on the west.

BY CAR You don't need a car to see Philadelphia. Parking is difficult and expensive downtown. Illegally parked cars are ticketed and towed. If you do have a car with you, leave it in the hotel garage and travel around downtown by public transportation or on foot.

BY BUS Philadelphia has a good network of buses, trolleys, and subways. The fare is $1.50; 40¢ for a transfer. Senior citizens (with a valid ID card) ride free during off-peak hours and holidays. A Day Pass ($4) entitles you to unlimited rides within a 24-hour period on all SEPTA buses, streetcars, subways, and elevated lines in the city, plus a one-way lift to the airport. Call SEPTA (tel. 215/574–7800) for route information.

BY TRAIN Commuter trains are your best bet for reaching outlying destinations such as Germantown, Chestnut Hill, Merion Station (site of the Barnes Foundation), and other suburbs. Call SEPTA (tel. 215/574–7800) for route information.

BY TAXI Cabs are plentiful downtown during the day. It's harder to get one at night, though they can usually be found at the hotels, train stations, and along Broad Street or South Street. It's $1.80 initially and then $1.80 per mile. A 10%–15% tip is standard. The main cab companies are Yellow (tel. 215/922–8400), United Cab (tel. 215/625–2881), and Quaker City Cab (tel. 215/728–8000).

REST STOPS You don't have to pay over $200 a night to enjoy the elegance and comfort of one of Philadelphia's luxury hotels—just visit the lobby. The Rittenhouse (210 W. Rittenhouse Sq.), the Four Seasons (18th and the Parkway), and the Sheraton–Society Hill (2nd and Walnut Sts.) are the three best for lobby lounging—and the bathrooms are terrific.

Good public lavatories include Borders Bookstore (1727 Walnut St.); Free Library (Rittenhouse Sq. West); Visitors Center (3rd St. below Chestnut St.); and Wanamaker's Department Store (13th and Market Sts.). Most major department stores and hotels should have rest rooms available.

GUIDED TOURS Philadelphia has no orientation tours per se, but Gray Line Tours (tel. 215/569–3666) has full-size bus tours of the historic and cultural areas. **Walking:** Audio Walk and Tour (tel. 215/925–1234) offers go-at-your-own-pace tours of the historic area, with cassette and tape player for rent and an accompanying map. Theme tours from the Foundation for Architecture Tours (tel. 215/569–3187) focus on architecture but touch on the history and development of each area covered. **Boats:** Sightseeing cruises on the Delaware River are offered by the Spirit of Philadelphia (tel. 215/923–1419) and

Philadelphia Water Taxi, Inc. (tel. 215/351–4170).

EXPLORING

The National Park Service administers **Independence National Historical Park** and calls it "the most historic square mile in America." The first eight sights are located in the park area. All have free admission and the same telephone number (tel. 215/597–8974).

Start your tour at the **Visitor Center** (3rd and Chestnut Sts). The park rangers behind the counter will answer your questions and supply maps and brochures. Catch the 28-minute movie, *Independence,* dramatizing the events surrounding the birth of the nation.

Directly across 3rd Street is the **First Bank of the United States** (3rd and Chestnut Sts.). The carving on the pediment is one of the few remaining examples of 18th-century wood carving. Next to the bank is a wrought-iron gateway topped by an eagle. Pass through it and you step out of modern-day Philadelphia and into Colonial America.

At the gateway begins a redbrick path that leads past a dozen important historic buildings. **Carpenter's Hall** (320 Chestnut St.) is where the first Continental Congress convened in 1774 and addressed a declaration of rights and grievances to King George III. Next door is the **Pemberton House** (the Army-Navy Museum) depicting highlights of the Revolutionary War, and **New Hall** (the Marine Corps Memorial Museum) displaying weapons, uniforms, and medals dating from 1775 to 1815.

As you continue west and cross 5th Street, you'll arrive at **Independence Square,** where on July 8, 1776, the Declaration of Independence was first read in public. A few more steps and you're at **Independence Hall** (Chestnut St. between 5th and 6th Sts.) where on July 4, 1776, the Declaration of Independence was adopted; in 1778, the Articles of Confederation was signed; and in 1787, the Constitution was formally adopted. Tours start from the east wing (Old City Hall) and last about 35 minutes.

One block north of Independence Hall is Philadelphia's best-known symbol, the **Liberty Bell** (Market St. between 5th and 6th Sts.). You can touch the 2,080-pound bell and read its biblical inscription: "Proclaim liberty throughout all the land unto all the inhabitants thereof." Rangers will tell you stories about the bell, including the tale of its famous crack. After hours, you can still see the bell in its glass-enclosed pavilion and press a button on the outside wall to hear a recorded account of its history.

From here you can walk two blocks east out of the Historical Park district to the Delaware River and **Penn's Landing**—the spot where William Penn stepped ashore in 1682—now a 37-acre park. Attractions here include the **USS *Olympia*** (tel. 215/922–1898), Commodore George Dewey's flagship at the battle of Manila in the Spanish-American War; and the **USS *Becuna*** (tel. 215/922–1898), a World War II "search and destroy" submarine. *Park admission free. Open daily. Admission charged for ships.*

Other sites you'll be walking near on this tour include **Christ Church** (2nd St. above Market St., tel. 215/922–1695, open daily, admission free), where 15 signers of the Declaration worshiped; **Elfreth's Alley** (off Front and 2nd Sts. between Arch and Race Sts., tel. 215/574– 0560), the oldest continuously occupied street in America; **Betsy Ross House** (239 Arch St., tel. 215/627–5343; open Tues.–Sun.; admission free); the **United States Mint** (5th and Arch Sts., tel. 215/597–7350; open Mon.–Sat.; admission free); the **Philadelphia Maritime Museum** (321 Chestnut St., tel. 215/925–5439; open Tues.–Sun.; admission free); and the **Graff House** (7th and Market Sts., tel. 215/597–8974; open daily; admission free), where Thomas Jefferson wrote the Declaration of Independence.

Stroll west down Market Street, turn right on 12th Street, and walk one block north. Here's what has the whole city abuzz these days— the brand-new **Philadelphia Convention Center** (1101 Market St., tel. 215/574–2070),

a brick-and-granite complex that absorbs four city blocks, including the Reading Terminal Train Shed. The second-largest convention center in the United States opened in June 1993 with much fanfare (Vice President Gore cut the ribbon), and, with a main exhibit hall that could swallow up seven football fields, is expected to draw the biggest exhibitors in the nation.

Return to Market Street and head toward Broad Street and City Hall. Walk around the north side of the building and continue two blocks north on Broad Street to the **Pennsylvania Academy of the Fine Arts.** This architecturally extravagant building (designed by Philadelphian Frank Furness) is the oldest art institution in the United States (founded in 1804) and houses a collection that ranges from Winslow Homer to Andrew Wyeth to Red Grooms. *Broad and Cherry Sts., tel. 215/972–7600. Open daily. Admission charged.*

Head west on Cherry Street for two blocks and you'll come to the **Benjamin Franklin Parkway,** which angles across the city's grid system from City Hall to Fairmount Park. This 250-foot-wide boulevard, inspired by Paris's Champs-Elysées, is adorned with fountains, statues, trees, and flags of every country.

Walk northwest one block to **Logan Circle,** where you'll see the beautiful **Swann Fountain.** Cross Logan Circle to the south for the **Academy of Natural Sciences** (19th St. and Benjamin Franklin Pkwy., tel. 215/299–1020; open daily; admission charged), America's first museum of natural history, founded in 1812. On the east side of Logan Circle is the **Cathedral of Saints Peter and Paul** (18th and Race Sts., tel. 215/561–1313; open daily; admission free), the basilica of the Archdiocese of Philadelphia. On the north side is the **Free Library of Philadelphia** (19th St. and Benjamin Franklin Pkwy., tel. 215/686– 5322; open daily; admission free), a Greek Revival building housing over 2 million volumes.

On the west side is the **Franklin Institute.** The Institute is actually four major attractions, including the Science Center, the Fels Planetarium, and, opened in 1990, the $72 million Futures Center and Omniverse Theater with its 79-foot domed screen. *20th St. and Benjamin Franklin Pkwy., tel. 215/448–1200. Open daily. Admission charged.*

Go two blocks farther up the Parkway to the **Rodin Museum,** a jewel box of a museum housing the best collection of Auguste Rodin's works outside of France. Even if you don't go in, walk up to the door and marvel at the 21-foot sculpture *The Gates of Hell. 22nd St. and Benjamin Franklin Pkwy., tel. 215/787–5431. Open Tues.–Sun. Donations requested.*

Crowning the top of the Parkway is Philadelphia's cultural triumph, the **Philadelphia Museum of Art.** Walk or run up the 98 steps, made famous in the movie *Rocky,* to the massive Greek temple–style building, covering 10 acres, with 200 galleries and over 300,000 works. Pick up a map of the museum at the door and wander around on your own or choose from a variety of guided tours. *26th St. and Benjamin Franklin Pkwy., tel. 215/763–8100. Open Tues.–Sun. Admission charged.*

And finally, just over the city line at Merion Station (Montgomery County) is one of the great collections of paintings in the world. The **Barnes Foundation** contains more than 1,000 works—including 175 Renoirs, 66 Cézannes, 65 Matisses, and numerous works by van Gogh, Rousseau, Degas, El Greco, and many others. Due to a two-year renovation and the art collection's international tour to Washington, D.C., Paris, and Tokyo, visitors will have to wait until 1995 to view the magnificent artwork again; however, the highly-touted arboretum and greenhouse that surround the mansion will remain open. Take the Main Line Local commuter train to Merion Station, and it's a pleasant 10-minute walk east from the station. *300 Latch's La., Merion Station, tel. 215/667–0290. Open Jan.–June and Sept.–Dec., Fri.– Sun. Admission charged.*

HOTELS AND INNS

Although the number of rooms—13,500—is small for a city of nearly a million and a half, a 1,200-room Marriott opening in January 1995—linked to the new Philadelphia Convention Center via a pedestrian walkway— will boost the room count substantially. For the time being, hotel reservations are advised. The city has no central reservation office.

Most of the hotels in downtown Philadelphia are located in three areas: the main shopping/theater district that encompasses a few blocks on either side of Broad Street, near Walnut Street; the Parkway/museum area that runs along the Benjamin Franklin Parkway from 16th Street to the Philadelphia Museum of Art; and the historic district on the east side of downtown that centers on Independence Hall and the Liberty Bell and extends to the Delaware River.

Price categories for double occupancy, without 11% tax, are *Expensive,* over $100; *Moderate,* $60–$100; and *Inexpensive,* under $60.

EXPENSIVE **The Barclay.** Rittenhouse Square (Philadelphia's poshest downtown park) is right outside your door when you stay in this elegant 1929 hotel with four-poster or canopied beds. *Rittenhouse Sq. E, 19103, tel. 215/545–0300 or 800/421–6662. 240 rooms. Restaurant, lobby lounge with jazz pianist, concierge. AE, D, DC, MC, V.*

Holiday Inn–Independence Mall. As the name indicates, the location is most convenient to the historic district (it's around the corner from the Liberty Bell). Colonial furniture, including poster beds and wing chairs, adds to the appeal of this family-oriented hotel. *4th and Arch Sts., 19106, tel. 215/923– 8660 or 800/HOLIDAY. 367 rooms. Restaurant, outdoor pool, gift shop, video-game room. AE, D, DC, MC, V.*

Holiday Inn–Midtown. This 1964-vintage hotel has spacious rooms decorated with prints of Philadelphia scenes or floral motifs; it also has an excellent central location in the theater and shopping district. *1305 Walnut St., 19107, tel. 215/735–9300 or 800/HOLI-*

DAY. 161 rooms. Restaurant, lounge, outdoor pool, no-smoking rooms. AE, D, DC, MC, V.

The Warwick. Guests stay in spacious rooms decorated in "English country–style" and mix in the bright, busy lobby with those who live in the apartments that make up half of the rooms in this stylish hotel. Capricco, the European-style café, serves desserts and espresso until the wee hours. *17th and Locust Sts., 19103, tel. 215/735–6000 or 800/523–4210. 200 rooms. Restaurant/bar, business center, weekend theater package. AE, DC, MC, V.*

MODERATE **Comfort Inn at Penn's Landing.** The location has more noise than charm (tucked between the Benjamin Franklin Bridge, Delaware Avenue, and I–95), but this 10-story hotel, opened in 1987, gives fine basic rooms and service at a good price. *100 N. Delaware Ave., 19106, tel. 215/627–7900 or 800/228–5150. 185 rooms, including 3 suites with hot tubs. Continental breakfast included, lobby lounge, free parking. AE, D, DC, MC, V.*

Quality Inn–Historic Downtown Suites. Because of the slightly out-of-the-way location in Chinatown, you get suite accommodations (with kitchen, exposed brick, and overhead wooden beams) at hotel-room prices in this historically certified building that was once a rocking-chair factory. *1010 Race St., 19107, tel. 215/922–1730 or 800/221–2222. 92 suites. Buffet breakfast included, lobby lounge, limited free parking. AE, D, DC, MC, V.*

Ramada Inn–Center City. If you're willing to stay just a bit away from downtown (though still near the Benjamin Franklin Parkway and the museums), rooms in this three-story, Y-shaped building are a good buy, especially those facing the parkway. *501 N. 22nd St., 19130, tel. 215/568–8300. 278 rooms, including 4 suites. Restaurant, outdoor pool and café, free parking. AE, D, DC, MC, V.*

Society Hill Hotel. This 1832 former longshoremen's house is one of the smallest hotels in the city. All 12 of the rooms are uniquely furnished with antiques and brass beds. *301 Chestnut St., 19106, tel. 215/925–1394. 12*

rooms, including 6 suites. Restaurant/piano bar, outdoor café. AE, DC, MC, V.

Thomas Bond House. This 1769, four-story house in the heart of Old City, has been faithfully restored with 18th-century features, from the molding and wall sconces to the marble fireplaces and four-poster beds. *129 S. 2nd St., 19106, tel. 215/923–8523. 12 rooms, including 2 suites. Parlor, complimentary wet bar. AE, DC, MC, V.*

INEXPENSIVE Bed-and-breakfasts, which follow the European tradition of a room and meal in a private house, are often a less expensive alternative to hotels. Most operate under the auspices of central booking agencies that screen and match guests and homes. Host homes offer considerable diversity and range in price from $30 to $150 a night.

Bed and Breakfast Connections. Its selection of more than 45 host homes includes a Colonial town house, an English Tudor mansion in Chestnut Hill, and an 18th-century farmhouse on the Main Line. Prices range from $35 to $125. *Box 21, Devon 19333, tel. 215/687–3565 or 800/448–3619. AE, MC, V.*

DINING

Since the "restaurant renaissance" of the early 1970s, Philadelphia has become a first-class restaurant city. There is no specific Philadelphia cuisine—unless you count soft pretzels, cheese steaks, hoagies, and Tastykakes.

All restaurant locations listed as "Center City" are within a 10-minute walk from Broad and Walnut streets. Society Hill and Old City are in the Historic District of downtown near the Delaware River. Price categories per person, not including 6% tax, service, and drinks, are *Moderate*, $15–$25, and *Inexpensive*, under $15.

MODERATE **Carolina's.** Cobb salad (a flaky tortilla shell stuffed with chicken, avocado, bleu cheese, black olives, tomato, and romaine lettuce) is one of the popular dishes at this Center City favorite, offering good-size portions from a large menu of sandwiches, pastas, and a dozen entrées that change daily. *261 S. 20th St., near Rittenhouse Sq., tel. 215/545–1000. AE, D, DC, MC. V.*

Downey's. There's Irish memorabilia on the walls, Irish stew on the menu, and always a lively crowd on hand at this popular South Street bar and restaurant. *Front and South Sts., Society Hill, tel. 215/629–0525. AE, D, DC, MC, V.*

Middle East. This Old City favorite is as well known for its sultan's-palace decor and belly dancers as for its first-rate menu—filled with dishes from Lebanon and other Middle Eastern countries. *126 Chestnut St., Old City, tel. 215/922–1003. AE, DC, MC, V.*

Sansom Street Oyster House. This unpretentious place, with the family collection of oyster plates lining the walls, serves some of Philly's best raw oysters, plus clams, fish, shellfish, and grilled and blackened dishes. *1516 Sansom St., Center City, tel. 215/567–7683. AE, D, DC, MC, V.*

Tequila's. This is the place to go in Philadelphia for Mexican food: From the lemon-based seviche (a favorite is the lobster stuffed with pineapple) to the crepes with goat's milk syrup for dessert, Tequila's puts a creative twist on authentic Mexican dishes. *1511 Locust St., Center City, tel. 215/546–0181. AE, DC, MC, V.*

Victor Cafe. If you like northern Italian cuisine—and if you love opera—the Victor Cafe offers a changing menu of pastas and grilled meats, plus operatic waiters and waitresses who burst into song at regular intervals. *1303 Dickinson St., South Philadelphia, tel. 215/468–3040. AE, DC, MC, V.*

White Dog Café. Perhaps the best restaurant in the city, the White Dog presents top-flight, organically grown cuisine in an intimate Victorian row house near the University of Pennsylvania. The decor is pleasant but not fancy, and the clientele includes students, businesspeople, tourists, and hip Philadelphians on their way into town for evening entertainment. *3420 Sansom St., tel. 215/386–9224. AE, DC, MC, V.*

INEXPENSIVE **Chef Theodore.** Here's the best Greek food in town, and lots of it, including the bargain-priced *meze*—a combination plate of eight delicacies, including marinated octopus and stuffed grape leaves. *1100 S. Delaware Ave., South Philadelphia, tel. 215/271–6800. AE, DC, MC, V.*

Joe's Peking Duck. Philadelphia's Chinatown has more than 50 restaurants, and this is the best—friendly atmosphere, plain decor, and great food. *925 Race St., Chinatown, tel. 215/922–3277. No credit cards.*

Melrose Diner. This classic Philadelphia diner serves nothing elaborate but offers top-quality diner meals—burgers and steaks, soups and cherry pie—at bargain prices. It's also open 24 hours. *1501 Snyder Ave., tel. 215/467–6644. No credit cards.*

Reading Terminal Market. If you're hungry and not sure what you want to eat, this is the place. A one-square-block market with more than 70 food shops, stalls, and lunch counters gives you a choice of Chinese, Greek, Mexican, Japanese, Italian, Pennsylvania Dutch, seafood, soul food, and hoagies. A Philadelphia treasure. *12th and Arch Sts., Center City, tel. 215/922–2317.*

Van's Garden. This is the least expensive Asian restaurant in Philadelphia—a variety of traditional noodle dishes topped with barbecued pork or beef can be had for $4.25—yet the food is definitely first-rate. *121 N. 11th St., Chinatown, tel. 215/923–2439. No credit cards.*

SHOPPING

Philadelphia has a wide array of stores and shopping areas. It has an upscale shopping district centered on 17th and Walnut streets, a jewelers' row (Sansom St., between 7th and 8th Sts.), an antiques row (Pine St., between 9th and 12th Sts.), and three enclosed downtown shopping malls (*see* Malls, *below*). Bargains are available, too, from discount stores, street vendors, and factory outlets.

MAIN SHOPPING DISTRICTS **Walnut Street.** The leading shopping area is Walnut Street between Broad Street and Rittenhouse Square, and the intersecting streets just north and south. These blocks are filled with boutiques, art galleries, jewelers, fine-clothing stores, and many other shops. A new addition to Walnut Street is Borders Book Shop (1727 Walnut St., tel. 215/568–7400), the biggest, best, and friendliest bookstore in town, complete with espresso bar.

South Street. From Front Street to 8th Street you'll find more than 180 unusual stores—new-wave and high-fashion clothing, New Age books, avant-garde art galleries, and 70 restaurants. It's a great street for window-shopping and people-watching, especially in the evenings.

MALLS The Gallery at Market East (Market St. from 8th to 11th Sts., tel. 215/925–7162) is America's first enclosed downtown shopping mall. The four-level, glass-roofed structure contains 220 shops and restaurants and three department stores—Stern's (tel. 215/922–3399), Strawbridge and Clothier (tel. 215/629–6000), and JC Penny (tel. 215/238–9100). And the newest downtown mall is The Shops at Liberty Place (17th and Chestnut Sts., tel. 215/851–9000), 60 shops and a food court placed around two levels of a circular 90-foot glass atrium.

DEPARTMENT STORES The granddaddy of local department stores is John Wanamaker (13th and Market Sts., tel. 215/422–2000). It occupies an entire city block, has a nine-story grand hall, boutiques, designer shops, a travel agency, ticket office, beauty salon, and post office.

SOUVENIR AND GIFT SHOPS The bookstore/gift shop at the Visitor Center (3rd and Chestnut Sts., tel. 215/597–8974) specializes in items related to Colonial Philadelphia and the Revolution. Destination Philadelphia (Bourse Bldg., 21 S. 5th St., tel. 215/440–0233) is a clothing store where every item bears some form of Philadelphia logo or design.

OUTDOOR ACTIVITIES

BIKING A treat for bikers is to ride out on the east side of the Schuylkill River, cross Falls Bridge, and return on the west side of the river. The scenic 8.2-mile loop has no hills and takes about an hour of casual pedaling. Rent bikes at 1 Boathouse Row, behind the Art Museum (tel. 215/225–3560).

GOLF Philadelphia has six city golf courses open to the public. The most difficult is Cobbs Creek (7800 Landsdowne Ave., tel. 215/877–8707) and the shortest is Walnut Lane (Walnut La. and Henry Ave., tel. 215/482–3370). Try to call a few days ahead to reserve tee times.

JOGGING AND HIKING The best locale for jogging and hiking is Forbidden Drive in the Wissahickon Valley in Fairmount Park, with more than 5 miles through a beautiful forested gorge, with no automobile traffic allowed.

ENTERTAINMENT

BALLET AND DANCE The Pennsylvania Ballet (tel. 215/551–7014) dances at the Academy of Music from September to June. Philadanco, Philadelphia Dance Company (tel. 215/387–8200), performs modern dance at the Annenberg Center (3680 Walnut St., tel. 215/898–6791) and other locations.

CONCERTS The world-renowned Philadelphia Orchestra performs at the Academy of Music (Broad and Locust Sts., tel. 215/893–1930) from September to May and at the Mann Music Center (West Fairmount Park, tel. 215/878–7707) in the summer. The Curtis Institute of Music (1726 Locust St., tel. 215/893–7902) presents free student recitals every Monday, Wednesday, and Friday of the school year.

OPERA The Opera Company of Philadelphia (tel. 215/981–1450) stages full-scale productions in original languages, with English supertitles, from November to April at the Academy of Music.

THEATER The Forrest Theater (1114 Walnut St., tel. 215/923–1515) has major Broadway productions. The Walnut Street Theater (9th and Walnut Sts., tel. 215/574–3550) has comedies, musicals, and dramas in an auditorium where almost every seat is a good one. The Wilma Theater (2030 Sansom St., tel. 215/963–0345) is a smaller theater that has gained critical acclaim for its innovative work.

DINNER SHOWS Riverfront Dinner Theater (Poplar St. and Delaware Ave., tel. 215/925–7000) specializes in Broadway musicals.

Cavanaugh's Restaurant (119 S. 39th St., tel. 215/386–4889) concentrates on comedy-mystery performances.

SPECTATOR SPORTS The major league holds home games in the sports complex at Broad Street and Pattison Avenue. The Phillies baseball team (tel. 215/463–1000) and the Eagles football team (tel. 215/463–5500) play at Veterans Stadium. The 76ers basketball team (tel. 215/339–7676) and the Flyers hockey team (tel. 215/755–9700) play at the Spectrum.

Rocky Mountain National Park
Colorado

ithin a single hour's drive, you ascend from 7,800 feet, at park headquarters, to 12,183 feet at the apex of Trail Ridge Road. Sweeping vistas from atop this vantage, the highest continuous paved road in the United States, assemble high-country lakes and meadows flushed with wildflowers, rushing mountain streams, and cool, dense forests of lodgepole pines and blue spruce below; above, view snow-dusted peaks that float in the sky, small glaciers, patches of blue Colorado columbine, and finally, the fragile, treeless ecosystem of alpine tundra seldom found outside the Arctic. Rocky Mountain National Park in Colorado isn't a pretty passage; it's a moment of grandeur.

Today, the visitor can see evidence of the park's long (1.8 billion years) and varied past. Scientists estimate that 530 million years ago the park was covered by water, which eventually receded and left tropical plains inhabited by dinosaurs. Erupting volcanoes came next—violent uplifts that created the Rocky Mountains. The glaciers that followed left the park as it looks now, full of valleys and peaks carved by ice.

With 18 official hiking trails, trail rides, bus tours, rock-climbing, golf courses, bike routes, fishing, and fine dining—the region delights both mountain explorers and those to whom roughing it is staying at an elegant country hotel. In Rocky, as the locals call it, you won't feel that you're just visiting the mountains; you'll be living up in the sky, too.

ESSENTIAL INFORMATION

WHEN TO GO The great advantage of traveling to Rocky in the summertime is that conditions are gentle and you can see and hike through much more of the park. The one drawback is the people; they are everywhere, and so are their cars, trucks, and RVs. In the summer, be up and about before 8 AM and you'll have a much better chance of getting a

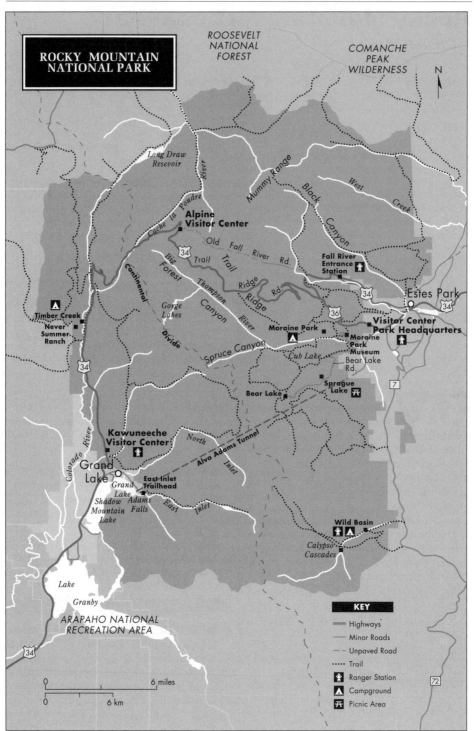

ROOSEVELT
NATIONAL
FOREST

COMANCHE
PEAK
WILDERNESS

N

**ROCKY MOUNTAIN
NATIONAL PARK**

*Long Draw
Resevoir*

Cache la Poudre River

Mummy Range

Black Canyon

West Creek

**Alpine
Visitor Center**

Old Fall River Rd.

**Fall River
Entrance
Station**

34

Estes Park

Big Forest

Trail

Thompson River

Ridge

Ridge

Rd

36

34

Continental

*Gorge
Lakes*

Spruce Canyon

Moraine Park

**Visitor Center
Park Headquarters**

Timber Creek

**Never
Summer
Ranch**

Divide

Cub Lake

**Moraine
Park
Museum**

Bear Lake
Rd.

7

34

Colorado River

**Kawuneeche
Visitor Center**

North

Inlet

Bear Lake

**Sprague
Lake**

**Grand
Lake**

*Grand
Lake*

**East Inlet
Trailhead**

Alva Adams Tunnel

*Shadow
Mountain
Lake*

*Adams
Falls*

East Inlet

Wild Basin

*Calypso
Cascades*

*Lake
Granby*

**ARAPAHO NATIONAL
RECREATION AREA**

34

72

0   6 miles

0   6 km

KEY

━━━ Highways
──── Minor Roads
- - - Unpaved Road
······· Trail
🚹 Ranger Station
⛺ Campground
⛩ Picnic Area

true wilderness experience. Summer is the only time of year that you'll be able to drive across the 50-mile Trail Ridge Road; the road closes with the first heavy snowfall—sometime between the end of September and Thanksgiving—and does not reopen until Memorial Day.

The best time to come here is early fall—after the crush of people and cars has gone and before the cold weather sets in—although some parts of Rocky remain crowded into the leaf-gazing season in early fall.

In wintertime, the east slope of the park at lower elevations is usually free of snow, but higher up there are blizzards and impassable drifts. Unless you want to downhill ski (often available only on weekends), cross-country ski, or take on the frozen backcountry on foot, Rocky is essentially a warm-weather getaway.

Due to the altitude, weather in the park is very changeable. Most of the improved campgrounds are below 9,400 feet, and conditions there are usually better than at higher elevations (on Trail Ridge Road it can snow even in July). Spring comes late, but by May much of the snow has melted and the wildflowers are in bloom. Summer days often reach into the 70s or 80s but drop into the 40s at night. July is the warmest month, with frequent late-day showers. August is the wettest period, and cold fronts arrive late in the month. September sees rain and snow, with temperatures in the 70s in the daytime and falling into the 30s at night. October is colder and snowier, particularly on the west side, but November's snowfall is usually light, and skiing is not yet satisfactory. December and January are cold, and at high elevations the windchill factor can be nasty. For the park's recorded weather forecast, call 303/586–2385.

TOURIST OFFICES Park Headquarters (Superintendent, Rocky Mountain National Park, Estes Park 80517, tel. 303/586–2371); Estes Park Chamber of Commerce (500 Big Thompson Ave., Estes Park 80517, tel. 800/44–ESTES).

EMERGENCIES Police, fire, and **ambulance:** Dial 911. **Doctors:** Estes Park Medical Center

(555 Prospect Ave., Estes Park, tel. 303/586–2317).

ARRIVING AND DEPARTING

BY PLANE The nearest airport is Denver International Airport (tel. 303/270–1300) in Denver, 83 miles southeast of the park. In summertime, allow two hours to drive from the airport to Rocky—the roads are generally two-lane and traffic can be heavy.

BY CAR From the east the best way to reach the park is on U.S. 34 or U.S. 36. Inside the park, U.S. 34 becomes Trail Ridge Road, which carries you across the Continental Divide and into Grand Lake. If you want to come in on the western, more scenic side of Rocky but you're in Denver, take I–70 to U.S. 40 and turn north. Just past Granby go north on U.S. 34 toward the park. Grand Lake is about 100 miles northwest of Denver. The western route is more scenic.

BY TRAIN Amtrak (tel. 800/USA–RAIL) trains from around the country stop at Union Station in Denver, but there is no train service to Estes Park or Grand Lake.

BY BUS Charles Tour and Travel (tel. 303/586–5151) operates charter buses between Denver and Estes Park from late April until late September. Tickets are $24 and the bus drops you off at your lodging. Charles Tour and Travel also offers tour packages through the park.

GETTING AROUND

BY CAR Since Rocky has only three paved roads, the driving options are limited.

ON FOOT The sweeping vistas are stupendous from inside an automobile or bus but even better when you leave your car and take a hike. Small trails are plentiful in every direction.

BY BUS In the summertime, a free shuttle bus runs daily from the Glacier Basin parking lot to Bear Lake. Buses leave every half hour from 8 AM to 9:30 AM and approximately every 12–15 minutes from 9:30 AM to 5:30 PM. From mid-August to mid-September it runs only on weekends.

REST STOPS Rocky has many public rest rooms at rest stops along Trail Ridge Road, at the Longs Peak campground, and at the visitor centers at Rocky's eastern and western entrances.

GUIDED TOURS Free ranger-led tours covering different aspects and areas of the park are offered regularly. One of the best tours is "Rocky after Dark," in which a ranger leads visitors into the park after sundown to observe the animals' nocturnal habits. Tundra walks are also recommended, but they are rigorous, involving two to three hours of hiking at high altitudes. *High Country Headlines,* a free publication found at the park's visitor centers and ranger stations, has a listing of tours with meeting times and places.

EXPLORING

Summer entrance fees are $5 per week per vehicle. There is no charge to enter the park in winter, except on weekends and holidays. The park's Annual Area Pass costs $15. The "Golden Eagle Pass," which lets you enter any national park in America for a calendar year, costs $25. People entering the park on bicycles, buses, or on foot pay $3 for a weekly pass.

Trail Ridge Road is the main paved road cutting through the park. In normal summer traffic, Trail Ridge Road is about a two-hour drive from the west to the east side. There are many gradual climbs and turnoffs, and the grade does not exceed 7%.

Begin your tour at the **Kawuneeche Visitor Center** on U.S. 34 at the west entrance to the park, and watch the 20-minute film on Rocky. The center also has exhibits, maps, and booklets on virtually every aspect of the park. *Tel. 303/586-2371. Open daily. Admission free.*

Backtrack on U.S. 34 and make a left on Highway 278 to reach the **East Inlet Trailhead.** From here, it's a pleasant 3/10-mile walk to **Adams Falls,** an excellent spot for a picnic.

Head back up U.S. 34 past the Kawuneeche Visitor Center. About 7¹/₂ miles up the road on the west side is a turnoff called **Never Summer Ranch,** a working ranch in the 1800s. From the road it's a short walk to the ranch, which has the only historic buildings within the park. *Tel. 303/627-3652. Open June 15–Labor Day, daily. Admission free.*

Continue along U.S. 34 to the **Alpine Visitor Center.** Nearby is Trail Ridge Store, the only snack bar in the park and a good place to stop for lunch. After eating, attend one of the ranger-led programs at the center. Then take Trail Ridge Road back toward Estes Park. *Tel. 303/586-2371. Open daily, except when Trail Ridge Rd. is closed (mid-Oct.–Memorial Day). Admission free.*

Old Fall River Road runs for 9.4 miles, from Horseshoe Park west to Fall River Pass. The original road crossing the mountains, Old Fall River Road, is one-way and uphill and features a gravel surface and many switchbacks. For the best one-day driving tour, drive up the road to the Alpine Visitor Center.

Along the 10-mile **Bear Lake Road,** the newly renovated **Moraine Park Museum** houses natural-history exhibits, including a depiction of the process of glaciation in the area. Adjacent to the museum is another building that can be viewed from a distance—the **William Allen White Cabin,** named after the famous Kansas journalist who wrote here during the summers. Visiting artisans now use the cabin in the warm months, so it's not open to the public. *Museum: tel. 303/586-2327. Open Memorial Day–Labor Day, daily; weekends through fall. Admission free.*

The road leading west off Bear Lake Road, across from the museum, leads to the **Cub Lake area.** The 4.6-mile trek is a moderate one, providing the best hiking experience for one day.

Farther down Bear Lake Road, stop at **Sprague Lake** and walk the half-mile around it. At the end of Bear Lake Road is **Bear Lake,** a good place to spot magpies. The half-mile walk to Nymph Lake is an even one, with only a 20-foot climb in elevation.

THE NATURAL WORLD The park is divided into three zones, which correspond to elevation. The first is the Montane Zone—from 7,000 to 9,000 feet above sea level—featuring slopes, valleys, and stands of evergreens. The second, the Subalpine Zone—from 9,500 to 11,500 feet—is both above and below the tree line. The third is the Alpine Zone— anything over 11,500 feet—which offers arctic temperatures, barren stretches, and nasty winds.

The park's ecosystem has great variety: 25 species of mammals, 250 species of birds, and 900 species of plants. A few black bears remain in Rocky. Mountain lions and bobcats are seldom seen. Bighorn sheep are a more common sight, especially along Big Thompson Canyon, near the Fall River Entrance Station. Moose have been spied in the willows of the Kawuneeche Valley. In autumn, herds of elk wander down to lower elevations and are most often visible at early morning or evening. The beavers usually work at night. Squirrels, chipmunks, and marmots are seen everywhere. Some people find these small mammals cute, but they can carry rabies and should not be befriended or fed.

Broad-tailed hummingbirds, woodpeckers, peregrine falcons, mountain jays, Steller's jays, and scores of other birds add color to the park. The white-tailed ptarmigan—pure white in its winter feathers—spends the cold months on the alpine tundra. At visitor centers and park information booths, employees will tell you the best sites for bird-watching. Vegetation includes such wildflowers as the wood lily, the wild iris, and the yellow lady's slipper orchid.

HOTELS AND INNS

There are no hotels within Rocky itself, but the surrounding area offers a range of everything from upscale hotels and resorts to bed-and-breakfasts, cabins by the river, vacation homes and condominiums, and guest ranches. The Estes Park area alone has nearly 75 different overnight options, and Grand Lake offers numerous other possibilities. For a complete guide to accommodations in Estes Park, call the Chamber of Commerce Lodging Referral Service at 303/586–4431 or 800/443–7837. Price categories for double occupancy, without 7% tax, are *Expensive*, over $100; *Moderate*, $50–$100; and *Inexpensive*, under $50.

ESTES PARK **The Aspen Lodge.** Located 8 miles south of Estes Park on Highway 7, the "ultimate family resort" has your pick of family reunion packages. Whether you stay in the main lodge or in an adjoining cabin, the decor is rugged alpine all the way. *6120 Hwy. 7, 80517, tel. 303/586–8133 or 800/332–6867. 36 rooms, 20 cabins. Meals included in summer, 2-night weekend stay required. Pool, sauna, hot tub. AE, D, DC, MC, V. Expensive.*

Estes Park Center/YMCA of the Rockies. Cabins on this huge, bucolic property have kitchens with stoves and refrigerators; most cabins also have fireplaces. *2515 Tunnel Rd., 80511–2800, tel. 303/586– 3341. 200 cabins. Restaurant, library, museum. No credit cards. Inexpensive–Moderate.*

Riversong Bed and Breakfast. The bedrooms in this elegant, romantic hideaway feature antique furniture and fireplaces. Some even have sunken bathtubs. *Box 1910, 80517, tel. 303/586–4666. 9 rooms with bath. MC, V. Moderate–Expensive.*

The Stanley Hotel. The classiest of the local hotels, The Stanley features both 19th-century elegance and modern conveniences. The hotel exterior is of old-fashioned, white-painted wood; the guest rooms, continually renovated and redone to their original 19th-century decor, match the exquisite public rooms. *333 Wonderview, Box 1767, 80517, tel. 303/586–3371 or 800/ROCKIES, fax 303/586–3673. 92 rooms. Heated outdoor pool, Jacuzzi, tennis courts. AE, D, MC, V. Moderate–Expensive.*

The Telemark Resort. Located just west of Estes Park, this resort borders the Big Thompson River. Its rustic cabins have screened-in porches and fireplaces. *Box 100 AC, 80517, tel. 303/586–4343 or 800/669–0650. 17 cabins. AE, MC, V. Moderate.*

Tyrol Motor Inn. All units have picture windows and panoramic views of the mountains. *Box 1570 AC, 80517, tel. 303/586–3382. 53 rooms. Heated pool, therapeutic pool, sauna. AE, D, MC, V. Inexpensive–Moderate.*

Trappers Inn. Just two blocks from downtown Estes Park, this quiet, squeaky-clean motel has fishing just across the road in Fall River. *Box 487 AC, 80517, tel. 303/586–2833. 20 rooms. AE, D, MC, V. Inexpensive.*

Whispering Pines Cottages. Located among the pines and alongside the Big Thompson River, these cottages give you the chance to hook a trout from your deck or patio. *Box 877 AC, 80517, tel. 303/586–5258. 15 cottages. Fully equipped kitchens, outside grills. AE, D, DC, MC, V. Inexpensive–Moderate.*

GRAND LAKE **Lemmon Lodge.** This Grand Lake favorite on the banks of the lake itself offers seclusion, a sandy beach, and a private dock for those who bring along their boats. *Box 514, 80447, tel. 303/627–3314 in summer; 303/595–3733 in winter. 5-bedroom lodge, 21 cabins for 4–10 people. Open Memorial Day–Oct. MC, V. Moderate–Expensive.*

Grand Lake Lodge. Built of lodgepole pine in 1925, this lodge is known as Colorado's favorite front porch because of the view of both Grand Lake and Shadow Mountain Lake. *Box 569, 80447, tel. 303/627–3967 or 303/759–5848 in the off-season. 66 cabins. Restaurant, swimming pool, horse rental, playground. AE, MC, V. Moderate.*

Shadowcliff Lodge. This Grand Lake retreat offers privacy and spectacular views, and with one double bed and two bunk beds in each room, it's perfect for large groups. *Box 658, 80447, tel. 303/627–9220. 12-room lodge and 7-room lodge, all with shared bath. $2 towel and linen fee. No credit cards. Inexpensive.*

CAMPGROUNDS

Rocky has five designated drive-in campgrounds. During the summer, reservations are required at Moraine Park and Glacier Basin, but Longs Peak, Timber Creek, and As-

penglen have first-come, first-served policies. Longs Peak allows tents only; the others accommodate RVs.

Most of the park's 520 RV spaces are paved. There are no gas hookups; bottled LP gas is available at the campgrounds. From June 1 to September 30, camping at the five park campgrounds is limited to seven days (three days at Longs Peak). Advance reservations can be made through MISTIX (tel. 800/365–2267).

Camping fees vary with the season. If the water is turned on, sites cost $7 per night at Longs Peak, Timber Creek, and Aspenglen, $10 per night at Moraine Park and Glacier Basin. Group sites at Glacier Basin cost $20–$50 per week. If water is unavailable, camping is free.

If you are planning an overnight trek into the backcountry, you must have a permit. These are free and can be picked up just east of Park Headquarters, at the Kawuneeche Visitor Center, and at the Wild Basin or Longs Peak ranger stations. To obtain a permit in advance, contact the Superintendent of Park Headquarters (Rocky Mountain National Park, Estes Park 80517–8397, tel. 303/586–4459). Reservations made by telephone for a permit must be made before June 1.

Outside the park, Estes Park has private camping facilities, and there are many sites near Grand Lake in the Arapaho National Recreation Area (Box 10, Granby, 80446, tel. 303/887–3331).

DINING

With nearly 100 different dining options in and around Estes Park and Grand Lake, you can sample everything from Mexican fare to Cajun, French, and Chinese cuisines. Many restaurants offer not only fine cuisine but great views of Rocky. Price categories per person, not including 7% tax, service, and drinks, are *Expensive,* over $15; *Moderate,* $10–$15; and *Inexpensive,* under $10.

ESTES PARK **The Fawn Brook Inn.** This romantic, secluded restaurant is a local favorite for elegant dining in an informal, relaxed atmosphere. The kitchen prides itself on its veal, lamb, and duck. *15 mi south of Estes Park on Hwy. 7, tel. 303/747–2556. AE, MC, V. Expensive.*

The Dunraven Grille at the Stanley Hotel. If you want to splurge, this restaurant offers excellent trout and filet mignon in an elegant resort setting. *333 Wonderview, tel. 303/586–3371. AE, D, DC, MC, V. Moderate–Expensive.*

Molly B's. The atmosphere here is homespun and friendly, and the menu offers fresh seafood, crepes, steaks, and homemade desserts. *200 Moraine Ave., tel. 303/586–2766. AE, MC, V. Moderate.*

Big Horn Restaurant. Its breakfast has been voted the best in Estes Park, but its steaks make it a popular lunch and dinner spot as well. *401 W. Elkhorn Ave., tel. 303/586–2792. No credit cards. Moderate.*

The Dunraven Inn. This local favorite features homemade Italian cooking, a dark interior, and walls pasted with autographed dollar bills. *2470 Hwy. 66, tel. 303/586–6409. MC, V. Moderate.*

Johnson's Cafe. Estes Park is full of good breakfast spots, but Johnson's Swedish pancakes, potato pancakes, and waffles are truly exceptional. *Stanley Village Shopping Center, 1 block from downtown, tel. 303/586–6624. No credit cards. Inexpensive.*

La Casa. This Mexican/Cajun restaurant on Estes Park's main street has a cozy back room with broad picture windows; frame your face in sunshine or simply relax to the sounds of the river flowing by La Casa's outdoor garden. *222 E. Elkhorn Ave., tel. 303/586–2807. AE, D, DC, MC, V. Moderate.*

GRAND LAKE **Corner Cupboard Inn.** This historic landmark in not-so-urban Grand Lake features Alaskan salmon steak, prime rib, and an overflowing salad bar. *1028 Grand Ave., tel. 303/627–3813. MC, V. Inexpensive–Moderate.*

The Grand Lake Lodge Restaurant. This restaurant offers a wonderful view of Grand Lake as well as numerous mesquite-grilled special-

ties, such as grilled chicken glazed with honey or grilled beef brushed with tangy barbecue sauce. *Off U.S. 34 north of Grand Lake, tel. 303/627–3967. MC, V. Moderate.*

SHOPPING

The park has only one snack bar and souvenir shop, known as Trail Ridge Store (tel. 303/222–3097), located near the Alpine Visitor Center. Elkhorn Avenue, the main street of Estes Park, is lined with novelty shops selling everything from western clothes to taffy.

OUTDOOR ACTIVITIES

BIKING Biking is the best in the early morning, before the roads are overrun with cars. The roads don't have much shoulder to accommodate the mountain bicyclist, and there are no bike paths. Rentals are not available in the park, but you can rent bicycles in Estes Park from Colorado Bicycling Adventures (184 E. Elkhorn Ave., tel. 303/586–4241).

BOATING There is no motorized boating inside the park. Nearly all of the lakes within Rocky are accessible only by hiking in, so you must carry your inflatable boating gear with you. (Not even inflatable boats are allowed on Bear Lake.) Lily Lake, at the eastern boundary of the park west of Twin Sisters, is right by the road and good for boating. Sprague Lake is also a good choice for boating, and it's an easy walk in. Fan Lake is recommended, but it's smaller.

FISHING Inside Rocky, you'll need a Colorado fishing license, and special regulations apply within the park. In some areas, you must release the fish you have caught. The town of Grand Lake is known for its fishing; big brown trout, 20-pound mackinaw, and modest kokanee salmon are regularly pulled from these waters. With Grand Lake itself, Lake Granby, Shadow Mountain Lake, and the nearby Colorado River, an angler can keep busy. Fishing licenses can be purchased in Estes Park at Scot's Sporting Goods (870 Moraine Ave., U.S. 36, tel. 303/586–2877).

GOLF The Grand Lake Golf Course (tel. 303/627–8008) offers outstanding views and moderate greens fees. The Estes Park Golf Club (tel. 303/586–8146), just south of downtown on Highway 7, is shorter but more challenging. Lake Estes Executive Course (tel. 303/586–8176) is nine holes.

HIKING For brilliant views of the Rockies, hike the 1.8 miles of steep terrain from the Wild Basin Ranger Station to Calypso Cascades, at the southwest corner of the park.

HORSEBACK RIDING Glacier Creek Stables (tel. 303/586–3244), near Sprague Lake, and Moraine Park Stables (tel. 303/586–2327) offer two-hour rides for about $25. Other trips range from from two to eight hours to overnight.

SKIING Never Summer Mountain Sports (tel. 303/627–8008) in Grand Lake rents backcountry skis for $12. On Rocky's east side, the summer trail at Bear Lake is the point of departure for many winter activities. On the west side of the park is the Tonahutu Creek Trail. Leave your car at the Kawuneeche Visitor Center and ski east from the parking lot. Skiers should always beware of high winds (up to 100 miles per hour) and avalanches.

SWIMMING Rocky's streams and lakes, fed by melting snow, are always cold. The Lake Estes Marina (1170 E. Big Thompson Ave., tel. 303/586–2011) rents wet suits. The YMCA (tel. 303/586–3341) just outside Estes Park has a swimming pool. The Estes Park Aquatic Center (tel. 303/586–2340) has an indoor pool.

TENNIS There are public courts in Grand Lake at Town Park and at the Metropolitan Recreation District (tel. 303/627–8328). The Estes Valley Recreation and Park District (tel. 303/586–8191) has six courts in Stanley Park.

WATER SPORTS The park's rivers are generally too shallow for rafting, and the main location for water sports is not inside the park but at Grand Lake or in the nearby Arapaho National Recreation Area. The Area's headquarters is in Granby (Box 10, Granby, 80446, tel. 303/887–3331).

San Antonio and Austin
Texas

sk a Texan to name the state's most charming city, and he will inevitably pick San Antonio, which has a historic setting that never fails to impress first-time visitors with its easy grace. Here Mexican traditions can be most readily felt, tempered by the influence of the German immigrants who settled in the nearby Hill Country. Although the city's namesake river may be an impediment to highway engineers, its twisting way has given San Antonio a priceless gift: *Paseo del Rio,* or the River Walk. Sequestered 20 feet below street level, this natural waterway winds through the middle of the downtown business district; it's laced over with stone arches, bordered by a subtropical terrain of lush plants, cypress trees, and flowers. All of San Antonio comes here to dine, shop, and meet friends.

If San Antonio is the most soothing of Texas cities, Austin is surely the most mellow. North on I–35 about 80 miles, this city is the seat of Texas government as well as home to the University of Texas. Austin has always been a progressive college town, and today it is testament to the efforts of environmentalists, with numerous parks and lakes that are used year-round by scullers and pleasure boaters. If sociology is more your style than outdoor life, the city will delight you with its people-watching possibilities, including a mix of university students, aging hippies, musicians, and Texas politicians. Austin also serves as the heart of the Texas music industry and is justly famous for its 6th Street nightclubs and other venues where such musicians as Willie Nelson and Lyle Lovett sometimes stop in.

ESSENTIAL INFORMATION

WHEN TO GO Central Texas summers are hot, usually in the 90s and sometimes more than 100°. Fortunately, the humidity in San Antonio and Austin is not as suffocating as

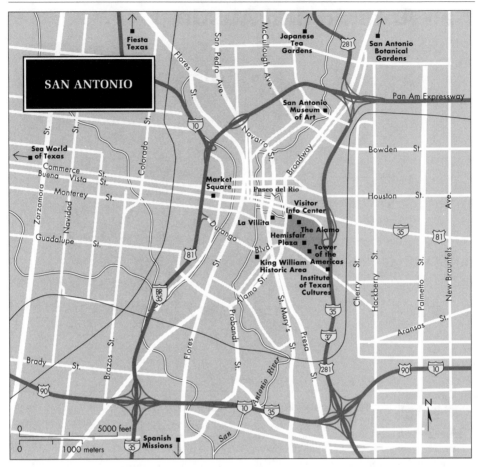

on the coast. Weatherwise, spring and fall are most comfortable, with average daytime temperatures in the 70s. A spring trip offers the additional attraction of wildflower season. Although winter can be chancy, with occasional cold snaps and rain, daytime temperatures in the 50s are more like it.

FESTIVALS AND SPECIAL EVENTS San Antonio offers many *fiestas* (festivals) throughout the year. **Christmas** is absolutely magical (and crowded), with a month of holiday celebrations, including the **Holiday River Festival** that illuminates the trees and bridges along the River Walk from the night after Thanksgiving until New Year's Eve. Thousands of candles glow softly inside paper bags and line the River Walk during **Fiesta de Las Lumi-**

narias (Festival of Lights), held the first three weekends in December. The poignant **Las Posadas** (The Inns), a reenactment of the Holy Family's search for an inn, winds along the River Walk the second Sunday of December.

San Antonio heralds the arrival of spring with its biggest celebration of the year, the century-old **Fiesta San Antonio** (tel., 210/227–5191), 10 days of parades, street fairs, festivals, art shows, sporting events, and elegant social balls. Held in April, Fiesta's dates vary each year but always include San Jacinto Day, April 21, commemorating the 1836 date when Texas defeated Mexico to win its freedom as an independent nation.

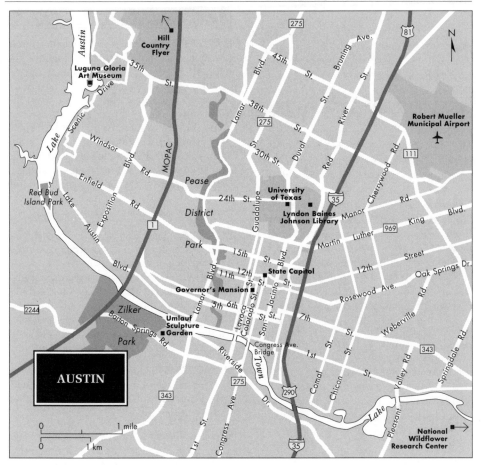

BARGAINS San Antonio offers many free attractions. Moreover, there seems to be a fiesta for every occasion, so you're likely to find free entertainment, such as mariachi bands, dancers, and street entertainers, especially in Market Square and on the River Walk.

Austin's bargains include free tours of the State Capitol, the Governor's Mansion, and the Lyndon Baines Johnson Library. The University of Texas schedules concerts, recitals, and speakers throughout the year; tickets are often free or cost just a few dollars. Free concerts and dance performances are plentiful in Zilker Park and at Auditorium Shores along Town Lake, especially during the summer.

TOURIST OFFICES San Antonio Convention & Visitors Bureau (121 Alamo Plaza, Box 2277, San Antonio 78298, tel. 210/270–8700 or 800/447–3372, fax 210/270–8782). Austin Convention and Visitors Bureau (201 East 2nd St., Austin 78701, tel. 512/474–5171 or 800/888–8AUS), or stop by Austin Visitor Information (201-B East 2nd St., Austin 78701, tel. 512/478–0098). For a free Texas State Travel Guide, write: Texas Department of Transportation (Travel and Information Division, Box 5064, Austin 78763, tel. 800/452–9292).

EMERGENCIES Police, fire, and ambulance: Dial 911. Hospitals: In San Antonio, the Nix River Walk Clinic (408 Navarro St., tel. 210/271–1841) and Santa Rosa Health Care

Corp. (519 W. Houston St., tel. 210/228–2011), and in Austin, the emergency room at Brackenridge Hospital (601 E. 15th St., tel. 512/476–6461) are open 24 hours for medical emergencies.

ARRIVING AND DEPARTING

BY PLANE San Antonio International Airport (tel. 210/821–3411) has two terminals hosting a dozen or so airlines. Ground transportation to downtown takes about 15 minutes when traffic is normal, and an average cab fare is about $12, plus tip. Star Shuttle (tel. 210/366–3183) offers 24-hour service from the airport and serves major downtown hotels ($7 one-way, $4 each additional person traveling with full-paying passenger; 24 hrs. advance reservation recommended). If you rent a car, take U.S. 281 south (McAllister Freeway) from the airport to downtown.

Austin's main airport is the Robert Mueller Municipal Airport (tel. 512/472–3321, paging and passenger information). A cab ride from the airport to downtown (5 miles) is $7–$10, plus tip. If you rent a car, take I–35 south from the airport to downtown. No airport shuttle service is available. Many of the larger hotels offer courtesy van service to and from the airport.

BY CAR San Antonio has interstate highways leading into it from every direction, including I–10 (from Houston) and I–35 (from Austin and Dallas); major highways pass through or nearby the central downtown area. The city is surrounded by Loop 410, which bypasses some, but not all, traffic.

Austin's major north–south arteries include I–35 to the east, and, to the west, Loop 360 (also known as Capital of Texas Highway) and MoPac Expressway (Loop 1).

BY TRAIN Amtrak (tel. 800/USA–RAIL) serves both Austin and San Antonio.

BY BUS Greyhound Lines (tel. 800/231–2222) and Kerrville Bus Company (tel. 512/389–1068) serve both San Antonio and Austin.

GETTING AROUND

SAN ANTONIO The best way to enjoy the city is on foot. Should you tire, VIA Metropolitan Transit Service (112 W. Soledad St., tel. 210/227–2020) has 94 regular bus routes (fare: 40¢) and four trolley routes (fare: 10¢) downtown. A Day Tripper Pass allows you to ride the VIA system all day for $2; this includes the VIA Vistas Cultural Route, which stops at more than a dozen museums and other attractions, including the historic missions. Express routes are also available from downtown to Sea World (fare: 85¢, one-way) and Fiesta Texas (fare: $1, one-way).

AUSTIN The 6th Street cabaret district and the University of Texas campus can be explored on foot, but otherwise Austin is better seen by car. The city has a regular city bus system, Capital Metro (tel. 512/474–1200), which runs a number of routes (fare: 50¢) as well as the free Armadillo Express downtown trolley buses between the University of Texas, Capitol complex, and convention center.

REST STOPS There's a gas station at practically every city intersection and virtually every freeway interchange, and all of them have rest rooms.

GUIDED TOURS San Antonio tour companies offer shopping trips to Mexico, nature hikes at various state parks, and tours of historic sites. Gray Line (tel. 210/226–1706 or 800/GRAYLINE, fax 210/226–2515) schedules daily bus tours around the city and a 40-minute, narrated water tour ($3) of the river.

In Austin, Gray Line (tel. 512/345–6789) covers the basic sights. Around Austin (tel. 512/345–6552) provides personalized tours of the city and can arrange a weekend Hill Country tour. The Lone Star Riverboat (tel. 512/327–1388) takes passengers on a 90-minute cruise of Town Lake (Mar.–Nov.).

EXPLORING

SAN ANTONIO Downtown San Antonio is a tourist mecca. If you begin each day with breakfast at one of the several restaurants on

Paseo del Rio, you'll be within minutes of many places you will want to visit. You will also want to browse along Commerce Street, Houston Street, and Alamo Plaza.

The Alamo. This former mission was established in 1718 by Spanish Franciscan friars, but it's remembered for the 1836 battle in which Lt. Col. William B. Travis, Davy Crockett, Jim Bowie, and more than 180 other Texans died fighting Mexico's General Antonio Lopez de Santa Anna. The Alamo became the symbol of Texas's fight for independence from Mexico, and 46 days after the massacre there, Santa Anna himself was captured and the Republic of Texas came into being. The adobe chapel looks much the same today as it did 150 years ago. The plaza out front tends to be a busy meeting place. *300 Alamo Plaza, tel. 210/225–1391. Open daily, except Christmas Eve and Christmas Day. Admission free. No hats, cameras, or video-recording devices inside.*

Fiesta Texas. Situated in an abandoned quarry at the base of sheer, 100-foot-tall limestone cliffs, this musical theme park managed by Opryland celebrates the state's diverse cultures with four entertainment theme areas—Hispanic, German, Old West, and 1950s Rock 'n Roll. Thrill-seekers venture aboard The Rattler, billed as the world's tallest and fastest wooden roller coaster, for the ride of their lives. *17000 I–10 West at Loop 1604, tel. 210/697–5443. Open Mar.–Memorial Day and Labor Day–November, weekends; Memorial Day–Labor Day, daily. Admission charged (children under 7 free).*

HemisFair Park. The site of the 1968 World's Fair is now home to the 750-foot-tall Tower of the Americas. The waterfall-filled park also features the Institute of Texan Cultures, a museum providing a fascinating, hands-on interpretation of Texas history and folk culture. The institute hosts the annual Texas Folklife Festival the first weekend of August. *Park: 200 S. Alamo St., tel. 210/299–8572. Open daily. Admission free. Institute: 801 S. Bowie St., tel. 210/226–7651. Open Tues.–Sun., except Thanksgiving and Christmas. Donations accepted.*

Japanese Tea Gardens. Goldfish-stocked ponds, pebble pathways, and outstanding floral displays make this a relaxing spot. *3800 N. St. Mary's St., tel. 210/821–3000. Open daily. Admission free.*

King William Historic Area. In the late 1800s, the 25-block King William District on the south bank of the San Antonio River was the most elegant residential area in the city. Today, many of the stately mansions have been restored and about a dozen operate as bed-and-breakfast inns. A map for a self-guided walking tour is available from the San Antonio Conservation Society (107 King William St., tel. 210/224–6163).

La Villita. Located right on the River Walk, this mid-18th-century Texas settlement and the city's original town site has been restored, with the houses and buildings providing spaces for artists and craftsmen. You can watch glassblowers, boot makers, painters, and jewelers, or dine at one of its three restaurants. *418 Villita at the River Walk, tel. 210/299–8610. Open daily, except Thanksgiving, Christmas and New Year's days. Admission free.*

Paseo del Rio (River Walk). Locals as well as visitors are drawn to this special 2^1/$_2$-mile promenade with European-style sidewalk cafés, specialty boutiques, and nightclubs—all fronted by cobblestone paths. At one narrow bend in the river, the Arneson River Theatre is carved right into the riverbank so that spectators can applaud shows being staged across the river. Extensions to the original WPA-built walkway lead to Rivercenter Festival Marketplace and to the San Antonio Convention Center.

San Antonio Botanical Gardens and Lucile Halsell Conservatory. This 38-acre garden blooms year-round with a profusion of colorful, thematic planting areas. You can "Walk Through Texas," discovering the state's native flora, or visit the Biblical Garden filled with fig trees, date palms, and other plant life mentioned in the Bible. The conservatory's futuristic-style glass pavilions re-create environments from around the world for some 2,000 different plants. *555 Funston Pl. at N.*

New Braunfels, tel. 210/821–5115. Open Tues.–Sun. Admission charged.

San Antonio Museum of Art. The collections, housed in the former Lone Star Brewing Company's castlelike building, range from pre-Columbian treasures and Mexican folk art to American masterpieces and antiquities from ancient Greece, Rome, and Egypt. 200 W. Jones Ave., tel. 210/829–SAMA. Open daily, except Thanksgiving and Christmas. Admission charged.

Sea World of Texas. The largest marine-life theme park in the world features water rides, a beach and wave pool, daily shows, and exhibits devoted to killer whales, penguins, walruses, dolphins, sea lions, and other aquatic life. 10500 Sea World Dr. at the intersection of Ellison Dr. and Westover Hills Blvd. off Texas Hwy. 151, tel. 210/523–3611 or 800/527–4757. Open daily June–Labor Day; weekends only Mar.–May and Sept.–Dec. 1. Admission charged (children under 3 free).

Spanish Missions. San Antonio's debt to the Spanish crown can be seen at five Franciscan missions established in the early 18th century. Except for the Alamo, the missions still serve active parishes. The best way to see the missions is aboard VIA's Vistas Cultural route, as the Mission Trail road signs are difficult to follow. The largest and best-restored building is Mission San Jose, where a mariachi mass is held at noon every Sunday. San Jose: 6539 San Jose Dr. at Mission Rd., tel. 210/229–4770. Open daily. Admission free.

AUSTIN You need not rush to see everything in Austin. A favorite pastime here is spending a lazy afternoon at a spring-fed swimming hole or at an outdoor garden, sipping a cool beverage.

State Capitol Building. This grand Renaissance Revival structure is the largest U.S. state capitol, actually nine feet taller than the national Capitol building in Washington, D.C. Austin's capitol features 7 miles of exquisite wainscoting, 500 doors, and 900 windows. A recent underground expansion added another 650,000 square feet to the original building. You can take a free tour or guide yourself around with a free pamphlet, "Texas Capitol Guide," available at the visitors desk. Ongoing renovations means that parts of the Capitol building are closed until January 1995. 11th St. and Congress Ave., tel. 512/463–0063. Open daily. Admission free.

Governor's Mansion. Since 1856, this elegant Greek Revival mansion has housed the Texas head of state. Each governor and his or her family have left their unique mark on the house, and you'll hear plenty of entertaining anecdotes on the short guided tour (Mon.–Fri.; tours leave every 20 minutes from the mansion's front gate). 1010 Colorado St., tel 512/463–5518. Call for hours. Admission free.

Hill Country. West of Austin and San Antonio, the Hill Country area has many little 19th-century German towns and runs from Dimebox and Flatonia to Fredericksburg and New Braunfels. These towns are known for their delightful country inns, old-fashioned restaurants, antiques shops, wurst makers, dude ranches, and many festivals. In Johnson City, the Lyndon B. Johnson National Historical Park includes the former president's boyhood home, a visitor center, the Johnson Ranch, and Texas White House. The Hill Country is popular among nature lovers and outdoorsmen, with a chain of seven Highland Lakes that wind for 150 miles. If you only have time for a quick look at the scenery, get on Loop 360 (Capital of Texas Highway) from South Lamar Boulevard or MoPac (Loop 1), and head north. Loop 360 swings around the west side of Austin, allowing views of violet-colored hills. Loop 360 runs into Loop 1 south for the return to downtown.

Hill Country Flyer. All aboard on restored steam engine No. 786 for a half-day, weekend-only excursion between Cedar Park (30 miles north of downtown Austin) and Burnet. The journey—in vintage coaches— and the roar of the powerful engine returns riders to a nostalgic bygone era. Depot in Cedar Park, just north of FM 1431 and U.S. 183 North, tel. 512/259–9368. Call for hours. Reservations required. Admission charged.

Laguna Gloria Art Museum. The collection here includes works by regional and nationally known artists and photographers. Be sure to stroll the lovely landscaped grounds facing Lake Austin. *3809 W. 35th St., tel. 512/458–8191. Open Tues.–Sun. Admission charged.*

Lyndon Baines Johnson Library. Located on the University of Texas campus, this presidential library houses more than 36 million personal and official documents as well as historical and cultural exhibits. *2313 Red River St. near E. 23rd St., tel. 512/482–5279. Open daily. Admission free.*

National Wildflower Research Center. Founded by Lady Bird Johnson, this is the only institution in the country dedicated exclusively to conserving and promoting the use of native plants in North America; it's situated on 60 acres along the Colorado River, east of Austin. *2600 FM 973 North, tel. 512/929–3600. Open weekdays with extended weekend hours in spring. Admission free.*

Umlauf Sculpture Garden. More than 100 sculptures by internationally known artist Charles Umlauf are exhibited in a small museum and throughout the site's landscaped gardens, set overlooking Zilker Park. *605 Robert E. Lee Rd. (off Barton Springs Rd.), tel. 512/445–5582. Open Thurs.–Sun. Admission charged.*

Wineries. The hills and lakes in this part of Texas create the perfect environment for grapevines. Among the wineries in the area open to visitors are Fall Creek (Tow, near Llano, tel. 512/476–4477), Bell Mountain/Oberhellmann Vineyards (Fredericksburg, tel. 512/685–3297), Moyer Champagne Company (San Marcos, tel. 512/396–1600), Hill Country Cellars (Cedar Park, tel. 512/259–2000), and Slaughter-Leftwich Vineyards (Austin, on Lake Travis, tel. 512/266–3331). Hours of operation change according to the season, so call ahead. For a free wine-country tour guide, contact the Texas Department of Agriculture, Box 12847, Austin 78711 (tel. 512/463–7624).

THE NATURAL WORLD The rugged hills near San Antonio and Austin are honeycombed with more than 2,500 caves, most of them wild and undeveloped. One of the most striking is Natural Bridge Caverns, where formations continue to form from constant water activity. *8 mi west of Natural Bridge Caverns Exit off I-35, tel. 210/651–6101. Open daily. Admission charged.*

The world's largest urban bat colony—750,000 Mexican free-tailed bats—hangs out beneath Austin's Congress Avenue Bridge April through October. It's become popular to find a spot just before dusk and watch their dramatic departures against the setting sun. The best vantage spots are from the hike-and-bike trail by the bridge or from the patio of Shoreline Grill restaurant.

McKinney Falls State Park, 7 miles southeast of Austin, features tree-lined Onion Creek and its two waterfalls. The park has good bird-watching, campgrounds, shady picnic areas, and playgrounds as well as 19th-century ruins scattered along the 1.7 miles of winding shoreline. Swimming is not allowed in the swimming hole when the bacteria count is high; call the park's hotline (tel. 512/243–0848) for the latest water conditions. *Scenic Rd., 2 mi west of U.S. 183, tel. 512/243–1643. Open daily. Admission charged.*

In Central Texas, the Colorado River forms a 150-mile chain of lakes that run from Burnet County to Austin. Along the Highland Lakes you can find great fishing, spectacular scenery, and an endless array of water recreation. Several luxury resorts, including Horseshoe Bay on Lake LBJ in Marble Falls and Lakeway Resort on Lake Travis near Austin, border the lakes. Along the shores of Lake Austin sits Lake Austin Spa Resort, a world-class health and fitness spa. At Lake Buchanan, the Vanishing Texas River Cruise ventures through miles of backwater wilderness for scenic views of towering limestone cliffs, beautiful waterfalls, and majestic eagles in flight during the winter. *Vanishing Texas River Cruise, RR 2341 (3¹/2 mi northwest of Burnet), tel.*

512/756–6986. Daily cruises. Admission charged.

HOTELS AND INNS

San Antonio accommodates visitors with numerous historic hotels and a wide range of bed-and-breakfast inns. In Austin, several downtown hotels border Town Lake, where frequent outdoor concerts add to the ambience. Both cities have fancier modern hotels and chain motels. Make your reservations well in advance: One of the nation's top convention destinations, San Antonio's rooms always seem to be booked to capacity, and Austin is packed with alumni during the University of Texas football season.

The reservation service Bed & Breakfast Hosts of San Antonio (tel. 210/824–8036 or 800/356–1605, fax 210/824–8036) lists nearly 50 bed-and-breakfast properties in the San Antonio area, with more than a dozen in the historic King William District. Lodging ranges from the grand, antebellum Ogé House to the Beckmann Inn and Carriage House, a charming, six-bedroom Victorian home.

Price categories for double occupancy, including 8% tax, are Expensive, $90–$110; Moderate, $70–$90; and Inexpensive, under $70. All rates are also subject to a 13% occupancy tax in San Antonio, 7% in Austin.

SAN ANTONIO **Menger Hotel and Motor Inn.** Ask for one of the Texana-furnished rooms in the original wing of the city's oldest hotel, located directly across the alley from the Alamo; be sure to visit the famous Menger Bar, where Teddy Roosevelt recruited his Rough Riders in 1898. 204 Alamo Plaza, 78205, tel. 210/223–4361 or 800/345–9285, fax 210/228–0022. 320 rooms, 18 suites. Restaurant, entertainment, pool, health club. AE, D, DC, MC, V. Moderate–Expensive.

La Mansion del Rio. This Spanish Colonial hotel, originally built in 1852 as a private boys' school, overlooks the Paseo del Rio and has a graceful, Old World charm that captures the ambience of the city. 112 College, 78205, tel. 210/225–2581 or 800/531–7208, fax 210/226–0389. 337 rooms, 11 suites. Restau-

rants, entertainment, pool. AE, D, DC, MC, V. Expensive.

Emily Morgan Hotel. The triangular shape of this Art Deco gem makes it one of the most distinctive buildings on the city's skyline. Located next door to the Alamo, the hotel is convenient to the River Walk and other downtown attractions. 705 E. Houston St., 78205, tel. 210/225–8486 or 800/824–6674. 177 rooms, 1 suite. Restaurant, pool, health club. AE, D, DC, MC, V. Inexpensive–Moderate.

Hyatt Regency Hill Country Resort. Located directly across the highway from Sea World, this 200-acre resort is a destination in itself. Settled on the site of a historic Texas ranch, it spreads across rolling Hill Country terrain. Among the amenities is a 950-foot-long Ramblin' River for tubing. 9800 Resort Dr. (off Hwy. 151), 78251, tel. 210/647–1234 or 800/233–1234, fax 210/681–9681. 500 rooms, 46 suites. Restaurant, pool, tennis, golf, health club, jogging and biking trails. AE, D, MC, V. Expensive.

AUSTIN **Guest Quarters Suite Hotel.** This modern high-rise hotel is conveniently located downtown; many of the one- and two-bedroom suites have views of the Capitol, two blocks away. 303 W. 15th St., 78701, tel. 512/478–7000 or 800/424–2900. 189 suites. Restaurant, lounge, pool. AE, D, DC, MC, V. Expensive.

Driskill Hotel. Since opening on Christmas Eve 1885, the grande dame of Austin hotels has been the gathering spot for politicians and other big-name decision makers. Recent renovations restored the original beauty of the Driskill's lavish lobby and rooms. 604 Brazos Street (at 6th Street), 78701, tel. 512/474–5911 or 800/527–2008, fax 512/474–2214. Restaurant, entertainment. AE, D, DC, MC, V. Moderate–Expensive.

Fairview. This early 20th-century Colonial Revival mansion offers guest rooms, all with private baths, in either the main or adjoining carriage house. Overlooking a quiet, tree-lined street, the main house with its massive white columns and delightful Victorian furnishings makes for a wonderful weekend get-away. *1304 Newning Ave. (near South Congress and Riverside Drive), 78704, tel. 512/444–4746. 3 rooms, 3 suites, all with kitchenettes. Full breakfast included. AE, DC, MC, V. Expensive.*

MOTELS

The following motels are in the *Inexpensive* price category.

SAN ANTONIO **Drury Inn/Airport** (143 N.E. Loop 410, 78216, tel. 210/366–4300 or 800/325–8300; fax 210/366–4300). 125 rooms, 12 suites; pool. **Hampton Inn/Airport** (8818 Jones Maltsberger, 78216, tel. 210/366–1800 or 800/HAMPTON, fax 210/366–1800). 121 rooms; pool. **Holiday Inn Downtown/Market Square** (318 W. Durango St., 78204, tel. 210/225–3211 or 800/HOLIDAY, fax 210/225–1125). 318 rooms, 2 suites; restaurant, pool. **La Quinta Convention Center** (1001 E. Commerce St., 78205, tel. 210/222–9181 or 800/531–5900, fax 210/228–9816). 140 rooms; pool. **La Quinta Market Square** (900 Dolorosa, 78207, tel. 210/271–0001 or 800/531–5900, fax 210/228–0663). 124 rooms, 2 suites; pool. **Rodeway Inn Fiesta Park** (19793 I–10 W., 78257, tel. 210/698–3991). 76 rooms, 1 suite; restaurant, pool.

AUSTIN **Capitol Motor Inn** (2525 S. I–35, 78741, tel. 512/441–0143). 80 rooms; Continental breakfast included, pool. **Drury Inns** (919 E. Koenig Lane, 78751, tel. 512/454–1144 or 800/325–8300). 137 rooms; breakfast served, pool. **Holiday Inn–Austin Town Lake** (20 N. I–35, 78701, tel. 512/472–8211 or 800/HOLIDAY, fax 512/472–4636). 321 rooms; restaurant, pool, health club. **La Quinta Inn** (5812 I–35 North, 78751, tel. 512/459–4381 or 800/531–5900, fax 512/452–3917). 59 rooms; pool. **Quality Inn Airport** (909 E. Koenig La., 78751, tel. 512/452–4200 or 800/221–2222, fax 512/452–4200). 91 rooms; breakfast served, pool.

DINING

When in Texas, dine as Texans do, and that usually means eating Mexican. Both San Antonio and Austin have hundreds of Tex-Mex restaurants.

Despite the Texas tradition of eating beef, you'll easily find restaurants that cater to the health-conscious with salads, light pastas, seafood, and fresh vegetables on the menu. Visitors who want sauces on the side or fish cooked without butter need only ask, and many menus highlight heart-healthy selections. Price categories per person, excluding sales tax, service, and drinks, are *Moderate,* $15–$25, and *Inexpensive,* under $15.

SAN ANTONIO **Boudro's on the River.** On the River Walk, this sidewalk café serves seafood and southwestern food, such as crab and shrimp tamales, pecan-grilled fish, and its trademark corn pudding. *421 E. Commerce St., tel. 210/224–8484. AE, DC, MC, V. Moderate.*

Cappy's. Changing exhibits by local artists add to the refreshing atmosphere of this Broadway landmark. The menu offers a varied selection of pasta dishes and mesquite-grilled fish, along with such tempting desserts as apple pie with butter-rum sauce and chocolate cake served warm and topped with Bluebell ice cream. *5011 Broadway, tel. 210/828–9669. AE, DC, MC, V. Inexpensive–Moderate.*

La Margarita. This restaurant receives credit for introducing the world to fajitas—grilled steak served with peppers and onions in a flour tortilla. Eat outdoors and watch the Market Square action or dine indoors (which is only slightly less frenetic) at the Cortez family's popular Tex-Mex cantina. *120 Produce Row in Market Sq., tel. 512/227–7140. AE, DC, MC, V. Inexpensive–Moderate.*

L'Etoile. While children are welcomed at this upscale French venue, they don't distract from a pleasurable evening out, as the restaurant provides baby-sitting next door. You can't go wrong with the delectably creamy lobster bisque or the veal, roast lamb, and grilled fish entrées. *6106 Broadway, tel. 210/826–4551. AE, DC, MC, V. Moderate.*

Rio Rio Cantina. A lively, youthful atmosphere and generous servings of *mole* (a chili- and chocolate-based sauce) chicken, enchiladas suiza, and other traditional Mexican dishes make this one of the best Tex-Mex choices on the River Walk. *421 E. Commerce, tel. 210/226–8462. AE, D, DC, MC, V. Inexpensive.*

AUSTIN **Fonda San Miguel.** Like a lush garden from a Mexican villa, the dining room makes a beautiful setting for dining on ceviche, chicken in mole, fish coated with achiote (a reddish, earthy-tasting seed), and other Mexican specialties. *2330 W. North Loop, tel. 512/459–4121. AE, D, DC, MC, V. Moderate.*

Mezzaluna. This trendy spot near downtown specializes in contemporary Italian cuisine— goat-cheese fritters, sautéed shrimp with smoked tomato-basil sauce, veal scaloppine, and the chef's signature dish, smoked-chicken lasagna. *310 Colorado St., tel. 512/472–6770. AE, DC, MC, V. Moderate.*

Shoreline Grill. With a spectacular view of Town Lake, diners find the cuisine to be as inviting as the scenery. The regional menu borrows heavily from the Creole cooking of neighboring Louisiana; try the Shoreline's blackened fish specialties, crab cakes with remoulade sauce, or the carmelized crème brûlée. Steak lovers should try the prime rib, slowly roasted on the grill. *98 San Jacinto Blvd., tel. 512/477–3300. AE, D, DC, MC, V. Moderate.*

Chuy's Hula Hut. Mix together a little Polynesian, Caribbean, and Mexican and you've got the Hula Hut, an eclectic eatery along the shores of Lake Austin just west of downtown. Order an appetizer, *tapas* (small samplings), or a pu-pu platter large enough to feed two. A popular choice at Chuy's is the Polynesian pescado platter, with coconut fried shrimp, grilled salmon fillet, and shrimp flautas with orange-mustard sauce. *3826 Lake Austin Blvd., tel. 512/476–HULA. AE, D, DC, MC, V. Inexpensive.*

Salt Lick. For a taste of true Texan barbecue, head about 25 miles southwest of downtown Austin to Driftwood and the Salt Lick. Ribs, brisket, sausage, and chicken cook slowly over an open pit and are served family style with all the trimmings. There's no air-conditioning, but fans and the shade of huge oak trees help to cool the place. If you want a cold beer to wash down the barbecue, bring your own—the Salt Lick is in a dry county. *FM 1826 (off U.S. Hwy. 290 West), tel. 512/858–4959. Open Wed.–Sun. No credit cards. Inexpensive.*

Threadgills. In this converted old service station, the late Kenneth Threadgill, a yodeler and music lover, created an Austin legend when he began inviting his friends over to play music (among those aspiring musicians was a University of Texas student named Janis Joplin). The restaurant also enjoys a reputation for its good home-style cooking. Some say the chicken fried steaks are the best in town. *6416 N. Lamar, tel. 512/451–5440. MC, V. Inexpensive.*

SHOPPING

San Antonio's Market Square (514 West Commerce St., tel. 210/299–8600) offers shops, restaurants, and a farmers market where you can buy dried-chili wreaths or fresh-made tortillas. El Mercado at the square is a large indoor shopping area, with stalls selling wrought iron, pottery, and Mexican dresses.

The newest extension of the River Walk leads to Rivercenter (849 E. Commerce St., tel. 210/225–0000), an entertainment, hotel, and shopping complex, anchored by the luxurious Marriott Rivercenter and Dillard's department store. Small specialty boutiques, along with national retail chains rise along three levels. An IMAX Theatre (483 Rivercenter Mall, tel. 210/225–4629 or 800/354–IMAX) shows *Alamo: The Price of Freedom* on a six-story screen.

Austin's distinctive shopping district is The Drag, which means Guadalupe Street from Martin Luther King Boulevard to 26th Street across from the University of Texas campus.

Here you'll find Bevo's Book Store (2304 Guadalupe St., tel. 512/476–7642), the university's souvenir store, and the People's Renaissance Market (W. 23rd and Guadalupe Sts.), an open-air bazaar. Elsewhere in Austin, visit Bluebonnet Markets (310 Neches, tel. 512/476–3484), where about a dozen artisans ply their mostly Texana handicrafts under one roof. The Travis County Farmers' Market (6701 Burnet Rd., tel. 512/454–1002) features fresh produce and crafts. For upscale shopping, The Arboretum (10000 Research Blvd. and Great Hills Trail, tel. 512/338–4437) features a number of boutiques, art galleries, Simon David gourmet grocery store and Amy's Ice Cream.

The area between San Antonio and Austin is a bargain hunter's mecca. In New Braunfels, the Mill Store Plaza (I–35 North, exit 189, tel. 210/625–5289), anchored by WestPoint Pepperell, features more than 50 name-brand factory stores where shoppers save 20% to 70% off retail prices. The San Marcos Factory Shops (tel. 512/396–2200) and Tanger Factory Outlet Center (tel. 512/396–7444) offer discount prices at several hundred showrooms, which include Liz Claiborne, Donna Karan, Guess, Brooks Brothers, and Mikasa. Both centers are located at I–35 and Center Point Road, via exit 200, in San Marcos.

OUTDOOR ACTIVITIES

BIKING Austin's scenic back roads offer gently rolling hills and tempting diversions, from tucked-away waterfalls to country antique emporia to barbecue joints. Loop 360 provides a grueling workout, while the hike-and-bike trail around Town Lake is more leisurely. The Bicycle Sport Shop (1426 Toomey Rd., tel. 512/477–3472) rents bikes.

CANOEING AND RAFTING You can canoe on any of the lakes in and around Austin. Within the city, rent a canoe by the hour or day at Zilker Park Boat Rentals (2000 Barton Springs Rd., tel. 512/478–3852). Serious adventurers go to New Braunfels and the neighboring village of Gruene (pronounced "Green"), where they pick up a raft, canoe, or tube from Rockin' "R" River Rides (1405 Gruene Rd.,

tel. 800/55–FLOAT) to float down the Guadalupe River.

GOLF In San Antonio, Mission del Lago (1250 Mission Grande, tel. 210/627–2522), Brackenridge (2315 Ave. B, tel. 210/226–5612), and Cedar Creek (8250 Vista Colina, tel. 210/695–5050) are recommended 18-hole golf courses. In Austin, check out Jimmy Clay Municipal Golf Course (5400 Jimmy Clay, east of I–35 at Stassney La., tel. 512/444–0999), or championship courses at Circle C Golf Club (11511 FM 1826, tel. 512/288–4297) and River Place (4207 River Place Blvd., off FM 2222 West, tel. 512/346–6784).

JOGGING AND WALKING Austin has 20 miles of hike-and-bike trails. The most popular is the 8½-mile trail that runs along the north and south shores of Town Lake.

SWIMMING Austin's favorite swimming hole is the naturally spring-fed Barton Springs in Zilker Park (Barton Springs Rd. between Robert E. Lee and Loop 1, tel. 512/476–9044); a 997-foot-long pool has chilly waters (a constant 68°).

ENTERTAINMENT

NIGHTLIFE The River Walk is a good place to sample San Antonio's fine restaurants and sometimes rowdy nightlife. Topping the list of fun places is Dick's Last Resort (River level, Navarro St. Bldg., tel. 210/224–0026), with Dixieland jazz and would-be comedians doubling as waiters. The Landing (Hyatt Regency river level, 123 Losoya and River Walk, tel. 210/222–1234) is home to Jim Cullum's Jazz Band. Sing-alongs keep the atmosphere boisterous at Durty Nelly's (Hilton Palacio del Rio river level, 200 Alamo and River Walk, tel. 210/222–1400).

THEATER The Majestic Theatre (212 E. Houston St., tel. 210/226–3333), built in 1929 and renovated in the late 1980s, is home to the San Antonio Symphony and the most popular venue for touring Broadway shows and concerts.

MUSIC If you like a lively music scene, Austin's 6th Street district is world-famous, with some two dozen nightclubs and music halls clustered within a few blocks. Elsewhere in town, traditional country fans flock to the Broken Spoke (3201 S. Lamar Blvd., tel. 512/442–6189). For blues, try Antone's (2915 Guadalupe St., tel. 512/474–5314). Jazz lovers enjoy Top of the Marc (618 W. 6th St., tel. 512/472–9849), an upscale night spot upstairs from Katz's Deli. Symphony Square (E. 11th and Red River Sts., tel. 512/476–6090), on the banks of Waller Creek, is home to the Austin Symphony and other music groups. A traditional gathering spot for politicians (a must on presidential campaign stops) and University of Texas alumni, Scholz Garten (1607 San Jacinto St., 512/477–4171) is one of the best places in town to hear good Texas music from the likes of Asleep at the Wheel, Gary P. Nunn, or Jerry Jeff Walker. Piano-playing Marcia Ball, the musician in residence, attracts other zydeco and blues buddies to the stage at her husband's La Zona Rosa (612 W. 4th St., 512/482–0662). The Backyard (13101 Hwy. 71 West, 512/263–4146) primarily books national touring acts for its 25,000-square-foot natural amphitheater where massive oak trees, a creek and waterfall provide the backdrop.

SPECTATOR SPORTS The San Antonio Spurs (tel. 210/224–9578) play basketball November through April at the Alamodome, a new 65,000-seat sports arena located downtown just east of I–35.

San Diego
California

Each year San Diego, California, absorbs thousands of visitors who are drawn by the climate: sunny, dry, and warm nearly year-round. Sunshine and crisp ocean air give San Diego—a city where snow falls maybe *once* a decade—the trappings of a temperate, tropical paradise: oases of lazy palms, sheltered bays fringed by golden pampas grass, and far-ranging parklands blossoming with brilliant bougainvillea, jasmine, ice plant, and birds of paradise. Ask San Diegans what they enjoy most, but don't be surprised by the consistency of their response: communing with sea and sand on one of the city's long, powdery beaches, maybe swimming, maybe napping, maybe watching the whales, seals, and dolphins swim offshore.

Visitors can run, bike, and walk for hours down the city's wide, lively streets or along coastal paths planned for the city's seemingly endless supply of fit, well-tanned denizens. Or you can drive by Mission Bay, a 4,600-acre aquatic park, where dozens of colorful, intricate kites fly over hundreds of picnickers lounging in the sun. Downtown you can wander the crowded streets and soak up the colorful lunchtime scene: mimes and musicians hamming it up for the parade of sailors, shoppers, and skateboarders. For a real San Diego experience, blend in with the masses streaming from steel-and-glass office towers to grab a quick lunch at the fanciful Horton Plaza shopping center, which serves as San Diego's de facto city center, with theaters, restaurants, and endless shops.

San Diego has always been recognized as an environmental utopia—reflected in everything from the city's unique modern architecture to its miles of immaculate public beaches. The city is a hodgepodge in the best sense due to its mix of military personnel and beach bums, immigrants and gays. Today, San Diego retains its sense of a western frontier as it develops into a major cosmopolitan centerpiece for the nation.

Torrey Pines
State Beach

Miramar

Mira Mesa Blvd.

S21

N. Torrey

Genesee Ave.

Pines Rd.

805

Miramar

Escondido Rd.

MIRAMAR

NAVAL
SYCAM

15

N

University of California
San Diego (UCSD)

*La Jolla
Cove*

MIRAMAR
NAVAL AIR
STATION

Gilman Dr.

San Diego Fwy.

*Ellen Browning
Scripps Park*

Torrey Pines Rd.

Ardath Rd.

San Diego
Museum of
Contemporary Art

LA JOLLA

52

Clairemont   Mesa   Blvd.

163

Murphy Canyon Rd.

La Jolla Blvd.

5

Clairemont Dr.

Balboa   Ave.

Genesee

Aero Dr.

8

Montezuma R

**PACIFIC
BEACH**

Mission Blvd.

Grand Ave.

Ingraham St.

*Mission
Bay
Park*

Ave.

Rd.

Cabrillo Fwy.

805

**MISSION
BEACH**

Mission   Bay

**LINDA
VISTA**

Linda   Vista   Rd.

P A C I F I C

Mission Bay Dr.

Sea World

Friars   Rd.

Adams Ave.

15

**OCEAN
BEACH**

Nimitz Blvd.

Rosecrans Blvd.

8

**OLD
TOWN**

163

University   Ave.

BUS
8

El Cajon Blvd.

Con

Fairmount Ave.

Euclid   Ave.

O C E A N

Sunset Cliffs Blvd.

Catalina   Blvd.

San Diego
Int'l Airport

Harbor   Dr.

Pacific Hwy.

San Diego Zoo

El Prado   *Balboa Park*

94

47th St.

94

209

**POINT
LOMA**

Embarcadero

Seaport
Village

Broadway
Market St.

DOWNTOWN

Imperial   Ave.

National Ave.

Cabrillo Memorial Dr.

North Island

U.S. NAVAL
AIR STATION
CORONADO

Old Ferry
Landing

Harbor Dr.

75

San Diego-
Coronado Bay
Bridge

National City Blvd.

8th   St.

18th   St.

Highland Ave.

Cabrillo
National
Monument

*Coronado
Beach*

Hotel Del
Coronado

San Diego Bay

**NATIONAL
CITY**

**CHULA
VISTA**

Montgomery Blvd.

E St.

8

SAN DIEGO

*Silver Strand
State Beach*

Strand   Blvd.

*Chula Vista
Wildlife
Reserve*

Broadway

J St.

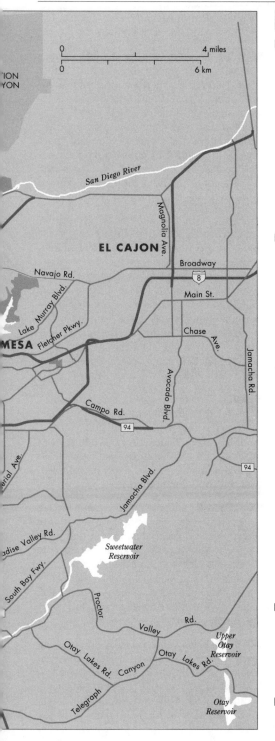

ESSENTIAL INFORMATION

WHEN TO GO San Diego's climate is as close to perfection as one can imagine, with an average annual high temperature of 70°, an average annual low of 55°, and an average annual rainfall of less than 10 inches. The 70 miles of coastline becomes foggy during June. The ocean water doesn't warm up until August, when it hits the high 60s. Santa Ana winds whip the trees in the fall, but that's about as extreme as the weather gets. As far as San Diegans are concerned, September is their town's best month: The water is still warm and the beaches are blessedly empty.

BARGAINS Mimes, jugglers, magicians, and musicians perform for free in Balboa Park, and an endless stream of skateboarders, roller skaters, and bicyclists show off along the beaches and bays. Seaport Village is another great spot for impromptu performances.

The San Diego Symphony gives free evening concerts June through August at Seaport Village, complete with fireworks. Sea World also has fireworks on summer nights—Mission Bay and Ocean Beach are the best spots from which to watch them. Navy ships docked downtown are sometimes open for free tours.

Balboa Park's museums offer free admission on Tuesdays on a rotating basis; the Information Center (House of Hospitality, tel. 619/239–0512) has a posted list. The Information Center also sells the "Passport to Balboa Park," with coupons and reduced rates for admission to the museums. Free organ concerts take place in the Organ Pavilion on Sunday afternoons, and a variety of choral groups and bands perform here for free on summer evenings.

TOURIST OFFICES International Information Center (Horton Plaza, corner of 1st Ave. and F St., San Diego 92101, tel. 619/236–1212). Mission Bay Visitor Information (2688 E. Mission Bay Dr., San Diego 92109, tel. 619/276–8200).

EMERGENCIES Police, fire, and ambulance: Dial 911. Hospitals: UCSD Medical Center (225 Dickinson St., tel. 619/543–6400) and

Mercy Hospital (4077 5th Ave., tel. 619/260–7000) have emergency rooms with 24-hour service. **Doctors:** The San Diego County Medical Society (tel. 619/565–8161) has a referral service, as do all the major hospitals. **Dentists:** Referral Service (tel. 619/235–4546). **Pharmacies:** The large chains—Longs, Sav-On, and Thrifty—stay open until 9 PM; Hillcrest Pharmacy (tel. 619/297–3993) delivers throughout the county.

ARRIVING AND DEPARTING

BY PLANE Most major airlines serve San Diego International Airport (tel. 619/231–5220), also known as Lindbergh Field, 3 miles northwest of downtown. San Diego Transit (tel. 619/233–3004) runs the No. 2 bus between the airport and downtown, where you can transfer to another bus or a trolley; the fare is $1, including transfer. Many hotels also have airport shuttle services. A taxi from the airport to a downtown hotel is $5–$6. Taxis are lined up by the baggage claim areas.

BY CAR I–5 runs south from Los Angeles (actually, from Washington State) to San Diego and is the fastest route to the coastal towns and downtown; Route 1 (the Pacific Coast Highway) travels through the coastal towns and is a more scenic, and congested, route. I–805 is the inland north–south route. I–8 travels west from Arizona and ends at the Pacific Ocean in Ocean Beach.

BY BUS Greyhound/Trailways Lines (tel. 619/239–9171 or 800/231–2222) operates frequent daily service between San Diego's downtown terminal (120 W. Broadway) and Los Angeles, with connections to other U.S. cities.

BY TRAIN Amtrak (tel. 800/USA–RAIL) makes eight trips daily between San Diego and Los Angeles.

GETTING AROUND

San Diego attractions are spread out, and public transportation among them is less than satisfactory. If you travel by bus, visit attractions that are close to one another; for exam-ple, visit downtown and Balboa Park, or Sea World and Mission Bay, on the same day.

BY CAR I–5 connects most of the beach towns, Old Town, downtown, and Balboa Park. Harbor Drive is a beautiful route along downtown's waterfront, Mission Bay Drive and Ingraham Street travel by most of the Mission Bay Park's popular areas, and Mission Boulevard is a must if you want to see the classic southern California beach scene. Scenic drives are marked by road signs with pictures of sea gulls or flowers. The nicest ones go through La Jolla and Point Loma.

Several parking lots around the downtown Embarcadero and Seaport Village charge $3–$5 a day. Parking meters charge 50¢ an hour and are usually good for two hours; don't bother running back to the meter to throw in more change—the space is good for two hours only, and you'll be ticketed if you stay longer (even if there's money in the meter). The lots at Balboa Park and the beach areas are free. From May through Labor Day, parking spots at most beaches are scarce; be prepared to cruise side streets if you arrive after 11 AM.

BY BUS The San Diego Transit Information Line (tel. 619/233–3004), open daily 5:30 AM–8:25 PM, has operators who will help you plan your route. The **Transit Store** (449 Broadway, tel. 619/234–1060) sells the Day Tripper Pass, a $4 investment good for a day of unlimited travel on buses and the trolley.

BY TROLLEY The bright-red electric San Diego Trolley travels along the waterfront in downtown to the Tijuana border and to El Cajon in East San Diego County. The fare is 50¢–$1.50 each way, and tickets can be purchased at vending machines at the trolley stops; exact change is required at many machines. The trolley runs approximately every 15 minutes from 5 AM to 1 AM.

BY TAXI Rates vary according to the company. Radio-dispatched cab companies include Coast Cab (tel. 619/226–8294), Yellow Cab (tel. 619/234–6161), and Orange Cab (tel. 619/291–3333). Cabs cruise the streets downtown, but they're hard to come by at the beaches.

REST STOPS Benches and public rest rooms are common downtown along the waterfront and in Horton Plaza. Public rest rooms at the beaches and Mission Bay sometimes do not have doors on the stalls, and they tend to have slippery floors from all the sand and water tracked in. The House of Hospitality (El Prado, Balboa Park) has large public rest rooms by the Information Center.

GUIDED TOURS One of the best ways to become acquainted with the city is on the Old Town Trolley (tel. 619/298–8687). Open-air, trackless trolleys are used for the 30-mile, two-hour, narrated city tour. You can get on or off the trolley at any of the 10 stops. The fare is $15. On Mondays, senior citizens are entitled to a discounted fare of $12.

EXPLORING

You could easily spend a week and not see all that San Diego has to offer, but you can hit the highlights in about three days. For culture, architecture, shopping, and a quick survey of the top sights, stick to downtown or Old Town, Balboa Park's museums, and the San Diego Zoo. For a more relaxing vacation of swimming, fishing, and sunbathing, stay in Mission Bay or one of the beach towns and make side trips to other attractions.

Balboa Park, with its Spanish-Moorish buildings, gardens, and museums clustered along El Prado (the central walkway), is San Diego's cultural center. Its most outstanding museums are the **Museum of Man** (tel. 619/239–2001), with exhibits of early world cultures, the **Museum of Photographic Arts** (tel. 619/239–5262), with varying shows from photographic greats and unknowns, and the **Reuben H. Fleet Space Theater and Science Center** (tel. 619/238–1168), with an Omnimax theater and hands-on science exhibits. Most are open daily and charge admission. Also in the park is the Botanical Building (next to the Lily Pond), the Japanese Garden, and the Simon Edison Center for Performing Arts.

Cabrillo National Monument, a park at the very tip of Point Loma, commemorates the first European discovery of San Diego in 1542. The view of the Navy and civilian vessels in the harbor is spectacular, and in January or February you might even glimpse a whale spouting during the gray whales' winter migration. *Cabrillo Dr., tel. 619/557–5450. Open daily. Parking fee.*

Coronado's 2.2-mile-long Coronado Bridge looks magnificent as you cross San Diego Bay on the Coronado Ferry—which sails from downtown. The ferry docks at the Old Ferry Landing, where there is a collection of specialty shops and restaurants. From here, tour buses or a trackless trolley take you to the **Hotel Del Coronado** (1500 Orange Ave., tel. 619/435–6611), a huge gingerbread palace with cupolas, terraces, towers, and the grandest lobby in town.

The **Embarcadero** (waterfront), an array of restaurants and cruise-ship piers lining Harbor Drive downtown, is a great place to walk. Begin at the B Street Pier, where cruise ships dock, passengers embark on harbor excursions, and the **Coronado Ferry** (B St. Pier, tel. 619/234–4111) and the **Maritime Museum** (B St. Pier, tel. 619/234–9153)—a collection of historic vessels—have their headquarters. The Embarcadero's pedestrian path curves by Navy vessels and parklands to Seaport Village, at Harbor Drive and Market Street. Wander through the shops and landscaped grounds of this 14-acre shopping, dining, and entertainment center that has become the cornerstone of the waterfront. Across Market Street, a nightlife and restaurant court is under construction. Continuing south along the waterfront you'll see the mirrored towers of the San Diego Marriott Hotel and Marina and the San Diego Convention Center. The Convention Center has an imaginative design that juts out over the water like a sailing vessel. Climb the center's back stairs for a smashing view across the bay.

The **Gaslamp Quarter,** a 16-block national historic district in downtown, contains restored Victorian buildings from the 19th century. Some interesting structures are the **William Heath Davis House** (410 Island Ave.), the headquarters of the Gaslamp Quarter Association, and the **Horton Grand Hotel** (311 Island Ave.) across the street. The **Gaslamp Foundation** (tel. 619/233–5227) gives 1¹/₂-hour guided walks of the historic Gaslamp Quarter, downtown, on Saturdays at 11 AM ($5 donation requested, children under 12 free).

Horton Plaza (4th Ave. and Broadway, downtown, tel. 619/239–8180), a large, colorful, modern shopping plaza with a tiled dome and a copper roof, houses several tiers of shops, restaurants, and theaters overlooking a central courtyard. If you drive to the plaza, have your parking stub validated for three hours of free parking.

La Jolla, often called the Monte Carlo of California, is the address of San Diego's wealthiest and most prestigious residents. Its natural highlight is Ellen Browning Scripps Park and the La Jolla Cove. Towering palms line the sidewalk from the cove's small beach (where divers and snorkelers congregate at the underwater preserve) for about a mile south to the Children's Pool, a safe, protected bay. Prospect and Girard streets are fun for people-watching and window shopping. Stop by the **San Diego Museum of Contemporary Art** for imaginative exhibits of painting, sculpture, and furnishings by modern artists, and another view of the cove. *700 Prospect St., tel. 619/454–3541. Open daily. Admission charged.*

Mission Bay, a 4,600-acre aquatic park, is San Diego's best biking, running, walking, and picnicking spot. Its **Visitor Information Center** (2688 Mission Bay Dr., tel. 619/276–8200) is stocked with information on all of San Diego's attractions.

Old Town best illustrates San Diego's Spanish and Mexican history and heritage. Clustered around Old Town Plaza (where art shows are often held), in Old Town San Diego Historical Park, the houses date back to San Diego's earliest settlements, in the early 1800s. **Old Town's Visitors Center** (San Diego Ave. at Mason St., tel. 619/237–6770) has maps for a walking tour of the neighborhood's historic buildings. At the north end of the park, the **Bazaar del Mundo** is a pseudo-Mexican village shopping and restaurant complex. The historic buildings and shops are open daily, and admission is free. Heritage Park, east of the Bazaar del Mundo, is home to a group of restored Victorian structures (moved from other parts of the city), and in Presidio Park the **Junipero Serra Museum** sits on a hill to the northeast above Old Town. *Presidio Dr., tel. 619/297–3258. Open daily. Admission charged.*

San Diego Zoo, Balboa Park's most heavily visited attraction, has more than 3,200 animals—including several endangered species. Among the new exhibits are Gorilla Tropics, Tiger River, and Sun Bear Forest, designed as bioclimatic zones where animals live much as they would in the wild. *Zoo Way at Park Blvd., tel. 619/234–3153. Open daily. Admission charged.*

Sea World, in Mission Bay, is the world's largest marine-life park. You have to be a big fan of sea creatures to spring for the $25.95 admission fee for adults, but if you love penguins, killer whales, sharks, and sea lions, it's worth it. To get the most for your money, spend a whole day here—this will give you plenty of time to browse through the indoor aquariums and see all the shows. *Sea World Dr., tel. 619/226–3901. Open daily. Admission charged.*

HOTELS AND INNS

Because public transportation is less than efficient, it's best to stay near the things you most want to see and do. New restaurants and hotels are springing up all the time in downtown to serve the new convention center; if you stay here, you'll be near the boats in the bay, downtown's dining and shopping scene, and Balboa Park. San Diego's traditional hotel zone is Mission Valley's Hotel Circle, where chain hotels and motels crowd both sides of I–8. Hotel Circle is convenient if you have a car (all the major freeways intersect here), but it's a terrible spot if you don't, and it has no natural beauty whatsoever. Several new budget hotels and motels have opened in Old Town along I–5, with good freeway access. Mission Bay and Pacific Beach along the coast have a few budget hotels, as does La Jolla, although for the most part lodging in La Jolla is more expensive. Stay in Coronado if you want to relax, walk through charming neighborhoods, and go to the beach, but keep in mind that it's removed from San Diego's other attractions.

Ask about specials, weekday rates, packages, and discounts for senior citizens and retired military personnel. Hotel rates are higher during the summer and at Christmas and Easter. Price categories for double occupancy, without 16% tax, are *Moderate,* $60–$100, and *Inexpensive,* under $60.

CORONADO **Coronado Motor Inn.** This spotless and peaceful motel is about 10 blocks from Coronado's main attractions. *266 Orange Ave., 92118, tel. 619/435–4121. 24 rooms. Pool, parking. AE, MC, V. Inexpensive.*

DOWNTOWN **Holiday Inn Harborview.** This round high rise (built in 1969) on the northern outskirts of downtown offers standard Holiday Inn–quality rooms with spectacular views. *1617 First Ave., 92101, tel. 619/239–6171. 205 rooms. Restaurant, lounge, pool. AE, MC, V. Moderate.*

Hotel Churchill. Originally built in 1915, this hotel has an interior resembling an English castle—each room is decorated in its own motif complete with a special name plaque on the door. The bright-red trolley stops right outside the front door. *827 C St., 92101, tel. 619/234–5186. 92 rooms. AE, MC, V. Inexpensive.*

La Pensione. This new budget hotel, with a central courtyard and kitchenettes in every room, is near all the downtown sights. *1546 2nd Ave., 92101, tel. 619/236–9292. 20 rooms. Kitchenettes. MC, V. Inexpensive.*

LA JOLLA **La Jolla Cove Motel.** Reserve far in advance for this popular motel: It overlooks the famous La Jolla Cove beach and has studios and suites (some with spacious oceanfront balconies) at the lowest rates in the area. *1155 Coast Blvd., 92037, tel. 619/459–2621. 120 rooms. Pool. AE, MC, V. Moderate.*

La Jolla Palms Inn. This modest motel, with fairly large rooms done in green, blue, and beige, is in a quiet neighborhood south of downtown La Jolla, within walking distance of good beaches and restaurants. *6705 La Jolla Blvd., 92037, tel. 619/454–7101. 58 rooms. Restaurant, pool, hot tub, complimentary Continental breakfast. AE, MC, V. Inexpensive–Moderate.*

MISSION BAY/BEACHES **Dana Inn & Marina.** This series of low-rise buildings is sprawled along lawns near Sea World and some of Mission Bay's best biking trails. *1710 W. Mission Bay Dr., 92109, tel. 619/222–6440 or 800/345–9995. 171 rooms. Restaurant, pool, marina. AE, MC, V. Moderate.*

Surfer Motor Lodge. The neighborhood is noisy but fun, and the ocean view from this high rise is wonderful. *711 Pacific Beach Dr., 92109, tel. 619/483–7070. 52 rooms. Restaurant, pool. AE, MC, V. Moderate.*

Mission Bay Motel. The streets around this motel swarm night and day with beach revelers—so the neighborhood is rowdy—but this is as close as you can get to staying right on the water. *4221 Mission Blvd., 92109, tel. 619/483–6440. 50 rooms. Pool. AE, MC, V. Inexpensive–Moderate.*

Padre Trails Inn. This low-key motel, just southwest of Mission Valley, is within walking distance of Old Town. *4200 Taylor St., 92110, tel. 619/297–3291. 100 rooms. Restaurant, lounge, pool. AE, MC, V. Inexpensive.*

OLD TOWN/MISSION VALLEY/HOTEL CIRCLE
Best Western Seven Seas Lodge. One of the better values in Hotel Circle, this hotel is within walking distance of Fashion Valley Shopping Center, Mission Valley's major bus stop. *411 Hotel Circle S, 92108, tel. 619/291–1300 or 800/421–6662. 309 rooms. Restaurant, pool. AE, MC, V. Moderate.*

The Ramada–Old Town. Old Town's Mexican hacienda–style architecture is present in this low-rise building along the freeway, with its tiled fountains, flowering courtyards, and Southwestern touches in the rooms. *2435 Jefferson St., 92110, tel. 619/260–8500 or*

800/2–RAMADA. 151 rooms. Restaurant, heated pool, hot tub. AE, MC, V. Moderate.

King's Inn. This sprawling, motel-like complex is a property of Atlas Hotels, and guests have access to the health clubs and sports facilities at the more expensive Atlas hotels in the valley. *1333 Hotel Circle S, tel. 619/297–2231. 135 rooms. Restaurant, pool. AE, MC, V. Inexpensive–Moderate.*

MOTELS

MODERATE Howard Johnson's (1430 7th Ave., 92101, tel. 619/696–0911). 136 rooms; restaurant, pool. **Super 8 of Mission Bay** (4540 Mission Bay Dr., 92109, tel. 619/274–7888). 117 rooms; pool.

INEXPENSIVE Downtown Budget Motel (1835 Columbia St., 92101, tel. 619/544–0164). 101 rooms. **Travelodge Balboa Park** (840 Ash St., 92101, tel. 619/234–8277). 28 rooms; restaurant, pool.

DINING

It's not hard to eat healthily in San Diego. Seafood is abundant, though more expensive than you might think. Fresh lobster from local waters is available from October to March, fresh abalone from March to October. Good values can be found for shark (which tastes much like swordfish but is half the price), dorado (also called mahimahi), halibut, yellowtail, and fresh yellowfin and albacore tuna. Other local specialties are avocados and fresh citrus.

Mexican food is everywhere in San Diego. Take-out stands—try one of the countless Roberto's, Royberto's, Alberto's, or Aliberto's—are delicious and cheap. Most of San Diego's inexpensive restaurants have some Mexican items on their menus; other bargains are Greek and Japanese restaurants. Price categories per person, not including 6½% tax, service, and drinks, are *Moderate,* $10–$15, and *Inexpensive,* under $10.

BEACHES Qwiigs. Lunch or dinner at this second-story restaurant across the street from the Ocean Beach Pier entails excellent ocean views and fresh, simply served seafood. *5083 Santa Monica Ave., Ocean Beach, tel. 619/222–1101. Moderate.*

The Rusty Pelican. This is the best place on Mission Beach Boardwalk for seafood and grilled chicken; budget-priced early-bird dinners make it easier to enjoy the second-story view of the sunset over the Pacific. *4325 Ocean Blvd., tel. 619/274–3474. AE, MC, V. Moderate.*

Point Loma Seafoods. Don't miss this fish market and take-out restaurant with sublime crab-salad sandwiches, ceviche, and seafood cocktails; seating is at a premium in the glassed-in dining areas. *2805 Emerson St., Point Loma, tel. 619/223–1109. MC, V. Inexpensive.*

Souplantation. Diners at this all-you-can-eat salad bar fill their plates with fresh vegetables and marinated salads, their bowls with chili and several varieties of soups, and more plates still with fresh fruit and bran muffins. The meal is a bargain at lunch. *3960 West Point Loma Blvd., W. Point Loma, tel. 619/222–7404. MC, V. Inexpensive.*

DOWNTOWN The Fish Market. Choose the oyster bar, the sushi bar, or restaurant seating at this spacious new fish house (with free parking after 6 PM) on the waterfront, great for mesquite-grilled fish and pasta dishes. *750 N. Harbor Dr., tel. 619/232–3474. AE, MC, V. Moderate.*

Panda Inn. Often voted the best Chinese restaurant in San Diego, this elegant dining spot offers low-priced Szechuan vegetable dishes and outdoor seating; if you can splurge, try the Peking duck. *506 Horton Plaza, tel. 619/233–7800. AE, MC, V. Moderate.*

Greek Town. Baked lemon chicken, bountiful salads, and hunks of baked moussaka make this family-run restaurant perfect for casual lunches or dinner with friends. *431 E St., tel. 619/232–0461. MC, V. Inexpensive–Moderate.*

Sushi Deli. This very casual restaurant—with two downtown locations (the newer one is called Sushi Deli Too)—is probably the greatest bargain in town. Try the California rolls, the teriyaki chicken platter, or any of the reasonably priced sushi combinations. Both locations are closed between lunch and dinner, from 2 PM to 5 PM. *828 Broadway, tel. 619/231–9597; 339 W. Broadway, tel. 619/233–3072. MC, V. Inexpensive.*

LA JOLLA **Alfonso's.** The oldest sidewalk café in La Jolla serves an outstanding carne asada burrito and a large tostada salad. *1251 Prospect St., tel. 619/454–2232. AE, MC, V. Moderate.*

Sammy's California Woodfired Pizza. For a taste of southern California, stop here for grilled Jamaican jerk chicken salad, Thai shrimp, and more than 20 versions of gourmet pizza (with such exotic toppings as goat cheese and sun-dried tomatoes). *702 Pearl St., tel. 619/456–5222. AE, MC, V. Moderate.*

MISSION VALLEY/HOTEL CIRCLE **Willy's American Bistro.** One of the few outstanding restaurants in the valley, Willy's serves salads, sandwiches, and grilled items in a warm setting with oak furnishings and stained-glass windows. *911 Camino del Rio S, tel. 619/692–0094. AE, MC, V. Inexpensive–Moderate.*

Adam's Steak and Eggs. Generous American and Mexican breakfasts include wonderful omelets and such hard-to-find delicacies as grits and corn fritters, all prepared with the freshest ingredients. *1201 Hotel Circle S, tel. 619/291–1103. MC, V. Inexpensive.*

OLD TOWN **Old Town Mexican Café.** Watch the tortilla-makers slap the dough around in the open-air kitchen while you wait for a table at the most popular Mexican restaurant in town, serving up such fare as tostadas loaded with lettuce and grilled chicken. *2489 San Diego Ave., tel. 619/297–4330. AE, MC, V. Inexpensive–Moderate.*

SHOPPING

SHOPPING DISTRICTS **Coronado:** The Old Ferry Landing (1201 1st St., tel. 619/435–8895) is a small shop and restaurant complex. **Downtown:** Horton Plaza (4th Ave. and

Broadway, tel. 619/239–8180) and Seaport Village (Harbor Dr. at Market St., tel. 619/235–4013) house shops and restaurants amid a festive atmosphere. **Hotel Circle:** Fashion Valley Shopping Center (352 Fashion Valley Rd., Mission Valley, tel. 619/297–3381) and Mission Valley Center (1640 Camino del Rio N., Mission Valley, tel. 619/296–6375) are sprawling, outdoor malls, great for people-watching and getting a sense of southern California style. **La Jolla:** University Towne Center (4545 La Jolla Village Dr., tel. 619/546–8858) is an open-air village featuring department stores, specialty shops, sportswear chains, restaurants, and cinemas. **Old Town:** The Bazaar del Mundo (2754 Calhoun St., Old Town, tel. 619/296–3161), a group of shops specializing in high-quality jewelry, fabrics, housewares, gifts, and books, is built around a Mexican courtyard with brightly colored flowers and squawking parrots.

DEPARTMENT STORES Department-store chains with branches at the malls are The Broadway (at Fashion Valley, Horton Plaza, and University Towne Center), May Company (at Mission Valley and University Towne Center), and Nordstrom (at Fashion Valley, University Towne Center, and Horton Plaza). Other department stores are Robinson's (at Horton Plaza and Fashion Valley), Neiman Marcus (Fashion Valley, tel. 619/692–9100), and Saks (Mission Valley Center, tel. 619/260–0030; 7600 Girard Ave., La Jolla, tel. 619/459–4123). For bargains, try Nordstrom Rack (Mission Valley West, tel. 619/296–0143), where discards from Nordstrom's larger stores are sold at great reductions.

OUTDOOR ACTIVITIES

BEACHES Public city beaches—Coronado Beach, Ocean Beach, Mission Beach, Pacific Beach, and La Jolla Shores—have lifeguards (in summer), rest rooms, and fire rings. Silver Strand State Beach (between Imperial Beach and Coronado) is a state park with RV camping facilities; parking for day use is $6. Torrey Pines State Beach (between La Jolla and Del Mar) is also a state park, but without camping facilities. The beach lies under sandstone cliffs topped by treasured Torrey pine trees and hiking trails. Parking is $6, but free parking is available along the streets. The beaches at Mission Bay are best for sunbathing and boating; there have been problems with water pollution—look for signs warning you to stay out of the water. La Jolla Cove is an underwater nature preserve perfect for snorkeling and diving; Scripps Canyon and Black's Beach are also excellent for diving.

BIKING The Embarcadero and Mission Bay are popular biking areas. The California Department of Transportation (tel. 619/688–6699) publishes a free map of San Diego's extensive network of bike trails. Bicycle helmets are common.

FISHING You don't need a license to fish from the piers in Ocean Beach and Imperial Beach, but you do need one (available at all bait-and-tackle shops) for fishing from the shoreline (the Silver Strand is a good spot). Full-day deep-sea fishing trips for tuna, marlin, dorado, and halibut (depending on the season) are offered April through October by Fisherman's Landing (tel. 619/221–8500) and Seaforth (tel. 619/224–3383). Freshwater fishing is available at several stocked lakes in East San Diego County. For general information about area lakes, call 619/465–3474.

GOLF Popular public golf courses are Balboa Park Municipal Golf Course (Golf Course Dr., tel. 619/570–1234), Coronado Golf Course (2000 Visalia Rd., Coronado, tel. 619/435–3121), Mission Bay Golf Center (2702 N. Mission Bay Dr., tel. 619/490-3370), and Torrey Pines Municipal Golf Course (11480 N. Torrey Pines Rd., La Jolla, tel. 619/570-1234).

JOGGING AND WALKING Popular areas for long runs or walks include the Embarcadero (waterfront) downtown, all of Mission Bay,

the Mission Beach boardwalk (which gets very crowded on weekends), Balboa Park, and most beaches at low tide.

TENNIS Public courts are available at Morley Field (tel. 619/295–9278) in Balboa Park, Robb Field (tel. 619/226–3407) in Ocean Beach, and the La Jolla Recreation Center (tel. 619/552–1658; courts available on a first-come, first-served basis only).

ENTERTAINMENT

THEATER San Diego has become a theater town, with acclaimed productions at the Old Globe Theatre at Simon Edison Centre for the Performing Arts (Balboa Park, tel. 619/239–2255), the La Jolla Playhouse at Mandell Weiss Center for the Performing Arts (University of California at San Diego, tel. 619/534–3960), the San Diego Repertory Theatre (Lyceum Theatre, 79 Horton Plaza, tel. 619/235–8025), the Gaslamp Quarter Theatre (playhouse: 547 4th Ave., tel. 619/234–9583; showcase: 444 4th Ave., tel. 619/232–9608), and several smaller theater company venues. Half-price tickets are available on the day of the performance from TIMES ARTS TIX (Broadway Circle, Horton Plaza, downtown, tel. 619/238–3810). Tickets are also available here for the San Diego Symphony, the opera, and other cultural events.

SPECTATOR SPORTS The San Diego Padres play baseball April through September for the National League West at San Diego Jack Murphy Stadium (Stadium Way at Friar's Rd., tel. 619/280–4636). The San Diego Chargers (tel. 619/280–2111) take over the stadium for the National Football League August through December. The San Diego Sockers (tel. 619/224–GOAL) play indoor soccer at the San Diego Sports Arena (3500 Sports Arena Blvd., tel. 619/224–4171) October through May.

San Francisco
California

ordered by the Pacific Ocean, the Golden Gate Strait, and San Francisco Bay, San Francisco encompasses only about 46 square miles. But it is packed with sights: the majestic Golden Gate and San Francisco–Oakland bridges; the hills and steep streets with cable cars rattling up and down; and exuberant architecture, including pastel-colored Victorian houses, stately mansions, and ultramodern downtown high rises. Its temperate climate nutures lush vegetation; and its restaurants are some of the best in the country.

Never a small town, San Francisco went from a settlement of cabins and tents to an instant metropolis during the 1840s gold rush. Since then, this port city has attracted generations of immigrants from around the world, including European, Asian, and Latin American countries. This unusually large number of residents with ties to other cultures flavors the cuisine, commerce, and tenor of the place; it also encourages a tolerance for diversity in customs, beliefs, and lifestyles. As a result, the city's neighborhoods are self-aware and retain strong cultural, political, and ethnic identities. Russian bakeries can still be found in the Richmond District, Irish bars dot the streets of Noe Valley, and taquerias send their enticing smells through the Mission District.

San Francisco's steep hills are notorious, but they do provide spectacular vistas all over town—the crests of the city's seven main hills offer variations on a theme of astounding beauty. From the top of Telegraph Hill you might see jewel-like Angel Island glittering in the sun or the clouds rolling in to cover the bay in a blanket of fog.

ESSENTIAL INFORMATION

WHEN TO GO Anytime of the year is the right time to visit San Francisco. Its temperate marine climate is characterized by winters that rarely reach the freezing point, with average maximum and minimum temperatures

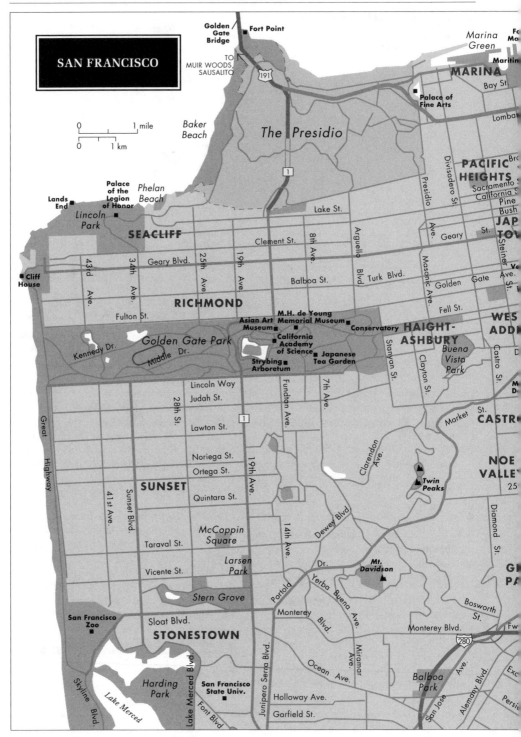

SAN FRANCISCO

0 — 1 mile
0 — 1 km

Golden Gate Bridge
Fort Point
TO MUIR WOODS, SAUSALITO
191
Marina Green
Fo Ma
Maritime
MARINA
Bay St.
Lomba
Palace of Fine Arts
Baker Beach
The Presidio
1
PACIFIC HEIGHTS
Bro
Sacramento
California St.
Pine
Bush
Divisadero St.
Palace of the Legion of Honor
Phelan Beach
Lands End
Lincoln Park
Lake St.
Presidio Ave.
Geary
St.
JAP TO
Ve
SEACLIFF
Clement St.
8th Ave.
Arguello Blvd.
Steiner
Cliff House
43rd Ave.
34th Ave.
Geary Blvd.
25th Ave.
19th Ave.
Balboa St.
Turk Blvd.
Masonic Ave.
Golden Gate Ave.
St.
Fulton St.
RICHMOND
M.H. de Young Memorial Museum
Fell St.
Asian Art Museum
Conservatory
HAIGHT-ASHBURY
WES ADD
Kennedy Dr.
Golden Gate Park
Middle Dr.
California Academy of Science
Japanese Tea Garden
Strybing Arboretum
Stanyan St.
Clayton St.
Buena Vista Park
Castro St.
Lincoln Way
Judah St.
Lawton St.
28th St.
1
Funston Ave.
7th Ave.
Clarendon Ave.
Market St.
CASTRO
M D
NOE VALLE
25
Noriega St.
Ortega St.
SUNSET
41st Ave.
Sunset Blvd.
Quintara St.
19th Ave.
14th Ave.
Dewey Blvd.
Twin Peaks
Diamond St.
Great Highway
McCoppin Square
Taraval St.
Larsen Park
Vicente St.
Dr.
Mt. Davidson
Yerba Buena Ave.
GI PA
Stern Grove
Portola Dr.
Monterey
Miramar Ave.
Bosworth St.
San Francisco Zoo
Sloat Blvd.
STONESTOWN
Monterey Blvd.
280
Fw
Junipero Serra Blvd.
Lake Merced Blvd.
Font Blvd.
Skyline Blvd.
Lake Merced
Harding Park
San Francisco State Univ.
Ocean Ave.
Holloway Ave.
Garfield St.
Balboa Park
San Jose Ave.
Alemany Blvd.
Exc
Persi

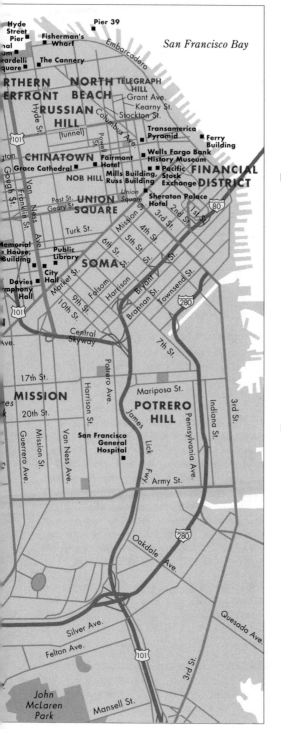

Hyde Street Pier
Pier 39
Fisherman's Wharf
Embarcadero
The Cannery
San Francisco Bay
RTHERN WATERFRONT
NORTH BEACH
TELEGRAPH HILL
Grant Ave.
Kearny St.
Stockton St.
RUSSIAN HILL
Hyde St.
(tunnel)
Columbus Ave.
Powell St.
Transamerica Pyramid
Ferry Building
CHINATOWN
Fairmont Hotel
Wells Fargo Bank History Museum
Grace Cathedral
Mills Building, Russ Building
Pacific Stock Exchange
FINANCIAL DISTRICT
NOB HILL
Union Square
Sheraton Palace Hotel
UNION SQUARE
Post St.
Geary St.
80
Van Ness Ave.
Franklin St.
Gough St.
Turk St.
Mission St.
2nd St.
3rd St.
4th St.
5th St.
6th St.
Memorial House, Building
Public Library
SOMA
Davies Symphony Hall
City Hall
Market St.
9th St.
10th St.
Folsom
Harrison
Bryant St.
Brannan St.
Townsend St.
280
Central Skyway
7th St.
17th St.
MISSION
20th St.
Guerrero Ave.
Mission St.
Van Ness Ave.
Harrison St.
Potrero Ave.
San Francisco General Hospital
Mariposa St.
James
Lick Fwy.
POTRERO HILL
Pennsylvania Ave.
Indiana St.
3rd St.
Army St.
Oakdale Ave.
280
Quesada Ave.
Silver Ave.
Felton Ave.
101
3rd St.
John McLaren Park
Mansell St.

in January at 55° and 41°. Summers are cooler than visitors might expect, with average maximum and minimum temperatures in July of 69° and 51°. Fog usually rolls in from the ocean during summer mornings (and evenings), normally clearing by midmorning. The city's residents most enjoy September, October, and November, when the weather is relatively warm, the fog has usually dispelled, and tour buses have thinned out. Spring has highs in the 60s and lows in the mid-40s.

FESTIVALS AND SPECIAL EVENTS **Feb.:** Chinese New Year celebration runs a week and culminates with the Golden Dragon Parade through downtown and Chinatown. **Apr.:** The Cherry Blossom Festival, a presentation of Japanese culture, includes a parade in Japantown. **May–June:** Carnaval in the Mission District includes a parade, a street festival, and a costume contest. The Lesbian, Gay, and Bisexual Freedom Day Parade takes up most of Market Street for an entire day in June and is usually as entertaining as it is long. **Sept.:** San Francisco Blues Festival takes place on the Great Meadow in Fort Mason. Check the San Francisco Convention and Visitors Bureau (see Tourist Offices, below) for information relating to these and other events.

BARGAINS Many of San Francisco's favorite attractions are free, including a walk across the Golden Gate Bridge, a visit to the Wells Fargo History Museum, and the view from Coit Tower (see Exploring, below). Free summer concerts take place in the Golden Gate Park Music Concourse (tel. 415/666–7107) and on summer Sundays in Stern Grove amphitheater (tel. 415/666–7107) on Sloat Boulevard. To get around, take advantage of the Municipal Railway's Passport ($6 a day, $10 for three days) for buses, cable cars, and the Muni Metro rail system. Half-price tickets to many stage shows go on sale at 11 AM Tuesday–Saturday at the TIX booth (tel. 415/433–7827) on the Stockton Street side of Union Square, between Geary and Post streets. Good areas for inexpensive dining are North Beach, Chinatown, and Clement Street between 2nd and 14th avenues.

For shopping bargains, try the area South of Market Street (SoMa), where you'll find factory outlets at Yerba Buena Square (5th and Howard Sts., tel. 415/543–1275), two blocks from Market Street, and at Six Sixty Center (660 3rd St. at Townsend, tel. 415/227–0464). For souvenirs, try the tourist-oriented shopping area along Fisherman's Wharf.

TOURIST OFFICES San Francisco Convention and Visitors Bureau (201 3rd St., Suite 900, 94103, tel. 415/974–6900) has a Visitors' Information Center on the lower level at Hallidie Plaza, at Market and Powell streets, that is open daily.

EMERGENCIES Police, fire, and ambulance: Dial 911. Hospitals: San Francisco General Hospital (1001 Potrero Ave., tel. 415/206–8000) and University of California Medical Center (505 Parnassus Ave., tel. 415/476–1000) have 24-hour emergency rooms. Doctors: Medical Society Referral Service (tel. 415/561–0853).

ARRIVING AND DEPARTING

BY PLANE Most major U.S. and international airlines serve the city's major airport, San Francisco International Airport (tel. 415/761–0800), which is located about 15 miles south of the city, between Highway 101 and San Francisco Bay. Allow a half-hour driving time from downtown.

Between the Airport and Downtown: SFO Airporter (tel. 415/495–8404) provides bus service ($8) between the airport and many downtown hotels. Supershuttle (airport tel. 415/871–7800, city tel. 415/558–8500) offers van service ($11) between the airport and any destination within San Francisco. Taxis will cost $25–$30 for the half-hour trip from the airport to downtown.

BY TRAIN Amtrak (tel. 800/USA–RAIL) trains stop at the Oakland Depot at 17th and Wood streets; from there, buses will take you across the Bay Bridge to the Transbay Terminal in San Francisco.

BY BUS Greyhound Lines (800/231–2222) serves the city from the Transbay Terminal (1st and Mission Sts.).

GETTING AROUND

Because the city is relatively compact and parking can be difficult to find, you will probably want to explore on foot or by public transportation as much as possible. You may not need a car at all, except perhaps for exploring the Presidio, the Golden Gate Bridge and Golden Gate Park, the Cliff House, or out-of-town destinations.

BY BUS, TROLLEY, AND STREETCAR The San Francisco Municipal Railway, or Muni (tel. 415/673–MUNI), operates the city's transit systems. Diesel and electric trolley buses serve most of the routes on city streets. The Muni Metro trains run underground along Market Street from the Embarcadero westward, then aboveground into the neighborhoods. (Fare: $1, 25¢ for senior citizens.) Exact change is required (bills and tokens may be used on some lines) and free transfers are available.

BY CABLE CAR San Francisco's rolling landmarks have been clattering up and down the hills since 1873; today a ride on a cable car can be just as exciting as a theme-park thrill ride. Two lines begin at Powell and Market streets: The Powell–Hyde line (No. 60), the most spectacular ride, ends up near Ghirardelli Square, while the Powell–Mason line (No. 59) terminates near Fisherman's Wharf. To avoid crowds and long waits in line, try the scenic California Street line (No. 61) that runs from Market and Drumm streets to Van Ness Avenue. Tickets are sold from machines at cable-car terminals and the Nob Hill intersection. Exact change is required. *Tel. 415/673–MUNI. Tickets: $3 adults, $1 children 5–17, $1 for age 65 and older.*

BY BART Bay Area Rapid Transit trains (tel. 415/788–BART) travel under San Francisco Bay from Market Street stations to Oakland, Berkeley, and other East Bay cities (fare: 80¢–$3).

BY CAR A car is not a necessity for getting around San Francisco. Driving is a challenge because of the city's hills, many one-way streets, and heavy daytime traffic. Parking is also a problem; downtown parking lots are often full and always expensive. Note that since the 1989 earthquake, most maps of the city are out of date. The Embarcadero freeway between I–80 (the Bay Bridge approach) and Broadway was demolished in 1991, and traffic returned to street level along the Embarcadero. Highway 101 south freeway access is available at Oak Street; exits and entrances beyond that have been demolished.

BY TAXI Fares are high in San Francisco ($3.50 for the first mile, $1.80 for each additional mile), although most trips are relatively short. Hailing a passing cab is usually possible only downtown and in the Civic Center area, so you may need to phone ahead or use the nearest hotel taxi stand to grab a taxi. Major cab companies include Yellow (tel. 415/626–2345) and Veteran's (tel. 415/552–1300).

REST STOPS Although the city maintains few public bathrooms, you can find accessible rest rooms at the shopping complexes on the Northern Waterfront, at the San Francisco Public Library in the Civic Center, and downtown at major department stores and hotels.

GUIDED TOURS Orientation: Golden Gate Tours (tel. 415/788–5775) offers van and bus tours in and around the city; senior-citizen discounts are available. The Gray Line (tel. 415/558–9400) uses double-decker buses for tours of the city and beyond. The Great Pacific Tour (tel. 415/626–4499) provides 13-passenger vans for sightseeing in the area.

Walking: The Friends of the San Francisco Public Library (tel. 415/558–3981) conducts free city walking tours, lasting 1–1¹/₂ hours. The Friends of Recreation and Parks (tel. 415/221–1311) offers free, guided 1¹/₂- to 2-hour walking tours of Golden Gate Park May–October.

EXPLORING

Few cities in the world pack so much diversity into so little space as San Francisco does. Though most of San Francisco's attractions are located in the northeastern quarter of the city, the outlying neighborhoods provide their own kinds of entertainment. The city's

legendary hills may slow you down a bit, but steps replace sidewalks on the steepest slopes, and the views from the top of the streets are breathtaking. (And, of course, it's only uphill halfway.) The San Francisco Municipal Railway's Street and Transit Map, available at newsstands and bookstores, charts all the city routes.

Bay Cruises and Alcatraz. A ferry ride on San Francisco Bay provides a fresh perspective of the city's skyline, the East Bay, and Marin County. The least expensive trip is on one of the Golden Gate ferries (tel. 415/332–6600), leaving from the Ferry Building at the foot of Market Street to Sausalito. Red and White Fleet (at Pier 41 and 43¹/₂ on Fisherman's Wharf, tel. 415/546–2628) offers a variety of bay cruises, including a ride under the Golden Gate Bridge; it also provides service to Alcatraz Island, where National Park Service guides lead excellent tours of the isle's infamous prison, now partly in ruins, which closed in 1963. (Dress warmly and wear comfortable shoes for the tour.) Advance reservations are recommended for the Alcatraz trip (tel. 415/546–2628).

California Academy of Sciences. This excellent attraction contains a natural-history museum, a planetarium, and the Steinhart Aquarium, which has a dramatic 100,000-gallon tank housing 14,000 creatures. *Golden Gate Park, tel. 415/750–7145. Open daily. Admission charged. Free 1st Wed. of each month.*

Chinatown. The largest Chinese settlement outside Asia, this neighborhood was established in the 1850s and now extends from the dragon-crowned gateway spanning Grant Avenue at Bush Street north to Broadway. Grant and Stockton streets may get crowded, but they have bountiful food markets, bakeries, restaurants, and souvenir shops, as well as pagoda roofs and Chinese street signs. A walk along Waverly Place (which parallels Grant Ave. from Sacramento to Washington Sts.) will give you a sense of Chinatown's past. The **Chinese Cultural Center** offers art exhibitions and neighborhood walking tours on Saturdays. *750 Kearny St. in Holiday Inn,* tel. 415/986–1822. Open Tues.–Sat. Admission free.

Civic Center. This area incorporates adjoining cultural institutions in an impressive building complex. The French Renaissance–style **City Hall** (filling the block bounded by Van Ness Avenue and Polk, Grove, and McAllister streets) dominates the area, with its dome higher than the Capitol's in Washington, D.C. Completed in 1915, City Hall was gradually surrounded by other civic buildings: the opulent **War Memorial Opera House** (Van Ness Ave. at Grove St.); the **Veterans' Building** (Van Ness Ave. and McAllister St.), which houses the **Museum of Modern Art** with permanent and traveling collections of contemporary artists and a café; the **Public Library** (McAllister and Larkin Sts.), with a third-floor history museum; and the glass-fronted **Davies Symphony Hall** (Van Ness Ave. and Grove St.). Nearby the Civic Center is a row of art galleries, crafts shops, and cafés on Hayes Street (between Franklin and Gough Sts.). Museum of Modern Art: tel. 415/863–8800. Open Tues.–Sun. Admission charged. Library museum: tel. 415/557–4567. Open Tues.–Sat. Admission free. Symphony Hall and Opera House tour information, tel. 415/552–8338.

Financial District. Once called "Wall Street West," this area, which bustles during weekdays, runs north along Montgomery Street from Market Street. You might want to begin your walk at the grand **Sheraton Palace Hotel** (2 New Montgomery St., tel. 415/543–0671) with its elegant Garden Court restaurant. Architectural highlights in the area include the **Mills Building** (220 Montgomery St.), which survived the 1906 earthquake; the Gothic-style **Russ Building** (235 Montgomery); and the **Pacific Stock Exchange** (Pine and Sansome Sts., tel. 415/393–7969), with monumental sculptures from the 1930s and free tours by advance reservation. The 853-foot **Transamerica Pyramid** (Montgomery and Clay Sts.) has a free observation area on the 27th floor (open weekdays) and a relaxing redwood grove on its east side. The **Wells Fargo Bank History Museum** displays gold nuggets, original Western art, a bandit's mementos, and an 1850s red stagecoach. 420 Montgomery St., tel. 415/396–2619. Open weekdays, except bank holidays. Admission free.

Fisherman's Wharf and the Northern Waterfront. You'll see more tourists and souvenir stands than fishing boats along the Wharf (Piers 43–47 at Taylor and Jefferson Sts.), but a stroll here can be rewarding as you pass by numerous seafood restaurants, craftsmen selling their wares, and street performers. East of the Wharf looms **Pier 39,** which includes a mall with shops, eateries, and free entertainment. South of the Wharf is **The Cannery** (Leavenworth and Beach Sts.), a three-story structure packed with shops and cafés. Another block west on Beach Street stands **Ghirardelli Square,** a charming complex of renovated 19th-century brick factory buildings with unusual gift shops, galleries, and restaurants. Across the street from the complex, the **National Maritime Museum** offers exhibits relating to maritime history and a collection of historic boats and ships at the **Hyde Street Pier.** Aquatic Park at the foot of Polk St. (Pier is 2 blocks east), tel. 415/556–3002. Open daily. Admission charged to Pier.

Golden Gate Bridge and Fort Mason. Built in the late 1930s, the **Golden Gate** is a 2-mile, Art Deco–style orange suspension bridge that connects the city to Marin County. A city Muni bus (No. 28) reaches the toll plaza on the San Francisco side, where there is also a parking lot for motorists. Though it can often be foggy and windy during the free walk across the bridge (warm clothing is needed), you'll have unparalleled views of the Bay Area on the east and west walkways and on the Marin side. Below the toll plaza, down a path and stairs (also accessible by car from Long Ave.) is the handsome **Fort Point** (tel. 415/556–1693), built in the 1850s to protect the city during the Civil War from sea invaders; the site is now a military museum with a superb bay view from the top floor (open daily; admission free). From here, hardy walkers may elect to stroll about 3$\frac{1}{2}$ miles along the **Golden Gate Promenade** to **Fort Mason** and the Northern Waterfront area (see above). The bridge is situated just north of the

Presidio, with more than 1,500 acres of hills, woods, and picnic sites that also allow walking and jogging. *Main entrance: Lombard and Lyon Sts. Open daily. Admission free.*

Golden Gate Park. Developed from sand dunes and weeds at the end of the 19th century, this park encompasses 1,000 acres of greenery, lakes, playgrounds, and museums stretching from Stanyan Street in the Haight–Ashbury neighborhood west to the Pacific Ocean. Although most visitors visit the park by car, Muni buses also provide service from downtown. Joggers, bicyclists, skaters, and picnickers flock here, and lawns and benches are available for relaxing. The oldest building is the ornate copy of London's Kew Gardens greenhouse, the Victorian **Conservatory of Flowers,** with a tropical garden and many rare flowers. Several of the park's major attractions are located in its eastern section: the **M. H. de Young Museum** and the **Asian Art Museum** (*see below*); the serene **Japanese Tea Garden,** with small ponds, flowering shrubs, and a teahouse; the **California Academy of Sciences** (*see above*); and the lovely **Strybing Arboretum.** Just beyond the park's western edge, where the Great Highway meets Point Lobos Avenue, is the Cliff House, a historic restaurant complex (and part of the Golden Gate National Recreation Area) overlooking the Pacific and Seal Rocks. To reach the park by public transportation, take the Muni 21-Hayes or 5-Fulton bus westbound at downtown Market St. to 10th Ave., and walk south into the park. *Conservatory: tel. 415/666–7017. Open daily. Admission charged. Japanese Garden: tel. 415/666–7017. Open daily. Admission charged. Arboretum: tel. 415/661–0688. Open daily. Admission free.*

M. H. de Young Memorial Museum and the Asian Art Museum. One of the West Coast's best art museums, the de Young features American art, with special collections of painting, sculpture, textiles, and decorative arts from Colonial times through the 20th century. It also has a fine shop and a pleasant café. The de Young adjoins the Asian Art Museum, with more than 10,000 sculptures, paintings, and ceramics. *Golden Gate Park. de Young Museum: tel. 415/863–3330. Asian*

Art Museum: tel. 415/668–8921. Open Wed.– Sun. One admission charge allows entrance to both museums. Free 1st Wed. of each month.

Mission Dolores. Begun in 1782, this adobe building, the 6th of 21 missions founded by the Franciscans, has a small museum and an adjacent cemetery with more than 5,000 Indian graves. For public transportation, take the Muni Metro J–Church car to 16th Street. *Dolores and 16th Sts., tel. 415/621–8203. Open daily. Admission charged.*

Muir Woods National Monument. Located 17 miles northwest of San Francisco, this 550-acre park contains majestic redwood groves. Some trees are nearly 250 feet tall and 1,000 years old. The weather is usually cool and often wet. By car, take Highway 101 north to the Mill Valley–Muir Woods Exit; note that traffic into the park can be heavy during summer, so this is one excursion worth taking by bus. For Golden Gate Transit bus information, call 415/332–6600; for Gray Line bus tour information, call 415/558–9400.

Nob Hill. A cable-car ride, or steep hike, up Powell Street from Union Square, this neighborhood was once the site of the estates belonging to the city's most prominent 19th-century robber barons; it is still home to many of the city's elite. The Gothic **Grace Cathedral** (1051 Taylor St.), the city seat of the Episcopal Church, is notable for its gilded bronze doors. Other landmarks in the area are the regal **Fairmont Hotel** (California and Mason Sts.), with its flamboyant red, black, and gold lobby, and the stately **Mark Hopkins Hotel** across the street. For a relaxing stop, visit the well-kept **Huntington Park** (California and Mason Sts.). From Nob Hill, you can hop on a Hyde Street cable car and ride to Lombard Street for a stroll down the brick-paved and flower-lined "crookedest street in the world," which leads to North Beach (*see below*).

North Beach and Telegraph Hill. Centered around Washington Square Park at Powell and Union streets and also around Columbus Avenue north of Broadway, this easygoing neighborhood, originally settled by Italians during the gold rush era, has several reasonably priced Italian restaurants, and a few other ethnic dining spots as well. A few highlights include **Panelli Brothers** (1419 Stockton St.) and **Molinari's** (373 Columbus Ave.), two popular delicatessens, and **Caffe Puccini** (411 Columbus Ave.) and **Caffe Roma** (414 Columbus Ave.), for cappuccino and pastries. Farther south of these cafés is **City Lights Bookstore** (261 Columbus Ave.), a landmark from the 1950s bohemian years with a fine book selection for browsing. From Washington Square, you can proceed to **Coit Tower,** a legacy of eccentric millionaire Lillie Hitchcock Coit on the crest of Telegraph Hill; here you'll have unparalleled views of the neighborhood, the bay, and downtown. The east end of Lombard Street continues uphill to Coit Tower, but there can be a long waiting line for the small parking lot. If you don't have a car, you can reach Coit Tower from North Beach by walking up Grant Avenue and following the steps to the right on Filbert Street, or taking the Muni 39–Coit bus from Washington Square. The most memorable way down from the tower is along the Filbert Street steps that pass wooded gardens and Victorian cottages from Montgomery Street east to the base of the hill. *Coit Tower: tel. 415/362–0808. Open daily. Admission charged.*

Palace of Fine Arts. Reconstructed in the 1960s, this rose-colored Roman Classic–style structure with massive columns, a great rotunda, and a swan-filled lagoon is the sole survivor of a 1915 exposition. The interior houses the first-rate Exploratorium, a popular hands-on science museum with 600 exhibits. *Baker and Beach Sts., the Marina, tel. 415/563–7337. Open Wed.–Sun. Admission charged.*

Sausalito. This hillside town on a sheltered site along San Francisco Bay in Marin County is filled with shops, cafés, and seafood restaurants; its views across the bay to San Francisco, however, are the prime attractions. By car, cross the Golden Gate Bridge and take Highway 101 north to the Sausalito exit. The ferry ride from the Embarcadero is more enjoyable than the drive. *Golden Gate Ferry, tel.*

415/332–6600. Red and White Fleet, tel. 415/546–2628.

Union Square. Bounded by Geary, Stockton, Sutter, and Powell streets, this area, the heart of downtown, has been San Francisco's retail center for more than a century. Here you'll find the city's finest department stores and boutiques. About 40 hotels are situated within three blocks of the square, and the downtown theater district is also nearby. The square itself, planted with palms and flowers, attracts a mixed crowd. The biggest retail stores around the square include **Macy's** (Stockton and O'Farrell Sts., tel. 415/397–3333), **Neiman Marcus** (150 Stockton St., tel. 415/362–3900), **I. Magnin** (Stockton and Geary Sts., tel. 415/362–2100), and **Saks Fifth Avenue** (384 Post St., tel. 415/986–4300). A short walk from the square are the more reasonably priced **Emporium** (Market St. near Powell St., tel. 415/764–2222) department store with a complete stock of clothing and home furnishings; and the upscale **San Francisco Shopping Centre** at Powell and Market streets, which is topped by **Nordstrom** (tel. 415/243–8500), with designer clothing and first-rate service. The following are worth a visit: the ornate atrium from the old City of Paris department store installed within Neiman Marcus; **Gump's** (250 Post St.), the elegant importer; the only San Francisco building designed by Frank Lloyd Wright (140 Maiden La., just east of the square); the glass-roofed **Crocker Galleria** (Post and Kearny Sts.), with 50 shops, restaurants, and services; and the art galleries upstairs in buildings around the intersection of Grant and Sutter streets.

HOTELS AND INNS

The recent construction and restoration of plush grand hotels in San Francisco has been matched by the extensive transformation of smaller properties into distinctive, European-style lodgings that offer warm personal service—often at half the price of the expensive hotels. The city also has a good selection of bed-and-breakfasts, often located in Victorian-style structures. Many of the city's budget accommodations are found a block or two west of Union Square and around the Civic Center, though some are also located in the downtown area alongside the pricier establishments. Because of the city's year-round appeal, few hotels offer off-season rates. Most motels are located along Lombard Street between Van Ness Avenue and the Golden Gate Bridge approach.

Reservation services include San Francisco Reservations (22 2nd St., 4th Floor, 94105, tel. 415/227–1500 or 800/667–1550). You can save money by staying in private homes and apartments, available by contacting Bed & Breakfast San Francisco (Box 420009, 94142, tel. 415/931–3083) and Bed & Breakfast International San Francisco (Box 282910, 94128–2910, tel. 415/696–1690 or 800/872–4500; fax 415/696–1699).

Price categories for double occupancy, excluding 11% tax, are *Expensive*, $110–$175; *Moderate*, $75–$110; and *Inexpensive*, under $75.

UNION SQUARE/DOWNTOWN **Petit Auberge.** The French countryside was imported to downtown San Francisco to create this charming bed-and-breakfast. Calico-printed wallpaper, fluffy down comforters, and French reproduction antiques decorate the rooms. *863 Bush St., 94108, tel. 415/928–6000, fax 415/775–5717. 26 rooms. Breakfast room, afternoon tea, working fireplaces in some rooms. AE, MC, V. Moderate–Expensive.*

York Hotel. This carefully renovated hotel located between Union Square and the Polk Street shopping area boasts its own cabaret— the stylish Plush Room—and complimentary breakfast. *940 Sutter St., 94109, tel. 415/885–6800 or 800/227–3608, fax 415/885–2115. 96 rooms. Fitness center, limousine service, valet/laundry service. AE, DC, MC, V. Moderate–Expensive.*

Bedford. Cheerful floral prints and canopy beds dominate the rooms in this stylishly renovated 17-story hotel, four blocks from Union Square. *761 Post St., 94109, tel. 415/673–6040; 800/227–5642; or in CA,* 800/652–1889, fax 415/563–6739. 144 rooms. *Restaurant, complimentary wine in afternoon, laundry service. AE, DC, MC, V. Moderate.*

Beresford Arms. Built in 1910 and full of Old World charm, the Beresford earns high marks for the complimentary wine and cheese served afternoons in the grand lobby. Standard rooms have queen-size beds and small refrigerators, while the suites with whirlpool baths and full kitchens are perfect for families. *701 Post St., 94109, tel. 415/673–2600 or 800/533–6533, fax 415/474–0449. 96 rooms. Valet/laundry service. AE, DC, MC, V. Moderate.*

Cartwright. Antiques, fresh flowers, and afternoon tea add to the distinctive surroundings of this friendly, family-owned hotel just off Union Square; rooms feature brass or wood-carved beds and refrigerators. *524 Sutter St., 94102, tel. 415/421–2865 or 800/227–3844, fax 415/421–2865. 114 rooms. Restaurant, concierge, valet/laundry service. AE, DC, MC, V. Moderate.*

Chancellor Hotel. This venerable hotel near the cable-car line has been attracting a loyal clientele since it was built in 1914; the rooms have been elegantly redecorated with cherry-wood furniture. *433 Powell St., 94102, tel. 415/362–2004 or 800/428–4748, fax 415/362–1403. 140 rooms, 6 suites. Restaurant, lounge. AE, DC, MC, V. Moderate.*

King George. Built to welcome visitors to the 1915 Panama Pacific International Exposition, this elegantly refurbished Georgian-style hotel in the theater district has a quaint Bread and Honey tearoom. *334 Mason St., 94102, tel. 415/781–5050 or 800/288–6005, fax 415/391–6976. 143 rooms. Bellman, 24-hr room service, special package rates. AE, DC, MC, V. Moderate.*

Mark Twain. Cheerfully decorated rooms with refrigerators, an attentive staff, and a location just two blocks from Union Square make this hotel a good choice. *345 Taylor St., 94102, tel. 415/673–2332, 800/227–4074, or 800/622–0873 in CA, fax 415/398–0733. 116 rooms. Restaurant, lobby bar, valet/laundry* service, sun deck, 24-hr service/security, special package rates. AE, DC, MC, V. Moderate.

The Aston Pickwick. A renovation in 1991 dramatically upgraded the rooms in this Gothic-style brick hotel across from the historic Old Mint and a half block from the elegant San Francisco Shopping Centre. 85 5th St., 94103, tel. 415/421–7500 or 800/227–3282, fax 415/243–8066. 190 rooms. Restaurant, lounge, valet/laundry service, special package rates. AE, DC, MC, V. Inexpensive–Moderate.

Adelaide Inn. Although the bedspreads and drapes may not always match, this cozy bargain offers clean rooms, an amiable staff, and complimentary Continental breakfast. 5 Isadora Duncan Court, off Taylor St. between Geary and Post Sts., 94102, tel. 415/441–2474. 16 rooms, all share bath. MC, V. Inexpensive.

Amsterdam. This European-style bed-and-breakfast inn with clean, bright rooms looking out from a prim Victorian building is a good value for its location between Union Square and Nob Hill. 749 Taylor St., 94108, tel. 415/673–3277 or 800/637–3444, fax 415/673–0453. 32 rooms, 5 with shared bath. Breakfast included, cable TV, some kitchens. AE, MC, V. Inexpensive.

Grant Plaza. This bargain-priced hotel at the entrance of Chinatown has small but clean rooms with plain, whitewashed furniture and a lovely stained-glass dome on the sixth floor. 465 Grant Ave., 94108, tel. 415/434–3883 or 800/472–6899, fax 415/434–3886. 72 rooms. AE, MC, V. Inexpensive.

CIVIC CENTER **Hotel Richelieu.** The Richelieu's rooms acquired new beds, furniture, and carpeting in an extensive 1988 renovation that helped re-create a Victorian-style atmosphere. The hotel is convenient to public transportation. 1050 Van Ness Ave., 94109, tel. 415/673–4711 or 800/227–3608, fax 415/673–9362. No-smoking rooms available, 24-hr restaurant adjacent. AE, DC, MC, V. Moderate.

Pensione San Francisco. This European-style hotel offers smartly decorated rooms and lobby areas, plus excellent facilities, at bargain prices. 1668 Market St., 94102, tel. 415/864–1271 or 800/886–1271. 36 rooms, all share baths. 24-hr concierge, laundry/dry cleaning service, color TVs and VCRs. V. Inexpensive.

FISHERMAN'S WHARF **Columbus Motor Inn.** Refurbished in 1991, this attractive motel between North Beach and Fisherman's Wharf has airy rooms with bay windows and two-bedroom suites that are ideal for families. 1075 Columbus Ave., 94133, tel. 415/885–1492. 45 rooms. No-smoking rooms, cable TV, parking. AE, DC, MC, V. Moderate.

LOMBARD STREET/MARINA DISTRICT **Cow Hollow Motor Inn.** This large, modern motel balances clean, recently renovated rooms with a convenient Marina area location—only four blocks from the bay. 2190 Lombard St., 94123, tel. 415/921–5800, fax 415/922–8515. 129 rooms. Restaurant, access to health club, kitchens. AE, DC, MC, V. Moderate.

Marina Inn. Dainty flowered wallpaper, poster beds, country pine furniture, and fresh flowers give the rooms here an English country air. 3110 Octavia St. at Lombard St., 94123, tel. 415/928–1000. 40 rooms. AE, MC, V. Moderate.

Vagabond Inn. The Vagabond offers comfortable bed-and-breakfast accommodations at motel prices. Continental breakfast is served in a cozy central sitting room, while turned-down beds and chocolate greet guests at the end of each day. 2550 Van Ness Ave. near Lombard St., 94109, tel. 415/776–7500 or 800/522–1555. 132 rooms. Continental breakfast included, restaurant, valet/laundry service, kitchens. AE, DC, MC, V. Moderate.

Town House Motel. This appealing two-story wood-and-stucco motel is one of the best values on Lombard Street. All the rooms have been recently renovated. 1650 Lombard St., 94123, tel. 415/885–5163 or 800/255–1516, fax 415/992–7090. Parking, TV with 24-hr movie channel, shuttle from airport. AE, DC, MC, V. Inexpensive–Moderate.

LOWER PACIFIC HEIGHTS **Laurel Motor Inn.** This relaxed, vaguely Southwestern-style motel is conveniently situated near cafés, antiques stores, and public transportation. *444 Presidio Ave. at California St., 94115, tel. 415/567–8467 or 800/552–8735, fax 415/928–1866. 49 rooms. Kitchens, parking. AE, DC, MC, V. Moderate.*

NOB HILL **Nob Hill Motel.** The Nob Hill is an easygoing—but efficient—family-run motel centrally located between Van Ness Avenue and Polk Street, on a quiet spot just off "motel row." *1630 Pacific Ave., 94109, tel. 415/775–8160 or 800/343–6900. 29 rooms. Refrigerators, parking. AE, DC, MC, V. Inexpensive.*

MOTELS

MODERATE **Bel Aire Travelodge** (3201 Steiner St., 94123, tel. 415/921–5162 or 800/255–3050). 32 rooms; parking. **Comfort Inn** (240 7th St., 94103, tel. 415/861–6469 or 800/544–0502). 68 rooms; parking. **Days Inn at the Wharf** (2358 Lombard St., 94123, tel. 415/922–2010, 800/325–2525, fax 415/563–7958). 22 rooms; parking. **S.F. Central Travelodge** (1707 Market St., 94103, tel. 415/621–6775 or 800/255–3050). 84 rooms; coffee shop, parking, valet/laundry service. **Valu Inn by Nendels** (900 Franklin St., 94109, tel. 415/885–6865, 800/843–4021, or 800/223–9626 in CA, fax 415/474–1652). 59 rooms; parking, health club.

DINING

The signature style of San Francisco has become "California cuisine," which emphasizes lightly grilled fish and poultry and fresh seasonal produce from nearby farms. Chinese dining spots feature steamed dishes, and vegetarian food is available in almost every restaurant, even in the Mission District's smallest family-run Mexican eatery. Most restaurants are usually willing to serve sauces on the side and comply with dietary requests. Visitors may eat well here without straining their budgets. Price categories per person, excluding 8.5% tax, service, and drinks, are

Expensive, over $25; *Moderate,* $15–$25; and *Inexpensive,* under $15.

UNION SQUARE/DOWNTOWN **Bentley's Oyster Bar & Restaurant.** The bustling bar here serves 12 different types of oysters, while the quiet dining room upstairs offers grilled fish in a variety of creative sauces, as well as crab cakes and New Orleans–style gumbo. There's live piano music during the week and live jazz on Friday and Saturday nights downstairs in the bar. *185 Sutter St., tel. 415/989–6895. AE, DC, MC, V. Moderate.*

Corona Bar & Grill. This sleek, very stylish restaurant offers a light and creative menu that draws heavily from Mexican and southwestern cuisines. Specialties include corn pasta ravioli, Petaluma duck burritos, and corn-and-shiitake-mushroom quesadillas. *88 Cyril Magnin St. north of Market St., tel. 415/392–5500. AE, DC, MC, V. Moderate.*

Janot's. This redbrick brasserie, located in an alley near Union Square, is presided over by a French owner and French chefs. Specialties include calves' liver sautéed with bacon and onions, and cassoulet of lingo beans with prawns, scallops, and house-made seafood sausage. *44 Campton Pl. east of Union Sq., tel. 415/392–5373. AE, MC, V. Moderate.*

Les Joulins. This friendly, unpretentious French bistro near Union Square serves a fresh salad of the day, as well as daily specials of fish, shellfish, chicken, and pasta. *44 Ellis St. near Stockton St., tel. 415/397–5397. AE, DC, MC, V. Moderate.*

Salmagundi. The soups and fresh salads change daily at this no-nonsense downtown cafeteria, which also prepares sandwiches. *442 Geary St., tel. 415/441–0894. No credit cards. Inexpensive.*

Souper Salad. Imaginative salads and hearty soups are the highlights at this comfortable café on the lower level of the San Francisco Shopping Centre. *865 Market St., tel. 415/777–9922. No credit cards. Inexpensive.*

EMBARCADERO **Ciao.** Light, contemporary Italian food is served in a bright high-tech setting accented by bronze and chrome. Specialties include squid-ink half-moon pasta stuffed with white fish in a shrimp sauce, osso buco (veal roast), and *crespelle all' aragosta* (crepes with lobster in a lobster sauce). *230 Jackson St. north of the Financial District, tel. 415/982–9500. AE, DC, MC, V. Moderate.*

Harbor Village. This beautifully designed branch of a Hong Kong restaurant, with antiques and teak furnishings, prepares subtly seasoned Cantonese cuisine, dim sum lunches, and fresh seafood from the restaurant's own tanks. *Embarcadero Center 4, Sacramento and Drumm Sts., tel. 415/781–8833. AE, MC, V. Moderate.*

Splendido's. Mediterranean cooking is the focus at this stylish dining spot. Specialties include shellfish soup and warm goat-cheese-and-ratatouille salad; for tamer gourmets there are hearty homemade soups and pizzas topped with fresh vegetables. *Embarcadero 4, Sacramento and Drumm Sts., tel. 415/986–3222. AE, DC, MC, V. Moderate.*

CIVIC CENTER Zuni Cafe Grill. Zuni's Italian–Mediterranean menu and its unpretentious atmosphere pack in the crowds from morning to late evening. Grilled fish and chicken are among the specialties, and even the hamburgers have an Italian accent: They're served on herbed focaccia buns. *1658 Market St. west of the Civic Center, tel. 415/552–2522. AE, MC, V. Moderate.*

Max's Opera Cafe. At this lively, cheerful restaurant in an upscale condo complex, deli sandwiches, salads, and grilled fish and chicken are served by singing waiters. *601 Van Ness Ave., tel. 415/771–7300. AE, MC, V. Inexpensive–Moderate.*

Stars Café. Stars Café is affiliated with the adjacent, upscale Stars restaurant but without the exorbitant prices; for the moment, the Café is also one of the city's more "hip" eating places. The never-dull menu adds a healthy, exotic edge to its soups, gourmet salads, and fresh pastas. *555 Golden Gate Ave. in the Civic Center, tel. 415/861–4344. AE, MC, V. Inexpensive.*

Vicolo. This downtown restaurant is perfect for lunch or a light dinner and is conveniently located near the Opera House and Symphony Hall. Besides the crisp salad selections, the menu features cornmeal-crust pizzas with some very imaginative (and *very* California) toppings. *201 Ivy St. off Franklin St., tel. 415/863–2382. No credit cards. Inexpensive.*

FINANCIAL DISTRICT Yank Sing. This tea house has grown by leaps and bounds with the popularity of dim sum, those small steamed or fried dumplings filled with shrimp, meat, or vegetables. A wider choice of Chinese cuisine is also offered. *427 Battery St. north of the Financial District, tel. 415/362–1640; 49 Stevenson St., south of Market near 1st St., tel. 415/495–4510. AE, DC, MC, V. Inexpensive.*

FISHERMAN'S WHARF/NORTHERN WATERFRONT

Gaylord's. Succulent Indian meals are served with polite efficiency at the popular—and sometimes impossibly crowded—Gaylord's. Choose from a selection of mildly spiced northern Indian food as well as from meats and breads baked in Gaylord's tandoori oven. There's also a wide choice of vegetarian dishes. *Ghirardelli Sq., tel. 415/771–8822; Embarcadero 1, Sacramento and Battery Sts., tel. 415/397–7775. AE, DC, MC, V. Moderate.*

JAPANTOWN Mifune. This amiable café in Japan Center specializes in the Japanese version of fast food: wheat or buckwheat noodles in steaming broth, with egg, seafood, and vegetable toppings. Tempura and grilled entrées are also available. *1737 Post St. near Fillmore St., tel. 415/922–0337. AE, DC, MC, V. Inexpensive.*

MARINA Greens at Fort Mason. Even resolute carnivores enjoy the wide range of creative vegetarian dishes at this celebrated dining spot; homemade breads and desserts are as exceptional as the bay views. *Building A, Fort Mason, Marina Blvd. at Laguna St., tel. 415/771–6222. MC, V. Moderate–Expensive.*

Scott's Seafood Grill and Bar. This pleasant restaurant has made its reputation on fresh fish—usually about a dozen choices—simply but delicately prepared. *2400 Lombard St.*

(try to arrive by 6:30 PM), tel. 415/563–8988; Embarcadero 3, Sacramento and Davis Sts., tel. 415/981–0622. AE, DC, MC, V. Moderate.

MIDTOWN **Golden Turtle.** This popular Vietnamese café has an extensive menu, including stir-fried and heart-healthy steamed dishes and a variety of salads and first-course vegetables. *2211 Van Ness Ave. near Broadway, tel. 415/441–4419. AE, MC, V. Inexpensive.*

NORTH BEACH **Buca Giovanni.** In a romantic subterranean dining room, you can sample a fine selection of Italian Tuscan cuisine, including house-made pasta and a selection of heart-healthy chicken and fish dishes. *800 Greenwich St., tel. 415/776–7766. AE, MC, V. Moderate.*

Capp's Corner. This is one of the last of North Beach's family-style Italian restaurants—the sort of place where diners sit at long Formica tables and feast on serious servings of soup, salad, roast chicken, and pasta. *1600 Powell St., tel. 415/989–2589. AE, DC, MC, V. Inexpensive.*

PACIFIC HEIGHTS **North India.** This cozy Indian restaurant specializes in chicken, prawns, and lamb quickly cooked in the heat of tandoori ovens, as well as curries and vegetarian dishes. *3131 Webster St. near Lombard St., tel. 415/931–1556. AE, DC, MC, V. Moderate.*

SOUTH OF MARKET **Chevy's.** This big, boisterous Mexican establishment stakes its reputation on using the freshest ingredients and sauces, and offers a good selection of grilled chicken and fish dishes in addition to more traditional Mexican creations. *4th and Howard Sts. near Moscone Convention Center, tel. 415/543–8060. MC, V. Inexpensive.*

SHOPPING

San Francisco's famous sourdough bread will be fresher and probably less costly from a North Beach bakery or neighborhood grocery store than from the airport gift shop. (The most authentic loaf is wrapped in a paper bag, not plastic.) For a variety of chocolate gifts, try the Ghirardelli Chocolate Shop (900 North Point, Ghirardelli Sq., tel. 412/474–3938) and the downtown shop Ghirardelli Chocolate (44 Stockton St. at Union Sq., tel. 415/397–3615). The city is known for Asian imports, and everything from trinkets to silk brocade can be found in Chinatown and Japantown. Cost Plus (Taylor St. between Beach and Bay Sts., tel. 415/885–5100) near Fisherman's Wharf is a good place to buy inexpensive imported gifts. Specialized books about San Francisco and the Bay Area can be found at the National Maritime Museum and Hyde Street Pier (Aquatic Park, tel. 415/556–3002) and at the City Lights Bookstore (261 Columbus Ave., tel. 415/362–8193) in North Beach.

MAJOR SHOPPING DISTRICTS Downtown's Union Square is flanked by the city's best department stores as well as expensive boutiques (*see* Exploring, *above*). Also downtown is South of Market Street (SoMa), where you'll find discount outlets (*see* Bargains, *above*). Chinatown, which is north of Union Square, has a seemingly endless choice of shops selling Chinese silks and jewelry, toy trinkets, pottery, baskets, and groceries (*see* Exploring, *above*). Nearby North Beach offers small clothing stores, antiques shops, or eccentric specialty shops (*see* Exploring, *above*). Fisherman's Wharf and the Northern Waterfront have Pier 39, the Anchorage, Ghirardelli Square, and The Cannery, four renovated complexes full of shops, restaurants, and outdoor entertainment (*see* Exploring, *above*).

Between Gough and Fillmore streets and south of the Marina and Fort Mason, Union Street shines with contemporary apparel, jewelry, and antiques shops; more antiques can be found on Sacramento Street near Presidio Avenue. Under one roof, the Japan Center (Geary and Post Sts.) in Japantown is usually uncrowded; it has crafts and houseware shops, where you can find antique kimonos, tansu chests, and fine porcelains. Once the nation's hippie headquarters in the '60s, the Haight Street area, stretching from Central Avenue to Stanyan Street, now features vintage fashions from the '40s and '50s, Mexican art, and collectibles. Nearby Castro

Street is the focus of the city's gay and lesbian communities; stores along the lively avenue feature crafts, health foods, clothes, and some very interesting clothing accessories.

OUTDOOR ACTIVITIES

BIKING Bike routes (tel. 415/666–7201) in Golden Gate Park (*see* Exploring, *above*) include one route through the park to Lake Merced and another from the south end of the city to the Golden Gate Bridge. Many bike-rental shops are located on Stanyan Street across from Golden Gate Park; major streets in the park are closed to cars on Sundays.

BOATING Stow Lake (tel. 415/752–0347) in Golden Gate Park has rowboat, pedal boat, and electric boat rentals.

FISHING Fishing boats leave from Fisherman's Wharf for salmon outside the bay or striped bass and giant sturgeon within the bay. Licenses can be bought at sporting-goods stores. Temporary licenses are available on charters, such as Capt. Ron's Pacific Charters (tel. 415/285–2000), Capt. Fred Morini (tel. 415/ 924–5575), Muny Sport Fishing (tel. 415/871–4445), and Wacky Jacky (tel. 415/586–9800).

GOLF The city maintains three easily accessible golf courses: the 18-hole Lincoln Park (34th Ave. and Clement St., tel. 415/221–9911), the 9-hole Golden Gate Park (47th and Fulton Sts., tel. 415/751–8987), and the 18-hole Harding Park (Lake Merced and Skyline Blvds., tel. 415/664–4690) on the city's western edge.

TENNIS The San Francisco Recreation and Park Department maintains 130 free tennis courts throughout the city (tel. 415/753–7101), including some in Golden Gate Park and Mission Dolores Park.

ENTERTAINMENT

CONCERTS The city has an extensive year-round concert schedule; check the "Datebook" section of the Sunday *San Francisco Examiner* and *Chronicle* for details. San Francisco Symphony (Davies Symphony Hall, Van Ness Ave. at Grove St., tel. 415/431–5400) performs September–May. The Symphony also presents pops concerts in July, at modest prices, at the nearby 7,000-seat Civic Auditorium (Polk and Grove Sts., tel. 415/431–5400).

DANCE San Francisco Ballet (War Memorial Opera House, Van Ness Ave. at Grove St., tel. 415/703–9400) performs *The Nutcracker* in December, and classic ballets and more contemporary works February–May.

FILM First-run theaters are scattered throughout the city but concentrated along Van Ness Avenue north of the Civic Center. The Castro Theater (429 Castro St. near Market St., tel. 415/621–6120), the city's last remaining movie palace from the 1920s, has an extensive schedule of classic revivals.

SKYLINE LOUNGES Carnelian Room (top of the Bank of America Bldg., 555 California St., tel. 415/433–7500) has dinner or cocktails on the 52nd floor; Starlite Roof (Sir Francis Drake Hotel, Powell and Sutter Sts., tel. 415/392–7755) offers band music and dancing on the 21st floor; Top of the Mark (Mark Hopkins Hotel, California and Mason Sts., tel. 415/392–3434) has fabulous views on the 19th floor.

SPECTATOR SPORTS Baseball's San Francisco Giants play spring and summer at Candlestick Park (tel. 415/467–8000), and the Oakland A's play at the Oakland Coliseum (tel. 510/638–0500). The Golden State Warriors play basketball at the Oakland Coliseum Arena (tel. 510/638–6300) October–April. Football's San Francisco 49ers (tel. 415/468–2249) appear at Candlestick Park.

Santa Fe and Taos
New Mexico

With crisp, clear air and bright, sunny weather, Santa Fe and Taos, its trendy satellite 60 miles to the north, couldn't be more welcoming. These two New Mexican towns are both situated at an invigorating altitude of more than 7,000 feet. The predominance of adobe architecture in these communities vaguely suggests the military compounds that both settlements were at one time. Santa Fe's Paseo de Peralta—a paved loop that approximates the former walls of the original Spanish colonial outpost established in 1609—still surrounds the vital core of the city. Taos, where the Coronado Expedition pushed north in 1598, echoes with reminders of those early days of Spanish colonization.

The populations of Santa Fe (60,000) and Taos (4,000) come from three separate cultures—Native American, Spanish, and Anglo (a term in northern New Mexico designating anyone who's not Native American or Spanish, regardless of race or ethnic background).

The combination of a stunning location, dramatic lanscapes, and a rich historical and cultural background have lured artists and writers for centuries. Visitors to these towns can appreciate streets filled with art galleries and outstanding museums; shops showcasing the finest Native American, Mexican, and Southwestern arts and crafts; restaurants offering distinctive regional cuisine; and hotels—both elegant and simple—decorated with regional handmade, hand-painted furnishings that have inspired "Santa Fe" and "Taos" decorative style trends throughout the United States.

ESSENTIAL INFORMATION

WHEN TO GO Santa Fe has a fairly mild climate, even in the winter; Taos can get much colder. The summer is a pleasant time to visit, but in July and August the area becomes crowded with tourists. Average daily minimum and maximum temperatures range from

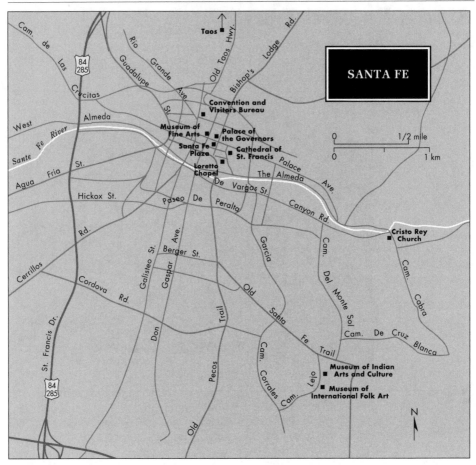

the mid-50s to the 90s. The sun is often intense because of the high altitude, but low humidity makes high temperatures bearable. Even when days are warm, evenings can become chilly or cold. The winter ski season attracts plenty of visitors beginning in late November until as late as April. Average daily minimum and maximum temperatures in Santa Fe fall between 19° and 45°; in Taos, the thermometer sometimes reads as low as 10°. Spring and fall are less crowded times for tourists. Average temperatures in the area range from 35° to 70° in the spring; 28° to 70° in the fall.

FESTIVALS AND SEASONAL EVENTS **New Year's Day:** For Indian New Year's celebrations, there's a Turtle Dance at the Taos Pueblo.

Mid-May: Taos Spring Arts Celebration runs during the last two weeks of the month. **Mid-July:** Rodeo De Santa Fe provides a taste of the Old West with cattle shows and roping contests. **Late July:** Spanish Market is held on the Santa Fe Plaza during the last weekend in July, with Spanish arts and crafts. **Mid-Aug.:** Indian Market on the Santa Fe Plaza showcases Indian arts and crafts. **Early Sept:** Las Fiestas De Santa Fe, beginning on the first Friday after Labor Day, celebrates the reconquest of Santa Fe in 1692, with parades, dancing, and fireworks. **October:** Cooler temperatures usher in the annual Wool Festival at Kit Carson Park in Taos, and the southern Rockies make a spectacular backdrop for the Taos Mountain Balloon Rally held late in

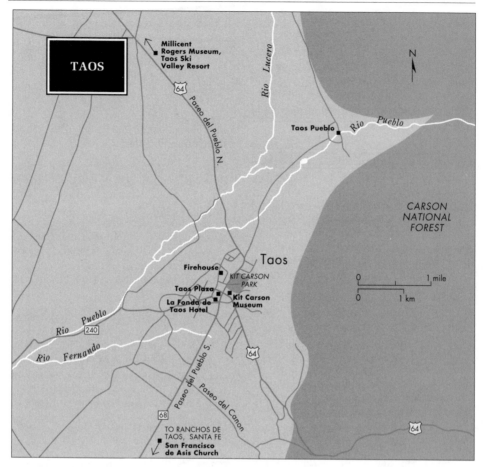

the month. **Christmas:** Christmas Eve in Santa Fe is festive, with carols at the Palace of the Governors and farolitos and luminarias (minibonfires) burning throughout the city. Christmas Day Indian dances take place at the Taos Pueblo.

BARGAINS Santa Fe Summerscene is a series of free concerts, dance performances, and storytelling sessions on the Santa Fe Plaza (July–Aug.). Shakespeare in Santa Fe presents the Bard's classics at the John Meem Library courtyard, St. John's College (tel. 505/982–2910; July and Aug.).

Entrance to the Indian pueblos outside of Santa Fe with ceremonial dances and crafts shops is free, excluding fees charged for parking and camera permits.

TOURIST OFFICES The Santa Fe Convention & Visitors Bureau (201 W. Marcy St., Box 909, Santa Fe 87504, tel. 505/984–6760 or 800/777–2489). Taos County Chamber of Commerce (229 Paseo Del Pueblo Sur, Drawer I, Taos 87571, tel. 505/758–3873 or 800/732–8267). New Mexico Tourism Department (Joseph M. Montoya Bldg., 1100 St. Francis Dr., Santa Fe 87503, tel. 505/827–0300). Indian Pueblo Cultural Center (2401 12th St. NW, Albuquerque 87102, tel. 505/843–7270).

EMERGENCIES **Santa Fe: Police, fire,** and **ambulance:** Dial 911. **Hospitals:** St. Vincent Hospital (455 St. Michaels Dr., tel. 505/983–

3361; 24-hour hotline, tel. 505/989–5242). **Doctors:** Lovelace Urgent Care Centers (901 W. Alameda, tel. 505/986–3666; 440 St. Michaels Drive, tel. 505/986–3566).

Taos: Police: tel. 505/758–4656. **Fire:** tel. 505/758–3386. **Ambulance:** tel. 505/758–1911. **Hospitals:** Holy Cross Hospital (Paseo del Pueblo Sur, tel. 505/758–8883).

ARRIVING AND DEPARTING

BY PLANE To reach Santa Fe and Taos, you fly into Albuquerque International Airport (tel. 505/842–4366), which is 65 miles southwest of Santa Fe and 130 miles south of Taos.

Mesa Airlines (tel. 800/637–2247) provides air shuttles between Albuquerque and Santa Fe Municipal Airport (tel. 505/473–7243). Flying time takes 25 minutes.

Because of the spectacular scenery, you may wish to rent a car and drive from the airport to your destination. From the Albuquerque airport, I–25 north goes directly to Santa Fe; from there, U.S. 84/285 goes north to Espanola, where you get on Route 68 to Taos (65 miles); all the major car-rental services have desks at the airport.

Greyhound Lines (tel. 800/231–2222) provides buses between Albuquerque and the two cities. Shuttlejack (tel. 505/982–4311 or 800/452–2665) offers bus service between Albuquerque and Santa Fe. Taos-based Faust's Transportation (tel. 505/758–3410) and Pride of Taos (tel. 505/758–8340) make airport pickups.

Amtrak (tel. 800/USA–RAIL) serves Santa Fe via the village of Lamy, 17 miles from Santa Fe.

BY BUS Greyhound Lines (858 St. Michaels Dr., tel. 505/471–0008 or 800/231–2222) serves Santa Fe and Taos throughout the day.

BY CAR Santa Fe is less than a day's drive from several metropolitan areas via I–25 (from El Paso, TX; Denver, CO) and I–40 (from Oklahoma City; Flagstaff, AZ). Taos is reached from Santa Fe via U.S. 84/285, connecting with Route 68 at Espanola.

GETTING AROUND

SANTA FE Downtown Santa Fe is easily explored by foot, with the majority of its museums, galleries, shops, and restaurants located within a comfortable radius of the famous Santa Fe Plaza. But you'll need a car, bus, or taxi for the city's outer reaches, and even a walk along Canyon Road can be a hilly 2-mile stretch from the plaza.

Santa Fe's main thoroughfares are St. Francis Drive, St. Michael's Drive, and Cerrillos Road (which connects with Route 14 and I–25 from Albuquerque). Paseo de Peralta encircles most of downtown Santa Fe with the central historic plaza sandwiched between San Francisco Street and Palace Avenue. Local car-rental services include Avis (tel. 505/982–4361), Budget (tel. 505/984–8028), and Hertz (tel. 505/982–1844).

Santa Fe Trails (tel. 505/984–6730) operates six bus routes from Sheridan Avenue in downtown Santa Fe (one block west of the Plaza and the Museum of Fine Arts) to various points throughout the city. Schedules can be obtained at the public library (145 Washington Ave.) and some downtown hotels.

Citywide taxi service is available via Capital City Cab Company (tel. 505/438–0000).

TAOS Like Santa Fe, Taos radiates around its famous Central Plaza, and a walk through downtown will only take a few minutes. Many of the top restaurants, stores, and galleries are all on or within the immediate vicinity of the plaza.

The Pride of Taos (next to the Chamber of Commerce office on Paseo Del Pueblo Sur, tel. 505/758–8340) provides taxi service to various points within town. Faust Tours (tel. 505/758–3410) offers radio-dispatched taxis to ski areas and other points in the vicinity. Taos's main streets are Paseo del Pueblo Norte and Paseo del Pueblo Sur, which skirts historic Taos Plaza. Bent Street and Kit Carson Road are the principal shopping areas. Local car-rental services include: Hertz (tel. 505/758–1668) and Payless (tel. 505/758–9501).

REST STOPS In Santa Fe there are public rest rooms in the Sweeny Convention Center (201 W. Marcy Street) about 2¹/₂ blocks north of the Plaza. There are public rest rooms in Kit Carson Park (just off Paseo del Pueblo Norte) several blocks north of the Taos Plaza. In addition, Santa Fe and Taos are adequately supplied with rest rooms in restaurants, hotels, museums, galleries, and even supermarkets—although they are normally for patrons' use only. During festivals or citywide celebrations, portable facilities are made available.

GUIDED TOURS Santa Fe: Gray Line of Santa Fe (229 N. Guadalupe St., tel. 505/983– 9491) features a variety of orientation tours. Afoot in Santa Fe Walking Tours (211 Old Santa Fe Trail, tel. 505/983–3701) offers a close-up look at the city with resident guides. Recursos (826 Camino de Monte Rey, tel. 505/982– 9301) provides tours centered around pueblos, history, culture, and nature. Santa Fe Detours (La Fonda Hotel Lobby, 100 E. San Francisco St., tel. 505/983–6565) has city walks, trail rides, and ski packages. Art Tours of Santa Fe (301 E. Alameda St., tel. 505/988– 3527) specializes in art-related trips. Southwest Adventure Group (142 Lincoln Ave., tel. 505/984–2080 or 800/723–9815) takes evening travelers through "haunted" parts of downtown Santa Fe. They also offer river rafting, hot-air balloon, and horseback riding trips.

Taos: Pride of Taos Tours (Box 1192, tel. 505/758–0762) provides bus tours of Taos highlights. Taos Historic Walking Tours (Box 2466, tel. 505/758–3861) covers all of the historically famous homes and sites.

EXPLORING

SANTA FE Santa Fe Plaza is the best place for a get-acquainted stroll of the city. First laid out in 1609–1610, this area was formerly a bull ring, the site of fiestas and fandangos, and the actual "End of the Santa Fe Trail." Today the plaza still remains the heart of the city, lined with a wide selection of shops, art galleries, and restaurants.

The Palace of the Governors, the oldest public building in the United States, borders the north side of the Plaza on Palace Avenue. Built in pueblo style at the same time that the Plaza was designed, it has been a New Mexican history museum since 1913. *100 Palace Ave., tel. 505/827–6483. Open Mar.–Dec., daily; Jan.–Feb., Tues.–Sun. Admission charged.*

The Museum of Fine Arts is across the street from Palace of the Governors on the corner of Palace and Lincoln avenues. Its outstanding 8,000-piece permanent collection concentrates on regional artists, such as Georgia O'Keeffe and Indian and Mexican masters. *107 Palace Ave., tel. 505/827–4455. Open Mar.–Dec., daily; Jan.–Feb., Tues.–Sun. Admission charged.*

The Cathedral of St. Francis, a block east of the Plaza, was built in 1869 by French architects in a French Romanesque style. Italian stonemasons added the finishing touches. It was founded by Santa Fe's first archbishop, French-born Jean Baptiste Lamy, who inspired Willa Cather's novel *Death Comes for the Archbishop*. *131 Cathedral Pl., tel. 505/982–5619. Open daily. Admission free.*

Loretto Chapel is next to the Inn at Loretto behind the landmark La Fonda Hotel. This handsome 1873 structure is known for the 20-foot "Miraculous Staircase" that leads to the choir loft, built by an itinerant carpenter who some believe was St. Joseph himself. *208 Old Santa Fe Trail, tel. 505/984–7971. Open daily. Admission charged.*

The Museum of International Folk Art is perched on a hillside 2 miles from the Plaza and near the southeastern edge of the city. The museum's main attraction is the Girard wing, containing thousands of examples of colorful folk-art creations from around the world, with miniature dioramas, religious imagery, and Mexican patios. The Hispanic Heritage wing is also worth a visit. *706 Camino Lejo, tel. 505/827–6350. Open daily (closed Mon. Jan.–Feb.). Admission charged.*

The Museum of Indian Arts and Culture, located next door, focuses on the history and contemporary culture of the state's Pueblo, Navajo, and Apache Indians. *710 Camino Lejo, tel. 505/827–6344. Open daily, except major holidays. Admission charged.*

Canyon Road is reached by bearing right from the St. Francis Cathedral to the end of Cathedral Place, turning left on Alameda Street, and then crossing the Paseo de Peralta. Canyon Road's 2-mile stretch from the center of town is now the city's most fashionable street, lined with many of the city's art galleries, shops, and restaurants. A shopping complex at the lower end (225 Canyon Rd.) provides parking and rest rooms for customers only.

Cristo Rey Church (Christ the King Church), at the corner of Upper Canyon Road (1¹/₂ miles from the Plaza) was constructed in 1939 to commemorate the 400th anniversary of Coronado's exploration of the Southwest. Built the old-fashioned way, with parishioners making the mud-and-straw bricks themselves, this is the largest adobe structure in the United States. *1107 Cristo Rey, tel. 505/983–8528. Open daily. Admission free.*

TAOS While the **Taos Plaza** does not possess the grace and dignity of Santa Fe's Plaza, it has its own small-town charm. The Spanish established the community around the Taos Plaza in 1617, and it remains the center of town life today, with assorted shops, galleries, and restaurants.

La Fonda de Taos Hotel, on the south side of the Plaza, has its own eccentric charm and houses erotic paintings by D. H. Lawrence in the manager's office. The paintings were once banned in London but are hardly scandalous by today's standards. *5 Plaza, tel. 505/758–7199.*

The Kit Carson Museum, located near the main intersection of town, where Paseo del Pueblo Norte and Paseo del Pueblo Sur meet, is the former home of the famous mountain man, trapper, and scout. Carson purchased the 12-room adobe building in 1843 as a wedding gift for his young bride. *East Kit Carson Rd., tel. 505/758–0505. Open daily. Admission charged.*

Taos Pueblo, one of the area's top attractions, is situated about 2 miles north of town. The largest existing multistoried pueblo structure in the United States, it has been continuously inhabited for centuries. Within its mud-and-straw walls, the Indian way of life has changed little over time. The site can get very crowded during summer weekends. *Off Rte. 3, tel. 505/758–9593. Open daily, except during a funeral or religious ceremony. Admission free. Charge for parking and camera permits.*

San Francisco de Asis Church lies 4 miles east of Taos in a Spanish Colonial ranching and farming community. This 18th-century monumental adobe masterpiece was rebuilt by community volunteers in 1979. It contains the painting *Shadow of the Cross,* in which the cross on Christ's shoulder can only be viewed at night. *Ranchos de Taos, tel. 505/758–2754. Open daily. Admission free.*

The Millicent Rogers Museum (4 miles north of the Plaza) contains more than 5,000 marvelous pieces of Native American and Hispanic art. *North of El Prado Rd., tel. 505/758–2462. Open daily except major holidays. Admission charged.*

THE NATURAL WORLD The Dome Wilderness comprises 5,200 acres in the volcanically formed Jemez Mountains, reached from Santa Fe by NM 4, intersecting with forest road 289. The Pecos Wilderness—223,333 acres of high mountains, forests, and meadows at the end of the Rocky Mountain chain—is reached from the city by NM 475 north. For information on camping in either wilderness area, contact the Santa Fe National Forest Office (tel. 505/988–6940). Forest maps are available for $2 and specific wilderness maps range from $1 to $4.

HOTELS AND INNS

Santa Fe and Taos are popular destinations that attract upscale travelers who are lured to their sophistication and stunning scenery. In recent years, room prices have escalated steadily. Low season hotel rates fluctuate considerably from place to place, but they are generally in effect from the beginning of November until the end of April (excluding the Thanksgiving and Christmas holidays). Price categories for double occupancy, excluding 10% tax, are *Expensive,* $125 and up; *Moderate,* $60–$125; and *Inexpensive,* under $60.

SANTA FE **Alexander's Inn.** This 1903 Victorian house exudes all the charm of an old country inn, with American country-style wooden furnishings, lots of open space, and a generous Continental breakfast. *529 E. Palace Ave., 87501, tel. 505/986–1431. 5 rooms. MC, V. Moderate.*

The Grant Corner Inn. This delightful, 13-room, downtown colonial B&B combines antique and American country furnishings with potted greens and rabbit knickknacks everywhere. Breakfasts here are popular with guests and locals alike. *122 Grant Ave., 87501, tel. 505/983–6678. 13 rooms. MC, V. Moderate.*

Hotel Santa Fe. This three-story hotel near downtown is operated by the Picuris Pueblo Indians, and offers rooms and suites decorated in the traditional Southwestern style, with local handmade furniture and Native American paintings. Many of the arresting bronzes throughout the hotel are by renowned sculptor Allan Houser. *1501 Paseo de Peralta, 87504, tel. 505/982–1200 or 800/825–9876. 40 rooms, 91 suites. Bar, deli. AE, D, DC, MC, V. Moderate–Expensive.*

Inn of the Animal Tracks. Three blocks east of the Plaza, this 90-year-old, restored eastside adobe has beamed ceilings, hardwood floors, handcrafted furniture, and fireplaces. Full breakfast and high tea are served. *707 Paseo de Peralta, 87504, tel. 505/988–1546. 6 rooms. AE, D, MC, V. Moderate.*

Preston House. This 1886 Queen Anne house, a rarity in a city of adobe structures, is tucked away in a quiet garden setting not far from the Plaza. *106 Faithway St., 87501, tel. 505/982–3465. 15 rooms. AE, MC, V. Moderate.*

Pueblo Bonito B&B Inn. This century-old adobe compound retains a Southwest pueblo

design throughout; all rooms have fireplaces. *138 W. Manhattan St., 87501, tel. 505/984–8001. 11 rooms, 7 suites. MC, V. Moderate.*

Territorial Inn. Creature comforts are a high priority in this elegant 100-year-old, two-story brick structure. The stylish decor is Victorian throughout, and Continental breakfast, afternoon treats, and brandy nightcaps are offered. *215 Washington Ave., 87501, tel. 505/989–7737. 10 rooms. MC, V. Moderate–Expensive.*

TAOS **Casa de Milagros.** A single-story turn-of-the-century adobe house, located a ¹/₂ mile east of the Taos Plaza, this pleasant B&B offers a large breakfast with bread baked in Indian ovens. *321 Kit Carson Rd., Box 2983, 87571, tel. 505/758–8001. 4 rooms, 1 suite. No smoking. Fireplaces. MC, V. Moderate.*

Don Fernando de Taos Holiday Inn. One mile south of the Plaza, this 1989 hotel is built in a distinct pueblo-style design, with rooms grouped around central courtyards. *1005 Paseo del Pueblo Sur, Drawer V, 87571, tel. 505/758–4444 or 800/HOLIDAY. 126 rooms. Restaurant, bar, pool. AE, MC, V. Moderate.*

El Monte Lodge. Nestled among cottonwoods in a quiet residential area east of the Plaza, this lodge has been in business for more than 50 years, and its owners, George and Pat Schumacher, know the area well. *317 Kit Carson Rd., Box 22, 87571, tel. 505/758–3171 or 800/828–TAOS. AE, DC, MC, V. Moderate.*

Hotel La Fonda de Taos. This historic lodging on the Plaza is a bit run-down at the seams, but it has a certain offbeat appeal. Cinema buffs take note: Rudolph Valentino once stayed here. *Taos Plaza, Box 1447, 87571, tel. 505/758–2211 or 800/833–2211. 24 rooms. MC, V. Moderate.*

The Blue Door. Located in the foothills between Taos and Ranchos de Taos, this 100-year-old adobe farmhouse, situated amid orchids, flower gardens, and lawns, provides an exceptional breakfast with local and Indian favorites. *La Mirada Rd., 87571, tel. 505/758–8360. 2 rooms. MC, V. Moderate.*

The Koshari Inn. Owners Denise and Bill Lin have lovingly converted a motel into a traditional, restful, Southwestern inn. *Kit Carson Rd., Box 6612, 87571, tel. 505/758–7199. 12 rooms. Pool, trout stream, bicycles. MC, V. Inexpensive.*

MOTELS

The following motels all fall in the Inexpensive price category.

SANTA FE **Alamo Lodge** (1842 Cerrillos Rd., 87501, tel. 505/982–1841). 19 rooms, 2 suites. **Budget Inn of Santa Fe** (725 Cerrillos Rd., 87501, tel. 505/982–5952). 160 rooms; pool. **Motel 6** (3695 Cerrillos Rd., 87501, tel. 505/471–4140). 121 rooms; pool. **Super 8 Motel** (3358 Cerrillos Rd., 87501, tel. 505/471–8811 or 800/843–1991). 59 rooms.

TAOS **Quality Inn** (E. Kit Carson Rd., 87571, tel. 505/758–7199). 99 rooms; bicycles, free local calls. **Taos Super 8 Motel** (1347 S. Hwy. 68, 87557, tel. 505/758–1088 or 800/848–8888). 41 rooms; RV parking. For those who don't mind sacrificing homey atmosphere and a high level of cleanliness in order to salvage the vacation budget, the **Taos Motel** has some of the least expensive rooms in Taos (4175 Paseo del Pueblo Sur, Hwy. 68, 87557, tel. 505/758–2524 or 800/323–6009). 28 rooms; senior-citizen discounts.

CAMPGROUNDS

Sante Fe has several nearby campground sites, including Apache Canyon KOA (I–25 north, tel. 505/982–1419), Los Campos RV Park (3570 Cerrillos Rd., tel. 505/473–1949), and Rancheros de Santa Fe Camping Park (Las Vegas Hwy., tel. 505/983–3482). Campers near Taos have access to the Orilla Verde Recreation Area (BLM, Santa Cruz Rd., tel. 505/758–8851) along the banks of the Rio Grande, approximately 10 miles south of Taos along NM 570.

DINING

Santa Fe and Taos cuisine is like no other: a delicious and extraordinary mixture of Pueblo Indian, Spanish colonial, Mexican, and American frontier cooking, all steeped and bubbled over the centuries. Recipes from Spain via Mexico were adapted generations ago for local ingredients—chilies, corn, pork, beans, honey, apples, piñon nuts, jicama, and leaves of the prickly pear cactus—and have remained much the same ever since. Chilies contain an entire storehouse of vitamins and minerals, and are loaded with vitamin C, while-corn tortillas provide protein and calcium. Besides the ever-popular Mexican hangouts, the area has numerous ethnic, health-food, and vegetarian restaurants that serve steamed and low-cholesterol entrées. A number of restaurants now serve buffalo stew, steaks, and burgers for those allergic to beef or on low-cholesterol diets. Many of the local, family-owned establishments are happy to cater to special dietary needs. Price categories per person, excluding 5.8% tax, service and drinks, are *Moderate,* $15–$25, and *Inexpensive,* under $15.

SANTA FE **The Bull Ring.** Set in a rambling old Spanish adobe (circa 1886), this is where New Mexico politicians gossip over steaks, seafood, and regional dishes. On weekends, local bands perform, turning the restaurant into a popular night spot. *414 Old Santa Fe Trail, tel. 505/983–3328. AE, MC, V. Moderate.*

Coyote Cafe. Restaurateur Mark Miller is known nationwide for the innovative menu (it changes daily) he created for this downtown establishment, formerly a Greyhound bus depot. *132 W. Water St., tel. 505/983–1615. AE, D, MC, V. Moderate.*

El Nido. This Santa Fe institution has been serving fine prime rib, succulent cuts of salmon and swordfish, and regional New Mexican specialties in its intimate, firelit rooms for over 50 years. *Bishops Lodge Rd., 1 mi from Tesuque (exit at Tesuque on NM 285 north), tel. 505/988–4340. MC, V. Moderate.*

La Tertulia. The lofty waiting room is reason enough to visit La Tertulia, housed in a converted 19th-century convent highlighted with pieces of Spanish colonial art. The creative New Mexican menu also features the excellent house sangria. *416 Agua Fria, tel. 505/988–2769. AE, MC, V. Moderate.*

Ore House on the Plaza. The Ore House has a perfect location, with a heated dining balcony overlooking Santa Fe's main plaza. Salmon, swordfish, and lobster are all artfully prepared, and margaritas come in 64 flavors. *50 Lincoln Ave., tel. 505/983–8687. AE, DC, MC, V. Moderate.*

Guadalupe Cafe. Even the most demanding diners will not be disappointed with the portions and the quality of the fare at this casual northern New Mexican establishment. *313 Guadalupe, tel. 505/982–9762. MC, V. Inexpensive.*

Shohko-Cafe. At this popular Japanese-Chinese restaurant, you can sample tempura, sushi, sukiyaki, and teriyaki, alongside vegetarian and seafood specials. *321 Johnson St. at Guadalupe, tel. 505/983–7288. AE, MC, V. Moderate.*

Tecolote Cafe. If you love brunch, come here for superb *huevos rancheros*—eggs served on a tortilla, with hot sauce and refried beans. The atmosphere at this breakfast-and-lunch eatery is casual; the coffee is all you can drink. *1203 Cerrillos Rd., tel. 505/988–1362. AE, DC, MC, V. No dinner. Inexpensive.*

Cafe Pasqual's. Only a block from the Plaza, this cozy, informal restaurant serves regional specialties and breakfast all day for sleepyheads. People sometimes stand in line outside, lured by thoughts of a *chorizo* burrito (sausage, scrambled eggs, home fries, and scallions wrapped in a flour tortilla). *121 Don Gaspar Ave., tel. 505/983–9340. MC, V. Inexpensive.*

Maria's New Mexico Kitchen. You can see fresh tortillas being made right in from of your eyes at this landmark restaurant, in business for over 40 years. Choose among traditional Mexican specialties, plus typical local favorites: homemade tamales, rellenos, blue-corn tamales, green chili stew, and sizzling fajitas. Don't leave without eating *at least* one

meal here. *555 W. Cordova Rd., tel. 505/983–7929. AE, D, MC, V. Inexpensive.*

TAOS **Apple Tree.** One of Taos' most popular dining spots, this restaurant gives New Mexican dishes a gourmet twist. *123 Bent St., tel. 505/758–1900. AE, DC, MC, V. Inexpensive–Moderate.*

Casa de Valdez. Two and a half miles south of the Plaza, this restaurant in a rustic A-frame building specializes in hickory-smoke barbecue and regional cuisine. *Paseo del Pueblo Sur, tel. 505/758– 8777. AE, MC, V. Inexpensive–Moderate.*

Chili Connection. Housed in a sprawling ranch-style adobe building with a large patio offering stunning mountain views, this dining sport serves up blue-corn tortillas, homemade salsa, buffalo burgers, and fajitas. *Ski Valley Rd., tel. 505/776–8787. AE, D, DC, MC, V. Inexpensive–Moderate.*

El Taoseno. What this eatery lacks in ambience it makes up for in its ample portions and down-home New Mexican food. Locals swear by it. *817 Paseo del Pueblo Sur, tel. 505/758–4142. No credit cards. Inexpensive.*

Amigos Natural Grocery and Juice Bar. With a health-food store in front, you'll find this natural-food café and juice bar in the rear a delight. *325 Paseo del Pueblo Sur, tel. 505/758–8493. No credit cards. Inexpensive.*

Bent Street Deli and Cafe. Simple and unpretentious, this is the place for you if you're yearning for a good sandwich; deli food, cappuccino, soups, and salads are also available. *120 Bent St., tel. 505/758–5787. No credit cards. Inexpensive.*

Michael's Kitchen. This family-run coffee shop and bakery specializes in both American and Spanish dishes, and offers plenty of choices—over 15 types of pancakes and 25 types of sandwiches alone. *304 Paseo del Pueblo Norte, tel. 505/758–4178. MC, V. Inexpensive.*

SHOPPING

SANTA FE Santa Fe may strike newcomers as one massive mall, with stores and shopping nooks sprouting up in the least likely of places. The downtown district offers a mix of shops, galleries, restaurants within a five-block radius of the Plaza. Under the shaded portals of the Palace of the Governors (*see* Exploring, *above*), local Indian vendors display their wares. Items are all handmade or hand-strung in Indian households; silver jewelry is either sterling or coin silver; all metal jewelry bears the maker's mark, registered with the Museum of New Mexico. Canyon Road is certainly Santa Fe's most famous shopping area, and the most expensive. At the southwest perimeter of town, the Guadalupe neighborhood is great for shopping, strolling, or relaxing at a sidewalk café. The local museums each have a gift shop carrying original folk-art pieces, fine-art reproductions, postcards, posters, books, and T-shirts.

Shops: Act 2 (410-B Old Santa Fe Trail, tel. 505/983–8585) carries vintage and modern clothing. Artesanos (222 Galisteo St., tel. 505/983–5563) is a large showroom for Mexican crafts. Old Santa Fe Trail Books (613 Old Santa Fe Trail, tel. 505/988–8878) is a bookstore and café. Cerrillos Road Mercantile and Trading Company (3741 Cerrillos Rd., tel. 505/471–6329) carries western memorabilia. Kachina House and Gallery (236 Delgado Rd., tel. 505/982–8415) features an incomparable collection of authentic Hopi Kachina dolls and Navajo arts and crafts. Sanbusco Outfitters (550 Montezuma Ave., tel. 505/988–1664) and Santa Fe Western Mercantile (6820 Cerrillos Rd., tel. 505/471–3655) have a complete line of western wear.

Art Galleries: Fenn Galleries (1075 Paseo de Peralta, tel. 505/982- 4631) carries original work by Georgia O'Keeffe and regional painters. 21st Century Fox Fine Art (215 W. Water St., tel. 505/983–2002) is a showroom of regional art.

Flea Markets: Trader Jack's Flea Market (7 miles north of Santa Fe on U.S. 84/285, look for the Santa Fe Opera, which is next door, tel. 505/455–7874) draws up to 400 dealers and thousands of buyers.

TAOS The main concentration of shops is directly on or just off the historic Central Plaza. That includes the John Dunn boardwalk on Bent Street, running parallel to the Plaza on the north, and Kit Carson Road, extending east off the northeast corner.

Tony Reyna's Indian Shops (outside arcade at the Kachina Lodge, tel. 505/758–2142; Taos Pueblo, tel. 505/758–3835) carry authentic Indian arts and crafts. El Rincon (114 E. Kit Carson Rd., tel. 505/758–9188) is the oldest trading post in Taos. The Taos Book Shop (122 E. Kit Carson Rd., tel. 505/758–3733) is the oldest bookstore in New Mexico. The Navajo Gallery (210 Ledoux St., tel. 505/758–3250) is home base for the prolific local painter, R. C. Gorman.

OUTDOOR ACTIVITIES

FISHING The following are fine for fishing: the San Juan River, located just below Navajo Dam in the northwest corner of the state; the Rio Chama, about 100 miles east of the San Juan River, west of NM 112; the Rio Grande, which passes 30 miles west of Santa Fe; Abiquiu Lake, 40 miles northwest of Santa Fe; Heron Lake, 23 miles southwest of Chama via U.S. 64/84 and NM 95; and Bluewater Lake, also in the northwest, 28 miles west of Grants via NM 371. For additional information, contact the Game and Fish Department (Villagra Bldg., 408 Galisteo St., Santa Fe 87503, tel. 505/827–7911).

GOLF **Santa Fe:** Cochiti Lake Golf Course (5200 Cochiti Hwy., Cochiti Lake, tel. 505/465–2239) or Santa Fe Country Club (Airport Rd., tel. 505/471–0601). **Taos:** Angel Fire Resort and Country Club (22 mi east of Taos on NM 484, tel. 505/377–6401 or 800/633–7463).

HORSEBACK RIDING The following all rent horses in the Santa Fe area: Camel Rock Ranch (10 minutes north of Santa Fe on U.S. 285, tel. 505/986–0408), Mountain Moma Packing and Riding Company (10 miles north of Santa Fe off U.S. 285, tel. 505/986–1924);

Rocking S Ranch (Madrid Hwy. south of Santa Fe, tel. 505/438–7333).

RIVER RAFTING The following Santa Fe companies offer river trips on the Rio Chama near Santa Fe and on the upper Rio Grande near Taos: Los Rios River Runners (La Fonda Hotel, tel. 505/983–6565, New Wave Rafting Company (107 Washington Ave., tel. 505/984–1444), Rio Bravo River Tours (1412 Cerrillos Rd., tel. 505/988–1153), and Rocky Mountain Tours (1323 Paseo De Peralta, tel. 505/984–1684).

SKIING The ski season in Santa Fe and Taos runs from Thanksgiving through early April. The Santa Fe Ski Area (tel. 505/982–4429 or Santa Fe Central Reservations, tel. 505/983–8200 or 800/982–SNOW) has a 1,650-foot vertical drop, 40 trails, 6 lifts, and a restaurant. The New Mexico Tourism and Travel Division offers a free packet of ski information (tel. 505/827–0291), and during the season current snow-condition information is available by calling 505/984–0606. For cross-country skiing information, contact the Santa Fe National Forest office (tel. 505/988–6940).

With the development of the Taos Ski Valley and several other nearby resorts, Taos is one of the premier ski destinations in the country. Taos Ski Valley Resort (tel. 505/776–2291) alone boasts a 2,600-foot vertical drop, 71 runs, 8 lifts, lodging for 1,000 guests, and several restaurants. For queries and reservations, contact Taos Valley Resort Association (Box 85, Taos Ski Valley 87525, tel. 505/776–2233 or 800/776–1111).

ENTERTAINMENT

SANTA FE **Music:** The acclaimed Santa Fe Opera performs July through August in a spectacular indoor/outdoor amphitheater (U.S. 84/285, 7 mi north of Santa Fe, tel. 505/982–3855). The Santa Fe Symphony Orchestra appears September through May at the Sweeny Center (Marcy and Grant Sts., tel. 505/983–3530). The Orchestra of Santa Fe, a professional chamber orchestra, performs September through May at the Lensic Theater (211 W. San Francisco St., tel. 505/988–4640).

Theater: Greer Garson Theater (College of Santa Fe, St. Michael's Dr., tel. 505/473–6511 or 505/473–6439) stages comedies, dramas and musicals. Other local companies include New Mexico Repertory Theater (tel. 505/983–2382) and Santa Fe Actors' Theater (tel. 505/982–8309).

Horse Racing: The Santa Fe Downs (off I–25, six minutes west of town, tel. 505/471–3311) attracts nearly a quarter-million spectators June through Labor Day.

TAOS **Music:** The Taos Community Auditorium (Paseo del Pueblo Norte, tel. 505/758–4677) offers modern dance, concerts, and movies. Taos Chamber Music Festival presents concerts on Paseo del Pueblo Norte (tel. 505/776–2388) and at the Hotel St. Bernard (Taos Ski Valley, tel. 505/776–2251). Music from Angel Fire (tel. 505/758–4667) is a free classical and jazz series (mid-Aug.–Sept.) at the Community Auditorium.

The Sagebrush Inn (South Santa Fe Rd., tel. 505/758–2254) offers live entertainment—mostly of the country-and-western variety—nightly in its spacious lobby lounge. During the ski season, Thunderbird Lodge (Taos Ski Valley, tel. 505/776–2280) offers its Jazz Legends series.

Savannah and the Golden Isles
Georgia

Savannah . . . the Golden Isles. . . . The very sound of these words conjures up misty images of mint juleps, live oaks dripping with Spanish moss, handsome mansions, and life lived at a leisurely southern pace. The mint juleps are still there, along with the moss and the mansion and the easygoing ways, but these popular destinations have their own up-to-date surprises.

On February 12, 1733, the English general James Edward Oglethorpe and 120 colonists arrived at Yamacraw Bluff on the Savannah River to found the 13th and last colony in the New World. As the port city grew, Scots, Huguenots, Germans, Salzburgers, Sephardic Jews from Spain and Portugal, Moravians, Italians, Swiss, Welsh, and Irish all arrived, creating in a rich gumbo the diverse mixture of cultures that shaped the city's character. Today, in the historic district, a wealth of restored mansions and other landmark buildings survives, many open to the public.

An hour south of the city begins the chain of Golden Isles: a string of lush, subtropical barrier islands meandering down the coast to the Florida border. Here, Indian relics have been found that date from about 2500 BC. English settlers who came to farm cleared the low-lying land and grew prosperous off cotton. In the early 20th century, Rockefellers, Morgans, Pulitzers, and Astors maintained vacation homes on Jekyll Island.

From the causeways and bridges leading to Jekyll Island, Sea Island, and St. Simons Island, you'll see a sea of flat, marshy grassland, but the islands are punctuated by stands of pines and live oaks (so called because the nondeciduous trees are green, or "live," all winter). One drives along roads shaded by oaks hung with Spanish moss. Cumberland Island is a National Seashore reached by ferry from St. Marys, and Little St. Simons Island is a privately owned retreat with a guest lodge. Each island, shaped by its history and ecology, has a character all its own.

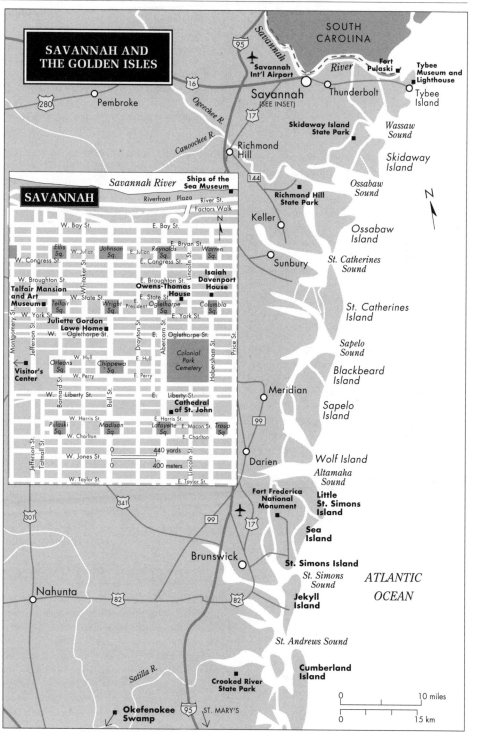

ESSENTIAL INFORMATION

WHEN TO GO Mild weather prevails here year-round; temperatures remain in the mid-50s during late fall and early winter and only occasionally fall below freezing. The thermometer climbs to the mid-60s and 70s by March, rising throughout April and into May, to hit 80 through most of June. Summer is typically humid, with temperatures in the high 80s and mid-90s. The hurricane season stretches from mid-August through most of September. Spring and early summer and fall are ideal times to come: Both Savannah and the Golden Isles are less crowded, the weather is at its best, and the mosquitoes are relatively inactive (they increase as summer progresses). Mid-spring and early fall are good times to catch lower lodging prices. If you are bothered by crowds, avoid Savannah around St. Patrick's Day—the city annually holds one of the country's largest outdoor bashes.

FESTIVALS AND SEASONAL EVENTS **Feb.:** Georgia Heritage Celebration in Savannah is a 12-day festival of the performing arts as well as arts and crafts. **Early Mar.:** Savannah's St. Patrick's Day celebration kicks off with a midmorning parade through downtown, and other events take place along the riverfront and on the streets and squares. **Apr.:** The Savannah Seafood Festival allows you to sample tasty native specialties like low-country shrimp boil, oyster roasts, and seafood casseroles. **Mid-May:** Brunswick Harborfest brings displays of good food and crafts and live music to the Brunswick waterfront. **Aug.:** Beach Music Festival on Jekyll Island is a "shaggin' in the sand" blowout that attracts large crowds. Sea Island Festival, held on St. Simons Island, is a regional cultural event at the pier, highlighted by the acclaimed Sea Island Singers and the art and crafts for sale at the booths of local artists and artisans. **Dec.:** Jekyll's Christmas Island begins on the first weekend and continues throughout the month. Historic houses, decorated for the holidays, are open for tours.

BARGAINS Free concerts by various music groups are held in Savannah's Johnson Square in summer on Wednesday and Friday from 11:30 AM to 1:30 PM. Seafood is a regional bargain. Fleets of shrimp boats troll up and down the coastal waterways, and dockside distributors and small businesses buy and sell all types of seafood directly off the boats. It is even possible to collect oysters, net crabs, and catch your own shrimp along the shoreline.

Discounted clothing, athletic equipment, housewares, luggage, books, and shoes are found at factory outlets and shopping centers. Bargain rates at local hotels and motels are usually in effect from late September to mid-February.

TOURIST OFFICES Brunswick–Golden Isles Chamber of Commerce (4 Glynn Ave., Brunswick 31520, tel. 912/265–0620). Jekyll Island Convention and Visitors Bureau (Box 3186, Jekyll Island 31520, tel. 912/635–3400, 800/841– 6586, or 800/342–1042 in GA). St. Simons Island Chamber of Commerce (Neptune Park, St. Simons Island 31522, tel. 912/638–9014). Savannah Area Chamber of Commerce (222 W. Oglethorpe Ave., Savannah 31499, tel. 912/944–0456 or 800/444–CHARM). Savannah Visitors Center (301 W. Broad St., Savannah 31499, tel. 912/944–0455).

EMERGENCIES **State Police:** Brunswick (tel. 912/265–6050), Jekyll Island (tel. 912/635–2303), or Savannah (tel. 912/232–6414). **Hospitals:** Savannah Chandler Hospital (5353 Reynolds St., tel. 912/356–6037). **Doctors:** Glynn County Walk-in Clinic (3400 Parkwood Dr., Brunswick, tel. 912/267–7600).

ARRIVING AND DEPARTING

BY PLANE Savannah International Airport (10 miles west of town) is served by American, Delta, Northwest, United, and USAir. McCall's Limousine Service (tel. 912/966–5364 or 800/673–9365) runs a shuttle van service between the airport and the city ($12 one-way; $22 round-trip). For the Golden Isles, Glynco Jetport, 6 miles north of Brunswick, is served daily by Atlantic Southeast Airline (tel. 404/765–2000), whose flights connect with Delta in Atlanta. You can also fly into Savannah or Jacksonville International Airport in Jacksonville, Florida, both an hour away, and make the commute into the area by car or shuttle.

BY CAR The north–south I–95 and east–west I–16 intersect just outside Savannah. I–16 leads into Savannah and dead-ends downtown. Follow I–95 south to the Golden Isles. U.S. 17, the Coastal Highway, also runs from Savannah to the Golden Isles and is more scenic.

BY TRAIN Amtrak's (tel. 800/USA–RAIL) *Palmetto, Silver Meteor,* and *Silver Star* serve Savannah, arriving at the station off Old Louisville Road (tel. 912/234–2611), 7 miles west of the historic district. Hotels run shuttle service to downtown, and taxis are plentiful.

BY BUS Greyhound Lines (tel. 800/231–2222) serves both Savannah and the Golden Isles with daily schedules.

GETTING AROUND

BY CAR Although the sights of Savannah can be seen on walking tours, a car is a necessity in this southern corner of Georgia. You can locate points of interest on display maps and pick up driving maps in the Chamber of Commerce offices and the Savannah Visitors Center.

REST STOPS Most restaurants, convenience stores, shops, and roadside markets in this area allow the public to use their rest rooms. The Savannah Visitors Center has public rest rooms. A boardwalk with gazebos and benches facing the Savannah River runs along the River Street area. Fort Pulaski has a visitor center with rest rooms as well as picnic areas. Welcome centers with rest rooms and travel information are on I–95 between Exits 8 and 9 south of Savannah, at the start of the F. J. Torras Causeway, on the causeway leading to Jekyll Island, and at the Neptune Park area on St. Simons's south end, which also has shaded picnic tables. More public rest rooms are in the bathhouses dotting the Jekyll Island shore.

GUIDED TOURS Black Heritage Tour (tel. 912/233–2027) offers three walking or driving tours that highlight significant sites linked to the area's rich black history. Tours by BJ (tel. 912/233–2335) has costumed guides that conduct small and large groups on morning, afternoon, and evening walks through the historic area. Carriage Tours of Savannah (tel. 912/236–6756 or 800/442–5933) runs modestly priced daytime horse and buggy tours, and upscale champagne evening tours of the historic district, from City Market, Madison Square, the Hyatt Regency Hotel, and the Savannah Visitors Center. Gray Line of Savannah/Landmark Tours (tel. 912/234–8687) conducts short, informative tours of the historic and Victorian districts and makes four-hour excursions outside the city to stately mansions, a historic fishing village and plantation, and a notable Savannah cemetery. Sea Island Boat Tours (tel. 912/638–3611 or 912/638–9354) offers daily two-hour tours of the surrounding marshes, narrated by a trained naturalist, that depart from the fishing dock in the morning and in the afternoon. Old Savannah Tours (tel. 912/354–7913) offers bus and trolley city tours as well as evening candlelight tours.

EXPLORING

SAVANNAH The city's high points can be seen in a fast-paced two days, though the seductive powers of its 22 lushly landscaped squares and cobblestone streets, draped in the shade of 200-year-old live oaks, might compel you to spend a leisurely week. History and architecture buffs can occupy themselves touring the many period houses in town, while others will contentedly cruise the spirited River Street area, a renovated warehouse district where Dixieland music wafts across a nine-block stretch of boutiques and taverns.

Cathedral of St. John the Baptist. Two blocks south from the historic Colonial Park Cemetery, this French Gothic building with impressive pointed arches is Georgia's oldest Roman Catholic church (1874); it faces Lafayette Square and its graceful fountain. *222 E. Harris St., tel. 912/233–4709. Open daily.*

Isaiah Davenport House. This stately house, just a short walk south on Abercorn Street from Reynolds Square, is one of the city's finest examples of Georgian architecture. It is furnished with Chippendale, Hepplewhite, and Sheraton antiques. *324 E. State St., tel. 912/236–8097. Closed Thurs. Admission charged.*

Juliette Gordon Lowe Home. Completed in 1821, this Regency-style mansion is the birthplace of Juliette Gordon Lowe, who founded the Girl Scouts of America in 1912. The home is filled with original Gordon family furnishings and is noted for its large Tuscan-style columns and decorative plasterwork. *142 Bull St., tel. 912/233–4501. Closed Wed. Admission charged.*

Owens-Thomas House. This was the first Regency mansion the English architect William Jay built in the city. Constructed of local materials, including tabby (a mixture of lime, sand, and ground oyster shell used in the 17th and 18th centuries), it was a showcase house, where the Marquis de Lafayette delivered his farewell speech in 1825. *124 Abercorn St., tel. 912/233–9743. Open daily. Admission charged.*

Scarbrough House. Headquarters for the Historic Savannah Foundation, this Regency mansion was built during the 1819 cotton boom by William Jay. Works by local artists are displayed throughout the house. *41 W. Broad St., tel. 912/233–7787. Open daily. Admission charged.*

The Ships of the Sea Museum houses a large collection of maritime memorabilia including models of sailing ships, steamships, nuclear vessels, and Christopher Columbus's *Niña, Pinta,* and *Santa Maria. 503 E. River St., tel. 912/232–1511. Open daily except major holidays. Admission charged.*

Telfair Mansion and Art Museum, the South's oldest public art museum, is housed in another William Jay masterpiece. There are American, French, and German Impressionist paintings; a collection of works by Kahlil Gibran; and Regency furniture and decorations in three period rooms. *121 Barnard St., tel. 912/232–1177. Closed Mon. Admission charged.*

Fort Pulaski. This restored fort 15 miles outside Savannah is a must for Civil War buffs. Operated by the National Park Service, it is complete with moats, drawbridges, massive ramparts, and towering walls. *U.S. 80, tel. 912/786–5787. Open daily except Christmas. Admission charged.*

Tybee Museum and Lighthouse are outside Savannah, 3 miles beyond Fort Pulaski. The lighthouse is Georgia's oldest, dating from 1773. The ocean view from the 145-foot-high deck is well worth the climb. The museum is devoted to the history of the surrounding four-state area. *Meddin Dr., tel. 912/786–4077. Closed Tues. Admission charged.*

THE GOLDEN ISLES Though Georgia's coast is strung with islands along its entire length, many of them are undeveloped and not open to the public. Of the islands where visitors can stay, Jekyll, Sea Island, and St. Simons are accessible by car from Brunswick; Cumberland Island National Seashore, by ferry from St. Marys; and Little St. Simons, by launch from St. Simons.

Cumberland Island is a largely undeveloped natural sanctuary for wild horses, deer, bobcats, and stressed-out vacationers. Remote expanses of sun-drenched beaches and sand dunes make it ideal for day trips and camping. The island has no transportation, nothing to buy, and all trash must be packed back to the mainland. Contact the National Park Service (Cumberland Island National Seashore, Box 806, St. Marys, 31588, tel. 912/882–4335) for ferry reservations and schedules and for camping information.

Jekyll Island, a vast playground flanked by the Intracoastal Waterway and the Atlantic, offers 63 holes of golf, 10 miles of beach, fishing, tennis, biking, and walking. Between 1886 and 1942, America's rich and famous wintered here, and today the **Jekyll Island Club Historic District** contains many of their brick, shingle, and tabby mansions. Tours of the district and buildings are conducted in open-air trolleys. *Exit 35, tel. 912/635–2236.*

Tours Labor Day–Memorial Day, daily. Admission charged.

St. Simons Island, as wide and as long as Manhattan, has 14,000 year-round residents and is the most developed of these islands. Its southern tip is rimmed by beaches, and a network of bike paths extends through the surrounding marshland and onto the island. At **Fort Frederica** national monument, built in the 1730s by the English to protect against a Spanish invasion from Florida, the fort's tabby ruins and many building foundations still stand. *St. Simons Island, tel. 912/638–3639. Open daily. Admission charged.*

Little St. Simons is a small, privately owned island with three (very expensive) lodges for overnight guests. Day trips by boat from St. Simons (tel. 912/638–7472, $60 per person) include a naturalist-led tour of the secluded island (Tues., Thurs., and Sat. only), lunch, and swimming.

Sea Island, linked by bridge to St. Simons, has been the domain of the Cloister (tel. 912/638–3611), a famous hotel and resort, since 1928. The public is free to admire the hotel grounds, drive by the houses along Sea Island Drive, use the golf course, space permitting, and dine in the main dining room by reservation.

THE NATURAL WORLD The low-lying marshes, beaches, and wooded thickets of the coastal islands support a vast network of wildlife. In the early morning and evening hours, rabbits are easy to spot along roadsides. Predawn low tides in spring are the prime time to walk any of the area's beaches to watch female turtles crawl ashore to lay their eggs. Twilight draws deer, raccoons, armadillos, and owls out of their hiding places. On beach walks, you'll see quick-footed sandpipers running along the water's edge and sea gulls and pairs of pelicans flying low across the ocean's surface. Regal egrets and herons stalk the marshes, while schools of dolphins and lone alligators swim the waterways. Ghost crabs are frequently seen at night during low tides, scurrying above the waterline.

The stands of majestic live oaks are heavily draped in Spanish moss. Palms of all sizes—from clumps of fan-shaped palmetto undergrowth to manicured rows of magnificent date palms—are also native to the area.

HOTELS AND INNS

Savannah has a diverse selection of charming accommodations steeped in history as well as more affordable hotels and chain motels outside the historic districts on main thoroughfares. Brunswick, St. Simons Island, Sea Island, and Jekyll Island offer both value and luxury. Prices for double occupancy, without 6% sales and 5% hotel tax, are *Expensive,* $90–$120; *Moderate,* $50–$90; and *Inexpensive,* under $50.

SAVANNAH **Ballastone Inn.** Genteel elegance reminiscent of the Old South pervades this 1850s brick town house in the historic district, with rooms painted in authentic Savannah colors and furnished with rice-carved four-poster and canopy beds. *14 E. Oglethorpe Ave., 31401, tel. 912/236–1484 or 800/822–4553. 18 rooms. Continental breakfast included, fresh fruit, library, landscaped courtyard, tennis, golf. AE, MC, V. Moderate–Expensive.*

Comer House. The polished pine floors, spacious rooms, sweeping verandas, and walled garden of this four-story Victorian were (in 1978) restored to the elegance they displayed when Confederate president Jefferson Davis spent a week here. *2 E. Taylor St., 31401, tel. 912/234–2923 or 800/262–4667. 2 rooms. Continental breakfast included, free use of bicycles, convenient to restaurants. Moderate–Expensive.*

Eliza Thompson House. Nestled in a peaceful residential area in the historic district, this lovely Federal-style Inn offers a full breakfast and afternoon wine and cheese in a beautiful garden courtyard. Rooms are decorated with period antiques, reproductions, and poster beds. *5 West Jones St., 31401, tel. 912/236–3620 or 800/348–9378. 25 rooms. Breakfast included, afternoon wine and cheese, land-*

scaped courtyard. AE, MC, V. Moderate–Expensive.

East Bay Inn. This charming restored cotton warehouse is located on the doorstep of Savannah's waterfront district. Antiques-filled rooms include poster rice beds or brass beds, and you can enjoy evening cordials in the parlor. *225 East Bay St., 31401, tel. 912/238–1225 or 800/500–1225. 28 rooms. Continental breakfast included, full-service restaurant in basement, free parking. AE, D, DC, MC, V. Moderate–Expensive.*

The Gastonian. You'll step back in time when you enter these two houses, where finely crafted details, well-kept Savannah antiques, working fireplaces, and southern hospitality create an intimate atmosphere. *220 E. Gaston St., 31401, tel. 912/232–2869. 13 rooms. Hot tub on sun deck, whirlpool baths, off-street parking. AE, MC, V. Moderate–Expensive.*

Pulaski Square Inn. The traditional rooms of this 1853 town house (one of the historic district's treasures) have kitchens and are furnished with a mix of antiques and reproductions. *203 W. Charlton St., 31401, tel. 912/233–8055 or 800/227–0650. 7 rooms, 6 with baths. Formal garden. AE, MC, V. Inexpensive–Moderate.*

BRUNSWICK AND THE ISLANDS **Greyfield Inn.** Cumberland Island is home to this charming inn built by the Carnegies in 1901. Wide, airy porches surround the majestic southern-style mansion, which, combined with the island's natural beauty, provides an ideal getaway. *Box 900, Fernandina Beach, FL 32035, tel. 904/261–6408. 11 rooms. Rates include meals, boat transportation to island, outings with naturalist guide, bicycles. MC, V. Expensive.*

King & Prince. St. Simon's premier resort has sprung up around a turreted, castlelike structure, which contains some of its guest rooms; housekeeping villas are in contemporary tiered buildings adjoining it. *102 Arnold Dr., St. Simons Island 31522, tel. 912/638–3631 or 800/342–0212. 125 rooms, 48 2- and 3-bedroom villas. Restaurant, indoor/outdoor*

pool, tennis, bike and sailboat rentals, gift shop. AE, DC, MC, V. Expensive.*

Jekyll Island Club Hotel. The restored turreted building, built by 19th-century financiers as a private retreat, is now a Radisson Resort property that offers turn-of-the-century elegance in a charming, updated historic setting. *371 Riverview Dr., Jekyll Island 31527, tel. 912/635–2600 or 800/333–3333. 134 rooms, 15 suites, 8 with whirlpools. 2 restaurants, pool, croquet court, gift shops, tennis. AE, DC, MC, V. Moderate–Expensive.*

Shipwatch Oceanfront Condominiums. Stay a day or a month in these well-established units with a nautical look and porthole windows, in one of the island's quieter residential neighborhoods. *1524 Wood Ave., St. Simons Island 31522, tel. 912/638–5450 or 800/627–6850. 42 2-bedroom, 2-bath units. MC, V. Moderate–Expensive.*

Jekyll Inn. The two-level villas perched on the edge of the ocean have balconies and patios that give beachcombers direct access to their rooms. *975 N. Beachview Dr., Jekyll Island 31527, tel. 912/635–2531 or 800/736–1046. 188 guest rooms, 74 town-house villas with kitchens. Restaurant, lobby bar, cocktail lounge, pool. AE, MC, V. Inexpensive–Expensive.*

Sea Gate Inn. In this orange-and-white U-shaped motel constructed with a '30s modern Jetsons flair (and with an elevator), you can stay in beachfront or poolside rooms or suites with private balconies. *1014 Ocean Blvd., St. Simons Island 31522, tel. 912/638–8661 or 800/562–8812. 18 rooms, 8 with kitchenettes; 2 suites. Pool. AE, MC, V. Inexpensive–Expensive.*

Brunswick Manor–Major Downing House. High tea is an afternoon tradition in this restored Victorian (circa 1886), furnished with antiques, that overlooks a square in the Old Towne district. *825 Egmont St., Brunswick 31520, tel. 912/265–6889. 4 rooms, 2 suites. 2 guest kitchenettes. Continental breakfast and afternoon tea included, boat charters available. MC, V. Moderate.*

The Clarion-Buccaneer. This centrally located oceanfront motel offers more amenities (including kitchenettes and private balconies and patios), at a better price than most of the island's other motels. *85 S. Beachview Dr., Jekyll Island 31527, tel. 912/635–2261. 206 rooms. Restaurant, pool, whirlpool, playground, tennis court, paddle-tennis court. AE, D, DC, MC, V. Inexpensive–Moderate.*

Rose Manor Guest House. Restored in the style of an English manor house, this circa-1890 Victorian bungalow offers the charm of formal gardens and rooms with Victorian furniture and antique linens. *1108 Richmond St., Brunswick 31520, tel. 912/267–6369. 2 rooms with shared bath, 4 suites. Airport shuttle service. No credit cards. Inexpensive–Moderate.*

Gaubert Bed & Breakfast is a comfortable, older, informally decorated house in the shadow of a historic lighthouse, just a block off the beach and steps away from popular restaurants, clubs, and shops. *521 Oglethorpe Rd., St. Simons Island 31522, tel. 912/638–9424. Inexpensive.*

Queens Court. In the heart of St. Simons's quaint village area, within walking distance of shops, restaurants, nightlife, and beaches, this small motel is a very good bargain. *437 Kings Way, St. Simons Island 31522, tel. 912/638–8459. 19 rooms, 9 with kitchenettes; 4 suites. Pool. MC, V. Inexpensive–Moderate.*

MOTELS

MODERATE **Best Western–Savannah Riverfront Inn** (412 W. Bay St., Savannah 31401, tel. 912/233–1011). 142 rooms; restaurant, pool, shuttle service. **Clubhouse Inn** (6800 Abercorn, Savannah 31405, tel. 912/356–1234 or 800/258–2466). 138 rooms; Continental breakfast, pool, kitchenettes. **Days Inn–Historic District** (201 W. Bay St., Savannah 31401, tel. 912/236–4440 or 800/325–2525). 195 rooms; restaurant, pool, fitness facilities, shuttle service, kitchenettes. **Days Inn–St. Simons** (1701 Frederica Rd., St. Simons Island 31522, tel. 912/634–0660). 101 rooms; complimentary happy hour (Tues.,

Wed., Thurs.), microwaves, refrigerators. **Glynn Place Mall Suites Hotel** (500 Mall Blvd., Brunswick 31522, tel. 912/264–6100 or 800/432–3229). 133 rooms; restaurant, lounge, pool, health club, shuttle service. **La Quinta Motor Inn** (6805 Abercorn St., Savannah 31405, tel. 912/355–3004). 154 rooms; pool, shuttle service. **Quality Inn–Downtown** (231 W. Boundary St., Savannah 31401, tel. 912/232–3200 or 800/637–5505). 172 rooms; restaurant, pool, lounge. **Riverwatch Inn** (100 Marina Dr., St. Simons Island 31522, tel. 912/638–4092). 20 rooms; restaurants, lounge, shops, dock slips.

INEXPENSIVE **Comfort Inn** (490 New Jesup Hwy., Brunswick 31525, tel. 912/264–6540). 118 rooms; restaurant, pool, lounge. **Days Inn–Abercorn** (11750 Abercorn St., Savannah 31419, tel. 912/927–7720 or 800/325–2525). 114 rooms; Continental breakfast included, Jacuzzi. **Hampton Inn Hotel** (201 Stephenson Ave., Savannah 31405, tel. 912/355–4100 or 800/HAMPTON). 129 rooms; Continental breakfast included, pool. **Super 8 Motel** (472 New Jesup Hwy., Brunswick 31525, tel. 912/264–8800). 62 rooms.

CAMPGROUNDS

Camping facilities in this area are extremely limited, though there's an occasional chain-operated KOA Kampground and mobile-home park where recreational vehicles can find hookups. The Golden Isles has two popular campgrounds connected to national and regional parks that are in more pleasant settings.

Blythe Island Campground. This medium-size, waterfront facility outside Brunswick is isolated in a natural setting among oaks and pine trees. The maximum stay is 14 nights from Memorial Day to Labor Day. *Blythe Island Regional Park, Rte. 6, Box 224, Brunswick 31525, tel. 912/261–3805. 40 RV sites with full hookups ($15.50), 30 with water and electric connections ($13.50), 27 tent sites ($10); showers, toilets, laundry, cable TV, picnic tables and barbecue areas. Reservations by phone or mail. MC, V.*

Jekyll Island Campground. Just off the ocean on 18 shady acres, this campground is a few minutes' walk from an uncrowded beach and a bicycle ride to four golf courses, tennis, and the historic district. Maximum stay is 14 nights, March–Labor Day. *North Beachview Dr., Jekyll Island 31527, tel. 912/635–3021. 80 RV sites with full hookups ($15.75), 64 with water and electric connections ($13.65), 76 tent sites ($10.50); picnic tables, showers, toilets, laundry, store. Reservations by phone or mail. D, MC, V.*

Skidaway Island State Park. Located eight miles southeast of Savannah, this 533-acre barrier island is comprised of marshlands and estuaries and offers a wide variety of activities. *Skidaway Island State Park, Savannah 31411, tel. 912/598–2300. 88 combination tent and trailer sites with water and electrical hookups; picnic tables, grills, 4 comfort stations providing hot showers, flush toilets, electrical outlets, automatic laundry; $10 per site per night; $2 entrance fee. No credit cards.*

DINING

People come to the coast for the freshly caught shrimp, fish, crabs, and oysters. Although seafood is still served deep-fried or with heavy cream sauce, growing health concerns have brought more broiled, boiled, and lightly sautéed dishes to the menus of even the established restaurants. Price categories per person, not including 6% tax, service, and drinks, are *Moderate,* $15–$25, and *Inexpensive,* under $15.

SAVANNAH **Crystal Beer Parlor.** Located in the historic district, this casual and longtime Savannah favorite is famous for its crab stew, shrimp salad, and "Crystalburger" served with thick french fries. *301 W. Jones St., tel. 912/232–1153. AE, D, MC, V. Inexpensive–Moderate.*

Elizabeth on 37th. An elegant mansion in the historic district with an old-Savannah decor is where Elizabeth Terry, one of the city's top chefs, prepares delicately sauced seafood dishes and a variety of meats. *105 E. 37th St., tel. 912/236–5547. AE, MC, V. Moderate.*

45 South. This popular southside eatery serves a range of well-prepared dishes acclaimed by local critics—from grilled swordfish to breast of duck to pork tenderloin—in a stylish, up-to-date setting with glass and mirrors. *20 E. Broad St., tel. 912/233–1881. AE, DC MC, V. Moderate.*

Pirates' House. This local dining legend with a piratical flair emphasizes all types of seafood—shrimp, fish, crab, and oysters—and serves more than 40 different desserts. *20 E. Broad St., tel. 912/233–5757. AE, DC, MC, V. Inexpensive–Moderate.*

Huey's. This riverfront New Orleans–style bistro serves authentic regional specialties, including heaping plates of red beans and rice, and fresh sugar-dusted beignets. *115 E. River St., tel. 912/234–7385. AE, DC, MC, V. Inexpensive.*

Mrs. Wilkes Boarding House. The fine, family-style, southern fare served in this understated basement restaurant has attracted the likes of David Brinkley and Charles Kuralt. *107 W. Jones St., tel. 912/232–5997. No credit cards. Inexpensive.*

Pearl's Elegant Pelican. There's a nautical theme to the decor of this restaurant in the historic district, which specializes in boiled, fried, or steamed seafood served family style. *152 Montgomery St., tel. 912/234–8972. AE, MC, V. Inexpensive.*

Seashell House. This no-frills establishment on the road to Skidaway Island serves all types of seafood dishes, including a tasty low-country Boil and a first-rate seafood platter. *3111 Skidaway Rd., tel. 912/352–8116. AE, MC, V. Inexpensive.*

GOLDEN ISLES **Alfonza's Olde Plantation Supper Club.** Seafood, superb steaks, and fried chicken are served by friendly waiters and waitresses in a low-key, come-as-you-are atmosphere. *Harrington La., St. Simons Island, tel. 912/638–9883. MC, V. Inexpensive–Moderate.*

Bennie's Red Barn. A converted barn with massive stone fireplace and balcony seating lends a clublike atmosphere to this long-standing restaurant that specializes in seafood and steaks. *Frederica Rd., St. Simons Island, tel. 912/638–2844. MC, V. Moderate.*

Kyoto Restaurant. The evening's entertainment begins as tableside chefs cook your meal to order in this sleek, contemporary restaurant done in black with polished wood. *224 Retreat Rd., St. Simons Island, tel. 912/638–0885. AE, DC, MC, V. Moderate.*

Crabdaddy's. Freshly grilled, blackened, or steamed seafood are the house specialty of this fun and informal restaurant a few blocks from the beach. *1217 Ocean Blvd., St. Simons Island, tel. 912/634–1120. MC, V. Inexpensive–Moderate.*

Birdie's. This casual and quaint diner in the village serves a healthier than usual selection—Cajun oysters, sautéed fish, soft-shell crabs—with fresh vegetables. *407 Mallery St., St. Simons Island, tel. 912/638–4852. MC, V. Inexpensive.*

The Crab Trap. This popular restaurant's rustic nautical theme and informal atmosphere complement a straightforward selection of broiled and fried seafood. *1209 Ocean Blvd., St. Simons Island, tel. 912/638–3552. MC, V. Inexpensive.*

Grapevine Cafe. The King and I in downtown Brunswick? Well, yes, if your definition includes petite filet mignon; there's also a South Pacific dinner of soft-shell crab plus the Porgy and Bess with fresh coastal crab cakes. When waiters aren't busy serving the all-inclusive prix-fixe dinners ($14.95), they'll sing tunes from popular musicals. *1519 Newcastle St., Brunswick, tel. 912/265–0115. Mon.– Thurs. lunch only; Fri. and Sat. dinner only. No credit cards. Inexpensive–Moderate.*

Mullet Bay. Wide verandas provide outside dining at this upbeat, brand-new eatery on St. Simons. The informal menu offers burgers, sandwiches, seafood, and pasta dishes. *500 Ocean Blvd., St. Simons Island, tel. 912/634–9977. AE, D, DC, MC, V. Inexpensive.*

Spanky's. A trendy restaurant and bar in the Golden Isles Marina, this popular spot with a waterfront view serves pizza, salads, and sandwiches. *225 Marina Dr., St. Simons Island, 912/638–0918. AE, D, MC, V. Inexpensive.*

SHOPPING

Souvenir shops in Savannah and the Golden Isles sell T-shirts and beachwear. In the nine cobblestone blocks of River Street along the Savannah River, you can find everything from pottery to paintings. Several antiques shops are just above this level off Bay Street, and there are more in the historic district. Two major suburban malls house a wide variety of regional and national chains, such as Belk's and Abercrombie & Fitch. Frederica Road on St. Simons Island is lined with fine clothing stores and gift shops; beachwear, gift, and souvenir stores thrive in the small commercial district in St. Simons village.

OUTDOOR ACTIVITIES

BEACHES Although natives rarely swim between September and March, the water temperatures remain relatively warm much longer. Some hardy souls swim as late as January. Tybee Island, 18 miles east of downtown Savannah, has wide-open stretches of public beaches, and all the beach areas rimming St. Simons and Jekyll islands are easily accessible.

BIKING St. Simons Island and Jekyll Island offer miles and miles of flat, well-paved biking trails, and their wide beaches are actually hard enough to bike on. The trail over the elevated bridges and across stretches of the F. J. Torras Causeway is more challenging. Contact the Chamber of Commerce (Brunswick, tel. 912/265–0620) for information about daily or weekly bike rentals.

BOATING AND SAILING All these coastal areas offer both sailboat and powerboat rentals. Try Barry's Beach Service (St. Simons Island, tel.

912/638–8053) for sailboats, Captain Jeanne (St. Simons Island, tel. 912/638–3611, ext. 5202) for charters with a captain, or Taylor's Fish Camp (St. Simons Island, tel. 912/638–7690) for captained or bareboat charters.

FISHING The Georgia Department of Natural Resources (1 Conservation Way, Brunswick 31520, tel. 912/264–7218) is the best source for current information on fishing regulations. Fishing charters operate out of St. Simons Island and Jekyll Island.

GOLF This is a golfer's paradise. The mild climate makes it a year-round sport, and there's a wide selection of challenging public and resort-operated courses to choose from. Contact local chambers of commerce for more information (*see* Tourist Offices, *above*).

WALKING In Savannah's Forsyth Park, oak trees generously shade a network of trails through the 20 lushly groomed acres. Tybee Island's wide beaches and seashore vistas make it another favorite walking spot. The flat beaches rimming St. Simons and Jekyll islands are ideal for jogging and walking, and there's an extensive system of paved paths that connects inland areas to the coastal islands over bridges and causeways.

ENTERTAINMENT

CONCERTS Local and traveling productions of theatrical, musical, and dance events are held at the Savannah Civic Center (Liberty and Montgomery Sts., Savannah, tel. 912/651–6550 or 912/651–6556 for ticket information).

DANCE Ballet South (201 Barn Dr., Savannah, tel. 912/354–3899), the city's resident classical dance company, appears at the Savannah Civic Center and other theaters.

MUSIC The Savannah Symphony Orchestra (225 Abercorn St., Savannah, tel. 912/236–9536) maintains an annual performance schedule. Coastal Jazz Association (224 W. Congress St., Savannah, tel. 912/232–2222) puts on concerts by local and national artists in and around the historic district.

THEATER Island Players (Neptune Park, St. Simons Island, tel. 912/638–3031) presents musicals and plays from January through June and children's plays in summer.

The Jekyll Island Musical Theater Festival (tel. 912/635–4060) presents outdoor musicals performed by professional actors from June through mid-August in the amphitheater of Jekyll Island.

Seattle
Washington

 eattle is defined by water. There's no use denying the city's damp weather, or the fact that its skies are cloudy for much of the year. People in Seattle don't tan—goes the joke—they rust.

But Seattle is also defined by a different kind of water. A variety of rivers, lakes, and canals bisect steep hills, creating a series of distinctive areas along the water's edge, where fishing boats and floating homes, swank yacht clubs and waterfront restaurants exist side by side.

The city is also defined by its people; the half million in the city proper and the 2 million in the surrounding Puget Sound region are a diversified bunch. Seattle has long had an active Asian and Asian-American population, and also includes well-established communities of Scandinavians, African-Americans, Jews, Native Americans, Hispanics, and other ethnic groups.

Seattle's wet climate tends to foster an easy-going, indoor lifestyle. Overcast days and long winter nights help make the city a haven for movie goers and book readers (per capita book purchases are among the highest in the country). At the same time, Seattleites are serious about the outdoors—whether it's hiking in the Cascade Mountains to the east, the Olympics to the west, or strolling in the city's extensive park system (designed by Frederick Law Olmsted, creator of New York City's Central Park).

Shedding it's sleepy-town image, Seattle is one of the fastest-growing cities in the United States and an important Pacific Rim seaport. The town that Sir Thomas Beacham once described as a "cultural wasteland" now has all the artistic trappings of a full-blown big city, with ad agencies and artists' co-ops, symphonies and ballet companies, plus a youthful music scene that introduced the word "grunge" into the national lexicon. Locals may berate this wet and misty city, but there's plenty of reasons why Seattle consistently ranks high on lists of the country's best places in which to live.

ESSENTIAL INFORMATION

WHEN TO GO Seattleites may gripe about the weather, but with raincoats and umbrellas, they have adapted to this damp, gray climate where it rains about 45 inches per year. In any season, several days of overcast and light showers are not unusual. Summer daytime temperatures are generally in the 70s, but there is usually a week of extremely hot weather, when temperatures hit the high 80s or low 90s. Even on those days, evening temperatures cool to the point where a sweater may be necessary. Fall may be the best time to visit—summer crowds are gone and blue skies and sunshine often persist, with temperatures in the 60s. Spring, with showers mixed with sunshine, and temperatures in the high 50s to low 60s, brings beautiful garden displays. The average temperature in January is 38°—freezing temperatures are rare, with only two or three snowfalls a season.

FESTIVALS AND SEASONAL EVENTS **Memorial Day Weekend:** The Folklife Festival showcases some of the region's best folk singers, jugglers, and bands, along with crafts and food vendors at the Seattle Center. **Late July–early Aug.:** Seafair (tel. 206/728–0123) salutes Seattle's marine heritage with a parade in downtown and hydroplane races on Lake Washington near Seward Park. **Labor Day Weekend:** Bumbershoot offers four days of music, including classical, blues, reggae, zydeco, and popular at Seattle Center.

BARGAINS Seattle's greatest asset—its spectacular scenery—is free. Another visual treat is the Pike Place Market (1st Ave. at Pike St.), where vendors hawk fresh seafood and produce, and craftspeople offer their wares. Just across the street at Victor Steinbreuck Park, you can take a picnic, listen to street musicians, and watch ferries crossing Puget Sound. Another city park with great views of Elliott Bay is Myrtle Edwards Park. Take the Hillclimb stairs from the market down to the

waterfront and walk or take the trolley north to the park, where there is a walking and bicycle trail along the shores of Elliott Bay.

Seattle's Out to Lunch summer concert series (tel. 206/623–0340) runs from mid-June to early September every weekday at noon in various parks, plazas, and atriums in downtown.

The Seattle Art Museum is free on the first Tuesday of the month. The Elliott Bay Book Company (101 S. Main St., tel. 206/624–6600) hosts lectures and readings by authors of local and international acclaim. Most are free, but phone ahead to be sure.

Ticket/Ticket (401 Broadway E on the second floor inside the Broadway Market, tel. 206/324–2744) sells half-price tickets for most theater, music, and dance events on the day of the performance. Prices for movies that have just left downtown theaters are always affordable at $2 at the Crest Cinema (16505 5th Ave. NE, tel. 206/363–6338).

The Pavilion Outlet Center just south of Southcenter Mall in Tukwila (17100 Southcenter Pkwy., tel. 206/575–8090) has a number of stores with discounted merchandise.

TOURIST OFFICES The Seattle/King County Convention and Visitors Bureau (800 Convention Pl., Seattle 98101, tel. 206/461–5840), at the I–5 end of Pike Street, can provide you with maps and information about lodging, restaurants, and attractions throughout the city.

EMERGENCIES Police, fire, and ambulance: Dial 911. Hospitals: Area hospitals with emergency rooms include Harborview Medical Center (325 9th Ave., tel. 206/223–3074) and Virginia Mason Hospital (925 Seneca St., tel. 206/624–1144).

ARRIVING AND DEPARTING

BY PLANE Seattle-Tacoma International Airport is 20 miles from downtown Seattle and is served by most major U.S. and international airlines. Allow 30–45 minutes' driving time to or from downtown.

Between the Airport and Downtown. Visitors can take Gray Line Airport Express (tel. 206/626–6088) buses from 6:10 AM to 11:45 PM, with departures every 20–30 minutes depending on the location of your hotel (fare: $7 one-way, $12 round-trip for adults). Shuttle Express (tel. 206/622–1424) offers service to and from the airport (fare: $14 for singles one-way or $21 for two one-way tickets).

BY CAR I–5 enters Seattle from the north and south, I–90 from the east.

BY BUS Seattle is served by **Greyhound** (tel. 800/231–2222) from its 8th Avenue and Stewart Street depot.

BY TRAIN **Amtrak** (303 S. Jackson St., tel. 800/USA–RAIL) provides rail transportation from Seattle.

GETTING AROUND

BY BUS Metropolitan Transit (821 2nd Ave., tel. 206/553–3000) provides a free-ride service in the downtown-waterfront area. Fares to other destinations range from 85¢ to $1.60 depending on the zone and time of day.

BY MONORAIL The Monorail (tel. 206/684–7200), built for the 1962 World's Fair, runs from Westlake Center to the Seattle Center every 15 minutes. Hours are Sunday–Thursday 9–9 and Friday and Saturday 9 AM–midnight. The fare is 80¢ each way for adults, 25¢ for seniors and children.

BY TAXI The taxi fare is $1.80 at flag fall and $1.80 per mile. Major companies are Farwest (tel. 206/622–1717) and Yellow Cab (tel. 206/622–6500).

BY TROLLEY Waterfront trolleys (tel. 206/553–3000) run from Pier 70 into Pioneer Square. Fares are 85¢ nonpeak and $1.10 for travel during peak hours (5:30 AM–8:30 AM and 3–6 PM).

REST STOPS Good for putting your feet up are atriums such as the one inside Columbia Center Court or Westlake Mall. The cleanest rest rooms are in these indoor centers and in department stores.

GUIDED TOURS **Orientation:** From Pier 55, Seattle Harbor Tours (Pier 55, Suite 201, 98101, tel. 206/623–1445) offers one-hour tours exploring Elliott Bay and the Port of Seattle. Gray Line, which departs from the downtown Sheraton (1400 6th Ave., tel. 206/626–5208), offers guided bus tours of the city and environs ranging in scope from a daily 2¹/₂-hour spin to a 6-hour "Grand City Tour."

Special-Interest: Tillicum Village (Pier 55–56, tel. 206/443–1244) sails from Pier 55–56 across Puget Sound to Blake Island for a four-hour experience of traditional Northwest Indian life, including a dinner of steamed clams and salmon and the Dance of the Wind performance. Underground Tours (610 1st Ave., tel. 206/682–4646 for reservations or 206/682–1511 for information) offers a 90-minute walking tour of the below-ground sections of Pioneer Square with tongue-in-cheek narration.

Self-guided: "A Directory of Seattle's Public Art," an illustrated brochure by the Seattle Arts Commission (312 1st Ave. N. tel. 206/684–7171), describes walks and drives to see more than 256 innovative works of art in public places.

EXPLORING

International District. Located south and east of the Kingdome, the International District is about one-third Chinese, one-third Filipino, and one-third residents from all over Asia. The district began as a haven for Chinese workers after they finished the Transcontinental Railroad; it contains many Chinese, Japanese, and Korean restaurants as well as herbalists, massage parlors, acupuncturists, and about 30 private clubs for gambling and socializing. Uwajimaya (519 6th Ave. S, tel. 206/624–6248), possibly the largest Japanese store on the West Coast, stocks china, gifts, fabrics, housewares, and a complete supermarket with an array of Asian foods. Also in this area is the Nippon Kan Theater (628 S. Washington St., tel. 206/467–6807), a national historic site that presents many Asian-interest productions, including the Japanese

Performing arts series, which runs from October through May.

Kingdome. Seattle's covered stadium is the home of the Seattle Seahawks NFL team and the Seattle Mariners baseball team. The 650-foot-diameter stadium was built in 1976 and has the world's largest self-supporting roof, which is 250 feet high. If you're interested in the inner workings, take the one-hour guided tour. *201 S. King St., tel. 206/296–3111. Opening hours vary. Admission charged.*

Museum of Flight. The Red Barn, the original Boeing airplane factory, houses an exhibit on the history of aviation. The Great Gallery, a dramatic structure designed by Seattle architect Ibsen Nelson, contains more than 20 airplanes—suspended from the ceiling and on the ground—dating back to the Wright brothers. There's a free, hour-long Boeing tour. *9404 E. Marginal Way S, tel. 206/764–5720. Open daily, except Christmas. Admission charged.*

Pike Place Market. This Seattle institution began in 1907 when the city issued permits to farmers allowing them to sell produce from their wagons parked at Pike Place. In 1911, the city built stalls that were allotted to the farmers on a daily basis. Urban renewal almost killed the market, but city voters led by the late architect Victor Steinbrueck rallied and voted it to be a historical asset. Many of the buildings have been restored, and the project is connected by stairs and an elevator to the waterfront. You can still purchase fresh seafood (which can be packed in dry ice for your flight home), produce, cheese, Northwest wines, bulk spices, tea, coffee, and arts and crafts. *1st Ave. at Pike St., tel. 206/682–7453. Open daily. Admission free.*

Pioneer Square. To get a sense of how Seattle has changed through the years, take a look at the old section of the city with its cobblestone streets and brick buildings. Start at Pioneer Park (Yesler Way and 1st Ave. S), where an ornate iron-and-glass pergola stands. This was the site of Seattle's original business district. In 1889, a fire destroyed many of the wood-frame buildings in the area, but the industrious residents and businesspeople rebuilt them with brick and mortar. The term "Skid Row" originated here, when timber was logged off the hill and sent to the sawmill. The skid road was made of small logs laid down and greased so the freshly cut timber could slide down to the mill. With the Klondike gold rush, this area became populated with saloons and brothels and the old pioneering area deteriorated. Eventually drunks and bums hung out on Skid Road, and the term changed to Skid Row. Today, Pioneer Square encompasses about 18 blocks and includes restaurants, bars, shops, the city's largest concentration of art galleries (*see* Shopping, *below*), and the **Klondike Gold Rush National Historical Park,** with a center showing film presentations, permanent exhibits, and summer gold-panning demonstrations. *117 S. Main St., tel. 206/442–7220. Open daily. Admission free.*

Seattle Aquarium. Sea otters and seals swim and dive in their pools, and the "State of the Sound" exhibit shows aquatic life and the ecology of Puget Sound. Just next door is the **Omnidome Film Experience,** which showcases large-scale OMNIMAX films such as the one showing the eruption of Mt. St. Helens. *Pier 59. Aquarium: tel. 206/386–4320; Omnidome: tel. 206/622–1868. Open daily. Admission charged.*

Seattle Center. This 74-acre complex built for the 1962 Seattle World's Fair includes an amusement park, theaters, the Coliseum, exhibition halls, museums, shops, and the city's most famous landmark, the **Space Needle,** with its lounge, restaurant (tel. 206/443–2100 or 800/937–9582), and observation deck. The 605-foot-tall symbol of the city is easily recognized from almost anywhere in the downtown area. The glass elevator to the observation deck offers an impressive view of the city.

University of Washington. Some 33,500 students attend the university, which was founded in 1861. On the northwestern corner of the beautifully landscaped campus is the **Burke Museum** (17th Ave. NE and N.E. 45th St., tel. 206/543–5590; open daily; donation requested), Washington's natural-history and anthropological museum. Nearby, the **Henry Art Gallery** (15th Ave. NE and N.E. 41st St., tel. 206/543–2280; open daily, except Monday; admission charged) displays paintings from the 19th and 20th centuries, textiles, and traveling exhibits.

Washington Park Arboretum, just south of the campus, offers self-guided walking tours of its lush grounds. A visitor center at the north end of the park is open to instruct you on the species of flora and fauna you'll see here. *2300 Arboretum Dr. E, tel. 206/543–8800. Open daily.*

Woodland Park Zoo. Many of the animals are free to roam their section of a total of 92 acres. The African Savanna, the Elephant Forest, and the Tropical Rain Forest are popular features. *N. 59th St. and Frement Ave., tel. 206/684–4800. Open daily. Admission charged.*

Just 85 miles southeast of Seattle is **Mt. Rainier National Park.** At 14,411 feet, Mt. Rainier is the fifth-highest mountain in the lower 48 states. In addition to the mountain with its glaciers and ice caves, the park includes some 400 square miles of wilderness, 300 miles of hiking trails, cross-country skiing trails, lakes and rivers for fishing, and camping facilities. Wildlife includes bears, mountain goats, deer, elk, eagles, beavers, and mountain lions. At an altitude of 5,400 feet, Paradise is the usual starting point for climbs to the summit during the summer, but mountain climbing is serious business and best suited for very physically fit individuals who have adequately trained and are accompanied by an experienced guide. At Paradise, the **Henry M. Jackson Visitor's Center,** the starting point for many hikes, has exhibits, films, and a 360-degree view of the summit and surrounding peaks. At 6,400 feet, the **Sunrise Visitor's Center** is the highest point accessible by car at Rainier. *To reach Mt. Rainier from Seattle, follow I–5, Hwy. 7, and Hwy. 706 south and east or Hwy. 410 east and south. Henry M. Jackson Visitor's Center: tel. 206/569–2211. Jackson is open Memorial Day–Labor Day, daily; Sunrise is open July 4th weekend–Labor Day, daily.*

HOTELS AND INNS

Downtown hotels are the most convenient, and most expensive. More economical are accommodations near the Seattle Center, where you can board the monorail for the short trip downtown. For recommendations regarding bed-and-breakfast accommodations, contact the Washington State Bed & Breakfast Guild (tel. 509/548–6224) or Pacific Bed & Breakfast Agency (tel. 206/784–0539). Price categories for double occupancy, excluding 15.2% tax, are *Expensive,* over $90; *Moderate,* $60–$90; and *Inexpensive,* less than $60.

DOWNTOWN **Mayflower Park Hotel.** Brass fixtures and antiques give a muted Oriental feel to this pleasant older hotel, built in 1927. Although it is quieter than most modern downtown hotels, its guest rooms are somewhat smaller. *405 Olive Way, 98101, tel. 206/623–8700, fax 206/382–6997. 164 rooms, 14 suites; no-smoking rooms available. Restaurant, lounge, access to health club. AE, DC, MC, V. Moderate–Expensive.*

Inn at Virginia Mason. Located east of the I–5 freeway from downtown, this mid-size inn was renovated in 1989 and now has attractively decorated rooms and ample parking. *1006 Spring St., 98104, tel. 206/583–6453. 79 rooms. Restaurant. MC, V. Moderate.*

Pacific Plaza. Built in 1928 and refurbished in 1989, this ideally located downtown hotel reflects its original character, with rooms and furnishings reminiscent of the '20s and '30s. Guest rooms are sized adequately for couples but not for families. *400 Spring St., 98104, tel. 206/623–3900 or 800/426–1165, fax 206/623–2059. 160 rooms. Continental breakfast included, 2 restaurants. AE, DC, MC, V. Moderate.*

West Coast Camlin Hotel. This recently remodeled 1926 Seattle hotel/motor inn, on the edge of downtown but close to the convention center, features spacious rooms slightly blemished by the noisy heating system. Rooms ending with 10 are best because they feature windows on three sides. *1619 9th Ave., 98101, tel. 206/682–0100 or 800/426–*0670, fax 206/682–7415. 136 rooms. Restaurant, lounge, outdoor pool. AE, D, DC, MC, V. Moderate.*

Seattle YMCA. These downtown rooms are clean and plainly furnished with a bed, phone, desk, and lamp. The building is a member of the American Youth Hostels Association, and four people can sleep in each dorm unit. *909 4th Ave., 98104, tel. 206/382–5000. 198 units. Pool, health club. MC, V. Inexpensive.*

SEATTLE CENTER **Sixth Avenue Inn.** This small but comfortable motor hotel, built in the 1960s and renovated around 1985, is located a few blocks between downtown and the Seattle Center. Suitable for families, the property has unexceptional but well-maintained decor and color schemes. *2000 6th Ave., 98121, tel. 206/441–8300, fax 206/441–9903. 166 rooms, no-smoking rooms available. Restaurant, lounge. AE, DC, MC, V. Moderate.*

Park Inn. Just a couple of blocks from the Seattle Center and the monorail for access to downtown, this 1960s-vintage motel has appealing, but not fancy, decor. *225 Aurora Ave. N, 98107, tel. 206/728–7666. 160 rooms, no-smoking rooms available. Indoor pool, whirlpool, parking. AE, MC, V. Inexpensive–Moderate.*

NORTH END **Meany Tower Hotel.** Built in 1931 and completely remodeled several times, this pleasant hotel, just a few blocks from the University of Washington, has retained much of its old-fashioned charm; the rooms on the upper floors have views of Lake Washington and Lake Union. *4507 Brooklyn Ave. NE, 98105, tel. 206/634–2000, fax 206/634–2000. 155 rooms; no-smoking rooms available. Restaurant, lounge. AE, DC, MC, V. Moderate.*

University Plaza Hotel. This is a full-service motor hotel on the west side of I–5 from the University of Washington. There is slightly out-of-date mock Tudor decor in the public areas, but rooms are spacious and pleasantly decorated with teak furniture; rooms near the freeway can be noisy. *400 N.E. 45th St.,*

98105, tel. 206/634–0100, fax 206/633–2743. 135 rooms; no-smoking rooms available. Restaurant, lounge, outside heated pool, fitness room, beauty parlor. AE, D, DC, MC, V. Inexpensive.

SEATTLE–TACOMA AIRPORT **Seattle Marriott–SeaTac.** The Marriott is surprisingly luxurious for being so far away from downtown. Built in 1981, the hotel features a five-story-high, 20,000-square-foot tropical atrium with newly renovated guest rooms. *3201 S. 176th St., 98188, tel. 206/241–2000, fax 206/248–0789. 459 rooms; no-smoking rooms available. Restaurant, 2 whirlpools, health club, game room, concierge service, airport shuttle. AE, D, DC, MC, V. Moderate–Expensive.*

Holiday Inn Sea-Tac. This hotel, built in 1970, has been remodeled with an atrium lobby and a garden room. The Top of the Inn revolving-view restaurant features singing waiters. *17338 Pacific Hwy. S, 98188, tel. 206/248–1000 or 800/HOLIDAY, fax 206/242–7089. 260 rooms. Restaurant, coffee shop, lounge, indoor pool, whirlpool, health club. AE, DC, MC, V. Moderate.*

MOTELS

MODERATE **Black Angus Motor Inn** (12245 Aurora Ave. N, 98133, tel. 206/363–3035). 53 rooms; restaurant, lounge, coffee shop, pool, no-smoking rooms. **University Inn** (4140 Roosevelt Way NE, 98105, tel. 206/632–5055). 42 rooms; outdoor pool, complimentary coffee and newspapers.

INEXPENSIVE **Commodore Motor Hotel** (2013 2nd Ave., 98121, tel. 206/448–8868). 100 rooms; downtown location. **Nendels Valu Inn** (2106 5th Ave., 98121, tel. 800/547–0106). 68 rooms. **Max-Ivor Motel** (6188 4th Ave. S, 98108, tel. 206/762–8194). 41 rooms; restaurant next door.

DINING

Dining in Seattle means many things. One of them is seafood—salmon, halibut, crab, shrimp, you name it. Another is dining with outstanding views—Elliott Bay in down-town, the Olympic Mountains and Shilshole Bay to the west, and Lake Washington and the Cascade Mountains to the east.

Dining out is a popular activity in this city, and one can eat healthily. Seafood can often be ordered steamed or poached for an especially low-fat source of protein. Vegetables are in plentiful supply in Seattle restaurants, especially in Chinese, Thai, Vietnamese, and East Indian establishments. Skip one of the decadent desserts on local menus and head down to the Pike Place Market for a fresh Washington apple. Price categories per person, excluding 8.2% tax, service, and drinks, are *Moderate,* $15–$25, and *Inexpensive,* under $15.

MODERATE **Cafe Sport.** This Pike Place Market restaurant serves a variety of cuisines—one day it may be Italian, another it may be Thai—but whatever it is, the food is excellent and the portions are hearty. *2020 Western Ave., tel. 206/443–6000. AE, DC, MC, V.*

Cucina! Cucina! Enjoy basic Italian fare—lightly sauced pasta and seafood dishes and one-person pizzas—in the restaurant or on the large deck overlooking Lake Union. But take note, this place can get noisy. *901 Fairview Ave. N, tel. 206/447–2782. AE, MC, V.*

Kells. This traditional Irish pub is tucked into an old brick building along the Pike Place Market. The menu is simple but satisfying—choose from Irish stew, leg of lamb, and meat pies, and wash it all down with a pint of Guinness. On some nights there's live Irish music here. *1916 Post Alley, tel. 206/728–1916. MC, V.*

Linyen. This comfortable restaurant offers a new, light style of Cantonese food. Most nights you'll find clams in black-bean sauce, spicy chicken, and fresh fish on the blackboard menu of specials. *424 7th Ave. S, tel. 206/622–8181. AE, DC, MC, V.*

Rover's. This is French cooking at its best, with a daily menu based on what's locally available. The atmosphere, too, is intoxicating: You eat in a romantic, converted private home built around a small garden. *2808 E. Madison St., tel. 206/325–7442. AE, DC MC, V.*

Takara. Sushi and sashimi are the hallmarks of this popular, classical Japanese restaurant. The salmon teriyaki is superb, as is the steamed black cod. *1501 Western Ave., tel. 206/682–8609. AE, MC, V.*

Wild Ginger. This restaurant's specialty is Pacific Rim cookery—primarily tasty and eclectic Asian fare—including southern Chinese, Vietnamese, Thai, and Malaysian dishes served in an intimate dining room. *1400 Western Ave., tel. 206/623–4450. AE, D, DC, MC, V.*

INEXPENSIVE **A. Jay's Eatery.** Good sandwiches, omelets, soups, and dinner entreés are served at this deli that lets you linger over coffee. *2619 1st Ave., tel. 206/441–1511. AE, MC, V.*

Bahn Thai. Because of the variety of dishes and the quality of the preparations, the Bahn Thai is still one of the best and most popular Thai places in Seattle, but it can get noisy in the evening. *409 Roy St., tel. 206/283–0444. AE, DC, MC, V.*

Chau's Chinese Restaurant. This small, plain place on the edge of Chinatown serves great seafood and specials as an alternative to the standard Cantonese fare. *310 4th Ave. S, tel. 206/621–0006. MC, V.*

El Puerco Lloron. There's a pink awning and a pig outside this steel-and-glass building, and fresh, handmade tortillas with great texture and flavorful fillings inside. *Pike Place Market Hillclimb, 1501 Western Ave., tel. 206/624–0541. AE, MC, V.*

Han II. This upstairs, upscale Korean restaurant serves great lunch specials and classic Korean barbecue, all prepared on gas burners at your table and accompanied by a troop of side dishes and dipping sauces. *409 Maynard Ave. S, tel. 206/587–0464. MC, V.*

Hien Vuong. An unpretentious place that serves up great Vietnamese food, making it one of the best lunch places in town. *502 S. King St., tel. 206/624–2611. No credit cards.*

Salvatore Ristorante Italiano. You may have to wait at this small place, but most people believe it's worth it when they taste the individual pizzas, pasta dishes, or one of the meat and fish courses chalked onto the blackboard above the kitchen window. *6100 Roosevelt Way NE, tel. 206/527–9301. MC, V.*

Sunlight Cafe. The Sunlight Cafe continues to draw an easygoing crowd for its steady and flavorful vegetarian dishes, such as hearty soups, stir-fried vegetables with a yogurt-cheese sauce, and bountiful vegetable salads with sesame-tahini dressing. *6403 Roosevelt Way NE, tel. 206/522–9060. No credit cards.*

Three Girls Bakery. This tiny, 13-seat lunch counter behind a Pike Place Market bakery serves good sandwiches, soups, chili, and great bread—try the sourdough. *1514 Pike Pl., tel. 206/622–1045. No credit cards.*

SHOPPING

With fresh and natural ingredients in abundance, Seattleites are excited to share the bounty. They do so by offering smoked salmon, jams, jellies, honey, and syrups made from fresh, local ingredients. Several people have been entrepreneurial and taken the ash resulting from the destructive eruption of Mt. St. Helens and fashioning it into glass for jewelry, vases, and other art objects. Artists and photographers make good use of the splendid scenery all around the region and offer their creations for sale through galleries and the Pike Place Market.

MALLS Westlake Center (400 Pine St., tel. 206/467–1600) lies in the middle of downtown Seattle. The three-story steel-and-glass building contains 80 shops as well as covered walkways to Seattle's two major department stores, Nordstrom's and The Bon. Northgate Mall (I–5 and Northgate Way, tel. 206/362–4777), located 10 miles north of downtown, encompasses 118 shops, including Nordstrom's, The Bon, Lamonts, and JC Penny.

ANTIQUES Seattle's antiques shops offer everything from expensive, high-quality pieces to the wacky, way-out, and eminently affordable. To see the former, browse at David Reed Weatherford (133 14th Ave. E, tel. 206/329–6533), specializing in 17th- and 18th-century English, French, and Oriental pieces. Pioneer Square Mall features 85 stalls of antique glassware, jewelry, and furniture (602 1st Ave. S, tel. 206/624–1164). Antique Importers (640 Alaskan Way, tel. 206/628–8905) offers 14,000 square feet of pieces from Victoriana to Art Deco.

SPECIALTY SHOPS **Books:** Elliott Bay Book Company (101 S. Main St., tel. 206/624–6600) is a great place for browsing, especially for children's, Northwest, and travel books. The University Book Store (4326 University Way NE, tel. 206/634–3400) is among the largest general bookstores in the country. **Crafts, Souvenirs, Toys:** Pike Place Market (*see* Exploring, *above*). **Menswear:** For discounted men's clothing, go to The Men's Wearhouse (16971 Southcenter Pkwy., Tukwila, tel. 206/575–4393). **Women's Clothing:** For supreme bargains, visit Loehmann's (3620 128th St. SE, Bellevue, tel. 206/641–7596) just across the I–90 bridge from Seattle.

OUTDOOR ACTIVITIES

BIKING The Burke-Gilman Trail is a city-maintained trail extending 12.1 miles from Lake Washington nearly to Salmon Bay. Myrtle Edwards Park, north of Pier 70, has a two-lane path for jogging and cycling. Bikes can be rented at Gregg's Greenlake Cycle (7007 Woodlawn Ave. N, tel. 206/523–1822).

FISHING There are good spots for fishing on Lake Washington, Green Lake, and Lake Union, and there are several fishing piers along the Elliott Bay waterfront. A couple of the many Seattle-based charter companies that offer trips for catching salmon, rock cod, flounder, and sea bass are Ballard Salmon Charter (tel. 206/789–6202) and Seattle Salmon and Bottle Fishing (tel. 206/292–0595).

GOLF There are almost 50 public golf courses in the Seattle area. Among the most popular municipally run courses are Jackson Park (100 N.E. 135th St., tel. 206/363–4747) and Jefferson Park (4101 Beacon Ave. S, tel. 206/762–4513).

HIKING Lincoln Park in West Seattle or Discovery Park in the Magnolia area both have inspiring walks along the beach or up on the bluff, with fabulous views of the Olympic Mountains, ferries, and sea life.

JOGGING Green Lake is a favorite destination for cyclists, joggers, race walkers, strollers, and roller skaters. Several outlets along the east side offer skate and cycle rentals. Other good areas for jogging and walking are the Burke-Gilman Trail, around the reservoir at Volunteer Park, and at Myrtle Edwards Park, north of the waterfront.

SKIING Snoqualmie Pass in the Cascade Mountains, about an hour's drive east of Seattle on I–90, has a number of fine resorts offering downhill and cross-country skiing trails. Among them: Alpental, Ski Acres, Snoqualmie Summit (for all areas: 3010 77th St. SE, Mercer Island 98040, tel. 206/232–8182).

TENNIS There are public tennis courts in many parks around the Seattle area. For information, contact the King County Parks Division (tel. 206/296–4258).

ENTERTAINMENT

The Weekly has detailed arts, movie, and music reviews; it hits the newsstands every Wednesday. You can order tickets by phone from Ticketmaster (tel. 206/628–0888) or Ticket/Ticket (401 Broadway E inside the Broadway Market, tel. 206/324–2744), which sells half-price tickets for most theater, music, and dance events on the day of the performance.

CONCERTS Seattle Symphony (Opera House at Seattle Center, tel. 206/443–4747) continues to uphold its long tradition of excellence. Most live rock and country-western concerts are held at the Paramount Theater (901 Pine St., tel. 206/682-1414) and the Moore Theater

(1932 2nd Ave., tel. 206/443–1744), both elegant former movie/music halls.

DANCE Pacific Northwest Ballet (Opera House at Seattle Center, tel. 206/547–5920) is the city's resident company. Meany Hall for the Performing Arts (University of Washington campus, tel. 206/543–4880) presents important national and international companies with an emphasis on modern and jazz dance.

DINNER SHOWS Dimitriou's Jazz Alley (2033 6th Ave., tel. 206/441–9729) is a downtown club with nationally known, high-quality performers and dinner service.

NIGHTCLUBS Bars with waterfront views include Hiram's at the Locks (5300 34th Ave. NW, tel. 206/784–1733), Ray's Boathouse (6049 Seaview Ave. NW, tel. 206/789–3770) and Anthony's Home Port (6135 Seaview Ave. W, tel. 206/783–0780) at Shilshole Bay.

OPERA Seattle Opera (Opera House at Seattle Center, Mercer St. at 3rd Ave., tel. 206/443–4711) is a world-class opera company, considered to be one of the top organizations in the country.

THEATER Seattle Repertory Theater (Bagley Wright Theater at Seattle Center, 155 Mercer St., tel. 206/443–2222) presents a variety of high-quality programming from classics to new plays October–May. Intiman Theater (Playhouse at Seattle Center, 2nd and Mercer Sts., tel. 206/626–0782 presents classic world drama in an intimate, high-quality setting May–November. The Fifth Avenue Musical Theater Company (Fifth Avenue Theater, 1308 5th Ave., tel. 206/625–1418) is a resident professional troupe that mounts four lavish musicals October–May each year.

SPECTATOR SPORTS The Seattle Mariners baseball team (Kingdome, 201 S. King St., tel. 206/628–3555) plays April through early October. The Seattle SuperSonics basketball team (Seattle Center Coliseum, 1st Ave. N, tel. 206/281–5850) plays October through April. The NFL Seahawks (Kingdome, 201 S. King St., tel. 206/827–9777) play August through December.

Sequoia and Kings Canyon National Parks
California

When famed naturalist John Muir first laid eyes on this region of the Sierra, he called it a sublime wilderness. Contemporary visitors to California's Sequoia and Kings Canyon national parks still walk awed among the silent giants—the sequoias, the earth's largest living things—and they still marvel at the deep granite canyons and the snow-capped peaks. The two parks share a boundary and are administered as one park. They now encompass 1,300 square miles that are rivaled only by Yosemite National Park, to the north, in terms of rugged Sierra beauty. The topography runs from foothill chaparrals in the west, to the Giant Sequoia belt at 5,000 to 7,000 feet, to the towering peaks of the Great Western Divide; 14,494-foot Mt. Whitney, the highest point in the contiguous United States, is the crown jewel of the east side.

Most of the major attractions in both parks can be reached by automobile, but the majority of acreage is without roads. If you expect to simply drive through, you will probably be disappointed: The panoramic views and striking geological features found in other national parks exist here, but they are less accessible. If you want to explore these parks, you will have to hike; and you'll have 900 miles of trails from which to choose.

Today 2 million people visit the parks annually. They come to wile away peaceful hours on uncrowded trails, or to trek into the rugged grandeur of the backcountry. But there was a time, beginning in the 1860s, when people came to these timberlands to cut trees, and in some places the scars are still evident. By 1890, however, the area's beauty was officially recognized and the destruction was put in check by the establishment of Sequoia National Park, the country's second national park. In 1940 the adjacent General Grant Park was expanded to include the South Fork Kings River and renamed Kings Canyon National Park.

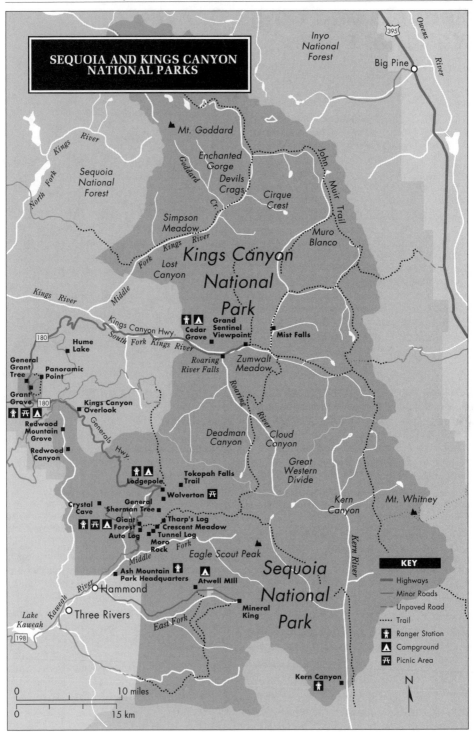

SEQUOIA AND KINGS CANYON
NATIONAL PARKS

Inyo
National
Forest

Big Pine

Owens River

395

Mt. Goddard

Kings River

North Fork

Sequoia
National
Forest

Goddard Cr.

Enchanted
Gorge

Devils
Crags

Cirque
Crest

John Muir Trail

Simpson
Meadow

Kings River

South Fork Kings River

Muro
Blanco

Lost
Canyon

Kings Canyon
National
Park

Kings River

Middle Fork

Kings Canyon Hwy.

Cedar
Grove

Grand
Sentinel
Viewpoint

Mist Falls

180

Hume
Lake

General
Grant
Tree

Panoramic
Point

Grant
Grove

180

Kings Canyon
Overlook

Roaring
River Falls

Zumwalt
Meadow

Roaring River

Redwood
Mountain
Grove

Redwood
Canyon

Generals Hwy.

Deadman
Canyon

Cloud
Canyon

Great
Western
Divide

Kern
Canyon

Mt. Whitney

Tokopah Falls
Trail

Lodgepole

Wolverton

Crystal
Cave

General
Sherman Tree

Giant
Forest

Auto Log

Tharp's Log

Crescent Meadow

Tunnel Log

Moro
Rock

Middle Fork

Eagle Scout Peak

Sequoia
National
Park

Kern River

Ash Mountain
Park Headquarters

Atwell Mill

Hammond

Kaweah River

Three Rivers

Lake
Kaweah

198

East Fork

Mineral
King

KEY

Highways
Minor Roads
Unpaved Road
Trail
Ranger Station
Campground
Picnic Area

Kern Canyon

N

0 _____ 10 miles

0 _____ 15 km

ESSENTIAL INFORMATION

WHEN TO GO During the summer months, daytime highs usually run from the 70s to low 80s in the middle elevations, where the park's most popular attractions are located. The lower elevations often experience temperatures above 100°. Overnight lows average 46° to 53°. Visitors should bear in mind that summer thundershowers are not uncommon, and that the weather can change quickly in the mountains.

In winter, temperatures usually range from the low 20s to mid-40s, with overnight lows down into the single digits. Much of the area is covered with a deep blanket of snow from December to May. The roads to Giant Forest and Grant's Grove and the Generals Highway, which connects the two areas, are open year-round but are subject to closures or chain restrictions because of snowfall.

The best times to visit the parks are during late spring and early fall, when the temperatures are still moderate and the crowds thin. The parks draw their heaviest crowds during the month of August and over holiday weekends. Summer visitors should remember that they will be approaching the park from the west, across the San Joaquin Valley, where temperatures often exceed 100° from late May through early September. In May, June, September, and October, lodging rates within the park are reduced by about 20%; from November through April, they are reduced by more than 30%.

FESTIVALS AND SEASONAL EVENTS **Apr.:** The Jazz Affair, held in the town of Three Rivers, is mostly swing jazz, held at several locations, with shuttle buses between sites. **Early May:** The Red Bud Festival, in Three Rivers, is a two-day arts and crafts festival. The Woodlake Rodeo, in Woodlake, is a weekend event that draws large crowds. **Dec. 25:** Carolers gather at the base of the General Grant Tree, the Nation's official Christmas tree.

TOURIST OFFICES Park Headquarters (Superintendent, Sequoia and Kings Canyon National Parks, Three Rivers 93271, tel. 209/565-3134). Fresno Visitor and Conven-

tion Bureau (808 M St., Fresno 93721, tel. 209/233-0836). Visalia Chamber of Commerce (720 West Mineral King, Visalia 93291, tel. 209/734-5876).

EMERGENCIES For **police, fire,** and **ambulance:** Dial 911.

ARRIVING AND DEPARTING

BY PLANE Sequoia and Kings Canyon national parks are serviced by the Fresno Airport (tel. 209/498-4700), located 5 miles from downtown Fresno and 55 miles from the parks. At the Visalia Airport (tel. 209/738-3201), commercial passengers may arrive on American Eagle, which makes connections in Los Angeles and San Jose.

BETWEEN THE AIRPORT AND THE PARKS **By Car or RV:** Only two roads lead into the parks and both approach from the west: Highway 180 from Fresno and Highway 198 from Visalia.

By Train: Amtrak (tel. 800/USA-RAIL) has stations in Fresno and Hanford, which is located 15 miles from Visalia. A shuttle bus (included in the fare) takes train passengers from Hanford to Visalia.

By Bus: Both Fresno and Visalia have Greyhound Lines (tel. 800/231-2222), with buses that come in from San Francisco and Los Angeles. Typically, it costs $44 for a round-trip ticket from Los Angeles and $55 from San Francisco.

GETTING AROUND

BY CAR Highway 180 from Fresno passes through the peninsulalike Grant Grove in the southwestern section of Kings Canyon, travels north through the national forest, reenters the park as the Kings Canyon Highway, then dead-ends. Highway 198 travels 59 miles from Visalia, entering Sequoia from the southwest at Ash Mountain. The Generals Highway connects the two highways, thereby linking the two parks. No roads enter the parks from the east. Vehicles longer than 22 feet are strongly advised to enter the park via Highway 180. Be warned that the National Park Service is currently in the midst of a long-term road-improvement program: sporadic delays are a possibility for the next few years. At park entrances visitors are given a free informational brochure, which includes a map of the parks.

BY BUS An hourly shuttle ($2) connects Lodgepole to Moro Rock by way of Giant Forest.

REST STOPS Approaching the park on Highway 198, Kaweah Lake, located 5 miles west of Three Rivers, offers boating, swimming, fishing, picnic facilities, camping, and public rest rooms.

GUIDED TOURS Guided tours of the park are available only through private tour companies. Call Park Headquarters (209/565–3134) for information.

EXPLORING

There are three centers of interest in the two parks: In Kings Canyon, there is the eponymous river and its surrounding Cedar Grove, and there is Grant Grove; in Sequoia, most people flock to the Giant Forest. From early May through October all the roads in the parks are open, providing access to some spectacular scenery. But the nature of these parks is best appreciated by including at least a few short walks in your tour. If you have only one or two days and want to see all three of these areas, it is best to stay in Grant Grove, which is a one-hour drive from both Cedar Grove and Giant Forest (along the Generals Highway). If you do not plan on extensive hikes, two or three days is ample time to acquaint yourself with these two parks.

The **Lodgepole Visitor Center** (Sequoia) or the **Grant Grove Visitor Center** (Kings Canyon), located at the parks' entrances, are excellent places to begin a visit. Exhibits and audiovisual programs provide a natural and cultural history of the parks, from their geological development to man's impact. Rangers are on duty to answer questions, and a large selection of printed materials is available.

From the Lodgepole Visitor Center, backtrack on General's Highway just under 4 miles to the **General Sherman Tree,** the largest living tree in the world. A sequoia slab nearby illustrates the big trees' dependence on fire for their existence. Nearby, the easy, 2-mile Congress Trail is a paved loop through the heart of the sequoia forest that takes one to two hours to complete.

Next, head farther south and turn off on the **Moro Rock–Crescent Meadow Road,** a 3-mile spur road that begins at the Cedar Grove Village and explores the southwest portion of the Giant Forest. The road is closed in winter, when it may be used as a ski trail, and is not recommended for RVs or trailers any time of the year. Among the odd attractions on this road is the **Auto Log,** a fallen giant sequoia on top of which you can drive your car, and the **Tunnel Log,** a sequoia that you drive through (there is a bypass for larger vehicles). Make the effort to climb the steep, 1/4-mile staircase to the summit of **Moro Rock,** a large granite dome that offers excellent views of the Great Western Divide and the western half of Sequoia National Park. About 100 yards from the end of the road is **Crescent Meadow,** John Muir's "gem of the Sierra," where brilliant wildflowers bloom in midsummer. Many trails begin here, including the 1-mile route to **Tharp's Log** (a home built in a fallen tree) and the High Sierra trail, which runs 71 miles to the summit of Mt. Whitney.

In summer you can take a 45-minute walking tour through **Crystal Cave** every day from 10 AM to 3 PM, on the hour. The marble cavern is full of stalagmites and stalactites. Bring a sweater, as the temperatures are in the 50s. It is at least a 45-minute drive from Giant Forest Village to the parking lot, and it will take you an additional 15 minutes to walk to the cave entrance. No trailers, RVs, or buses are allowed on Crystal Cave Road, which has a weight limit of 6,000 pounds. (Admission charged.)

The **Kings Canyon Highway** winds alongside the powerful Kings River, below the towering granite cliffs and past the tumbling waterfalls of a canyon John Muir called a rival to Yosemite. One mile east past the Cedar Grove Village turnoff is a turnoff allowing a wonderful vista of the glacial past of the U-shaped canyon, everything from the valley floor to where the forks in the Kings River come together. Four miles farther along is the Grand Sentinel Viewpoint, where you will see the 3,500-foot tall granite monolith and some of the most interesting rock formations in the canyon. The drive takes about one hour each way. Take Highway 190 east from Grant Grove.

Back on Generals Highway, head north to Grant Grove and the **General Grant Tree,** the third-largest living tree in the world, believed to have been standing for 3,000 years. A designated National Shrine, it is the Nation's Christmas Tree and the only living memorial to American soldiers who have died while fighting for the United States in its wars. To reach the tree, take the short trail, which also passes the historic Gamlin Cabin, a cabin built in 1867, and the Fallen Monarch, a hollowed, fallen giant sequoia early explorers used for shelter. This trail begins 1 mile northwest of the Grant Grove Visitor Center.

Nearby, a steep and narrow spur road (not recommended for trailers and RVs) heads east through the visitor center parking lot, curves left around the meadow, splits to the right, and leads 2.3 miles to **Panoramic Point.** A $1/4$-mile walk from the parking lot, the viewpoint offers a spectacular vista of the High Sierra. You can see from Mt. Goddard in northern Kings Canyon Park to Eagle Scout Peak in Sequoia Park. Unfortunately, Mt. Whitney can't be seen from the west side of the park because of the height of the Great Western Divide. The Park Ridge Trail, a 4-mile round-trip, begins here.

About 8 miles southeast of Grant Grove on Generals Highway, there is another turnoff. This one is unpaved and bumpy; it dead-ends after about 2 miles at Redwood Saddle, where you'll find the trailhead to **Redwood Canyon.** Here there are miles of trails leading through the world's largest grove of the world's tallest tree. Take in the cascades and quiet pools of Redwood Creek on a short walk, day hike, or overnight backpacking trip.

The sandy **Mist Falls Trail** follows the glaciated South Fork Canyon through forest and chaparral, past several rapids and cascades, to one of the largest waterfalls in the two parks. This 8-mile round-trip hike is relatively flat but climbs 600 feet in the last mile. It takes four to five hours to complete. The trailhead is at Road's End, $5^1/2$ miles east of the Cedar Grove Village turnoff.

HOTELS AND INNS

All of the parks' lodges and cabins are open during the summer months, but in winter only those in Giant Forest and Grant Grove remain open. A variety of accommodations are offered at Giant Forest and Grant Grove, from rustic cabins without baths to a deluxe motel. From November through April, excluding holiday periods, low-season rates are in effect, resulting in savings of 20%–30%.

All of the lodging facilities within the park are operated by Sequoia Guest Services, an authorized concessionaire of the National Park Service, and each of the areas has a simple, inexpensive restaurant. Most of the accommodations do not have formal names; when calling for reservations, describe the room using the guidelines below. For information and reservations, contact Sequoia Guest Services (Box 789, Three Rivers 93271, tel. 209/561–3314, fax 203/561–3135). Price categories for double occupancy, without $16^1/2$% tax, are *Expensive,* over $85; *Moderate,* $50–$85; and *Inexpensive,* under $50. All hotels accept MC and V.

INSIDE THE PARK **Giant Forest.** The deluxe motel is the finest accommodation available in the park, with two queen-size beds, carpeted floors, and private showers. There are no low-season rates available. *Expensive.*

There are a variety of family cabins: a cozy cabin with two double beds and carpeted floors; two rooms with bed space for six and carpeting; or smaller units with one double and one single bed and wood floors. All have private tub or shower bath. *Moderate.*

There is a standard motel with simple, comfortable rooms with two double beds, carpeted floors, private tub/shower bath, and a large picture window. Some special motel units have an outdoor balcony. *Moderate.*

There are very rustic cabins that don't have baths, and some do not have electricity, in which case kerosene lamps are provided. Some have wood stoves for cooking (utensils not included) and tent roofs. All are closed in the winter. *Inexpensive.*

Grant Grove. The most luxurious accommodations here are carpeted cabins with private bath, electric wall heaters, and twin-size beds. Most of these units, however, are in twos, and the adjoining walls are a little thin. Other cabins are even simpler, with woodstoves providing heat and kerosene lamps providing light. A central rest room and shower facility is nearby. *Inexpensive.*

CEDAR GROVE **Cedar Grove Motel.** This is a small, 18-room motel/lodge, with rooms featuring two queen-size beds, carpeted floors, private showers, and air-conditioning. Open late May through September; rooms should be booked well in advance. *Moderate.*

STONY CREEK **Stony Creek Motel.** Open late May to September, the quiet motel/lodge here is actually on national forest land between Grant Grove and Giant Forest. The rooms are carpeted and have private showers. *Moderate.*

MOTELS

The following accommodations are outside the park perimeter.

MODERATE **Best Western** (40105 Sierra Dr., Three Rivers 93271, tel. 209/561–4119). 44 rooms; pool, spa. **Buckeye Tree Lodge** (46000 Sierra Dr., Three Rivers 93271, tel. 209/561–5900). 12 rooms, all with view of river; close to park. **Lazy J Motel** (39625 Sierra Dr., Three Rivers 93271, tel. 209/561–4449). 18 small cabins, 6 kitchenettes; swimming pool, river access, recommended for families.

CAMPGROUNDS

Staying in a campground is by far the most economical way to stay in Sequoia/Kings national parks. Campgrounds are located near each of the major centers, and most have all the basic facilities. Those planning to camp should note the various seasonal temperatures and be prepared for precipitation at any time of the year. The only campground offering reservations is Lodgepole in Sequoia National Park. All other campgrounds are on a first-come, first-served basis, and they often fill by Friday afternoon in July and August. More information on campgrounds is available through the Park Superintendent (Sequoia and Kings National Parks, Three Rivers 93271, tel. 209/565–3134).

KINGS CANYON **Cedar Grove Area. Sentinel, Moraine,** and **Sheep Creek** have a total of 314 sites, with immediate access to the views and trails of Kings Canyon and the Kings River. *$10. Showers, bathrooms, coin laundry, picnic tables, store, pay phone, short-order food service, service station. Closed mid-Oct.–mid-May.*

Grant Grove Area. Azalea (118 sites), **Sunset** (184 sites), and **Crystal Springs** (67 sites)— with a total of 369 sites—are all situated among the giant sequoias and close to restaurants and stores. These areas draw a lot of families. *$10. Pay showers, bathrooms, store, phones, restaurant, service station, dump station in Azalea.*

SEQUOIA **Foothills Area. Potwisha, Buckeye Flat,** and **South Fork** is in the 2,100- to 3,600-foot elevation area, located within a half-hour's drive of the Giant Forest, and have a total of 85 sites. Buckeye Flat and South Fork are not recommended for RVs or trailers, and Potwisha has a sanitary disposal station. South Fork tends to draw an older crowd and remains fairly quiet, largely because of its isolated location. *$8–$12. Potwisha has bathrooms and phone, while Buckeye Flat has bathrooms and South Fork has only pit latrines. Buckeye Flat is open mid-Apr.–mid-Oct. and South Fork mid-May–Oct.*

Giant Forest/Lodgepole Area. Dorst and **Lodgepole** campgrounds are located 12 miles north of Giant Forest Village, at an elevation of 6,800 feet. Together they have 478 campsites. Lodgepole is located within a half-mile of the visitor center and a 10-minute drive from the shops and restaurants in the Giant Forest Village. *Lodgepole: $12 during reservation season, $8 at other times. Limited facilities and no fees after heavy snow accumulates. Bathrooms, coin laundry, dump station, store, phone service station. Dorst: $10. Dorst has bathrooms, picnic tables, phone. Open Memorial Day–Labor Day.*

Mineral King Area. Atwell Mill (23 sites) and **Cold Springs** (37 sites) are located about 20 miles up a steep and very curvy road from the Generals Highway. The road is not recommended for trailers or RVs, and trailers are not permitted in the campgrounds. These are the quietest, most remote campgrounds, and they offer easy access to a number of hiking and backpacking trails. Campground elevations are 6,650 feet to 7,500 feet. *$10. Pit latrines, phones. At Silver City Resort (2 mi away) there are pay showers, and a restaurant, but gas and ice are not always available. Open Memorial Day–Sept.*

DINING

Each of the major areas within the park has only one restaurant, serving breakfast, lunch, and dinner. These are simple, no-frills eateries where basic American fare is well prepared and prices are reasonable. Health-conscious eaters will find a limited selection of foods, including salads, fruit platters, and fresh-frozen fish. All of the restaurants within the parks are managed by Guest Services (Giant Forest, Box A, Sequoia National Park 93262, tel. 209/565–3381). There are several restaurants on the way in or out of the park that are worth a visit. Price categories per person, not including 6¹/₂% tax, service, and drinks, are *Moderate,* $15–$25, and *Inexpensive,* under $15. All restaurants within the parks accept MC and V.

WITHIN THE PARK **Cedar Grove Restaurant.** As in many fast-food restaurants, patrons here order their food at a counter and then carry it to a table themselves. The limited menu includes hamburgers, hot dogs, and sandwiches for lunch and dinner; eggs and toast for breakfast. *Open when the snow melts–Labor Day. Inexpensive.*

Giant Forest Lodge Dining Room. This is the fanciest restaurant in the two parks, with table cloths, soft lighting, and a quiet atmosphere. The dinner menu features soups, salads, chicken, and fish. Breakfast and lunch are served every day, and there is a Sunday morning buffet brunch. *Open when the snow melts–mid-Oct. Inexpensive.*

Grant Grove Restaurant. This spacious restaurant serves up American fare for breakfast, lunch, and dinner. Among the tasty specials is a delicious red snapper in lemon-mushroom sauce. Chef's salad, fruit platters, and several other fish dishes are also offered. *Inexpensive.*

Lodgepole Delicatessen. For a quick lunch or dinner try this deli for hot and cold sandwiches, hamburgers, pizza, and other short-order items. *Open when the snow melts–mid-Oct. Inexpensive.*

Stony Creek Coffee Shop. At this sit-down coffee shop you can have eggs and toast in the morning, sandwiches for lunch, and burgers for dinner. The menu is similar to that of the coffee shop in Grant Grove. *Open when the snow melts–Labor Day. Inexpensive.*

The Village Cafeteria in Giant Forest. Breakfast, lunch, and dinner are served in a cafeteria-style setting, with dishes such as fish, chicken, and vegetable stir-fry for the health-conscious. *Inexpensive.*

OUTSIDE THE PARK **White Horse Inn.** Locals consider this the finest dining in town. Filled with antiques and bedecked with draperies and mirrors, the White Horse retains an English atmosphere. The house special is prime rib. Other choices are teriyaki chicken, the fresh fish, or duck à la Montmorency, which is half of a roasted duck in a cherry sauce. *42975 Sierra Dr., Three Rivers, tel. 209/561–*

4185. AE, D, MC, V. Closed Mon. and Tues. Moderate.

Clingen's Junction Restaurant. If you're anywhere near this place when you get hungry, make the drive. For breakfast you'll be treated to omelets or strawberry waffles with potatoes; at lunch try the turkey-breast sandwich with mushrooms. Dinner might start with homemade soup and fresh-baked breads. There is a dieter's special, and if you don't see what you want on the menu, just ask. *35591 E. Kings Canyon Hwy. (Hwy. 180), Clingen's Junction, tel. 209/338–2559. AE, MC, V. Inexpensive.*

The Noisy Water. Yet another casual establishment, The Noisy Water is named for the North Fork Kaweah River, which flows within view of the restaurant's large windows. Several menu selections are aimed toward vegetarians and health-conscious diners. *41775 Sierra Dr., Three Rivers, tel. 209/561–4517. AE, MC, V. Inexpensive.*

Staff of Life. The sunny atmosphere in this local hangout allows the many indoor plants to flourish. Lunch, served from 11 AM to 4 PM, includes soups, salads, and sandwiches, ranging from roast beef to vegetarian fave. Try the yogurt smoothies for dessert. *41651 Sierra Dr., Three Rivers, tel. 209/561–4937. Inexpensive.*

OUTDOOR ACTIVITIES

CROSS-COUNTRY SKIING There are cross-country touring centers and marked trails at Giant Forest (tel. 209/565–3435) and Grant Grove (tel. 209/335–2314). Qualified instructors, lessons, and rentals (touring and backcountry skis and snowshoes) are available. The centers operate weekdays 9 AM–5 PM, weekends and holidays 8 AM–6 PM.

FISHING There is a limited amount of trout fishing available in the parks' creeks and rivers from late April through mid-November, primarily in the Kings and Kaweah rivers. A California fishing license is required for persons 16 and older, and anglers should check the state and park fishing regulations for special closures and restrictions. Licenses

and fishing tackle are available in Lodgepole, Stony Creek, Grant Grove, and Cedar Grove.

HORSEBACK RIDING A number of private operators offer everything from one-hour trips to full-service, multiday pack trips into the backcountry. Popular one-day destinations are Mist Falls and Upper Bubb's Creek. Horseback rides are available through Cedar Grove Pack Station (tel. 209/565–3464), Grant Grove Stables (tel. 209/335–2374), Mineral King Pack Station (tel. 209/561–3404), or Wolverton Pack Station (tel. 209/565–3445).

SNOWSHOE WALKS Naturalist-guided snowshoe walks are offered on weekends and holidays, as conditions permit (usually mid-Dec.–mid-Mar.). It is recommended that you make reservations through the visitor centers (tel. 209/335–2315 in Grant Grove; 209/565–3341, ext. 631 in Giant Forest/Lodgepole).

WALKING AND HIKING The most popular trails within the parks are well marked and well maintained. Walkers should remember that at many times of the year, snow and ice can make for treacherous footing on the trails. In each of the areas, a variety of trail options allows walkers and hikers to pick the length of their walks. The Redwood Canyon trail offers miles of easy walking through the world's largest grove of redwoods; the Buena Vista Peak trail provides an overview of the high Sierra; the Congress Trail is a 2-mile stroll on a paved loop trail through the heart of the Sequoia Forest; the Hazelwood Nature trail is a 1-mile loop featuring trailside information about sequoias and man's impact on them; the Crescent Meadow trail has an excellent midsummer wildflower show; the Trail for All People is a paved trail that forms a $^2/_3$-mile loop around Round Meadow. Information on longer, more strenuous trails is available at the parks' visitor centers.

ENTERTAINMENT

During the summer months, evening campfire programs are held at many of the parks' campgrounds. In winter, programs are held at the Lodgepole Visitor Center, the Beetle Rock

Center, and the Grant Grove Visitor Center on Fridays and Saturdays. Additional programs are sometimes offered during holidays. A full schedule of evening programs is published in the *Sequoia Bark,* the free park newspaper handed to each visitor at the entrance gates. The program schedules are also posted on visitor-center bulletin boards.

Shenandoah Valley and Charlottesville

Virginia

Slanting southwesterly through Virginia between the gentle Blue Ridge and the rugged Appalachian Mountains is the lush Shenandoah Valley. Once the route blazed by European settlers from the coastal colonies into Kentucky, it was long covered with wheat and cornfields, but now its green acres offer more diversity. Today, the valley is sought out by travelers for its picturesque Skyline Drive and Blue Ridge Parkway, its colorful old towns founded by Germans and Scotch-Irish, its early crafts, and its old inns and eating places.

East of the valley—over well-traveled Afton Mountain in the Blue Ridge chain—lies Thomas Jefferson's hometown of Charlottesville, site of the University of Virginia. That city and the valley fit neatly into Virginia's most popular tourist package: a triangular tour beginning in Washington, D.C., and continuing to Williamsburg, Richmond, Charlottesville, Lexington, and then back to D.C.

through the valley and the northern Virginia horse country.

Three other towns of unusual interest in up-country Virginia are Lexington, where Lee and Jackson lie buried near educational institutions they served; Winchester, where Washington embarked in youth on his military career; and Staunton, Woodrow Wilson's birthplace. Other highlights are Natural Bridge; the hunt country around Warrenton and Middleburg, where fox hunts, races, and horse shows enliven weekends; and Abingdon, near the southwest tip of the state, with its famous Barter Theater and music festivals.

ESSENTIAL INFORMATION

WHEN TO GO June, July, and August are the best months to visit, because temperatures then average in the upper 70s to mid-80s. October is also a favorite with many valley visitors, when turning leaves brighten the lowlands with red and yellow. May and June

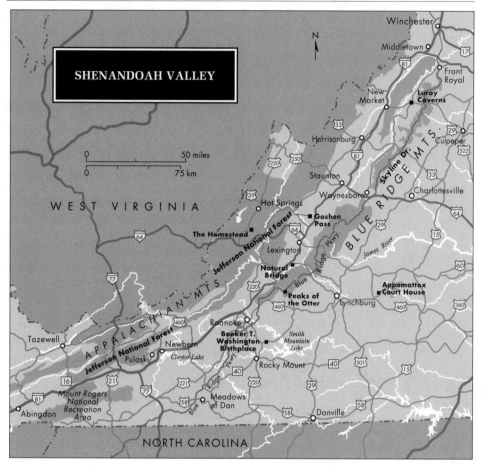

are blooming time for mountain laurel and rhododendron, which illumine upland hills with their pink-white blossoms. In addition, April is Garden Month in Virginia, and local garden tours are a highlight of this cool yet often rainy month.

BARGAINS The biggest bargain in the region is the Blue Ridge Parkway, the Park Service's free scenic skyway through part of Virginia's mountains. The 469-mile parkway connects the Shenandoah National Park in Virginia with the Great Smoky Mountains National Park in North Carolina and Tennessee. Virginia's 216-mile section begins near Waynesboro at Rockfish Gap, at the southern end of the Skyline Drive. Also free is historic Goshen Pass, a picturesque upland river

gorge near Lexington and Staunton. Free admittance to grounds and historic buildings is offered by Washington and Lee University, Virginia Military Institute, and the University of Virginia. Also free to visitors is the Cyrus McCormick Farm and Workshop at Steele's Tavern, where the McCormick reaper was invented. Numerous Charlottesville and Shenandoah Valley wineries offer free wine tasting; contact the local chambers of commerce and visitor information centers (*see below*) for advance information on local wineries.

TOURIST OFFICES Charlottesville-Albemarle Convention and Visitors' Bureau (Box 161, Charlottesville 22902, tel. 804/977–1783). Lexington Visitor Center (102 E. Washington St., Lexington 24450, tel. 703/463–3777).

Roanoke Valley Convention and Visitors' Bureau (114 Market St., Box 1710, 24088, tel. 703/342–6025 or 800/635–5535). Shenandoah Valley Tourist Information Center (off I–81 at Exit 67, Box 1040, New Market 22844, tel. 703/740–3132). Staunton Tourist Information Center (Richmond Rd. [Rte. 250] at I–81, Exit 222, Staunton 24402, tel. 703/332-3972). In addition, the Rockfish Gap Visitor Information Center, located just off I–64 at the intersection of the Skyline Drive and Blue Ridge Parkway on Afton Mountain, is staffed by some very knowledgeable volunteers.

EMERGENCIES **Police, fire,** and **ambulance:** Dial 911. In Shenandoah National Park, dial 703/999–2227 or 800/732–0911; on Blue Ridge Parkway, 800/727–5928. **Hospitals:** In Charlottesville, emergency rooms are at Martha Jefferson Hospital (459 Locust Ave., tel. 804/982–7150) and the University of Virginia Hospital (Jefferson Park Ave., tel. 804/924–2231). Both are open 24 hours. In Lexington, phone 703/463–2112 for the police or rescue squad.

ARRIVING AND DEPARTING

BY PLANE Frequent service to northern Virginia by major airlines is available through Washington National and Dulles International airports, Roanoke Municipal Airport, and Charlottesville-Albemarle Airport.

BY BUS Greyhound Lines (tel. 800/231–2222) serves Abingdon (465 W. Main St., tel. 703/628–6622), Charlottesville (310 W. Main St., tel. 804/295–5131), Lexington (631 Waddell St., tel. 703/463–2424), Roanoke (26 Salem Ave., tel. 703/342–6761), and Staunton (100 S. New St., tel. 703/886–2424).

BY CAR The valley is served by I–81 from the north, I–66 from Washington, D.C., I–64 from the eastern part of Virginia and from the west, and by I–77, which runs north–south through the southwest tip of the valley. For weather and road conditions in Virginia, call 800/367–ROAD.

BY TRAIN Amtrak (tel. 800/USA–RAIL) stops daily at Charlottesville (Union Station, 810 W. Main St.) on its New York–New Orleans run and also has service three days a week at Staunton (1 Middlebrook Ave.) and at Charlottesville en route between New York and Chicago. The same train stops at Clifton Forge (Ridgeway St.) for The Homestead.

GETTING AROUND

BY CAR The easiest way to visit the Shenandoah Valley and Charlottesville is by car. I–81 and U.S. 11 run through the entire valley, intertwined with each other and connecting with I–64 at Staunton and at Lexington. A car is needed in Charlottesville and, of course, to take the scenic Skyline Drive and connecting Blue Ridge Parkway.

REST STOPS There are rest rooms at Fairfield Information Center, on I–81 southbound in Rockbridge County, near Lexington; at Buchanan Information Center on I–81 southbound near Buchanan; at Harrisonburg Information Center on I–81 northbound near Harrisonburg; at the picnic area off I–81 at the Cyrus McCormick Birthplace Farm at Steele's Tavern; and at the Thomas Jefferson Visitors Center off I–64 at Route 20 South.

GUIDED TOURS Washington and Lee University at Lexington offers a free guided tour of Lee Chapel, where Lee is buried and portraits of founders are shown. The Virginia Military Institute at Lexington (tel. 703/464–7326) runs free guided tours from September till June at 11 AM and 3 PM daily and at 10 AM and 1 PM on Saturdays; during the summer, tours are offered Monday–Friday. For $6, the Lexington Carriage Company (tel. 703/463–3777 or 703/463–5647) will take you around town in a horse-drawn carriage for 35 minutes, April to October. A walking-tour brochure is available at the Lexington Visitor Center (tel. 703/463–3777). The Historic Staunton Foundation (tel. 703/885–7676) offers free one-hour guided tours of the town Saturday morning at 11, Memorial Day through October, departing from the Woodrow Wilson Birthplace (24 N. Coalter St.). A brochure is available for a self-guided tour. The University of Virginia at Charlottesville (tel. 804/924–3239 or 804/924–7969) gives five free guided tours daily (at 10 and

11 AM and 2, 3, and 4 PM) of the Rotunda and Lawn. A map of the university—plus parking and general information—is available at the university of Virginia Visitor Information Center/Police Station (tel. 804/924–7969).

EXPLORING

It's helpful to think of Virginia's Shenandoah Valley as a carrot-shaped region with Winchester and Front Royal at the top and Abingdon close to its bottom. One side is delineated by the mountaintop Skyline Drive and Blue Ridge Parkway, which run in splendor along the heights from Front Royal southwesterly into North Carolina. Paralleling the mountains is I–81, which follows the valley bottom from the Maryland border into Tennessee, tracing the route blazed long ago by European settlers. In the 18th century, it was called the Great Wagon Road, while a western branch from Roanoke was the Wilderness Road, made famous by Daniel Boone.

Present-day visitors may combine both the Skyline Drive/Blue Ridge Parkway and I–81 in their circuit of the valley, enjoying both nature and history. The parkways, designed for taking in the scenery at a leisurely pace, have two lanes and a 45 mph speed limit that's strictly enforced. On weekends in good weather, traffic can be abominable, so be warned. We cover the valley's highlights from north to south.

About 10 miles south of the South West Virginia Pine on I–81 is **Winchester,** gateway city to the Shenandoah Valley, center of apple production. Founded in 1732 and still full of Colonial buildings, the city has always been an important intersection. Washington worked as a surveyor here (his office is now a museum), and during the Civil War, the town changed hands 72 times.

Shenandoah National Park is the upland mountain empire surrounding the 105-mile **Skyline Drive.** It offers hundreds of miles of hiking trails, including part of the Appalachian Trail, plus campgrounds and trout fishing in white-water streams. Pick up *Shenandoah Overlook,* a free newspaper,

when you enter the park. (For information, call 703/999–3483, 703/999–2266 or 800/828–1140.)

Luray Caverns are the largest of the valley's spectacular lighted caves. Underground rock formations are illumined to eerie effect. A "Stalacpipe Organ" made of stalactites is played from a keyboard. A one-hour tour starts every 20 minutes. *West of Rte. 211 from Skyline Dr. at Luray, tel. 703/743–6551. Open daily. Admission charged. Hours vary by season.*

New Market, on I–81 not far from the parkway, is the site of a Civil War battle in which teenage Virginia Military Institute cadets fought Union soldiers. It is today the New Market Battlefield Historical Park and the Hall of Valor Civil War Museum. *I–81 at New Market, tel. 703/740–3101. Open daily except Thanksgiving, Christmas, and New Year's. Admission charged.*

Staunton, pronounced "Stanton," is the seat of once-huge Augusta County, originally including all of West Virginia, Kentucky, Ohio, and Indiana. Here, in the now-restored Woodrow Wilson House, the 28th president was born in 1856. *18–24 N. Coalter St., tel. 703/885– 0897. Open daily except Thanksgiving, Christmas, and New Year's. Admission charged.*

Just outside town is the **Museum of American Frontier Culture,** with re-created farms from Northern Ireland, England, Germany, and upland Virginia. *1250 Richmond Rd. off I–81 at Exit 222, tel. 703/332– 7850. Open daily except Thanksgiving, Christmas, and New Year's. Admission charged.*

Charlottesville lies just outside the Shenandoah Valley in rolling and beautiful Albemarle County. Here, at Monticello, Jefferson's mountaintop home and avocation, one can get a clear picture of the third president. *Rte. 53 (off Rte. 20), 2 mi southeast of Charlottesville, tel. 804/295–8181 or 295–2657. Open daily except Christmas. Admission charged. Stop at the Thomas Jefferson Visitors Center just off I–64 at Rte. 20S for a free movie, permanent exhibition, bathroom facilities,* *gift shops, information and tickets for Monticello, Ash Lawn-Highland, and Michie Tavern.*

Jefferson's idyllic **University of Virginia** can be seen on free tours, starting at the Rotunda (tel. 804/924–3239). Nearby is **Ash Lawn,** one-time farm of James Monroe, which survives as a plantation house and arts center. *Rte. 795 (off Rte. 53), 2 mi past Monticello, tel. 804/293–9539. Open daily except Thanksgiving, Christmas, and New Year's. Admission charged.*

Blue Ridge Parkway, free to all users, is a mountaintop scenic drive (and a national park) that diverges from Skyline Drive. From the majestic mountaintop of Afton, it curves gracefully for 469 miles southwest into North Carolina and Tennessee. Its **Peaks of Otter Recreation Center** (tel. 703/586–4357), near Roanoke, has a variety of lodges, waysides, and guided nature walks, plus a section of the Appalachian Trail. *For parkway information, call 703/982–6213 or 703/982–6458.*

Goshen Pass is a picturesque 3-mile scenic drive that follows the white-water Maury River through the Allegheny Mountains. The Pass lies along Route 39, which branches westward from I–81 and I–64 just north of Lexington. The route leads into Bath County, a mountainous recreational oasis and spa area—Warm Springs, Bolar Springs, and Hot Springs, site of the 15,000-acre **Homestead** (tel. 800/542–5734), the country's oldest resort, known for its old-fashioned luxury and its golf courses, bridle paths, and hiking trails.

Lexington is a must for travelers with an interest in history. A center of early Scotch-Irish settlement in the valley, it is the home of **Washington and Lee University.** Endowed by George Washington and presided over by Robert E. Lee, W & L is the sixth-oldest college in the nation. Visit its ancient colonnaded campus and its Lee Chapel and Museum. *Tel. 703/463–8768. Open daily except Thanksgiving and the following day, Dec. 24–26 and 31. Admission free.*

Next door is **Virginia Military Institute,** founded in 1839. The **VMI Museum** contains much about Stonewall Jackson, who taught there. *Tel. 703/464–7232. Open daily except Thanksgiving and Dec. 24–Jan. 1. Admission free.*

On the VMI grounds is the **George C. Marshall Museum,** honoring the Nobel Prize-winning alumnus who was U.S. chief of staff in World War II, world leader, and designer of the Marshall Plan. *Tel. 703/463–7103. Open daily except Thanksgiving, Christmas, and New Year's. Admission free.*

The **Stonewall Jackson House,** near the two schools, is preserved much as he left it to serve the Confederate army in 1861. *8 E. Washington St., tel. 703/463–2552. Open daily except Easter, Thanksgiving, Christmas, and New Year's. Admission charged.*

Natural Bridge, 15 miles south of Lexington on I–81, is a world- famous arch 215 feet high and 90 feet long, carved out of Rockbridge County limestone by Cedar Creek below, and once owned by Thomas Jefferson. *I–81 to Exit 49 or 50, tel. 703/291–2121. Open daily. Admission charged.*

Roanoke is a modern railroad center 54 miles south of Lexington. It is also a center of educational institutions and of three museums and an art gallery, the **Roanoke Museum of Fine Arts** (tel. 703/342–5760; admission free), which chiefly shows works of regional artists. The **Science Museum of Western Virginia** (tel. 703/343–7876; admission charged) displays natural history and includes a planetarium and children's exhibits. The **Roanoke Valley Historical Society** (tel. 703/342–5760; admission free) displays relics of Virginia Indians, from whose name for wampum the word "Roanoke" comes.

The **Virginia Museum of Transportation** in Roanoke is devoted to trains. *303 Norfolk Ave., tel. 703/342–5670. Open daily except Thanksgiving, Christmas, and New Year's. Admission charged.*

Rocky Mount, 20 miles southeast of Roanoke, is Booker T. Washington's birthplace, now a national monument. Born in slavery, the brilliant educator and writer became an early leader of blacks and slaves, consultant to presidents, and founder of Tuskegee Institute in Alabama. *Rte. 116S to Burnt Chimney, then 6 mi east on Rte. 122N, tel. 703/721–2094. Open daily except Thanksgiving, Christmas, and New Year's. Admission charged.*

Abingdon, near the North Carolina border, is a cultural crossroads in the wilderness, with the famous Barter Theater (*see* Entertainment, *below*), the Virginia Highlands Festival (when 150,000 people come for the music, crafts exhibits, and antiques displays), and the Burley Tobacco Festival, whose stars are country-music performers and farm animals.

THE NATURAL WORLD The forested empires of federal park lands in the valley provide cover for many animals, birds, and plants. These holdings include not only Shenandoah National Park and Blue Ridge Parkway but also George Washington National Forest and Jefferson National Forest. Though the eastern buffalo no longer survives in these uplands, black bear and wildcats are common in the woods, and bald eagles not unknown. Even more visible are white-tailed deer, woodchucks, squirrels, foxes, rabbits, hawks, doves, owls, and songbirds. The region is noted for its concentration of geological phenomena, including Natural Bridge, the cascading riverbed of Goshen Pass, the many natural caverns, and mountain ranges varying in age from the ancient Blue Ridge to the more recent and rugged Appalachians. For a brochure on Virginia State Parks, call 800/866–9222.

HOTELS AND INNS

The scale of hotels in the Shenandoah Valley is small, like the valley towns themselves, except Roanoke. Motel chains offering standard amenities have one- or two-story structures close to exits in the towns along I–81, and a few old family-owned hotels and bed-and-breakfasts survive, especially in college towns like Charlottesville, Staunton, and Lexington. For information and bed-and-breakfast reservations, contact **Guesthouses,**

Bed & Breakfast, Inc. (Box 5737, Charlottesville, VA 22905, tel. 804/979–7264), a reservation service for the Charlottesville area. **Blue Ridge Bed & Breakfast Reservation Service** (Rock & Rills, Rte. 2, Box 3895, Berryville, VA 22611, tel. 703/955–1246 or 800/296–4204) provides the same service up and down the Shenandoah Valley, excluding the area around Charlottesville.

Price categories for double occupancy, without 4.5% sales tax, are *Expensive,* over $95; *Moderate,* $60–$95; and *Inexpensive,* under $60.

ABINGDON **Alpine Motel.** At this small, upland motel with pleasant, simple decor, you get a good view of Mount Rogers, Virginia's highest peak. The Barter Theater is nearby. *882 E. Main St., 24210, tel. 703/628– 3178. 19 rooms. AE, D, MC, V. Moderate.*

Martha Washington Inn. Built in 1832 by General Francis Preston, this exclusive inn across from the Barter Theatre is an elegant testimony to Virginia's aristocratic past. The inn underwent an $8 million renovation in 1985. Rooms are furnished with antiques and some have fireplaces, Jacuzzis, and steam showers. *150 W. Main St., 24210, tel. 703/628–3161 or 800/533–1014. 61 rooms and 15 suites. AE, D, DC, MC, V. Expensive.*

CHARLOTTESVILLE **Boar's Head Inn.** Located 2 miles outside town on Route 250 West, this quiet resort features both rooms and suites with simple but elegant furnishings, mostly antiques. Efficiencies, suites, and rooms with king- and queen-size beds are available. Hot-air-balloon rides are one of the inn's unique offerings. *Rte. 250 West, Box 5307, 22905, tel. 804/296–2181 or 800/476–1988. 173 rooms and 11 suites. AE, D, DC, MC, V. Expensive.*

English Inn. This convenient motel has a three-story atrium lobby with cascading plants and a bed-and-breakfast friendliness. *2000 Morton Dr. (junction of U.S. 29 and Rte. 250 bypass), 22901, tel. 804/971–9900 or 800/338–9900, fax 804/977–8008. 88 rooms and suites. Restaurant, indoor pool, sauna, exercise equipment. AE, D, DC, MC, V. Moderate.*

Omni Charlottesville. This relatively new hotel is located on the Downtown Mall, at the center of town and near a variety of shops and restaurants. The decor is a mixture of Colonial and modern, but don't expect too much Old World charm from this chain offering. *235 W. Main St., 22901, tel. 804/971–5500 or 800/843–6664. 208 rooms and 3 suites. AE, DC, MC, V. Expensive.*

The Osceola Mill Country Inn. At the Mill you'll find warm, friendly, unpretentious accommodations just off the Blue Ridge Parkway, about 15 miles outside Charlottesville at milepost 27 on Virginia Route 56. This country inn was once part of the McCormick Farm, where the McCormick reaper was invented, and the Victorian Farmhouse, Mill, and the Old Mill Store (a private honeymoon cottage) still offer a unique, pleasantly rural lodging experience. *Rte. 56, Steele's Tavern 24476, tel. and fax 703/377–6455, tel. 800/242–7352. 12 rooms, 1 cottage. Continental breakfast included. MC, V. Expensive.*

HOT SPRINGS **The Homestead.** Founded in 1891 at the source of natural mineral springs, the Homestead is the oldest and certainly one of the most luxurious resorts in the United States. All rooms are decorated elegantly with fine antiques and country memorabilia. As for facilities, the Homestead cannot be beat. *U.S. 220, Hot Springs 24445, tel. 703/839–5500 or 800/336–5771, fax 703/839–7656. 521 rooms, including 75 suites. 7 restaurants, tennis courts, 9 ski slopes, 3 18-hole golf courses, indoor/outdoor pools, spa, riding trails, fishing. AE, MC, V. Expensive.*

Roseloe Motel. This family-run hostelry has excellent views of Warm Springs Valley and is located near the Warm Springs pools. *Rte. 2, Box 590, 24445, tel. 703/839–5373. 14 rooms, some with kitchenette. AE, DC, MC, V. Inexpensive.*

LEXINGTON **Days Inn–Keydet–General Motel.** This one-story brick establishment, perched on a suburban hill, is a favorite with alumni of Lexington's famed schools. *Rte. 60W outside town, 24450, tel. 703/463–2143 or 800/325–2525. Restaurant, wet bars, refrig-*

erators in some rooms. Pets permitted. AE, D, DC, MC, V. Moderate.

MEADOWS OF DAN **Rocky Knob Cabins.** These refreshingly simple rustic cabins just off Blue Ridge Parkway have kitchens but no private baths. *Milepost 174, Rte. 1, Box 5, 24120, tel. 703/593–3503. AE, MC, V. Open Memorial Day–Labor Day. Inexpensive.*

MIDDLETOWN **Wayside Inn.** Once called Wilkerson's Tavern on the Black Bear Trail, it has a string of first-floor taprooms and dining rooms and is furnished with antiques and Victoriana. *7783 Main St. (junction of I–81 and U.S. 11), 22645, tel. 703/869–1797, fax 703/869–6038. 24 rooms and suites. Restaurant. AE, D, DC, MC, V. Moderate.*

NATURAL BRIDGE **Natural Bridge Resort and Conference Center.** Close to the bridge, this resort hostelry with old-fashioned decor and food offers good views of the Blue Ridge from porches and rocking chairs. *Exits 175 and 180 off I–81, Box 57, 24578, tel. 703/291–2121 or 800/533–1410. 180 rooms. Restaurant, lounge, deli/snack bar, pool, tennis courts, walking trails , indoor miniature golf course. AE, D, DC, MC, V. Moderate.*

PEAKS OF OTTER **Peaks of Otter Lodge.** This rustic, modern hotel is known for its cuisine and moderate prices. The elevated site offers a rare view of the Blue Ridge, Abbott Lake, and the valley. *Milepost 86, Blue Ridge Pkwy., north of Roanoke (Box 489, Bedford 24523), tel. 703/586–1081 or 800/542–5927 in VA, fax 703/586–4420. 62 rooms. Restaurant, coffee shop, bar. MC, V. Moderate.*

ROANOKE **Patrick Henry Hotel.** Renovated in 1991, this 1925 landmark is centrally located in Roanoke's downtown district and within walking distance of many sights. Oriental rugs, white-marble floors, and antique furniture create quite a presence in this beautiful old building. All of the guest rooms are large and include sitting areas as well as kitchenettes. *617 S. Jefferson St., 24011, tel. 703/345–8811 or 800/833–4567. 100 rooms with kitchenettes. AE, MC, V. Expensive.*

■STAUNTON■ Belle Grae Inn. Built in 1870, this restored Victorian mansion offers 14 uniquely decorated rooms with rocking chairs and canopied or brass beds. Complimentary breakfast and afternoon teas are served. *515 W. Frederick St., 24401, tel. 703/886–5151. 14 rooms. No children under 14. AE, DC, MC, V. Moderate.*

Frederick House. Five restored houses dating from 1810 form this inn in the historic downtown. All rooms are furnished with antiques, and a pub and restaurant are adjoining. Smoking is not allowed. *28 N. New St., 24401, tel. 703/885–4220 or 800/334–5575, fax 703/885–2217. 14 rooms. Full breakfast included. AE, D, DC, MC, V. Moderate.*

MOTELS

■MODERATE■ Boxwood Bed and Breakfast (Rte. 847, Harrisonburg 22801, tel. 703/867–5772). 4 rooms; no smoking. **Comfort Inn–Stephens City** (I–81 at Exit 78, Stephens City 22655, tel. 703/869–6500 or 800/228–5150). 60 rooms; Continental breakfast included, whirlpool baths. **Hamilton Motel** (Rte. 2, Box 78, Woodstock 22664, tel. 703/459–4086). 43 rooms; restaurant, pool, pets allowed. **Hampton Inn–Harrisonburg** (Rte. 33E on University Blvd., 22801, tel. 703/432–1111 or 800/HAMPTON). 126 rooms; Continental breakfast included. **Hampton Inn–Winchester** (west of town on U.S. 50 at 1655 Apple Blossom Dr., Winchester 22601, tel. 703/667–8011 or 800/HAMPTON). 103 rooms; Continental breakfast included, pool, elevators. **Holiday Inn–Staunton** (I–81 at Exit 58, Staunton 24401, tel. 703/248–5111 or 800/HOLIDAY). 100 rooms; restaurant and lounge. **Hotel Strasburg** (I–81 at Exit 74, 201 Holliday St., Strasburg 22657, tel. 703/465–3711). 21 rooms; whirlpool baths. **Sheraton Inn and Country Club** (I–81 at Exit 58, Woodrow Wilson Pkwy., Staunton 24401, tel. 703/248–6020 or 800/325–3535). 112 rooms; restaurant, golf and tennis privileges at country club.

■INEXPENSIVE■ Battlefield Motel (I–81 at Exit 67, New Market 22844, tel. 703/740–3105). 14 rooms; free coffee, basketball court. **Blue**

Ridge Motor Lodge (I–81 at Exit 67, New Market 22844, tel. 703/740–8088 or 800/545–8776). 18 rooms; free coffee, playground, basketball. **Bond's Motel** (I–81 at Exit 79, Winchester, 22601, tel. 703/667–8881). 16 rooms; free coffee. **Cardinal Motel** (U.S. 211, Luray 22835, tel. 703/743–5010). 24 rooms; playground. **Center City Motel** (I–81 at Exit 2, Front Royal 22630, tel. 703/635–4050). 18 rooms. **Echo Village Motel** (I–81 at Exit 79, Winchester 22601, tel. 703/869–1900). 66 rooms. **New Market Battlefield Days Inn** (I–81 at Exit 67, New Market 22844, tel. 703/740–4100 or 800/325–2525). 86 rooms. **Shenandoah Motel** (I–81 at Exit 76, Front Royal 22630, tel. 703/635–3181). 32 rooms. **Travelodge of Winchester** (I–81 at Exit 80, Winchester 22601, tel. 703/665–1685 or 800/255–3050). 149 rooms; free coffee, doughnuts.

CAMPGROUNDS

The two national parks and two national forests in the valley offer many opportunities for camping, as does Mount Rogers National Recreation Area in the southwest tip of the state. Shenandoah National Park (tel. 703/999–2266) has three campgrounds with showers, flush toilets, and coin laundries, but no hookups ($8–$10) at Big Meadows (MP 51 on the Skyline Drive; reservations), and at Lewis Mountain (MP 57.5) and Loft Mountain (MP 79.5), both first-come, first-served. Lewis Mountain also has a few rustic cabins run by a concessionaire (tel. 703/999–2255). Blue Ridge Parkway (tel. 703/982–6458) has four campgrounds in Virginia (Otter Creek, MP 60.9; Peaks of Otter, MP 86; Roanoke Mountain, MP 120.4; and Rocky Knob, MP 169), all first-come, first-served primitive sites with flush toilets and dumping stations but no showers or hookups ($8). George Washington National Forest (tel. 703/433–2491) has 21 campgrounds (5 take reservations, tel. 800/283–CAMP). Facilities and fees range from free for primitive sites with pit latrines, $6–$7 for some that have showers and bathrooms, to $12 for the few with electrical hookups. Jefferson National Forest (tel. 703/982–6270) has 16 campgrounds in its six districts, some primitive, some with bathrooms and showers, but no hookups. Fees range from free to $8. At Mount Rogers National Recreational Area (part of the Jefferson National Forest, tel. 703/783–5196) there are six campgrounds, all with flush toilets, some with showers, none with hookups, whose fees range from $2 to $8. Many privately owned campgrounds are also scattered throughout the region; try Yogi Bear's Jellystone Park Camp–Resort (Rte. 1, Box 275, Charlottesville 29943, tel. 703/456–6409 or 800/558–2954), located off Route 250 between Charlottesville and Waynesboro at the base of Afton Mountain. Fees for one of its 120 wooded and creekside campsites, including hookups, are $17.50–$24.

DINING

The ethnic roots of upland Virginia go back not only to England but also to Scotland and Germany, and the fare is apt to have a hearty Germanic flavor. Fresh, homemade rolls and German pancakes are popular, along with sauerkraut, sauerbraten, cottage cheese, and pastries made from local apples, peaches, and berries. Another favorite is shoofly pie, which got its name from its resemblance to cauliflower, or *choufleur,* the French word used in Alsace. The valley is also known for its locally cured hams and bacon. Virginia is one of the half-dozen leading wine producers of the nation. Wineries abound, especially in Albemarle County, around Charlottesville. Dinner price categories per person, not including 4.5% tax (plus any local tax), service, and drinks, are *Expensive,* over $25; *Moderate,* $15–$25; and *Inexpensive,* under $15.

ABINGDON **The Tavern.** Built in 1779, this cozy restaurant was a hospital in the Civil War. The menu includes rainbow trout from nearby waters. *222 E. Main St., tel. 703/628–1118. MC, V. Moderate–Expensive.*

CHARLOTTESVILLE **Amazona's.** This Brazilian restaurant offers first-rate South American cuisine: Black beans, fresh herbs, and exotic spices complement an assortment of beef, pork, poultry, seafood, and vegetarian dishes. *2244 Ivy Rd., tel. 804/977–8853. MC, V. Moderate.*

C & O Restaurant. Don't let the boarded-up storefront with the old Pepsi sign fool you. Downstairs is a lively bistro, upstairs a more formal dining room (jacket and tie required). C & O features excellent regional French cuisine and has a wine list with over 300 varieties. *515 E. Water St., tel. 804/971–7044. Reservations advised. MC, V. Expensive.*

Martha's Cafe. Try the crab cakes, enchiladas or vegetarian entrées at this local favorite near the University of Virginia. The shaded outdoor café is open from midspring to late fall. *11 Elliewood Ave., tel. 804/971–7530. No credit cards. Inexpensive.*

Southern Culture. There's a true mix of styles and influences at Southern Culture—everything from Tex-Mex to Cajun, Creole, and just plain southern. Try such delicacies as Cajun baby cakes—shrimp and scallops blended with spicy jalapeño peppers—before moving on to a substantial plate of Louisiana short stacks. The atmosphere here is reminiscent of the Florida Keys in the late '40s. *633 W. Main St., tel. 804/979–1990. MC, V. Moderate.*

LEXINGTON **Willson Walker House.** American cuisine is served in a handsome old house of the Jefferson period that's a favorite site for entertaining out-of-towners. *30. N. Maine St., tel. 703/463–3020. Closed Sun.– Mon. AE, MC, V. Moderate.*

MIDDLETOWN **Wayside Inn Dining Room.** This 18th-century inn in a village near Winchester is a survivor from George Washington's day, furnished in antiques. It serves such favorites as spoon bread, smothered chicken, and peanut soup. *7783 Main St., tel. 703/869–1797. AE, D, DC, MC, V. Moderate.*

PEAKS OF OTTER **Peaks of Otter Lodge.** This elevated inn near Roanoke and the Blue Ridge Parkway is celebrated for its Friday night seafood buffet and Sunday country buffet. *MP 86, Blue Ridge Pkwy. north of Roanoke, Bedford, tel. 703/586–1081 or 800/542–5927 in VA. AE, D, DC, MC, V. Moderate.*

ROANOKE **The Library.** This Continental restaurant with quiet, refined decor is known for its superbly prepared seafood dishes. If you're looking for a formal eatery in Roanoke—jackets are required for men—you've just found it. *3117 Franklin Rd. SW (Piccadilly Sq. shopping center), tel. 703/985–0811. Jacket required. Dinner only. Closed Sun. AE, DC, MC, V. Expensive.*

STAUNTON **The Restaurant at 23 Beverly.** Formerly a men's clothing store and hot dog haven, this unique restaurant in Staunton's historic district is decorated with the work of local artists and features modern American cuisine—mostly pastas and grilled meats. The wine cellar is stocked with over 120 Virginia varieties. *23 Beverly St., tel. 703/885–5053. AE, D, MC, V. Moderate.*

Rowe's Family Restaurant. This is a country place that has been in the same family since 1947. Its entrées include chicken and Virginia ham; the breads are home-baked. *I–81 at Exit 57, tel. 703/ 886–1833. D, MC, V. Inexpensive.*

WARM SPRINGS **Waterwheel Restaurant.** This former gristmill dates from 1700 and contains a fine French and regional restaurant with a refreshing mix of haute cuisine and old favorites. *Grist Mill Sq., tel. 703/839–2231. MC, V. Closed for lunch and Sun. and Mon. Moderate–Expensive.*

SHOPPING

Among the numerous discount outlets throughout the valley are the Waynesboro Village Factory Outlet at Waynesboro (with Liz Claiborne, London Fog, and Royal Doulton porcelain among its 40 exhibitors) and an Aileen Factory Outlet at Woodstock, with first-grade women's wear. For crafts and collectibles, try the amusing Tuttle and Spice General Store near New Market. The P. Buckley Moss Museum, at Waynesboro, sells prints by the popular local artist. Try the Roanoke Market Building for international foods and specialties. At Front Royal, the Bizarre Bazaar offers antiques, quilts, collectibles, folk art, and crafts. The Strasburg Emporium, a center for 55 dealers who sell under one roof, calls itself Virginia's largest antiques center. More sophisticated antiques are found in shops in Winchester, Charlottesville, and Roanoke.

OUTDOOR ACTIVITIES

BIKING All federal parks and forests in the valley permit biking over nearly all trails, though no separation is designated for bicyclists. The steep grades make mountain bikes desirable.

BOATING AND CANOEING One of the few water resorts in the valley is Smith's Mountain Lake, 45 miles southeast of Roanoke, where guests enjoy boating, sailing, fishing, and land sports. Bernard's Landing there also rents housekeeping cottages (Monita, VA 24121, tel. 703/721–8870 or 800/572–2048). The Smith Mountain Lake State Park (on the north shore, tel. 703/297–4062) has a beach, boat rentals, and the like. Other recreational waterways are Claytor Lake (tel. 703/674–5492), a state park south of Radford, and crystal-clear Lake Moomaw in George Washington National Forest, near Covington. Douthat State Park (tel. 703/862–7200) in nearby Clifton Forge has a 50-acre lake for swimming, trout fishing, and boating, plus hiking trails and campsites.

You can rent a canoe to negotiate the valley's cascading streams at Front Royal Canoe (Rte. 340 near Front Royal, tel. 703/635–5440), Downriver Canoe Company (Rte. 613 near Front Royal, tel. 703/635–5526), Shenandoah River Outfitters (Rte. 684 near Luray, tel. 703/743–4159), James River Basin Canoe Livery (Rte. 4, Box 125, Lexington 24450, tel. 703/261–7334), and James River Runners (Rte. 4, Box 106, Scottsville 24590, tel. 804/286–2338).

FISHING Several freshwater species are caught in the 500-mile trout streams in Jefferson National Forest and in 50 other streams. Be sure to obtain a five-day Virginia fishing license, available April through mid-October at concession stands along Skyline Drive and at sportsmen's shops.

GOLF Among golf courses open to the public are The Homestead in Hot Springs (tel. 703/839–5500 or 800/336–5771), with three 18-hole courses; Caverns Country Club Resort (Rte. 211 in Luray, tel. 703/743–6551), whose course is along a river; Greene Hills Golf Club (Rte. 33 in Stanardsville, tel. 804/985–7328); and The Links, adjoining Natural Bridge (tel. 703/291–2121). Wintergreen in Nellysford (tel. 804/325–2200 or 800/325–2200) has two courses, one in the mountains and one in the valley.

HIKING The famous Appalachian Trail runs through part of this area, and more than 500 miles of trails exist in Shenandoah National Park alone. They are shown in a guidebook available at the visitor centers at mileposts 4.6 and 51 on the Skyline Drive. There are others on the Blue Ridge Parkway, in Woods Creek Park, and Chessie Nature Trail (the latter two in and near Lexington). For a list, write the Virginia Department of Conservation and Recreation (203 Governor St., Richmond 23219).

HORSEBACK RIDING Trail riding through the Blue Ridge Parkway is offered by Stoney Run Trails from Rockbridge County, near Buena Vista (tel. 703/261–1910). At Troutdale near Roanoke, guided equestrian tours of Mount Rogers National Recreation Area are arranged by Fairwood Stables (tel. 703/677–3301). Horse shows and competitions are held March–November at the Virginia Horse Center, Lexington (tel. 703/463–7060). The Homestead in Hot Springs also has extensive riding trails (tel. 703/839–5500 or 800/336–5771).

SKIING Winter sports are popular at such upland Virginia sites as Wintergreen in Nelson County (tel. 800/325–2200). Ski-weekend packages are offered by The Homestead in Hot Springs (tel. 703/839–5500 or 800/336–5771) and by Massanutten Village Ski Resort (off Rte. 33 in McGaheysville, tel. 703/289–9441).

TENNIS The Homestead in Hot Springs (tel. 703/839–5500 or 800/336–5771) has 19 courts, including one all-weather; Wintergreen in Nellysford (tel. 804/325–2200 or 800/325–2200) has 25 outdoor courts. Four courts are available to the public at Caverns Country Club Resort (Rte. 211, in Luray, tel. 703/743–7111). Many other hostelries have courts, as do some of the towns, especially those with colleges or universities.

ENTERTAINMENT

CONCERTS Frequent musical events are offered by such sponsors as Shenandoah College and Conservatory (tel. 703/662–4118 or 703/662–4135) at Winchester, Ash Lawn-Highland Professional Opera Company (tel. 804/293–9539) in Charlottesville, Orkney Springs Music Festival (tel. 703/856–2141) near Harrisonburg, and the Garth Newell musicians (tel. 703/839–5018) at Warm Springs. A partial listing is available from the Virginia Division of Tourism (202 N. 9th St., Richmond 23219, tel. 804/768–4484 or 800/VISIT–VA).

THEATER The Barter Theater, one of America's leading professional companies, produces frequent plays at its theater in Abingdon (tel. 703/628–2281 or 800/368–3240). Nearby in Lexington, the popular Lime Kiln Theater (tel. 703/463–3074) revives memories of valley history with its *Stonewall Country* and other dramas. At Roanoke, Mill Mountain Theater (tel. 703/342–5740) performs throughout the year. For a listing, contact the Virginia Division of Tourism (202 N. 9th St., Richmond 23219, tel. 804/786–4484 or 800/VISIT–VA).

The Smoky Mountains
Tennessee and North Carolina

At the Great Smoky Mountains National Park, shared almost equally by North Carolina and Tennessee, the Southern Appalachians reach their ultimate grandeur as 16 peaks soar more than 6,000 feet. A grayish blue, smokelike haze often hovers about these magnificent peaks, given their name by the Cherokee Indians, the region's first human inhabitants. Established in 1934, the 520,000-acre park is about 60 miles long and 20 miles wide.

Mysterious and haunting, these mountains are teeming with wildlife. Because hunting is not permitted, many species have made their home in the park. You may spot deer in Cades Cove, and wild turkeys, ruffed grouse, quail, and black bears. More than 200 species of birds reside in the park at one season or another; they're especially visible during the spring and fall migrations and the summer nesting season.

Plant life in the Great Smoky Mountains National Park is among the United States' most varied. There are at least 130 native species of trees, and although much of the woodland is second growth, 110,000 acres of virgin forest remain, preserving a magnificent tract of red spruce, whose lives are measured in centuries. Wildflowers and shrubs bloom, rivers and streams are often bordered by thick stands of rhododendron, and on some "balds"—mountaintops covered only with grass or low-growing plants—there are dazzling displays of flame azalea in the spring. It is scarcely to be wondered, then, that the Great Smoky Mountains National Park is the most-visited national park.

ESSENTIAL INFORMATION

WHEN TO GO Dogwoods and hosts of wildflowers bloom from late April to mid-May. June and July bring mountain laurel, flame azalea, and rose, purple, and white rhodo-

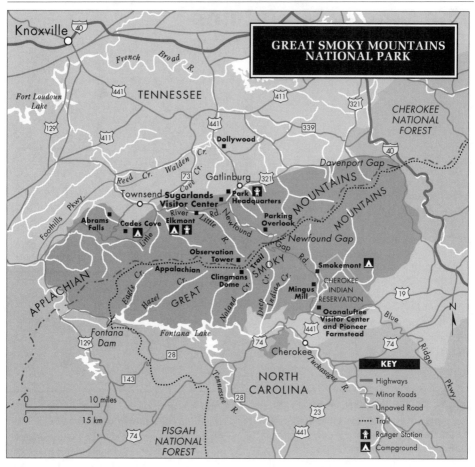

dendrons. The primrose, sweet shrub, Indian paintbrush, Queen Anne's lace, Turk's Cap lilies, and minuscule bluets last all summer and into September. Toward late September at higher elevations, the sumac turns deep scarlet, heralding the approach of autumn. Foliage generally peaks about mid-October in the higher altitudes and lasts into early November along the intermediate and lower slopes. Numerous varieties of hardwood trees produce brilliant colors—gold, red, russet, deep scarlet, and dazzling yellow.

There is no bad or wrong time of year to visit the park. However, during July, August, and October, you may want to avoid driving the Newfound Gap Road on weekends; traffic during these peak seasons can slow to a snail's pace. Even during the summer, the weather can be crisp and cool at higher elevations. Winter temperatures can vary from moderate to bitterly cold, but the Newfound Gap Road remains open unless there's ice and snow, and the park has a certain solitary beauty—and it's uncrowded.

BARGAINS The best bargain is the park itself; admission to the Great Smoky Mountains National Park is free. Seasonal nature programs are also free and are conducted by park rangers at visitor centers and campgrounds. These programs sometimes involve short walks (including sunset and twilight treks), while others are illustrated talks.

TOURIST OFFICES Superintendent, Great Smoky Mountains National Park (Gatlinburg, TN 37738, tel. 615/436–1200). North Carolina Travel & Tourism Division (430 N. Salisbury St., Raleigh, NC 27611, tel. 919/733–4171 or 800/847–4862 outside Raleigh). Tennessee Department of Tourist Development (Room T, Box 23170, Nashville, TN 37202, tel. 615/741–7994).

EMERGENCIES Police, fire, and ambulance: Dial 911 or call park headquarters at 615/436–1230.

ARRIVING AND DEPARTING

BY PLANE Tennessee's Knoxville Airport is approximately a one-hour drive from Gatlinburg, and the Asheville Airport in North Carolina is approximately a one-hour drive from Cherokee. Rental cars are available at both airports.

Between the Airports and the Park by Car: From Knoxville, follow U.S. 411/441 40 miles south to Gatlinburg, at the park's northern entrance. U.S. 441 (the Newfound Gap Road) runs through the park to exit outside Cherokee. From Asheville, North Carolina, take U.S. 19 west for 48 miles to the park's southern gateway town, Cherokee. From Cherokee, North Carolina, follow U.S. 441 4 miles north into the park's southern entrance. The Blue Ridge Parkway also leads westward from Asheville to its terminus just outside Cherokee.

BY BUS Greyhound Lines (tel. 800/231–2222) has service to Knoxville (100 Magnolia Ave., tel. 615/522–5144) and Asheville (2 Tunnel Rd., tel. 704/253–5353).

GETTING AROUND

BY CAR You'll need a car to tour the park. Pick up free maps and literature on the park at visitor centers near the Gatlinburg and Cherokee entrances.

REST STOPS Public rest rooms can be found at park visitor centers, campgrounds, and picnic areas.

GUIDED TOURS Bus tours—sights include Cades Cove, Newfound Gap, Clingmans Dome, and Roaring Fork—depart daily in summer from Cherokee and Gatlinburg and cost $12–$18. Contact Acorn Vacations Step-On Guide Service (Gatlinburg, tel. 615/436–8898 or 800/736–8898), Mountain Tours (Pigeon Forge, tel. 615/453–0864), and Smoky Mountain Tours (Gatlinburg, tel. 615/436–3471).

Backpack trips can be booked through Back of Beyond Expeditions (Gatlinburg, tel. 615/436–0481). Naturalist George Ellison (Bryson City, tel. 704/488–8782) offers guided wildflower hikes, while the Great Smoky Mountains Institute at Tremont (Townsend, tel. 615/448– 6709) offers two- to six-day courses in backpacking, crafts, and wildlife photography.

EXPLORING

The major highway traversing the park is U.S. 441, known within the park as Newfound Gap Road. This 35-mile stretch of road connects the major gateway cities of Gatlinburg, Tennessee, and Cherokee, North Carolina, and winds past overlooks, hiking and nature trails, and several historic attractions. To get a real feel for this mountain wilderness, plan to explore Newfound Gap Road, some spur roads, and some of the park's 900 miles of hiking or horseback trails.

Our tour runs southeast, from Gatlinburg to Cherokee. As an alternate route, however, you can enter the park from Townsend, Tennessee, driving east on Route 73, which connects with Little River Road. If you choose this route, it would make sense to visit Cades Cove first, and then drive east along Little River Road to Sugarlands Visitor Center.

Sugarlands Visitor Center and **the Great Smoky Mountains National Park Headquarters** are at the park entrance, 2 miles south of Gatlinburg, Tennessee, on U.S. 441. Here you can get an introduction to the park through an audiovisual presentation and displays highlighting the wildlife, plants, and geological formations of the Smokies. From mid-

April to October, rangers give campfire programs and other illustrated talks. *Tel. 615/436–1200. Open daily. Admission free.*

Cades Cove, west of the Sugarlands Visitor Center along Little River Road, is a carefully preserved historic area reflecting the heritage of pioneer settlers. For many years, families who lived here were virtually isolated from the rest of the world. You can follow an 11-mile loop road through the area, stopping at the visitor center where displays depict life here as it once was. Also along the way are hewn-log houses, small churches with their historic burial grounds, and a working gristmill. The loop road is open daily, weather permitting. *Tel. 615/448–2472. Visitor center and gristmill open mid-Apr.–Oct., daily. Admission free.*

You can also choose from about 70 miles of hiking trails at Cades Cove. Its elevation is slightly less than 2,000 feet, and if you want to head for 4,600-foot **Rich Gap,** you'll enjoy a fairly steep climb. It's especially scenic during spring wildflower season or in autumn, when the woods are aglow with color. For a more level hike, head west to **Abrams Falls,** quite dramatic if there have been recent heavy rainfalls.

The **Elkmont area,** east of Cades Cove off Little River Road, has more than 80 miles of trails. Among them are easy, relaxed walks along the Cucumber Gap and Husky Gap trails near Elkmont Campground.

Continue southeast along Newfound Gap Road, to find scenic overlooks where you can park your car and absorb the essence of these soaring forests of Canadian hemlock, red spruce, Fraser fir, yellow buckeye, and various oaks.

Along the route, too, you can explore a wealth of hiking trails, including **Alum Cave Bluffs Trail,** a 5-mile, round-trip trek (especially splendid about mid-June, when rose and purple rhododendrons usually reach peak bloom) beginning at the Alum Cave parking area and **Cove Hardwoods Self-Guided Nature Trail,** which will take you first through open areas where pioneers once farmed the land and then through virgin hardwood forest.

Newfound Gap, about midway along the Newfound Gap Road at a 5,048-foot elevation, marks the boundary dividing North Carolina and Tennessee. On a clear day, views from this majestic site on the crest of the Great Smokies are extraordinary.

The **Appalachian Trail** crosses the highway at Newfound Gap, and even if you're not a serious hiker, you'll enjoy a short walk along this famous pathway. Unfortunately, heavy usage and soil erosion have worn down the trail to solid rock in places. Serious hikers wishing to walk its entire stretch in the park can enter at Davenport Gap at the eastern end of the park or Fontana Dam at the southwestern end. It will take six to eight days to complete the trail, and there are shelters along the trail about a day's walk apart.

Clingmans Dome, the highest peak in Tennessee at 6,643 feet, can be reached by a 7-mile spur road from Newfound Gap, but keep in mind that this road is generally closed in winter. A rather steep pathway that is not too arduous leads to a mountaintop observation tower from which, good weather permitting, you'll see the mountains sweeping in every direction.

Oconaluftee Visitor Center, just inside the park's southern entrance, marks the end of your drive through the Great Smoky Mountains National Park. The adjacent Oconaluftee Pioneer Farmstead consists of a collection of vintage structures—main house, barn, storage bins, smokehouse—suggesting the rugged, self-sufficient lifestyle of mountain people during the late 19th century. During the peak visitor season, craftsfolk demonstrate pioneer skills. Half a mile north, off Newfound Gap Road, cornmeal is produced the old-fashioned way by water-powered wheels and may be purchased at Mingus Mill. *Visitor center: tel. 704/497–9146. Open daily. Admission free. Mingus Mill: no phone. Open mid-Mar.–mid-Nov., daily. Admission free.*

HOTELS AND INNS

Accommodations range from basic, limited facilities in the Great Smoky Mountains National Park to a wide range of motor inns, lodges, and hotels in every price category in the gateway resort towns of Gatlinburg, Tennessee, and Cherokee, North Carolina.

Price categories for double occupancy, without tax (11³/₄% in Tennessee, 7¹/₂% in North Carolina), are *Expensive*, $76–$96; *Moderate*, $50–$75; and *Inexpensive*, under $50.

CHEROKEE   **Best Western Great Smokies Inn.** This well-maintained affiliate of the international hotel group has colorful, spacious rooms and is set on gardenlike grounds landscaped with native plantings. *1 block off U.S. 441N, Box 189, 28719, tel. 704/497–2020 or 800/528–1234. 152 rooms. Dining room, lounge with entertainment, heated pool, playground. AE, D, DC, MC, V. Moderate.*

GATLINBURG   **Park Vista Hotel.** This lavish, circular tower hotel lacks the charm you'll find in some of the region's family-run Colonial inns, but there are striking mountain views from the rooms' private balconies. *³/₄ mi east off U.S. 441 via Airport Rd., Box 30, 37738, tel. 615/436–9211, 800/421–7275 or 800/526–1235 in TN. 315 rooms. Dining room, lounge, heated indoor pool, wading pool, whirlpool. AE, D, DC, MC, V. Expensive.*

Best Western Fabulous Chalet. In a quiet country setting overlooking Gatlinburg, this luxurious small inn has one- and two-bedroom town houses and suites, some with fireplaces and balconies. *516 Sunset Dr., Box 11, 37738–0427, tel. 615/436–5151 or 800/933–8675. 38 rooms. Continental breakfast included (in summer), heated pool. AE, D, DC, MC, V. Moderate–Expensive.*

Mid-Town Lodge. Chalet-style town houses are a favorite here: Each sports large fireplaces, loft bedrooms with king-size beds, and full bathrooms tucked under cathedral ceilings. Downstairs you'll find a well-equipped kitchen and queen-size sofa bed. Other options in this heart-of-downtown hotel include poolside rooms, luxury suites, and efficiencies. *805 Parkway, Gatlinburg, 37738, tel. · 615/436–5691 or 800/633–2446. 133 rooms, 25 town houses. Swimming pool, Jacuzzi. AE, MC, V. Moderate.*

NEAR THE PARK   **Fontana Village Resort.** Originally built in the 1940s to house construction workers from nearby Fontana Dam, this clustered community of cabins, cottages, and hotel rooms is far in the wild, untrammeled western reaches of the park. Rooms in the Fontana Inn are typical motel offerings; opt instead for one of the recently remodeled two-bedroom cottages, equipped with fireplaces and kitchens. *Fontana Dam, NC 28733, tel. 704/498–2211 or 800/849–2258. 80 rooms, 100 cottages. Restaurant, tennis courts, horses, boating, fishing. AE, D, MC, V. Inexpensive–Moderate.*

Wonderland Hotel. Those who loved the old Wonderland Hotel, which until 1992 was located inside the park at Elkmont, will not be disappointed by its replacement: This sprawling lodge with its rough-sawn, knotty-pine exterior adroitly re-creates the rustic appeal of the time-worn original. Rooms are furnished with reproduction antiques that seem out of place in these sylvan surroundings, but the Wonderland's location and remote setting are hard to beat. *3889 Wonderland Way, Sevierville, 37862, tel. 615/436–5490 or 615/428–0779, fax 615/429–4752. 29 rooms. Restaurant, horses. No TV or telephone in rooms. Closed Jan.–mid-March. MC, V. Moderate.*

MOTELS

MODERATE   **Comfort Inn** (Box 132, Cherokee, NC 28719, tel. 704/497–2411 or 800/228–5150). 54 rooms; pool, playground. **Comfort Inn South** (309 Oakley Dr., Gatlinburg, TN 37738, tel. 615/436–7813 or 800/228– 5150). 93 rooms; heated pool, whirlpool. **Days Inn** (Box 1865, Cherokee, NC 28719, tel. 704/497–9171 or 800/325–2525). 58 rooms; 2 pools, wading pool, playground, fishing. **Gazebo Inn** (417 Airport Rd., Box 435, Gatlinburg, TN 37738, tel. 615/436– 2222). 60 rooms; heated pool, whirlpool. **Gillette Motel** (235 Airport Rd., Box 231,

Gatlinburg, TN 37738, tel. 615/436–5601 or 800/437–0815). 80 rooms; heated pool. **Holiday Inn** (Box 1929, Cherokee, NC 28719, tel. 704/497–9181 or 800/465–4329). 154 rooms; dining room, indoor and outdoor pools, whirlpool, sauna, game room, playground, tennis, trout fishing. **Homestead House** (Box 367, Gatlinburg, TN 37738, tel. 615/436–6166 or 800/233–4663). 86 rooms; Continental breakfast in lobby included, conference room, tennis. **Howard Johnson's Motor Lodge** (559 Parkway, Box 408, Gatlinburg, TN 37738, tel. 615/436–5621 or 800/654–2000). 252 rooms; heated pool, wading pool, coin laundry. **Lloyd's on the River** (Box 429, Bryson City, NC 28713, tel. 704/488–3767). 21 rooms; pool. **Quality Inn Intown** (125 Le Conte Creek Dr., Gatlinburg, TN 37738, tel. 615/436–4865 or 800/473–8319). 71 rooms; heated pool, fishing. **Rocky Waters Motor Inn** (333 Parkway, Box 230, Gatlinburg, TN 37738, tel. 615/436–7861 or 800/824–1111, ext. C). 105 rooms; 2 heated pools, 2 wading pools, whirlpool, coin laundry, fishing.

INEXPENSIVE **Alpine Motel** (Box 523, Gatlinburg, TN 37738, tel. 615/436–5651). 37 rooms; heated pool, wading pool. **Cox's Gateway Motel** (1100 Parkway, Gatlinburg, TN 37738, tel. 615/436–5656 or 800/933–0777). 48 rooms; heated pool, wading pool. **Craig's Motel** (Box 1047, Cherokee, NC 28719, tel. 704/497–3821). 30 rooms; pool, wading pool, playground, fishing. **Creekstone Motel** (104 Oglewood Lane, Gatlinburg, TN 37738, tel. 615/436–4628). 25 rooms; heated pool, wading pool, pets accepted. **Pageant Hills Motel** (Box 172, Cherokee, NC 28719, tel. 704/497–5371). 42 rooms. **Spruce Flats Motel** (Box 94, Gatlinburg, TN 37738, tel. 615/436–4387 or 800/648–2895). 31 rooms; heated pool, wading pool.

CAMPGROUNDS

The three largest and most popular developed campgrounds in Great Smoky Mountains National Park are Cades Cove and Elkmont on the Tennessee side, and Smokemont in North Carolina. From May through October, reservations must be made through Ticketron. This can be done at any walk-in Ticketron outlet nationwide at least one day in advance or approximately six weeks in advance by mail. To make reservations by mail, write to Ticketron Reservations (Box 62429, Virginia Beach, VA 23462).

Cades Cove Campground. Cades Cove provides an excellent base for varied day hikes. Its ranger station can issue permits for backcountry camping; there are 17 backcountry campsites in the area. *10 mi southwest of Townsend, TN, via TN 73 and Laurel Creek Rd. (Gatlinburg, TN 37738, tel. 615/436–5615). 160 RV and tent sites. No hookups ($11). Dump station, picnic tables, grocery store, fishing, seasonal nature programs, rental horses and bicycles, fireplaces, flush toilets and cold running water. Stay limited to 7 days May–Oct.*

Elkmont. The park's largest campground, Elkmont is nestled in a scenic wooded swatch along the Little River. Backcountry camping permits are available, and there are 13 backcountry campsites. *8 mi west of Gatlinburg, TN, via Newfound Gap Rd., Little River Rd., Elkmont Rd. (Gatlinburg, TN 37738, tel. 615/436–5615). 220 RV and tent sites. No hookups ($11). Dump station, picnic tables, fishing, seasonal nature programs, fireplaces, flush toilets and cold running water. Stay limited to 7 days May–Oct.*

Smokemont. Just inside the park's North Carolina entrance, this heavily used campground along the Oconaluftee River is convenient to eastern segments of the park, which have numerous hiking and horseback trails. *6 mi north of Cherokee, NC, via Newfound Gap Rd. (Gatlinburg, TN 37738, tel. 615/436–5615). 152 RV and tent sites. No hookups ($11). Dump station, picnic tables, fishing, seasonal nature program, rental horses, fireplaces, flush toilets and cold running water. Stay limited to 7 days May–Oct.*

DINING

Except for the dining room of the Wonderland Hotel, there are no restaurants or food stands in Great Smoky Mountains National Park. Gatlinburg, Tennessee, however, has a wide variety of dining establishments in every price category, and Cherokee, North Carolina, has a selection as well. Freshly caught mountain trout and country ham with red-eye gravy and grits are featured on many mountain menus, and in Tennessee, sourwood honey is often served with breakfast, and you can buy jars to take home. Price categories, per person, not including tax ($7^3/4$% in Tennessee, $4^1/2$% in North Carolina), service, and drinks, are *Moderate,* $10–$20, and *Inexpensive,* under $10.

CHEROKEE **The Chestnut Tree.** A favorite with family vacationers, this large and airy dining room features steak, prime rib, and freshly caught mountain trout. *Holiday Inn, U.S. 19, tel. 704/497–9181. AE, D, DC, MC, V. Inexpensive–Moderate.*

GATLINBURG **Burning Bush Restaurant.** Antique-style furnishings evoke a Colonial atmosphere, and the menu features such dishes as broiled Tennessee quail. *1151 Parkway, tel. 615/436–4669. AE, DC, MC, V. Moderate.*

The Open Hearth. There's candlelight dining at the foot of the Smokies in this perennially popular restaurant, where specialties include aged charcoal beef and rainbow trout. *1138 Parkway, tel. 615/436–5648. AE, DC, MC, V. Moderate.*

Pioneer Inn Restaurant. In the charming, rustic atmosphere of this restored log cabin beside the river, you can order such distinctive dishes as game pie, country pork chops, and homemade soup with golden corn sticks. *373 Parkway, tel. 615/436–7592. AE, DC, MC, V. Inexpensive–Moderate.*

Smoky Mountain Trout House. This cozy restaurant serves trout prepared 12 different ways. *410 Parkway, tel. 615/436–5416. AE, DC, MC, V. Inexpensive–Moderate.*

Ogle's Buffet Restaurant. Buffet tables groan with five choices of country-style meats such as country ham, along with farm-fresh vegetables and 70 varieties of salad fixings. You can dine in the soft green-and-beige dining room or on the patio above a turbulent moun-

tain stream. *539 Parkway, tel. 615/436–4157. MC, V. Inexpensive.*

Pancake Pantry. Century-old brick, polished oak paneling, and copper accessories create a rustic ambience for enjoying such house delicacies as Austrian apple walnut pancakes. *628 Parkway, tel. 615/436–4724. No credit cards. Inexpensive.*

OUTDOOR ACTIVITIES

BIKING The flat floor of Cades Cove is excellent for bicycling, and you can rent bikes at the Cades Cove general store (across from Cades Cove Ranger Station). From early May to mid-September, the 11-mile Cades Cove Auto Loop is closed to automobile traffic until 10 AM. Mountain bike rentals and route maps are available at NOC Bryson City Store (Everett St., Bryson City, tel. 704/488–2446).

FISHING You can fish year-round in the park's 600 miles of open waters. Smallmouth and rock bass and brown and rainbow trout are frequent catches, but possession of brook trout is prohibited. Anglers must purchase North Carolina or Tennessee licenses.

HIKING The park has about 900 miles of hiking, nature, and horseback trails. You can choose from full-day hikes, rugged backcountry treks, or easy nature trails. Pick up trail guides at the park's visitor centers, where you can also obtain backcountry camping permits.

HORSEBACK RIDING During the peak spring through autumn vacation season, you can rent horses in the park from Cades Cove Riding Stables (Walland, tel. 615/448–6286), Deep Creek Riding Stables (Bryson City, tel. 704/488–8504), Davy Crockett Riding Stables (Townsend, tel. 615/448–6411), and Wonderland Stables (Sevierville, tel. 615/436–5490).

SKIING Outside the park, Ober Gatlinburg Ski Resort, reachable from downtown Gatlinburg, Tennessee, by car or aerial tramway, offers winter visitors the opportunity to ski 10 slopes and trails, ranging from novice to expert. *1001 Parkway, Gatlinburg, TN 37738, tel. 615/436–5423, 800/251–9202, or 800/843–6237 in TN.*

The Texas Gulf Coast

The Texas Gulf Coast has almost a thousand miles of sawtooth shoreline made up of barrier islands, river deltas, and bays. Some of its towns and villages have been developed as tourist resorts, primarily at the northern and southern ends of Padre Island. But by far the largest part of the coast is preserved as wetlands by state and federal edict, with large estuary tracts set aside for reptiles, mammals, and migratory birds.

The Gulf of Mexico is the common link among the coast's cities and towns, yet visitors who look beyond the obvious find many differences as they explore the Texas coast. There's Galveston, a sand barrier island that was once the home of Karankawa Indians and later grew into a prosperous shipping port (at one time it was the second-wealthiest city in the United States); the laid-back fishing village of Port Aransas; the artists' colony of Rockport; and at the state's far southern tip, South Padre Island, the sea-and-sand mecca for thousands of spring breakers, and the neighboring Rio Grande Valley, winter home to thousands of Canadians and midwesterners.

Resort-hoppers should know that Galveston, Corpus Christi, and South Padre Island have all become more cosmopolitan in recent years and are blooming with high-rise condos. Even so, none has quite outgrown the feeling of being a simple beach town, kind to budgets. Everywhere along the coast there are funky oyster bars, docks where you can see the "mosquito" fleet (so called because shrimp boats with their nets up look like giant mosquitoes), deep-sea fishing boats for charter, and inexpensive lodging.

Texans are famous for driving fast and talking slow. Here on the coast, far from the madding crowds of Dallas and Houston, life is leisurely and very casual. Folks strictly adhere to the motto "living on island time." So, meander gently here and leave schedules and deadlines at home.

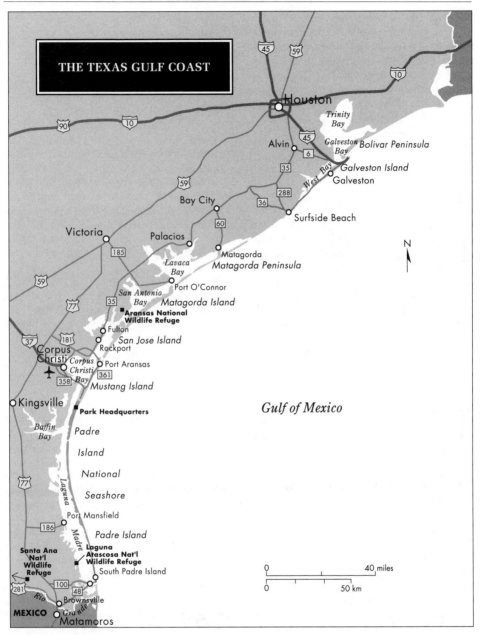

THE TEXAS GULF COAST

Trinity Bay

Houston

Alvin

Galveston Bay Bolivar Peninsula

Galveston Island

Galveston

West Bay

Bay City

Surfside Beach

Victoria

Palacios

N

Matagorda

Lavaca Bay Matagorda Peninsula

Port O'Connor

San Antonio Bay Matagorda Island

Aransas National Wildlife Refuge

Fulton

San Jose Island

Rockport

Corpus Christi *Corpus Christi Bay* Port Aransas

Mustang Island

Kingsville

Park Headquarters

Baffin Bay Padre

Island

Gulf of Mexico

National

Seashore

Port Mansfield

Padre Island

Laguna Madre

Santa Ana Nat'l Wildlife Refuge

Laguna Atascosa Nat'l Wildlife Refuge

South Padre Island

0   40 miles

0   50 km

MEXICO *Rio Grande* Brownsville

Matamoros

ESSENTIAL INFORMATION

WHEN TO GO   The humidity is so high all along the Texas coast that winters can be occasionally chilly (in Galveston temperatures sometimes hover in the 40s, though mid-50s is usually the average daily temperature), while the summers are muggy, usually in the high 80s. The temperate seasons, fall and spring, with average Galveston temperatures around 80° and 69°, respectively, are the most reliable, although many winter Texans contend that winter down in the Rio Grande Valley, with its average of 63°, is just about perfect. Travelers should keep in mind that Brownsville's summer heat can be unbearable, but the town is pleasant to visit in the winter. Hurricane season runs from June through September; storms are tracked well in advance of their landfall, giving coastal residents plenty of time to clear out. Birdwatching is usually best from early November through mid-March during the winter migration, but weather conditions may vary. Deepsea fishing is excellent year-round.

BARGAINS For offbeat shopping bargains in Galveston, try Colonel Bubbie's (2202 Strand, tel. 409/762–7397), a surplus store of military gear (no guns or ammunition) from around the world, and Hendley Market (2010 Strand, tel. 409/762–2610) with offbeat gift items, including antique postcards and maps, old linens and lace, and folk-art treasures. The Old Peanut Butter Warehouse is chock-full of antique furniture, depression glass, vintage jewelry, and a pantry offering homemade peanut butter. Also in Galveston, take a free ride on the Bolivar Ferry (tel. 409/763–2386); the ride is a great way to see dolphins during the day or view a full moon at night. To catch the ferry, take the Seawall east to Ferry Road until it ends.

You shouldn't leave south Texas without driving across the Mexican border for a day of shopping. Brownsville's sister city is Mexico's Matamoros, and you can cross the border easily via the bridge in downtown Brownsville. However, it is advisable to take a cab across the border rather than walking or driving your own vehicle. Also use common sense and don't venture away from the crowd or into deserted areas alone. As long as you stay within 25 miles of the border, you don't need a passport, visa, or other papers. The shopping markets and curio shops are popular for their Mexican embroidered clothing, jewelry, handicrafts, footwear, furniture, and guayaberas, a traditional men's shirt worn in south Texas. If spirited bargaining in the markets is not your style, you may want to shop at the government-run Centro Artesanal in

Matamoros, where the prices are fixed and the quality is high.

TOURIST OFFICES Brownsville Convention and Visitors Bureau (Box 4697, Brownsville 78523, tel. 210/546–3721 or 800/626–2639; fax 210/546–3972). Corpus Christi Area Convention and Tourist Bureau (1201 N. Shoreline Dr., Corpus Christi 78403, tel. 512/882–5603 or 800/678–6232; fax 512/882–4256). Galveston Island Convention and Visitors Bureau (2106 Seawall Blvd., Galveston 77550, tel. 409/763–4311, 800/351–4237 or 800/351–4236 in TX; fax 409/765–8611). Rockport-Fulton Area Chamber of Commerce (Box 1055, Rockport 78382, tel. 512/729–6445, 800/242–0071 or 800/826–6441 in TX). Port Aransas Chamber of Commerce (421 W. Cotter St., Port Aransas 78373, tel. 512/749–5919 or 800/45–COAST; fax 512/749–4672). South Padre Island Convention and Visitors Bureau (600 Padre Blvd., South Padre Island 78597, tel., 210/761–6433 or 800/343–2368; fax 210/761–9462). For information on Padre Island National Seashore, contact the National Park Service (9405 Padre Island Dr., Corpus Christi 78418, tel. 512/937–2621).

EMERGENCIES Police, fire, and ambulance: Dial 911. **Hospitals:** AMI Brownsville Medical Center (1040 W. Jefferson St., Brownsville, tel. 210/544–1400) has a 24-hour emergency room. In Galveston, there is a 24-hour emergency room at the University of Texas Medical Branch (6th St. and the Strand, tel. 409/772–1521). Corpus Christi's Memorial Medical Center caters to out-of-town visitors with ExpressCare, a walk-in treatment center open daily from noon until midnight (2606 Hospital Blvd. at Morgan exit off Crosstown Expressway, tel. 512/881–4000).

ARRIVING AND DEPARTING

BY PLANE Galveston is not served by any major airlines, so plan to fly into either of Houston's two airports. Intercontinental Airport (tel. 713/230–3000), the larger of the two, is in the far north of Houston, about 1½–2 hours from Galveston, depending on traffic; the more manageable Hobby Airport (tel.

713/643–4597) is on the south side of the city and about an hour from the island. Call the Galveston Limousine Service (tel. 409/765–5288) for a pickup, or your Galveston hotel may have a courtesy car. Be sure to call ahead to make arrangements so you are not left stranded.

Corpus Christi and the Rio Grande Valley (which includes the Brownsville and South Padre Island areas) are both served by a number of airlines, although lower-priced Southwest Airlines is the most frequent flyer between Texas cities. For more information, call Corpus Christi International Airport (tel. 512/289–2675) or Valley International Airport (tel. 210/430–8600) at Harlingen.

BY CAR There is no coastal highway as such along the Gulf Coast, so plan on detours to see some of the smaller seaside towns. From Galveston, take County Road 3005 out the west end of the island and cross over the toll bridge to the mainland at Surfside Beach. Pick your way over to Highway 35, then follow it south along the coast to Corpus Christi. It's a well-maintained road that offers plenty of local color and frequently winds along the coast. U.S. 77, which runs from just north of Rockport south to Brownsville, is a straight shot, but about 20 miles inland from the sea.

BY TRAIN Texas Limited (tel. 713/629–3700 or 409/765–5700) links downtown Houston to Galveston Friday–Sunday with its restored antique railroad cars.

GETTING AROUND

Given the large distances involved, a car is the most practical way to travel the Texas Coast. RV centers dot the coast, especially down near the border (most RV parks rent hookups by the night, week, or month). Pleasure boaters also have safe access with the many marinas and protected waterways along the coast.

The Galveston Island trolley runs daily from the beachfront to The Strand (round-trip fare: $2 adults, $1 children). A motorized trolley connects Corpus Christi's major hotels to the Bayfront, and the Tide, a brightly painted bus,

takes you from downtown to the aquarium and beaches; both services cost 50¢. A water taxi also shuttles passengers from downtown to Corpus Christi Beach ($1).

On South Padre Island, you can rent a dune buggy at Starcade (3305 Padre Blvd., tel. 210/761–2247). The WAVE coastline trolley daily runs up and down the island's main street, Padre Boulevard (cost: 50¢ one-way, or $1 all day).

REST STOPS The coast's many service stations are usually reliable rest stops, and many are noted by highway signs. In the cities, towns, and wildlife refuges, the visitor centers (*see* Tourist Offices, *above;* The Natural World, *below*) offer dependable facilities.

GUIDED TOURS **Galveston:** The Galveston Historical Foundation (2016 Strand, tel. 409/765–7834) offers tours of the area. Island Tours Unlimited (tel. 409/762–8605) arranges custom tours. The *Colonel* (tel. 409/763–4900), a Victorian-style paddlewheel boat, offers day and dinner cruises. Treasure Island Tour Train provides a 90-minute tour around the city; board the train at Moody Center (Seawall Blvd. at 21st St., tel. 409/765–9564).

Aransas Wildlife Refuge: While in the Rockport area, you can view the celebrated whooping cranes that winter in the Aransas National Wildlife Refuge. Four boats leave from Rockport Harbor and carry up to 250 passengers each to visit the nesting grounds every day. Reservations should be made at least a day in advance with the vessels *Captain Ted's* (tel. 800/338–4551), *Wharf Cat* (tel. 800/782–2473), *New Pelican* (tel. 512/729–8448), or *Pisces* (tel. 800/245–9324).

Corpus Christi: You can view the city from the water on the 265-passenger *Flagship* (tel. 512/884–1693); it docks at the Peoples Street marina.

South Padre Island: Boats depart daily from Sea Ranch Marina for two-hour narrated cruises of the Gulf of Mexico; the highlight is spying bottlenose dolphins frolicking in the waters (tel. 210/761–7646).

Brownsville: Historic trolley tours depart from Brownsville Convention Center twice daily, Thursday–Saturday (tel. 210/546–3721).

EXPLORING

The following highlights main attractions along the coast from north to south.

GALVESTON Texas is a state of large landscapes, best explored by car, but historical Galveston can be easily explored on foot. Start on the waterfront at **Pier 21.** A new seven-acre harbor development along Pier 21 includes retail shops, restaurants, a hotel, and the **Pier 21 Theatre,** which shows *The Great Storm,* a documentary about the 1900 hurricane that nearly wiped Galveston off the map. Nearby, the *Elissa,* an 1877 three-masted iron barque, has been restored as an operational sailing ship and is part of the adjacent **Texas Seaport Museum,** which has historical exhibits of 19th-century Galveston and observation decks. *Pier 21, 1 block off the Strand, tel. 409/763–1877. Open daily. Admission charged to ship, museum, and theater.*

The Railroad Museum, housed in an Art Deco station on the Strand near the *Elissa,* re-creates a people-filled train station lobby with lifelike statuary. It also features an extensive collection of vintage railroad cars. *The Strand at 25th St., tel. 409/765–5700. Open daily. Admission charged.*

Several blocks of the **Strand Historic District** between the *Elissa* and Railroad Museum are lined with fine, old, 19th-century iron-fronted buildings, once part of a financial hub known as the "Wall Street of the Southwest." Most have been restored and today house boutiques, restaurants, bars, art galleries, and several manufacturers' outlet stores.

The East End Historical District, 6 blocks from the Strand, is a 40-block area between 19th and 11th streets and Broadway to Market Street; here you'll find examples of Greek Revival, Gothic, Victorian, and other architectural styles of the last century. A free brochure available at the Strand Visitor Center

(2016 Strand, tel. 409/765–7834) has a map that suggests a walking tour of the district. A companion audio tour (fee charged) is also available. Several grand homes, such as **Aston Villa** (2328 Broadway; admission charged) and the **Bishop's Palace** (1402 Broadway; admission charged) are open daily. Others, privately owned, are open only for the annual homes tour in early May and early December.

Moody Gardens, a 142-acre property landscaped with some 20,000 plants and trees, creates a lush environment for the 10-story Rainforest Pyramid, a white-sand beach and lagoon, an IMAX theater, and an exotic animal petting zoo. *1 Hope Blvd., tel. 409/744–4673 or 800/582–4673. Open daily. Admission charged.*

ROCKPORT-FULTON These two small towns are the jumping-off point for viewing the whooping cranes and exploring the Aransas National Wildlife Refuge (*see* Guided Tours, *above;* the Natural World, *below*). Rockport is also known as an artists' colony, and you'll find seascape paintings for sale in galleries, such as the **Estelle Stair Gallery,** along Austin Street. The **Rockport Arts Center** (901 Broadway, tel. 512/729–5519; admission free) also features changing exhibits from local artists. The town has a good beach—Rockport Beach Park—as well as excellent deep-sea game fishing. Just off Hwy. 35 between Rockport and Fulton sits the **Fulton Mansion** (Henderson St. and Fulton Beach Road, tel. 512/729–0386; admission charged), a beautifully restored French Second Empire mansion built in 1874.

CORPUS CHRISTI The gleaming white Philip Johnson–designed **Art Museum of South Texas** has collections of pre-Columbian figures and modern painting; it stands at the Corpus Christi–side entrance to the ship channel turning basin. *1902 N. Shoreline Dr., tel. 512/884–3844. Open Tues.–Sun. Admission charged.*

Directly across the channel is the **Texas State Aquarium,** which showcases more than 250 species of aquatic life from the Gulf of Mexico. *2710 N. Shoreline Dr. (Corpus Christi*

Beach), tel. 512/881–1200 or 800/477–GULF. Open daily. Admission charged.

Docked next door to the aquarium is the **USS Lexington**, a naval aircraft carrier nicknamed the "Blue Ghost" during World War II, when it served in the South Pacific. It now houses a floating naval museum. *Corpus Christi Beach, tel. 512/888–4873. Open daily. Admission charged.*

The **Corpus Christi Museum of Science & History** features an exceptional exhibit with artifacts and sunken treasures from a Spanish galleon that wrecked on Padre Island in 1554. *1900 N. Chaparrel St., tel. 512/883–2862. Open Tues.–Sun. Admission charged.*

Following the quincentennial celebration of Columbus's visit to the Americas, the **Columbus Fleet**—authentic reproductions of the *Niña, Pinta,* and *Santa Maria*—is now permanently anchored at Cargo Dock 1, adjacent to Corpus Christi Museum. *1901 N. Chaparrel St., tel. 512/883–2863. Open daily. Admission charged.*

Corpus Christi offers some of the best water sports on the coast, from windsurfing to fishing to skiing. Either stay on the mainland and enjoy the protected bay beaches (including Corpus Christi Beach, McGee Beach, and Cole Park) or take the causeway over to Padre Island's Malaquite Beach or Mustang Island State Park. A number of concessions along the seawall and marina offer other recreational activities, such as three-wheeled surreys and water trikes.

BROWNSVILLE Aviation history takes flight at the **Confederate Air Force's Rio Grande Valley Wing Museum,** where hangars at Brownsville International Airport shelter vintage World War II aircraft and combat memorabilia. The CAF stages air shows in early March and late October. *922 Minnesota St., Brownsville Airport, tel. 210/541–8585. Open daily. Admission charged.*

The Audubon Society's 32-acre **Sabal Palm Grove Sanctuary** welcomes bird-watchers to explore one of the last remaining Sabal palm woodlands in the region. Bobcats, coyotes

and the endangered oscelot are also found here. *Southmost Rd. on Rabb Plantation south of Brownsville, tel. 210/541–8034. Open Nov.–Apr., Thurs.–Mon.; May–Oct., weekends. Admission charged.*

Gladys Porter Zoo, rated as one of the 10 best zoos in the nation, has more than 1,750 uncaged mammals, birds, and reptiles, many of them among the world's rarest endangered species. *500 Ringgold, tel. 210/546–2177. Open daily. Admission charged.*

Few American visitors leave Brownsville without going over the bridge into Matamoros, Mexico, to shop (*see* Bargains, *above*).

SOUTH PADRE ISLAND At **Sea Turtle Incorporated** the endearing Ila Loetscher, recognized worldwide for her campaign to save the endangered Ridley sea turtle, stages Turtle Lady Shows each Tuesday and Saturday morning. *5805 Gulf Blvd., tel. 210/761–2544. Admission charged.*

THE NATURAL WORLD Positioned at the convergence of two major flyways, the Texas Coast is well known for its bird sanctuaries. In the Rio Grande Valley, both Santa Ana and Laguna Atascosa, known for their many rare animals and birds, offer self-guided auto tours, miles of walking trails, and several photography blinds. Just 3 degrees north of the Tropic of Cancer, **Santa Ana** is a 2,000-acre remnant of a subtropical forest where you can view many plants and animals seldom seen anywhere else in the country. Located on a bend of the Rio Grande River, the junglelike refuge is famous for more than 300 documented species of birds, many of Mexican origin. *South and east of McAllen off U.S. 281 along Military Hwy., tel. 210/787–3079. Open daily to pedestrians dawn–dusk; tour road open to vehicles weekdays. A guided tram runs in the winter. Admission free.*

The **Laguna Atascosa** wildlife refuge contains 46,000 acres, composed of coastal prairies, salt flats, and brushlands, that attract large flocks of waterfowl. Javelina, white-tailed deer, and alligators are also among the inhabitants. *On the coast just north of Port*

Isabel, off FM 106, tel. 210/748–3607. Open daily. Admission charged.

The 54,829-acre **Aransas National Wildlife Refuge,** crisscrossed with hiking trails and roads for cars, is home to whooping cranes (mid-Oct.–late-Mar.; see Guided Tours, above, for information on boat tours). The area also features some 500 species of waterfowl, songbirds, and hummingbirds as well as wild boars, alligators, bobcats, wolves, and deer. 38 mi north of Rockport near Hwy. 35, tel. 512/286–3559. Open daily. Admission charged.

Padre Island National Seashore is a protected, primitive area where you can hike, camp, and collect shells. (Remember that there is no potable water in the area for 110 miles, so bring your own.) From the tops of some sand dunes, you can look at the Gulf of Mexico to the east and the Laguna Madre to the west. You can tour the pristine barrier island in a four-wheel-drive vehicle, but first consult with park rangers about tides and weather conditions. You can reach Padre Island National Seashore from I–37 in Corpus Christi by taking Hwy. 358 to Park Rd. 22. The park road leads to the Malaquite Beach visitor center (tel. 512/949–9368), with informative rangers. Open daily. Admission charged.

HOTELS AND INNS

Bed-and-breakfasts have caught on in Texas in recent years and are good alternatives to the chain motels if you're on a tight budget. Moderately priced Galveston bed-and-breakfasts include the **Gilded Thistle** (1805 Broadway, tel. 409/763–0194) and the **Virginia Point Inn** (2327 Ave. K, tel. 409/763–2450). Galveston has the greatest variety of accommodations, but prices run a little higher here than farther south. Condos are also available for short-term leases. Any local chamber of commerce (see Tourist Offices, above) can steer you toward a real-estate agent eager to send you listings and brochures.

Most Texas cities levy a hefty local room tax, which can raise your tariff rather dramatically. At most coastal properties, rates double

during spring break (late-Feb.–mid-Mar.); summer rates average 30% higher than winter rates. Price categories for double occupancy, excluding 8% tax, are Expensive, $90–$110; Moderate, $70–$90; and Inexpensive, under $70.

BROWNSVILLE **Rancho Viejo Resort.** One of south Texas's most stunning resorts is also a golfer's paradise, with two 18-hole courses; choose between one of the Spanish-style villas right on the golf course or a room in the main lodge. 6 mi north of Brownsville on Expressway 77/83 (Box 3918), 78520, tel. 210/350–4000 or 800/531–7400. 58 rooms, 31 suites with kitchenettes. Restaurant, pool, tennis. AE, DC, MC, V. Moderate–Expensive.

Fort Brown Hotel & Resort. This lovely motor inn, surrounded by a resaca (lagoon) with tropical gardens and waterfalls, has a great location—you can walk to Mexico. 1900 E. Elizabeth St., 78520, tel. 210/546–2201 or 800/582–3333. 278 rooms, 12 suites. Restaurant, pool, tennis. AE, D, DC, MC, V. Inexpensive–Moderate.

CORPUS CHRISTI **Best Western Sandy Shores.** Ask for a room facing the gulf at this pleasant, beachside, high-rise hotel near the Texas State Aquarium. 3200 Surfside, 78403, tel. 512/883–7456 or 800/242–5814, fax 512/883–1437. 252 rooms, 7 suites. Restaurant, pool, gift shop, kite museum. AE, D, DC, MC, V. Inexpensive–Moderate.

Corpus Christi Marriott Bayfront. Overlooking the bay and sitting across the street from People's Street T-head, this luxurious hotel is convenient to all downtown attractions. 900 N. Shoreline Blvd., 78401, tel. 512/886–1600 or 800/874–4585, fax 512/887–6715. 450 rooms, 28 suites. Restaurant, indoor and outdoor pool, health club. AE, D, DC, MC, V. Expensive.

GALVESTON **Tremont House.** A soaring atrium lobby, white-lace linens on the beds, a fine restaurant, and a convenient Strand location make this elegant restoration of a 19th-century mercantile building one of the city's most popular hotels. 2300 Ship's Mechanic Row, 77550, tel. 409/763–0300 or

800/874–2300, fax 409/763–1539. 117 rooms, 9 suites. Dining room, room service, concierge, gift shop, limo, passes to Galveston Racquet Club. AE, DC, MC, V. Expensive.

Hotel Galvez. This 1911 Spanish-style stucco hotel, across from the Gulf of Mexico, hosts many celebrities and places visitors in the middle of the beachfront action. *2024 Seawall Blvd., 77550, tel. 409/765–7721 or 800/392–4285, fax 409/765–7721, ext. 667. 225 rooms, 3 suites. Restaurant, 2 pools, room service, guest membership in Galveston Country Club. AE, D, DC, MC, V. Moderate–Expensive.*

Victorian Inn. Located in the East End Historical District near the Strand, Galveston's first bed-and-breakfast, an Italian-Victorian beauty, features antique furnishings throughout. *511 17th St., 77550, tel. 409/762–3235. 4 rooms, 1 suite. AE, DC, MC, V. Moderate.*

Harbor House. The anchor attraction of a new waterfront development, this comfortable but plain inn is settled into a former steamship terminal and features nautical-theme decor. The inn's greatest asset may be its waterfront views. *Pier 21, No. 28, 77550, tel. 409/763–3321 or 800/874–3721, fax 409/765–6421. 42 rooms, 3 suites. Restaurant. AE, DC, MC, V. Expensive.*

■PORT ARANSAS■ Tarpon Inn. It's been called seaside tacky, but this Hemingwayesque hotel, built in 1886 and on the National Register of Historic Places, appeals to anglers out to catch big game fish. Creatures of comfort note: Rooms do not have televisions or phones. *200 E. Cotter St. (Box 8), 78373, tel. 512/749–5555 or 800/365–6784. 22 rooms, 2 suites. Nearby restaurant, free parking. AE, MC, V. Inexpensive.*

Port Royal. A destination in itself, this condominium resort on Mustang Island gives guests the option of lounging on the beach, just outside your door, or on the banks of the largest lagoon in Texas. *Hwy. 361, Box 336, 78373, tel. 512/749–5011 or 800/242–1034, fax 512/749–6399. 170 rental units. Restaurant, pool, tennis courts, convenience store, gift shop. AE, D, DC, MC, V. Expensive.*

■ROCKPORT-FULTON■ Sandollar Resort. Birdwatchers and fishermen alike flock to this relaxed bargain motel nestled amid live oak trees on a hill overlooking the sea. *Fulton Beach Rd. at Hwy. 35, Box 30, 78382, tel. 512/729–2381. 27 rooms, some with kitchenettes; 2 suites. Restaurant, pool, RV spaces, marina. MC, V. Inexpensive.*

■SOUTH PADRE ISLAND■ Sheraton Beach Resort. Every room has an ocean view at this beautiful 12-story resort, with lavish landscaping and an inviting beach. *310 Padre Island Blvd., 78597, tel. 512/761–6551 or 800/222–4010, fax 512/761–6570. 200 rooms, 50 suites. Restaurant, pool, gift shop, water sports. AE, D, DC, MC, V. Moderate.*

Bahia Mar Resort. One of the first hotel-condo developments on the island, this beachfront property offers wonderful views of the water and access to miles of pristine beach. *6300 Padre Island Blvd., 78597, tel. 210/761–1343 or 800/292–7502, fax 210/761–6287. 200 rooms, 20 suites, 50 condominium units. Restaurant, pool, nightclub, tennis courts, putting green, gift shop. AE, D, DC, MC, V. Moderate–Expensive.*

MOTELS

■MODERATE■ Holiday Inn on the Beach (5002 Seawall Blvd., Galveston 77550, tel. 409/740–3581 or 800/465–4329). 178 rooms; restaurant, gift shop, pool, ocean view. **Ramada Inn** (600 Strand, Galveston 77550, tel. 409/765–5544 or 800/228–2828). 232 rooms; restaurant, water view.

■INEXPENSIVE■ Days Inn Corpus Christi (901 Navigation, Corpus Christi 78408, adjacent to Corpus Christi Greyhound Racetrack, tel. 512/888–8599 or 800/233–DAYS). 121 rooms; restaurant, pool. **Days Inn Rockport** (1212 Laurel, Rockport 78382, tel. 512/729–6379 or 800/325–2525). 25 rooms, 5 suites; pool. **Gaido's Seaside Inn** (3800 Seawall Blvd., Galveston 77550, tel. 409/762–9625). 108 rooms, pool, restaurant. **Gulfview Hotel** (2300 Seawall Blvd., Galveston 77550, tel. 409/762–1166). 124 rooms; pool. **Holiday Inn** (1945 North Expressway, Brownsville 78520, tel. 210/546–4591). 159 rooms, 3 suites; restaurant, pool. **La Quinta Motor Inn** (55 Sam Perl Blvd., Brownsville 78520, tel. 210/546–0381). 137 rooms, 6 suites; restaurant, pool. **Sandcastle** (200 W. Kingfish, South Padre Island 78597, tel. 210/761–1321 or 800/221–5218). 50 condo units; kitchens, pool, fishing, boat slips. **Sea Shell Inn** (202 Kleberg Pl., Corpus Christi 78402, tel. 512/888–5391). 26 rooms; pool, beach. **Travelers Inn** (6805 South Padre Island Dr. at Nile Dr., Corpus Christi 78412, tel. 512/992–9222 or 800/663–8300). 119 rooms, 3 suites; pool.

DINING

The trinity of Texas cuisine are Tex-Mex, chicken-fried steak, and barbecue—all delicious, and heavy, foods. However, fresh seafood contributes a fourth, lighter component to the regional cooking. The Gulf of Mexico boasts some of the most fertile fishing grounds in the world, yielding black drum, yellowfin tuna, gulf mahimahi, flounder, snapper, grouper, redfish, swordfish, and pompano. The coast's warm waters also yield sweet shrimp, blue crabs (excellent barbecued), and mild-flavored oysters. Frying is still the preparation of choice along the gulf, but that is changing. Today health-conscious diners can get grilled seafood almost everywhere. You will find the Tex-Mex food down around Brownsville especially good. Price categories per person, excluding 8% tax, service, and drinks, are *Moderate*, $15–$25, and *Inexpensive*, under $15.

BROWNSVILLE **Palm Court.** The relaxed setting and tropical foliage blend well with the health-minded menu (there are a couple of Pritikin items), but even serious epicureans will not be disappointed by the shrimp crepes, lasagna, terrific soups, and fresh daily specials. *2235 Boca Chica Blvd., tel. 210/542–3575. AE, MC, V. Inexpensive.*

Los Camperos. Strolling mariachi bands add to the festive atmosphere of this Mexican-style steak house that offers steak *al carbón* (grilled) along with enchiladas, fajitas, and other Tex-Mex favorites. *1400 International Blvd., tel. 210/546–8172. AE, MC, V. Inexpensive.*

CORPUS CHRISTI **Elmo's City Diner & Oyster Bar.** This '50s-style diner offers Coastal Bend delicacies, such as King Ranch chicken, guacamole, oysters-on-the-half-shell, and home-style hamburgers. *622 N. Water St., tel. 512/883–1643. AE, D, DC, MC, V. Inexpensive–Moderate.*

The Lighthouse. An easy walk from the downtown hotels, this marina restaurant offers a dramatic bay view along with seafood, pasta, and chicken. *Lawrence St. T-head, tel. 512/883–3982. AE, D, DC, MC, V. Moderate.*

La Pesca. This casual place features fresh seafood cooked with a Mexican flair, plus homemade breads and desserts. *701 N. Water St., tel. 512/887–4558. AE, D, DC, MC, V. Moderate.*

Water Street Oyster Bar. Amberjack steaks are grilled to perfection at this former garage turned restaurant; original brick walls and the concrete floor add to the lively atmosphere of this landmark eatery. House specialties include oysters and shrimp *en brochette* (wrapped in bacon, skewered and grilled) and blackened redfish. *309 N. Water St., tel. 512/881–9448. AE, DC, MC, V. Moderate.*

Rusty's. What's a trip to the beach without a thick, juicy "cheeseburger in paradise"? These are the best around. *1645 Airline Rd., tel. 512/993–5000. AE, MC, V. Inexpensive.*

GALVESTON **Gaido's.** This granddaddy of seafood houses in Galveston, known all over Texas for its changing menu, offers crabs, oysters, shrimp, and snapper prepared a dozen ways each. *3828 Seawall Blvd., tel. 409/762–9625. AE, MC, V. Moderate.*

The Wentletrap. The beautiful three-story Renaissance Revival restoration, Continental food, and gracious service all make dining here special; try the salads at lunch and the seafood at dinner. *2301 Strand, tel. 409/765–5545. AE, DC, MC, V. Moderate.*

Mallory's Wharf. This popular restaurant at the Harbor House hotel offers delectable variations on traditional seafood specialties—try the blackened shrimp, chicken-fried catfish, or the house specialty, Wharf Chowder. *Pier 21, tel. 409/763–3321. AE, DC, MC, V. Moderate.*

Benno's on the Beach. Cajun-inspired seafood, including rich peppery crawfish etouffée, red beans and rice, and blackened oysters, are served in this open-air beachside shack. *1200 Seawall Blvd., tel. 409/762–4621. MC, V. Inexpensive.*

El Nopalito. Locals come to this colorful, ramshackle favorite for a cheap and funky Mexican breakfast and heaping platters at lunch. *614 42nd St. between Church St. and Broadway Ave., tel. 409/763–9815. No dinner. No credit cards. Inexpensive.*

Hill's Pier 19. Gumbo, oyster po'boys, and seafood are the standards at this dockside salty dog; eat outside at picnic tables where you can watch freighters, tugboats, and shrimp boats. *20th St. at the wharves, tel. 409/763–7087. AE, DC, MC, V. Inexpensive.*

PADRE ISLAND **Snoopy's Pier.** You can fill up on fried fish, shrimp, or oysters at this breezy, seaside café. Start with an order of crabmeat-stuffed jalapeños. Dine outside and watch the brown pelicans soar over the waves. *13313 S. Padre Island Dr., tel. 512/949-8815. No credit cards. Inexpensive.*

PORT ARANSAS **Seafood & Spaghetti Works.** While the building may resemble a spaceship gone off course, it's the delicious seafood and pasta dishes that draw diners back again and again for giant grilled shrimp, wonderful pasta dishes, and scrumptious desserts such as Butterfinger Cheesecake. *709 Alister St., tel. 512/749–5666. AE, DC, MC, V. Moderate.*

Quarterdeck. From the Quarterdeck you can watch fishing boats unload the catch of the day, only to find it reappear later on your own menu—grilled, fried, broiled, or stuffed. *914 Tarpon, Fisherman's Wharf, tel. 512/749–4119. AE, MC, V. Moderate.*

ROCKPORT-FULTON **The Big Fisherman.** A combination restaurant, zoo, and plant nursery, this local favorite offers seafood specials

and a close-up view of wild animals. *Fulton Beach Rd. at FM 1069 (turn away from the sea), tel. 512/729–1997. AE, MC, V. Inexpensive–Moderate.*

The Boiling Pot. Shrimp, crabs, corn-on-the-cob, and potatoes are all boiled together, Cajun style, and served right on the butcher-paper-covered tables at this lively dining spot. *Fulton Beach Rd. at Palmetto, tel. 512/729–6972. AE, D, MC, V. Inexpensive–Moderate.*

SOUTH PADRE ISLAND **Rovan's Restaurant and Bakery.** The lines are long, but the service is quick, the prices cheap, and the food plentiful at this popular homespun spot. Breakfast is served all day, and locals give Rovan's barbecued ribs a serious thumbs-up. Many locals also swear by the home-baked goods. *5300 Padre Blvd., tel. 210/761–6972. Closed Tuesdays. No credit cards. Inexpensive.*

OUTDOOR ACTIVITIES

BEACHES The 110-mile-long Padre Island has the best beaches in Texas, most of them protected as National Seashore, largely undeveloped and accessible only by four-wheel-drive vehicles. Malaquite Beach at the northern tip and South Padre Island to the south offer scenic stretches of beach. Other exceptional beaches include Mustang Island, the barrier island that protects Corpus Christi Bay and extends north from Padre Island to Port Aransas; Galveston's East Beach, the least eroded of Galveston's beaches; and Bolivar Peninsula, north of Galveston Island and accessible by ferry. Many Texas beaches are still relatively primitive, although some offer amenities. In Galveston, for example, Apffel Park has a pavilion with showers, a snack bar, and rest rooms.

FISHING You can charter a boat for a day of deep-sea fishing in almost any port along the coast. Most charters go out about 40 miles for kingfish, dorado, bluefish, shark, Spanish mackerel, tuna, wahoo, and barracuda. In Galveston, contact Aqua Safari Charters (tel. 409/935–4646 or 800/759–4547). In Port

Aransas, contact Fisherman's Wharf (tel. 512/749–5760), Woody's Sports Center (tel. 512/749–5252), or Deep Sea Headquarters (tel. 512/749–5597). The *Capt. Clark* departs from People Street T-head three times daily in Corpus Christi (tel. 512/884–4369 or 512/643–7128).

You will also find piers and jetties all along the coast. Most, but not all, are free. In Port Aransas, the Horace Caldwell fishing pier jets 1,240 feet into the Gulf of Mexico and permits anglers to hook tarpon, shark, and many other species. In addition, excellent surf fishing is found along the public beaches, especially at the north end of South Padre Island between Andy Bowie Park and the Mansfield jetties, and at San Luis Pass on the western tip of Galveston Island. If you plan to fish or gather oysters, check locally to make sure there is no red tide and that the waters are unpolluted.

A Texas fishing license is required for fishing persons aged 17 to 65, regardless of your state of residence. A special, three-day saltwater-sport fishing license is also available. Licenses may be purchased at most bait camps, sporting-goods and tackle stores, and convenience stores. For more information, contact the Texas Parks and Wildlife Department (tel. 800/792–1112).

GOLF The newly redesigned Galveston Island Municipal Golf Course (tel. 409/744–2366) has 18 holes and a large clubhouse. Galveston Country Club at Pirates Beach (tel. 409/737–2776) is a private facility, but area hotels offer guest membership privileges. Corpus Christi and the Valley also have many fine golf courses, including the Rancho Viejo Country Club (tel. 210/350–4000), north of Brownsville, with its two 18-hole courses.

HIKING The wildlife refuges and Padre Island National Seashore offer extensive trail systems and self-guided walking tours (*see* The Natural World, *above*).

WINDSURFING Windsurfers rank Corpus Christi as one of the top sailing spots in the country because of its constant strong winds (the average wind velocity is 12 mph). Colorful sails dot the waters most every day of the year beneath the **JFK Causeway** and at **Bird Island Basin** on Padre Island. Lessons and rentals are available from Wind & Wave (10721 South Padre Island Drive, Corpus Christi, tel. 512/937–WAVE).

SHELLING San Jose Island, or St. Jo to the locals, is a beachcomber's paradise. Uninhabited and accessible from the mainland only by ferry from Port Aransas, its secluded beaches sprawl for miles. Fall and winter are the best times for finding perfect, unbroken sand dollars and other fragile treasures that wash ashore. Woody's Boat Basin (114 Cotter St., Port Aransas, tel. 512/749–5252) has daily boat trips to St. Jo; don't forget your ice chest (lots of ice and cold drinks), picnic basket, umbrella, towels, fishing tackle, and sunscreen. There are no rest rooms or potable water on the island, and little shade.

Waikiki and Honolulu
Hawaii

tepping off the airplane at Honolulu International Airport, the sensation hits you. The warmth of the tropical air mixed with rain-forest musk and a slight taste of the surrounding sea make it clear that you've arrived in a place unlike any other in the United States.

That first impression usually stays with you, though Honolulu and Waikiki have grown far beyond the simple South Seas image created by the tourist brochures. The airport, for example, bustles just as it would in any other city of 400,000. The skyline stretching between the reef runway and distant Diamond Head Crater is lined with modern buildings, busy highways, and other vacationers.

Waikiki, snuggled in the shadow of Diamond Head, is a 2¹/₂-mile strip with 33,000 hotel and condominium rooms, scores of restaurants, and seemingly endless shopping opportunities. Waikiki is actually part of the City and County of Honolulu, a title that includes the entire island of Oahu. At only 3¹/₂ miles from downtown, the resort area makes a good base for exploring the 618 square miles of this, the third-largest island in the Hawaiian chain.

ESSENTIAL INFORMATION

WHEN TO GO Soaked in sunshine and cooled by trade winds, Hawaii boasts one of the most ideal climates in the world. Waikiki's year-round temperatures average 75°–80°. Summers, especially August and September, are slightly warmer and drier, while winters, particularly February and March, are slightly cooler, with more rainfall. Yet Waikiki is on the dry leeward shore and rarely has more than two or three consecutive days of precipitation. Waikiki's consistent climate means its peak season has more to do with the weather elsewhere. Crowds escaping cold winters begin to arrive in mid-De-

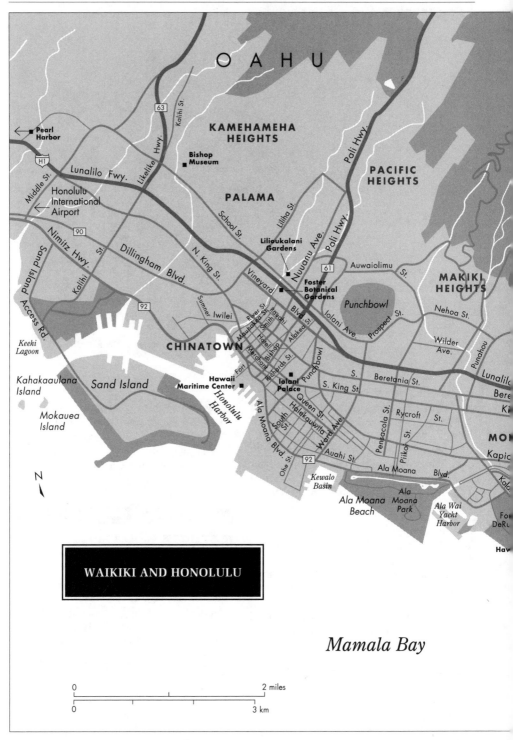

O A H U

KAMEHAMEHA
HEIGHTS

PACIFIC
HEIGHTS

PALAMA

MAKIKI
HEIGHTS

63

Kalihi St.

← Pearl
Harbor

Likelike Hwy.

Pali Hwy.

H1

Lunalilo Fwy.

Bishop
Museum

Middle St.

Honolulu
International
Airport

School St.

Liliha St.

Nuuanu Ave.

Pali Hwy.

Auwaiolimu

St.

Nehoa St.

Nimitz Hwy.

90

Sand Island

Dillingham   Blvd.

N. King St.

Lilioukalani
Gardens

61

Wilder
Ave.

Kalihi

Summer   Iwilei

Vineyard

Blvd.

Foster
Botanical
Gardens

Iolani Ave.

Punchbowl

Prospect St.

Punahou

Lunalilo

92

River St.

Maunakea St.

Smith

Pauahi

Alakea St.

Bere

Access Rd.

Keehi
Lagoon

CHINATOWN

Hotel

Bishop

Punchbowl

Beretania St.

Ki

Kahakaaulana
Island

Sand Island

Fort

Merchant St.

Nuuanu

Richbrid. St.

Iolani
Palace

S. King St.

Rycroft   St.

Mokauea
Island

Hawaii
Maritime Center

Honolulu
Harbor

Queen St.

S.

Pensacola St.

Piikoi St.

MO

Kapic

N

Ala Moana Blvd.

South
St.

Helekauwila
Ward Ave.

Auahi St.

Ala Moana

Kala

Ohe St.

92

Kewalo
Basin

Ala Moana
Beach

Ala
Moana
Park

Blvd.

Ala Wai
Yacht
Harbor

For
DeRu

Hav

WAIKIKI AND HONOLULU

Mamala Bay

0   2 miles

0   3 km

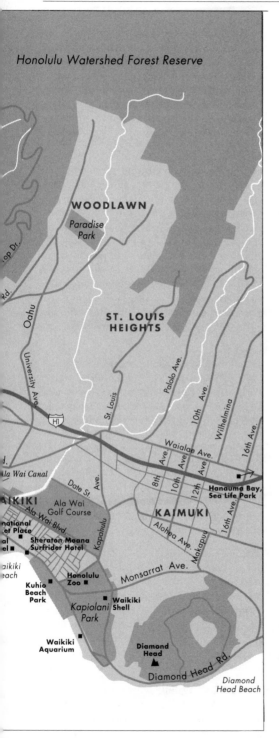

cember and usually don't thin until April. Room rates traditionally run 10%–15% higher during this period.

FESTIVALS AND SEASONAL EVENTS Jan.–Mar.: The Narcissus Festival welcomes the Chinese New Year with a beauty pageant and fireworks in Chinatown. **Mid-Jan.:** The Hawaiian Open Golf Tournament draws the nation's top golfers to the exclusive Waialae Country Club. **May 1:** Lei Day is Hawaii's version of May Day, with lei contests, music, and hula in Kapiolani Park. **Late June:** The King Kamehameha Hula Competition presents the best practitioners of the ancient dance. **Late Sept.:** The Aloha Festivals include major events such as Hawaiian pageantry, canoe races, and a grand parade.

BARGAINS Hawaii can be expensive, but you'll find plenty of enjoyable low-cost or free activities in Waikiki and Honolulu. You can start with a free stroll on Waikiki Beach, one of the best places to people-watch in the world. You can make yourself more comfortable sitting on the beach with a $1.49 grass beach mat available at **Woolworth's** (2224 Kalakaua Ave.) or the ubiquitous ABC Discount Stores. Several free, weekly visitor publications are offered at kiosks along Waikiki's streets; these booklets include the latest calendars and money-saving coupons, and list free tours.

Kapiolani Park offers free kite-flying demonstrations; tennis, soccer, and softball tournaments; and music concerts. The Zoo Fence Art Mart, located on the Diamond Head side of the **Honolulu Zoo** (Wed., Sat., Sun.; free), is a display of affordable artwork by local painters and photographers. The widely accepted "best deal" in all of Honolulu is **The-Bus,** the island's city-operated bus service. For a mere 60¢, you can ride completely around Oahu (*see* Getting Around, *below*).

TOURIST OFFICES The **Hawaii Visitor Bureau**'s main office is conveniently located in the Waikiki Business Plaza (2270 Kalakaua Ave., 8th Floor, Honolulu 96815, tel. 808/923–1811). One of the bureau's information booths can be found on the ground level of nearby Ala Moana Shopping Center on Ala Moana Boulevard.

EMERGENCIES Police, fire, and **ambulance:** Dial 911. **Suicide & Crisis Center:** Dial 521–4555. **Doctors:** Honolulu County Medical Society (tel. 808/536–6988) offers doctor referrals. Doctors on Call (Outrigger Waikiki Hotel, lobby level, 2335 Kalakaua Ave., tel. 808/971–6000) has a doctor and nurses on duty weekdays 8:45–5. **Pharmacies:** Kuhio Pharmacy (Outrigger West Hotel, 2330 Kuhio Ave., tel. 808/923–4466) and The Medicine Man (1113 Kapahulu Ave., tel. 734–1133) are both reliable.

ARRIVING AND DEPARTING

BY PLANE **Honolulu International Airport** (tel. 808/836–6411), 20 minutes from Waikiki, is the only airport available to travelers arriving from the U.S. mainland. Flight times from the West Coast average $4^1/_2$–5 hours.

Between the Airport and Waikiki: TheBus, Honolulu's municipal bus service, costs only 60¢ a ride. The drawback is that you're allowed only one bag and it must fit on your lap. A variety of car-rental companies offer their services just outside the main airport terminal. Among them are **Avis** (tel. 800/331–1212), **Budget** (tel. 800/527–7000), **Dollar** (tel. 800/367–7006), **Hertz** (tel. 800/654–3011), and **National** (tel. 800/CAR–RENT).

Taxi service is offered immediately adjacent to the airport's baggage claim areas. The fare to Waikiki runs approximately $20 plus tip. Drivers also charge 30¢ for each suitcase. Although expensive, taxis offer the fastest and easiest way to get to your hotel. **Terminal Transportation** (tel. 808/836–0317) operates an airport shuttle service into Waikiki for $6 per passenger. It's an inexpensive alternative to a taxi, but takes more time.

GETTING AROUND

ON FOOT Waikiki, at $2^1/_2$ miles long and a $^1/_2$ mile wide, is an easy walk for most. You'll find rest stops everywhere, from beach side

benches to shaded spots in the parks. The main thoroughfares of Kalakaua and Kuhio avenues, paralleling the beach on one side and the Ala Wai Canal on the other, run nearly the length of Waikiki. A beachfront stroll from Diamond Head to the Ala Wai Yacht Harbor gives a nice overview of the action. You'll find free maps in all the visitor publications.

BY BUS **TheBus,** Honolulu's city bus system, provides air-conditioned, comfortable transportation throughout the island. For a mere 60¢, you can circle Oahu in a few hours, depending on how often you hop off. Exact change is required. A $15 senior-citizen (65 or older with proof of age) bus pass, good for four years, may be obtained in person at the bus office (811 Middle St., 7:30 AM–4 PM Mon.–Fri.). Privately published bus-route maps are available at drugstores and other convenience outlets, or call TheBus schedule office (tel. 808/848–5555) for directions.

BY CAR Car-rental companies abound both at Honolulu International Airport (*see* Arriving and Departing, *above*) and in Waikiki. Wear your seat belt—it's the law. Streets and highways are well marked. Detailed maps can be found in the free visitor publications found in Waikiki's streetside kiosks.

BY TAXI Taxis are available throughout Waikiki and Honolulu. Call **Charley's** (tel. 808/531–1333) or **SIDA of Hawaii, Inc.** (tel. 808/836–0011). Prices for trips of any length can be steep, beginning at $1.75 start-up, plus 25¢ for each $^1/_7$ mile.

BY TROLLEY An open bus, modeled after an old-fashioned trolley, plies the streets of Waikiki, Ala Moana Shopping Center, and downtown. Some 20 stops are made along the 90-minute route. The driver/conductor narrates the tour, pointing out sights, shopping, and dining. Call the Waikiki Trolley office (tel. 808/526–0112) for all-day passes ($15 adults; $5 children).

REST STOPS Waikiki is a place on the go, but living on "island time" means spending a few minutes here and there to relax and enjoy the tropical surroundings. Throughout Waikiki, walkers will find a variety of palm-shaded benches, beaches, and other restful stopping points.

GUIDED TOURS **Orientation:** A variety of tour companies offer excursions around and to various locations throughout the island. Vehicles range from small vans to full-size buses. Nearly all are air-conditioned. Van tours are smaller, spend less time loading and unloading, and may be more personal. Among the most reliable and popular tour companies are American Express (tel. 808/921–6300), Gray Line Hawaii (tel. 808/833–8000), E. Noa Tours (tel. 808/599–2561), Polynesian Adventure Tours (tel. 808/833–3000), Polynesian Hospitality (tel. 808/526–3565), Roberts Hawaii (tel. 808/523–7750), and Trans Hawaiian Services (tel. 808/735–6467).

Walking Tours: Join one of these informative walks for a chance to get some exercise while learning about Honolulu. The Chinatown Walking Tour (tel. 808/533–3181), held each Tuesday, gives a fascinating peek into the area's herbal shops, an acupuncturist's shop, and specialty stores and markets. The tour costs $5. History is also the focus of the three-hour Historic Downtown Walking Tour, operated by the Mission Houses Museum (tel. 808/531–0481). Reservations are required for the $7 museum/downtown tour, which is held twice a week. Passport Hawaii (tel. 808/924–1911) leads historic and cultural tours of Waikiki, with stops at significant landmarks along the way. The tour touches on the events that have made Waikiki what it is today. Held twice monthly, it costs $7. Reservations are required.

EXPLORING

Waikiki and Honolulu have much to offer, as does the entire island of Oahu. Closely grouped attractions, such as those in Waikiki, can be seen in one or two days. Allow more time—and possibly a rental car—to see those in downtown and around Oahu. Starting from Diamond Head and working your way clockwise around the island, you can see:

Diamond Head, perhaps Hawaii's greatest landmark, offers a marvelous view of Waikiki from its summit. A tunnel passes through the crater's wall and delivers you to the center itself. From there, it's a .7-mile hike to the summit. Wear comfortable walking shoes and allow 40–60 minutes to reach the top. *Open daily. Admission free.*

The Honolulu Zoo, on the opposite side of Kapiolani Park from Diamond Head, offers 40 green acres and more than 2,000 furry and finned creatures. *151 Kapahulu Ave., tel. 808/971–7171. Open daily. Admission charged.*

The Kodak Hula Show, performed at an outdoor stage in Kapiolani Park, has captivated more hula lovers and learners in its 50 years than any other Hawaii show. It's colorful, lively, and photogenic. *Adjacent to the Waikiki Shell, tel. 808/833–1661. Shows Tues.–Thurs. Admission free.*

The Waikiki Aquarium, on the waterfront near Kapiolani Park, is small for a city that's entirely surrounded by ocean. Nevertheless, the aquarium has an interesting assortment of displays and sea life. *2777 Kalakaua Ave., tel. 808/923–9741. Open daily. Admission charged.*

Kuhio Beach Park is one of the more popular of the many small beaches making up what's collectively called Waikiki Beach. Kuhio Beach is marked by a seawall jutting into the ocean across from the zoo entrance. The wall acts as a breakwater and keeps the shoreside pools calm. Beyond the wall, boogieboarders and surfers ride the waves. *Extending from Waikiki Beach Center to the wall.*

The Sheraton Moana Surfrider, on the National Register of Historic Places, ranks as the matriarch of Hawaii hotels and is actually the oldest lodging (1901) in Waikiki. Following a $50 million renovation, the grand dame is back in style with period furnishings, historical exhibits, and spotless woodwork. Robert Louis Stevenson is said to have sat beneath the giant banyan tree in the hotel courtyard. *2365 Kalakaua Ave., tel. 808/922–3111.*

The International Market Place, in the heart of Waikiki, overflows with two-wheeled push carts, wood-carvers, basket-weavers, and other Pacific artisans. *2330 Kalakaua Ave., tel. 808/923–9871. Open daily. Admission free.*

The Royal Hawaiian Hotel, Waikiki's pink palace, still maintains its charms next to its modern glass-and-concrete neighbors. Take a stroll through the gracious lobby and great hallways, then out into the gardens filled with coconut trees and brilliant flowers. *2259 Kalakaua Ave., tel. 808/923–7311. Open daily. Admission free.*

Iolani Palace, built in Victorian style by King David Kalakaua, represents America's only royal palace. It contains the thrones of Kalakaua and his successor and sister, Queen Liliuokalani. On the grounds you can also see the Iolani Barracks and the Kalakaua Coronation Bandstand, still used most Friday afternoons for free Royal Hawaiian Band concerts. *King St. and Richards St., tel. 808/522–0832. Open Wed.–Sat. Admission charged.*

Chinatown is undergoing a renaissance of sorts. Trendy galleries, studios, and cafés have started to join the acupuncture shops, noodle factories, and sidewalk food markets. Also look for the colorful Oahu Market, an open-air emporium with hanging pig heads, display cases of fresh fish, and row after row of exotic fruits. Chinatown is best explored during the day; at night it becomes a bit tawdry. *Between King, Kekaulike, Pauahi, and Nuuanu Sts.*

The Hawaii Maritime Center, located on the edge of the very active Honolulu Harbor, includes the *Falls of Clyde,* a century-old four-masted, full-rigged ship; the Hokulea Polynesian voyaging canoe; and the Kalakaua Boat House. The boathouse is an engaging museum filled with displays, videos, and other exhibits that bring Hawaii's ocean-related past to life. *Pier 7 across Nimitz Hwy. from Alakea St., tel. 808/536–6373. Open daily. Admission charged.*

The Bishop Museum, inland from downtown, has achieved international fame as a center for Polynesian archaeology, ethnology, and history. You'll find the skeleton of a giant sperm whale, feather capes, and an authentic grass hut. An adjacent planetarium spotlights the "Polynesian Skies." *1525 Bernice St., tel. 808/848–4129. Open daily except Christmas. Admission charged.*

Pearl Harbor, specifically the USS *Arizona* Memorial located there, receives more visitors than any other sight in the Aloha State. The tour begins with a 20-minute documentary and shuttleboat ride to the memorial. The monument straddles the hulk of the USS *Arizona,* which sank with 1,102 men aboard when the Japanese attacked the harbor-bound fleet on December 7, 1941. *U.S. Naval Reservation, Pearl Harbor, tel. 808/422–0561. Open daily. Admission free.*

The North Shore of Oahu represents a long, wild stretch of shoreline with plenty of sights. In Mokuleia, stop to watch the gliders and sky divers take off and land at Dillingham Airfield. The nearby town of Haleiwa holds a funky collection of boutiques, galleries, restaurants, and surf shops. Continuing up the coast, you'll come upon Waimea Bay, home of monster surf during the winter months, and Waimea Falls Park, a collection of gardens, pools, and remnants from ancient Hawaiian civilizations that once occupied the valley. Your next stop should be Sunset Beach, famed among surfing aficionados worldwide. Look for the biggest waves in the winter, but stay on shore where it's safe.

Sea Life Park makes for an enticing marine attraction. Located near Waimanalo, its waterborne menagerie includes penguins, killer whales, and the world's only "wholphin," the offspring of a whale and a dolphin. *Makapuu Point, Waimanalo, tel. 808/259–7933. Open daily. Admission charged.*

Hanauma Bay, near Hawaii Kai, has introduced more travelers to snorkeling than any other swimming spot in Hawaii. Look beneath the waves for an abundance of tropical fish in this marine preserve. Rainbow-colored tangs, angelfish, and parrotfish are just a few of the many species you'll spot. Try for a morning visit for the clearest water conditions. *Kalanianaole Hwy. (Hwy. 72), on the east side of Diamond Head.*

THE NATURAL WORLD Waikiki provides an interesting collection of flora, fauna, and natural landscapes. You'll see trees ranging from tall coconut palms to spreading banyans. Look for huge samples of the latter in front of the Honolulu Zoo and in the courtyard of the Sheraton Moana Surfrider hotel.

Among the most common flowers are red and white anthuriums, exotic bird of paradise, multicolored bougainvillea, red and yellow gingers, and hibiscus. Flitting among them are a variety of birds. Bird-watchers will spot barred doves, Indian mynahs, and the red-headed Brazilian cardinals. Frigate birds are the most common seabirds cruising over the coasts.

Hawaii's reefs sport a rainbow of undersea life. Don a mask and snorkel to see butterfly fish, wrasses, parrotfish, moray eels, Moorish idols, and the impressive *humuhumunukunuku-a-pua'a,* a small triggerfish that's the official state fish. Deeper waters host the Pacific blue marlin, mahimahi (dolphin fish), rays, and a variety of tuna.

Don't be surprised to run into two common critters in your hotel: cockroaches and geckos. The former thrives in Hawaii's moist environment. The latter is a small lizard that eats insects and emits a chirping bark. Having a gecko in your island home is considered good luck.

HOTELS AND INNS

Waikiki boasts some 33,000 hotel and condominium rooms, ranging in price from $30 to more than $3,000 a night. Despite an increasing number of upscale accommodations, the area remains one of the most affordable destinations in the Aloha State. Look for a room right in the thick of Waikiki if you want to be where the action is.

If you want to save on food costs, an assortment of condominiums and some hotels offer full or partial kitchens in their units.

It's wise to book your accommodations in advance. January, February, and August are peak months, and booking then may be difficult if you don't begin early. Ask about package deals, which may include room and car, transfers, and other extras.

Price categories for double occupancy, excluding 9.17% tax, are *Moderate,* $75–$120, and *Inexpensive,* under $75.

WAIKIKI **Hawaiiana Hotel.** One of Hawaii's cherished old-timers, this sectioned two- and three-story hotel is within a block of the beach and surrounded by a lush tropical garden. Open your door, and the gardens and pools are right there. All rooms are equipped with air-conditioners and kitchenettes. *260 Beach Walk, Honolulu 96815, tel. 808/923–3811 or 800/367–5122. 95 rooms. Pool, free washers and dryers. AE, MC, V. Moderate.*

Hawaiian Waikiki Beach Hotel. Rooms here have rattan furniture, private lanais, and views over the ocean and nearby Kapiolani Park. The seawall in front of the hotel gives stupefying sunset views. *2570 Kalakaua Ave., Honolulu 96815, tel. 808/922–2511 or 800/877–7666. 716 rooms, 2 restaurants, 2 lounges, shops, pool. AE, DC, MC, V. Moderate.*

New Otani Kaimana Beach Hotel. On the beach at the quiet end of Waikiki near Kapiolani Park, this polished lodging is bright, clean, and open to the trade winds. The on-site Hau Tree Lanai restaurant is first-rate. *2863 Kalakaua Ave., Honolulu 96815, tel. 808/923–1555 or 800/733–7949. 125 rooms. 2 restaurants, lounge, shops, meeting rooms. AE, DC, MC, V. Moderate.*

Outrigger Reef Hotel. This hotel, right on the beach next to Ft. DeRussy Park, offers renovated rooms (many with lanais) and cheerful public areas. Be sure to ask for a room with an ocean view. *2169 Kalia Rd., Honolulu 96815, tel. 808/923–3111 or 800/733–7777. 883 rooms. 2 restaurants, 4 lounges, nightclub, shops, meeting rooms, pool. AE, DC, MC, V. Moderate.*

Waikiki Hana. The hotel has no pool, but you're only a short walk from the beach (and a short walk from the Hyatt Regency Waikiki). Most rooms come equipped with kitchenettes and air-conditioners. *2424 Koa Ave., Honolulu 96815, tel. 808/926–8841 or 800/367–5004. 73 rooms. Restaurant, lounge. AE, DC, MC, V. Moderate.*

Continental Surf Hotel. Two blocks from the ocean and convenient to shopping and dining options, this Kuhio Avenue high rise offers good value and the option of a kitchenette. *2426 Kuhio Ave., Honolulu 96815, tel. 808/922–2755 or 800/367–5004. 140 rooms. Facilities: lounge, laundry. AE, DC, MC, V. Inexpensive.*

Edmunds Hotel Apartments. Four blocks from the ocean, on the Ala Wai Canal, this hotel is wrapped by a long lanai, offering fine views of the canal and glorious Manoa Valley beyond. The studio rooms are small and nondescript, but many have kitchenettes. Light sleepers may find the occasional traffic noise annoying. *2411 Ala Wai Blvd., Honolulu 96815, tel. 808/923–8381. 12 rooms. No credit cards. Inexpensive.*

Outrigger Royal Islander. Studios, one-bedrooms, and suites can be had in this Polynesian-decorated hotel just two minutes from a nice stretch of Waikiki Beach. Guests may use the swimming pools at other Outrigger hotels. *2164 Kalia Rd., Honolulu 96815, tel. 808/922–1961 or 800/733–7777. 101 rooms. Restaurant. AE, DC, MC, V. Inexpensive.*

Waikiki Lei Apartments. Set in the middle of Waikiki but still only minutes from the beach, this affordable, well-maintained lodging has studios with kitchenettes and refrigerators. *241 Kaiulani Ave., Honolulu 96815, tel. 808/923–6656 or 808/734–8588. 19 rooms. Pool, coin laundry. No credit cards. Inexpensive.*

AROUND THE ISLAND **Laniloa Lodge.** An hour from Waikiki, near the Polynesian Cultural Center in Laie, the lodge sports a Polynesian motif and quiet atmosphere. Five separate wings form a circle around the central swimming pool. *55–109 Laniloa St., Laie*

96762, tel. 808/293–9282 or 800/LANILOA. 46 rooms. Pool. AE, DC, MC, V. Moderate.

Manoa Valley Inn. Built in 1919, this stately hotel 2 miles inland from Waikiki offers Continental-breakfast buffets on a shady lanai and fresh tropical fruit and cheese in the afternoon. Be sure to specify if you want a room with a private bath. *2001 Vancouver Dr., Honolulu 96822, tel. 808/947–6019 or 800/634–5115. 8 rooms. TV and VCR in the reading room. MC, V. Moderate.*

Pagoda Hotel. Just minutes from Ala Moana Shopping Center and Ala Moana Park, this quiet hotel offers studios with full kitchen facilities and a free shuttle into Waikiki. *1525 Rycroft St., Honolulu 96814, tel. 808/941–6611 or 800/367–6060. 361 rooms. 2 restaurants, shops, pool. AE, DC, MC, V. Moderate.*

Pat's at Punaluu. This unpretentious condominium, located between the island's windward side and the North Shore, includes units with full kitchens and dishwashers. *53–567 Kamehameha Hwy., Hauula 96717, tel. 808/293–8111 or 800/845–8799. 142 rooms. Restaurant, shops, pool, saunas, gym, recreational areas. MC, V. Inexpensive.*

Schrader's Windward Marine Resort. This rural resort overlooking Kaneohe Bay has one-, two-, and three-bedroom units—some with kitchens—and offers a variety of water sports and activities. *47–039 Lihikai Dr., Kaneohe 96744, tel. 808/239–5711 or 800/735–5711. 55 rooms. Pool, spa, boats. AE, DC, MC, V. Moderate.*

BED–AND–BREAKFASTS

Bed and Breakfast Hawaii. This reliable booking agency offers homestays around Oahu and the Neighbor Islands. *Box 449, Kapaa 96746, tel. 808/822–7771 or 800/733–1632.*

Bed and Breakfast Honolulu. This company sports an especially good selection of rooms in Honolulu, including lodgings in one of Waikiki's few remaining private homes. *3242 Kaohinani Dr., Honolulu 96817, tel. 808/595–7533 or 800/288–4666.*

Pacific Hawaii Bed and Breakfast. This booking company will help arrange a B&B in the moderate range. *19 Kai Nani Pl., Kailua 96743, tel. 808/262–6026 or 800/254–5030.*

DINING

Hawaii's ethnic melting-pot population—Hawaiian, American, Japanese, Chinese, Korean, European, Vietnamese, and Thai, among others—results in an unusually diverse dining scene. Specialties include delectable fish—such as mahimahi and opakapaka (blue snapper)—sushi, kalua (roasted) pig, poi (a starchy pudding), sweet-and-sour spareribs, and tempura.

Fine (but expensive) dining takes on an international flair here, with culinary masters staffing the better hotel restaurants. Splurge on at least one dinner or less expensive lunch. To save money on the balance of your meals, take advantage of hotels and condominiums that offer in-room kitchens. Breakfast bargains, full meals for less than $3, are offered at many restaurants. Traditional Hawaiian luaus tend to be sold as packages and are on the expensive side. Check with your hotel and the free visitor publications to find the best bargain.

Restaurant price categories per person, not including 4.17% tax, service, and drinks, are *Moderate,* $20–$40, and *Inexpensive,* under $20.

WAIKIKI Bon Appetit. This European-style bistro provides a menu of fresh fish, lamb, and other entrées—some on a fixed-price plan—in a pink-and-black setting highlighted by eye-catching paintings. *Discovery Bay, 1778 Ala Moana Blvd., tel. 808/942–3837. AE, DC, MC, V. Moderate.*

Castagnola's. Opened by a New Jersey transplant who missed his home state's hearty Italian cooking, this second-story spot features such traditional fare as veal sorrentino and baked stuffed eggplant. *Inn-On-The-Park, 1920 Ala Moana Blvd., tel. 808/949–6277. MC, V. Moderate.*

The Chart House. With its decor of varnished wood, saltwater aquariums, and photos of racing sailboats, this respected seafood spot fits in well with its harborside location and the yachting enthusiasts who frequent it. *1765 Ala Moana Blvd., tel. 808/941–6669. AE, DC, MC, V. Moderate.*

Golden Dragon. Some of Honolulu's best Szechuan, Cantonese, and nouvelle Chinese cuisine can be had for dinner in this waterfront eatery, presided over for the last 30 years by chef Dai Hoi Chang. *Hilton Hawaiian Village, 2005 Kalia Rd., tel. 808/946–5336. AE, DC, MC, V. Moderate.*

Orchids. You can't beat the setting, right beside the sea in the airy Halekulani Hotel, with Diamond Head looming in the distance and fresh orchids everywhere. The menu features mammoth popovers and creative salads; the hearty Sunday brunch is also popular. *2199 Kalia Rd., tel. 808/923–2311. AE, D, MC, V. Moderate.*

Restaurant Suntory. Japanese dining here comes in four areas: a sushi bar, a teppanyaki (food prepared on an iron grill) room, a shabu shabu (thinly sliced beef boiled in broth) room, or a private dining room. *Royal Hawaiian Shopping Center, 2233 Kalakaua Ave., tel. 808/922–5511. AE, DC, MC, V. Moderate.*

Eggs and Things. With a breakfast-only menu, this eatery attracts late-night revelers thanks to its unusual hours (11 PM–2 PM). Omelets are as huge as your plate and come with all sorts of fillings. *1911 Kalakaua Ave., tel. 808/949–0820. No credit cards. Inexpensive.*

Perry's Smorgy. Perry's ranks as one of Waikiki's true dining bargains: One low price buys you all the lunch or dinner you can eat from the long buffets of this garden-style cafeteria. *2380 Kuhio Ave., tel. 808/926–0184. AE, MC, V. Inexpensive.*

NEAR WAIKIKI Keo's Thai Cuisine. This twinkling nook, with tables set amid lighted trees and large paper umbrellas, attracts couples of all ages who savor delicately seasoned Thai specialties, including chicken in lemon sauce and rice noodles sautéed with shrimp and peanuts. *625 Kapahulu Ave., tel. 808/737–8240. AE, DC, MC, V. Moderate.*

The Willows. Dine with a local crowd in thatched huts overlooking a koi pond and waterfall at this local favorite. The menu includes a wide range of Hawaiian and other Polynesian specialties. *901 Hausten St., tel. 808/946–4808. AE, DC, MC, V. Moderate.*

Hard Rock Cafe. Music fans of all ages savor great salads and sandwiches amid rock 'n' roll memorabilia, a Cadillac "woodie" over the bar, and the famous collector T-shirts of this close-to-Waikiki diner. *1837 Kapiolani Blvd., tel. 808/955–7383. AE, MC, V. Inexpensive.*

Maple Garden. Spicy Szechuan cuisine, such as eggplant in a tantalizing hot garlic sauce, is served to a predominantly local crowd at this simply decorated restaurant. *909 Isenberg St., tel. 808/941–6641. AE, DC, MC, V. Inexpensive.*

Ono Hawaiian Foods. A local, no-frills hangout for Island-style foods, including *poi* (taro paste), *laulau* (fish and meat steamed in ti leaves), and *kalua* (roasted pig). *726 Kapahulu Ave., tel. 808/737–2275. No credit cards. Inexpensive.*

SHOPPING

Shopping in Waikiki and Honolulu can be as simple as picking up pineapples and aloha wear at Woolworth's, or as adventurous as a buying expedition into the nooks and crannies of Chinatown. Along the way, you'll find clothes in brilliant floral patterns, Asian antiques, designer jewelry, tacky tiki statues, and exotic imports from Indonesia. Prices range from dirt-cheap to sky-high.

MAJOR SHOPPING DISTRICTS Waikiki seems to have almost as many shops as it does hotel rooms. Most of them fall along the main thoroughfares of Kuhio and Kalakaua avenues; nearly all of the large hotels offer boutique shopping of one sort or another. The **Royal Hawaiian Shopping Center** (2201 Kalakaua Ave., tel. 808/922–0588) offers everything from Hawaiian crafts to the best from Paris.

Ala Moana Shopping Center (1450 Ala Moana Blvd., tel. 808/946–2811), once the world's largest open-air shopping center, is minutes from Waikiki. There you'll find departments stores such as Sears and Liberty House, as well as a growing collection of designer boutiques. **Ward Centre** (1200 Ala Moana Blvd., tel. 808/531–6411) and **Ward Warehouse** (1050 Ala Moana Blvd., tel. 808/531–6411) provide a side-by-side mix of eclectic specialty shops, boutiques, and restaurants. Shopped-out spouses can visit Ala Moana Park and Kewalo Basin's sportfishing and sightseeing fleets during the buying sprees. **Kahala Mall** (4211 Waialae Ave., tel. 808/732–7736) can be found 10 minutes from Waikiki on the far side of Diamond Head. Look for upscale clothing shops, a Waldenbooks, and several restaurants there.

FLEA MARKETS Put on your walking shoes and sunscreen and head for Honolulu's **Aloha Stadium** (Kamehameha Hwy. near Pearl Harbor, tel. 808/732–9611) for the **Aloha Swap Meet.** For less than 50¢ a person, you can spend several hours on Wednesday or the weekend perusing the local crafts, food stalls, wholesale goods, and secondhand items sold in the stadium parking lot. The market's not only a good place for bargains, but the people-watching opportunities are nearly unbeatable.

OUTDOOR ACTIVITIES

BEACHES Sandy strands rim Oahu, and all of the beaches are open to the public. Waikiki Beach, actually a collection of individually named stretches, provides protected waters for swimming, snorkeling, and sunbathing. Come prepared for the sun's intensity, and use caution around the ocean. Other nearby beaches include Ala Moana Beach Park, also protected by a large reef, and Hanauma Bay, one of the best snorkeling sites in the Hawaiian Islands.

BOATING A fleet of excursion boats regularly plies the waters off Waikiki, offering sunset and dinner cruises, whale-watching voyages during winter and spring months, and sightseeing trips. Companies such as Aikane Catamarans (tel. 808/522–1533) and Windjammer Cruises (tel. 808/922–1200) take passengers on motorized trips aboard large-capacity vessels. Honolulu Sailing Co. (tel. 808/239–3900) and Tradewind Charters (tel. 808/973–0311) actually raise their sails for tradewind-driven tours.

DEEP-SEA FISHING A sportfishing fleet is based at Honolulu's Kewalo Basin, just opposite the Ward Warehouse shopping center. Although fishing trips are expensive, half-day and shared excursions are available. Fishing gear is included. Try Coreen-C Charters (tel. 808/536–7472), ELO Sportfishing (tel. 808/947–5208), or Island Charters (tel. 808/536–1555).

GOLF Oahu has more golf courses than any other Hawaiian island, and more than 15 of them are open to the public. Closest to Waikiki is the Ala Wai Golf Course (404 Kapahulu Ave., tel. 808/296–4653), across the Ala Wai Canal. The 18-hole course is par 70 on 6,424 yards and has a pro shop and a restaurant.

HORSEBACK RIDING Saddle up for a beach or trail ride with three stables on Oahu. Kualoa Ranch (49–560 Kamehameha Hwy., tel. 808/237–8515) offers escorted rides across 4,000 acres. Sheraton Makaha Lio Stables (84–626 Makaha Valley Rd., tel. 808/695–9511) gives rides through an old plantation. Turtle Bay Hilton & Country Club (57–91 Kamehameha Hwy., tel. 808/293–8811) takes riders along the 75 acres of hotel property and beach.

JOGGING/HIKING Hawaii's climate makes for year-round jogging and hiking opportunities. Waikiki's Kapiolani Park (at Kalakaua and Kapahulu avenues) and Ala Moana Park (Ala Wai Blvd. across from Ala Moana Shopping Center) offer trails and paved areas for foot-pounding fun. Avoid Ala Moana Park late at night. Diamond Head offers a .7-mile hike from the center of the crater to its summit.

SURFING Age truly is no barrier in learning to ride the waves off Waikiki Beach. Several beach operators offer large stable boards and instruction.

TENNIS Several Waikiki hotels offer rooftop tennis courts. The Ilikai (1777 Ala Moana Blvd., tel. 808/949–3811) sports six courts, a pro shop, and instruction; the Pacific Beach Hotel (2490 Kalakaua Ave., tel. 808/922–1233) has two courts. Additional courts may be found in nearby Kapiolani and Ala Moana parks.

ENTERTAINMENT

BALLET AND DANCE The Honolulu Symphony (tel. 808/537–6191) imports a nationally-renowned ballet troupe each autumn, and the locally based Ballet Hawaii (tel. 808/988–7578) performs throughout the year. To see examples of Hawaiian hula, check out the Kodak Hula Show (held weekly in Waikiki's Kapiolani Park) or the frequent free demonstrations performed at Waikiki's Royal Hawaiian Shopping Center (2201 Kalakaua Ave., tel. 808/922–0588).

CONCERTS The Honolulu Symphony (tel. 808/537–6191) holds its season from September to April at Blaisdell Concert Hall (Ward Ave. at King St.). Members offer Symphony on the Light Side concerts as well. A summer Starlight Series is held at the Waikiki Shell in Kapiolani Park. The Royal Hawaiian Band (tel. 808/922–5331) gives free Friday-afternoon concerts on the lawn of the Iolani Palace (King St. and Richards St.). Additional Hawaiian music, such as slack-key guitar and ukulele, can be heard at frequent demonstrations in front of the Royal Hawaiian Shopping Center (2201 Kalakaua Ave., tel. 808/922–0588).

THEATER Diamond Head Theater (520 Makapuu Ave., tel. 808/734–0274) can be reached from Waikiki in five minutes. Musicals, dramas, contemporary, and classical shows are among its repertoire. The Manoa Valley Theater (2833 E. Manoa Rd., tel. 808/988–6131) offers nonprofessional productions in an intimate theater in Manoa Valley, within 15 minutes of Waikiki.

COCKTAIL AND DINNER SHOWS Honolulu's dinner shows have broadened in recent years to include Las Vegas–style entertainment as well the standard Polynesian extravaganzas. One of the newer offerings is Legends in Concert (Royal Hawaiian Shopping Ctr., 2233 Kalakaua Ave., tel. 808/971–1400), a musical presentation of superstar look- and sound-alikes such as Elvis and Marilyn Monroe. Among Waikiki's long-standing shows are the Brothers Cazimero (Monarch Room, Royal Hawaiian Hotel, 2259 Kalakaua Ave., tel. 808/923–7311), Don Ho (Polynesian Palace, Outrigger Reef Towers Hotel, 227 Lewers St., tel. 808/923–9861), Charo! (Tropics Surf Club, Hilton Hawaiian Village, 2005 Kalia Rd., tel. 808/949–4321), Danny Kaleikini (Kahala Hilton, 5000 Kahala Ave., tel. 808/734–2211), and the Sheraton's Spectacular Polynesian Revue (Ainahau Showroom, Sheraton Princess Kaiulani Hotel, 120 Kaiulani Ave., tel. 808/922–5811).

SPECTATOR SPORTS Hawaii has no professional sports teams and so must rely on visiting teams, staged tournaments, and amateur competitions for its spectator sports. Among those are: the Aloha Basketball Classic, held each spring at the Neal Blaisdell Center (Ward Ave. and Kapiolani Blvd.); the Pro Bowl, featuring the NFL's best players each January or February at Aloha Stadium (tel. 808/486–9300); the Hawaiian Open Golf Tournament, attracting the nation's golfing greats to the Waialae Country Club (4997 Kahala Ave., tel. 808/526–1232) early each year; and the Triple Crown Hawaiian Pro Surfing Championships (tel. 808/377–5850), held at the Banzai Pipeline and Sunset Beach during November and December.

Throughout the year, you also can watch amateur sports such as outrigger canoe racing along Waikiki's Ala Wai Canal, surfing and windsurfing from the lookout near the lighthouse on Diamond Head Road, and everything from soccer to kite-flying competitions in Kapiolani Park.

Washington, D.C.

Because many of us spent our childhoods in dreary classrooms learning about checks and balances and the three branches of the federal government, it's easy to think of Washington as little more than a civics book come to life. But that would be missing the rest of the curriculum. Washington is a science book, too, home to the Smithsonian Institution and 14 of its world-class museums. It's a coffee-table art book, with galleries holding some of the most beloved and historic works from America and beyond. And when the bell rings for recess, there's still plenty to do, from sampling creative ethnic cuisine in this melting-pot capital to frolicking on the lush banks of the Potomac.

And guess what? You own the school. If you mutter every April 15 when signing your name to an income-tax check, then you should come to town to see your tax dollars at work. Washington—from the organized free-for-all called Congress to the peaceful and contemplative Lincoln Memorial—truly is every American's city.

Don't let the politicians spoil Washington for you. Even native Washingtonians—and don't be fooled, there is such a thing—get fed up with their antics from time to time. But remember, those responsible for political high jinks don't come *from* Washington, they come *to* Washington. And once you visit, you'll see why.

ESSENTIAL INFORMATION

WHEN TO GO Washington was once a hardship posting for diplomats from certain European countries. And indeed the city's hot, humid summers can seem malarial. The maximum average temperature in August is 86°, but from June to September, heat waves can push the thermometer above 95°. Winters are less extreme (January's average high is 47°), but one or two snowstorms a year seem

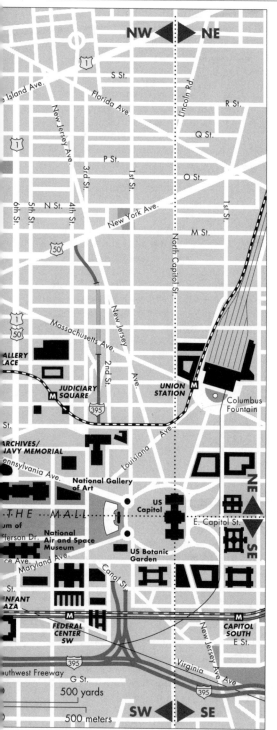

to paralyze the city. Spring and fall, however, are delightful.

You'll find cheaper hotel rates in winter and during the long summer recess (check with your local legislative office; the recess takes place at a different time each summer). Fall is when you'll find the city's museums and galleries the least crowded.

FESTIVALS AND SEASONAL EVENTS **Feb.:** Black History Month is celebrated at sites around the city. **Late Mar.–Early Apr.:** The National Cherry Blossom Festival celebrates the Japanese cherry trees that ring the Tidal Basin (though the festival almost never coincides with the trees' peak bloom). **Late June–early July:** The Festival of American Folklife on the Mall features music, food, and arts and crafts of various cultures. **July 4:** The Fourth of July offers a band concert and fireworks on the Mall. **Mid-Dec.:** The National Christmas Tree Lighting and Pageant starts the holiday season, as the president lights the national tree.

BARGAINS Washington is not cheap; however, many of its best-known sights are. All the memorials in the city, from the Jefferson to the Vietnam Veterans, are free of charge.

If you know well ahead of time that you'd like to visit some of Washington's federal sites, contact your senator or representative and get the special free tickets that allow you to wait in lines slightly shorter than those many of your fellow citizens will be standing in. Visitors with disabilities are entitled to go to the head of all lines when touring federal buildings and monuments.

The National Building Museum hosts free lunchtime concerts the fourth Wednesday of the month. There are free classical concerts in the National Gallery of Art West Building on Sunday evenings from October to June. The Sylvan Theater on the Washington Monument grounds is the site of big-band and military concerts from mid-June to August. You can get obstructed-view tickets to National Symphony Orchestra performances in the Kennedy Center Concert Hall for $6.

Half-price, day-of-performance theater tickets are available at TicketPlace (12th and F Sts. NW, tel. 202/TICKETS). The National Theatre (1321 Pennsylvania Ave. N, NW, tel. 202/783–3370) hosts a wide-ranging free-performance series each Monday night during most of the year.

TOURIST OFFICES For written information contact the Washington, D.C., Convention & Visitors Association (1212 New York Ave. NW, Washington, DC 20005). There is a walk-up visitor information center at 1455 Pennsylvania Ave. NW (tel. 202/789–7000, recorded information, tel. 202/737–8866). Dial-A-Park (tel. 202/619–PARK) is a recording of events at Park Service attractions around Washington.

EMERGENCIES **Police, fire,** and **ambulance:** Dial 911. **Hospitals:** There's an emergency room at George Washington University Hospital (901 23rd St. NW, tel. 202/994–3211). **Doctors and Dentists:** Prologue (tel. 202/DOCTORS) runs a physician and dentist referral. The DC Dental Society (tel. 202/547–7615) refers dentists. **Pharmacies:** Peoples Drug operates two 24-hour pharmacies (14th St. and Thomas Cir. NW, tel. 202/628–0720; 7 Dupont Cir. NW, tel. 202/785–1466).

ARRIVING AND DEPARTING

BY PLANE Three airports serve the Washington area: National Airport (tel. 703/685–8000), 4 miles south of downtown in Virginia; Dulles International Airport (tel. 703/471–4242), 26 miles west of the city; and Baltimore–Washington International Airport (BWI) (tel. 410/859–7111), about 30 miles northeast of Washington in Maryland.

National and Dulles airports are served by the buses of Washington Flyer (tel. 703/685–1400). Buses stop at numerous hotels as well as at a downtown terminal at 1517 K Street NW. The service runs daily from around 5:30 AM to midnight, with buses leaving roughly every half hour. The ride from National to downtown takes 20 minutes and costs $8. From Dulles, it's $16 for the hour-long ride. The Airport Connection (tel. 301/441–2345)

serves BWI with buses that leave roughly every 90 minutes from 7 AM to 10 PM for the 1517 K Street NW terminal with a stop in Greenbelt, Maryland. The hour-long ride costs $14.

If you are arriving at Washington National Airport, don't have much to carry, and are staying at a hotel near a subway stop, it makes sense to take the Metro downtown. The ride takes about 20 minutes and costs between $1 and $1.25, depending on the time of day.

Free shuttle bus service is provided between BWI airport terminals and the airport's train station, where Amtrak and MARC (Maryland Rail Commuter Service) trains stop. Trains depart BWI for Washington's Union Station from around 6 AM to midnight—but call for details. The cost for the 40-minute ride is $10 on an Amtrak train, $4.25 on a MARC train. MARC trains run weekdays only from 6 AM to 9 PM. (For Amtrak information, tel. 800/USA–RAIL; for MARC schedule information, call 800/325–RAIL and request information on Penn Line service.)

Taxis queue in front of the terminals at all three airports. If you're traveling alone, expect to pay about $8 to get from National Airport to downtown; from Dulles, $35; from BWI, $36. Big D.C. cab companies include Diamond (tel. 202/387–6200) and Capitol (tel. 202/546–2400).

BY CAR I–95 runs north and south and skirts Washington as part of the Beltway, the six- to eight-lane highway that encircles the city. Major routes for entering the city include I–395 from the south to the 14th Street Bridge and 14th Street; I–270 from the northwest to I–495 and Connecticut Avenue or 16th Street into the city; and I–66 from the southwest across the Theodore Roosevelt Bridge to Constitution Avenue. (*Note:* I–66 has weekday rush-hour high-occupancy vehicle (HOV) restrictions. From 6:30 to 9 AM, cars traveling eastbound inside the Beltway must have at least three people in them. A similar restriction applies westbound from 4 to 6:30 PM.) A more scenic route is joining the George Washington Parkway off I–495 in Virginia and following it east along the Potomac and then across the Arlington Memorial Bridge and past the Lincoln Memorial.

BY TRAIN More than 50 trains a day arrive at Washington's Union Station (50 Massachusetts Ave. NE, tel. 800/USA–RAIL).

BY BUS Washington is a major terminal for Greyhound Lines (1005 1st St. NE, tel. 800/231–2222).

GETTING AROUND

The District of Columbia is arranged, said Pierre L'Enfant, the Frenchman who designed it in 1791, "like a chessboard overlaid with a wagon wheel." Streets run north and south and east and west in a grid pattern; avenues— most named after states—run diagonally, connecting the various traffic circles scattered throughout the city. The District is divided into four sections: northwest, northeast, southwest, and southeast; the Capitol Building serves as the center of the north–south and east–west axes. North Capitol and South Capitol streets divide the city into east and west; the Mall and East Capitol Street divide the city into north and south. Streets that run north to south are numbered; those that extend east to west are lettered (until the letters run out, at which point alphabetical names are used: Adams, Belmont, and so forth). Make sure you have a destination's complete address, including quadrant (there are *four* 4th and D intersections in Washington: one each in NW, NE, SW, and SE). Bring a good map, too.

BY METRO Trains run weekdays 5:30 AM– midnight, Saturdays 8 AM–midnight, and Sundays 10 AM–midnight. The base fare is $1; the actual price depends on the time of day and distance traveled. You can buy your ticket at the computerized Farecard machines in each station. They take change as well as crisp one- and five-dollar bills (some also take tens and twenties). An $8 Metro Family/Tourist Pass entitles a family of four to one day of unlimited subway travel any Saturday, Sunday, or holiday (except July 4). Passes are available at Metro Sales Outlets (including the Metro Center station) and at many hotels.

BY BUS All Metrobus rides within the District are $1. Transfers, good for two hours, are available on buses and in Metro stations. Bus-to-bus transfers are accepted at designated Metrobus transfer points. Rail-to-bus transfers must be picked up before boarding the train. There may be a transfer charge when boarding the bus.

For general subway and bus travel information, call 202/637–7000. A helpful brochure—"All about the Metro System"—is available by calling the travel information number or writing to Office of Marketing, WMATA (600 5th St. NW, Washington, D.C. 20001).

BY TAXI Taxis in the District are not metered, operating instead on a curious zone system. The basic single rate for traveling within one zone is $3. It's more for additional passengers ($1.25 each), during the 4–7 PM rush hour ($1 extra), if you've called for a radio-dispatched cab ($1.50 extra), and/or if you have bulky suitcases or require personal services ($1.50 and up). A typical nonrush-hour ride for two from, say, Union Station to the National Gallery of Art, would be $4.25, excluding tip.

BY CAR A car can be a drawback in Washington. Traffic is horrendous, especially at rush hours, and driving is confusing, with many lanes and some entire streets changing direction suddenly at different times of day. Parking is also an adventure: at a premium and expensive (private lots downtown charge as much as $4 an hour and up to $13 a day). Since its major attractions—especially those on the Mall—are within easy walking distance of one another, see the city on foot and take the Metro to out-of-town sights such as Old Town Alexandria and Arlington National Cemetery.

If you do drive downtown, note that there is free, three-hour parking around the Mall on Madison and Jefferson drives. You can park free— in some spots all day—in parking areas south of the Lincoln Memorial on Ohio Drive and West Basin Drive in West Potomac Park. Both areas fill quickly.

Some peculiar Washington traffic idiosyncrasies: Traffic lights often hang down at the sides of intersections, not directly above them. Cars entering a traffic circle must yield to those already in it.

REST STOPS All Smithsonian Institution museums have free, clean, and safe public rest rooms. Metro stations don't have any.

GUIDED TOURS Tourmobile (tel. 202/554–7950) buses provide several narrated tours. One stops at 18 historic sites and museums between the Capitol and Arlington National Cemetery, arriving at each site every 15 or 20 minutes. In the spring and summer, for an additional fee, some buses also go to Mount Vernon or the Frederick Douglass Home. Tickets range from $5 to $16.50 for adults; $2.50 to $8 for children. The 90-minute, 14-stop Old Town Trolley tour (tel. 301/985–3020) takes in the main downtown sights and also ventures into Georgetown and Upper Northwest. Tickets are $15 for adults, $7 for children 5–12. Passengers on both tours can get on and off as often as they like. The Gray Line Tour offers a number of tours ranging from four hours (the Washington tour) to two days long (trips to nearby sites like Colonial Williamsburg). The Gray Line Tour's (tel. 301/386–8300) four-hour tour of Washington, Embassy Row, and Arlington National Cemetery leaves Union Station at 8:30 AM and 2:30 PM (2 PM only Nov.–Mar.). The cost is $18 and up ($9 and up for kids).

WALKING AND SPECIAL-INTEREST The Smithsonian's Resident Associate Program (tel. 202/357–3030) frequently sponsors weekend bus and walking tours of Washington's most interesting neighborhoods and sights at prices that start at around $11 per participant. The National Building Museum (tel. 202/272–2448) hosts tours with an architectural or construction bent ranging from $6 to $26. Scandal Tours (tel. 202/387–2253) snakes past locales like Gary Hart's Capitol Hill town house and, of course, the Watergate. The 90-minute tour is $27 per person. "Datebook" in the *Washington Post*'s Thursday "Home" section often lists other tours.

EXPLORING

You can say you've "done" Washington if you've walked from the Capitol Building to the Lincoln Memorial and visited the museums and monuments in between. The Mall is the city's tourist core and it's the place most visitors head for first. Spend a few days sampling its many offerings, then venture beyond the federal enclave and see the other side of the city.

The following tour outlines the Mall's highlights. Sights farther afield follow.

MUSEUMS It would be easy to spend a week on the Mall, where nine of the Smithsonian museums are located, with other attractions nearby. Smithsonian museums are free, and are open seven days a week from 10 AM to 5:30 PM. For help sorting out Mall exhibits and activities, stop at the Smithsonian Castle's high-tech information center, or in summer, visit the information kiosks along the Mall. *Smithsonian Castle: 1000 Jefferson Dr. SW, tel. 202/357–2700. Open daily. Admission free.*

Near the Smithsonian Castle, the **Freer** (Jefferson Drive at 12th St. SW, tel. 202/357–1967) and the **Sackler Gallery** (1050 Independence Ave. SW, tel. 202/357–1300) display Asian art; the **National Museum of African Art** (950 Independence Ave. SW, tel. 202/357–1300) is the only museum in the country that is exclusively dedicated to artifacts from sub-Saharan Africa.

Just a block away from the Freer is the **United States Holocaust Memorial Museum,** just opened in 1993. This museum's exhibits, public spaces, and architecture reflect and memorialize the tragedy, horror, and heroism that accompanied the Nazi rise to power. The very moving displays unfold chronologically from 1933 to 1945. *100 Raoul Wallenberg Pl. SW, 20024, tel. 202/488–0400. Open daily. Admission free but ticket reservations required.*

The **National Air and Space Museum** is the most-visited museum in Washington, with displays that follow aviation from its early days (the plane the Wright brothers flew) to its heady days (Charles Lindbergh's *Spirit of St. Louis*) to its extraterrestrial days (a backup model of the Skylab and a piece of moon rock). Films dealing with flight are shown on an IMAX screen that is so big (five stories high!), it might make you airsick. *Jefferson Dr. and 6th St. SW, tel. 202/357–2700. Open daily. Admission free.*

Washington is so full of things to see—and its blocks are so long—that you may need a break. For a restful pause, stop at the **U.S. Botanic Garden.** The oldest botanical garden in America, its first greenhouse was constructed in 1842. Though the central display is being redesigned, six galleries—plus terrace displays—make this garden well worth a visit. Permanent exhibits include New and Old World cacti and a Dinosaur Garden featuring prehistoric plants, and there are beautiful seasonal shows such as the annual Christmas poinsettia display. *1st St. and Maryland Ave. SW, tel. 202/225–8333. Open daily. Admission free.*

Back on the Mall, directly north from the Air and Space Museum, is the **National Gallery of Art,** a beautiful John Russell Pope–designed building that contains one of the most impressive art collections in the world. The soaring, angular East Building—across 4th Street NW—generally shows more modern works and is home to changing exhibits. *Madison Dr. and 4th St. NW, tel. 202/737–4215. Open daily. Admission free.*

West of the National Gallery lies the **National Museum of Natural History.** This is a museum's museum, with more than 118 million objects in its research collection. Highlights include dinosaur bones, plant and animal specimens, a living coral reef, the Insect Zoo, and the supposedly cursed Hope Diamond. *Madison St. between 12th and 14th Sts. NW, tel. 202/357–2700. Open daily. Admission free.*

GOVERNMENT BUILDINGS The governing of the country takes place in the massive, block-long buildings that surround the Mall. Many popular sites offer free daily tours, though in the summer you'll need to line up early for free tickets—usually at 8:30 AM. At federal buildings and monuments, people with disabilities are entitled to go to the head of the line.

Start with the **United States Capitol.** Newly cleaned and restored, the Capitol provides the best example of democracy in action that Washington has to offer. Its attractions aren't only political, though, since the building contains some of the finest art in town, including Constantino Brumidi's *Apotheosis of Washington* in the center of the Capitol dome and the lovingly restored Old Senate Chamber. To get a quick, free tour, join the line that forms in the Rotunda. And don't miss the main event: senators and representatives speechifying in their respective chambers. (See the *Washington Post*'s "Today in Congress" listings to find out what's happening where.) Ride the subway that runs beneath Capitol Hill's streets, connecting the Capitol Building to the various House and Senate office blocks where most of the real work gets done. *East end of the Mall, tel. 202/224–3121. Open daily. Admission free.*

From the Capitol walk west on Independence to 7th St., then continue four blocks north to the **National Archives.** The Declaration of Independence, Bill of Rights, and Constitution are displayed in the Archives in a bullet-proof case and bathed in protective green light and helium gas. Researchers can study immigrant documents, military records, government papers, and millions of other items stored here, while casual visitors can enjoy changing exhibits related to American history. *Constitution Ave. between 7th and 9th Sts. NW, tel. 202/501–5000. Open daily. Admission free.*

Head west four blocks on Constitution Avenue and turn north on 15th Street for two blocks. On the left is the **White House,** home to every U.S. president since John Adams. Queue at the blue-and-green ticket booth on the Ellipse, south of the White House below E Street. *1600 Pennsylvania Ave. NW, tel. 202/456–7041. Open Tues.–Sat. Admission free.*

MONUMENTS Washington's elegant, stately monuments are largely gathered at the western end of the Mall. The **Washington Monument** punctuates the city like a huge exclamation point. Finished in 1884, the 555-foot-tall obelisk is the largest masonry structure in the world. An elevator takes visitors to the top for a view unmatched in this largely horizontal city. The elevator stops running around 11:30 PM, so watch the time—unless you want to walk down 898 steps. South of the monument, on the banks of the Tidal Basin, is the John Russell Pope–designed **Jefferson Memorial,** dedicated in 1943. A 19-foot statue of the third president stands in a rotunda inscribed with his writings. A 10-minute walk away, across the Inlet Bridge and down West Basin and Ohio drives, is the **Lincoln Memorial,** considered by many to be the most moving monument in the city. The modified Greek temple, designed by Henry Bacon and completed in 1922, contains Daniel Chester French's peaceful statue of the 16th president. Northeast of the Lincoln Memorial, nestled in the ground past a grove of trees, is what has fast become one of the most visited sights in Washington, the **Vietnam Veterans Memorial.** The gentle black granite V is inscribed with the names of the more than 58,000 Americans who died in the Vietnam War. *Washington Monument: Constitution Ave. at 15th St. NW, tel. 202/426–6840. Open daily. Admission free. Jefferson Memorial: Tidal Basin, South bank, tel. 202/426–6821. Open daily. Admission free. Lincoln Memorial: West end of Mall, tel. 202/426–6895. Open daily. Admission free. Vietnam Veterans Memorial: 23rd St. and Constitution Ave. NW, tel. 202/634–1568. Open daily. Admission free.*

OTHER ATTRACTIONS Here are some of Washington's other top attractions, a few of which you can venture to on foot from the Mall. You'll want to take the Metro or drive to those that are farther away.

Old Town Alexandria. The colorful past of this once bustling Virginia tobacco port is still alive in restored 18th- and 19th-century homes, churches, and taverns. Start your tour at **Ramsay House,** home of the town's first postmaster and lord mayor and today headquarters of the Alexandria Convention & Visitors Bureau (221 King St., tel. 703/838–4200; open daily). Other stops should include **Gadsby's Tavern Museum** (134 N. Royal St., tel. 703/838–4242; open Tues.–Sun.), a center of political and social life in the 18th century; the **boyhood home of Robert E. Lee** (607 Oronoco St., tel. 703/548–8454; open daily, closed Dec.15–Feb. 1; admission $3), a fine example of a 19th-century Federal-style town house, filled with antique furnishings; and the **Torpedo Factory Arts Center** (105 N. Union St., tel. 703/838–4565; open daily; admission free), a former munitions plant that now serves as studio and gallery space for some 175 professional artists.

Arlington National Cemetery. More than 200,000 graves are spread out over these 612 acres of rolling Virginia hills. John F. Kennedy and his brother Robert are both buried here, as are the remains of the unknown soldiers from past American conflicts. *West end of Arlington Memorial Bridge, Arlington, VA, tel. 703/692–0931. Open daily. Admission free.*

Bureau of Engraving and Printing. A 20-minute, self-guided tour takes visitors past presses that turn out some $40 million a day. Self-guided tours run until 3 PM. In summer, line up by 8:30 AM for tickets to the guided tours that run until 2:30 PM. Sadly, there are no free samples. *14th and C Sts. SW, tel. 202/622–2000. Open daily. Admission free.*

Georgetown. Like Alexandria, Virginia, this community was an active port long before Washington became a city. Today, it's the capital's wealthiest neighborhood, a profusion of Georgian, Federal, and Victorian homes, and center of the best nightlife and shopping in town. The bustling crossroads is M Street and Wisconsin Avenue NW. To the south, below M Street, is the tranquil **C&O Canal** (hitch a National Park Service barge ride in warmer months at 1057 Thomas Jefferson St. NW, tel. 202/653–4190). **Fletcher's Boat House,** at the intersection of Reservoir and Canal roads, rents canoes and rowboats for use on the canal and the river (weather permitting) for $8 an hour or $15 a day. Fletcher's also sells fishing licenses and tackle. To the north, on N Street and above, are expensive homes and estates. One of the loveliest spots in town is **Dumbarton Oaks,** a sprawling property that has 10 acres of enchanting gardens and two museums: one of pre-Columbian works, another of Byzantine art. *Dumbarton Oaks: 31st and R Sts. NW, tel. 202/338–8278. Gardens open daily; admission charged. Museums open Tues.–Sun.; admission charged.*

The Phillips Collection. In 1921, Duncan Phillips turned two rooms of his Georgian Revival home in the fashionable Dupont Circle neighborhood into an art gallery, in the process creating the first permanent museum of modern art in the country. On display are works by such modern masters as Braque, Cezanne, Klee, Matisse, and Renoir as well as by American modernists. *1600–1612 21st St. NW, tel. 202/387–2151. Open Tues.–Sun. Admission charged.*

JUST FOR KIDS The Smithsonian museums put on a host of free children's programs. At the **Arts and Industries Building** (900 Jefferson Drive, SW, tel. 202/357–1500, admission charged), Discovery Theater presents performances for children. The **National Museum of Natural History** (*see above*) features an Insect Zoo, a Discovery Room full of touchable objects from nature, and, of course, the Dinosaur Hall with its fully reconstructed skeletons of prehistoric creatures of land and sea.

The **National Zoological Park** is home to more than 4,000 animals representing some 500 species, including the famously shy giant panda Hsing-Hsing, the only living panda in the United States. The ambitious new Amazonia exhibit re-creates a rain-forest ecosystem. *3001 Connecticut Ave. NW, tel. 202/673–4800. Open daily. Admission free.*

The **Washington National Cathedral** offers stone-carving and stained-glass workshops on Saturday mornings all year except August, and on Wednesday evenings in summer. *Wisconsin and Massachusetts Aves., tel. 202/537–2934. Donation requested.*

The **Capital Children's Museum** has everything to delight children, from bubble demonstrations to a crawl-through maze, plus a soon-to-be-opened animation exhibit. *800 3rd St. NE, tel. 202/543–8600. Open daily. Admission charged.*

The charmingly dilapidated **Glen Echo Park,** in Maryland, features two children's programs hosted by **Adventure Theatre** (tel. 301/320–5331) and the **Puppet Company** (tel. 301/320–6668). *7300 MacArthur Blvd., Glen Echo, MD. Park admission charged.*

HOTELS AND INNS

The nation's capital has been riding a hotel boom for more than a decade, with 49 new hotels built between 1976 and 1988 alone. That means visitors can expect variety and quantity. (It also means room rates are flexible.) Washington is small enough—and public transportation smooth enough—that you shouldn't feel "out of it" no matter where you stay. Still, Capitol Hill hotels will put you that much closer to federal attractions; hotels in Georgetown or near Dupont Circle will allow you a shorter walk home from restaurants and night spots. December and January and the stifling months of July and August are when you'll find the best off-season rates.

To find reasonably priced accommodations in small guest houses and private homes, contact either of the following bed-and-breakfast services: **Bed & Breakfast Accommodations, Ltd.** (Box 12011, 20005, tel. 202/328–3510, fax 202/332–3885) or **Bed and Breakfast League/Sweet Dreams and Toast** (Box 9490, 20016, tel. 202/363–7767).

Price categories for double occupancy, without 11% room and occupancy ($1.50 a night) tax, are *Moderate,* $100–$130, and *Inexpensive,* under $100.

MODERATE **Bellevue Hotel.** Charming and comfortable, this small Capitol Hill hotel is close to Union Station and within six blocks of the Smithsonian museums on the Mall. *15*

E St. NW, 20001, tel. 202/638–0900 or 800/327–6667, fax 202/333–5426. 140 rooms. Restaurant, bar, library, free overnight parking. AE, DC, MC, V.

Georgetown Dutch Inn. Tucked away on a side street in Georgetown near the C&O Canal, this hotel has a homey ambience, guest rooms complete with sofa beds, and walk-in kitchens. *1075 Thomas Jefferson St. NW, 20007, tel. 202/337–0900 or 800/388–2410, fax 202/638–5132. 47 rooms. Access to health club, free parking. AE, DC, MC, V.*

Latham Hotel. A small, elegant hotel located right in the middle of fashionable Georgetown, the Latham also offers a critically acclaimed restaurant. *3000 M St. NW, 20007, tel. 202/726–5000 or 800/368–5922, fax 202/337–4250. 143 rooms. Restaurant, bar, outdoor pool, health-club access, valet parking. AE, DC, MC, V.*

Omni Georgetown. Near the bohemian Dupont Circle (but, despite the name, not in Georgetown), this well-appointed hotel boasts some of the largest guest rooms in the city. *2121 P St. NW, 20037, tel. 202/293–3100 or 800/843–6664, fax 202/857–0134. 294 rooms. Restaurant, bar, pool, exercise room, sauna, gallery, valet parking. AE, D, DC, MC, V.*

Quality Hotel Capitol Hill. A good value for the budget-minded traveler, this hotel offers a Capitol Hill location with a view of the Capitol dome from some rooms. *415 New Jersey Ave. NW, 20001, tel. 202/638–1616 or 800/228–5151, fax 202/638–0707. 341 rooms. Restaurant, pool, free parking. AE, DC, MC, V.*

INEXPENSIVE Channel Inn. An informal waterside establishment south of the Mall on an inlet of the Potomac, the Channel Inn seems far from the city's hub but is convenient to the new Waterfront Metro station that will take you there. *650 Water St. SW, 20024, tel. 202/554–2400 or 800/368–5668, fax 202/863–1164. 100 rooms. Restaurant, bar, coffee shop, pool, free parking. AE, DC, MC, V.*

Days Inn Connecticut Avenue. On a wide street away from downtown but near such northwest Washington attractions as the zoo and the cathedral, the Days Inn offers standard hotel furnishings and a complimentary Continental breakfast. *4400 Connecticut Ave. NW, 20008, tel. 202/244–5600 or 800/952–3060, fax 202/244–6794 155 rooms. AE, D, DC, MC, V.*

Hotel Tabard Inn. Located in a set of Victorian town houses on a quiet street not far from Dupont Circle and downtown, this hundred-year-old inn's antique-filled rooms and gracious service make for an English-style experience. *1739 N St. NW, 20036, tel. 202/785–1277, fax 202/785–6173. 40 rooms, 27 with private bath. Restaurant, no TV in rooms. MC, V.*

Hotel Windsor Park. Near to (but cheaper than) the major convention hotels, the Windsor Park offers small, immaculate rooms and a residential setting a short walk away from Dupont Circle, Embassy Row, and Woodley Park. *2116 Kalorama Rd. NW, 20008, tel. 202/483–7700 or 800/247–3064, fax 202/332–4547. 43 rooms. AE, D, DC, MC, V.*

Howard Johnson Kennedy Center. This eight-story lodge offers reliability, large rooms with refrigerators, and a site near the Kennedy Center and Georgetown. *2601 Virginia Ave. NW, 20037, tel. 202/965–2700 or 800/654–2000. 192 rooms. Restaurant, rooftop pool, free parking for cars (no vans). AE, DC, MC, V.*

Kalorama Guest House. Reminiscent of Grandma's house, this quaint, Victorian town house in Adams-Morgan has a relaxed atmosphere and features a complimentary breakfast. A separate annex in Woodley Park is not far from the National Zoo. *1854 Mintwood Pl. NW, 20009, tel. 202/667–6369, fax 202/312–1262. Annex: 2700 Cathedral Ave., tel. 202/328–0860. 50 rooms, 30 with private bath. AE, DC, MC, V.*

Normandy Inn. A small, European-style hotel on a quiet street near many embassies, the Normandy offers comfortable rooms and a complimentary Continental breakfast. *2118*

Wyoming Ave. NW, 20008, tel. 202/483–1350 or 800/424–3729, fax 202/387–8241. 75 rooms. Underground parking. AE, DC, MC, V.

Quality Hotel Central. This high rise up the street from Dupont Circle is popular with visitors who can't find rooms at the more expensive Hilton across the street. 1900 Connecticut Ave. NW, 20009, tel. 202/332–9300 or 800/842–4211, fax 202/328–7039. 147 rooms. Restaurant, pool, access to health club. AE, D, DC, MC, V.

DINING

The District has weathered wave after wave of restaurant trends, from New American to Southwestern, from upscale Italian to postmodern Oriental. Somehow it's survived them all. Of course, some tastes are immune to fads, and Washington's location near the Chesapeake Bay and the Atlantic Ocean means seafood is usually fresh, none more so than the hallowed Chesapeake blue crab. As for favorite dining neighborhoods, there's a strong Latin and Ethiopian flavor in Adams-Morgan, especially on 18th Street south of Columbia Road. Dupont Circle boasts some of the city's best Italian eateries. Georgetown, around Wisconsin Avenue and M Street, is chockablock with restaurants. And Washington even has a compact Chinatown, centered around 7th and G streets NW.

Price categories per person, not including 9% tax, service, and drinks, are Expensive, $25–40; Moderate, $15–$25; and Inexpensive, under $15.

ADAMS-MORGAN **Belmont Kitchen.** On warm spring nights, customers flock to this neighborhood restaurant's outdoor dining area, enjoying upside-down pizzas, grilled fish and meat, and a low-calorie, three-course dinner that's always on the menu. 2400 18th St. NW, tel. 202/667–1200. DC, MC, V. Moderate.

La Fourchette. It looks the way a bistro should—with an exposed brick wall, tin ceiling, and bentwood chairs—and serves hearty entrées like bouillabaisse, rabbit, and lamb and veal shanks, all at a reasonable prices.

2429 18th St. NW, tel. 202/332–3077. AE, DC, MC, V. Moderate.

Cities. Periodically this restaurant changes both menu and decor to match the look and taste of such cities as Sicily, Mexico City, and Los Angeles. The chef has been called one of the best in Washington; weekend crowds confirm her popularity. 2424 18th St. NW, tel. 202/328–7194. AE, DC, MC, V. Moderate.

Meskerem. Adams-Morgan is a hotbed of Ethiopian restaurants, but none are as distinctive as this exotically decorated spot, where diners sit on cushions and sample watt (meat and vegetarian stews) scooped up in spongy injera bread. 2434 18th St. NW, tel. 202/462–4100. AE, MC, V. Inexpensive.

CAPITOL HILL **America.** A lively and attractive bar and restaurant in the soaring main hall of Union Station, America has a menu as broad as its name, from Minnesota scrambled eggs to New Mexico–style pasta. Union Station, 50 Massachusetts Ave. NE, tel. 202/682–9555. AE, DC, MC, V. Moderate.

DOWNTOWN **Bombay Palace.** A cosmopolitan setting provides the backdrop for authentic Indian dishes, from mild to scorching, with such entrées as chicken and prawns cooked in a tandoor oven, butter chicken (tandoori chicken in a tomato sauce), and gosht patiala (a stew of meat, potatoes, and onions in a ginger sauce). 2020 K St. NW, tel. 202/331–0111. AE, DC, MC, V. Moderate.

Primi Piatti. An exuberant Roman atmosphere underscores this Washington favorite almost as much as the light and healthful Italian dishes it serves, many of which—including lamb and veal chops and tuna with fresh mint sauce—are prepared on a woodburning grill. 2013 I St. NW, tel. 202/223–3600. Jacket and tie suggested. AE, DC, MC, V. Moderate.

DUPONT CIRCLE **Skewers.** Lamb with eggplant and chicken with roasted peppers are favorites at this avant-garde Middle Eastern restaurant, whose healthful, reasonably priced selections are popular with Ralph

Nader. *1633 P St. NW, tel. 202/387–7400. AE, DC, MC, V. Moderate.*

Sala Thai. The chef will honor requests for spicy food but is more interested in flavor than fire, preparing such subtly seasoned dishes as *panang goong* (shrimp in curry-peanut sauce), chicken sautéed with ginger and pineapple, and flounder with a choice of four sauces. *2016 P St. NW, tel. 202/872–1144. AE, DC, MC, V. Inexpensive.*

GEORGETOWN **Citronelle.** There's a wide window here with quite a view of a hectic kitchen in which white-clad chefs steadily turn out deliciously inventive nouvelle cuisine. Your palate will tingle all the way from the gingery abalone carpaccio appetizer through the gravity-free Napoleons with butterscotch sauce. *Latham Hotel, 3000 M St. NW, lower level, tel. 202/625–2150. Reservations advised. Jacket and tie recommended. AE, MC, V. Expensive.*

Bamiyan. Even the uninitiated can find something to enjoy on this restaurant's appealing Afghani menu, whether it's a chicken, beef, or lamb kebab, a plate of *aushak* (dumplings with scallions, meat sauce, and yogurt), or a side order of sautéed pumpkin. *3320 M St. NW, tel. 202/338–1896. AE, MC, V. Moderate.*

Sushi-Ko. It was Washington's first sushi bar and it remains one of the best, with a menu that extends beyond raw fish to encompass seafood and vegetable tempuras, fish teriyaki, and udonsuki noodles. *2309 Wisconsin Ave. NW, tel. 202/333–4187. AE, MC, V. Moderate.*

American Cafe. With 15 locations in the area, this is a D.C. success story; the secret is affordable, healthy food—croissant sandwiches, salads, fresh fish—in casual but sophisticated spaces. *1211 Wisconsin Ave. NW, tel. 202/944–9464. AE, DC, MC, V. Inexpensive.*

Austin Grill. A boom in Tex-Mex restaurants includes this bright, lively spot whose mesquite grill turns out fajitas, grilled fish, and cubed beef that goes into some of the best chili in town. *2404 Wisconsin Ave. NW, tel. 202/337–8080. AE, MC, V. Inexpensive.*

UPPER NORTHWEST **Dancing Crab.** Heaps of spicy, steaming crabs are piled high on the brown-paper-covered tables at this informal uptown spot, where a casual crowd uses wooden mallets to crack the shells of the tasty crustaceans. *4611 Wisconsin Ave. NW, tel. 202/244–1882. AE, DC, MC, V. Moderate.*

SHOPPING

When it comes to shopping, Washington has one unsung gem: the museum gift shop. Washington's museums, especially those of the Smithsonian Institution, offer high-grade selections based on the collections they display. At the National Gallery of Art, you'll find accurate copies of famous works both suitable for framing and suitably framed. You can take home a model of the space shuttle or an astronaut's freeze-dried ice cream sandwich from the National Air and Space Museum. Handsome handcrafts, ceramics, and glass are plentiful at the Renwick Gallery (Pennsylvania Ave. at 17th St. NW). And for a complete selection of books on America and Americana as well as blues, jazz, and folk music albums released by the Smithsonian, visit the massive store in the National Museum of American History (14th St. and Constitution Ave. NW).

MAJOR SHOPPING DISTRICTS Georgetown is probably Washington's favorite shopping area. The intersection of Wisconsin Avenue and M Street is the hub, and spread out from this nexus, you'll find shops that sell jewelry, antiques, foreign magazines, and designer fashions. The crossroads is also the location of Georgetown Park, a three-level, upscale mall that manages to be both Victorian and modern at the same time.

Dupont Circle, especially Connecticut Avenue north of Massachusetts, has some of the flavor of Georgetown but is a little on the funkier side, with book and record stores as well as shops selling coffee, stationery, clothing, and bric-a-brac.

Around the Metro Center metro station are two of the city's biggest department stores: Woodward & Lothrop (11th and F Sts. NW) and Hecht's (12th and G Sts. NW) as well as cut-price, low-quality shops selling everything from wigs to foundation garments. The Shops at National Place (13th and F Sts. NW, tel. 202/783–9090) is a glittering, three-story collection of stores, including Banana Republic and the Sharper Image.

Union Station (50 Massachusetts Ave. NE, tel. 202/371–9441) underwent a complete renovation in 1988, transforming it into a massive mall with lots of boutiques and special-interest shops.

Mazza Gallerie (5300 Wisconsin Ave. NW, tel. 202/966–6114) is an upmarket mall near the Maryland border that's anchored by the ritzy Nieman Marcus, Williams-Sonoma, and Pierre Deux.

Eastern Market (7th St. and North Carolina Ave. SE, tel. 202/543–7293), popular with locals, has an outdoor farmers market and, inside, established specialty shops that will intrigue most bargain hunters.

DEPARTMENT STORES Both Hecht's (12th and G Sts. NW, tel. 202/628–6661) and Woodward & Lothrop (11th and F Sts. NW, tel. 202/347–5300) are bright and spacious, with sensible groupings of merchandise that make shopping easy on the eyes and feet. "Woodies" is especially good for clothes in a variety of styles and price ranges.

If you're looking to spend a little more money, three stores near the Maryland border will be happy to accommodate you. Lord & Taylor (5255 Western Ave. NW, tel. 202/362–9600), Nieman Marcus (Mazza Gallerie, tel. 202/966–9700), and Saks Fifth Avenue (5555 Wisconsin Ave., Chevy Chase, tel. 301/657–9000).

OUTDOOR ACTIVITIES

BIKING Cyclists spin their wheels on flat, well-paved bike trails in Rock Creek Park along Rock Creek Parkway and Beach Drive, and around the monuments and into East Potomac Park, southeast of the Tidal Basin. There is a good 3-mile loop around the golf course in East Potomac Park. The entryway is near the Jefferson Memorial; the park is safe in the daytime, but avoid it after dark. There's also scenic biking on the towpath along the C&O Canal in Georgetown and north into Maryland. It's 15 miles on the occasionally rocky packed-earth surface up to Great Falls. You can rent bikes at Big Wheel Bikes (1034 33rd St. NW, Georgetown, tel. 202/337–0254; 7th and Pennsylvania SE, tel. 202/543–1600), Fletcher's Boat House (intersection of Reservoir Rd. and Canal St., tel. 202/244–0461), Metropolis Bikes (709 8th St. SE, Capitol Hill, tel. 202/543–8900), and Thompson's Boat House (Virginia Ave. and Rock Creek Pkwy. behind the Kennedy Center, tel. 202/333–4861). For further information, consult the Potomac Pedalers Touring Club (tel. 202/363–8687) or the Washington Area Bicyclists Association (tel. 202/872–9830).

JOGGING/HIKING Popular routes include looping around the Mall on the gravel walkways between the Lincoln Memorial and the Capitol. You can extend the 4.5-mile run by veering south of the Mall past the Jefferson Memorial and into East Potomac Park. Rock Creek Park has 15 miles of trails. A 4-mile loop starts at P Street in Georgetown and extends to the National Zoo. For information on group runs, call the D.C. Road Runners Club (tel. 703/241–0395).

SWIMMING Call the District of Columbia's Department of Recreation (tel. 202/576–6436) for information on the 8 indoor and 18 large outdoor pools it maintains.

TENNIS Hains Point (East Potomac Park, tel. 202/554–5962) and the Washington Tennis Center (16th and Kennedy Sts. NW, tel. 202/722– 5949) each have around two dozen outdoor courts and six indoor courts. Fees are $3.50–$14 an hour, depending on the season and type of court; call ahead to reserve.

ENTERTAINMENT

ARTS You can find just about anything you want at the Kennedy Center (New Hampshire Ave. and Rock Creek Pkwy. NW, tel. 202/467–4600 or 800/444–1324). There are four separate performance areas in which you can find anything from repertory film to opera. Be sure to call ahead—the center will undergo major renovation, and some theaters may close temporarily.

Tickets to many performance and sporting events are available through TicketMaster (tel. 202/432–7328). For information on various activities, consult the *Washington Post,* the free weekly *City Paper,* and *Washingtonian* magazine.

MUSIC **Classical:** The National Symphony Orchestra's season extends from September through June, with most performances at the Kennedy Center (tel. 202/416–8100). During the Armed Forces Concert Series (June– Aug.) there's free music nightly from military bands at sites around the city; for information call 202/767–5658 or 202/433–4011. Chamber groups from around the world perform on Sunday afternoons from September through May at the Phillips Collection art gallery (1600–1612 21st St. NW, tel. 202/387–2151). The Smithsonian Institution sponsors performances in the theaters of its various museums (tel. 202/357–2700 or 202/357–3030).

Contemporary: There's frequent jazz and rhythm-and-blues performers at Blues Alley (Wisconsin Ave. below M St., tel. 202/337–4141); jazz at the One Step Down (2517 Pennsylvania Ave. NW, tel. 202/331–8863); bluegrass at the Birchmere (3901 Mt. Vernon Ave. in Alexandria, tel. 703/549–5919); and alternative rock at the 9:30 Club (930 F St. NW, tel. 202/393–0930).

BALLET AND DANCE The Washington Ballet (tel. 202/362–3606) performs works by such masters as George Balanchine and Paul Taylor, mainly at the Kennedy Center.

OPERA The Washington Opera (tel. 202/416–7800) presents seven lavish operas at the Kennedy Center during its November-to-March season. Though it usually sells out by subscription, returned tickets are sometimes available. Cheaper, standing room tickets go on sale each Sunday. Other operatic choices include Mount Vernon College (2100 Foxhall Rd. NW, tel. 202/231–3467), which produces experimental operas in the spring and fall, and the Summer Opera Theater Company (Hartke Theater, on the campus of the Catholic University of America in northeast Washington, tel. 202/526–1669) and the two productions it mounts each July and August.

THEATER Arena Stage (6th St. and Maine Ave. SW, tel. 202/488–3300) is one of the country's leading repertory theaters. Ford's Theatre (511 10th St. NW, tel. 202/347–4833), the site of Lincoln's assassination, is both a museum (managed by the Park Service) and a functioning theater. The National Theatre (1321 E St. NW, tel. 202/628–6161) is the oldest in the city and is the home of many pre- and post-Broadway shows. The Shakespeare Theatre at The Lansburgh Theatre (450 the St. NW, tel. 202/393–2700) presents Elizabethan plays from September to May.

SPECTATOR SPORTS The closest major-league baseball team is the Baltimore Orioles, in their new Camden Yards home (Russell St., Baltimore, MD; tel. 410/685–9800); purchase tickets in Washington at the Orioles Baseball Store (914 17th St. NW, tel. 202/296–2473). The Capital Centre in suburban Maryland (1 Harry S. Truman Dr., Landover, MD; tel. 301/350–3400) hosts Washington Bullets basketball (Sept.–Apr.) and Washington Capitals Hockey (Oct.–Apr.). All Washington Redskins home football games at RFK Stadium (East Capitol and 22nd Sts. SE, tel. 202/546–2222) have been sold out since 1966 to season ticket holders. Seats to preseason games are usually available, though, and if you're willing to pay dearly, you can get regular season seats from ticket brokers who advertise in the *Washington Post* classifieds.

Waterton/Glacier International Peace Park
Montana and Alberta, Canada

Waterton/Glacier International Peace Park is like the frontier before it was altered by man. Formed of the United States' giant Glacier National Park and Canada's far smaller Waterton Lakes National Park, which meet at the U.S.–Canadian border in northwestern Montana, the area embodies the essence of the Rocky Mountains. Its massive peaks form the backbone of the Continental Divide. The huge ice sheets for which Glacier Park was named have retreated, but the wild terrain they created reveal their power, and the more than four dozen glaciers that remain give a sense of what they were like. Ribbons of pure, clear water streaming from these ice fields eventually flow into three oceans—the Pacific, via the Columbia River, the Atlantic, via the Mississippi, and the Arctic, via the St. Mary River. There are dozens of waterfalls, many large, deep lakes, and scores of smaller ones. Flora is profuse, and the coniferous forests, alpine mountainsides, thickly vegetated stream banks, and green-carpeted meadows provide homes and sustenance for abundant and varied wildlife; Glacier is one of the few parks with substantial numbers of grizzly bears. In Waterton, the rugged alpine scenery gives way to prairie grasslands.

Going-to-the-Sun Road, one of the most dizzying rides in North America, is just one of several scenic routes that showcase these natural wonders and provide access to nature centers and hiking trails that give a more intimate view. Assuring a comfortable stay is a wide variety of accommodations—campgrounds to castlelike hotels, basic diners to fine restaurants. You'll find these just outside the park in communities such as East Glacier Park and West Glacier, and in the small but busy commercial centers within park boundaries: Two Medicine, Apgar, Lake McDonald, Rising Sun, and Many Glacier in Glacier, and Watertown Townsite in Waterton.

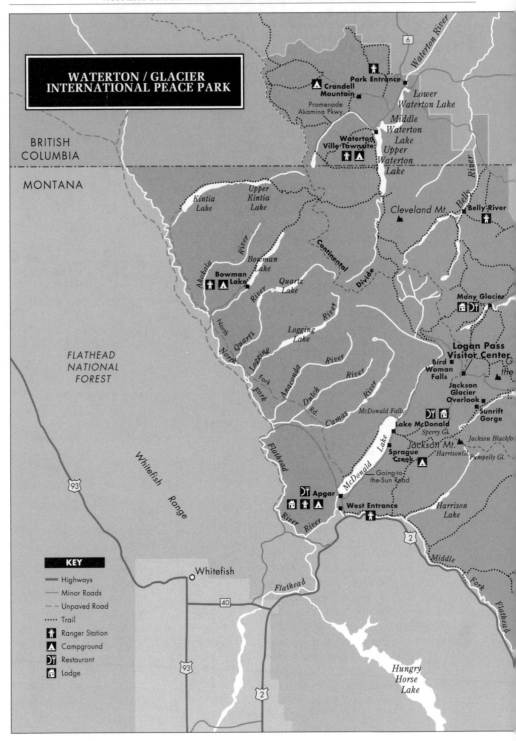

WATERTON / GLACIER INTERNATIONAL PEACE PARK

BRITISH COLUMBIA

MONTANA

Park Entrance

Crandell Mountain

Promenade Akamina Pkwy.

Lower Waterton Lake

Middle Waterton Lake

Waterton Ville·Townsite

Upper Waterton Lake

Kintla Lake

Upper Kintla Lake

Cleveland Mt.

Belly River

Belly River

Akokala River

Bowman Lake

Bowman Lake

Quartz Lake

Continental Divide

Many Glacier

North Quartz River

Logging Lake

Logan Pass Visitor Center

FLATHEAD NATIONAL FOREST

North Fork

Logging Fork

Anaconula

Dutch

Camas

River

River

River

Bird Woman Falls

the

Jackson Glacier Overlook

Sunrift Gorge

McDonald Falls

Lake McDonald

Sperry Gl.

Jackson Mt.

Jackson Blackfo

HarrisonGl. Pumpelly Gl.

Sprague Creek

Flathead

Going-to-the-Sun Road

McDonald Lake

Harrison Lake

Whitefish Range

93

Apgar

West Entrance

River

River

2

Middle Fork

Flathead

Whitefish

Flathead

40

93

2

Hungry Horse Lake

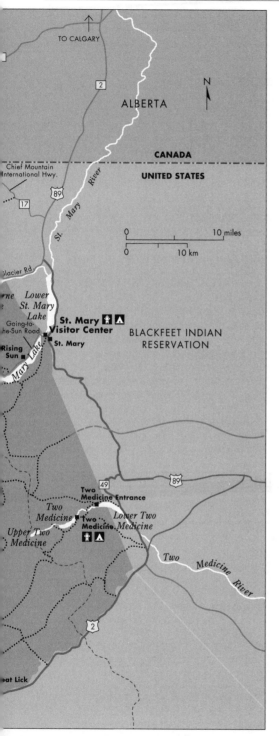

ESSENTIAL INFORMATION

WHEN TO GO Most people visit Waterton/Glacier in summer: Weather is warmest, flora freshest, wildlife best distributed, and the glacier-fed streams and waterfalls running full.

Temperatures average in the high 70s and low 80s by day in summer, 45°–50° at night; 20°–30° by day in winter, below zero at night; and 65°–70° by day in spring and fall, 35°–40° at night. However, weather on any day often varies more drastically. It is most consistently stable in early September, when crowds dissipate. It's a good time to visit. High-country winters last at least from September to June.

FESTIVALS AND SPECIAL EVENTS **Late Apr. or early May:** The opening of the Going-to-the-Sun Road, one of Glacier's big annual events, draws spectators as crews plow away tons of snow. **July 1 (Canadian Independence Day)– July 4 (U.S. Independence Day):** Days of Peace and Friendship offers special talks on the International Peace Park theme. **Third weekend in Aug.:** The Beargrass Festival has native dancers, cowboy poetry, storytelling, fiddling, golf, and chili-cooking competitions in Waterton Townsite.

BARGAINS The best activities are always free: hiking, picnicking, fishing, wildlife-watching, naturalist activities. Canada's 7% tax on rooms, meals, and purchases is refundable; inquire at the border.

TOURIST OFFICES Glacier National Park (West Glacier 59936, tel. 406/888–5441). Waterton Lakes National Park (Waterton Park, Alberta, Canada T0K 2M0, tel. 403/859–2224). Travel Montana (1424 9th Ave., Helena 59620–0401, tel. 406/444–2654). Travel Alberta (10065 Jasper Ave., Edmonton, Alberta, Canada T5J 0H4, tel. 800/661–8888). Waterton Park Townsite Chamber of Commerce (Box 55–6, Waterton Lakes National Park, Alberta, Canada T0K 2M0, tel. 403/859–2203). Glacier Park, Inc. (Box 147, East Glacier Park 59434–0147, tel. 406/226–5551 or 403/236–3400) mid-May–September. Dial Tower (Phoenix, AZ 85077, tel. 602/207–6000 or 403/236–3400) October–mid-May.

EMERGENCIES Stop in at a ranger station or dial 911 for **police, fire,** and **ambulance.** Or, in Glacier, call headquarters (tel. 406/888–5441; 888–5407; 732–4401 after hours). In Waterton, phone the ranger station (tel. 403/859–2636), park superintendent (tel. 403/859–2224), or Waterton Royal Canadian Mounted Police (tel. 403/859–2244). **Doctors and Hospitals:** Glacier resources include the Kalispell Regional Hospital, about 30 miles southwest of West Glacier (tel. 406/752–5111). Nearer Waterton, try Cardston, 20 miles west of the north park boundary (hospital, tel. 403/653–4411; clinic, tel. 403/653–3311), or Pincher Creek, 30 miles north of the north park boundary (hospital, tel. 403/627–3333; clinic, tel. 403/627– 3321).

ARRIVING AND DEPARTING

BY PLANE The nearest airport to Glacier is Glacier Park International Airport (tel. 406/257–5994), 30 miles southwest of the park between Kalispell and Whitefish. Flathead/Glacier Transportation (tel. 406/862–7733) runs vans from the airport, charging $32 to West Glacier, on the park's southwest border; $100 to East Glacier Park, just outside the southeast boundary; and $140 to Many Glacier, in the northeast. Fares are for one; you pay $2 per additional passenger.

BY CAR Uncrowded, two-lane U.S. 2 accesses Glacier Park from the east and west. It connects to I–90, which cuts through Butte and Missoula, via I–15 on the east, and U.S. 93 on the west.

BY TRAIN Amtrak (tel. 800/USA–RAIL) stops at West Glacier and East Glacier Park.

GETTING AROUND

BY CAR A car is the best transportation here. Roads are suitable for RVs, though caution is necessary and some vehicle-length restrictions apply. The North Fork Road, Going-to-the-Sun Road, Two Medicine Road, and Many Glacier Road travel deep into the park and access trailheads and points of interest. In winter, these close, and your sole option is U.S. 2, which runs just outside the south boundary, dipping into the park at the Goat Lick and passing the winter game range. In Waterton, Route 5 into Waterton Townsite is the only road that's open all year.

REST STOPS All park campgrounds and picnic areas accessible by car have rest rooms, as do all visitor centers. So do private businesses in Apgar Village, Lake McDonald, Two Medicine, Rising Sun, Swiftcurrent, Many Glacier, and Waterton Townsite. West Glacier, East Glacier Park, St. Mary, and Babb, just outside the Glacier Park boundary, also have rest rooms.

GUIDED TOURS **Bus Tours:** These can be exciting, especially the tours offered by Glacier Park, Inc. (*see* Tourist Offices, *above*), which uses vintage 1936, rolltop Scarlet Buses.

Narrated Cruises: Especially good are Waterton Lake Cruises (tel. 403/859–2362), which dock at Waterton Townsite and stop on both sides of the international border, venturing as far south as Goat Haunt. Or you can opt for Glacier National Park SceniCruises (tel. 406/888–5727 or 406/732–4430), 45 minutes to 1½ hours long, on Lake McDonald, Many Glacier, Two Medicine, or St. Mary Lake.

Naturalist Walks: Both parks have many ranger-guided walks. For details, contact headquarters (*see* Tourist Offices, *above*).

EXPLORING

It is possible to travel through this vast area in a single day. But it's a shame to hurry. And while park roads do showcase abundant scenery, it's important to make time for walks and picnics. Stop at visitor centers at Apgar, St. Mary, Logan Pass, and Waterton Townsite to find out about special programs scheduled during your visit.

The general public pays $5 for a seven-day ticket to visit Glacier ($3 for pedestrians, motorcyclists, or bicyclers), $4 per day ($9 for a four-day pass) to enter Waterton.

North Fork Road is narrow, unpaved, and one of the two (along with Two Medicine Road) least traveled roads in the park. It parallels the North Fork of the Flathead River for 43 miles and leads through lodgepole pine flats and other river-bottom terrain with the forested mountains of the Whitefish Range rising to the west. It also provides access to beautiful Bowman and Kintla lakes, where you'll find campgrounds and good trout fishing (though if you walk into Logging and Quartz lakes, the angling will probably be even better). Driving time is around two hours, excluding stops. You can pick up the road at the stop sign about a mile inside the park's west entrance; make a left turn.

Going-to-the-Sun Road, accessible by turning right at the stop sign, is probably the biggest single attraction in Glacier. Literally blasted out of solid rock, this 1930-era engineering feat climbs to Logan Pass, topping the Continental Divide at 6,664 feet, then drops downhill to St. Mary Lake on the east side. Along the way, it twists through conifer forests, past mountain peaks, and along grassy basins brightly dotted with summer flowers. To complement the breathtaking scenery, there are many opportunities for hikes, walks, and animal-watching both on and off the road. At rustic Lake McDonald Lodge, named for its location on the park's largest lake, you can have a bite, rent a small boat or canoe, embark on a guided cruise, go for a hike, or take a horseback ride. Beyond there, you can stop to view the McDonald Falls off the left side of the road or the treeless avalanche chutes on the mountainsides above. Bears are often visible there, especially in early summer, and Bird Woman Falls stripes the opposite canyon wall. At the panoramic visitor center atop Logan Pass, you can learn about the local alpine environment, or stroll the 1¹/₂-mile trail to Hidden Lake Overlook for a fine view of the deep-blue lake below. Across the road you could hike a short distance along the 35¹/₂-mile-long Highline Trail; carved out of a sheer cliff (but negotiable for most visitors), it overlooks a vast portion of southwest Glacier. On the trip down, on the east side of the Continental Divide, there's a vista of bald, 9,642-foot Going-to-the-Sun Mountain; a glimpse of Jackson Glacier looming in a rocky pass; sev-

eral waterfalls; and intriguing Sunrift Gorge, a miniature canyon just off the road.

The road is 50 miles long and should take about 1¹/₂ hours to drive, excluding stops. The last two or three hours before dark are best for the trip—with best lighting for photos, best wildlife-spotting, and smallest crowds.

Many Glacier Road parallels Sherburne Lake along a scrubby forest of lodgepole pines, aspens, and cottonwoods broken by meadows that come alive with flowers in the summer. It ends in a glacially carved valley surrounded by rugged mountains. Grinnell and Salamander glaciers, once a single ice mass, are clearly visible along the way. Access is from the northeast side of the park, southwest of Babb; the 20-mile road ends at Swiftcurrent, where you can fish, take a boat cruise, ride horseback, have a meal, and camp or check into a motel, then enjoy a ranger campfire talk. There are also good hikes, long and short, including the one to Grinnell Glacier, the largest in the park; the high basin on the north side of the valley is a good place to spot bears, mountain goats, sheep, and other wildlife.

Chief Mountain International Highway is another one of Waterton/Glacier's great drives. Moving from Glacier northwest to Waterton Townsite then down toward Waterton Lakes, it begins in the rolling hills at the edge of the prairie and climbs through open fields patched with cottonwoods and aspens, into thick forests—first of deciduous trees, then conifers, mostly lodgepole pine and spruce. Coming down, there's a panorama embracing almost all of Waterton Park and a view of the Lewis Overthrust—600-million-year-old rock that geological movements have thrust over 100-million-year-old rock—where grizzly bears, mountain goats, or other wildlife can often be spotted. To cover the 35 miles between St. Mary and Waterton, allow 1¹/₂ hours, excluding stops.

THE NATURAL WORLD You can almost always see goats and other wildlife at the Goat Lick, on the extreme southern tip of Glacier. Bighorn sheep and mule deer are usually present in and around Waterton Townsite. Deer and chipmunks are also easy to see. An astute observer can often pick out elk, black bears and grizzly bears, moose, and coyotes. Bobcats, lynxes, mountain lions, raccoons, foxes, wolverines, and martens are present but less common. Smaller animals include pikas, snowshoe hares, porcupines, beavers, marmots, and other rodents. A small number of bison reside in Waterton, and gray wolves live in both parks. Both parks shelter a wide variety of birds, including songbirds, waterfowl, and such predators as bald eagles and ospreys.

HOTELS AND INNS

Accommodations here range from plain to ornate, but a western-rustic mood prevails, and rates are reasonable, despite the demand. Reserve two months to a year in advance, especially for July and August—you can't count on cancellations. The most distinctive (and most expensive) properties are inside the Peace Park, but you don't have to spend a fortune to enjoy their convenience, since there are several less expensive options. Note: Unless otherwise noted, all properties in the Peace Park are run by Glacier Park, Inc. (see Tourist Offices, above).

Price categories for double occupancy, not including tax (4% in Montana, 12% in Canada), are *Expensive*, $80–$210; *Moderate*, $50–$80; and *Inexpensive*, under $50. Note that rates sometimes drop in June, before winter is fully dissipated. Unless otherwise noted, all hotels, inns, and motels are closed from September or October until May or June.

GLACIER **Glacier Park Lodge.** This grand old hotel at East Glacier Park was built in the 1920s with 500- to 800-year-old fir and cedar logs 3 feet in diameter as its main supports. *155 rooms. Restaurant, snack bar, lounge, evening entertainment, heated pool, 9-hole golf course. D, MC, V. Expensive.*

Many Glacier Hotel. The most isolated of the Peace Park's grand hotels, this vintage chalet on Swiftcurrent Lake in northeast Glacier is often considered the most scenic as well. *210 rooms. Restaurant, snack bar, lounge, evening entertainment, gas station. D, MC, V. Expensive.*

Lake McDonald Lodge. Set amid the cedars on the south side of the lake of the same name, this old lodge in the Lake McDonald area has a Wild West look to it, in part owing to the animal heads on the lobby walls. *100 rooms. Restaurant, coffee shop, lounge, evening entertainment, gas station, store. D, MC, V. Moderate–Expensive.*

Village Motor Inn. This two-story wooden lodge with balconies has a spectacular view of the mountains and the lake out front, where there's a beach—though swimming in such cold water is not for the faint of heart. *36 rooms, 12 with kitchenettes. D, MC, V. Moderate.*

Apgar Village Lodge. This establishment, built early in this century—one of the few in Glacier Park not run by Glacier Park, Inc.— stands out for its setting among big trees rather than for its somewhat plain, though meticulously clean, accommodations. *Box 398, West Glacier 59936, tel. 406/888–5484. 48 units (25 cabins), 23 with kitchenettes. D, MC, V. Open May 1–Oct. 15. Moderate.*

Granite Park Chalet and Sperry Chalet. These popular wilderness chalets, built around the time of World War I from rugged natural materials, are in a class by themselves—and an unforgettable experience— since accommodations are spartan and access is only via a long, steep trail. The chalets, however, are temporarily closed for repairs and not expected to reopen until early 1995; call for the latest details. *Belton Chalets, Inc., Box 188, West Glacier 59936, tel. 406/888– 5511. 18 rooms (single beds only) at Glacier Park Chalet, 20 rooms at Sperry. No showers or baths, though hot and cold running water is provided. Pit latrines. Hearty breakfasts and dinners included in rates; lunch available. No credit cards; full payment in advance required. Moderate.*

Rising Sun Motor Inn. Disregard the barracks-like appearance—the Rising Sun is clean, neat, and conveniently and prettily situated on Going-to-the-Sun Road at mountain-encircled St. Mary Lake. *72 units (25 cabins). Coffee shop, store. D, MC, V. Moderate.*

Swiftcurrent Motor Inn. This motel-and-cabin complex is plain but practical—and its location at the end of Many Glacier Road assures fine views. *88 units (26 cabins, some without bath). Coffee shop, coin laundry, store. D, MC, V. Inexpensive–Moderate.*

WATERTON **The Prince of Wales Hotel.** This grand establishment at Waterton Townsite, designed like a Swiss chalet, seems old-fashioned but offers a great look at the mountains, especially from the rooms facing south toward Upper Waterton Lake. *82 rooms. Restaurant, tea room, lounge, evening entertainment. D, MC, V. Expensive.*

Bayshore Inn. The L shape of this motel-style establishment, probably the most modern in the Peace Park, matches the shoreline of Upper Waterton Lake and parallels a gravel beach. *Box 38, Waterton Townsite, T0K 2M0, tel. 403/859–2211. 70 rooms (49 facing lake). Restaurant, coffee shop, lounge, evening entertainment, hot tub, room service, coin laundry. AE, MC, V (no credit card guarantees for reservations made more than 10 days in advance of stay). Moderate–Expensive.*

Kilmorey Lodge. The only year-round, full-service lodge in Waterton Park, this older, two-story structure faces the lake and is surrounded by trees. *Box 100, Waterton Townsite, T0K 2M0, tel. 403/859–2334. 25 rooms. Restaurant, gazebo-café, lounge, room service. AE, DC, MC, V. Moderate.*

MOTELS

MODERATE **Aspen-Windflower Motel** (Box 100, Waterton Townsite, T0K 2M0, tel. 403/859–2255). 50 rooms and cabins, 14 with kitchenettes; Jacuzzi. **Crandell Mountain Lodge** (Box 114, Waterton, T0K 2M0, tel. 403/859–2288). 13 rooms, 8 with kitchenettes. **Glacier Motel** (Box 93, East Glacier Park 59434, tel. 406/226–5593). 17 rooms and cabins, 7 with kitchenettes. **River Bend Motel** (Box 398, West Glacier 59936, tel. 406/888–

5662). 32 rooms and cabins, 4 with kitchenettes; restaurant, store, nearby coin laundry. **St. Mary Lodge Motel** (St. Mary 59417, tel. 406/732–4431 in summer; 208/726–6279 in winter). 70 rooms and creekside or deluxe cabins, 12 kitchenettes; restaurant, lounge, coin laundry. **Vista Motel** (Box 98, West Glacier 59936, tel. 406/888–5311 or 800/831–7101). 26 rooms, 6 with kitchenettes; heated pool.

INEXPENSIVE **Glacier Highland Motel** (Box 397, West Glacier 59434, tel. 406/888– 5427). 33 rooms, 3 with kitchenettes. **Jacobson's Cottages** (Box 216, East Glacier Park 59434, tel. 406/226–4422). 12 cabins, 1 with kitchen. **Mountain Pine Motel** (Box 260, East Glacier Park 59434, tel. 406/226–4403). 26 rooms. **Sears Motel and Campground** (Box 275, East Glacier Park 59434, tel. 406/226–4432). 16 rooms, 19 campsites (12 with full RV hookups); Rent-a-Wreck car rentals.

CAMPGROUNDS

There are more than a dozen campgrounds as well as several picnic areas in Glacier, and several others in Waterton; they range from busy areas with all services to quiet, rustic spots where you can enjoy a true woodland experience. All campgrounds are first-come, first-served and fill up by early afternoon during July and August. No credit cards are accepted.

In Glacier, none offer utility hookups, and none have showers (available for nominal fee at Rising Sun and Swiftcurrent Motor inns). Waterton campgrounds have more comprehensive facilities. For details, contact park headquarters (*see* Tourist Offices, *above*).

GLACIER **Apgar.** A short walk from Apgar Village and Lake McDonald, this campground is large, busy, and close to many activities and services. *Just inside Glacier's west entrance. 196 sites ($10). Bathrooms, dump station, picnic tables, boat access.*

Bowman Lake. Here, off a graveled road at Bowman Lake in northwest Glacier, you'll find a campground that doesn't feel crowded—though it lacks some of the amenities of bigger spots. *At the end of Bowman Lake Rd. near Polebridge. 48 sites ($8). Picnic tables, boat access.*

Many Glacier. This large, busy campground in a scenic valley in northeast Glacier is the departure point for hikes into the park's northern areas. *At the end of Many Glacier Rd. at Swiftcurrent. 117 sites ($10). Bathrooms, dump station, picnic tables, boat access.*

Rising Sun. This campground on the north side of Glacier's St. Mary Lake is almost as big and just as busy as Apgar. It offers such water sports as fishing, cruising, and paddling. *Located 5 mi west of Glacier's east entrance. 156 sites ($10). Bathrooms, dump station, picnic tables, boat access.*

Two Medicine. Though lacking the facilities you find at Apgar and Rising Sun, this campground on Two Medicine Lake in southeast Glacier is not only scenic but, happily, fills up later than the rest. *At the end of Two Medicine Rd., next to Two Medicine Store, 11 mi northwest of East Glacier Park. 99 sites ($10). Bathrooms, dump station, picnic tables, boat access.*

WATERTON **Belly River.** This small, wooded campground feels delightfully rustic. *Off Chief Mountain International Hwy., 17¹/₂ mi east of Waterton Townsite. 24 hike-in sites ($7.25). Picnic tables, playground.*

Crandell Mountain. The deep-woods location in the center of the park is far from any development. *Off Red Rock Rd., 11 mi from Waterton Townsite. 129 sites ($10.50). Showers, bathrooms, dump station, picnic tables, playground.*

Waterton Townsite. Within walking distance of this large, busy campground, you'll find all the facilities of the town. The trade-offs for such convenience are occasional crowds and noise. Ask about the waiting list if there's no site available when you arrive. *On the south end of Waterton Townsite. 95 sites with hookups ($17.50), 113 sites without hookups ($13), 30 walk-in sites ($13). Showers, bath-*

rooms, dump station, picnic tables, playground.

DINING

Though most cooking here is basic American fare, heart-smart fare is served in at least one area restaurant, and most will accommodate requests for special preparation. Price categories per person, not including tax (7% in Canada only), service, or drinks, are *Moderate*, $13–$25, and *Inexpensive*, under $13.

GLACIER AND ENVIRONS **Cedar Dining Room.** The straightforward cooking takes second place to the Old West atmosphere at this grand, circa-1914 lodge. *Lake McDonald Lodge off Going-to-the-Sun Rd., tel. 406/888–5431. D, MC, V. Moderate.*

Glacier Park Lodge. A gracious ambience prevails in the dining room of this giant log structure. The menu is strictly western—burgers, steaks, beans, and potatoes. *Rte. 49, East Glacier Park, tel. 406/226–9311. D, MC, V. Moderate.*

Interlaken Lounge. The turn-of-the-century chalet decor—and the fine view of Swiftcurrent Lake just outside—makes a fine backdrop for leisurely, hearty meals of steak, grilled chicken, pasta, and steaming stews. *Many Glacier Hotel, Many Glacier Rd., tel. 406/732– 4411, ext. 610. D, MC, V. Moderate.*

Cedar Tree Deli. The counter here dishes out sandwiches, ice cream, and yogurt to go—and there are picnic tables outside. *Going-to-the-Sun Rd., Apgar Village, tel. 406/888–5232. No credit cards. Inexpensive.*

Eddie's Café. This simple restaurant is a good bet for salads, chicken, rainbow trout, or western foods like beef. *Going-to-the-Sun Rd., Apgar Village, tel. 406/888–5361. MC, V. Inexpensive.*

WATERTON AND ENVIRONS **Garden Court.** This room in the spectacular hilltop Prince of Wales château-hotel makes a fine setting for special meals of local favorites—and the view of Waterton Lake out the windows will take your breath away. *Prince of Wales Hotel, Wa-*

terton Townsite, tel. 403/859–2231. D, MC, V. Moderate.

Kootenai Brown. In this dining area of a modern inn overlooking mountain-backed Waterton Lake, the focus is western fare, including salads, chicken, trout, and beef. *Bayshore Inn, Waterton Ave., Waterton Townsite, tel. 403/859–2211. AE, MC, V. Moderate.*

Lamp Post. Special low-fat, low-sodium entrées—such as grilled trout and skinless chicken—come as a welcome surprise in an area where heavy, old-fashioned American cooking predominates. *Kilmorey Lodge, Waterton Townsite, tel. 403/859–2334. AE, DC, MC, V. Moderate.*

Snow Goose Grill. For something special, this spot with western flair makes a good alternative to dining in the park. Steaks and pasta are specialties, as is whitefish caught by Native Americans in nearby St. Mary Lake. *St. Mary Lodge, St. Mary, tel. 406/732–4431. AE, MC, V. Moderate.*

Zum-M-M's. You can grab some fast food at the counter at this popular local spot—but you'll probably opt for its café or the somewhat fancier dining room, where you'll be treated to classic western cuisine (in other words, more beef and trout). *Waterton Ave., Waterton, tel. 403/859–2388. AE, MC, V. Inexpensive–Moderate.*

New Frank's Restaurant. This simple eatery is the only restaurant in the Peace Park where you can get Chinese as well as western fare. *Waterton Ave., Waterton Townsite, tel. 403/859–2240. AE, MC, V. Inexpensive.*

Pearl's. Pearl's, a squeaky-clean market and deli, is the place for fresh-made sandwiches and pasta. *Windflower Ave., Waterton Townsite, tel. 403/859–2284. MC, V. Inexpensive.*

OUTDOOR ACTIVITIES

BIKING Glacier's roads are narrow, and the Going-to-the-Sun Road is steep. However, North Fork and Many Glacier roads are good, easy rides. Waterton allows bicycling on designated trails; Red Rock Canyon Road would suit novice pedalers. For rentals, call the Village Inn (tel. 406/888–5632), on Lake McDonald at Apgar.

CROSS-COUNTRY SKIING Winter enthusiasts appreciate the relatively flat terrain on the North Fork Road and around Lake McDonald in Glacier, and in northern Waterton.

FISHING Local waters shelter ling, northern pike, whitefish, kokanee, grayling, and several types of trout—cutthroat, bull, brook, rainbow, and lake. You can catch fish in virtually all park waters; as elsewhere, the best is the hardest to get to. A license is necessary in Waterton but not Glacier.

GOLF It is not unusual to see moose, elk, deer, bighorn sheep, and other wildlife while playing 18 at Waterton Lakes Golf Course, at Waterton Townsite (tel. 403/859–2383; fee charged, reservations advised on weekends). Or try Glacier Park Lodge's 9-hole course (tel. 406/226– 9311; fee charged, no reservations) and West Glacier's 18-hole Glacier View Golf Course (tel. 406/888–5471; fee charged, reservations advised).

HIKING Roads in the Peace Park provide access to some 850 miles of marked trails that allow for short strolls, rough cross-country treks, and everything in between.

In Glacier, for instance, Going-to-the-Sun Road leads to the ¼-mile-long Trail of the Cedars, which cuts through an ancient cedar and hemlock forest and enters Avalanche Gorge. There you can pick up the 2-mile-long Avalanche Trail to Avalanche Lake, surrounded by Avalanche Basin, a huge natural amphitheater with a half-dozen waterfalls. Farther along, at Logan Pass, the short walk to Hidden Lake Overlook is popular.

Many Glacier Hotel (*see* Hotels and Inns, *above*) is a departure point for day hikes that take in glaciated canyons, steep mountains, profuse flora, and varied wildlife. From Two Medicine, trails head into southeast Glacier, to Paradise Point and Appistoki, and Rockwell Falls, among other sites.

North Fork Road (*see* Exploring, *above*) accesses trails to Logging, Quartz, Rogers, and Trout lakes.

In Waterton, Waterton Townsite is the starting point for several popular hikes: the steep 3/4-miler up to Bear's Hump, for a great view of Waterton Townsite, Waterton Lake, and the surrounding mountains; the Lakeshore Hike along Waterton Lake to Boundary Bay (3½ miles away) and Glacier's Goat Haunt (6½ miles away); and the 8-mile round-trip to Alderson Lake. In northwest Waterton, the Snowshoe and Blakiston Valley trails, which skirt the north and south sides of 8,803-foot Anderson Mountain, lead to meadows of wildflowers and sites rich in wildlife, particularly mountain goats. Note: Backcountry-use permits, available at ranger stations, are required for fires and backcountry camping.

HORSEBACK RIDING Look into short jaunts or overnight trips from Glacier Park Outfitters (tel. 406/732–5597 or 406/752–1237), or, in Waterton, Alpine Stables (tel. 403/859–2462).

TENNIS Public courts adjoin the Waterton Townsite campground.

SWIMMING Mountain lakes are cold. Try the beaches at Apgar Village on Lake McDonald and Waterton Townsite on Upper Waterton Lake—or the heated pool at Waterton Townsite campground.

WHITE-WATER RAFTING Several West Glacier outfitters stage trips on the pristine Flathead River: Glacier Raft Company (tel. 406/888–5454), Glacier Wilderness Guides (tel. 406/888–5466 or 800/521–RAFT), Great Northern Whitewater (tel. 406/387–5340 or 800/735–7897), Wild River Adventures (tel. 406/888–5539 or 800/826–2724).

The White Mountains
New Hampshire

orthern New Hampshire claims the highest mountains in New England, the 750,000 acres of White Mountain National Forest, as well as wilderness that stretches north into Canada. It's no wonder that hikers, climbers, and nature lovers call this God's country. New Hampshire's mountains are not only higher than those of neighboring Vermont and Maine, they are more rugged, more challenging to climb, and more unpredictable in terms of climate. Gorges slash through the rock-strewn mountain flanks, rivers rush south down the steep-sided valleys, and storms swirl around the summit of Mt. Washington with a powerful force unknown down below. But the White Mountains offer more than the harsh beauty of wilderness. Motorists can take in some of the region's most spectacular scenery by driving the Kancamagus Highway. Southeast of the national forest, on the eastern side of the state, North Conway lures shoppers to its miles of factory outlets and off-price designer boutiques. And when the White Mountains are white with snow, they offer some of the finest and most varied skiing east of the Rockies.

ESSENTIAL INFORMATION

WHEN TO GO Brisk nights are common even in midsummer, though the occasional muggy heat wave does settle over the region in July and August, sending temperatures into the high 80s and low 90s. Autumn, with daytime temperatures ranging from 50° to 70°, comes early. Unless you hunt, avoid the region during hunting season (early November–mid-December). Winters are long and often brutally cold in the mountains (daytime temperatures range from 12° to 34°), but snow is plentiful for skiing. Spring arrives slowly, first bringing mud season from late March to mid-April. Rates at motels and inns are considerably lower in spring, and they drop again after the fall foliage season.

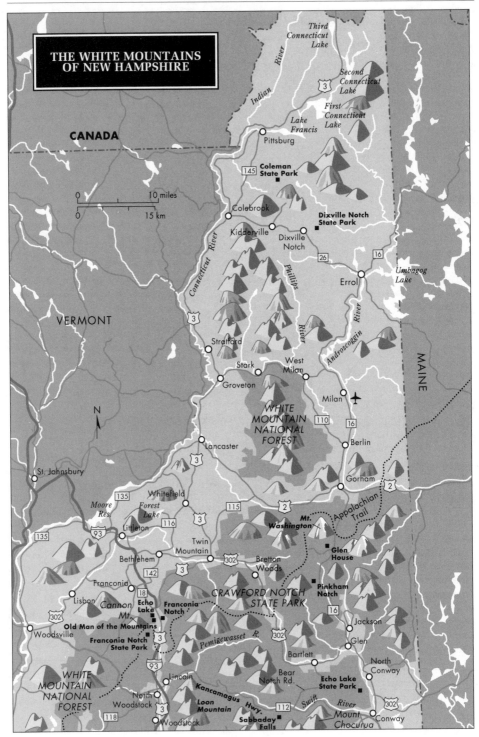

THE WHITE MOUNTAINS OF NEW HAMPSHIRE

CANADA

Third Connecticut Lake

Indian River

Second Connecticut Lake

First Connecticut Lake

Lake Francis

Pittsburg

145 **Coleman State Park**

Colebrook

Kidderville

Dixville Notch

Dixville Notch State Park

26

16

Errol

Umbagog Lake

Connecticut River

Phillips River

VERMONT

3

Stratford

Stark

Groveton

West Milan

Androscoggin River

Milan

MAINE

WHITE MOUNTAIN NATIONAL FOREST

110

16

Berlin

Lancaster

Gorham

2

St. Johnsbury

135

Whitefield

Moore Res.

Forest Lake

116

3

115

2

Mt. Washington

Appalachian Trail

135

93

Littleton

Twin Mountain

302

Bretton Woods

Glen House

Bethlehem

142

3

Franconia

18

Echo Lake

Franconia Notch

CRAWFORD NOTCH STATE PARK

Pinkham Notch

Lisbon

Cannon Mt.

Old Man of the Mountains

Pemigewasset R.

302

16

Jackson

302

Woodsville

Franconia Notch State Park

3

Glen

93

Bartlett

North Conway

Lincoln

Bear Notch Rd.

Echo Lake State Park

WHITE MOUNTAIN NATIONAL FOREST

North Woodstock

Loon Mountain

Kancamagus Hwy.

Swift River

302

118

3

Woodstock

112

Sabbaday Falls

Mount Chocurua

Conway

0   10 miles
0   15 km

N

TOURIST OFFICES White Mountains Attractions Association (Box 10, North Woodstock 03262, tel. 603/745–8720 or 800/FIND–MTS outside NH), Mt. Washington Valley Visitors Bureau (Box 2300VG, North Conway 03860, tel. 603/356–3171), White Mountain National Forest (Box 638, Laconia 03247, tel. 603/528–8721).

EMERGENCIES **State Police** (tel. 800/852–3411). **Hospital:** Memorial Hospital (Intervale Rd., North Conway, tel. 603/356–5461).

ARRIVING AND DEPARTING

BY PLANE Manchester Airport (tel. 603/624–6556) in southern New Hampshire is the state's principal airport. You'll need a car to proceed to the White Mountains area, which is accessible from the airport by driving north on I–93.

BY CAR I–93, the principal north–south route through Manchester, Concord, and central New Hampshire, takes you from eastern Massachusetts into the heart of the White Mountains. I–89 links Concord, south of the White Mountains, with central Vermont.

BY BUS Greyhound Lines (tel. 800/231–2222) and its subsidiary, Vermont Transit Lines (tel. 603/228–3300 or 800/451–3292), link the cities of New Hampshire with major eastern U.S. cities.

GETTING AROUND

BY CAR I–93 and Route 3 bisect the White Mountain National Forest on their south–north extent between Massachusetts and the Province of Quebec, Canada. On the eastern side of the area, Route 16 is the main artery from the coast, past the Mt. Washington valley and on toward Maine. The Kancamagus Highway (Rte. 112) is the east–west thoroughfare through the White Mountain National Forest.

BY BUS Concord Trailways (tel. 603/228–3523 or 800/639–3317 in NH).

REST STOPS North Conway at Routes 16 and 302 has a rest area with rest rooms, picnic facilities, and public phones. The visitors' center at Lincoln, I–93, Exit 32, has rest rooms.

GUIDED TOURS Otter Brook Wildlife Programs (Intervale, tel. 603/356–5045) offers naturalist-led walks in the area to groups of any size. Raven Interpretive Wildlife Programs (Conway, tel. 603/447–5796) provides guides who lead bird- and mammal-watching expeditions.

EXPLORING

The White Mountains region is compact enough geographically so that you can drive in a single morning from the discount shopping malls of North Conway to the rugged scenery of the presidential range, the spine of mountains running north from Mt. Jackson to Mt. Madison.

North Conway has a high concentration of hotels, motels, and restaurants, along with discount outlets. Here the Conway Scenic Railroad (Main St., tel. 603/356–5251) operates from May to October (admission charged). A steam engine pulls antique coaches, 11 miles in one hour, past forests, cornfields, and rocky rivers. From North Conway, take Route 16/302 north to Glen. If you want to drive up Mt. Washington, continue on Route 16 to Glen House, 16 miles north of Glen.

Mt. Washington, at 6,288 feet the highest mountain in the northeastern United States, has severe weather conditions practically year-round. The two-hour drive up the mountain should be taken with caution, as hairpin turns and sharp drop-offs without guardrails are common; you should use low gear all the way. At the top, the Sherman Adams Summit Building has a museum and glassed-in viewing area. Hired drivers are available at Glen House to take you on a tour up the mountain. You can also hike it or take the Cog Railway at Bretton Woods (*see below*). *Road: Tel. 603/466–3988. Open mid-May–mid-Oct., daily. Toll charged on road.*

Crawford Notch State Park (tel. 603/374–2272), west of Glen past Bartlett on Route 302, is a good place for a picnic and a hike along the well-trodden trails to Arethusa Falls or Silver and Flume cascades. A more strenuous hike is the 1.4-mile trail up Mt. Willard. The trail departs from the Crawford Notch Depot information center on the west side of Route 302.

Bretton Woods, north of the park on Route 302, is a secluded village that was a preferred retreat of wealthy vacationers at the turn of the century who stayed at the sumptuous Mt. Washington Hotel, which still welcomes guests today. The view of the presidential range towering over the immense white structure is memorable.

The Mt. Washington Cog Railway is a steam-powered, mountain-climbing railway, operating since 1869. To reach the railway from Bretton Woods, take the marked road 6 miles northeast from Route 302. Don't attempt the 3½-hour round-trip in poor weather. *Rte. 302, Bretton Woods, tel. 603/846–5404 or 800/922–8825, ext. 6, outside NH. Operates May–early Nov., daily, weather permitting. Admission charged. Reservations advised.*

Continue west on Route 302, then pick up Route 3 after Twin Mountain and drive southwest toward Franconia Notch. A short detour north on Route 18 takes you to the town of Franconia, and if you head south for a few miles on Route 116, you'll see signs for Robert Frost's home.

The Frost Place, the poet's 1915 home, contains memorabilia and signed editions of his books. *Ridge Rd., Franconia, tel. 603/823–5510. Open July and Aug., Wed.–Mon.; June, weekends; call for hours during fall foliage season. Admission charged.*

Return to Route 3 and drive south into Franconia Notch. From Route 3 you can pick up the **Franconia Notch State Parkway,** an 8-mile stretch of I–93 that cuts through this popular scenic area.

Echo Lake, off Exit 3 of the parkway, offers a pleasant sandy beach and swimming, fishing, and boating. Visitors have a view of Mt. Lafayette and nearby Cannon Mountain.

The Cannon Mountain Aerial Tramway, off Exit 2, lifts you 2,022 feet in five minutes to the 4,200-foot summit of the mountain. *Franconia Notch State Park, tel. 603/823–5563. Open mid-May–mid-Oct., daily; mid-Oct.–mid-May, weekends weather permitting. Admission charged.*

Old Man of the Mountains (Great Stone Face), the most famous attraction in the Franconia Notch area, lies about ½ mile south of the Cannon Mountain tramway. This natural granite formation in the side of Profile Mountain resembles a flinty-faced old gentleman; it has been immortalized in writings of Nathaniel Hawthorne and Daniel Webster.

The Flume is located off Exit 1 at the southern end of Franconia Notch State Park, south of the Cannon Mountain tramway. At the site of this 800-foot-long natural chasm at the base of Mt. Liberty, visitors make their way along a series of boardwalks and stairways, and they get a view of **Avalanche Falls.** The visitor center offers a historic exhibit about the area and a 20-minute film that serves as an introduction to all the major sights in Franconia Notch State Park. The center also marks the beginning of a 9-mile paved bicycle path through the park that is suitable for walking. *Tel. 603/823–5563 or 603/745–8391. Open mid-May–mid-Oct., daily. Admission charged to the Flume.*

The Kancamagus Highway, a 34-mile stretch interrupted by only one cutoff at Bear Notch Road, takes you through some of the east's most magnificent mountain scenery. It is the state's most popular (and crowded) route for viewing the fall foliage. The road takes you by Loon Mountain and follows the Hancock branch of the Pemigewasset River and the Swift River. About halfway through the drive, keep an eye out for the parking lot and picnic area at Sabbaday Falls. A ½-mile trail takes you to the multilevel cascade that plunges through two potholes and a flume. A few miles east you'll find the beginning of the self-guided Rail and River trail at the Passaconaway Information Center near the Bear Notch Road. About 5 miles farther east, the moderately demanding 2.8-mile Boulder

Loop trail begins opposite the Blackberry Crossing campground. The ledges offer good views of Mt. Chocorua and the Swift River Valley. The Kancamagus Highway ends at Route 16 in Conway.

THE NATURAL WORLD The presidential range contains the largest alpine area in the eastern United States. The exposed summits are ecologically fragile, tundralike areas that are home to many endangered plant species, such as dwarf cinquefoil, alpine avens, and cloudberry. Keep a lookout for moose in marshy, boggy areas along the eastern section of the Kancamagus Highway. Sharp-sighted bird-watchers may also spot bald eagles and peregrine falcons in the region.

HOTELS AND INNS

Resorts, motels, country inns, and bed-and-breakfasts are thick as snowflakes; only during foliage season should you hesitate to travel without reservations. (Getting into a special place requires advance calling in any season.) Reservation Service of the Country Inns in the White Mountains (tel. 603/356–9460 or 800/526–1300) will help you find a room. Price categories for double occupancy, excluding 8% tax, are *Expensive*, $100–$130; *Moderate*, $70–$100; and *Inexpensive*, under $70.

BARTLETT **Notchland Inn.** Overlooking the Saco River valley at the entrance to Crawford Notch, this unique, wood-paneled mansion dating from the 19th century features bedrooms furnished with armoires, wing chairs, afghans, and working fireplaces. *Rte. 302, Hart's Location, 03812, tel. 603/374–6131 or 800/866–6131. 9 rooms, 2 suites. Full breakfast included, dining room, pool, hot tub, hiking, cross-country ski trails. AE, MC, V. Moderate.*

BETHLEHEM **The Bells.** This pagoda-shaped bed-and-breakfast filled with family heirlooms and choice bits from the owners' antiques shop offers good value on a quiet residential side street. *Strawberry Hill St., 03574, tel. 603/869–2647. 4 rooms with bath.*

Full breakfast included. MC, V. Inexpensive– Moderate.

CONWAY **Tanglewood Motel & Cottages.** You can swim or fish in a mountain stream just outside the door of this neat, family-operated, one-floor motel, with rooms in a variety of sizes (some sleep up to six) and two-person cottages with fully equipped kitchens. *Rte. 16, 03818, tel. 603/447–5932. 13 rooms with bath. AE, MC, V. Inexpensive– Moderate.*

EAST MADISON **Purity Spring Resort.** Once a farm and sawmill situated on a private lake, Purity Spring has been run for a century as a four-season, American-plan resort. Whether you choose rooms in the main inn, adjacent lodge, or separate cottages, the decor is sturdy, old-fashioned New England. Skiers note: the King Pine Ski Area is on the property. *Rte. 153, 03849, tel. 603/367–8896 or 800/367–8897. 45 rooms, 35 with bath. Restaurant, private lake, tennis courts, volleyball. MC, V. Moderate.*

FRANCONIA **Franconia Inn.** Many of the rooms have canopy beds at this friendly white-clapboard bed-and-breakfast inn on 117 scenic acres, with access to various sports. *Easton Rd., 03580, tel. 603/823–5542 or 800/473–5299. 31 rooms, 3 suites. Full breakfast included, restaurant, pool, tennis court, cross-country skiing, riding stable, glider field. AE, MC, V. Moderate.*

GLEN **Covered Bridge House.** The second-floor bedrooms at this conveniently located inn—complete with its own authentic 1851 covered bridge—have lace curtains, period furniture, country-style accessories, and a selection of books for rainy-day relaxation. *Box 358, Rte. 302, 03838, tel. 603/383–9109 or 800/232–9109. 5 rooms. Full breakfast included, gift shop, private river beach. AE, MC, V. Inexpensive– Moderate.*

JACKSON **Inn at Thorn Hill.** This casually elegant, romantic hideaway with a main house (designed by Stanford White), a carriage house, and three cottages is convenient to shops, galleries, and sports; it's better suited to couples than families. *Thorn Hill*

Rd., 03846, tel. 603/383–4242 or 800/289–8990. 13 double rooms, 2 suites, 3 cottages. Full breakfast included, restaurant, pub, pool, cross-country ski trails. AE, MC, V. Moderate–Expensive.

■ **NORTH CONWAY** ■ **1785 Inn.** This striking white Colonial inn with blue trim offers mountain views, rooms with country-style furnishings and varied Colonial-to-Victorian antiques, and a prize-winning restaurant. *Box 1785, Rte. 16, 03860, tel. 603/356–9025 or 800/421–1785. 17 rooms, 12 with bath; 1 suite. Full breakfast included, restaurant, room service, pool, cross-country ski trails, tennis courts. AE, D, DC, MC, V. Moderate–Expensive.*

■ **SNOWVILLE** ■ **Snowvillage Inn.** Guest rooms furnished with four-posters and working fireplaces, and conservationist innkeepers who lead guided mountain walks with fine lunches, make this complex of three converted buildings an outstanding choice. *Box A-50, Snowville 03849, tel. 603/447–2818. 18 rooms with bath. Restaurant, cross-country trails, tennis. AE, MC, V. Choice of bed-and-breakfast or breakfast and dinner. Moderate–Expensive.*

MOTELS

■ **MODERATE** ■ **Briarcliff Motel** (North Conway 03860, tel. 603/356–5584 or 800/338–4291). 29 rooms; pool. **Covered Bridge Motor Lodge** (Box V, Jackson 03846, tel. 603/383–9151 or 800/634–2911). 32 rooms; pool, tennis courts, fishing. **The Lodge at Jackson Village** (Box 593, Jackson Village 03846, tel. 603/383–0999 or 800/233–5634). 32 rooms; pool, tennis courts, room refrigerators. **Swiss Chalets Motel** (RR 1, Box 91, Intervale 03845, tel. 603/356–2232 or 800/831–2727). 36 rooms; pool, cross-country trails.

■ **INEXPENSIVE** ■ **School House Motel** (Box 368, North Conway 03860, tel. 603/356–6829 or 800/638–6050). 25 rooms; pool. **Villager Motel** (Box 427, Barlett 03812, tel. 603/374–2742 or 800/334–6988). 18 rooms; pool, rooms available with kitchenettes and fireplaces. **The Will's Inn** (Box 359, Barlett

03812, tel. 603/383–6757 or 800/233–6780). 23 rooms; 9 rooms with kitchenettes.

CAMPGROUNDS

The New Hampshire Campground Owners Association (Box 320, Twin Mountain 03595, tel. 603/846–5511) will send a list of all private, state, and national-forest campgrounds.

The Appalachian Mountain Club runs eight mountain huts, where you can experience the wilderness with a roof over your head and meals prepared for you. The huts vary in size, with most of them sleeping about 40 people, mostly in bunk rooms. All have superb settings alongside the trails of the White Mountain National Forest; you can hike from one hut to the next. *Appalachian Mountain Club, Box 298, Gorham 03581, tel. 603/466–2727. Reservations recommended. MC, V.*

White Mountain National Forest (Box 638, Laconia 03247, tel. 603/528–8721) has 23 roadside campgrounds on a 14-day-limit basis. Two of the best campgrounds run by the forest service are:

Dolly Copp. In Pinkham North, this large area (6 mi south of Gorham and near Mt. Washington) offers a range of sites from wooded areas to campsites in an open field; some sites are located on the Peabody River. *White Mountain National Forest, Androscoggin Ranger District, 80 Glen Rd., Gorham 03581, tel. 603/466–2713. 176 tent and RV sites, no hookups, flush toilets, picnic tables and barbecue areas. Reservations for July and Aug. through MISTIX, tel. 800/283–CAMP. MC, V (accepted by MISTIX only).*

Jigger Johnson. Located near the middle of the Kancamagus Highway, this quiet campground is an isolated, wooded spot with some sites on the Swift River. *White Mountain National Forest, Saco Ranger District, RFD 1, Box 94, Conway 03818, tel. 603/447–5448. 75 RV and tent sites, no hookups, bathrooms, picnic tables and barbecue areas. No reservations.*

DINING

Dining opportunities in the White Mountains range from country inns serving fine dinners in hushed, candlelit dining rooms to simple, easygoing family restaurants specializing in generous portions and cheerful service; diners with special dietary demands will find most establishments sympathetic to their needs. Visitors should be aware that many inns in the area have their own restaurants that are open to nonguests. Only the very special dining rooms require reservations. Price categories per person, excluding 8% tax, service, and drinks, are *Moderate*, $15–$25, and *Inexpensive*, under $15.

CONWAY **Darby Field Inn.** At this delightful blue-clapboard mountain retreat, visitors can dine by candlelight as they sample the eclectic menu, featuring American and Continental cuisines, with attention paid to those seeking low-fat and vegetarian entrées. *Bald Hill, tel. 603/447–2181. AE, MC, V. Moderate.*

FRANCONIA **Franconia Inn.** The two brothers who own the Franconia Inn devote themselves to pleasing a variety of customers, from families with young children to health-conscious couples who dine on simply prepared veal and chicken dishes. *Easton Rd., tel. 603/823–5542. Reservations advised. AE, MC, V. Moderate.*

GLEN **The Bernerhof.** The dining room with its rubbed wood and flowers has an alpine ambience, and the cooking is primarily classic French, with veal dishes a specialty. *Rte. 302, tel. 603/383–4411. AE, MC, V. Moderate.*

Margaritaville. If you need a break from traditional New England cuisine, you'll find superbly prepared, authentic Mexican food at this appropriately named restaurant, presided over by five friendly sisters. *Rte. 302, tel. 603/383–6556. No credit cards. Inexpensive.*

NORTH CONWAY **The Scottish Lion.** You can sample such American-Scottish specialties as hot oatcakes in the cozy dining room of this part bed-and-breakfast inn and part tartan-pa-

pered pub, both overlooking meadows and mountains. *Rte. 16, tel. 603/356–6381. AE, DC, MC, V. Moderate.*

SNOWVILLE **Snowvillage Inn.** The influence of Austria turns up in the decor of the inn's wood-paneled, mountain-view dining room and in the single-entrée dinners, and the kitchen staff happily accommodates diners who request low-cholesterol or vegetarian meals. *Stuart Rd., tel. 603/447–2818. Reservations required. AE, MC, V. Moderate.*

SHOPPING

Custom-made hiking boots are the pride of the Mt. Washington Valley, but the area is also known for good family sportswear, especially ski clothes. North Conway has become a shopping mecca for its dense concentration of designer and factory outlets, but the town also offers less frantic specialty stores along Route 16/302, known locally as Main Street.

FACTORY OUTLETS AND MALLS Mt. Washington Valley Outlet Association (Box 2264, Conway, tel. 603/447–5295) answers questions about the more than 90 outlets in Mt. Washington Valley. On Route 16 in North Conway, look for names like Anne Klein, Dansk, L. L. Bean, Corning, Reebok, and Ralph Lauren. The Depot Factory Outlet Stores (Rte. 112, Lincoln) stock predominantly factory seconds. Millfront Marketplace, Mill at Loon Mountain (tel. 603/745–2245) is a clutch of specialty stores at the junction of I–93 and the Kancamagus Highway.

OUTDOOR ACTIVITIES

CANOEING White-water runs on the Swift River are fast and intricate. Contact Saco Bound-Downeast River Trips (Box 119, Center Conway 03812, tel. 603/447–3801), who offer canoe and kayak trips and white-water rafting on five rivers, as well as sales and rentals.

FISHING For serious trout and salmon fishing, try the Connecticut lakes, though any clear stream in the White Mountains will do.

Many are stocked, and there are 650 miles of them in the national forest alone. Some 45 lakes and ponds contain trout and bass.

■ HIKING ■ The Appalachian Trail runs across the state and is a popular route for backpackers. Short hikes in Franconia Notch State Park include Artist's Bluff, Lonesome Lake, and the Basin-Cascades Trail. Off the Kancamagus Highway, try the Boulder Loop or Greely Ponds trail or the more challenging Champney Falls and Piper trails to the summit of Mt. Chocorua. Sanguinari Ridge Trail in Dixville Notch is also a good, fairly easy hike. For further information about hiking, contact the Appalachian Mountain Club (Box 298, Pinkham Notch, Gorham 03581, tel. 603/466–2725), White Mountain National Forest (U.S. Forest Service, Box 638, Laconia 03246, tel. 603/524–6450 or 603/528–8721), and New England Hiking Holidays-White Mountains (Box 1648, North Conway 03860, tel. 603/356–9696 or 800/869–0949).

■ SKIING ■ Attitash (Rte. 302, Barlett 03812, tel. 603/374–2368) has downhill skiing on 22 miles of trails. Black Mountain (Rte. 16B, Jackson 03846, tel. 603/383–4490) has primarily easy to middling terrain on a mountain with a 1,100-foot vertical drop. Bretton Woods (Rte. 302, Bretton Woods 03575, tel. 603/278–5000) offers both downhill skiing on 26 trails and 62 miles of cross-country ski trails. Cannon Mountain (Franconia Notch State Park, Franconia 03580, tel. 603/823–5563) is one of the oldest New England ski areas and still one of the more challenging, with a 2,150-foot vertical drop. Loon Mountain (Kancamagus Hwy., Lincoln 03251, tel. 603/745–8111) specializes in wide, straight, and consistent intermediate trails, with 22 miles of cross-country trails. Mount Cranmore (Box 1640, North Conway 03860, tel. 603/356–5543) has a range of downhill slopes (mostly for intermediates) and 37 miles of cross-country trails. Wildcat Mountain (Pinkham Notch, Rte. 16, Jackson 03846, tel. 603/466–3326) is known for tough expert trails.

Williamsburg
Virginia

O f all our surviving Colonial American towns, none is more colorful or historic than Williamsburg, the capital of Virginia in the days of Washington, Jefferson, and Patrick Henry. It sits between the James and the York rivers, astride the busy Virginia Peninsula, preserving the exciting pace of 18th-century America.

The heart of Williamsburg is the mile-long Historic Area that the late John D. Rockefeller, Jr., quietly began buying up in 1926, now restored to its pre-Revolutionary luster. At one end is the College of William and Mary, founded in 1693, and at the other stands the Capitol, seat of the royal governor until 1776. Throughout the town are dozens of historic sites—Colonial homes, crafts shops, and taverns like the Raleigh, where Washington and fellow legislators talked revolt over ale and chicken pie.

Today, trained craftspeople make rifles and wigs and wagon wheels before your eyes. Costumed interpreters bring the Capitol and the Governor's Palace to life, and up and down Duke of Gloucester Street roll horse-drawn carriages as the bell clangs in Bruton Church's tower. Against the Colonial backdrop, reconstructed taverns serve 18th-century food, actors and musicians perform, and militia drills draw crowds to the village greens. Harpsichord concerts are held in the Governor's Palace, folk art is exhibited in the Abby Aldrich Rockefeller Folk Art Center, and 18th-century decorative arts in the DeWitt Wallace Gallery.

A scenic drive, the Colonial Parkway, connects Williamsburg with Jamestown, England's first permanent foothold in the New World, and Yorktown, site of the conclusive battle of the Revolution. Near Williamsburg lie several of the historic James River plantations, well worth a trip.

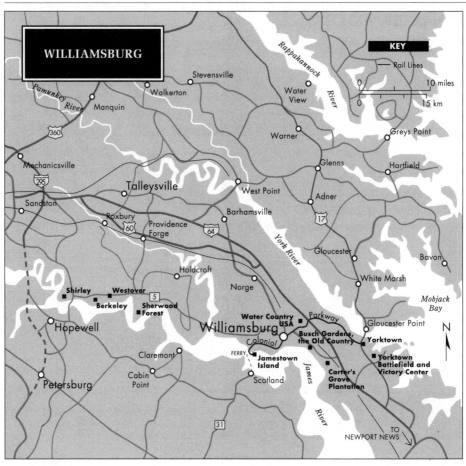

ESSENTIAL INFORMATION

WHEN TO GO Most visitors to Williamsburg come in July and August, when the temperature is frequently in the 90s; spring and fall have better weather and fewer people. From January to the end of March and from mid-September through November the crowds are thinnest; mild winters make for pleasant walking tours. The height of spring bloom comes at the end of April, when Virginia celebrates Historic Garden Week and many old homes are opened to the public. Rains sometimes mar June, but in July and August the sun usually shines. Autumn has special charm, for the scent of hickory smoke from the town's fireplaces hangs over the Historic Area on cold mornings, and dogwoods and maples are brilliantly yellow and red. Many visitors come for Christmas shopping on Merchants Square in town and at the Williamsburg Pottery and discount malls on Richmond Road.

FESTIVALS AND SPECIAL EVENTS **Feb.:** a five-day Antiques Forum. **Apr.:** a four-day Garden Symposium and Virginia Garden Week. **July–Aug.:** family programs abound and fife-and-drum parades march from the Capitol to Market Square. **Labor Day weekend:** Publick Times—children's songs and dances, militia encampments on Palace Green and Market Square, and old-time horse races. **Oct.:** An Occasion for the Arts (street fair with sales of arts and crafts). **Dec.:** The spectacular Grand Illumination, candlelight concerts, caroling, and tree-decoration workshops are some of the many holiday activities.

BARGAINS Frequent free concerts and lectures are held at William and Mary (tel. 804/221–2674), and street theater in the Historic Area takes the form of "character interpreters" dressed as 18th-century citizens who engage visitors in conversation about such "current" events as the infamous stamp tax. Among local wares that are good buys are peanuts from nearby farms, Smithfield and country hams, glassware reproductions from the Jamestown Glasshouse, and reproductions of the salt-glaze and brown-glaze pottery of the early settlers. At Yorktown, the National Park Service's Visitor Center and the battlefields are free. The Jamestown–Scotland Wharf toll ferry ($4 per car) will take you on a beautiful 2^1/$_2$-mile crossing of the James River.

TOURIST OFFICES Contact the Williamsburg Convention and Visitors Bureau (201 Penniman Rd., Williamsburg 23185, tel. 804/253–0192) for hotels; the Visitor Center (tel. 804/220–7659 or 800/HISTORY) for general information and Historic Area hotels. Colonial National Historical Park (tel. 804/898–3400 for Yorktown, and 804/229–1733 for Jamestown).

EMERGENCIES For Williamsburg **police, fire,** and **ambulance**, dial 911. Virginia State Police (tel. 800/582–8350). **Hospital:** Williamsburg Community Hospital (1238 Mount Vernon Ave., tel. 804/253–6000). **Pharmacies** are open Monday–Saturday 9–9 and Sunday 11–6; at other times, call the hospital.

ARRIVING AND DEPARTING

BY PLANE Newport News–Williamsburg International Airport (tel. 804/877–0924) is 20 miles from Williamsburg. Richmond International (tel. 804/226–3052) and Norfolk International (tel. 804/857–3351) are both 50 miles away. All airports are served by taxis and by VIP Limousine Service (tel. 804/220–1616; fax 804/253–1948).

BY CAR Most visitors arrive by car on I–64. Those coming from Richmond may want to take slower-paced Route 5, the John Tyler Highway, past the James River plantations.

BY TRAIN AND BUS Amtrak (tel. 800/USA–RAIL) has train service from Boston, New York, and Washington D.C. Greyhound Lines (468 N. Boundary St., tel. 800/231–2222) connect Williamsburg with all parts of the nation.

GETTING AROUND

Historic Area shuttle buses (free for ticket holders) make nine stops on a constant circuit of the area before returning to the Visitor Center. Williamsburg is best seen on foot and by using these buses, but a car is convenient for visiting outlying sights.

REST STOPS At the Visitor Center; at the ticket center at Duke of Gloucester and Henry streets; behind the Davidson Shop at Duke of Gloucester and Botetourt streets; between the Governor's Palace and the Brush-Everard House on Palace Green; in the Governor's Palace courtyard; between the Capitol and Waller Street; on Francis Street near the Magazine; at the Publick Hospital, DeWitt Wallace Gallery of Decorative Arts, Abby Aldrich Rockefeller Folk Art Center, and Bassett Hall Visitor Center on Francis Street.

GUIDED TOURS Williamsburg Limousines, Inc. (tel. 804/877–0279) conducts guided tours to Jamestown and Yorktown. It also runs shuttle buses from Williamsburg hotels and motels daily to Jamestown, Yorktown, Busch Gardens, and Carter's Grove plantation. Historic Air Tours (tel. 804/253–8185) runs flights over the Colonial settlements, James River plantations, and historic battlefields.

EXPLORING

Colonial Williamsburg. People usually go first to the **Visitor Center,** close to I–64, to buy tour passes, make dinner and entertainment reservations, and watch *The Patriot* orientation film (35 minutes). One-day, one-week, and one-year passes cost $24–$29; Bassett Hall admission ($8) is sold separately. Get a copy of the weekly "Visitors Companion," which lists programs and has a good map. To do the town justice, allow at least three days.

Duke of Gloucester Street, the spine of the pedestrian area, extends from the **Wren Building** at William and Mary to the **Capitol.** Both are exquisite buildings, and the Capitol will orient you historically. In between are the **Governor's Palace, Bruton Parish Church,** private houses and gardens, taverns of the period, and the functioning workshops of a wig maker, printer, tailor, wheelwright, silversmith, milliner, and the like. Here you can also see wonderful collections of folk art (at the Abby Aldrich Rockefeller Center) and decorative arts (at the DeWitt Wallace Gallery) as well as the Rockefellers' personal treasures, on view at Bassett Hall.

A day trip west of town along Route 5 will take you to four of the famous James River plantations. If your time is limited, go to Berkeley or Shirley.

Jamestown Island. The **Visitor Center** (tel. 804/229–1733) is a National Park Service museum that tells Jamestown's history and the story of John Smith, Pocahontas, and Chief Powhatan in diorama and archaeological exhibits. Nearby is the reconstructed Glasshouse of 1608, where costumed artisans blow glass. Admission to both is included in the park entrance fee ($5 per car). **Jamestown Settlement** (tel. 804/229–1607), adjoining Jamestown Island, is a 20-acre state park with full-scale replicas of the Jamestown settlers' three ships, *Susan Constant, Godspeed,* and *Discovery;* a reconstruction of a Powhatan Indian village and of the original triangular James Fort; and an indoor museum. *Glasshouse Point, open daily except Christmas and New Year's Day. Admission charged.*

Yorktown. The **Visitor Center Museum** (tel. 804/898–3400), near the actual 1781 siege lines, depicts on a relief map the siege that forced the British to surrender; it also depicts the Battle of the Capes, in which the French fleet halted British rescue ships. At the **Nelson House** in summer, a historical drama on the life of Thomas Nelson takes place every half hour. The **Yorktown Victory Center,** a state-run museum, focuses on events in the Revolution leading to the siege, with a film, replicas of an encampment and an 18th-century farm site, and an audio exhibit starring six talking plaster figures. *Tel. 804/887–1776. Open daily except Christmas and New Year's. Admission free to Visitor Center; admission charged to Victory Center.*

Busch Gardens. An open-air theme park celebrates the popular attractions of Great Britain, France, Germany, and Italy, with amusement-park rides, entertainments and shows, and hearty European food. *3 mi east of town, tel. 804/253–3360. Open mid-May–Labor Day, daily; other times, weekends; closed Nov.–Mar. Admission charged.*

Carter's Grove. At the Burwell estate, 5 miles east of town, the house is exhibited as restored in the 1930s by its last private owners. The grounds contain the **Winthrop Rockefeller Archaeological Museum** and remains of Wolstenholme Town, wiped out by Indians in 1622. *Rte. 60 at Grove, tel. 804/229–1000. Open mid-Mar.–Dec., daily. Admission charged.*

Shirley. The Colonial home of the Hill and Carter families was visited in the Civil War by Robert E. Lee, whose mother, Anne Carter Lee, lived here. *Rte. 5, in Charles City County, tel. 804/829–5121. Open daily, except Christmas. Admission charged.*

Berkeley. This plantation, settled in early Jamestown days, was later owned by the Harrisons. Benjamin Harrison V, who built much of the present house, signed the Declaration of Independence, served as governor, and fathered President William Henry Harrison. *Rte. 5, Charles City County, tel. 804/829–6018. Open daily except Christmas. Admission charged.*

Sherwood Forest. When John Tyler retired from the presidency in 1845, he enlarged this farmhouse for himself and his new wife and named it for Robin Hood's hideaway. *Rte. 5, Charles City County, tel. 804/829–5377. Open daily except Christmas and New Year's Day. Admission charged.*

Westover. William Byrd II, founder of Richmond, urbane scholar, and man of the world, built this mansion to be the seat of the Byrd dynasty. *Rte. 5, Charles City County, tel. 804/829–2882. Grounds and garden only; open daily except Christmas and New Year's Day. Admission charged.*

Mariner's Museum. Thirty miles east of town is a maritime park created in 1931, whose galleries are crammed with ship models, paintings, historic vessels, and artifacts of the seven seas. *Warwick Blvd. and J. Clyde Morris Blvd., Newport News, tel. 804/595–0368. Open daily except Christmas. Admission charged.*

Water Country USA. Although you can't swim in the huge wave pool, a dozen aquatic rides will get you delightfully wet. *Rte. 199 east of town, tel. 804/229–9300. Admission charged. Open Memorial Day–Labor Day, daily; late May and early Sept., weekends.*

THE NATURAL WORLD Williamsburg sits in flat tidewater farmland crisscrossed by creeks and punctuated by stands of tall pines. The town is a haven for songbirds, many resisting the urge to migrate because of the year-round bird-feeding. Livestock is kept in town pastures, as was done in early times, and visitors are greeted by the sight of browsing horses and dray oxen. Carp swim in the Governor's Palace pond, and adjoining the Golden Horseshoe Golf Course is another pond alive year-round with a flock of mallards. Jamestown Island (admission $5 per car), a federal game preserve inhabited by deer, possum, raccoon, rabbits, squirrels, and songbirds, is circuited by a 5-mile nature trail. In the early morning, bird-watchers stand with binoculars along the James, scanning the scene for the abundant wildlife.

HOTELS AND INNS

The most unique and convenient hostelries—the Williamsburg Inn, the Williamsburg Lodge, Woodlands, and the Governor's Inn—are run by Colonial Williamsburg (tel. 804/229–1000 or 800/HISTORY). Bed-and-breakfasts and motels outside the area are less expensive but have less Colonial atmosphere; you'll get even lower prices in Yorktown and Newport News. Price categories for double occupancy, without the 8¹/₂% sales tax, are *Expensive*, $95 and up; *Moderate*, $60–$95; and *Inexpensive*, under $60.

EXPENSIVE **Williamsburg Inn.** This prestigious inn adjacent to the Historic Area is decorated in the elegant Regency style and is known for its impeccable service. *Francis St., 23185, tel. 804/229–1000, fax 804/220–7798. 120 rooms. Dining room, bar, health club with indoor pool, outdoor pool, golf course. AE, MC, V.*

Williamsburg Hospitality House. This convenient, modern hotel within walking distance of the Historic Area has quiet service and sumptuous decor and offers off-street parking. *415 Richmond Rd., 23185, tel. 804/229–4020, fax 804/220–1560. 309 rooms. Dining room, bar, heated pool. AE, MC, V.*

Williamsburg Lodge. This well-known Early American–style hotel, part of Colonial Williamsburg's Conference Center, is in the Historic Area. *5 S. England St., 23185, tel. 804/229–1000, fax 804/220–7797. 315 rooms. Dining room, bar, exercise club with indoor pool, outdoor pool, bike rentals, golf course. AE, MC, V.*

MODERATE **Applewood Colonial Bed and Breakfast.** This pleasant brick house with Colonial decor, canopy beds, and an apple theme is a fine place for families, within walking distance of the Historic Area. *605 Richmond Rd., 23185, tel. 800/899–2753. 4 rooms. Continental breakfast and afternoon tea included. No credit cards.*

Heritage Inn. This charming and comfortable inn 1 mile from the Historic Area is a three-story building built in the mid-60s, decorated inside and out in true colonial style. *1324 Richmond Rd., 23185, tel. 804/229–6220 or 800/782–3800. 54 rooms. Restaurant, pool with patio. AE, DC, MC, V.*

Liberty Rose Bed and Breakfast. This pleasant clapboard-and-brick suburban house on wooded grounds has eclectic, romantic decor that combines Victorian with 18th-century antiques and reproductions. *1022 Jamestown Rd., 23185, tel. 804/253–1260. 4 rooms. Full breakfast included. MC, V.*

Williamsburg Woodlands. At this spacious facility adjoining the Visitor Center, some suites accommodate up to eight. Guests dine at the adjacent Woodlands Grill or the Cascades Restaurant. *102 Visitor Center Dr., tel. 804/220–5474, fax 804/220–7788. 315 rooms. 3 outdoor pools, picnic area, fitness trail, miniature golf. AE, MC, V.*

INEXPENSIVE–MODERATE **War Hill Inn.** This 1960s colonial, secluded amid pastures and orchards two miles from town, is full of family things and Colonial reproductions. *4560 Long Hill Rd., 23185, tel. 804/565–0248. 5 rooms, 2 sleep 4. Full breakfast included. AE, MC, V.*

MOTELS

MODERATE **Budget Host-Governor Spottswood** (1508 Richmond Rd., 23185, tel. 800/368–1244 or 800/572–4567 in VA). 80 rooms; pool, playground, coffee in rooms, cable TV. **Carolyn Motor Court** (1446 Richmond Rd., 23185, tel. 800/446–8930; fax 804/253–1372). 65 rooms; café, pool, cable TV. **Governor's Inn** (506 N. Henry St., 23185, tel. 804/220–7379; fax 804/220–7788). 200 rooms; free bus to Historic Area and Cascades restaurant; pool, Continental breakfast included, pets allowed. **Holiday Inn Express** (119 Bypass Rd., 23185, tel. 804/253–1663; fax 804/220–9117). 132 rooms; pool, Continental breakfast included, cable TV.

INEXPENSIVE **HoJo Inn** (824 Capitol Landing Rd., 23185, tel. 804/229–4933, 800/446–1041 or 800/336–6126 in VA). 183 rooms; pool, cable TV. **Quality Inn–Lord Paget** (901 Capitol Landing Rd., tel. 804/229–4444 or 800/537–2438; fax 804/220–0366). 95 rooms; café, pool, coin laundry, cable TV, putting green, fishing lake. **Westpark Hotel** (1600 Richmond Rd., 23185, tel. 804/229–1134; fax 804/229–1134). 181 rooms; restaurant, bar, indoor pool, video games, bellhops, valet service, cable TV.

CAMPGROUNDS

Most area campgrounds (around Jamestown and along I–64, at least 5 miles from Williamsburg) are open March–mid-November. Advance reservations for June–August are needed at all of them. Contact the Visitors Bureau (tel. 800/368–6511) for information.

First Settler's Campground of Williamsburg. This well-placed facility adjoins Powhatan Creek. *1890 Jamestown Rd., 23185, tel. 804/229–4900. 142 RV sites, full and partial hookups ($21–$25); 54 tent sites ($17 and $19), showers, bathrooms, laundry, swimming pool, rental boats, archery, miniature golf. AE, MC, V.*

Williamsburg KOA Kampground. This camp near a lake provides free van service to Williamsburg and discount tickets to the attractions. *Exit 55 from Rte. 646 at Lightfoot, 23188, tel. 804/565–2907 or 800/635–2717. 12 cabins that sleep 4 ($38), 65 RV sites, full and partial hookups ($24–$26), 75 tent sites ($19), showers, bathrooms, laundry, solar heated pool, lake fishing. MC, V.*

DINING

Chesapeake Bay yields seafood in abundance for the restaurants of Williamsburg. The beloved blue crab appears au gratin, in crab cakes, crab imperial, and crab ravigote. Oysters are served in stew, scalloped, and fried, and the delicate shad roe, caught fresh in March and April, is served with new potatoes and fresh asparagus. Traditional tidewater cooking shows up in the Smithfield ham, kale, turnip greens, and hot breads served in a few restaurants, and you can also find French, Chinese, Vietnamese, Italian, and Cajun cuisines.

At the Colonial Taverns, four authentic 18th-century eating places in the Historic Area, visitors dine in the atmosphere of Colonial times, with costumed waiters, and oversize napkins and cutlery. The fare is hearty early American and differs in each tavern. All are decorated in Colonial style; all offer outdoor dining and accept AE, MC, and V. Price categories per person, not including 8¹/₂% tax, service, and drinks, are *Moderate,* $15–$25, and *Inexpensive,* under $15.

MODERATE Colonial Taverns: **Christiana Campbell's** (Waller St., near Capitol, tel. 804/229-2141) features Virginia fish, crab, and oysters. **Chowning's** (Duke of Gloucester St. at Queen St., tel. 804/229–2141) specializes in Brunswick stew, duckling, and prime rib. **King's Arms** (Duke of Gloucester St., across from Raleigh Tavern, tel. 804/229–2141) offers game pie, peanut soup, Virginia ham. **Shields** (Duke of Gloucester St., near Capitol, tel. 804/229–2141) serves spit-roasted chicken and New York strip steak.

Golden Horseshoe Clubhouse Grill. Good, simple lunches and dinners are served to golfers and others on the second floor of a luxurious white-brick Georgian clubhouse with a porch that overlooks a pond. *S. England St., tel. 804/220–7696. AE, MC, V.*

Nick's Seafood Pavilion. This famous Mediterranean-style eatery in Yorktown offers fresh seafood and Greek specialties. Try their bluefish, flounder, spot (a delicate ocean fish), or crabmeat. *Water St., Rte. 238 at south end of Yorktown Bridge, tel. 804/887–5269. AE, MC, V.*

The Trellis. This California-style restaurant serves an unusual array of entrées (specializing in Chesapeake seafood) in the spacious, plant-filled restaurant or outdoors in good weather. *Merchants Sq., tel. 804/229–8610. AE, MC, V.*

INEXPENSIVE **Back Fin Seafood Restaurant.** This unpretentious family-type restaurant with booths and tables serves good fresh fish, clams, and chicken, to a nautical theme, with fishnets and oars on the walls. *1193 Jamestown Rd., tel. 804/220–2249. MC, V.*

Cap'n Bill's Fresh Seafood Market and Restaurant. This hard-to-find hideout is a favorite with locals. The homespun menu is familiar—fish, fish, and fish, all superbly prepared. *4391-A Ironbound Rd., tel. 804/220–1382. AE, MC, V. Closed Sun.*

Chickahominy House. Home-style southern breakfasts (Virginia ham, eggs, hominy grits) and Miss Melinda's Lunch (Brunswick stew, ham biscuits, and homemade pie) are served amid antique furnishings, which are for sale. *1211 Jamestown Rd., tel. 804/229–4689. V.*

Morrison's Cafeteria. This southern chain serves such varied daily fare as Florida shrimp, roast beef, spoon bread, fried okra, and sweet-potato pie, in a large, airy room with greenery and colorful Colonial decor. *1851 Richmond Rd., tel. 804/253–0292. AE, MC, V.*

Polo Club Restaurant and Tavern. Polo equipment decorates this stylish bistro, specializing in fresh fish, steaks, oversize burgers, and unusual sandwiches. *Colony Square Shopping Center on Jamestown Rd., tel. 804/229–1122. MC, V.*

SHOPPING

Bargain-hunters flock to the Williamsburg Pottery (tel. 804/564–3326), 4 miles west on Richmond Road. In a dozen warehouses are stacks of china, glassware, household goods, clothing, garden furniture, plants, and lots more—most of it at bargain prices. Near the Pottery are countless outlet malls and discount shops. More expensive reproduction 18th-century furnishings are sold at the Craft House at the Williamsburg Inn (tel. 804/220–7749) and at Merchants Square (tel. 804/220–7747).

OUTDOOR ACTIVITIES

BIKING The Historic Area limits auto traffic, thus affording space for pedestrians and bicyclists. Bicycles can be rented at the Williamsburg Lodge on South England Street (tel. 804/229–1000).

CARRIAGE RIDING For a leisurely view, ride through Williamsburg in an 18th-century horse-drawn carriage. Reserved tickets may be purchased on the day of the ride at the Greenhow Lumber store on Duke of Gloucester Street.

GOLF There are good courses in town at the Williamsburg Inn and Lodge (tel. 804/229–1000), at Fords Colony (240 Fords Colony Drive, tel. 804/258–4130), and at nearby Kingsmill Golf Club (100 Golf Club Rd., Kingsmill, tel. 804/253–3906).

HIKING The 5-mile nature trail on Jamestown Island is an ideal place for exercise, with the added possibility of seeing wildlife. At both the Jamestown and Yorktown ends of the Colonial Parkway, turnoffs lead to waterfront recreation areas, where people walk, picnic, or play volleyball. Walking is popular in the Historic Area's pedestrian zone, especially in the early morning.

SWIMMING The nearest surf bathing is at Virginia Beach, 50 miles east on I– 64; many area lodgings have pools.

ENTERTAINMENT

CONCERTS Folk singers, the Fife and Drum Corps, and folklorists perform frequently in the buildings and on the greens of Williamsburg (general information: tel. 804/220–7645). Many wonderful evening concerts and Colonial-style programs take place throughout the Historic Area. Professional and student performers also grace the boards of Phi Beta Kappa Hall (tel. 804/221–2674) at the College of William and Mary. Check the "Visitors Companion" to see what's going on, or call 804/220–7645 for special events.

Wisconsin Dells

Native American legend claims a giant serpent created Wisconsin Dells, one of the most scenic spots along the 400-mile-long Wisconsin River. Scientists say the 15-mile stretch of soaring rock formations was created over thousands of years by glacial waters cutting through soft Cambrian sandstone to a depth of 150 feet. Yet whatever their origin, the majestic dells of the Wisconsin River are one of the state's foremost natural attractions, and one of the Midwest's most popular tourist destinations.

In the 1850s, the community of Kilbourn City grew up at the Dells, and pioneer photographer H. H. Bennett settled here. Bennett's outstanding photographs of the Dells began to draw tourists as early as 1868, and to publicize the geologic novelty of the Dells, Kilbourn City was renamed Wisconsin Dells in 1931.

Once home to rivermen, trappers, lumberjacks, and Native Americans, the area today known as the Dells encompasses the small, adjacent communities of Lake Delton (on the west bank of the river) and Wisconsin Dells (on the east bank). Set some 3 miles apart, north to south, they are connected by Wisconsin Dells Parkway (U.S. 12/Rte. 23), a bustling, four-lane strip teeming with attractions. While the sandstone cliffs and majestic river remain the Dells' highlights, man-made enticements run a close second, and the region is filled with water parks, rides, stage shows, Indian ceremonials, specialty shops, and other amusements. And you'll have no trouble finding your way around—there are signs *everywhere*.

ESSENTIAL INFORMATION

WHEN TO GO While Wisconsin Dells holds the state's record-high temperature of 114°, the average temperature during peak tourist

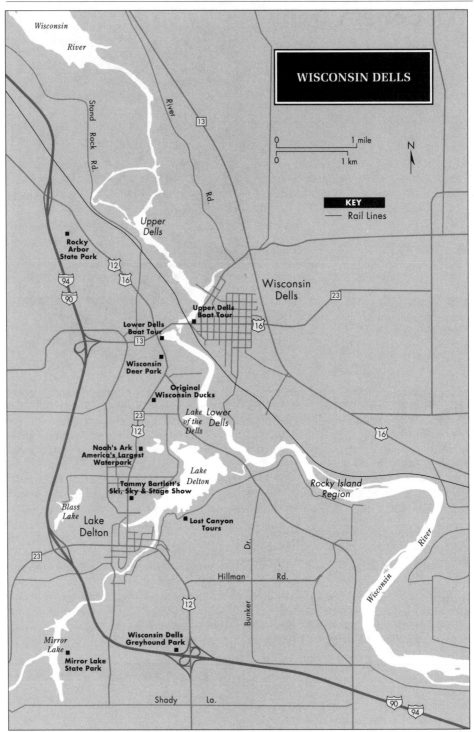

season (June–August) is just under 70°, and nights are pleasantly cool. The region is especially lovely from late September to mid-October, when the weather cools down, the foliage hits its peak of color, and the crowds of youngsters that throng the Dells' children-oriented attractions have returned to school. During the cold, snowy season (Nov.–Mar.), when nearly all attractions are closed, Wisconsin Dells becomes popular with skiers and snowmobilers.

TOURIST OFFICES Wisconsin Dells Visitor & Convention Bureau (701 Superior St., Wisconsin Dells 53965, tel. 608/254–8088 or 800/22–DELLS). Wisconsin Division of Tourism (Box 7606, Madison 53707, tel. 608/266–2161 or 800/432–TRIP).

EMERGENCIES **Police, fire,** and **ambulance:** Dial 911. **Doctors:** Dells Clinic (1310 Broadway, tel. 608/253–1171). **Hospitals:** St. Clair Hospital (707 14th St., Baraboo, tel. 608/356–5561).

ARRIVING AND DEPARTING

BY PLANE Madison's Dane County Regional Airport (tel. 608/246–3380), 45 miles southeast of the Dells (an hour's drive via I–90/94), has daily scheduled flights by major U.S. carriers.

BY CAR I–90/94, traversing the state from west to southeast and skirting the Dells, is the fastest route across southern Wisconsin. U.S. 12, which passes through rolling hills and river valleys as it travels north, is a favorite route with travelers arriving from the south.

BY BUS Greyhound Lines (tel. 800/231–2222) stops regularly in the Dells.

BY TRAIN Amtrak (tel. 608/254–7706 or 800/USA–RAIL) offers twice-daily rail service to the Dells.

GETTING AROUND

BY CAR AND RV You'll need a car for traveling along the strip (Wisconsin Dells Parkway). The major attractions offer ample parking for both cars and RVs. To avoid strip

traffic between Lake Delton and Wisconsin Dells, take I–90/94, using Exit 92 (U.S. 12) to reach Lake Delton and Exit 87 (Rte. 13) to reach Wisconsin Dells.

REST STOPS Public rest rooms can be found adjacent to the Wisconsin Dells Convention and Visitors Bureau (701 Superior St.). Rest rooms and picnic facilities are available at Rocky Arbor State Park (just north of the Dells on U.S. 12) and Mirror Lake State Park (just south of the Dells on Ferndell Road).

EXPLORING

You can "do" the Dells in a day or a week, depending on your pace and interests. A power dam on the Wisconsin River near the Route 13/23 bridge divides the river into the Upper Dells and Lower Dells. A number of tours cover the Dells' natural attractions, and Rocky Arbor State Park (with hiking trails) provides a respite from the crowds. If you're traveling with children, you'll want to spend time at the water parks, miniature golf courses, and the like.

Dells Boat Tours offers a 2½-hour Upper Dells tour (departing from the docks just east of the bridge in Wisconsin Dells), which includes stops to view the fantastic rock formations from up close and to stroll through fern-filled canyons and along nature trails. The one-hour, nonstop Lower Dells tour (leaving from the docks at the west end of the bridge), cruises by the Rocky Islands, caverns, and rock formations. You'll save money if you purchase a combination Upper and Lower Dells boat-tour ticket, but if you take only one boat tour, make it the Upper Dells tour—it's more scenic. *11 Broadway, tel. 608/254–8555. Tours mid-Apr.–Oct., daily. Admission charged.*

Lost Canyon Tours organizes horse-drawn wagon tours of this narrow, mile-long, 80-foot-high sandstone canyon in Lake Delton. In its deepest recesses, the canyon has not seen the sun for more than 50,000 years. Picnic facilities are available. *720 Lost Canyon Rd., tel. 608/253–2781. Tours mid-May–mid-Sept., daily. Admission charged.*

Noah's Ark, along the strip, bills itself as America's largest water park and offers water slides, wave pools, and raft rides, along with go-cart tracks, miniature golf, and a host of other diversions. *Wisconsin Dells Pkwy., 1¹/₂ mi south of the bridge, tel. 608/254–6351. Open Memorial Day–Labor Day, daily. Admission charged.*

Rocky Arbor State Park offers a break from the crowds and hubbub of the Dells. Tucked away among stands of white and Norway pines, this 225-acre park has picnic areas, a children's playground, campsites, a 1-mile, easy walking nature trail, and soaring rock formations dating back thousands of years. *U.S. 12, 1¹/₂ mi north of the Dells, tel. 608/254–2333. Open Memorial Day–Labor Day, daily. Admission charged.*

Tommy Bartlett's Ski, Sky, and Stage Show puts on three shows daily, featuring waterski acts, acrobats, racing speedboats, precision hang gliding, land other family entertainment. A laser light show is enacted at night. *560 Wisconsin Dells Pkwy., tel. 608/254–2525. Open late May–Labor Day, daily. Admission charged.*

Wisconsin Deer Park, on the strip in Wisconsin Dells, is a 28-acre wildlife exhibit in a forest setting. You might spot several varieties of deer, including rare white deer—many of which you can pet and feed—along with elk, buffalo, and other wildlife. *583 Wisconsin Dells Pkwy., tel. 608/253–2041. Open May–mid-Oct., daily. Admission charged.*

Wisconsin Dells Greyhound Racing Park is Wisconsin's first pari-mutuel betting facility. Dog-racing programs are held most evenings, with occasional matinees, and doubleheaders on many weekends. There is both indoor and outdoor seating. A Beginner's Welcome Booth offers help to novice bettors. *Winner's Way, U.S. 12 and I–90/94, Lake Delton, tel. 608/253–3647. Open Jan.–late Nov., daily. Admission charged.*

Original Wisconsin Ducks are not waterfowl but World War II amphibious vehicles that take you on an action-packed, 7¹/₂-mile land-and-water drive through Fern Dell, Red Bird Gorge, and the Lower Dells. *1890 Wisconsin Dells Pkwy., 1 mi south of the bridge, tel. 608/254–8751. Open May–Oct., daily. Admission charged.*

HOTELS AND INNS

Accommodations in the Dells range from bed-and-breakfasts in historic homes to modern resorts, housekeeping cottages, and motels, which frequently offer bargain rates. Off-season rates are generally in effect from mid-September to June 1 or later. Some two-thirds of the region's accommodations are closed November–April. Reservations for peak season (June–Aug.) should be made at least two months in advance, and some facilities require a minimum stay during this time. Price categories for double occupancy, without 10% tax, are *Moderate,* $50–$85, and *Inexpensive,* under $50.

MODERATE **Baker's Sunset Bay Resort.** Rooms in this tranquil, lakeside family resort feature kitchenettes and private decks. Large, modern, housekeeping cottages (some with fireplaces) have screened porches and views of Lake Delton. *921 Canyon Rd., Wisconsin Dells 53965, tel. 608/254–8406. 30 units. Beach, 2 heated pools, free rowboats, pontoon boat rental, fishing, outdoor game area. MC, V.*

Bennett House B & B. Listed on the National Register of Historic Places, this restored 1863 Greek Revival structure was the home of early Dells photographer H. H. Bennett. Filled with antiques, the house has a gazebo and a Victorian garden. *825 Oak St., Wisconsin Dells 53965, tel. 608/254–2500. 3 rooms, 1 with private bath. Full breakfast included, fireplace in country kitchen and dining room, screened porch. No credit cards.*

Monte Carlo Resort Motel. In a quiet, secluded wood only two blocks from the strip, this resort motel on the shores of Lake Delton is popular with families and offers rooms with lake views (some with kitchenettes), apartments, and cottages (some with fireplaces). *350 E. Hiawatha Dr., Wisconsin Dells 53965, tel. 608/254–8761. 40 units. Heated* *outdoor pool, beach, fishing boats, tennis courts, volleyball court, game room, playground, picnic facilities, some rooms with whirlpool baths. MC, V.*

Riviera Motel. The modern, spacious rooms in this motel located near Dells attractions include poolside rooms, family suites with fireplaces, and suites with kitchens. *811 Wisconsin Dells Pkwy., Wisconsin Dells 53965, tel. 608/253–1051 or 800/800–7109. 55 rooms. Indoor and outdoor heated pools, whirlpool, sauna, snowmobile trails, winter plug-ins. AE, MC, V.*

Sherman House B&B. This two-story, 14-room home with a large lawn, an adjacent park, triple bay windows, and views of the river was built by one of Frank Lloyd Wright's associates in 1904 and adheres to the clean, classic style of Wright's Prairie School architecture. *930 River Rd., Wisconsin Dells 53965, tel. 608/253–2721. 4 rooms, 2 with private bath. Continental breakfast and afternoon refreshments included, large veranda. No credit cards.*

Aloha Beach Resort & Suites. Formerly the Tiki Hawaiian Motel, this resort property overlooking Lake Delton has large, modern rooms, including family and efficiency units, as well as luxury suites with whirlpool baths. It's also close to attractions along the strip. *1370 E. Hiawatha Dr., Wisconsin Dells 53965, tel. 608/253–7441. 63 rooms, most with private bath. Heated indoor and outdoor pool, sauna, private beach, rowboats, playground. AE, D, MC, V.*

INEXPENSIVE **Gables Motel.** Centrally located in downtown Wisconsin Dells (one block north of Broadway), this two-story motel is within easy walking distance of the boat docks and downtown attractions, restaurants, and shopping. *822 Oak St., Wisconsin Dells 53965, tel. 608/253–3831. 30 rooms. Heated outdoor pool, winter plug-ins. AE, D, MC, V.*

Indian Trail Motel. Away from the Dells' hustle and bustle, but within pleasant strolling distance of downtown attractions, this quiet, family motel offers large, comfortable

rooms and suites, and the largest motel grounds in town. *1013 E. Broadway, Wisconsin Dells 53965, tel. 608/253–2641. 45 rooms. Heated indoor and outdoor pool, sauna, large playground, nature trail, some rooms with whirlpool bath and microwave ovens. AE, D, MC, V.*

CAMPGROUNDS

Three state parks near Wisconsin Dells offer camping and spectacular scenery: Devil's Lake State Park (near Baraboo), Mirror Lake State Park, and Rocky Arbor State Park. While each park offers a number of campsites on a first-come, first-served basis, you can't count on sites being available during peak travel times; reservations are necessary. Full payment for a campsite must be included with a reservation application, along with the $8 registration fee.

In addition to camping fees, a vehicle sticker is required for admission to all Wisconsin state parks; the daily fee for nonresidents is $6 per car. An annual sticker, which may be used at any Wisconsin state park, costs $28 and is the most economical option if you plan to camp for more than a few days.

Devil's Lake State Park. This 9,000-acre park is one of Wisconsin's oldest. These 500-foot bluffs, believed by scientists to be among the most ancient rock outcroppings in North America, ring a 360-acre lake offering two sand beaches with changing houses, fishing, and boating. Fifteen miles south of the Dells off U.S. 12, the park has 15 miles of hiking trails, several children's play areas, and is home to nearly 900 plant communities and more than 100 species of birds. *S5975 Park Rd., Baraboo 53913, tel. 608/356–8301. 415 RV and tent sites ($10 per night), 121 with electrical hookups ($11.75 per night). Showers, flush toilets, picnic tables and grills, wheelchair-accessible rest rooms and picnic and camping facilities, nature center, interpretive programs. Reservations by mail only.*

Mirror Lake State Park. Just a 10-minute drive from Wisconsin Dells, Mirror Lake is surrounded by sandstone bluffs and is frequented in autumn by migrating waterfowl, including several species of ducks, grebes, and great blue herons. White-tailed deer, rare pileated woodpeckers, mink, and beavers are also seen here. Hikers will find 20 miles of trails. Evening nature programs, guided nature hikes, and lectures by visiting naturalists are offered in summer. The park is ¹/₂ mile south of I–90/94 on U.S. 12 and 1¹/₂ miles west on Ferndell Road. The campgrounds are closed November through March. *E10320 Ferndell Rd., Baraboo 53913, tel. 608/254–2333. 144 RV and tent sites ($10 per night), 27 with electrical hookups ($11.75 per night). No showers, rustic toilets, sand beach, picnic tables and grills, wheelchair-accessible rest rooms and picnic and camping facilities, nature center, interpretive programs. Reservations by mail only.*

Rocky Arbor State Park. One-and-a-half miles north of the Dells on U.S. 12, Rocky Arbor State Park is tucked away among stands of towering white and Norway pines. The small (225 acres) park has soaring rock formations some 500 million years old and a 1-mile self-guided nature trail. Open Memorial Day–Labor Day, the park handles the overflow of campers from Devil's Lake and Mirror Lake. *Rocky Arbor State Park (c/o Mirror Lake State Park, E10320 Ferndell Rd., Baraboo 53913, tel. 608/254–2333). 89 wooded RV and tent sites ($9 per night), 18 with electrical hookups ($10.75 per night). No showers, rustic toilets, picnic tables and grills, wheelchair-accessible rest rooms and picnic and camping facilities. Reservations accepted by telephone June 1–Aug. 30 (tel. 608/254–8001) or by mail. MC, V required for phone reservations.*

DINING

Wisconsin is the dairy state—milk, butter, and cheese are among its most prolific products. In line with this rich character, the cuisine of the Dells tends to be hearty, stick-to-the-ribs fare, but menus usually include such lighter dishes as seafood, chicken, and veal—and salad bars are available in all but the smallest restaurants. Price categories per person, not including 5% tax, service, and drinks, are *Moderate,* $15–$25, and *Inexpensive,* under $15.

MODERATE **Fischer's Supper Club.** Newly remodeled, this longtime Dells favorite has a slick new "Northwoods" look with its dark oak and pine decor. For 45 years, lean steaks, seafood, and chicken dishes have been served in its two modern dining rooms. *441 Wisconsin Dells Pkwy., Lake Delton, tel. 608/253–7531. MC, V.*

House of Embers. Famous for its hickory-smoked ribs, prepared in the restaurant's own smokehouse, this northwoods-style dining spot's menu also includes fresh fish, veal, and flame-broiled steaks. Candlelight dinners are held in the garden gazebo. *935 Wisconsin Dells Pkwy., tel. 608/253–6411. AE, MC, V.*

Ishnala Supper Club. Giant Norway pines grow right through the dining room and cocktail lounge of this elegant restaurant and nightclub set atop a bluff overlooking secluded Mirror Lake. Waiters dressed in Native American costume serve prime rib, grilled steak, lobster, and other seafood dishes. *Ishnala Rd., Lake Delton, tel. 608/253–1771. AE, MC, V.*

Thunder Valley Inn. This rural restaurant serves daily breakfasts that feature fresh-baked breads and cinnamon rolls, and an old-fashioned Friday-night fish fry. Dining on Saturdays is by reservation only. *W15344 Waubeek Rd., tel. 608/254–4145. MC, V.*

INEXPENSIVE **Dells Grill.** This local favorite, with its Formica-and-chrome decor, serves up sandwiches, light plate lunches, and homemade soups and desserts to hungry crowds of locals. *318 Broadway, tel. 608/254–2727. No credit cards.*

Dick's Polish-American Smorgasbord. Ethnic-food lovers will want to try this fun, informal restaurant offering such Polish delicacies as pierogi, polish sausage, and sauerkraut, along with such lighter American specialties as chicken and seafood. *400 Hwy. A, tel. 608/253–4451. AE, D, DC, MC, V.*

The Patio Restaurant. Owned by the same family since 1925, this small, unpretentious restaurant is noted for its homemade soups, breakfast specials, and fresh cinnamon rolls and pies baked in its own bakery. *208 Broadway, tel. 608/254–7176. No credit cards.*

SHOPPING

Broadway Street, Wisconsin Dells' main shopping street, is lined with T-shirt emporiums, fudge shops, souvenir shops, and shops selling such local specialties as Wisconsin cheese and Indian crafts.

ANTIQUES AND GIFTS Oak Street Antiques Mall (725 Oak St., tel. 608/254–4200) specializes in antique dolls, jewelry, toys, prints, and furniture. The Loonery (714 Oak St., tel. 608/253–7131) has 24 crafts stores featuring wildlife items; Market Square Cheese (1150 Wisconsin Dells Pkwy., tel. 608/254–8388) has a large selection of cheeses and ships orders nationwide; and the Winnebago Indian Museum Gift Shop (Rte. 13 and River Rd., tel. 608/254–2268) sells low-priced Indian crafts and deerskin footwear.

OUTDOOR ACTIVITIES

BOATING One way to explore the Wisconsin River is to rent a canoe, paddleboat, or sailboat. Aqua Sports (1280 Hiawatha Dr., Lake Delton, tel. 608/254–6048), Holiday Shores (3900 River Rd., Wisconsin Dells, tel. 608/254–2878), Lake Delton Water Sports (U.S. 12, Lake Delton, tel. 608/254–8702), and Mirror Lake Canoe & Boat Rental (Ishnala Rd., Lake Delton, tel. 608/254–7001) provide safety equipment and instruction along with rentals.

GOLF Christmas Mountain (5944 Christmas Mountain Rd., tel. 608/254–3971) and Dell View Golf Course (511 E. Adams St., Wisconsin Dells, tel. 608/253–4653) are challenging 18-hole courses; Coldwater Canyon (4065 River Rd., tel. 608/254–8489) is a 9-hole course. Call ahead to arrange tee times.

HORSEBACK RIDING Christmas Mountain Ranch (5944 Christmas Mountain Rd., tel. 608/254–3935) offers English- and Western-style riding lessons and riding trails. Beginners are welcome. OK Corral Riding Stable (Hwy. 16, 1 mi south of Wisconsin Dells, tel. 608/254–2811) offers Western-style riding for adults and children on 100 acres of trails.

SKIING Mirror Lake State Park (tel. 608/254–2333), 1 mile south of I–90/94 on U.S. 12 and then east 1½ miles at E10320 Ferndell Road, has 18 miles of groomed cross-country trails; Christmas Mountain (5944 Christmas Mountain Rd., tel. 608/254–3971) has seven downhill runs ranging from beginner to intermediate and 12 miles of groomed, partially lighted cross-country trails ranging from beginner to expert.

ENTERTAINMENT

The weekly *Wisconsin Dells-Lake Delton Area Guide,* available free throughout the Dells area, lists regional events and activities.

CONCERTS The Wisconsin Opry (E10964 Moon Rd., tel. 608/254–7951) features nightly country cookouts and country-music shows Memorial Day–mid-September; nationally known country-and-western performers occasionally make appearances.

DINNER SHOWS Molly's Showplace (1540 Wisconsin Dells Pkwy., tel. 608/254–6222) presents breakfast entertainment, matinee stage shows, and live dinner shows, Memorial Day–Labor Day.

Yellowstone National Park
Wyoming

Where else but Yellowstone can you pull off an empty highway at dawn to see two bison bulls shaking the earth as they collide in battle before their herd, and, an hour later, be caught in an RV traffic jam? For 120 years, Yellowstone, the oldest national park in the United States, has been full of such contrasts that usually revolve around its twin role as America's preeminent wildlife preserve and its most accessible one.

Yellowstone is a high plateau, ringed by even higher mountains; the park lies mostly in northwestern Wyoming and extends into Montana and Idaho. Roadside elevations range from 5,314 feet at the North Entrance to 8,859 feet at Dunraven Pass. The Gallatin Range to the west and north, the Absaroka and Beartooth ranges to the north and east, and the Tetons to the south all have peaks higher than 10,000 feet. Scenery in the park ranges from near-high desert around the North Entrance to lodgepole pine forests around the South Entrance, and otherworldly landscapes of stunted pine and shrub around thermal areas.

From whichever direction you approach the Yellowstone plateau—larger than Delaware and Rhode Island combined—you'll see signs of the massive summer 1988 fires. Beyond the South Entrance along dizzying Lewis River Canyon, a landscape of charred trees to the west fit the media portrait of what happened: an unprecedented disaster to America's original natural preserve. Past the North Entrance along the Gallatin Range, the multicolored mosaic of burned and unburned pine and aspen offers the bigger Yellowstone picture. Right now, Yellowstone visitors have a rare chance to see nature's massive regeneration. Roadside exhibits near Lewis Lake, south of Tower Falls, and at five other locations explain that process.

ESSENTIAL INFORMATION

WHEN TO GO Yellowstone's midsummer average temperatures hover in the 70s at midday and around 40° at night. Snow is possible in high elevations year-round. June and September are often wet and cloudy in the park's lower elevations, but September, and to a lesser extent October, can also have delightfully sunny days—albeit 5° to 20° cooler than midsummer. Winter and spring are Yellowstone's best-kept secrets—the former for cross-country skiing, solitude, and wildlife encounters; the latter for viewing baby bison, moose, and other new arrivals. January afternoon highs average in the 20s, with nighttime average lows around zero.

The park's crowds can be daunting in July and August, when reservations are essential for most lodging. Only one stretch of road, from the North Entrance to Cooke City, Montana, on the northeast, is open year-round to wheeled vehicles; other roads open between early April and late May.

FESTIVALS AND SEASONAL EVENTS **Mid-Mar.:** The Rendezvous Ski Race in West Yellowstone is one of eight segments in the cross-country Great American Ski Chase. **Early Apr.:** Cowboy Range Ballads in Cody is a weekend of western entertainment.

Late June–early July: Plains Indian Pow-Wow and Cody Stampede in Cody celebrate the Indian and Cowboy heritages of the Northern Plains. **July 4:** Home of Champions Rodeo is a major rodeo circuit event in Red Lodge, 69 miles from Yellowstone's Northeast Entrance on the spectacular Beartooth Highway (other park gateway towns hold summer rodeos—check with tourist offices, listed below).

BARGAINS Free and varied ranger-led activities inside the park, usually held during summer months and listed daily at visitor centers, include photography workshops, map-and-compass workshops, and bird- and wildlife-watching. TW Recreational Services (*see* Tourist Offices, *below*), the park concessionaire for restaurants and lodging, offers some attractive deals if you're willing to

rough it a bit: "Budget," "Rough Rider," and "Rustic Shelter" cabins cost $19–$25 per night at Mammoth, Roosevelt, and Old Faithful. TW Services also offers a two-night winter package ($129 per couple) at Mammoth Hot Springs Hotel, including dinner and a half day of ice skating, plus discounts on guided ski and Snowcoach tours.

TOURIST OFFICES Yellowstone National Park Service information (tel. 307/344–7381). Information and reservations for lodging and activities: TW Recreational Services (Yellowstone National Park 82190–9989, tel. 307/344–7311). Wyoming Division of Tourism (tel. 307/777–7777 or 800/225–5996). Travel Montana (tel. 406/444–2654 or 800/541–1447). Bozeman Chamber of Commerce (Box B, Bozeman, MT 59715, tel. 406/586–5421). Cody Country Chamber of Commerce (Box 2777, Cody 82414, tel. 307/587–2297). Jackson Hole Chamber of Commerce (Box E, Jackson 83001, tel. 307/733–3316).

EMERGENCIES For **police, fire,** and **ambulance:** Dial 911. **Hospitals:** Yellowstone Lake (tel. 307/242–7241). **Doctors:** National Park Service emergency medical technicians and park medics are on duty at all times. Outpatient clinics operate Memorial Day through mid-September at Yellowstone Lake (tel. 307/242–7241) and Old Faithful (tel. 307/545–7325). Mammoth Hot Springs Clinic (tel. 307/344–7965) is open year-round.

ARRIVING AND DEPARTING

BY PLANE The two most convenient airports are Jackson Hole Airport (tel. 307/733–7682), outside Jackson, and Yellowstone Regional Airport (tel. 307/587–5096) in Cody, 50 and 52 miles from the South and East Entrances, respectively. Both have daily flights connecting to Denver or Salt Lake City on several national and commuter airlines. Gallatin Field (tel. 406/388–6632) in Bozeman, Montana, 90 miles from the West Entrance, also has daily flights connecting to Minneapolis or Denver. Some lodgings in the area offer free airport shuttles. From Yellow-

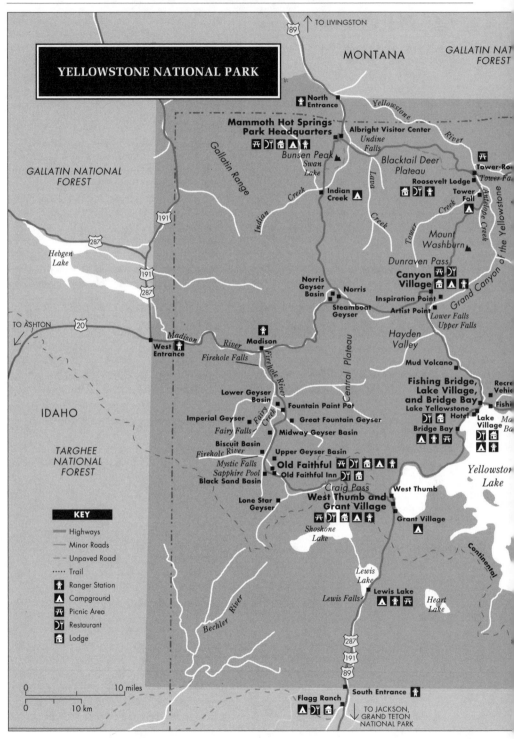

YELLOWSTONE NATIONAL PARK

TO LIVINGSTON

89

MONTANA

GALLATIN NATIONAL FOREST

GALLATIN NATIONAL FOREST

Gallatin Range

Hebgen Lake

191

287

TO ASHTON

20

IDAHO

TARGHEE NATIONAL FOREST

North Entrance

Mammoth Hot Springs Park Headquarters

Albright Visitor Center

Undine Falls

Bunsen Peak
Swan Lake

Indian Creek

Indian Creek

Lava Creek

Blacktail Deer Plateau

Roosevelt Lodge

Tower-Ro

Tower Fal

Tower Fall

Antelope Creek

Mount Washburn

Dunraven Pass

Norris Geyser Basin

Norris

Steamboat Geyser

Canyon Village

Inspiration Point

Artist Point

Grand Canyon of the Yellowstone

Lower Falls
Upper Falls

Hayden Valley

Central Plateau

Mud Volcano

Madison River

Madison

West Entrance

Firehole Falls

Firehole River

Lower Geyser Basin

Imperial Geyser

Fairy Falls

Fairy Creek

Fountain Paint Pot

Great Fountain Geyser

Midway Geyser Basin

Biscuit Basin

Firehole River

Mystic Falls

Sapphire Pool

Black Sand Basin

Upper Geyser Basin

Old Faithful

Old Faithful Inn

Fishing Bridge, Lake Village, and Bridge Bay

Lake Yellowstone

Hotel

Recre
Vehic

Fishi

Lake Village

Ma
Ba

Bridge Bay

Yellowstor Lake

West Thumb

Lone Star Geyser

Craig Pass

West Thumb and Grant Village

Shoshone Lake

Grant Village

Continental

Lewis Lake

Lewis Falls

Lewis Lake

Heart Lake

Bechler River

KEY

Highways
Minor Roads
Unpaved Road
Trail
Ranger Station
Campground
Picnic Area
Restaurant
Lodge

0   10 miles

0   10 km

Flagg Ranch

South Entrance

TO JACKSON, GRAND TETON NATIONAL PARK

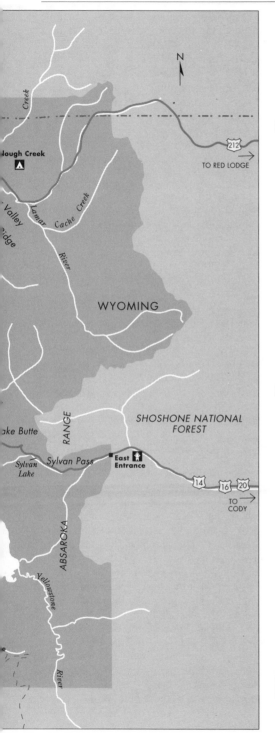

stone Regional Airport, Cody Connection Taxi (tel. 307/587–9292) takes passengers into town for about $5. One-way taxi fares from Bozeman's or Jackson Hole's airports are about $12; for a taxi in Jackson contact Buckboard Cab (tel. 307/733–1112) or Eagle (tel. 307/739–9999).

BY CAR All five park entrances join the Grand Loop Road. The most spectacular entry is from the northeast on U.S. 212, the Beartooth Highway. The 69 miles from Red Lodge, Montana, traverse the 11,000-foot-high Beartooth Pass, the nation's highest mountain highway pass with dizzying switchbacks. The northern approach on U.S. 89 is a straight shot through Paradise Valley, flanked by the Absaroka Range on the east and Gallatin Range on the west, to the original stone entry arch in the funky old tourist town of Gardiner, Montana. The South Entrance (U.S. 89), which is ideal for anyone also stopping at Grand Teton Park, the West Entrance on U.S. 20 through West Yellowstone, and the East Entrance on U.S. 14–16–20 from Cody are the most heavily trafficked.

BY BUS Greyhound Lines (tel. 800/231–2222) connects Bozeman, Montana, to points nationwide. From Bozeman, Karst Stage (tel. 406/586–8567) runs two routes daily into the park from mid-May through mid-September, with pickups at all Bozeman motels. Cody Bus Lines (tel. 800/733–2304) provides daily service from Billings. From downtown Cody, Powder River Transportation (tel. 307/527–6223) leaves daily for Old Faithful and other Loop lodgings.

From early December to early March, Karst Stage operates shuttles from Bozeman's airport to Mammoth and West Yellowstone. Holiday Tour and Travel (tel. 307/733–4152) offers a daily winter shuttle from downtown Jackson to Flagg Ranch near the South Entrance. These shuttles connect to Snowcoach tours into the park (*see* Guided Tours, *below*).

GETTING AROUND

Despite a few good bus connections in the park, a car remains the most practical way to see Yellowstone. Some Yellowstone roads are steep with sharp drop-offs: Be especially careful south of Mammoth Hot Springs near Bunsen Peak, north of Canyon Village at Dunraven Pass, and just past the South Entrance along the Lewis River Canyon. Off-road parking is plentiful at all major sites.

REST STOPS The park has 50 picnic areas, most with nonflush toilets. Rest rooms with flush toilets are provided at Grant Village, Old Faithful, Madison, Norris, Mammoth Hot Springs, Tower-Roosevelt, Canyon, Fishing-Bridge, and Yellowstone Lake visitor centers.

GUIDED TOURS TW Recreational Services (*see* Tourist Offices, *above*) schedules bus tours from various park locations between mid-May and mid-September and from the Gardiner, Montana, bus depot. In winter, it offers orientation tours on tractored Snowcoaches; a half-day snowmobile tour; cross-country ski tours; and a winter wildlife bus tour. Free ranger-led activities, listed at visitor centers, include guided walks ranging from a stroll through Old Faithful's geyser system to a strenuous hike up Specimen Ridge at Mammoth Hot Springs.

EXPLORING

Admission to Yellowstone Park also allows entrance into Grand Teton Park for up to one week; entry fee is $10 per vehicle or $4 per individual on foot or bicycle. National Park Service Golden Age and Golden Access Passports enable free entry to persons over 62 and blind and disabled persons.

You can drive the 142-mile Grand Loop in a day—but it's easier to explore it over a few days. Major park attractions can only be seen by driving to parking areas and walking to the features. If your time is limited, consider concentrating on just one area—the Grand Loop's two halves are ideal for segmenting a visit like this.

Yellowstone Lake, 22 miles from the South Entrance, is North America's largest mountain lake, with 110 miles of shoreline. **Fishing Bridge** at the lake's northern end was named for the thousands of anglers who were al-

lowed to fish from its rails until 1972. **Fishing Bridge Museum,** an example of early park architecture, contains bird displays; it's also an ideal place from which to start a lakeshore stroll. **Lake Butte,** a wooded promontory rising 615 feet above the lake, is reached by a 1-mile spur road 10 miles east of Fishing Bridge: try catching a sunset here. *Fishing Bridge Visitor Center, tel. 307/242–2450. Open late May–mid-Sept., daily. Scenicruiser tours leave Bridge Bay Marina daily early June–mid-Sept. Fee charged.*

Old Faithful, Yellowstone's most famous attraction, is part of the world's greatest concentration of thermal features, along a 50-mile stretch of road between Old Faithful and Mammoth Hot Springs. A lobby sign in historic Old Faithful Inn tells when the next eruption is due (approximately every 65–78 minutes); the inn's deck and benches around the geyser itself are the best viewpoints. Dozens of other thermal areas dot the immediate vicinity, accessible by boardwalks and trails. Observation Point Trail (1.1 mile) crosses bubbling Firehole River, passes Solitary Geyser, and returns to the Upper Geyser Basin Trail, which offers other walking options. The Three Senses Trail off Firehole Lake Drive is recommended. *Old Faithful Visitor Center, tel. 307/545–2750. Open early Apr.– Oct. 31, daily; winter season dates vary.*

Mammoth Hot Springs is the park headquarters. The Terrace, an eerily colored travertine (calcium carbonate) plateau, towers over the hot springs. Take the Upper Terrace Loop; drive 2 miles south of Mammoth, where you'll pass 500-year-old gnarled limber pine trees growing atop extinct thermal features. You can walk down from here to the Main Terrace past formations such as the Liberty Cap, with the aid of a 25¢ map available in the parking area. Five miles south of Mammoth, a rough, one-way dirt road circles Bunsen Peak. *Albright Visitor Center, tel. 307/344–2263. Open daily, with movie and slides throughout the day. Mammoth General Store open daily; service station open mid-May–mid-Oct., daily; hotel, fast food, horseback riding (fee charged), photo shop open May–Sept., daily.*

Tower-Roosevelt area, 18 miles east of Mammoth, centers around Roosevelt Lodge, another early park structure. Blacktail Plateau Drive, a one-way dirt road paralleling the main road eastward, traverses sagebrush hills, pine and aspen forests. A few miles south of the lodge is 132-foot-high Tower Falls, named for nearby volcanic pinnacles. *Roosevelt Store and Tower service station open early June–early Sept. Horseback rides, stagecoach rides, Old West cookout available early June–early Sept. (fee charged).*

Grand Canyon of the Yellowstone is reached driving south from Tower-Roosevelt. The road crosses Dunraven Pass (8,850 feet), covered in wildflowers and subalpine fir. At Canyon Village, a 2¹/₂-mile one-way loop road leads first to a spur road out to Inspiration Point, where the Yellowstone River plunges 1,000 feet below. The canyon's colors were created by hot water acting on volcanic rock. Next is Grandview Point, affording a distant view of 308-foot Lower Falls, and Lookout Point, with a steep trail descending close to the Falls. Back on the main road, turn left in .3 mile to view the edge of the 109-foot Upper Falls. Another .6 mile south, Artist Point Road's trails lead to views of both falls. Artist Point, at road's end, involves minimal walking and offers spectacular views of the canyon and Lower Falls. *Canyon Visitor Center, tel. 307/242–2550. Open mid-May–Sept., daily. Service station open early May–early Sept., daily; general store open late May–late Sept., daily; horseback rides (fee charged) available mid-June–Sept. 1.*

THE NATURAL WORLD Elk come right into Mammoth and the Old Faithful Geyser Basin, especially in early morning and evening—generally the best times to view Yellowstone's wildlife. Just below Tower Falls, as you drive up Mt. Washburn, look east, downslope, into prime grizzly bear country on Antelope Creek. This area is closed to human travel. The Hayden Valley between Fishing Bridge and Canyon is prime moose, bison, and waterfowl territory. Watch for elk, bison, antelope, and coyotes in the Lamar Valley. Bighorn sheep frequent Mt. Washburn in summer.

HOTELS AND INNS

While surrounding towns have plenty of accommodations (*see* Motels, *below*), staying in the park keeps you close to the action. It's wise to make reservations at least two months in advance for Old Faithful Inn, Lake Yellowstone Hotel, and Mammoth Hot Springs Hotel. Old Faithful Inn opens in early May, while most other park lodgings open in late May or early June; only the Inn and Old Faithful Snow Lodge stay open into October. Old Faithful Snow Lodge and Mammoth Hot Springs Hotel accommodate winter guests from mid-December to early March. Rates are slightly higher in summer. Price categories for double occupancy, excluding 2% tax, are *Moderate,* $40–$85, and *Inexpensive,* under $40.

Yellowstone visitor areas have a mix of Moderate and Inexpensive rooms. All reservations must be made through the Reservations Department of TW Recreational Services (*see* Tourist Offices, *above*). Guests arriving within 14 days of the date of the reservation may use credit cards.

GRAND CANYON AREA **Canyon Lodge.** This busy property, the park's largest, consists of uninspired, single-story plain pine-frame cabins in clusters of four or more. Its size, however, means Canyon Lodge is one of the last to fill up. *North Rim Dr. 580 units. 3 restaurants, cafeteria, gift shop. Inexpensive–Moderate.*

LAKE AREA **Grant Village.** The newest park lodging, built in 1984 at the south end of the lake, proves they don't make 'em like they used to: It's gray on the outside and dull on the inside. Still, half the rooms overlook the lake and have private baths. *Grant Village Rd. 299 rooms. 2 restaurants, gift shop. Moderate.*

Lake Yellowstone Hotel and Cabins. Extensively renovated in 1989, this elegant colonial-style building with 50-foot Ionic columns overlooks the lake and features some of the nicest rooms in the park, with peach carpeting, pine furniture, and brass beds. *On Yellowstone Lake. 250 rooms and* *cabins. Lakeview restaurant, lobby bar, gift shop, nearby marina. Moderate.*

Lake Lodge. This peaceful property has cabins nestled in the trees with good views of the lake. *Lake Village Rd. 186 rooms. Cafeteria, gift shop. Inexpensive–Moderate.*

MAMMOTH AREA **Mammoth Hot Springs Hotel and Cabins.** Built in 1937, with one wing dating from 1911, this hotel with a spacious lobby and smallish rooms is generally less crowded than the other two historic park hotels. Although it shares grounds with the park headquarters, this spot is a little far from some of the main attractions. *5 mi from park's north entrance. 235 rooms and cabins. 2 restaurants, gift shop. Inexpensive–Moderate.*

OLD FAITHFUL AREA **Old Faithful Inn.** With its soaring log-beam construction, four hanging balconies, and giant stone fireplace, this National Historic Landmark has rooms in the 1904 section with brass beds; newer upper-range rooms in the east and west wings with Victorian cherrywood furniture; and motel-style midrange rooms with ranch oak furniture. The east-wing rooms were renovated in 1993; all have baths, and an elevator serves the upper floors. *First left off Old Faithful Bypass Rd. 326 rooms. 2 restaurants, Native American crafts gift shop. Inexpensive–Moderate.*

Old Faithful Snow Lodge. This compact, drab-looking building, open in winter, is one of two Yellowstone properties that stay open in winter. The rooms are nondescript motel style, but the lobby's modern stone fireplace is a popular gathering spot on windy winter nights. *Old Faithful Bypass Rd. next to visitor center. 31 rooms, 34 cabins. Restaurant, gift shop. Inexpensive–Moderate.*

Roosevelt Lodge. Simple frame cabins surround a cozy two-fireplace log lodge with rocking chairs on the porch. In the dining room, big bowls of cole slaw, beans, and corn are passed around family style. *At Tower-Roosevelt Junction on Grand Loop Rd. 80 cabins. Restaurant, gift shop. Inexpensive–Moderate.*

Old Faithful Lodge and Cabins. This budget choice is nicer than some of the park's mid-range options; the lobby has a giant fireplace and a commanding view of Old Faithful. *At far end of Old Faithful Bypass Rd. 132 cabins. Cafeteria, 2 snack shops, gift shop. Inexpensive.*

MOTELS

MODERATE **Buffalo Bill Village** (1701 Sheridan Ave., Cody 82414, tel. 307/587–5544). 79 rooms; restaurant, pool. **Cedar Mountain Lodge** (803 Sheridan Ave., Cody 82414, tel. 307/587–2248). 45 rooms; pool. **Cody Motor Lodge** (1455 Sheridan Ave., Cody 82414, tel. 307/527–6291). 30 rooms. **Days Inn** (1321 N. 7th Ave., Bozeman, MT 59715, tel. 406/587–5251 or 800/325–2525). 80 rooms. **Pony Express Motel** (Box 972, Jackson 83001, tel. 307/733–2658). 41 rooms; pool. **Super 8 Motel** (730 Yellowstone Rd., Cody 82414, tel. 307/527–6214). 64 rooms. **Super 8 Motel** (1520 S. Hwy. 89, Jackson 83001, tel. 307/733–6833). 97 rooms.

INEXPENSIVE **Big Bear Motel** (Hwy 14–16–20, Box 2015, Cody 82414, tel. 307/587–3117 or 800/325–7063). 42 rooms; pool; pets allowed. **Motel 6** (1370 W. Broadway, Jackson 83001, tel. 307/733–1620). 155 rooms; pool.

CAMPGROUNDS

Yellowstone has 11 park-service campgrounds and one RV park operated by TW Recreational Services. All campsites are available on a first-come, first-served basis, except Bridge Bay, which is on the nationwide MISTIX (tel. 800/365–2267) reservation system from mid-June to Labor Day. Canyon Village is restricted to hard-sided units, because bears frequent the area.

Bridge Bay. The largest park campground, set back from the lake in a wooded grove 3 miles southwest of Lake Village, features a marina, rental boats, fishing, campfire talks, and guided walks. Don't expect solitude. *420 RV and tent sites ($8), no hookups; showers 4 mi away, bathrooms, picnic tables and barbecue areas.*

Canyon. One-quarter mile east of Canyon Village and near a laundry and visitor center, this area is popular with families and accessible to many short trails. *280 RV sites ($8), no hookups; showers, bathrooms, picnic tables and barbecue areas. No reservations.*

Fishing Bridge RV Park. This is the only full RV facility in the park, at Fishing Bridge junction. Trailers must be under 40 feet with no canvas. Make reservations through TW Recreational Services (*see* Tourist Offices, *above*). *345 RV sites ($19), hookups (no extra fee); showers, bathrooms, laundry nearby, picnic tables and barbecue areas, laundry nearby.*

Mammoth Hot Springs. The sites on a sagebrush hillside are also popular with elk and mule deer, just below the Mammoth complex and near its amphitheater, where rangers hold evening talks. *85 RV and tent sites ($8), no hookups; bathrooms, picnic tables and barbecue areas. No reservations.*

Slough Creek. A small, creekside campground 10 miles northeast of Tower Junction off a spur road, this is about as far from Yellowstone's beaten path as you can get without actually camping in the backcountry. *32 RV and tent sites ($6), no hookups; pit latrines, picnic tables and barbecue areas. No reservations.*

DINING

The Northern Rockies have come far from the days when roadside signs advised, "This is cow country—eat beef!" You'll still find some of the best steaks around, cut from grass-fed beef, but healthier eating habits have taken hold here, too. Rocky Mountain trout is served at several park restaurants, and pastas outnumber fried potatoes nowadays. Expect less formality than you'd find elsewhere, even in the fanciest restaurants. Along with the informality come better prices. Price categories per person, excluding 6% tax, service, and drinks, are *Moderate,* $10–$20, and *Inexpensive,* under $10. All park restaurants are operated by TW Recreational Services (tel.

307/344–7311). (For Jackson restaurants, *see* Grand Teton National Park chapter.)

INSIDE YELLOWSTONE **Old Faithful Inn Dining Room.** Lines form early at the park's premier restaurant—a big, friendly place that serves an impeccable trout almondine as well as a generous Sunday-brunch buffet. *Old Faithful Inn, tel. 307/344–7901, ext. 4999. Reservations required. AE, D, DC, MC, V. Moderate.*

Roosevelt Lodge Dining Room. Pine chairs and tables set the rustic tone at this popular restaurant with a "family menu"each entrée comes with bowls of coleslaw, mashed potatoes, corn, baked beans, and corn bread muffins. *Roosevelt Lodge, tel. 307/344–7311. AE, D, DC, MC, V. Moderate.*

Terrace Dining Room. Overlooking what was once the Army's parade and drill field at Mammoth Hot Springs, this restaurant serves excellent pastas and chicken dishes. *Across from Mammoth Hot Springs Hotel, tel. 307/344–7311. AE, D, DC, MC, V. Moderate.*

Canyon Lodge Cafeteria. You'll find long lines, but it's worth the wait for cheap and hearty soups, chili, and lasagna. *Canyon Lodge, tel. 307/344–7311. No credit cards. Inexpensive.*

Old Faithful Lodge Cafeteria. Lasagna, pizzas, and other staples are served here, but it's the tableside views of Old Faithful that draw the crowds. *Old Faithful Lodge, tel. 307/344–7311. No credit cards. Inexpensive.*

OUTSIDE YELLOWSTONE **Chico Hot Springs.** This lodge-saloon-hot springs resort also houses one of Montana's best restaurants; dinners can get expensive, but the more moderate, all-you-can-eat Sunday brunch features custom-made omelets, cereals, freshly baked rolls and breads, and fruits. *East River Rd. (follow signs on U.S. 89 35 mi north of North Entrance), Pray, MT, tel. 406/333–4933. D, MC, V. Moderate.*

Irma Hotel. Hearty breakfasts, a wide variety of lunchtime sandwiches, and hearty dinners (with a salad-bar option) is offered in this historic hotel named for Buffalo Bill's daughter. *1192 Sheridan Ave., Cody, tel. 307/587–4221. AE, D, DC, MC, V. Moderate.*

La Comida. This small restaurant in downtown Cody has shaded sidewalk tables—and plenty of indoor seating—where you can enjoy large servings of home-style Mexican dishes. *1385 Sheridan Ave., Cody, tel. 307/587–9556. AE, D, DC, MC, V. Moderate.*

Trapper's Inn. Amid pine furniture and mountain-man memorabilia, diners linger over thick soups, sourdough pancakes, biscuits and rolls, and hearty entrées such as grilled steak or chicken with potatoes and beans. *315 Madison Ave., West Yellowstone, MT, tel. 406/646–9375. AE, MC, V. Moderate.*

Casa Sanchez. The best Mexican food in Yellowstone—everything from tamales and burritos to beans, eggs, and tortillas—is served in three downstairs rooms of a converted house. *719 S. 9th Ave., Bozeman, MT, tel. 406/586–4516. D, DC, MC, V. Inexpensive.*

Patsy Ann's Pastry and Ladle. Come here for whole-grain baked goods, soups, and sandwiches. *1243 Beck Ave., Cody, tel. 307/527–6297. No credit cards. Inexpensive.*

SHOPPING

Yellowstone and its surroundings have two tiers of shopping possibilities for travelers: souvenirs and the real thing. Among the latter are genuine Northern Plains Indian beadwork, fine leather cowboy boots and coats, distinctive woolens, and local crafts. Souvenirs include rubber tomahawks and tom-toms that have acquired their own kitsch tradition, fake six-guns and other cowboy "paraphernalia," more Yellowstone sweatshirts and T-shirts than you could possibly imagine, and decorated mugs. (Some of the region's best shopping is in Jackson; *see* the Grand Teton National Park chapter.)

GIFT SHOPS Old Faithful Inn's gift shop offers Native American beadwork and western regional art, along with mugs, sweatshirts and calendars. Also at Old Faithful, the Hamilton General Store sells outdoor gear and souvenirs (some of the bear-related sweat-

shirts are truly funny). Mammoth Hot Springs Hotel has an interesting Christmas gift shop.

Outside Yellowstone, the Buffalo Bill Historical Center (720 Sheridan Ave., Cody, tel. 307/587–4771) has the region's preeminent gift shop for Plains Indian crafts and jewelry. The Country Bookshelf (28 W. Main, Bozeman, MT, tel. 406/587–0166) stocks a wide selection of contemporary and historical Western literature.

FACTORY OUTLETS The Montana Woolen Shop (3100 W. Main St., Bozeman, MT, tel. 406/587–5261) sells sweaters and other woolens, plus some expensive leathers. Benetton Factory Outlet (48 E. Broadway, Jackson, WY, tel. 307/733–8890) sells Italian clothing. London Fog Factory Store (485 W. Broadway, Jackson, WY, tel. 307/739–1819) specializes in men's and women's sportswear.

OUTDOOR ACTIVITIES

BIKING Some 300 miles of roadway are available to bicyclists; bikes are prohibited on trails and in the backcountry. If you bike on the Grand Loop Road, keep in mind its notable climbs at Craig Pass between Old Faithful and Grant Village; Sylvan Pass between East Entrance and Fishing Bridge; and Dunraven Pass between Tower and Canyon. The gravel Bunsen Peak Road near Mammoth and Blacktail Deer Plateau Road between Mammoth and Roosevelt Lodge allow two-way bike and one-way auto traffic. Some roads restricted to bicycle and foot travel are: the abandoned railroad bed paralleling the Yellowstone River near Mammoth (5 miles); the Riverside Trail starting at the West Entrance (1 mile); the paved trail from Old Faithful's Hamilton Store to Morning Glory Pool (2 miles); and Natural Bridge Road near Bridge Bay (1 mile). Bikes can be rented and repaired in the gateway towns of West Yellowstone, Livingston, and Bozeman, Gardiner, Montana, as well as Cody and Jackson, Wyoming.

FISHING Cutthroat, brook, lake, and rainbow trout, along with grayling and mountain whitefish, can all be caught in Yellowstone's waters. Catch and release is the general policy, though you can keep some of the cut-throat, rainbow, and brookies, and all of the whitefish—get a copy of the fishing regulations at any visitor center. No live bait is allowed. Prime fishing areas include the upper Yellowstone River (north of Canyon), and Yellowstone, Sylvan, and Shoshone lakes and their tributaries. Literally dozens of backcountry and roadside rivers and creeks throughout the park provide good fishing, too: Try the Lamar River (north), Madison River (west), and Lewis River (south). TW Recreational Services (tel. 307/344–7311) rents boats at Bridge Bay Marina; fishing supplies are available at all Hamilton Stores (Old Faithful, Bridge Bay, Fishing Bridge, Canyon, Tower-Roosevelt Lodge, Mammoth).

HORSEBACK RIDING TW Recreational Services (tel. 307/344–7311) runs easy one- and two-hour group trail rides from corrals at Roosevelt Lodge, Canyon Lodge, and Mammoth. Check at visitor center and park hotel activities desks for times and prices. A number of outfitters offer three-, five- and nine-day horseback trips into the backcountry; try Thorofare-Yellowstone Outfitting (Box 604, Cody, 82414, tel. 307/587–5929 or 800/326–5928).

SKIING Besides guided ski tours (*see* Guided Tours, *above*), individual cross-country skiing options are limited only by your ability. At Old Faithful, the easy Lone Star Geyser Trail (9 miles) passes thermal features and links to several other trails ranging from easy to difficult. The Riverside Trail starts at the West Entrance and follows the Madison River; it involves one traverse up a short, steep hill. The canyon area has several trails

for beginner to intermediate skiers, with some awesome rimside views as well as dangerous switchbacks for advanced skiers only. Detailed brochures and maps are available from visitor-center ranger desks. You can rent touring and telemark skis, or snowshoes, at Mammoth Hot Springs Hotel and Old Faithful Snow Lodge (*see* Hotels and Inns, *above*). Skier shuttles are available at both locations.

WALKING AND HIKING Possibilities abound in Yellowstone: Your only problem will be choosing walks to suit your ability. Always check at a visitor-center ranger desk before hiking to gauge a trail's difficulty (hikers should have Yellowstone topographical maps, available at visitor centers), and never wander out of sight of your trail. Beginners should concentrate on the many marked walkways at major attractions: The Upper Geyser Basin at Old Faithful can keep you busy for hours with fairly gentle boardwalk trails, as can the boardwalks at Norris Geyser Basin and Mammoth Hot Springs Terrace. Two easy backcountry hikes are the trail along the Lamar River Valley in the park's northeast and the 4-mile trail out to Shoshone Lake about 8 miles east of Old Faithful. A topographical map will forewarn you of difficulties on trails that might look easy on the maps handed out at the entrances: Both the Lost Lake Trail (which leaves from behind Roosevelt Lodge) and the Slough Creek Trail (departs the campground of that name) involve steep ½-mile opening climbs, followed by gentle terrain. If you're planning to camp as well as hike in the backcountry, you must obtain an overnight-use permit from a ranger station or visitor center.

Yosemite National Park
California

O n one compact California valley—only 7 miles long and 1 mile wide—are two of the world's 10 highest waterfalls, the largest single granite rock on Earth (El Capitan), and one of America's most recognized peaks (Half Dome). And this spectacular valley is just a small part of 750,000-acre Yosemite National Park, which also contains in its southern tip the Mariposa Grove of Big Trees, a stand of giant sequoias towering 20 stories above the forest floor.

Toward the east is Yosemite's high country, an untamed expanse of rolling meadows, pristine forest, hidden lakes, and rocky domes.

In 1890, President Theodore Roosevelt, at the urging of conservationist John Muir and many like him, designated Yosemite one of our first national parks. Visitors from around the world, including royalty from Italy, Sweden, and Denmark, came here. They entered near Mariposa, gleefully riding a stagecoach through a tunnel bored into the trunk of a single sequoia. At the top of the rise south of Yosemite Valley, they saw America's Shangri-la—a deep, green canyon with walls of stone rising 3,000 feet into the clouds and graceful waterfalls plummeting down from these angelic heights. It's the same vista that you will see today.

Millions of people visit Yosemite every year. There is no arguing with the claim that, especially in the summer, it's very crowded. Such extravagant praise has been written of this valley (by John Muir and others) and so many beautiful photographs taken (by Ansel Adams and others), that you may wonder if the reality can possibly measure up. For almost everyone, it does; Yosemite reminds them of what *breathtaking* and *marvelous* truly mean.

ESSENTIAL INFORMATION

WHEN TO GO Although the high country is snowed in from late fall to late spring, Yosemite Valley is open year-round. In winter, the valley is often dusted with snow, but temperatures remain in the 40s during the day, dipping down to the 20s at night. Autumn and early spring weather in the valley is surprisingly mild, with warm days (60s and 70s) and crisp nights (30s and 40s). Summer in the valley brings hot, dry days with temperatures in the 80s and pleasant evenings with temperatures in the 50s. The high country is cooler, with daytime temperatures in the 60s and nighttime temperatures that dip into the 30s.

Summer is Yosemite's most crowded season, especially in the valley. More than 3 million people visit the park each year, the bulk of them between June and August. Many activities are offered, but you will have to contend with traffic jams, noxious tour buses, and lodging that is almost impossible to obtain. We recommend visiting during the off-season, when the autumn leaves turn, snow highlights the mountaintops, and deer and coyote make their winter homes in the valley. Even spring, when the mighty waterfalls reach their peak and flowering trees bloom in the valley, is less crowded than summer. However, summer is the only time of year when the Tioga Road into the high country is sure to be open.

FESTIVALS AND SEASONAL EVENTS **Jan.:** Chefs' Holidays are free cooking demonstrations by well-known chefs for everything from exotic mushrooms to chocolate. Optional banquet dinner, $75, not including wine (tel. 209/454–2020). **Early May–late Oct.:** An Evening with a Tramp and Stickeen, one of Yosemite's best-loved evening activities, is a one-man show in which Lee Stetson portrays naturalist John Muir on Tuesdays, Thursdays, and Fridays for a nominal fee. **Mid-Nov.–mid-Dec.:** Vintners' Holidays, similar to Chefs' Holidays, are held during midweek in the grand parlor of the Ahwahnee Hotel and feature free seminars by California's prestigious vintners, culminating in an elegant, albeit pricey ($80 including wine) banquet dinner (tel. 209/454–2020). **Dec. 23:** Yosemite Pioneer Christmas is a free, old-fashioned program of caroling, candlelight tours, and stagecoach rides at the Wawona area of the park.

BARGAINS Yosemite National Park offers a myriad of free and low-cost activities throughout the year. The admission fee to this national treasure is a bargain in itself—$5 per car for a week's stay, or $3 per person if you don't arrive in a car.

Photo enthusiasts will delight in the free camera walks given each morning year-round by professional photographers. From March through October, professional artists offer free midday workshops in watercolor, etching, drawing, and other mediums. Bring your own materials or purchase them for about $10. Rangers lead free discovery walks throughout the year and free snowshoe walks in winter. Children can participate in the free Junior Ranger naturalist activities. Free evening activities include films and slide shows on Yosemite. In winter, you can find 25% discounts off lodging and bargain ski packages, especially in midweek.

TOURIST OFFICES National Park Service, Information Office (Box 577, Yosemite National Park 95389, tel. 209/372–0200 or 209/372–0264 for a 24-hr recording). Yosemite Area Road and Weather Conditions (tel. 209/372–0200). Northern California Road Conditions (tel. 800/427–ROAD). Camping and Recreation Information (tel. 209/372–0302). Valley Visitor Center (Box 577, Yosemite National Park 95389, tel. 209/372–0299).

EMERGENCIES **Doctors:** Yosemite Medical Clinic (Yosemite Village, tel. 209/372–4637) offers emergency care 24 hours daily. **Dentists:** The Dental Service (Yosemite Village, tel. 209/372–4200), next to the medical clinic, has been providing visitors with care since 1927.

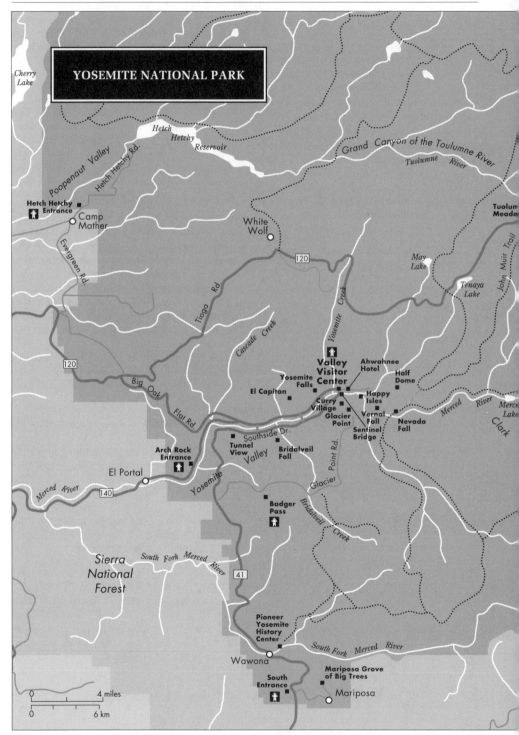

YOSEMITE NATIONAL PARK

Cherry Lake

Poopenaut Valley

Hetch Hetchy Rd.

Hetch Hetchy Reservoir

Grand Canyon of the Toulumne River

Tuolumne River

Hetch Hetchy Entrance

Camp Mather

White Wolf

120

Tuolumne Meadows

Evergreen Rd.

May Lake

Tioga Rd.

Tenaya Lake

John Muir Trail

120

Cascade Creek

Yosemite Creek

Big Oak

Flat Rd.

Valley Visitor Center

Ahwahnee Hotel

Half Dome

Yosemite Falls

El Capitan

Curry Village

Happy Isles

Merced River

Merced Lake

Glacier Point

Vernal Fall

Nevada Fall

Clark

Sentinel Bridge

Arch Rock Entrance

Southside Dr.

Tunnel View

Valley

Bridalveil Fall

Glacier Point Rd.

El Portal

140

Merced River

Yosemite

Badger Pass

Bridalveil Creek

Sierra National Forest

South Fork Merced River

41

Pioneer Yosemite History Center

South Fork Merced River

Wawona

Mariposa Grove of Big Trees

South Entrance

Mariposa

0   4 miles

0   6 km

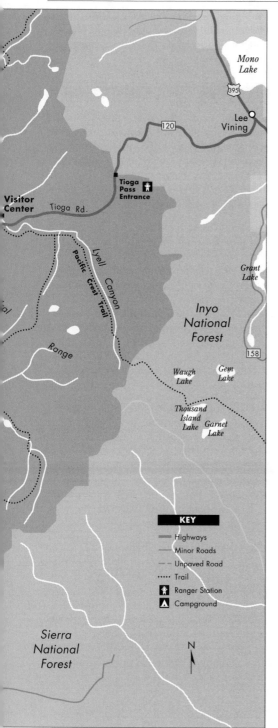

Mono Lake

[395]

Lee Vining

[120]

Tioga Pass Entrance

Visitor Center　Tioga Rd.

Pacific Crest Trail

Lyell Canyon

Grant Lake

Inyo National Forest

[158]

Range

Waugh Lake　Gem Lake

Thousand Island Lake　Garnet Lake

KEY

━━ Highways
── Minor Roads
┄┄ Unpaved Road
···· Trail
🚻 Ranger Station
⛺ Campground

Sierra National Forest

N

ARRIVING AND DEPARTING

BY PLANE If you're coming from out of state, you will most likely fly into San Francisco or Los Angeles and then drive. An alternative is to fly into Fresno, which is the closest airport (97 miles away) but is not as well serviced by major airlines.

Between the Airport and the Park by Car or RV. Yosemite is a four- to five-hour drive from San Francisco and a six-hour drive from Los Angeles. From the west, three highways come to Yosemite; all intersect with Highway 99, which runs north–south through the Central Valley. Highway 120 is the northernmost and most direct route from San Francisco, but it rises higher into the mountains, which can be snowy in winter. Highway 140 from Merced is the major route; Highway 41 from Fresno is the shortest route from Los Angeles and offers the most dramatic first look at Yosemite Valley.

Coming from the east, Highway 120, the Tioga Road (known as Tioga Pass Road), climbs over the Sierra crest, past Tuolumne Meadows, and down into the valley. It's scenic, but the mountain driving may be stressful and it's only open in the summer due to heavy snow in the upper elevations. Carry chains no matter what your approach to Yosemite. They are often mandatory on Sierra roads during snowstorms. If you get caught in the valley and need to buy chains there, you'll pay twice the normal price.

BY BUS Yosemite Gray Line (tel. 209/443–5240 or 800/640–6306 in CA) runs buses from Fresno ($40 round-trip) and Merced (north of Fresno on Hwy. 99, $30 round-trip) to Yosemite Valley. Yosemite Via (tel. 209/384–1315) runs buses from Merced to Yosemite ($30 round-trip plus $3 park entrance fee, 2½ hours one-way).

BY TRAIN Amtrak (tel. 800/USA–RAIL) has train service to Merced, where you can connect with bus transportation.

GETTING AROUND

Although the most convenient way to travel to Yosemite is by car, you won't need an automobile once you arrive. A free shuttle bus circles continually (7:30 AM–10 PM in summer, 9 AM–10 PM the rest of the year) to all valley destinations. In winter, a free bus carries skiers from the valley to Badger Pass. In summer, bus transportation to the high country is available for less than $20. If you do drive in the valley, parking lots are available at all major sites.

REST STOPS Rest rooms are few and far between on the forested mountain roads leading to Yosemite, but once in the park, you will find indoor bathrooms at the hotels and visitor centers. Portable toilets are available at the parking lots of major sites.

GUIDED TOURS Yosemite offers tours that are run by Yosemite Park and Curry Company to fit every schedule and a variety of interests. Tickets may be purchased at the hotels' tour desks. Prices quoted are for adults; children 12 and under are half the quoted rates; and children under 5 ride free. Advance reservations are recommended (tel. 209/372–1240). Tours are offered spring through fall, conditions permitting, unless otherwise stated. **Valley Floor Tour:** a 26-mile, two-hour tour of the valley's highlights with narration of the history, geology, and plant and animal life. **Moonlight Tour:** a late-evening version of the Valley Floor Tour offered on full-moon nights and the three nights prior, from June through September. **Glacier Point Tour:** a half-day trip to the vista at Glacier Point, 3,200 feet above the valley; operates approximately June 1 through Thanksgiving. **Big Trees Tram Tour:** a one-hour, open-air tram tour of the Mariposa Grove of Big Trees. **Tuolumne Meadows Tour:** a full day's outing across Tioga Pass Road to Mono Lake, with photo stops at highlights; operates July through Labor Day.

In addition to the commercial tours, rangers lead a variety of free tours ranging from snowshoeing at Badger Pass in winter to interpretive valley walks. For times, consult the visitor center (tel. 209/372–0299) or the *Yosemite Guide* newspaper, which is available for free at the park entrances and public buildings.

EXPLORING

The magnificent sites of Yosemite Valley are easily accessible by auto or free shuttle bus, with short trails to the bases of the powerful waterfalls. To experience the incomparable beauty of this national treasure, however, allow time for hikes off the well-beaten tourist paths (*see* Hiking, *below*).

Entering Yosemite Valley from the west: If you want to orient yourself, stop at the Valley Visitor Center, where a 20-minute slide show offers an entertaining overview of the park's history and beauty; rangers on duty are extremely helpful in recommending short hikes. You'll pass some of the vista points on the way to the visitor center, and if you're really pressed for time, stop at them before going on because the circle road around the valley is one way and it would mean doubling back.

Bridalveil Fall should be your first stop. The parking lot is about 20 yards up Highway 41 from the valley road (Southside Drive). A paved ¼-mile trail with a slight, 100-foot rise will take you to the base of this graceful 620-foot cascade. The Ahwahneechee Indians called it *Pohono,* or spirit of the puffing wind, as breezes blow this lacy waterfall sideways along the cliff face.

El Capitan, the largest single granite rock on Earth, rising 3,593 feet, will loom to your left as you head farther into the valley. Turnouts along the road provide unbeatable vistas of the rock—rising more than 350 stories above you. Shadows of cloud set off patterns of light on its vertical striations, creating an everchanging show. A pair of binoculars and keen eyes will allow you to spot rock climbers as they slowly ascend the sheer, vertical face of "El Cap."

Take a left over **Sentinel Bridge** and park. Walk to the center of the bridge for the best view of **Half Dome,** the most distinctive rock in the region, rising nearly 5,000 feet above the valley floor, and its reflection in the Merced River.

Drive back over the bridge and continue on Southside Drive. Hardy hikers may want to go straight to the Curry Village day-use lot, walk to the end of the shuttle bus road and climb the moderately steep (400-foot elevation gain) trail to the footbridge overlooking the 317-foot **Vernal Fall** (2¹/₂ miles round-trip, allow 1¹/₂ hours). Beyond Vernal Fall, the trail climbs up to the 594-foot Nevada Fall, then all the way to the top of Half Dome.

If you're not hiking, follow the road as it turns left across the Merced River. Take the short side road that dead-ends at the **Ahwahnee Hotel.** This stately 1927 lodge of granite-and-concrete beams, stained to look like redwood, is a perfect man-made complement to Yosemite's natural majesty. Visit the immense parlors with their walk-in hearths and priceless antique Indian rugs and baskets. The dining room is extraordinary, with high ceilings interlaced with massive sugar-pine beams.

Looping back toward the west, follow the signs for Yosemite Village. A large parking lot lends access to the gift stores, fast-food restaurants, and most important, the **Valley Visitor Center** (tel. 209/372–0299) with its exhibits on park geology and excellent selection of books on Yosemite. Behind the center is a small, re-created Ahwahneechee village as it might have appeared in 1872, 20 years after the first contact with non-Native Americans. Markers explain the lifestyle of Yosemite's first residents through the eyes of a young child. For more Indian lore, take a quick peak at the Indian Cultural Museum next door and its impressive collection of baskets.

Yosemite Falls is a short walk or drive from here. This is the highest waterfall in North America and the fifth-highest in the world. Though it looks like one cascade, Yosemite Falls is actually three waterfalls, a powerful chain of water twice the height of the Empire State Building. From the granite ridge high above you, Upper Fall drops 1,430 feet straight down. The Cascades, or Middle Fall, tumbles over another 675 feet, pouring into the steep 320-foot drop of the Lower Fall.

You can see the dizzying height of Yosemite Falls from the parking lot, but can only experience its power by following the ¹/₄-mile paved trail to its base. The path leads to a footbridge, often showered with the mist of the mighty falls, that crosses the rushing waters with Lower Yosemite Falls towering above you. Many return to the parking lot at this point, but the intrepid walker can continue across the bridge to a surprisingly little-traveled route. At this level, a wooded path winds through the cool forest, meandering several times over creeks via footbridges. In a secluded spot, you'll discover the site of John Muir's cabin, with Yosemite Falls as a backdrop. The trail circles back to the falls parking lot.

Tunnel View, up Highway 41 on the way out of the valley, is a must for those with more time. The parking lots for this vista point are on either side of the road just before the tunnel. Below, tucked into 7 miles of pure inspiration is Yosemite Valley, with Bridalveil Fall on the right, El Capitan on the left, and Half Dome forming the backdrop to this deep, green canyon.

Farther up Highway 41 is the turnoff for the road to **Glacier Point** (closed in winter), another spectacular panorama of Yosemite, taking in the valley below and high country peaks on the horizon.

Highway 41 curves through the mountains south to the **Pioneer Yosemite History Center** at Wawona (30 miles, allow 45 minutes). Cross the New England–style covered bridge to this collection of century-old log buildings that have been relocated here from their original sites around Yosemite. It is a vivid reminder of the park's first settlers and visitors, particularly in summer when costumed docents play the roles of the pioneers. The nearby Wawona Hotel, a whitewashed Victorian lodge built in 1879, is a pleasant stop for lunch.

Mariposa Grove of Big Trees is 6 miles south of Wawona. More than 20 giant sequoias are visible from the parking lot, but to get a true feel for the size of these trees, take the ³/₄-mile walk along the self-guiding nature trail to the Grizzly Giant. This gargantuan tree is 32 feet in diameter, 209 feet tall, and believed to be 2,700 years old.

Tuolumne Meadows is accessible in summer by driving east out of Yosemite Valley along Highway 120 (55 miles from the valley). This is the most extensive meadow system in the Sierra Nevada. Picnickers and day hikers enjoy the crystalline lakes, rolling fields, and rounded granite domes. Many hikers begin their journeys from here, but you'll need to get acclimated to the 8,575-foot altitude.

HOTELS AND INNS

Lodging in Yosemite ranges from the elegant Ahwahnee Hotel to spartan tent cabins. In the valley, Yosemite Lodge, made up of a variety of lodging alternatives, is the most populated area. It also has the most food, shopping, and restaurant services and is within easy walking distance of Yosemite Falls and the Valley Visitor Center. The secluded Ahwahnee Hotel is the only accommodation in Yosemite that offers color television and room service. Curry Village, a community of wooden and tent cabins, is within walking distance of the trails emanating from Happy Isles. In the summer, you can find rustic lodges at Tuolumne Meadows and White Wolf.

Reserve your room or cabin in Yosemite Valley as soon as possible. You can reserve exactly 366 days in advance of your arrival date. Hotel rooms and cabins with private bath are particularly popular. The Ahwahnee, Yosemite Lodge, and Wawona Hotel are regularly sold out on weekends, holiday periods, and all days between May and September within minutes after the reservation office opens. If you visit from November through March, especially midweek, you'll have a much easier time getting a reservation and will find rooms discounted up to 25%. All reservations for lodging in Yosemite are made through Yosemite Park and Curry Company (Central Reservations, 5410 E. Home Ave., Fresno 93727, tel. 209/252–4848).

Additional lodging is available in Yosemite's gateway cities, but the nearest town, El Portal, is still 14 curvy mountain miles from the Valley Visitor Center. The next nearest town, Midpines, is 36 miles away, and Mariposa, with the most lodging options, is a distant 43 miles away. The Mariposa County Chamber of Commerce (Box 425, Mariposa 95338, tel. 209/966–2456), covering El Portal, Fish Camp, and Mariposa, offers a free service brochure listing all county hotels, motels, bed-and-breakfast inns, restaurants, and sights.

Price categories for double occupancy, without 9% tax, are *Expensive,* over $85; *Moderate,* $50–$85; and *Inexpensive,* under $50.

YOSEMITE NATIONAL PARK **Awahnee Hotel.** This grand 1920s-style mountain lodge—the most sought-after lodging in Yosemite—is constructed of rocks and sugar-pine logs, with exposed timbers and spectacular views. The Grand Lounge and Solarium are decorated in a style that is a tribute to the local Miwok and Paiute Indians. The decor in the rooms continues that motif. *123 rooms. Restaurant, lounge, pool, tennis. AE, DC, MC, V. Expensive.*

Wawona Hotel. This circa-1879 National Historic Landmark, located at the southern end of Yosemite National Park near the Mariposa Grove of Big Trees, has rooms that reflect their era—most are small and do not have private bath. The Victorian parlor in the main hotel boasts a fireplace, board games, and a pianist who sings Cole Porter tunes on weekend evenings. *104 rooms. Restaurant, lounge, pool, tennis, stables, golf course adjacent. Open daily Easter week–Thanksgiving, during Christmas week and weekends year-round. AE, DC, MC, V. Moderate.*

Curry Village. This is a large community of spartan but adequately furnished one-room cabins and tent cabins (with wood frames and canvas walls and roof) in a woodland setting in the eastern end of Yosemite Valley. Those without bath share campground-style community bathrooms with showers available for a nominal fee. *183 cabins, 427 tent cabins, 18 hotel rooms. Fast-food restaurant, pool, skating rink, stables. AE, DC, MC, V. Inexpensive–Moderate.*

Yosemite Lodge. This property encompasses a variety of lodging alternatives, from rustic, one-room cabins (with electric heater) that share a camp-style bathroom with flush toilets to deluxe hotel rooms with cathedral ceilings and balconies overlooking Yosemite Falls. *495 rooms. 2 restaurants, cafeteria, lounge, pool, 2 gift shops. AE, DC, MC, V. Inexpensive–Moderate.*

MOTELS

OUTSIDE YOSEMITE NATIONAL PARK The following motels are 60–90 minutes by car from Yosemite Valley, unless otherwise noted.

Moderate: Berkshire Inn (19950 Hwy. 120, Groveland 95321, tel. 209/962–6744). 6 rooms; Continental breakfast included, Jacuzzi, 8 common rooms with television. **Best Western Yosemite Gateway Inn** (40530 Hwy. 41, Oakhurst 93644, tel. 209/683–2378 or 800/528–1234). 118 rooms; heated indoor/outdoor pool, sauna, whirlpool, exercise room. **Cedar Lodge** (9966 Hwy. 140, El Portal 95318, tel. 209/379–2612). 206 rooms; restaurant, pool, gift shop. 25 minutes from Yosemite Valley. **Shilo Inn** (40644 Hwy. 41, Oakhurst 93644, tel. 209/683–3555). 80 rooms; pool, sauna, whirlpool, steam room, exercise room. **Yosemite Gold Rush Inn** (4994 Bullion St., Box 1989, Mariposa 95338, tel. 209/966–4344 or 800/321–5261). 61 rooms; Continental breakfast included, pool, whirlpool, gift shop.

Inexpensive: Miners Inn (St. Rte. 140 at St. Rte. 49N, or Box 246, Mariposa 95338, tel. 209/742–7777). 64 rooms; pool, whirlpool, movies, coffee in room.

CAMPGROUNDS

Yosemite Valley campgrounds are well maintained but crowded, especially in summer. Lack of undergrowth between tent sites means there's not much privacy. The campgrounds in Yosemite Valley are all in the eastern end with similar environments by the Merced River and have communal bathrooms with flush toilets. Showers are available for a nominal fee at Curry Village and at valley swimming pools in season.

The Recreational Vehicle limit is 35 feet in Yosemite. Rangers accommodate large RVs by matching them with the larger tent sites in each campground. There are no hookups in the National Park, but LP gas is available at the service stations. Gravel and dirt RV sites are available in all park campgrounds except Upper River in the valley and the walk-in campgrounds.

All valley campgrounds, with the exception of Sunnyside Walk-in, must be reserved through Mistix (tel. 800/365–2267). You can reserve campsites no sooner than eight weeks in advance. Yosemite campgrounds consistently sell out within minutes of the time they become available during the high season. Call Mistix as soon as the office opens exactly eight weeks in advance to ensure a campsite for your visit. Campground choice is reserved, but individual sites are available only on a first-come, first-served basis, so arrive early for the best selection. Weather regulates the opening day of the seasonal campgrounds. Fees range from $2 per person to $12 per site.

Lower River and Upper River. Two similar campgrounds with some nice sites by the river; however, the road between the two has the heaviest traffic, which may be a consideration for families with young children. *262 sites ($12). Open Apr.–late Oct.*

North Pines. Easy access to the stables and Mirror Lake trail, but some sites can be too close to the horsey odor. *85 sites ($12). Open May–Oct.*

Sunnyside Walk-in. The only Valley campground available first-come, first-served and the only one west of Yosemite Lodge. It fills quickly and is typically sold out everyday from spring through fall. *35 sites ($2).*

Upper Pines. Ideal for tent campers who don't want to be next to RVs, this is the only drive-in valley campground for tents only. *124 sites ($12). Open Apr.–Nov.*

Wawona. A first-come, first-served family campground with sites by the river, it's across the street from the Wawona hotel in the south end of Yosemite National Park. *100 sites ($7).*

DINING

Yosemite is not known as a gourmand's delight. The food here is primarily basic American. Those on a budget should head for the cafeteria at Yosemite Lodge and the hamburger stand at Curry Village (open spring to fall). There are several year-round fast-food options near the Valley Visitor Center. Summer-only restaurants are located in the Tuolumne Meadows Lodge and White Wolf Lodge.

Choose the restaurant for the setting, since the menus are similar, with few exceptions, in all of them. All restaurants are run by Yosemite Park and Curry Company (Central Reservations, 5410 E. Home Ave., Fresno 93727, tel. 209/252–4848). Operating hours vary by season and are listed in the *Yosemite Guide* newspaper.

Price categories per person, not including 7.25% tax, service, and drinks, are *Expensive,* over $25; *Moderate,* $15–$25; and *Inexpensive,* under $15. All accept AE, DC, MC, V.

The Ahwahnee Dining Room. This is the most romantic and elegant setting in Yosemite, with its massive room, floor-to-ceiling windows, and soaring, 34-foot-high ceiling supported by immense sugar-pine beams. The restaurant glows with candlelight and serves such specialties as chicken piccata. *Tel. 209/372–1489. Jacket and tie recommended. Moderate–Expensive.*

Mountain Room Broiler. Conveniently located at Yosemite Lodge, this restaurant offers casual fine dining away from the noise and crowds of other Yosemite Valley dining areas but is not as formal or expensive as the Ahwahnee and serves simply prepared fish

such as salmon and trout. *Tel. 209/372–1281. Moderate.*

Wawona Hotel Dining Room. This is a romantic, nostalgic setting dating from the late 1800s, with white linen cloths, tabletop candles in hurricane lamps, and friendly service offering trout, daily chicken specials, a Szechuan vegetable platter with roast pork with plum sauce, a children's menu, and Sunday brunch. *Tel. 209/375–6556. Inexpensive–Moderate.*

Degnan's Deli. In an alpine-style building with fireplaces, Degnan's Deli offers sandwiches, salads, and gourmet cheeses, while Degnan's Fast Food serves pizza and ice cream. *Tel. 209/372–1454. Inexpensive.*

Four Seasons Restaurant. Next to the Mountain Room Broiler, this large, casual restaurant is ideal for families looking for something more relaxed than the cafeteria, with entrées including grilled trout almondine (fresh when available), steak, barbecued breast of chicken, vegetarian meals, and a children's menu. Sign up early for dinner or be prepared for a long wait in line in the busy seasons. *Tel. 209/372–1269. Inexpensive.*

The Village Grill. Open spring to fall, this casual, popular place serves hamburgers and sandwiches. *Tel. 209/372–1207. Inexpensive.*

SHOPPING

The Village Store (tel. 209/372–1253), near the Valley Visitor Center, offers the largest selection of goods, including groceries, magazines, film, clothing, camping supplies, postcards, gifts, and souvenirs. Nearby is Degnan's Nature Crafts (tel. 209/372–1453), a gift shop. The Ansel Adams Gallery (tel. 209/372–4413), next to the Valley Visitor Center, is the most elegant store in the park, with Ansel Adams prints, fine artwork, and top-quality Indian crafts.

At the Ahwahnee Hotel, the lobby Sweet Shop (tel. 209/372–1271) sells Ahwahnee logo merchandise, while the Gift Shop (tel. 209/372–1409) specializes in Indian jewelry and handicrafts. At the Yosemite Lodge, the Gift Store (tel. 209/372–1297) offers Yosemite souvenirs, picnic supplies, and film. The Indian Shop (tel. 209/372–1438) here features Indian artwork, handmade items, and moccasins. Curry Village has a year-round Mountain Shop (tel. 209/372–1296), with rock-climbing and backpacking supplies, and a Gift Store (tel. 209/372–1291). Badger Pass Ski Area offers a winter-only Ski Shop (tel. 209/372–1333) with ski clothing, sunglasses, and sun lotions.

OUTDOOR ACTIVITIES

BIKING Yosemite Valley is ideal for biking, with more than 8 miles of scenic, mostly level bikeways. Bike rentals, with helmets, are available at Yosemite Lodge (year-round, conditions permitting) and Curry Village (summer only).

FISHING In the Merced River in the valley and the Toulumne River in the high country, trout, mostly brown and rainbow, are available but not plentiful. Residents and nonresidents may purchase a one-day license at Yosemite Village Sport Shop (tel. 209/372–1286) next to the Village Store. For information, contact the Department of Fish and Game (3211 S St., Sacramento 95816, tel. 916/227–2244).

HIKING For an excellent map and description of the valley trails, invest in the colorful "Map & Guide to Yosemite Valley," available at the Visitor Center.

"A Changing Yosemite" is a self-guiding nature trail (pick up a pamphlet at the trailhead) that begins about 75 yards in front of the Valley Visitor Center. This level walk follows the road, then circles through Cook's Meadow. Allow at least 45 minutes for this 1-mile paved loop trail.

A popular, easy trail leads from Shuttle Bus Stop #17 (near the valley stables) to Mirror Lake. Allow one hour for this 2-mile hike. If you want to go farther, you can continue on the 3-mile Mirror Lake Loop for an added hour of pleasant hiking.

HORSEBACK RIDING All horses and pack animals must be accompanied by a guide. Scenic trail rides range from two-hour, half-day, and one- to six-day High Sierra saddle trips. Stables are open late spring through early fall in Yosemite Valley (tel. 209/372–1248) and during the summer only in Wawona (tel. 209/375–6502), White Wolf (tel. 209/372–1323), and Tuolumne Meadows (tel. 209/372–1327). Reservations must be made in person at the stables or at the hotel tour desks.

Walk & Lead Ponies are available per hour. Children ride on gentle ponies while adults lead them on trails near the stables.

ICE SKATING Skating is available from late October through mid-March depending upon seasonal conditions at an outdoor rink in Curry Village.

SKIING Yosemite offers both cross-country and alpine skiing at Badger Pass in the winter months. Its gentle terrain is ideal for novices. Senior citizens over 60 and everyone exactly 40 years old ski free every day. Both alpine and cross-country ski lessons and rentals are available.

SNOWSHOEING Park rangers offer free snowshoe tours at Badger Pass during the winter months when the ski area is operating. These 11/2-hour walks include rest stops when the ranger explains animal behavior in winter.

SWIMMING Several swimming holes with small, sandy beaches can be found along the Merced River at the eastern end of Yosemite Valley. Find gentle waters to swim; currents are deceptively strong and temperatures chilling. Do not attempt to swim above or near waterfalls or rapids—fatalities have occurred. Outdoor pools (summer only) are located at Curry Village and Yosemite Lodge.

ENTERTAINMENT

In the evenings, ranger talks, slide shows, and documentary films present unique perspectives on Yosemite. Programs vary according to season, but there is usually at least one activity per night in the valley.

Zion and Bryce Canyon National Parks

Utah

nly 84 miles separate two of the most dramatically scenic national parks in the United States, Zion and Bryce Canyon, both found in southern Utah. Zion is Utah's most developed and busiest national park, with more than 2 million annual visitors. Close to major interstates, the park has a large lodge, spacious campgrounds, and extensive programs and services, all contributing to its popularity. It also has paved roads and easy hiking trails that allow for quick visits. Still, anyone who ventures from the main park roads will discover rugged trails in a true canyon with towering sandstone walls reaching 2,000 feet as well as a complex desert ecology.

The Virgin River, a muddy little stream that can turn into a violent red torrent during the spring runoff or after a summer thunderstorm, shaped the mighty canyon and its tributaries. Under a bright sky, a hiker can enter a side canyon barely 20 feet across and be sandwiched between high walls washed in shades of crimson, vermilion, tan, and orange and often streaked with dark "desert varnish" (oxidized minerals).

Bryce Canyon, on the other hand, is not really a canyon at all but a number of pink and white amphitheaters carved by rain, snow, and ice from the encircling cliffs. At 9,100 feet in elevation at its highest point, the park experiences four distinct seasons. Its brilliant red, buff, and tan limestone cliffs in strange and wonderful shapes change color with the season, the time of day, and the weather. Except during the height of the summer season, Bryce is a relatively quiet place in which to enjoy nature.

ESSENTIAL INFORMATION

WHEN TO GO Though both parks experience distinct seasons, the changes are more pronounced at Bryce Canyon, where its high elevation means more extreme temperatures.

At Bryce, for example, the average high in January is 39° and the average low is 9°. In the summer, highs generally average in the low 80s, evenings in the mid-40s. January highs at Zion, on the other hand, range from 39° to 60°, with lows usually in the mid-20s. In April, the highs range between 62° and 80°, and lows from 37° to 59°. Summer heat can present problems to hikers, with temperatures between 93° and 103° in the middle of the day not uncommon.

About 75% of the visitors at both parks arrive during the summer, when trails can be crowded and lodging scarce. Spring and fall are the best times to visit Zion, when temperatures are moderate and crowds are smaller. Fall is probably the best season to visit Bryce; weather is clearer than at other times and the aspens begin to turn gold. For lower hotel rates, visit either park during the winter.

BARGAINS In both parks, ranger-naturalists sometimes offer free talks and guided nature walks; check park visitor centers for these activities. The Utah Shakespearean Festival (tel. 801/586–7880) is held July 1–early September at Southern Utah State College in Cedar City near Zion National Park. Many of the activities surrounding the theater festival are free, including Greenshow, featuring puppets, storytellers, and musicians. You can also shop for unusual and rare rocks at fairly inexpensive prices at several shops in Springdale, near the entrance to Zion National Park or in small towns between the two parks on U.S. 89.

TOURIST OFFICES Superintendent, Zion National Park (Springdale 84767, tel. 801/772–3256). The Zion Canyon Visitor Center is near the park's south entrance, and the Kolob Canyons Visitor Center is in the northwest corner of the park just off I–15. Bryce Canyon National Park (Bryce Canyon 84717, tel. 801/834–5322). The visitor center is located near the park's main entrance.

EMERGENCIES **Zion:** For medical emergencies, dial 911, contact a park ranger, or call 801/772–3256 from 8 to 5; 801/772–3322 or 800/624–9447 after hours. Outside the park,

contact Zion Medical Clinic (Springdale, tel. 801/772–3226) or Dixie Regional Medical Center (St. George, tel. 801/634–4200). **Bryce Canyon:** For medical emergencies, contact a park ranger or call 801/834–5322; first aid is available at the visitor center. Outside the park, contact Garfield Medical Center (Panguitch, tel. 801/676–8842).

ARRIVING AND DEPARTING

BY PLANE SkyWest Airlines, the Delta Connection (tel. 800/453–9417), has regular flights from Salt Lake City and Las Vegas to St. George Municipal Airport, located 43 miles from Zion and 126 miles from Bryce, and to Cedar City Municipal Airport, located 59 miles from Zion and 78 miles from Bryce. Air Nevada (tel. 800/634–6377) flies April– mid-November, daily, from Las Vegas to Bryce, offering a package that includes airfare, a guide, and rim stops at Bryce.

From the Airport to the Parks: The easiest way to get to the parks from the airport is by car. In Cedar City, you can rent a car from Avis (Municipal Airport, tel. 801/586–3033), Hertz (tel. 801/586–6096), National (tel. 801/586–7056), and Speedy (tel. 801/586–RENT). In St. George, you can rent from A-1 (tel. 801/673–8811), Avis (Municipal Airport, tel. 801/673–3686), Budget (tel. 801/673–6825), Dollar (tel. 801/628–6549), and National (Municipal Airport, tel. 801/673–5098). For limousine service in St. George, call Toraco Enterprises (tel. 801/628–8687).

BY CAR Salt Lake City and Las Vegas are the closest major cities to Zion and Bryce. I–15 runs from Salt Lake City, northeast of Zion, and from Las Vegas, to the southwest, and connects to Zion's Kolob Canyons Road entrance. The park's south and east entrances are located on Route 9, which branches off I–15 near St. George. A more scenic but slower route from Salt Lake City to the east entrances is U.S. 89, which also links Zion to Bryce Canyon and Grand Canyon parks. To reach the main entrance of Bryce, take U.S. 89 from the south via Kanab and Hatch or from the north via Panguitch. You'll have to

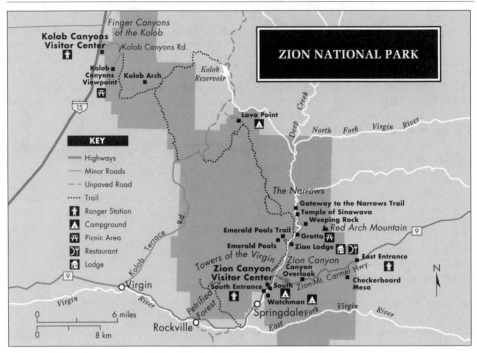

ZION NATIONAL PARK

Finger Canyons of the Kolob

Kolob Canyons Visitor Center

Kolob Canyons Rd.

Kolob Canyons Viewpoint

Kolob Arch

Kolob Reservoir

15

Lava Point

Deep Creek

North Fork Virgin River

KEY

▬ Highways

— Minor Roads

-- Unpaved Road

···· Trail

Ranger Station

Campground

Picnic Area

Restaurant

Lodge

Kolob Terrace Rd.

The Narrows

Gateway to the Narrows Trail

Temple of Sinawava

Weeping Rock

Emerald Pools Trail

Red Arch Mountain

Grotto

Emerald Pools

Zion Lodge

Towers of the Virgin

Zion Canyon Overlook

East Entrance

Zion Canyon Visitor Center

South Entrance

South

Zion-Mt. Carmel Hwy.

Checkerboard Mesa

9

Virgin

Watchman

9

Virgin River

Petrified Forest

Springdale

East Fork

Rockville

0   6 miles

0   8 km

N

turn east on UT 12 and south on Highway 63, which leads to the entrance (from U.S. 89 to the entrance is about 21 miles).

The drive from Las Vegas to Zion is 158 miles; to Bryce, 237 miles. The drive from Salt Lake City to Zion is 309 miles; to Bryce, 256 miles.

BY TRAIN Amtrak (tel. 800/USA–RAIL) stops at both Salt Lake City and Las Vegas, where car rentals and bus tours are available.

BY BUS Greyhound Lines (tel. 800/231–2222) services St. George and Cedar City.

GETTING AROUND

Both parks are easily explored by car and allow opportunities for walking and hiking.

REST STOPS Public rest rooms at Zion and Bryce are found at the visitor centers. At Bryce, the only visitor center is right near the park entrance. At Zion, visitor centers are located near the south entrance and the Kolob Canyons entrance. The Grotto picnic area in Zion canyon near the lodge also has rest

rooms. Another small rest stop is located at the end of the Kolob Canyons Road.

GUIDED TOURS The Utah Travel Council (Council Hall/Capitol Hill, Salt Lake City 84114, tel. 801/538–1030) compiles an annual list of motorcoach tours into Utah from across the United States. Scenic West Tours (tel. 800/723–6429) offers regular and specialized package tours to the parks from Salt Lake City. Other companies offering more flexible schedules and personalized tours include R&R Tours (St. George, tel. 801/628–3643), Scenic American Tours (Springdale, tel. 801/772–3473 or 586–9496), and Toraco Enterprises (St. George, tel. 801/628–8687).

EXPLORING

Entrance fees for both parks for a seven-day pass are $5 per vehicle and $3 per person arriving on a bus, on foot, or on a bicycle. Entry is free to holders of Golden Eagle, Golden Age, and Golden Access Passports.

Zion and Bryce Canyon can both easily be seen by simply driving to major overlooks located off the highways that wind through both parks. Try to allow time for at least one or two short hikes on the park trails.

ZION **Zion Canyon Visitor Center.** The short multimedia program at this center has slides covering every season accompanied by narration by people who have lived and worked in the park. Rangers are available with helpful information on hiking, rock-climbing, and other outdoor activities in the area.

Zion Canyon Scenic Drive. This 13-mile round-trip drive takes you along the floor of Zion Canyon, with brilliantly colored cliffs towering above you. The drive begins at the south entrance and proceeds north to the Temple of Sinawa parking area. Stop at the historic Zion Lodge about halfway on the drive for a snack or lunch. North of the lodge, past Red Arch Mountain, is the Grotto picnic area. Along this drive, you'll have access to several walking and hiking trails, including the following (from south to north on the drive).

Emerald Pools Trail. This relatively easy one-hour, 1.2-mile round-trip hike begins opposite the Zion Lodge and ends at the Lower Emerald Pool, where three waterfalls cascade off the red cliffs. Another mile and a bit more energy will take you to the larger Upper Emerald Pool, at the base of some high cliffs.

Weeping Rock Trail. Beginning at the Weeping Rock parking lot, this easy half-hour, 1/2-mile round-trip trail leads to a spring that issues from a rock, with hanging gardens in spring and summer.

Gateway to the Narrows Trail. An especially beautiful route in spring and summer, when colorful wildflowers hang from canyon walls, the easy 90-minute, 2-mile round-trip trail follows the Virgin River to Zion Canyon Narrows. The way is shaded and the river keeps things cool; interpretive signs relate the natural history of the canyon.

Zion–Mt. Carmel Highway. This segment of Route 9 climbs 13 miles one-way from the bottom of the canyon at the south entrance up winding switchbacks and through tunnels carved out of the rock. It passes the petrified sand dunes of the Checkerboard Mesa before reaching the east entrance. This is the road that connects Zion to Bryce Canyon and the Grand Canyon. The easy, one-hour, 1.2-mile round-trip Canyon Overlook Trail, just east of the long tunnel, is one of the most attractive hikes off this road, ending at an awesome view of lower Zion Canyon.

Two other drives in the remote areas of Zion include the 15-mile round-trip journey along Kolob Canyons Road, from the **Kolob Canyons** Visitor Center to the Kolob Canyons Viewpoint, entering the red-rock walled Finger Canyons and the 50-mile round-trip drive from the town of Virgin north along the Kolob Terrace Road to Lava Point and **Kolob Reservoir.** The latter route runs along the western edge of the park, offering great views from the top of the canyon and passing farmhouses and bright green fields.

BRYCE CANYON The best time to explore the park is in the very early morning and the late afternoon, when the sun sets the rocks ablaze with color.

Visitor Center. Located near the park entrance, the center has a 10-minute slide show introducing the park. Rangers offer interpretative programs, and exhibits describe park flora and fauna.

Overlooks. You can drive on two main roads in the park—a section of Highway 12 in the northern end of the park and Highway 63, which leads south from the main entrance into the heart of Bryce and dead-ends after 18 miles at Rainbow Point, with a superb 270° view of surrounding canyon country. The park has 13 overlook points; Fairyland, Sunrise, Sunset, Inspiration, and Bryce Points offer some of the best views of the unusual pinnacles, spires, and other rock formations.

Queen's Garden Trail. This short, one-hour, 1¹/₂-mile round-trip hike, beginning at Sunset Point, involves a moderately strenuous descent—and subsequent ascent—of 320 feet. Still, it allows you a closer view of the unique landscape.

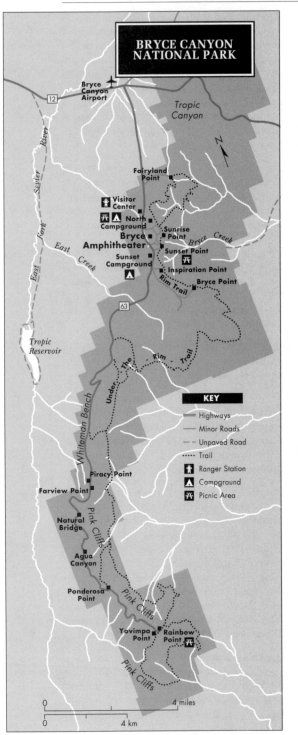

BRYCE CANYON NATIONAL PARK

Bryce Canyon Airport

Tropic Canyon

12

Sevier River

East Fork

Fairyland Point

Visitor Center

North Campground

Bryce Amphitheater

East Creek

Sunset Campground

Sunrise Point

Bryce Creek

Sunset Point

Inspiration Point

Rim Trail

Bryce Point

63

Tropic Reservoir

The Rim Trail

Under the

Whiteman Bench

KEY

Highways

Minor Roads

Unpaved Road

Trail

Ranger Station

Campground

Picnic Area

Piracy Point

Farview Point

Natural Bridge

Pink Cliffs

Agua Canyon

Ponderosa Point

Pink Cliffs

Yovimpa Point

Rainbow Point

Pink Cliffs

0   4 miles

0   4 km

Rim Trail. Although this easy to moderate trail stretches 11 miles along the rim of the amphitheater, hikers or cross-country skiers in the winter can access it at many different points. You can take a quiet stroll anywhere along the trail, which is paved between Sunrise and Sunset points.

HOTELS AND INNS

Lodging inside and near both parks is somewhat limited, making reservations almost a must during the busy tourist season of June–August and on any three-day holiday weekend.

The most convenient places to stay outside Zion are in Springdale, just outside the south entrance, or in neighboring Rockville. Bed-and-breakfasts in Springdale are surprisingly reasonable and allow visitors a taste of the local culture. The nearest town to Bryce of any consequence is Panguitch, 24 miles from the park entrance. Besides the historic lodges inside the two parks, the other accommodations near the parks, though clean, are simple motel rooms with two double beds and ordinary amenities. Price categories for double occupancy, excluding 6% tax, are *Moderate,* $50–$85, and *Inexpensive,* under $50.

ZION Cliffrose Lodge and Gardens. A quarter of a mile from the park's south entrance and surrounded by botanical gardens and acres of lawns and trees, this serene hotel has spacious rooms and balconies with views of Zion Canyon and Watchman Mountain. *281 Zion Park Blvd., Springdale 84767, tel. 801/772–3234 or 800/243–8824. 36 rooms. Pool. AE, D, MC, V. Moderate.*

Handcart House Bed and Breakfast. This Mormon pioneer–style stucco home is filled with antiques; breakfast is generous. *244 W. Main St., Box 146, Rockville 84763, tel. 801/772–3867. 3 rooms. AE, MC, V. Moderate.*

Harvest House Bed and Breakfast. The first-rate Harvest House ranked as Utah's top B&B in recent surveys. A hot tub makes it an inviting place to return to after a long hike. Reservations are strongly suggested. *29 Can-*

yon View Dr., Box 125, Springdale 84767, tel. 801/772–3880. 4 rooms. MC, V. Moderate.

Zion Lodge. All rooms at the motel-like lodge have balconies that open onto splendid canyon views, but gas-burning fireplaces make the cabins more popular. *Zion National Park, Box 400, Cedar City 84720, tel. 801/586–7686 for reservations, 801/772–3213 to reach the lodge; fax 801/586–3157. 121 rooms and cabins (no phones or TVs). Restaurant, snack bar, gift shop. AE, DC, MC, V. Moderate.*

Best Western Driftwood Lodge. This standard motel has well-manicured grounds and perhaps the best swimming pool in Springdale. *1515 Zion Park Blvd., Box 98, Springdale 84767, tel. 801/772–3262. 47 rooms. Restaurant, pool. AE, D, DC, MC, V. Moderate.*

Blue House Bed and Breakfast. This blue frame house with white trim is pleasantly decorated with plush carpets, floral bedspreads in the rooms, and wicker and oak furnishings. *125 E. Main St., Box 176, Rockville 84763, tel. 801/772–3912. 4 rooms, 2 with private bath. MC, V. Inexpensive–Moderate.*

Canyon Ranch Motel. The individual cabin units are unremarkable, but those with kitchenettes book up quickly. *668 Zion Park Blvd., Box 175, Springdale 84767, tel. 801/772–3357. 21 rooms, 5 have kitchenettes. Pool. D, MC, V. Inexpensive–Moderate.*

Flanigans. Kelly-green carpets and pastel southwestern furnishings contribute to the appeal of this modern wood-and-glass property. The most modern units resemble a big log cabin. *428 Zion Park Blvd., Box 100, Springdale 84767, tel. 801/772–3244 or 800/765–7787. 36 rooms. Restaurant, pool. AE, D, DC, MC, V. Inexpensive–Moderate.*

Under the Eaves Guest House. This small guest house, built of sandstone blocks cut from the canyon walls in 1935, offers rooms with antique furniture and a full breakfast. *980 Zion Park Blvd., Box 29, Springdale 84767, tel. 801/772–3457. 5 rooms, 3 with private bath. MC, V. Inexpensive–Moderate.*

BRYCE CANYON **Bryce Canyon Lodge.** This historic hostelry features lodgepole pine cabins with cathedral ceilings and stone fireplaces, and more contemporary rooms in the lodge. Reservations must be made at least three months in advance. *Bryce Canyon, Box 400, Cedar City 84721, tel. 801/586–7686, fax 801/586–3157. 114 rooms. Facilities: restaurant, shop. AE, DC, MC, V. Moderate.*

Ruby's Inn. A member of the Best Western chain, Ruby's is the largest lodging in the area, with a post office, a service station, a shopping complex, a nightly rodeo in summer, horseback riding, and skiing in the winter. *1 mi north of the park entrance. Hwy. 63, Box 1, Bryce 84717, tel. 801/834–5341 or 800/528–1234, fax 801/834–5265. 216 rooms. Restaurant, pool, gift shop, RV park. AE, D, DC, MC, V. Moderate.*

Bryce Canyon Pines Motel. This quiet, modern motel complex is situated 6 miles from the park entrance. *Hwy. 12, Box 43, Bryce 84764, tel. 801/834–5441. 52 rooms. Restaurant, pool, RV park. D, DC, MC, V. Moderate.*

Bryce Valley Inn. This relatively new motel features large rooms decorated with southwestern touches. It also provides shuttles to the park for guests. *200 North Main, Box 8, Tropic 84776 801/679–8811. 63 rooms. Restaurant, laundry, AE, MC, V. Moderate–Inexpensive.*

CAMPGROUNDS

For a complete listing of both public and private campgrounds in the area, send for a Utah Travel Guide from the Utah Travel Council (Council Hall–Capitol Hill, Salt Lake City 84114, tel. 801/538–1030). To make reservations in any Utah State Park, call 800/322–3770.

ZION During the summer months, Zion's main campgrounds, South and Watchman, fill almost every night. The best sites are closest to the Virgin River and farthest from the road. Neither campground takes reservations. For information, call 801/772–3256.

South Campground. Open from April 15 to September 15, this area near the south entrance is situated along the Virgin River and surrounded by large cottonwood trees. *140 RV and tent sites, no hookups ($7). Running water, bathrooms, picnic tables and barbecue areas.*

Watchman Campground. This large area flanked by towering red cliffs is located near the south entrance. *270 RV and tent sites, no hookups ($7). Running water, bathrooms, picnic tables and barbecue areas.*

Outside the park, some of the best campgrounds near Zion, especially for tenters, are found in nearby state parks. In contrast to the Zion Park campgrounds, those at **Coral Pink Sand Dunes State Park** (tel. 801/874–2408) and **Snow Canyon State Park** (tel. 801/628–2255) are rarely crowded. A bit out of the way, these parks with showers and bathrooms are best for stopovers on the way into or out of Zion. Coral Pink Sand Dunes, near the town of Kanab on Highway 89, is a natural place to break during a journey between Zion and the Grand Canyon's North Rim. Snow Canyon is located to the east of Zion, not far from I–15 and St. George. The camping sites are set in pretty sandstone coves, surrounded by juniper trees. For RV hookups as well as tent sites, the closest private facility is the **Zion Canyon Campground** (tel. 801/772–3237), about 1/2 mile south of the south entrance, with showers, bathrooms, coin laundry, game room, and swimming.

BRYCE CANYON Bryce Canyon's two campgrounds, North and Sunset, generally fill every night from mid-May–mid-September; neither accept reservations, so you'll need to arrive by 2 PM the day you wish to stay. Both campgrounds are fine for tenters and maximum RV length is 30 feet. A store, laundry, and showers are located near Sunrise Point. For information, call 801/834–5322.

North Campground. Located east of the visitor center, this area, nestled under pine trees at an elevation of 8,000 feet, is open year-round, with one loop winterized for the cold temperatures. *55 RV and tent sites, no hookups ($6). Running water, bathrooms.*

Sunset Campground. Open from May 15 to October 1, this area, situated 2 miles south of the visitor center, has a setting similar to North Campground. *50 RV and tent sites, no hookups ($6). Running water, bathrooms.*

Outside the park are two relatively primitive but spectacular U.S. Forest Service camping areas: **Red Canyon** (tel. 801/676–8815 or 800/283–CAMP) on Highway 12, about 8 miles from Bryce, and **White Bridge** (tel. 801/865–3200) on Highway 143, 2 1/2 miles from Panguitch and about 30 miles from Bryce.

Tenters will enjoy the alpine setting of **King's Creek Campground** (tel. 801/676–8815) in Dixie National Forest, about 11 miles west of Bryce. To get here, turn off Highway 12 west of the junction with Highway 63 and drive south for 7 miles down a dirt road.

Kodachrome Basin State Park (tel. 801/679–8562), 9 miles southeast of the town of Cannonville and about 23 miles east of Bryce, is an excellent campground with showers.

Private campgrounds close to the park include **Ruby's Inn** (tel. 801/834–5341), 1 mile from Bryce on Highway 63, with RV hookups, showers, coin laundry, and a pool; and **Bryce Canyon Pines** (tel. 801/834–5441), 6 miles from Bryce on Highway 12, with shady sites, a laundry, and horseback riding.

Bryce/Zion KOA (tel. 801/648–2490), 5 miles north of Glendale on Highway 89, is a good place to stop between Bryce and Zion, with tent sites and RV hookups, showers, bathrooms, coin laundry, and a pool.

DINING

Eating out in this corner of Utah is a down-home American affair; restaurants are neither fancy nor high-priced, but the food served is wholesome, filling, and western style. Menus tend to favor barbecue entrées and red meat, yet health-conscious diners should be able to find chicken and salad entrées that are prepared to their liking. The restaurants listed below are in the price category *Inexpensive,* under $15 per person, excluding tax, service, and drinks.

ZION **Bit and Spur.** The popular Bit and Spur, one of the best Mexican restaurants in Utah, serves innovative and healthy southwestern-style dishes such as fajitas and seafood enchiladas. *1212 Zion Park Blvd., Springdale, tel. 801/772–3498. MC, V.*

Driftwood Lodge. This establishment, with rustic ranch decor and picture windows framing a pasture and red cliffs, serves roasted chicken, trout, and homemade bread. *1515 Zion Park Blvd., Springdale, tel. 801/772–3262. AE, D, DC, MC, V.*

Electric Jims. This fast-food dining spot has the look of a '50s diner with a southwestern touch. Enjoy broiled chicken breast served with sprouts and Swiss cheese and a vegetarian sandwich with bean sprouts, pickles, tomatoes, cucumbers, and ortega chili. Jims is sometimes closed during winter; call for current hours. *Near the park's south entrance on Zion Park Blvd., Springdale, tel. 801/772–3838. No credit cards.*

Flanigans. This pleasant place with southwestern pastel decor serves American and Continental cuisines, including pastas, trout, and grilled chicken. *428 Zion Park Blvd., Springdale, tel. 801/772–3244. AE, D, DC, MC, V.*

Pioneer Lodge and Restaurant. American food and a full salad bar are offered at this local favorite with an old fireplace. *838 Zion Park Blvd., Springdale, tel. 801/772–3233. AE, D, MC, V.*

Zion Lodge. In the park, fine American cuisine is served in a western-style dining room, with a wood-beamed ceiling, historic photos, and a wall of windows overlooking the canyon. *Zion Park, tel. 801/772–3213. AE, DC, MC, V.*

BRYCE CANYON **Bryce Canyon Lodge.** For the best food in the area, come to this rustic old stone-and-wood lodge, which serves such specialties as lamb stew and savory barbecued ribs. *Bryce Canyon Park, tel. 801/834–5361. AE, DC, MC, V.*

Bryce Canyon Pines Restaurant. Popular with families, this small establishment serves uncomplicated dishes such as fish-and-chips, homemade soup, and chili. *Hwy. 12 (6 mi from the park), tel. 801/834–5441. D, DC, MC, V.*

Doug's Place. Doug's is located in the tiny hamlet of Tropic, east of Bryce. Typical diner fare is punctuated with taco salads and sticky sweet rolls. *141 North Main St., Tropic, tel. 801/679–8633. AE, D, DC, MC, V.*

Hungry Coyote. Stop in for hearty southwestern dishes—grilled chicken and fajitas, among them—served in an atmosphere thick with antiques and faded old pictures. The Hungry Coyote is located inside the Bryce Valley Inn in Tropic, east of the park. *200 North Main, Tropic, tel. 801/679–8811. AE, MC, V.*

Fosters Family Steakhouse. This clean, relatively quiet and modern steak house—with a stone fireplace and bright picture windows—features a standard menu of chicken and seafood. *Hwy. 12 (4 mi from the park), tel. 801/834–5227. AE, D, MC, V.*

Ruby's Inn. This historic motel, store, and dining complex has a good soup and salad bar and an all-you-can-eat buffet. *Hwy. 63 (1 mi from the park), tel. 801/834–5341. AE, D, DC, MC, V.*

OUTDOOR ACTIVITIES

BIKING Zion is not recommended for biking because its roads are often crowded and quite narrow. Bryce Canyon's roads are wide enough, however, to accommodate cyclists safely. Ruby's Inn (tel. 801/834–5341), a mile from the park's entrance, rents bicycles. Backcountry Bicycle Tours (Box 4029, Bozeman, MT, 59722, tel. 406/586–3556) and Backroads Bicycle Touring (1516 5th St., Dept. Q612, Berkeley, CA 94710, tel. 800/245–3874) organize bicycle trips to both parks.

BIRD-WATCHING May–July is the best time to observe birds in the parks. More than 270 species of birds have been identified at Zion;

170 species at Bryce. The park visitor centers carry a checklist for bird-watchers.

HORSEBACK RIDING Canyon Trail Rides (Box 128, Tropic 84736, tel. 801/834–5291 or 801/679–8665 after June 1) offers guided horseback trips from mid-March through October in Zion and April 1–October 1 at Bryce.

SKIING AND SNOWSHOEING Some cross-country skiing and snowshoeing is available on Zion's higher plateau; Wildcat Canyon and the upper West Rim Trail have the best conditions.

Bryce is an excellent winter-sports area, with cross-country skiing available both inside and directly outside the park. You can rent skis from Ruby's Inn (tel. 801/834–5341). Free snowshoes can be obtained at the Bryce visitor center; Queen's Garden and Navajo Loop trails are recommended for snowshoers.